CHRISTIANS IN THE TWENTY-FIRST CENTURY

Christians in the Twenty-First Century

George D. Chryssides
and
Margaret Z. Wilkins

SHEFFIELD OAKVILLE

Published by Equinox Publishing Ltd.
UK: Unit S3, Kelham House, 3, Lancaster Street, Sheffield S3 8AF
USA: DBBC, 28 Main Street, Oakville, CT 06779

www.equinoxpub.com

First published 2011

British Library Cataloguing-in-Publication Data
A catalogue record for this book is available from the British Library.

ISBN-13 978 1 84553 212 3 (hardback)
       978 1 84553 213 0 (paperback)

Library of Congress Cataloging-in-Publication Data
  Christians in the twenty-first century/George D. Chryssides
and Margaret Z. Wilkins.
    p. cm.
  Includes bibliographical references (p.) and index.
  ISBN 978-1-84553-212-3 (hb)—ISBN 978-1-84553-213-0 (pb) 1.
Christianity. I. Wilkins, Margaret Z. II. Title. BR121.3.C49 2011
270.8'3—dc22
                  2010042253

Typeset by S.J.I. Services, New Delhi
Printed and bound in the UK by the MPG Books Group

To Ali

Contents

List of Illustrations

Preface

As its title suggests, *Christians in the Twenty-first Century* is about people and about the present. The present, however, is a moving target, and quickly becomes the past as the Christian faith changes. We have only witnessed just over a tenth of the twenty-first century, and even as we write, events are happening which are likely to have an important impact on its practitioners, and which are not wholly resolved. The issue of women bishops in the Church of England is but one example, and books on contemporary religion would never see the light of day if their authors waited to determine the outcomes. It is inevitable therefore that some details of this book will become superseded by events, as the twenty-first century progresses. We leave it to future authors to update the story.

This book began from the authors' attempts to explain Christianity to students from a wide range of backgrounds and religions. Since both the authors were brought up in staunchly Christian backgrounds, many of the religion's ideas either seemed obvious, or else needed explanations that are difficult to articulate for 'outsiders'. We are therefore grateful to students over the years who have asked probing and challenging questions, and thus helped to develop the material that we offer here. With so many religious communities (not merely Christian ones) in the English West Midlands, where the authors have lived for many years, it seemed very limiting merely to draw on written resources, such as historical documents and complex theological writings that are unknown to the majority of practitioners of the Christian faith. We have therefore attempted to present Christianity as it is practised, rather than as Christian history or Christian doctrine. Obviously, one cannot explain present practice without commenting on its roots in historical figures such as Jesus, Paul, the Church Fathers, Christian saints, popes and Protestant Reformers. Our aim, however, is to present a wide spectrum of Christianity as it is practised, rather than in its intellectu-alized or idealized forms.

The book's methodology is discussed at length in the first chapter. While methodology is important to students, general readers who are less patient with abstract academic discussions may prefer to embark at the second chapter rather than the first. It is not possible to compress the whole of Christianity into a single volume, or even a whole library, so readers will inevitably find omissions. One student once commented that some of our teaching material lacked Christianity's key element, namely how to become a Christian and find salvation. While it may be important to find answers to such questions, not all readers will necessarily feel that they can be discovered in the Christian faith, and this book does not aim either to commend or to criticize Christianity. Readers who want to find faith must seek it either amdist the plethora of resources that are readily found in Christian book stores and websites, or in the Christian communities that abound worldwide.

Some practicalities merit brief mention. First, the book's subject-matter is broad, and of course it is not possible to paint a full picture of even a tenth of a century within a single volume. We have tried to avoid constantly saying that we cannot do justice to a theme within a section or a chapter: readers must take this as read, and use the bibliographical and other resources to pursue topics further. Second, the use of inclusive language is always an issue for present-day authors. While the main text seeks to be gender-inclusive, some important quotations—particularly from old sources—do not observe this practice. It would of course be wrong to alter or to ignore important source material. Many writers use the feminine gender to refer to the Church. We have not followed this practice, which we regard as somewhat arcane, and possibly confusing to those who are unfamiliar with Christianity, although again many sources adopt this convention.

The authors would like to express their thanks to all those who have made this book possible: colleagues, students, Christian leaders and their congregations. There are too many to name individually, but particular thanks are due to Dr Stephen Jacobs (University of Wolverhampton), who commented a draft of the first chapter. We should also like to thank Equinox Publishing, especially Janet Joyce and Valerie Hall, for their management of the product throughout its preparation.

George D. Chryssides
Margaret Z. Wilkins

Abbreviations and Acronyms

3C	Christian Community Church
ACLU	American Civil Liberties Union
AIDS	acquired immune deficiency syndrome
ECUSA	Episcopal Church of the USA
EHAIA	Ecumenical HIV and AIDS Initiative in Africa
ASV	American Standard Version
BCE	Before Common Era
BFBS	British and Foreign Bible Society
BMS	Baptist Missionary Society
CAFOD	Catholic Agency for Overseas Development
CCBI	Churches Together in Britain and Ireland
CCCC	Conservative Congregational Christian Conference
CCJ	Council for Christians and Jews
CCND	Christian Campaign for Nuclear Disarmament
CE	Christian Endeavour
CE	Common Era
CIM	China Inland Mission
CMJ	Church's Ministry among Jewish People
CND	Campaign for Nuclear Disarmament
CoC	Cost of Conscience
CoG	Children of God
ELCA	Evangelical Lutheran Church in America
FF-ing	'flirty fishing'
FFWPU	Family Federation for World Peace and Unification
GAFCON	Global Anglican Future Conference
HIV	human immunodeficiency virus
IARF	International Association for Religious Freedom
IBRA	International Bible Reading Association
IBSA	International Bible Students' Association
ICC	International Churches of Christ
ICoC	International Churches of Christ

IIC	International Interfaith Council
IIOC	International Interfaith Organisations Network
IMC	International Missionary Council
ISKCON	International Society for Krishna Consciousness
KJV	King James Version
LCMS	Lutheran Church Missouri Synod
LGBT	lesbian, gay, bisexual and transexual
LXX	Septuagint
MCU	Modern Churchpeople's Union
MEPI	Middle East Peace Initiative
MLP	More Light Presbyterians
NACCC	National Association of Congregational Christian Churches
NASB	New American Standard Bible
NEB	New English Bible
NFS	National Federation of Spiritualists
NRM	new religious movement
NSAC	National Spiritualist Association of Churches
OCA	Orthodox Church in America
OMF	Overseas Missionary Fellowship
PEV	provincial episcopal visitor
PKs	Promise Keepers
ROCOR	Russian Orthodox Church Outside Russia
RSV	Revised Standard Version
SALT	Strategic Arms Limitation Talks
SBC	Southern Baptist Convention
SDA	Seventh-day Adventist
SNU	Spiritualists' National Union
SPUC	Society for the Protection of Unborn Children
SSPX	Society of St Pius X
ToU	Temple of Understanding
UC	Unification Church
URC	United Reformed Church
WARC	World Alliance of Reformed Churches
WCC	World Council of Churches
WCF	World Congress of Faiths
WMC	World Missionary Conference
YMCA	Young Men's Christian Association
YUSMALOS	Jupiter, Uranus, Saturn, Mars, Luna, Orion and Sirius
YWCA	Young Women's Christian Association

1

Studying Christianity

This book approaches Christianity in a new way. The existing literature on Christianity tends to fall into three categories. Academic literature principally consists, firstly, of histories of the Christian faith, and, secondly, there is Christian theology. The third category is popular literature, offering guidance on how to practise Christianity, normally focused on a particular Christian tradition, such as evangelical Protestantism or Roman Catholicism. This book seeks to adopt a different approach, exploring how Christianity is practised in its multitudinous forms. The authors adopt a 'religious studies' approach, rather than a theological or a historical one, and the book aims at understanding the varieties of the Christian faith, rather than to commend any particular expression of it.

Academic studies of religion tend to treat world religions unevenly. Christianity and Buddhism tend to receive historical and philosophical treatment, while introductions to Judaism emphasize its practices. Hinduism, on the other hand, has been explored both by scholars who have studied its religious texts, and by anthropologists who have observed the way in which it is practised in everyday life, usually in one particular society. There is nothing inherently wrong with any of these approaches, but it is important to draw on such studies, to explain how religions are actually practised by ordinary people. It is certainly true that Christianity would not be practised as it is today without the great ecumenical councils of the fourth and fifth centuries that led to the formation of the Nicene Creed, or without Martin Luther, John Calvin, the other Protestant Reformers and the Catholic Counter-Reformation, or without the Second Vatican Council and the present-day ecumenical movement. However, few rank-and-file Christian believers, if asked, would be very articulate about these landmarks in Christian history. To present Christianity, therefore, in terms of its doctrinal history, is to leave the average Christian unacknowledged. This book seeks to redress the balance by presenting an account of the Christian faith, which reflects the beliefs and practices of Christian believers.

This approach encounters a number of initial problems. First, such an account cannot legitimately be the account of any single believer, for to do so would fail to acknowledge the multifaceted nature of the Christian faith. The World Council of Churches has some 350 denominations that are affiliated to it, and does not by any means encompass every mainstream expression of Christianity. Of necessity, the authors have adopted an eclectic approach to the subject-matter: Christianity's three major strands—Roman Catholicism, Eastern Orthodoxy and Protestantism—are identified and explained, but the emphasis remains on how the ordinary believer experiences these traditions, and how it affects their lifestyle. In addition, a number of key themes are identified, such as the Church, the sacraments, ethics and Christian festivals, all of which have a significant impact on the practising Christian.

The relationship between individual believers and this type of academic account of their religion can perhaps best be explained by an analogy. Consider the example of students reading their university or college prospectus. The information it gives will not describe what any one student is doing, but rather a totality of activities within the institution, and thus goes beyond any single person's individual experience. At the same time, it should be recognizable by individual members as an accurate and reasonably balanced account of the university or college. It will no doubt contain material that goes beyond the main activity of studying one's subject. Most higher education establishments, for example, will provide brief information about their origins and history, together with other generic data such as mission statements, aims and policies. Student life goes beyond academic study, and needs other dimensions to support it: accommodation, library facilities, information technology and less academic-centred activities such sports, recreation and social life. Exactly what proportions of these varied types of material find their way into a prospectus is a matter of judgement. There is no one correct recipe, although it would be an impoverished prospectus if it were simply like the old-style ones, encountered many years ago by the present authors, where only academic syllabuses, staff lists and a brief history of one's institution were the staple diet of the prospective student. Applying this analogy to the study of the Christian faith, one roughly might compare the older-style prospectuses with the traditional historical and theological accounts of the Christianity. While not denying the value of the history and the substance of the Christian religion, these traditional accounts omit a great deal that ought to be of interest, and, most importantly, they leave well behind the average believer.

A second problem is how an author should give an account of everyday belief and practice. A series of real or imagined mini-biographies of believers who belong to the various traditions would run the risk of trivializing the subject-matter, and relegating the book to a somewhat lower intellectual level than is here intended. Serious academic writing must explain as well as describe, and hence do rather more than tell the story of how various believers live their lives. As Ninian Smart stated, accounts of religion must 'transcend the informative', and explanations must be given that justify the differences that exist between the faith of an Orthodox believer, and that of a Roman Catholic or a Protestant. Any such attempt to explain such differences immediately throws one back on historical and theological controversies. After all, how can one explain Eastern Orthodoxy without discussing the issue of the *filioque* clause (the phrase 'and the Son') in the Nicene Creed? How can one understand Protestantism without referring to Martin Luther's break with the Roman Church, and his theological teaching that one is 'justified by faith alone'? And can one really understand the Christian faith without referring back to its founder Jesus of Nazareth and its early missionary-theologian Paul of Tarsus?

Christianity is a historical religion, and a heavily doctrinal one. It teaches that, to bring salvation to humankind, God has broken into history in the form of Jesus Christ, his Son, who, together with the Holy Spirit, form an undivided Trinity. More than any other world religion, Christianity has taken pains carefully to formulate its doctrines in the form of numerous creeds and confessions, and to safeguard its teachings against heresy. While some reference must necessarily be made to Christianity's history and doctrines, the central focus will be the belief and practice with which the average believer is familiar. Believers (even clergy) may not be well able to expound the doctrine of the Trinity, but it is not possible to belong to the Christian faith without knowing of its existence. Most Christians may lack theological understanding of the ancient creeds, but the Apostles' Creed and the Nicene Creed are recited liturgically, at least in Orthodoxy, Roman Catholicism and Anglicanism, and hence a congregation is inevitably aware of them. Some explanation will be given to what they mean, but it is important to note how they used, and the purpose they typically serve in today's Church.

If pressed on matters of theology, most Christians would undoubtedly be aware, however they cared to express it, that Christianity is about sin and redemption. Whatever disagreements may exist between different traditions, denominations and schools of theology, it would be generally agreed that humanity suffers from the condition of sin and that Jesus Christ, the Son of God, had a pivotal role in securing humankind's salvation, whereby all who believe are offered eternal life. In Eastern religions, such as Hinduism, Buddhism and Jainism, the spiritual seeker's final goal is presented as a distant and difficult prospect. Even the Buddha himself, it is taught, lived some 530 lives before finally reaching the state of nirvana, and all these three religions have tended to advocate a somewhat austere spiritual path in order to make significant progress towards the final goal of *moksha* (liberation) or *nirvana* (enlightenment). In one of the major strands of Jainism, monks renounce all their possessions, including even their clothing, in a single-minded endeavour towards enlightenment. The severity of the path of the religious adept in these traditions has caused most believers to adopt a supportive role towards the monastic life, rather than to become a permanent part of it; consequently, most practitioners are only theoretically rather than practically committed to attaining the religion's final goal.

This observation has caused Simon Weightman, a scholar of Hinduism, to suggest a scheme that recognizes that different Hindus can seek to gain somewhat different benefits from their tradition. He identifies three 'complexes' (as he calls them). First there is the 'transcendental complex' in which the Hindu seeks the highest spiritual goal of liberation. For most Hindus, such a quest is not practical—at least in their present existence—and therefore they may decide to aim for a better reincarnation. Weightman characterizes such an aim as the 'dharmic complex'. (*Dharma* in Hinduism means, roughly speaking, one's spiritual obligations, and these relate to the law of karma—the effects of one's deeds—which dictates that good and bad spiritual and moral practice have respectively beneficial or deleterious repercussions.) The third complex is the 'pragmatic complex', and by identifying this complex, Weightman acknowledges that many Hindus do not seek either liberation or better rebirth, but are more concerned with surviving in their day-to-day existence. The farmer may want a good crop; a family may want to fend off illness; there may be a ghost that needs exorcism; and so on. Of course, one does not have to choose only one of the three complexes; most practitioners will combine the three in different degrees. Weightman represents the complexes by a triangle, placing the names 'transcendental', 'dharmic' and 'pragmatic' at each corner, and suggesting that individuals place themselves within the triangle, according to their engagement with each complex.

Weightman's model is a useful one, but it cannot be transposed directly on to Christianity, for two reasons. First, Christianity does not teach reincarnation, but that believers enjoy one single life, which is decisive with their eternal destiny. Second, the Christian faith does not present the quest for salvation as something that involves a world-renouncing lifestyle and severe austerity that only a few can endure. Christianity offers salvation to all: it is given by divine grace to all who will accept it, and hence eternal life is a realistic possibility for everyone. The present authors therefore employ an adaptation of Weightman's scheme: for the purposes of the present study, Christianity's three aspects will be defined as the transcendental, the ethical and the pragmatic. It is not proposed to deal with each of these sequentially in the course of this book, but rather to acknowledge the importance of all three within Christian belief and practice.

These three categories require explanation. The 'transcendental' relates to the final goal of Christianity, towards which the believer strives, variously known as 'salvation', 'eternal life', 'the kingdom of God' and 'the kingdom of heaven'. As Francis Clark has pointed out, all the major world's religions identify a predicament, a purpose and a path. As he puts it, they answer three questions: 'From what?', 'To what?' and 'By what?' (Clarke 1977: 9). Religions are singularly uncomplimentary about the situation in which humans are reckoned to be in. For the Hindu it is *maya* ('illusion'), for the Buddhist it is *dukkha* ('unsatisfactoriness', often misleadingly rendered as 'suffering'), and for the Jew and the Christian it is 'sin'. This condition is endemic, indeed embedded in the nature and fabric of the world, and the fact that Christianity uses a word that is not normally employed in everyday speech ('sin') serves to highlight its seriousness. Paul writes, 'All have sinned and fall short of the glory of God' (Rom. 3:23) and 'The wages of sin is death' (Rom. 6:23). The better news is that humanity does not need to remain in this condition. Religions offer a much superior state to aim for: *moksha*, nirvana, eternal life (the 'To what?). Further, they offer a path to the supreme goal, which may be meditation, insight, devotion or deeds.

The various aspects of Christianity that surround the themes of sin and salvation form the 'transcendental' part of the faith. This is this part that has attracted the greatest attention in the study of the Christian religion, and the nature of sin, redemption and eternal life have been the subject-matter of much theological speculation. Controversies such as the appropriateness of faith or works in securing salvation lie at the heart of Protestantism's historical roots, and mark an important division between the Roman Catholic and Protestant traditions. The fact that such matters belong to the theological and historical dimensions of Christianity does not mean that they are distanced from the faith of the ordinary believer. On the contrary: not only do the historical disputes explain important differences between traditions; many believers, particularly in the evangelical Protestant tradition, are thoroughly conscious of the need for salvation, and indeed frequently claim to have gained it. The familiar question, 'Are you saved?', remains at the forefront of the mission of such Christians.

Religions typically offer guidance for living. This aspect of religion—the ethical—differs from the transcendental in that it is not necessarily connected directly to the salvific process. The respective roles of faith and work in securing salvation continue to divide Christians. Whatever the relationship between one's deeds and attaining eternal life, some Christians will acknowledge the role of their faith in enabling them to make moral decisions, improving their personal integrity and empowering them to face life more confidently. The ethical dimension spans both the Church's teachings on ethical matters, as well as the effect one's faith has on one's life. Some Christians will sometimes make remarks like, 'I learned to manage my anger after I became a Christian', and not merely recognize that Jesus taught the importance of restraining one's anger (Mt. 5:22) and loving one's enemies as well as one's friends (Mt. 5:43-48).

Christianity's pragmatic dimension is probably the most neglected in academic literature. Religion can be used pragmatically, to achieve physical rather than spiritual benefits. It is not uncommon, for example, to install a Saint Christopher medallion in one's car, in the belief that this saint offers protection to travellers. Some believers aver that a brief prayer to Saint Anthony is effective in enabling them to locate lost property. Although Christians in the Protestant tradition are less likely to subscribe to the belief that patron saints can intercede on one's behalf, the notion that various saints have special jurisdiction over specific aspects of human affairs is acknowledged, at least to some degree, in most forms of Christianity. Even in Scotland, where the Protestant Reformation had far-reaching effects, Saint Andrew is revered as the country's patron saint. Other examples of the pragmatic role of religion might include the use of intercessory prayer to assist with worldly benefits; thus, a student might pray for success in an examination, and a congregation might typically pray for the needy, the sick and the suffering. Some Christians are familiar with the use of 'arrow prayers': according to some popular Christian teaching, an effective way of dealing with problems in life is to put up a quick extempore prayer when one is faced with a difficult or unexpected situation, such as encountering a bully or undergoing a job interview.

Another area of popular practice which serves no obvious spiritual or ethical purpose is the celebration of festivals such as Christmas and Easter. Despite the prevalent belief that religion in the USA and Britain is increasingly losing its hold on people, Gordon Heald, writing in the Roman Catholic journal *The Tablet* in 2001, presented the findings of a British survey on Christmas customs, in which it was claimed that only one per cent of the British population did not celebrate Christmas in any way. However much Christian clergy may preach against the secularization and commercialization of Christmas, one cannot deny that the festival is associated with the birth of Jesus Christ, and that few, if any, are ignorant of the fact. It would be incorrect to suggest that Santa Claus has nothing to do with Christianity: whatever the origins of the ever-popular figure, Saint Nicholas is a Christian saint (the patron saint of children), and the exchanging of presents at the festive season is associated with the Magi (or 'wise men') who brought their gifts of gold, frankincense and myrrh to the child Jesus.

It may be objected that Christmas trees, hot cross buns and Easter eggs have nothing to do with Christianity as a religion, but are folk practices rather than truly religious activities. Such an objection raises the question of what religion is—a concept that continues to be contested among scholars of religion. If one takes the view that religion is about belief in supernatural beings—a notion espoused a century ago by E. B. Tylor, and reinforced by phenomenologists such as Rudolf Otto and Mircea Eliade, who defined the essence of religion respectively as 'the numinous' and 'the sacred'—then plainly these popular activities would have no place in accounts of the Christian religion. (Who ever encountered God while eating a Christmas pudding?)

However, the view that religion is about finding the sacred is precisely the view that the present authors wish to question. If we were to concede that religion was about beliefs in supernatural beings and a quest to experience the 'numinous', then we would be thrown back into the traditional historical-theological account of Christianity, which we wish to reject. We would also have an unbalanced account of the Christian faith, which might suggest that all Christians held beliefs that could be clearly articulated, and that they had direct acquaintance with 'the sacred'. We would be limiting ourselves to what Ninian Smart calls the doctrinal and experiential dimensions of religion, when in fact he identifies seven: doctrinal, experiential, narrative ('mythological'), ethical, ritual, institutional ('social'), and 'material'. (The last of these relates to the way in which religions typically transform ordinary materials, such as brick or metal, or bread and wine, and transform them into special sacred objects or substances.) Arguably, there are additional 'dimensions' of religion; in a recent publication the present authors distinguish nine key components of religious institutions: origins, scriptures, predicament, worldviews, lifestyle, spiritual practice, societal issues, organizational structure and their ultimate goal (Chryssides and Wilkins 2006).

Although there is some reason to believe that religious experiences are more common than is often thought, such phenomena are only experienced by a minority of people. In a National Opinion Poll survey in 1976, 36 per cent of respondents gave an affirmative answer to the question, 'Have you ever felt as though you were very close to a powerful spiritual force that seemed to lift you out of yourself?' (Hay 1982: 124). While this may be unexpectedly high, it still leaves behind 64 per cent of the British population. Even if all the respondents were Christians, there would still remain a majority bereft of any such religious experience.

Similarly, if one defines Christianity in terms of its doctrines, a theological account of the Christian faith does not reflect the standpoint of the average believer. Even clergy have been known to express concern when they are obliged to preach a relevant sermon on Trinity Sunday, and the vast majority of Christians, if asked, would be able to explain what was meant by substantial sections of the Nicene Creed. Even one clergyman who is known to the authors expressed a total lack of recognition of the name Arius, despite his crucial role in causing Bishop Athanasius, the champion of 'orthodoxy', to formulate his doctrine of the person of Christ, which secured acceptance in the great Ecumenical Councils of the third and fourth centuries, and became enshrined in the Nicene Creed. Arius's name features in every book on early Christianity and early Christian doctrine that is known to the authors: no doubt Christianity would not be as it is without the influence of these early Christian leaders, yet these debates on Christ's nature are at a distance from Christianity as it is commonly known. Much as theology may form a substantial part of the clergy's training, and loom large in many ecumenical debates, Christian congregations have a singular lack of interest in the subject. Indeed, to accuse a preacher of delivering a sermon that is 'too theological' is quite a damning criticism.

In order to provide an account of Christianity as it is practised, it is necessary to abandon the notion that was presupposed in 'supernaturalist' definitions of religion, which seeks to identify a religion's essence in its belief in supernatural beings, and the idea that religion consists of the 'numinous' or the 'sacred'. As Smart has shown, religion is to be defined in more varied forms, and not merely the doctrinal and experiential, important though these are.

'Cultural Christians'

It may be asked whether the authors' concept of Christianity is not unduly wide. In suggesting that we should regard Christmas and Easter celebrations as part of Christianity, are we not dealing with folk customs rather than serious religion, or at best what some writers commonly refer to as 'cultural Christianity'? Several responses need to be made to this objection.

First, it would be wrong to suppose that all of Christianity is practised within the context of a church. Religions have a tendency to pervade all of life, and to regard Christianity as equivalent to 'Church Christianity' would result in a somewhat curtailed account of the Christian faith. Certainly, as has already been argued, few Christians would maintain that they can achieve salvation through celebrating the popular festivals, but we have already suggested that to confine religion to the salvific is to provide only a partial view. While many Christians might like to see a greater emphasis on Christianity's salvific power (the 'transcendental'), there are degrees of allegiance to any religion, and the different ways in which it is practised.

In the British census of 2001, some 71.6 per cent of the British population defined themselves as 'Christian'. This result surprised many, since on any one Sunday only about 4 per cent attend a service of worship. (Some other polls have arrived at an even higher proportion of those claiming a Christian identity: 73 per cent, according to Opinion Research Business, in the same year; Thomas 2003: 18). The shortfall between the 71.6 per cent and the 4 per cent cannot simply be dismissed on the grounds that the respondents were merely 'nominally Christian', 'fringe Christians', 'cultural Christians' or adherents to a 'folk religion'. Unlike the rest of the census form, there was no obligation for citizens to answer the religious question, and there was provision for respondents to define themselves in terms of another major religious tradition, an 'other religion', or as 'no religion'. So presumably they meant something by their self-description as 'Christian'.

In his book *Counting People In* (2003) Richard Thomas argues for a new approach to thinking about who belong to the Christian faith and who do not. Thomas contends that it is not simply 'participant' members who should be 'counted in' as adherents to the Christian faith, on the grounds that the Church has a 'servant' role to a community, who may draw on Christianity for a variety of purposes, spanning rites of passage, celebration of major festivals, education and social services. One might also add that Christianity has performed a major role in shaping culture, in a multiplicity of ways, encompassing law, custom, literature, art and architecture. Moreover, the Church's emphasis on attendance as the expression of commitment is not mirrored in other religious traditions. The notion of a holy day and congregational worship finds expression principally in the semitic (sometimes called 'Abrahamic') religions. In other traditions, such as Buddhism, Hinduism and Sikhism, there is no day of the week that is specially marked out for religious activity; there is less emphasis on congregational worship, and the precise mode of expression of devotion is left to individuals.

Second, it is difficult to draw a distinction between 'folk religion' and whatever one regards as its contrast. Instinctively, it might seem as if there is a contrast between the Christian monk who commits his life to devotional activity and the seemingly uncommitted layperson who puts up a Christmas tree once a year. However, various scholarly attempts to make such distinctions have invariably encountered insuperable problems. One such attempt was by Robert Redfield, who sought to distinguish between a 'great' and a 'little' tradition—a distinction that first appeared in his *Peasant Society and Culture* (1956). Redfield's thesis was that there was a distinction between religion in urban societies, which is presided over by accredited religious specialists, is centrally controlled, relies on sacred texts and practises officially prescribed rites in accordance with set liturgical procedures. By contrast, the 'little tradition' belongs to 'peasant populations', who are typically non-literate, geographically remote, and have pragmatic interests, which often differ from those people who are involved in urban life. Such interests include rituals relating to crops (planting, growing, harvesting), which are associated with the calendar year of solstices and equinoxes, as well as fending off evil—typically in the form of disease, famine, and the 'evil eye'. The countryside provides an environment in which the pre-existent indigenous religions can thrive, having trees, waterfalls, rivers, caves and so on, all of which provide locations for local shrines. Being more remote, Redfield argued, the practices of this rural tradition ('folk religion' or 'little tradition') were more likely to live on. Since these rural communities are geographically fairly isolated, they are not subject to any central controlling authority, and can therefore maintain their own practices without hindrance. These practices are not prescribed by any manual of liturgy, and the communities, being non-literate, simply act out, rather than think out their practices.

Redfield's distinction is no longer widely accepted, and its problems regarding the Christian tradition should be evident. The so-called 'folk practices' of erecting Christmas trees and giving presents are undertaken by the rural and the urban population alike, and, with few exceptions, both sectors of the population (at least in the West) are literate. In addition, the clergy are involved in the more spiritual and the more popular expressions of Christianity alike. The local vicar will quite often accompany local carol singers round the parish or distribute Easter eggs to worshippers on Easter morning. He or she will frequently baptize children or officiate at weddings where the parents or couples involved have no obvious church connection, and may have a variety of motives, not necessarily spiritual, in desiring these rites of passage. It is not unknown for clergy to bless new homes or religious paraphernalia such as Saint Christopher medallions. Although believers may seldom talk of ghosts and spectres, the present authors have personally encountered those who have reportedly experienced them in their local church. Should such entities prove troublesome, arrangements can be made for exorcism. Although this not a common rite, provision is typically made for it: each diocese in the Church of England has a member of clergy who is officially given the role of dealing with such matters.

Similar objections can be made to attempts to distinguish between 'orthodox' and 'popular' religion. Christianity has become enmeshed in all sorts of practices that have proved popular, but involve religious officialdom: the crowning of a May queen, a pilgrimage to Lourdes, the honouring of war heroes on Remembrance Day at a cenotaph. It is not straightforwardly the case that numerous Roman Catholic lay pilgrims seek healing at Lourdes, while their priesthood offers salvation through the Mass. The Lourdes shrine is both popular and official: not only does it attract large numbers of pilgrims, but Saint Bernadette's claims to have seen visions of the Virgin Mary in 1858 were officially accredited by the Roman Catholic Church, leading to her canonization in 1933. Clergy as well as laity visit her shrine. The memorabilia that are sold at Lourdes may vary in aesthetic quality, but they are simultaneously popular and official. The miracles that are alleged to take place at Lourdes are both popularly believed and officially endorsed. It is therefore not possible to say that Lourdes exists as a form of popular religion, in contrast to 'official' Catholicism, or that it is part of a 'folk religion' that rivals a mainstream tradition. Rather than assert the existence of two contrasting traditions ('great/little', 'orthodox/popular', 'folk/mainstream'), we believe it is preferable to identify different strands that intertwine within the same single religion, enabling its members to derive different benefits from it, such as the attainment of salvation, ethical guidance and pragmatic benefits such as healing or prosperity.

The Multifaceted Nature of Christianity

Rather than presupposing that there are two contrasting traditions within Christianity, in what follows, the authors treat Christianity as a single religion, but with a large variety of expressions. It is an enormously complex religion, yet, despite its many divisions, Christians frequently proclaim that it is one faith, and that there is 'one Church, one faith, one Lord' (that is, Jesus Christ, who is proclaimed as 'Lord'). There is no neat, simple way of explaining Christianity, and it would probably be unduly restricting to rely on one set of academic tools to unravel its complexity. A scheme such as Ninian Smart's 'dimensions' of religion would involve simultaneously treating Christianity's various strands under each single heading, while an approach that explored Christianity by sequentially exploring its three major traditions runs the risk of becoming the historical-theological type of account, which we are seeking to avoid.

Instead, the account we offer draws on three different ways of classifying religion: by tradition, by dimension, and by its functions (Weightman's 'complexes'). Any general book on Christianity must acknowledge its three major traditions: Roman Catholicism, Eastern Orthodoxy and Protestantism. All the traditions acknowledge their faith's 'narrative' dimension, drawing on the stories of the Hebrew scriptures, culminating in the Gospel accounts of Jesus of Nazareth. They draw substantially on the founder-leaders—Jesus of Nazareth and Paul of Tarsus—whose teachings are enshrined in Christian scriptures. The canon of Scripture forms an important dimension of the Christian faith, and will occupy a chapter in its own right, exploring its function as well as some of its content.

Christianity's narrative and scriptural dimensions raise questions about the historicity of its subject-matter. While seeking to avoid a historical approach to the subject matter, issues of the historicity of the Bible arose as products of the European Enlightenment. Clearly it would be unrealistic to provide substantial coverage of the recent 'Jesus debate', but some reference must be to it, since some of the literature has percolated down to a popular level, and issues relating to the different roles of myth and history continue to divide present-day Christians. Such issues form part of Christianity's doctrinal dimension—an aspect of the religion which can by no means be ignored, and which relates to key themes such as the professed oneness of the Church, and to its creeds. Christianity's ritual dimension assumes an importance, particularly in its sacraments—rites that are singled out as having special importance beyond regular prayer and worship.

In addition to the three ways of classifying religion mentioned above, Christianity is a religion which has given rise to much debate, and it is therefore important to make reference to a number of controversies that have arisen in recent times. Debates such as those between Darwinists and creationists continue to divide Christians, as does the related rift between fundamentalists and liberals. Issues such as the ordination of women and attitudes concerning sexual orientation and particularly gay clergy continue to cause controversy and to cause division. Whether Christianity should continue to pursue its role as a missionary religion, or whether it has a different mission in the present-day world is a further theme on which comment will be made. It is often said that contemporary Western society has succumbed to a process of secularization. Again, although it is not possible to explore in depth a topic on which numerous entire books have been written, it is important to comment on some of the important social processes that have been identified as impinging on the Christian faith. Allied to this topic is the issue, which has not yet been adequately explored, of how the majority of the British population, who describe themselves as Christian but do not substantially practise Christianity within the context of a church congregation, express their faith. The issue of how Christianity expresses itself outside of its congregational life is one which will be examined. Traditions, dimensions, 'complexes' and issues inextricably intertwine, and it is not possible to treat them discretely or sequentially. The authors intend to sacrifice academic tidiness in the interests of an inclusive account of the Christian faith, which examines Christian life as it is practised by present-day believers.

Insiders and Outsiders

Something should be said about the standpoint of the authors and the way in which the book came into being. There are differences of opinion among scholars on whether one's colours should show. The school of phenomenology recommended a focus on the 'phenomenon', whether this is to be construed as the sacred, or whether—as with Ninian Smart and James L. Cox—as the worldview and the people who espouse it. The postmodernist critics of phenomenology contend that it is not possible to identify an objective phenomenon that exists independently of an author's standpoint. Everything is 'coming from somewhere', and hence there are only perspectives, not objective phenomena. Writers should therefore 'come clean' and, rather than make a pretence of objectivity, identify the standpoint from which they write. Some evangelical Christians have maintained that the phenomenologist's neutrality is not so much impossible, but undesirable. One should not sit on the fence, maintaining methodological agnosticism, where important matters of truth, and indeed eternal salvation, are concerned.

These are large issues, and only brief rejoinders are possible here. In response to the postmodernist, it can be replied that the existence of authors' standpoints does not imply that all standpoints are equally valid, or equally interesting, nor does it imply that it is unnecessary for authors to compensate for standpoints that may make their writing unbalanced, prejudiced or inaccurate. If it is believed that any standpoint is equally valid, then this would negate the point of all academic study, since prejudice and ignorance would be just as valid standpoints as those of the experienced and conscientious researcher. The raw fresher would have as much right to claim expertise on Christianity as his or her tutors, who may have made the study of Christianity their lives' work.

Researchers have backgrounds, interests and no doubt prejudices that cause them to present their material in a certain way. In the case of the present authors, George Chryssides trained many years ago in a Protestant seminary, where emphasis was placed on the Protestant Reformation, the writings of Calvin, and subsequently the more radical Protestant scholars such as Rudolf Bultmann in biblical studies and Paul Tillich in systematic theology. Roman Catholicism was little mentioned, except by way of declaring it erroneous, and, as far as he recalls, Eastern Orthodoxy was never mentioned. Margaret Wilkins began her career with the study of classics, focusing on Christianity as an emergent religion within the Roman Empire. Her religious background is predominantly in the Church of England, although she attended Quaker meetings regularly for a year, and belonged to an Orthodox choir for some time. Both authors have had extended contact with the Unitarian Church. While it would be possible to write from these standpoints, unvarnished, doing so would hardly have produced a book that could claim to be balanced or inclusive.

Obviously there remain ways in which the researcher and the object of research remain inseparable. One cannot simply 'bracket one's assumptions' and view 'the phenomenon' with the eidetic vision that the phenomenologists recommended. It is not possible even to realize what all one's prejudices and biases are, let alone shake them off. Further, this book inevitably reflects the authors' own personal choices about what is important and interesting, and it reflects our own personal academic history, in that it is the totality of what the authors themselves encountered in the course of their researches. The material one reads and the informants one uses are always those that are available to the researcher. One's informants are invariably people who are known to the authors, and hence part of the authors' world, and subject to the authors' evaluation. In this sense any piece of writing is going to be the consequence of one's own personal history. It is always possible that one's research would have benefited by the appraisal of inaccessible believers or academics, or that a book may have ignored some important aspect of the subject matter, where this was unknown to the author. While authors have a duty of care to ensure that their material is researched as comprehensively as possible, omissions and biases are frequently matters of regret, rather than standpoints that should simply be identified.

By contrast to the postmodernist, there are certain Christians—indeed some of them are students—who hold that their own brand of Christianity is the only one that bears the truth. More often than not, such Christians belong to the Protestant evangelical tradition, which will be explored in a later chapter, although it has also been characteristic of Roman Catholic and Orthodox Christians to claim to belong to the one and only true Church. Whether such Christians are right is a theological judgement, which lies beyond the scope of this book. It is not the authors who will be presiding over the Last Judgement: maybe God will provide humankind with the answer at the end of time. In the meantime, however, the agenda for students who are pursuing the study of religion is to gain 'empathetic understanding', not to grade forms of religion in terms of their presumed proximity to the truth or their ability to offer true salvation. If students, tutors or textbook authors wish to evangelize, they have the right to propagate their beliefs and endeavour to persuade others, but this is not part of the academic study of religion, and must be done outside the context of the classroom, the essay and the textbook. There is an important sense in which students of religion are not interested in truth. Whether or not the study of Christianity's various forms assists one's personal quest for religious truth, academic study of this kind aims not at ascertaining who has 'got it right', but rather at achieving an understanding of the various traditions and denominations within Christianity.

It is not the authors' role even to determine what *is* a legitimate expression of Christianity. This is an issue that Christians themselves must decide, not academics or students of religion. Each religion has its own ways of setting its boundaries and determining who can be acknowledged to be within the tradition, who are outsiders, and who remain on the edges. In the case of Christianity, there are various national Councils of Churches, as well as the World Council of Churches, to which denominations can apply for membership, and who gain acceptance, or in some cases rejection. Such acknowledgement or lack of it serves as a litmus test to establish Christianity's boundaries. While our present study includes a chapter on Mormons, Jehovah's Witnesses, the Unification Church and others, this is to demonstrate Christianity's edges rather than its scope. We make no claims about whether or not they offer genuine salvation, but merely acknowledge that, at least at present, mainstream Christianity does not regard them as a legitimate part.

Making the Familiar Strange and the Strange Familiar

The students to whom the authors have taught Christianity have come from a variety of backgrounds. This book started life as teaching material for students in a multi-cultural multi-faith tradition at the University of Wolverhampton, England. Some students have been Christian, and familiar—perhaps overfamiliar—with their own brand of Christianity; others have been professed atheists and agnostics; others have been 'interested inquirers', either interested in widening their knowledge of religion, or else studying the varieties of Christianity as part of their own spiritual quest. Roughly a third of students belonged to some other faith altogether, usually Islam, Sikhism or Hinduism, and occasionally were Buddhists or Jains. Most of them were commencing their study of Christianity from scratch, and many had never been inside a church, let alone attended a Christian service of worship. For them, studying

Christianity was rather like the authors' own initial acquaintance with these other world religions—an endeavour to make the unknown known and the unfamiliar familiar. One of the authors inherited the module title 'Christianity as a world religion' from his predecessor, the implication being that this was a module that sought to expound Christianity in the same kind of way as one would teach Hinduism, Buddhism or Islam—that is, non-confessionally, assuming no prior knowledge, identifying and doing justice to its various major strands. This was not an easy task: suddenly one had to distance oneself from the religion with which one was overfamiliar, and try to see it through the eyes of those for whom it was unfamiliar. As the teaching of the module progressed, it became apparent that it was not simply Asian students who lacked familiarity with the Christian faith; there are white European students who claim never to have attended a church service, not even for a wedding for a funeral.

Distancing oneself from one's own tradition was greatly helped by the presence of students from other traditions. Having to give apparently simple pieces of briefing advice, such as knowing to expect the giving of the peace and the offertory at an Anglican Eucharist, what options the participant-observer had during the distribution of the sacrament, and when to stand, sit or kneel, all served to highlight what was unfamiliar to the outsider. Explaining how 'high' Anglicanism differed from Roman Catholicism was not an easy task, and raised questions of which tradition the Church of England really belonged to, when considering the Catholic-Protestant divide. Reactions from students also proved salutary: one of them found the worship very formal, lacking spontaneity and exuberance, while others said that the highlight of the entire module was receiving a blessing from the celebrant during the Eucharist. Others identified the strong creedal emphasis in Christianity, which appeared to emphasize right belief rather than guidance for living.

The principle of making the strange familiar and the familiar strange is frequently invoked by ethnographers, but also applies to the study of religions. The sheer complexity of Christianity can create bewilderment to those who start out from the standpoint of unfamiliarity. For example, over and above denominational labels such as 'Methodist', 'Baptist' and 'United Reformed', Christians use terms like 'evangelical', 'fundamentalist' and 'charismatic'. The latter are unofficial terms, frequently used to describe the ethos of congregations and can span a variety of denominations (usually, but not always, Protestant), although, confusingly, there are minor denominations that include these names, for example, the Evangelical Church (an American Wesleyan denomination), the Charismatic Episcopal Church, and—outside the mainstream—the Fundamentalist Church of Jesus Christ of Latter Day Saints. Seemingly minute points of nomenclature can often cause problems, even offence, for the unwary. For example, what is the difference between a church and a chapel? Should a congregation's leader be referred to as a priest, a vicar, a minister or a pastor? Should the sacrament be referred to as the Mass, the Eucharist or Holy Communion? Is the central table an altar, or should one call it a communion table? Making such distinctions is not academic pedantry. All these terms carry much historical and theological baggage, and one can genuinely cause offence by using them inappropriately. (If readers doubt this, let them try suggesting to the Revd Ian Paisley that he is a priest who celebrates the Mass!)

Whether the 'insider' or the 'outsider' understands a religion better is an issue that aroused considerable discussion among academics. Without entering into the complexity of this debate, it can be noted that there are advantages and disadvantages in both standpoints. Outsiders can lack empathy: it is not immediately obvious why Christians should want to participate in a 'meal'—which hardly resembles a conventional meal—in which the officiant claims that they are eating and drinking the body and blood of their saviour. Lack of empathy is therefore associated with a further problem: a possible failure to grasp the meaning of events and practices, rather than simply their spatio-temporal aspects. The student who once introduced her account of a field visit to a Roman Catholic Mass by writing, 'A man in a pink robe walked up to the front', was not bringing out anything distinctively religious in her field notes: this could equally have been an account of a Christmas pantomime!

A further problem for the outsider (which may occasionally also be shared by insiders) is the temptation to pass off simplistic accounts of the religion as the definitive ones. The authors have frequently encountered student portrayals of Christian belief in an afterlife, which read, 'Christians expect to go to heaven when they die.' Such a description is flawed on at least two counts. First, it is—bluntly—a somewhat infantile description of life after death, rather reminiscent of the infants' hymn, the last lines of which run:

> Take me when I die to heaven,
> Happy there with thee to dwell.

The word 'heaven' in isolation is seldom used in the Church's liturgy, or even in the vocabulary of rank-and-file believers. Much more favoured are terms like 'eternal life', 'the world to come', the communion of saints, the kingdom of God, the kingdom of heaven, or the (general) resurrection. Second, Christianity admits a variety of beliefs about life after death. Some Christians may believe that eternal life is a kind of family reunion in a spiritual realm, where the faithful will be immediately recognizable to each other; others might hold that there is a soul that is distinct from the body, and is the eternal aspect of the self that survives the destruction of the physical body. Others again may question whether eternity is simply an infinite continuity of time, following the end of one's time on earth. There are also Christians who question whether one can expect any after-life state, arguing that eternal life is something here and now. After all, Jesus said, 'The kingdom of God has come upon you' (Mt. 12:18), as if it had already happened. Just as one should not attribute naivety to the believer, equally one should avoid attributing undue theological sophistication to the average Christian. There are many Christians who simply do not know what, if anything, to expect after death, and focus on living their present life with faith and hope. Any student who writes, 'Christians believe that...' has probably failed to grasp the complexity of the faith.

If the student is an 'insider', he or she already has a start in understanding the Christian religion. However, a number of 'insider' problems are worth noting. Insiders can be tempted to assume that their own faith is the normative, or even the only version of Christianity. One has to allow, not only for the existence of other forms of the Christian faith, but to treat them in as impartial and objective a way as possible. The authors have come across several writers in the Protestant evangelical tradition who view Roman Catholicism as a modern-day 'heresy'. While students may have their own personal views about where religious truth lies, and while there are different ideas on what counts as an 'authentic' form of a religion, it is a requirement of belonging to the World Council of Churches that its members recognize the authenticity of each other. It is only where it is apparent to the majority of mainstream Christians that a movement is outside the mainstream that scholars and students of religion are entitled to regard it as such. (A number of such examples will be considered in chapter 17.)

A further hazard of 'insiders' can be thinking that they understand the Christian faith in greater depth than they actually do. When teaching classes on Christianity that have prerequisites attached to them, the authors have occasionally encountered students who want such prerequisites to be waived, on the grounds that they are Sunday School teachers

19

or even pastors. No doubt such potential students are doing an excellent job, and of course there are instances where alternative entry qualifications are permissible, even welcome. However, the evangelical Christian's maxim, 'You only need to know the Lord', is one that applies to gaining salvation, not to gaining academic qualifications. The two are different: just as a student who simply has faith may not necessarily have academic expertise, likewise the scholar is not necessarily someone who can be sure of salvation. Indeed, there are some Christians that would hold that academic study can be a serious impediment to one's faith, since it can inculcate doubt, and since Jesus said that God had 'hidden these things from the wise and learned, and revealed them to little children' (Mt. 11:25). Jesus was no doubt making a statement about having faith, rather than about academic study, but if anyone were to suppose the latter, this would be an argument against the academic study of religion, rather than an argument that the possession of faith is sufficient for scholarly understanding.

Classifying Christian Organizations

We have noted Christianity's variety of forms, and the need to acknowledge and understand them. As a prelude to doing so, a number of tools exist to help the student. One such instrument is the creation of typologies, whose function is to organize complex subject matter into more manageable proportions. However, even the usual sociological typologies of religious organizations do not appear to apply uncontroversially to Christian organizations. Max Weber proposed the model of 'church' contrasting with 'sect', contending that the former designated the dominant religion (Christianity in the Germany of Weber's era), into which the majority of citizens are born, which supports societal values, and to which belonging is the normal expectation. By contrast, the 'sect' deviates from the more conventional religious and societal values, and membership is typically by choice (or 'conversion') rather than by upbringing. Much discussion has been given to Weber's church/sect typology, and the authors have discussed this elsewhere (Chryssides and Geaves 2007: 135-37). For the purposes of the present study, we propose to use the following scheme: Church, tradition, denomination, sect, cult and new religious movement (NRM).

The concept of 'Church' will be developed in a separate chapter. In brief, we use the term to refer to the entirety of Christendom worldwide. 'Tradition' denotes the three major strands within Christendom:

Roman Catholicism—Eastern Orthodoxy and Protestantism—which have already been mentioned. The word 'denomination' denotes sub-categories of the major traditions, for example Baptists, Church of Scotland, Congregational, and United Reformed within Protestantism, and organizations like the Ukrainian Catholic Church within Roman Catholicism. The term 'sect' is little used in this volume, and where it appears it is mainly used adjectivally ('sectarian'), denoting Christian groups that have either consciously broken away from the mainstream or attempted to claim a special uniqueness that allegedly makes them the sole custodians of truth or salvation. Examples of sects in this sense might be the Jehovah's Witnesses and the Unification Church (popularly known as the 'Moonies'). The term 'new religious movement' has a wider application than 'sect': the NRM has not necessarily originated through splintering off from mainstream Christianity, but can derive from other traditions; for example, the International Society for Krishna Consciousness (ISKCON) is Hindu-derived. The use of the term 'NRM' is contested among sociologists and scholars of religion, and we have discussed its application elsewhere (Chryssides and Wilkins 2006); in brief, we take it to denote those organizations which have been set up within roughly the last two centuries, which possess the salient features associated with religion, and which lie outside mainstream religion. The word 'cult' is not used as synonymous with 'NRM', contrary to popular and media usage, but denotes a loosely organized movement with a central focus. Thus one might speak of the 'cult of the Virgin Mary' or a cult of venerating relics: devotion to Mary spans a number of Christian traditions—Roman Catholicism, Eastern Orthodoxy, some forms of Anglicanism—and paying homage to Mary can take a variety of forms, spanning incorporation into formal Christian liturgy, an interest in visionary apparitions, roadside shrines and pilgrimage centres such as Lourdes and Nock.

This typology may seem reasonably straightforward, but it runs into problems when the terms are employed by certain Christians. Roman Catholicism, for example, has traditionally rejected being classed as a denomination, or even one tradition among several, claiming, as it does, to be the one and only true Church. (A similar claim is sometimes made within Eastern Orthodoxy.) The Anglican Church does not fit comfortably into the tradition-denomination distinction. Is it a form of Protestantism, or does it lie outside the Protestant tradition? It claims to be 'catholic and reformed'—a description that will be discussed in a later chapter—but it is certainly not part of Roman Catholicism. Typologies invariably have their problems, but even when there are problem cases—as with the examples mentioned here—the typology usefully serves to highlight the controversial issues that arise in such instances.

Methodology

Issues regarding the collection of data are paramount in the study of the religion. The subject employs a variety of methods of data collection, including primary and secondary written source material (including Internet and other electronic sources), field work (observation and participant-observation) survey work (including interviews and questionnaires). Normally a researcher begins by defining a set of aims and then ascertaining which research tools are appropriate in order to achieve them. Unlike more narrowly focused research projects, however, this book is the culmination of the authors' lifetime acquaintance with the Christian religion, with much of the information already gathered through reading, and personal acquaintance with its multiplicity of forms. The authors' stance combines having belonged to the Christian faith in various locations, and having visited various denominations for a variety of reasons—professional, ecumenical, social and at times out of sheer curiosity. Working with students has involved accompanying them on field visits to various branches of the Christian Church.

We have resisted the tendency to collect data systematically through interviews and questionnaires. Apart from being inordinately time-consuming, working with human participants generally involves specific and narrow foci, running contrary to the authors' intention of producing a survey of Christianity that is as broad as possible. Although the book seeks to examine what Christians actually do, rather than what the extant literature says they do, it is doubtful whether the former can be determined by formal survey work. In any case, the book's aim is not to elicit opinion, but to present a factual account of a variety of forms of Christianity.

The sheer size and complexity of Christianity makes it difficult to handle within the covers of a single volume, and this book cannot claim to be anything remotely approaching a comprehensive account. Christianity is the religion of approximately one third of the world's population, having around 2.1 billion adherents at the turn of the twenty-first century. It is estimated that there are some 34,000 denominations worldwide, plus a further 194.4 million individuals who remain unaffiliated to any institutional form of the religion (Avis, in Bowden 2005: 229;

Johnson and Mandryk 2001). Obviously, exact statistics depend on which organizations one counts as examples of Christianity, but the figure is not greatly affected if one subtracts Latter-day Saints (Mormons), Jehovah's Witnesses, Unitarians, Nestorians, Christian Scientists, and other groups that lie on Christianity's edges. These staggering statistics create obvious problems for compiling a single book. In deciding which organizations to cover, the authors have used the two criteria of size and significance. We have given coverage to examples of all three major traditions, perhaps with slightly more extended treatment of Protestant groups, since the major ones are more diverse than Roman Catholic and Orthodox ones. Where smaller groups are featured, they have been included either because of interest they have aroused, or because they help to shed light on the wider phenomenon of Christianity or issues that have affected it. For example, the Amish probably account for little more than 100,000 of Christianity's 2.1 billion followers—a minuscule proportion—yet they are well known, and highlight some of the issues relating to religion and modernity.

We do not pretend to have resolved all the methodological issues relating to the present study—typologies, research tools, approaches, standpoints. Methodology is a current preoccupation in the study of religion, and at times appears to be discussed as if it were an end in itself. The ultimate purpose of methodology is to provide the scholar with the tools of the trade, and tools exist, not for their own sake, but to get work done. Having discussed some of the tools that the study of Christianity involves, we now move on to utilizing them in the study of the varieties and complexities of the Christian faith.

2

Christianity's Many Faces

An outsider looking at Christianity for the first time might well be bewildered by its many varieties. The Roman Catholic priest, in fine vestments, presides over the Mass, follows a very formal set liturgy, in which he (never she) pronounces that a communion wafer and a cup of wine have truly become the body and blood of Christ. At a Quaker meeting, the assembled people sit for an hour in complete silence, occasionally interrupted by an attendee who feels moved by the Spirit to give a brief message to the gathering. The Salvation Army come to worship at a 'corps' or a 'citadel' in quasi-military uniform, and have brass bands, which play regularly to the public. At a Pentecostalist meeting, there are no professional clergy, and worship leaders do not wear special religious attire; most of the worship is spontaneous, with Bible readings, testimonies, a sermon, and prayer that builds up in intensity, often culminating in members 'speaking in tongues'. Meanwhile, in the Church of Scotland, the minister (who is definitely not to be called a priest) dons black robes, ascends a pulpit, from which he or she conducts a service that includes prayers, Bible readings and a sermon, interspersed with hymns. What, if anything, do these different forms of religion have in common? Indeed, should we really consider them to be one single religion at all, rather than several?

Despite the enormous varieties of Christianity, one obvious common factor is that all of them would claim to have their origins in Jesus of Nazareth, to whom Christians accord the title 'Christ'. The title derives from the Greek word *christos*, meaning 'anointed', and used to translate the Hebrew word *mashiach*, or 'messiah'. In basing their faith on Jesus Christ, Christians claim that he is more than a historical figure, who taught in first-century Palestine. To claim that he is the messiah designates him as God's chosen one, sent to save his people. If asked to summarize his or her faith in a single sentence, most—if not all—Christians would be happy to subscribe to Paul's statement, 'Christ died for our sins' (1 Cor. 15:3). In all the many forms of the religion, it would be rare to find a Christian who was not familiar with the broad outline of the Christian story, and who would summarize it by something like the following.

God made humanity the culmination point of the world's creation. Adam and Eve, the primordial man and woman, were placed in the Garden of Eden, in a state of perfection, and invited to eat all of the fruit of the garden, apart from one tree—the tree of the knowledge of good and evil. Adam and Eve disobeyed God by eating the forbidden fruit, and were expelled from the garden, never to return. Their descendents, the Israelites, wandered in the desert in search of a new promised land, under the leadership of Moses, who received God's law—including the Ten Commandments—at Mount Sinai. The Jewish people persisted in disregarding the law, and various prophets were sent to urge them to mend their ways, which they failed to do. Finally, God sent his only son, Jesus Christ, to be more than a prophet, but a saviour, who would redeem the world from sin.

The distinctive part of the Christian story describes Jesus' birth as miraculous. His mother Mary was a virgin when she became pregnant, and Jesus' birth in a stable in Bethlehem was heralded by angels appearing to nearby shepherds, and by a bright star, which guided kings from the orient to find the infant Jesus. Jesus was brought up in Nazareth, his parents' home town, where his father worked as a carpenter. At around the age of 30 he began a ministry of preaching and miracle working (especially healing), in Galilee and in Jerusalem, aided by twelve disciples whom he chose. His teaching proved controversial with the Jewish authorities of his time, and he was particularly opposed by the Pharisees, who are portrayed as legalists, concerned with the precise letter of the Mosaic Law, but having lost its true spirit of love and compassion. After celebrating a final meal in an upper room with his disciples, he went out into the Garden of Gethsemane, where he was arrested, having been betrayed by Judas Iscariot, one of the twelve. He stood trial by Pontius Pilate, the Roman governor, and was condemned to death by crucifixion.

For the Christian, however, Jesus' death was not the end. The Christian story maintains that Jesus was buried in a garden tomb, but rose again from the dead some three days later. After making various appearances to his disciples, he ascended into heaven after 40 days. Having promised to send the Holy Spirit to his disciples, they met together in the upper room on the Jewish Day of Pentecost, and experienced the descent of the Holy Spirit, who enabled them to speak boldly in public, proclaiming Jesus Christ as saviour and Lord. The Pentecost experience is held to mark the birth of the Christian Church, which proclaimed Jesus as more than an itinerant rabbi who was sentenced to death: Jesus' death was a sacrificial one, in which he paid the price for the world's sin, and secured salvation for humanity.

The final part of the Christian story is still awaited. At Jesus' ascension, two men dressed in white appear, and announce that Jesus will return 'in the same way you have seen him go into heaven' (Acts 1:11). There is an expectation, therefore, that Jesus will return on the clouds, taking his faithful servants up into heaven, bringing an end to human history, with a final judgement of the living and dead, which will result in an eternal separation of the righteous and the wicked with the righteous living and reigning with Christ, while the wicked are consigned eternally to the fires of hell.

This is the fundamental Christian story, and most, if not all, Christians would recognize the summary above as their own religion's story. However, it cannot straightforwardly be presented as an account of what all Christians believe—for several reasons. While Christian fundamentalists would believe these details literally (or something very like them), there can be disagreements about some points of detail. In particular, there is disagreement about end-time events—for example, whether Christ will return before or after Armageddon (the final battle between Christ and Satan), or whether the 'rapture' (Christ's seizing of his followers to meet him in the air) precedes or follows a 'great tribulation' that those who remain on earth will experience.

Fundamentalism is only one school of thought within Christianity. Other Christians—particularly scholars within the Protestant tradition—regard many of the details of the story as 'myth' rather than history. By using the word 'myth' they do not mean that the stories are worthless, but rather that their importance lies not in their claim to report incidents relating to Jesus' life that they find hard to believe, but in their spiritual meaning. For example, they might argue that there is little point in one's being told that Jesus turned water into wine (Jn 2:1-11): Jesus' followers can perform no such amazing feats today, and hence at a literal level the story lacks significance. What is more important, arguably, is the meaning of the story—for example, that Jesus transforms the Jewish law into the newness of the gospel. It is worth noting that the author of John's Gospel never uses the word *dunamis* ('power' or 'miracle'), like the other three Gospel writers, but instead employs the word *semeion* ('sign'). For

John, the wondrous deeds attributed to Jesus are to be understood as signs of something beyond their physical manifestations.

Relatively few Christians, of course, are familiar with the range and complexity of contemporary scholarship in Christianity, and most are relatively unaware of the scholarly literature in theology and biblical studies. The question of popular belief among Christians has been somewhat under-researched in academic circles. One recent non-academic, but nonetheless significant, study was conducted in the USA by the Barna Group. This organization carries out primary research relating to present-day Christian ministry. In December 2007 the group conducted a survey of 1,005 subjects, selected at random. With regard to ten Bible stories, they were asked whether 'they trusted those stories to be factually accurate' or whether they were 'narratives that were not factually accurate but were designed to teach principles'. It should be remembered that the interview was conducted with the public at large, rather than Christians in particular; hence a slightly higher proportion of Christians would believe the stories to be true. The proportion of the US population who are Christian is reckoned to be 84.5 per cent, although it is likely that other sectors of the population might also accept the literal veracity of the stories. However, the poll provides at least a rough indication of where Christians might stand on such matters. The stories, and the per centage that agreed that they were 'factually accurate', are as follows.

Jesus physically rose from the dead	75%
Jesus was born of Mary, who was a virgin	75%
Jesus turned water into wine at a wedding at Cana	69%
Jesus fed 5,000 people with five loaves and two fish	68%
Noah built an ark which saved his family and animals from	
a great flood	64%
The devil tempted Eve in the Garden of Eden	56%
Samson lost his phenomenal strength by having his hair shorn	49%
Daniel was miraculously unharmed in the den of lions	65%
Moses parted the Red Sea, letting the Israelites across	64%
Peter walked on the water with Jesus	60%
The world was created in six days	60%

(Barna Group 2007)

The full set of statistical information is unpublished. However, the Barna Group claims that 'born again' Christians are 40 per cent more likely to believe these stories than non-Christians, and that Republicans are 26 per cent more likely to believe them than Democrats. Black Christians are significantly more likely to believe them that the white or Hispanic population, and the more educated, and those on higher earnings are less likely to entertain them literally.

It is significant, of course, that the key events that are enshrined in Christianity's creeds (Christ's resurrection and the virgin birth) receive the highest acceptance. (Some 83 per cent of mainline Protestants claimed to accept the resurrection story, as compared with 95 per cent non-mainline Protestants, and 82 per cent Roman Catholics.) The Barna Group fails to comment that the US population seems to find it easier to accept New Testament incidents than Old Testament ones. The single exception is Peter walking on the water: the report does not say how the question was phrased, but respondents may have recalled that Peter was unsuccessful in this endeavour, and that Jesus had to rescue him (Mt. 14:30). It is also possible that respondents had problems with the word 'day' in the example of the six-day creation: there is disagreement among Christians as to whether six days means six literal periods of twenty-four hours, particularly since the sun, whose relation to the earth defines the earth's day, was not created until the fourth day (Gen. 1:14-19).

The Barna Survey, of course, only relates to the USA, which is predominantly Christian, and most evident in its Protestant variety. It would therefore be wrong to assume that its findings necessarily applied to other countries, where knowledge of the Bible's contents might not be as strong. Yet, however much one wants to question the data, several fairly definite conclusions can be drawn. First, it is evident that most Christians are more prone to accept a conservative form of the Christian story, believing it literally rather than in its mythological or symbolic meaning. Second, the Bible story forms part of the 'rhetorical' version of Christianity. In other words, it is the form that is typically preached from the Church's pulpits, where the preacher usually expounds the Bible as if it were literally true, and without calling into question the historical veracity of the Bible story, even though his or her training frequently involves examining historical-critical issues relating to Scripture. At a Greek Orthodox Eucharist, it is quite common for the priest to deliver a short homily, in which he does little more than simply re-tell the story of the Bible passage that has been read moments before. Although it may seem initially surprising that preachers appear to shed their scholarship as soon as they enter a pulpit, it should be remembered that the function of preaching is not to provide a history or a theology lesson to the congregation, but to draw on Scripture's power as 'myth'. The Christian message goes beyond any literal history that the Bible may contain, providing spiritual meaning, offering guidance for living, and—more importantly—the path to salvation.

The Festival Calendar

The Christian story is not simply a story to be believed or interpreted. The Church's festival year enables Christians to participate actively in the story, as if it were occurring in their own lifetime. They believe it is important to appropriate this story, and to make it their own. With the exception of the Quakers, whose silent worship precludes any preconceived intention to celebrate specific festivals, all Christians celebrate the major festivals of Christmas, Easter and Pentecost. Protestantism is less likely to acknowledge other festivals, partly because its worship is less rule-governed, and partly because of its aversion to venerating saints and the Virgin Mary, the reasons for which will be explored in a subsequent chapter. Protestants will certainly celebrate Palm Sunday, give some acknowledgement to Advent, and possibly—at their discretion—mark Trinity Sunday.

Advent, Christmas and Epiphany

The Church's liturgical year begins in Advent, not, as one might expect, with Christmas or with the calendrical new year. Advent begins on the fourth Sunday before Christmas. For most Christians it is a period of anticipation, heralding the birth of Christ. In many churches—even in the Protestant tradition, despite its typical aversion to candles—four 'advent candles' are placed in the chancel, with a central candle for Christmas. Three of them are normally purple—the liturgical colour for the season—and are progressively lit for each Sunday of the Advent period. The fourth candle is typically blue, and is lit on the fourth Sunday, which commemorates the Virgin Mary and her role in Christ's incarnation. The final candle is lit on Christmas Day, completing the display. Although most Christians tend to associate Advent with the run-up to Christmas, Advent reminds the Church of Christ's second advent—his return to earth to wind up human history, to judge the world, and to take his followers to their eternal abode. Most of the hymns and Bible passages that are read during the Advent season tend to take up this theme, rather than the stories that tell of Christ's first coming.

Christmas, of course, together with Easter, is a high point in the Christian calendar, marking Christ's incarnation. Christianity teaches that the birth of Jesus marked the entering of God into human history, assuming human form, to begin his redemptive work to expiate sin. Many people who do not normally frequent churches like to participate in the many carol services that are held in Western countries. Particularly popular are 'Midnight Masses', which typically begin in the closing hours of Christmas Eve, and bring in the new Christmas Day. The popular carol 'O come, all ye faithful' is usually sung without its final verse, when used at carol services before Christmas, allowing the congregation to affirm at the opening hours of Christmas morning:

> Yea, Lord, we greet thee,
> Born this happy morning,
> Jesus, to thee be glory given.
> Son of the Father,
> Now in flesh appearing,
> O come let us adore him,
> Christ the Lord.

One particular Christmas service merits brief comment: the Christingle Service, which has increased in popularity in recent times in the West. The service was devised by a Pastor John, of the Moravian Church in Germany, in 1747. Pastor John wanted to find a symbol to explain Christ's love to children. As he sat in front of his fire, he came on the idea of giving each child a candle, wrapped in a red ribbon, with the prayer, 'Lord Jesus, kindle a flame in these dear children's hearts.' The idea was taken up many years later by John Pensom of The Children's Society who introduced it to Anglican churches in 1968. The service consists of carols, readings and prayers, and culminates with each member of the congregation being given an orange, into which a candle with a red ribbon has been inserted, together with sweets and small pieces of fruit (often raisins and dolly mixtures) on four cocktail sticks. The orange represents the world, the red ribbon signifies Christ's blood, the four sweets and fruits mark the earth's four seasons, and the candle represents Jesus Christ, who is the light of world. Towards the end of the service, the candles are lit, and the church lights dimmed, and the congregation stands in a circle around the chancel, singing carols. The popularity of Christingle has caused it to be celebrated in other Christian traditions, not merely within Anglicanism.

The Bible gives no indication about the time of year at which Jesus was born, and many Christians realise that 25 December may not have been the precise date of Jesus' birth. The Christmas carol mentioning that

> Snow had fallen,
> snow on snow...
> In the bleak mid-winter
> Long ago

is a figment of the imagination of those Christians who live in colder climates and experience Christmas themselves in this way. There is no indication that Christmas was celebrated in the early Church, and there are various theories concerning the assignation of the December date to it. One theory is that 25 December was the date of the winter solstice in the Julian calendar. A slightly more sophisticated theory is that the date was set to coincide with the festival of Sol Invictus—'the unconquered sun', denoting the Roman sun god—which was held on that date. Christianity was therefore deliberately rivalling Roman 'pagan' religion by offering an alternative festival. This date is observed by all except the Armenian Church, who continue to celebrate Christmas on 6 January.

The festival that almost immediately follows Christmas is Epiphany. Epiphany was originally associated with Christ's baptism, with which it is still associated in the Eastern churches. From the fourth century onwards in the West, it has marked the visit of the Magi ('wise men') to the infant Jesus. Epiphany is the 'manifestation of Christ to the Gentiles': the word is derived from the Greek word *epiphaneia*, meaning 'to show forth'. The Bible records that they came from the East, and—although there were diaspora Jews living in foreign lands—we are to understand that they were Gentiles, not Jews. They are not described as kings in the Bible: more likely we are to think of them as astrologers, since they appear to have studied the stars as portents of significant events on earth. The early church father Tertullian (c. 160–c. 225) described them as *fere reges*—'almost kings'—and Origen (c. 185–c. 254) affirmed that there were three of them. Their number is not stated in the Bible, but it probably assumed that there were three, because three gifts are mentioned: gold, frankincense and myrrh. These gifts have symbolic significance: gold to indicate kingship, frankincense priesthood, and myrrh death. The story serves to indicate that Christ's kingship and priestly sacrifice are for all of humanity, and not merely for God's chosen people, the Jews.

Lent and Easter

The next major festival, Easter, is heralded by the six-week period of Lent. Lent commemorates the 40-day period in which, as the Gospel writers claim, Jesus was in the desert, and underwent temptation by the devil before embarking on his ministry. (In reality, Lent lasts for 46 days, not 40; 40 is the number of weekdays in the period.) Since Easter Day is invariably a Sunday, the beginning of Lent is always a Wednesday—'Ash Wednesday'. The preceding day, Shrove Tuesday, is so-called because of the ancient practice of 'shriving'—confessing one's sins to a priest and being granted absolution (assurance of forgiveness). Few Christians are aware of this association, and in Britain, Ireland and Australia Shrove Tuesday is celebrated with the secular 'pancake day' celebrations. (See chapter 16.)

Ash Wednesday marks the beginning of Lent, and the name relates to the Roman Catholic Church's practice of placing ash on the heads of worshippers, as a sign of penitence. The donning of 'sackcloth and ashes' was a symbol of repentance in ancient Hebrew society (Dan. 9:3). Lent is traditionally a time of fasting in Roman Catholicism and Eastern Orthodoxy, a reminder that Jesus is said to have fasted in the desert during his 40-day temptation. Fasting also serves to demonstrate that believers are able to control their bodies, and are not simply the servants of their appetites and desires. Fasting is also believed to bring the practitioner closer to God, whose spiritual nature makes him independent of fleshly desires; to fast is therefore to become more God-like. Protestants, by contrast, often regard fasting as a mere external observance, asserting that salvation can only be gained through faith, not through works or physical manifestations of penitence.

Lenten fasting does not entail going without food altogether. Traditionally, it has entailed the avoidance of meat and alcohol, and the substitution of fish or a vegetarian diet on fast days. Apart from Christian vegetarians, who will avoid fish as well as meat at all times, most Christians are not as stringent in their spiritual practice. More realistically they will give up some small luxury during Lent—perhaps alcohol, or chocolate, or tobacco (if they smoke)—as a form of self-discipline, and as an encouragement to themselves to give up some practice that is potentially harmful. Some Christians view Lent as a time when they can discipline themselves positively to take up some good practice, rather than give up a reprehensible one.

The final week of Lent, which leads on to Easter, is known as Holy Week. Many churches will organize additional services during this week, often one each day, in which the story of Christ's passion is progressively recounted. The week begins with Palm Sunday, commemorating the day in which Jesus is believed to have rode into Jerusalem on a donkey, hailed by the crowds as the coming king. The use of a donkey rather than a horse—the normal steed of a conquering hero—was to indicate that Jesus came in peace rather than as a military conqueror: a title frequently ascribed to Jesus is the 'prince of peace' (Isa. 9:6). Many churches mark the occasion by having a 'procession of palms', in which clergy bless palm branches or crosses made out of palm leaves, and distribute them to the congregation, who ceremonially process around the church's premises, to re-enact Jesus' triumphant entry into Jerusalem, holding the palms as a symbol of victory of Satan, which also serves to recapitulate the theme of Jesus' overcoming Satan's temptation in this period. In Jerusalem, the tradition of holding a Palm Sunday procession goes back at least to the fourth century: pilgrims assemble at Bethany, above the Mount of Olives and high above the city, and process down to the Old City below—a journey of about a mile. Many churches burn the palms after the Palm Sunday celebrations, and the ash is used on Ash Wednesday the following year.

The Sunday preceding Palm Sunday has traditionally been named 'Passion Sunday', although Christ's 'passion' has traditionally been defined as a single week leading up to his crucifixion. In 1970, the Roman Catholic Church transferred this name to Palm Sunday, designating the day as 'Palm Sunday of the Lord's Passion'. The juxtaposition of the two labels serves to highlight the two seemingly conflicting themes associated with the festival. On the one hand, it is triumphant celebration, celebrating Christ's conquest and kingship, but on the other hand it anticipates the bitter events of the coming week. At a human level, Jesus' victory was short-lived.

Palm Sunday procession at St Michael the Archangel, Rushall, England.
Photograph: Mark Duffus

The four Gospels attribute a rather large number of events to the last week of Jesus' life. Scholars typically refer to these sections of the Gospels as the 'passion narrative', noting that the Gospel writers, understandably, attach particular importance to Jesus' death. Whether it was possible for so many incidents in Jesus' life to have taken place in such a short time is debateable, but most Christians accept their accounts, and many churches will use Holy Week as an opportunity to reflect on some of the stories, which are read and which form the subject-matter of homilies. Two days are particularly significant in Holy Week: Maundy Thursday and Good Friday.

Maundy Thursday marks the occasion when Jesus brought his disciples to an 'upper room' in Jerusalem to celebrate the Jewish Passover. The Bible records that, on arrival, none of the disciples volunteered for the customary practice of washing the guests' feet, whereupon Jesus himself took a towel and a bowl of water, assuming a servant's role, and performed this task on everyone's behalf. The incident highlights Jesus' role as 'servant', rather than the kingly role he assumed at the triumphal entry. Christians regard Jesus as God's servant, mentioned in Isaiah's prophecy (Isa. 42:1-7; 49:1-6; 50:49; 52:13–53:12), fulfilling God's will on behalf of humankind. Some churches re-enact the event with the celebrant washing the feet of members of the congregation (sometimes a representative twelve members are selected, representing the twelve disciples). The name 'Maundy Thursday' derives from the first antiphon (*mandatum novum*) of the foot-washing ceremony, as celebrated in the ancient Church.

The Gospel story recounts that, after the foot-washing, Jesus and his disciples celebrated their last meal together. Whether or not this was the Passover meal, a *kiddush* (a Jewish thanksgiving), or simply an ordinary meal before Passover time, has been much debated among biblical scholars, with no agreed conclusion. However, Christians appropriate the Passover theme, and Jesus Christ is typically referred to as the 'lamb of God'—an allusion to Jn 1:29, where John the Baptist (sometimes called John the Baptizer) gives him this title. The Eucharist, which is typically celebrated as part of the Maundy Thursday, is part of the re-enactment of the Last Supper, at which Jesus distributed bread and wine with the instruction, 'Do this in remembrance of me' (1 Cor. 11:23). In some churches, a small garden scene is displayed beneath the altar, signifying the Garden of Gethsemane. According to the Gospel story, Jesus led his disciples to this garden, on the border of Jerusalem, and asked Peter, James and John, his three closest disciples, to keep a watch with him while he prayed (Mk 14:32). These disciples were unable to keep their watch, and Jesus returned to find them asleep. This incident immediately preceded his arrest in the garden, when an armed mob entered, having been sent by the Jewish authorities. Members of the congregation are invited to recapitulate the disciples' failed vigil, by sitting in silence in front of the altar, in an attempt to demonstrate that they are able to carry out Jesus' instruction to the disciples, 'Watch and pray' (Mk 14:38).

Good Friday, the day that follows, is a solemn occasion, since it commemorates Jesus' death. Some churches hold a three-hour vigil, from noon until three o'clock in the afternoon—the period during which Jesus was on the cross (Mk 15:33). Especially in the Roman Catholic tradition, congregations use the 'stations of the cross' as a means of recapturing the various scenes of Jesus' last hours. The practice is also followed, although to a lesser extent, in Anglicanism and Lutheranism. The stations of the cross comprise 14 locations on the Via Dolorosa (literally 'sad street') in Jerusalem's old city, each of which commemorates a scene relating to Jesus' trial and crucifixion. The stations are characteristically used for prayer and devotion during Lent, and especially Good Friday, and it is common for pilgrims to carry life-size crosses along the way, as a re-enactment of the events of the passion. At each station, the ancient canticle 'Adoremus Te' ('Thee we adore') is typically recited or sung:

> *Leader:* We adore you, O Christ, and we praise you.
> *All:* Because by your holy cross You have redeemed the world.
> (Catholic Online 2010)

> Traditionally, the 14 stations are:
> (1) Jesus is condemned to death.
> (2) Jesus carries his cross.
> (3) Jesus falls for the first time.
> (4) Jesus meets his mother.
> (5) Simon of Cyrene helps to carry Jesus' cross.
> (6) Veronica wipes the face of Jesus.
> (7) Jesus falls for the second time.
> (8) Jesus meets the women of Jerusalem.
> (9) Jesus falls for the third time.
> (10) Jesus is stripped of his clothing.
> (11) Jesus is nailed to the cross.
> (12) Jesus dies on the cross.
> (13) Jesus' body is taken down from the cross.
> (14) Jesus is laid in the tomb.

The events listed above form the traditional set of stations, although there have been variations. Some churches portray the resurrection as a fifteenth 'station'. The Ukrainian Greek Catholic Church, which accepts the authority of Rome, but uses the Greek liturgy, has abandoned the use of these 'stations', along with rosaries and monstrances, in its attempts to de-Latinize its practices. The thirteenth station typically depicts Mary lifting Jesus down from the cross, as if he were an infant being cradled: such an artistic portrayal is known as a Pieta.

Twelve out of these 14 stations depict scenes described in the Bible. However, there is no biblical account of Jesus meeting his mother on the way to the cross, and the story of Veronica comes from a later tradition. According to Roman Catholic piety, Veronica was a woman in the crowd who stepped out with a cloth to wipe Jesus' brow as he made his way to the cross. Jesus' face became miraculously imprinted on the cloth, which is known as the Veil of Veronica. Veronica is alternatively known as Berenice, and is credited with the name Seraphia in Mel Gibson's controversial film, *The Passion of the Christ* (2004), although the script does not refer to her by name. The apocryphal *Acts of Pilate* identifies her with the woman whom Jesus cured of a haemorrhage (Mt. 9:20), and the early Church historian Eusebius tells us she lived in Caesarea Philippae. According to mediaeval legend, Veronica took the veil to Rome; St Peter's Basilica houses a veil that is claimed to be the original, but there are five other 'rival' veils on display in other churches and monasteries. The name Veronica is popularly held to mean 'true icon' (Latin *vera* + icon), and wherever any original veil may be housed, the picture of the veil is well known, and copies are used iconically in many churches and private homes.

Pope John Paul II defined a slightly revised set of stations of the cross, removing the non-biblical incidents. The list runs as follows:

(1) Jesus in the Garden of Olives.
(2) Jesus is betrayed by Judas and arrested.
(3) Jesus is condemned by the Sanhedrin.
(4) Jesus is denied by Peter.
(5) Jesus is judged by Pilate.
(6) Jesus is scourged and crowned with thorns.
(7) Jesus takes up his cross.
(8) Jesus is helped by the Cyrenean to carry his cross.
(9) Jesus meets the women of Jerusalem.
(10) Jesus is crucified.
(11) Jesus promises his kingdom to the good thief.
(12) Jesus and his mother and disciple.
(13) Jesus dies on the cross.
(14) Jesus is laid in the tomb.

The first public celebration of the stations was in Rome's Coliseum in 1991. Initially the Pope himself carried the cross in procession but, as his strength progressively failed during his last years before his death in 2005, others assumed this task. In 2007, Pope Benedict XVI formally approved the new stations for public celebration and private meditation. Most churches in the Roman Catholic, High Anglican and Lutheran traditions have the stations of the cross displayed pictorially or in bas-relief form around their interior walls, and thus the stations can be used locally for devotion, without the necessity of visiting a place of pilgrimage.

The Protestant tradition finds difficulty with the stations of the cross, for several reasons. Their association with Roman liturgy creates initial resistance, as does the fact that they involve the use of images, which is regarded as idolatrous. (The reasons for this belief will be explained in a later chapter.) Additionally, as mentioned above, two of the incidents are unbiblical. Many Protestant churches therefore prefer to celebrate Good Friday by reflecting on the 'seven words of the cross'. Taken collectively, the four canonical Gospels report seven sayings of Jesus while he was hanging on the cross. (Lk. 23:34, 43; Jn 19:26; Mt. 27:46 // Mk 15:34; Jn 19:29, 30; Lk. 23:46). Some or all of these passages might be read, with homilies on one or more—even all—of them.

Another method of re-enacting Christ's passion has been the 'passion play'. This originated from the Church's practice of extensively reading the key passages from the biblical passion narrative during public worship—a practice that continues in many churches today, with designated readers for specific characters, and the congregation reading words attributed to the crowd in the story. The passion play took its rise in the fifteenth century, but experienced a revival in the nineteenth after a decline as a consequence of the European Enlightenment. As the name implies, it is a dramatization of the Gospel narrative, frequently using contemporary costume, without regard for historical authenticity. The most famous passion play is that of Oberammergau, performed every ten years, on the last year of each decade. The Oberammergau play originated in 1634 from a vow made by members of the town, that, if they were spared from the prevalent epidemic of bubonic plague, they would perform this regular passion play. Performances last for five months in the designated year, and consist of dramatization, music and choral singing, and *tableaux vivants*, in which performers depict scenes from both the Old and New Testaments, as a means of demonstrating how the entire Bible points to Christ, not merely the Gospel narrative.

Passion plays are performed in various cities worldwide. Some churches may put on their own lower-scale dramatisations of the Passion, although it would be misleading to suggest that this was a particularly prevalent practice. In recent times, Christians have resorted to more modern media. Denys Arcand's *Jésus de Montréal* (1989) was an attempt to reinterpret Christ's passion in a modern idiom, while Mel Gibson's *The Passion of the Christ* (2004) attempted to be a more traditional portrayal.

The observance of Lent and the somewhat melancholy nature of Holy Week serve to intensify the exuberance of Easter, which is the high point of the Christian calendar. Easter Sunday marks the day of Christ's resurrection, demonstrating his victory over death and his conquest of sin. Although Jesus' penultimate words on the cross are recorded as 'It is accomplished' (Jn 19:30), indicating that it was Christ's sacrificial death that atoned for sin, the resurrection highlights the triumph of Christ's work. The Bible teaches that Adam and Eve were destined to live for ever in the Garden of Eden, but forfeited their immortality as a consequence of their sin. Jesus is regarded as the 'Second Adam', the one who comes into the world as a perfect being, but who, unlike Adam, succeeds in living a perfect life, and whose sacrifices atone for the sin of Adam and subsequently humanity, thus enabling humankind to enjoy eternal life. Easter worship highlights the theme of the conquest of death; one famous ancient hymn, frequently used at Easter, begins:

> Jesus lives! thy terrors now
> can O death, no more, appal us;
> Jesus lives! by this we know
> thou, O grave, canst not enthrall us.
> Alleluia!

As St Paul wrote, 'Christ has indeed been raised from the dead, the firstfruits of those who have fallen asleep. For since death came through a man, the resurrection of the dead comes also through a man. For as in Adam all die, so in Christ all will be made alive' (1 Cor. 15:20-22).

In the various traditions and denominations, the main service on Easter Sunday will normally have the same format, but with the readings focused on the resurrection theme. Some congregations will hold an Easter vigil. This is a service that is held either on the previous evening, often spanning the midnight hour heralding Easter morning, or else at dawn, ushering in the daylight of Easter Sunday. According to Matthew's Gospel, soldiers were placed at Jesus' tomb, to prevent his disciples from stealing his body and feigning a resurrection; they witnessed the momentous event of Jesus emerging the tomb, but were bribed to maintain silence about it. Easter vigils thus recall this precise moment of Christ's resurrection.

Some explanation of the dating of Easter may be appropriate. Easter is known as a 'moveable feast'—that is to say, it always occurs on the same day of the week, but the calendrical date varies. (The term 'moveable' does not mean that Church authorities can move the date of the festival at will, unlike some minor festivals, where clergy can 'transfer' the date, for example when two festivals happen to coincide.) The festival is associated with spring in several ways. The name itself is probably connected with the Celtic goddess of spring, known as Eostre or Estera, to whom offerings were made at the vernal equinox. The Jewish Passover, which arguably originates from ancient vernal rites, was the occasion for Jesus' visit to Jerusalem, during which his arrest, trial and crucifixion took place. The timing of Easter picks up on both sets of events, the date of which related to the phases of the moon and the spring equinox. In the Western Churches, Easter is reckoned to fall on the Sunday after the full moon which follows the equinox, allowing the festival to fall some time between 22 March and 25 April. There is a mathematical way of calculating Easter, which is set out in the Church of England's *Book of Common Prayer*, among other sources. This involves taking the year number, and arithmetically deriving 'golden numbers' and 'year letters'. Few Christians understand such a system, however, and, since Easter dates are well publicized by civil and ecclesiastical authorities, find no need to use it. Eastern Orthodoxy has a different method of determining the date of Easter, since the Orthodox Easter therefore usually (but not always) falls on a different date. (See chapter 10.)

Eastern churches do not use the Gregorian calendar, introduced by Pope Gregory XIII in 1582. Their dating relates to the Hebrew calendar, usually—but not always—giving a date that falls a week later than the Western one.

From Easter to Trinity Sunday

Because of the 'movability' of Easter, other festivals that depend on its timing move accordingly. Not only is the timing of Lent tied to Easter, commencing 46 days before it, together with its associated festivals, but also three important ensuing festivals: Ascension Day, Pentecost and Trinity Sunday. According to the Gospels, Jesus appeared to his disciples during a 40-day period after his resurrection, at the end of which he led them out to Bethany, a high point about a mile outside Jerusalem, where a cloud descended and received him back up into heaven. Two men, dressed in white, appeared (possibly angels, or perhaps Moses and Elijah—we are not told) and announced that Jesus would return again to earth in the same way as he ascended into heaven. The presumed site of the Ascension is Mount Olivet, where the Russian Orthodox Church has its Convent of the Ascension, and which is a popular pilgrimage site.

Being precisely 40 days after Easter, Ascension Day always falls on a Thursday, when the festival is typically celebrated. The Ascension is celebrated once more on the ensuing Sunday. In the Orthodox tradition, the festival is known as *Analepsis* ('taking up'), and is frequently heralded by all night vigils. In England, Ascension Day was often celebrated by the carrying in procession of a banner bearing an image of a lion (representing Christ, the 'lion of Judah') surmounting a dragon (representing Satan), thus showing Christ's triumph over the forces of evil. The symbolism also connoted the victory of the English over the Welsh, since the lion and dragon are those countries' respective national symbols! Other customs included the elevation of an image of Christ through an opening in a church's roof, while an image of a dragon was made to descend. Such practices are now rare, although the emphasis on the theme of height continues. For example, in Oxford, England, it is customary for choristers to assemble on the top of the Magdalen College tower in the early hours of Ascension Day morning, to sing Ascension hymns.

The emphasis on physical height at Ascension time does not imply, of course, that Christians believe that Jesus literally rode up in a cloud to a place above the sky. Although most Christians would not claim an ability to articulate the doctrine of the Ascension with any degree of theological sophistication, many are certainly familiar with the discourse in which Jesus tells his disciples that his departure from the world is necessary for him to send the Holy Spirit to them (Jn 14:15-21). The Ascension also serves to demonstrate Jesus' authority. Orthodox theology in particular sees the Ascension as the culmination of Christ's incarnation: Christ did not lose his divine status by becoming human, but resumed his authority at God's right hand, where he reigns with the Father, and will judge the world at the end of time. The Ascension, Orthodoxy emphasizes, highlights the expectation that humanity's redeemed state will be superior to the paradisiacal state from which Adam and Eve fell. In the Protestant tradition, Christ's position in heaven assures the believer that he is there as an advocate on behalf of the faithful—a particularly important idea, since Protestants typically reject the belief that saints should be prayed to, and that they intercede on one's behalf.

In the Orthodox tradition, the Sunday after Ascension is the Sunday of Holy Fathers of the First Ecumenical Council at Nicaea. This was the first of four major ecumenical councils, and was held in 325 CE, to formulate what became the Nicene Creed. (See chapter 6.) The last words of the creed, as defined at Nicaea, were: 'He ascended into heaven, and sits at the right hand of the Father; and shall come again, with glory, to judge the living and the dead; Whose kingdom shall have no end.'

Fifty days after Easter comes Pentecost. The name literally means 'fifty days' and was a Jewish festival before becoming appropriated by Christianity. Jews continue to celebrate Pentecost (*Shavuoth* or 'Weeks'), celebrating the firstfruits of the harvest and also the giving of the Law to Moses at Mount Sinai. The Christian festival relates to the event described in Acts 2, where Jesus' disciples are gathered in the upper room at the time of this Jewish festival, when they experienced the sound of a strong wind and 'tongues of fire' descending on their heads. The experience emboldened them, and it is reported that Peter addressed the large crowd that had assembled in Jerusalem for the festival, securing some three thousand converts, who were baptized.

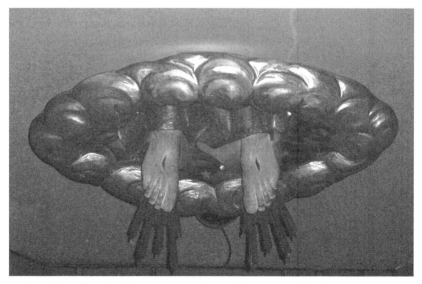

Ceiling of the Chapel of the Ascension, Shrine of Our Lady of Walsingham, England. Jesus' Ascension is here portrayed in a literal fashion.
Photograph: Margaret Wilkins

Pentecost has therefore been associated with baptism, and Easter and Pentecost have traditionally been regarded as particularly appropriate occasions to administer the rite. The alternative name 'Whitsun' or 'Whit Sunday', used in Britain, may derive from the early Christian baptismal practice in which candidates for baptism donned white robes. Alternatively, the source of the term may not be 'White Sunday', but 'Wit Sunday', 'wit' meaning 'wisdom', a gift with which the Holy Spirit is traditionally associated. Many churches in the Greek Orthodox tradition are named 'Saint Sophia', meaning 'holy wisdom'. The first official use of the term 'Whitsunday' was in the first Prayer Book of Edward VI in 1549. Apart from references to the theme of Pentecost, there are no special liturgical celebrations for Pentecost. In many countries the day following the festival (sometimes the entire week) is a public holiday, and Eastern Orthodoxy ensures that the faithful have a fast-free week following Pentecost, since the birth of Christ's Church is a cause for celebration rather than self-denial.

Trinity Sunday immediately follows Pentecost. Like Pentecost, no special services or liturgy are involved, but the Sunday serves to highlight the completeness of the godhead. God the Father, as the Orthodox churches put it, is the 'fount of divinity'; Christmas has emphasized how the Father sent his Son into the world; Easter has highlighted his sacrificial death and resurrection; and Pentecost has marked the sending of the Holy Spirit. Trinity Sunday sums up these previous festivals, presenting the deity as one complete and undivided unity. Christianity teaches the triune nature of God—a topic to which we shall return.

Christian Sundays are designated by their position within the main calendrical seasons (Advent, Epiphany, Lent, Easter and Pentecost/Trinity). Thus a Sunday is described as 'First in Advent', 'Second after Epiphany', 'Fourth in Lent' or whatever. Anglicans and Lutherans use Trinity as the pivotal point for the Sundays between Pentecost and Advent, whereas Roman Catholicism numbers Sundays after Pentecost. The period of Pentecost/Trinity is a lengthy one, spanning approximately 25 Sundays—almost half the entire year. It is part of 'ordinary time', in contrast with the special periods of Advent, Lent and Easter. The long period of ordinary time does not entail that the liturgical calendar is dull and uneventful, however, for it is marked by a number of smaller festivals. The festival of All Saints falls on 1 November, and is celebrated by Roman Catholics and several other Western churches. (Eastern Orthodoxy celebrates it on the Sunday after Pentecost.) The festival commemorates not only those saints who have been canonized by the Church, but all of the faithful who are presumed to have attained God's kingdom in heaven. It is a celebration of their attainment, and a reminder that the Church consists of both the living and the dead. The ensuing day is All Souls' Day, commemorating all the faithful departed: in Roman Catholic thought, this includes the dead who have not yet attained God's kingdom, but who are completing their passage through purgatory.

The last Sunday before Advent marks the end of the liturgical year, and is designated by the Roman Catholic Church and some Protestant churches as the Feast of Christ the King. The Church's year has made reference to the key incidents in Jesus' life and his accomplishment in redeeming humanity from sin. This final Sunday sums up his attainment, and honours him as the Lord who rules over the earth. Many churches bear a saint's name (such as Saint Michael, Saint Mary, Saint John, Saint Paul), and hence make a particular point of celebrating the festival of their patron saint, but those who do not will use the Feast of Christ the King as their patronal festival.

In the Roman Catholic and Anglican traditions, different colours are used to indicate the relevant season of the liturgical calendar. The clergy's vestments and the drapery used to adorn altars and pulpits is changed periodically: green for 'ordinary time', dark blue or purple for Advent, gold or white for Christmas, purple for Lent, gold or yellow for the Easter period up to Ascensiontide, red for Pentecost and All Saints' Day, and black for Good Friday. (There can be variations to this scheme, according to local practice.)

The purpose of the liturgical calendar

Those who do not belong to a religious tradition may wonder why Christian communities take such pains to observe this complex variety of festivals, and to perform these sometimes dramatized re-enactments of the Christian story. Keeping these festivals performs an obvious didactic function: together with other aids, such as stained glass windows, statues and pictures, the festival year is a constant reminder of the sequence of events in Jesus' ministry and the story of the Church. Their observance, too, keeps up a tradition: while few Christian rites can be traced back to Jesus himself, the Christian Church has been observing them for many centuries, and their observance identifies the present-day Christian with the wider Church, past as well as present.

There is a further important reason for celebrating festivals. Christianity teaches that Jesus was more than a great figure in human history. According to Christian teaching, Jesus' importance only partly lies in his human ministry; his accomplishment is reckoned to be something in which all generations of believers can share. If Jesus were simply a Jewish rabbi who lived and taught in first-century Palestine, present-day Christians would be at second remove from his ministry—people who could only hear and read about a life that his contemporaries experienced in reality. Central to Christianity is the message that Jesus is the Christ—a cosmic figure who transcends his historical manifestation—who died for the sins of the world and who offers eternal life to all believers—past, present and future. By re-enacting the events of the Christian story, believers place themselves in the position of Jesus and his contemporaries. However, the re-enactment of these events differs significantly from those who re-enact past events like historical battles. Such re-creators of the past take pains to ascertain the precise location of the battle-scene, the costumes that would be worn, and the exact sequence of the events that took place, in an endeavour to re-create the scene that took place centuries previously. By contrast, this is not what Christians endeavour to achieve with these liturgical re-eanctments. The passing of nearly 21 centuries since his life on earth make no difference to Christ's soteriological work, and by placing themselves in the original Christian story, believers are demonstrating that Christ's work is for them, as well as for his immediate circle of followers. The idea of appropriating the salvific events for one's own generation is underlined in the practice of many classical artists, such as Raphael and Botticelli, who portrayed biblical scenes such as Christ's nativity against a background of mediaeval European buildings. It is irrelevant to point out that such depictions are inauthentic or un-researched: the artist's purpose is to demonstrate that Christ's incarnation, death and resurrection offer salvation to all.

Christianity is complex, and it is not possible to outline a liturgical calendar that applies to all of the Christian tradition. Some Christians are more comfortable than others with overt physical enactments of these biblical events. Roman Catholicism and Eastern Orthodoxy are more prone towards these overt external demonstrations of solidarity with biblical events. Protestantism, by contrast, tends to dislike elaborate ritual, emphasizing the need for appropriation of Christ's redeeming work to come from the heart of the believer. Despite its complex diversity, however, all Christians hold Jesus Christ as their central focus, believing in him as the divine saviour, who redeemed the world from sin.

3

Jesus

However much Christianity may have developed its beliefs and practices over the centuries, there can be little doubt that it owes its origins to Jesus of Nazareth. Of all the characters in human history, Jesus is undoubtedly the most discussed, and the one who has given rise to the greatest number of theories and speculations. It would be impossible to do justice to the 'Jesus debate' within a single chapter: the best we can hope to do is to offer a brief overview of the background against which Jesus lived and taught, what most Christians believe about him, and finally the current debates about who Jesus really was.

One writer provides us with the following description of Jesus:

> There hath appeared in these times...a man of great power named Jesus Christ, who is called by the Gentiles (peoples) the prophet of truth, whom his disciples call the Son of God: raising the dead and healing diseases, a man in stature middling tall, and comely, having a reverend countenance, which they that look upon may love and fear; having hair of the hue of an unripe hazel-nut and smooth almost down to his ears, but from the ears in curling locks somewhat darker and more shining, waving over (from) his shoulders; having a parting at the middle of the head according to the fashion of the Nazareans; a brow which a moderate colour (red) makes beautiful; with the nose and mouth no fault at all can be found; having a full beard of the colour of his hair, not long, but a little forked at the chin; having an expression simple and mature, the eyes grey, glancing...and clear; in rebuke terrible, in admonition kind and lovable, cheerful yet keep gravity; sometimes he hath wept, but never laughed; in stature of body tall and straight, with hands and arms fair to look upon; in talk grave, reserved and modest (so that he was rightly called by the prophet) fairer than the children of men. (Lentulus, thirteenth century, quoted in James 1924: 477-78.)

Alas, Lentulus was writing in the thirteenth century, and does not indicate his sources of information. In all probability, his description of

Jesus is a reflection of medieval Christian piety, rather than historical authenticity. Western attempts to portray Jesus often depict him as if he were a Westerner, with white skin and grey-blue eyes. It is interesting to note Lentulus' comment that Jesus could weep, yet never laughed. Lentulus is thinking of the Gospel accounts of Jesus weeping at his friend Lazarus' tomb (Jn 11:35) and his lament over Jerusalem, whose destruction was imminent (Lk. 19:41). However, Jesus' teaching was not without its humour: sayings like, 'If your hand causes you to sin, cut it off' (Mk 9:43) would probably have been met with laughter from his audience. (If we do not find such remarks funny in the twenty-first century West, it is only because standards of humour vary according to time and place.)

There is a considerable gap between the average Christian's image of Jesus and the various ones that present-day historians have suggested. Believers' understanding of who Jesus was comes essentially from the Bible, which they regard as a special divinely-inspired book. They rely on the four canonical Gospels, together with one or two other fragments we find in the Book of Acts and occasionally in Paul's writings, as an accurate portrayal. For the historian, however, there are no 'special books' that have absolute authority, and the Gospel accounts must be assessed for authenticity, reliability and corroboration, like any other historical document. The gap between the believer and the scholar is often one of ignorance: many Christians are unfamiliar with the findings of modern historical research on Jesus, and are not interested in them. However, the recent 'Jesus Seminar', which we shall discuss later, has received media publicity and aroused interest, as has the work of N. T. ('Tom') Wright (b.1948), Bishop of Durham since 2003, who has done much to popularize the debate in Britain. For other Christians, particularly fundamentalists, the gap is one of standpoint: they are diametrically opposed to 'advances' in biblical scholarship, and seek to re-assert the veracity of the Bible. Several evangelical publishers have produced a significant amount of literature that seeks to combat twentieth and twenty-first century scholarship.

The External Evidence

What do we know about the historical Jesus? There can be little doubt that Jesus of Nazareth was a genuine historical figure. A small handful of historians have called his existence into question, but there must have been someone who was responsible for transforming a distinctive version of Judaism into what became Christianity. Although the greatest source of information about Jesus is by far the canonical Gospels, there is a small but significant amount of external corroboration. The Samaritan historian Thallus (52 CE) and the Roman author Tacitus (75–140 CE) confirm that he was put to death under the Roman governor Pontius Pilate. We have some information from Josephus, the Jewish historian, although this is somewhat more problematical. Josephus describes him as 'a wise man, if it be lawful to call him a man, for he was a doer of wonderful works—a teacher of such men as receive the truth with pleasure' and affirms that 'He was Christ' and that he rose from the dead. This seems strange, since Josephus was not one of Jesus' followers, remaining a Jew throughout his life, and some historians think these remarks may be a later interpolation by a Christian scribe. Josephus does affirm, however, that the Jewish Sanhedrin condemned Jesus to be stoned, but that Pontius Pilate ordered his crucifixion. Josephus also provides an additional point of detail: Jesus, he tells us, had a brother called James.

In addition to the four New Testament Gospels there are a number of apocryphal gospels, attributed to disciples such as Peter, James, Philip and Nicodemus. It is unlikely that the claimed authors genuinely belonged to Jesus' immediate following. Unlike the canonical Gospels, they show an interest in the childhood of Jesus—a topic on which Matthew, Mark, Luke and John have little to say. The childhood stories, however, lack credibility as genuine accounts of incidents in Jesus' early years; for example, one story records that Jesus made birds out of clay, and imbued them with the breath of life, so that they were able to fly away. Such stories give us little insight into the historical Jesus, although the naivety of such tales may indicate that they belong to an earlier period than the four biblical Gospels. Understandably, the apocryphal gospels are little known to the average Christian, and are rarely studied, even in theological seminaries. Many of these Christian apocryphal writings have been collected in a volume entitled *The Apocryphal New Testament*, published in 1924 by M. R. James. (James is better known to the public for his ghost stories, an area in which he also excelled.)

Greater attention has been given to the Gospel of Thomas, however. It was discovered in 1945 in Nag Hammadi, Egypt, and is a short work consisting entirely of sayings attributed to Jesus; there is no attempt to recount any incidents in his life. There is significant overlap between Thomas's material and sayings in the canonical Gospels. For example:

> Jesus said:
> You see the splinter in your brother's eye;
>> but you do not see the beam in your own eye.
> When you cast out the beam from your own eye,
> then you will see to cast out the splinter
>> from your brother's eye.
>> (Gospel of Thomas 86:12-17; Grant and Freedman 1960: 139)

This closely parallels a passage in Matthew and Luke (Mt. 7:3, 5; Lk. 6:41-42) and is one of numerous such examples. The apparent authenticity of such sayings has caused one writer to include extracts from the Gospel of Thomas in an edited anthology of New Testament scripture (Henson 2004). The clear overlap between Thomas and the synoptic Gospels raises the question of which source came first, and scholars are not agreed on this matter. Some believe in the primacy of Thomas, since it is a shorter, simpler source, and date it at around 60 CE. Others believe that is much later, possibly as late as 140 CE. (Most scholars date Mark, generally agreed to be the earliest canonical Gospel, at around 70 CE.) Although the Gospel of Thomas is an important discovery, unfortunately it does little to shed additional light on who Jesus was.

What about the Dead Sea Scrolls? It is a popular but erroneous belief that they shed remarkable new evidence about Jesus' life and teaching. Such beliefs are fuelled by popular writers such as Dan Brown in his controversial *The Da Vinci Code*, where his fictional character Sir Leigh Teabing explains, 'The Dead Sea Scrolls were found in the 1950s hidden in a cave near Qumran in the Judaean desert... In addition to telling the true Grail story, these documents speak of Christ's ministry in very human terms' (Brown 2003: 317).

Some comment is needed to set the record straight on the scrolls. The Dead Sea Scrolls were discovered at Qumran, at the side of the Dead Sea, in 1947 by a shepherd boy who threw a stone into a cave and heard the sound of breaking pottery. Subsequent discoveries in nearby caves continued up to 1956. On investigation he found a number of clay pots containing ancient scrolls. On gaining access to the scrolls, scholars discovered that they contained copies of almost all of the entire Hebrew scriptures—the most ancient to be found—together with distinctive documents relating to an ancient Jewish community who lived an isolated existence on the banks of the Dead Sea. This second group of documents contains the group's *Manual of Discipline*, as well as a book of psalms and an apocalyptic text. The group is believed to have taken its rise around 125 BCE and the documents date from 20 BCE to 70 CE. The

Qumran community may have consisted of Essenes, an austere Jewish group who observed a strict rule of life, but this is unproven. Some have suggested that John the Baptist may have belonged to the Qumran sect, or been an Essene, but this is sheer conjecture.

Although the Scrolls do not shed new light on Jesus of Nazareth, they provide some insight into one Jewish community which was in existence during the time of Jesus. Whatever uncertainties may surround Jesus himself, his cultural and religious background can be clearly ascertained. The Jews had been the victims of various foreign invasions. When Nebuchadnezzar's armies invaded Judaea, their central focus of worship, the Jerusalem Temple, was destroyed, and the Jews were exiled to Babylon in 687 BCE. King Cyrus of Persia had permitted a return from captivity, and work on the rebuilding of the city and its Temple began under Nehemiah and Ezra during the fifth century BCE. The Temple was completed in 516 BCE and dedicated the following year. When Antiochus Epiphanes, ruler of the Seleucid Empire, conquered Judaea, he plundered and desecrated the Temple in 169 BCE. This prompted the Maccabean rebellion, enabling the Jerusalem Temple to be returned to the Jews in 162 BCE and re-consecrated. During the subsequent Roman occupation, King Herod, who was Governor of Judaea, allowed further renovation and expansion of the Temple—a project that took 40 years to reach completion in 20 CE. When Jesus began his ministry, this newly refurbished Temple would be a source of national pride.

Not all Jews used the Temple for their main acts of worship, however. For many it was too far from home: the distance between Jerusalem and Nazareth—Jesus' home town—is around 80 miles. Some other Jews—the diaspora—worked abroad, and hence did not have access to the Temple's facilities. As a consequence, the synagogue movement arose. Its origins may have been the result of the Babylonian captivity, when worship in the absence of a temple was needed; however, synagogues were certainly in existence by the third century BCE. The word 'synagogue' means 'meeting house', and synagogues were places where prayers were said collectively and scriptures were read and expounded. The Gospels record Jesus as using synagogues on several occasions, and Luke recounts an incident when Jesus is given a scroll of the prophet Isaiah, reads a short extract and offers brief comment (Lk. 4:14-20). The religious leader who presided over the synagogue was the rabbi.

The co-existence of the Temple and the synagogues resulted in two types of religious leaders. The Sadducees were the governors of the Temple, with the priests as its officiants. The Pharisees constituted a rival camp, being the supporters of the synagogue movement, and also the interpreters of the Jewish Law. The Pharisees tend to get a bad press in the Gospels, and in subsequent Christianity, being portrayed as legalistic nit-pickers, constantly taken to task by Jesus. This perception by Christians may be somewhat unfair, although it still continues. The Pharisees attempted to encourage the Jews to relate the Law to everyday living, and not simply to regard fulfilling Temple obligations as sufficient. They were theological innovators, for example in their championing the belief that there is life after death—a doctrine that the Sadducees denied. Interestingly, where Jesus comments on controversies between the Sadducees and the Pharisees, he appears to be on the side of the latter (for example Mk 12:18-27).

Another emergent idea at the time of Jesus was messianism. The coming of a messiah is not explicitly referred to in Hebrew scripture, although Christians have subsequently interpreted biblical prophecies and other material as alluding to it. The place of messianism in Jewish thought has been somewhat exaggerated by Christians: the coming of a messiah was a common, but by no means universal belief among first-century Jews, and messianic ideology probably arose in the 150 years or so before Jesus' birth. As Michael Hinton argues, messianism tended to gain prominence in later Jewish thinking because of Jewish-Christian disputes that were prompted by the Christians' claim that Jesus was the messiah. The messiah that the Jews expected was not conceived of as a supernatural figure: the messiah would be born as a normal human being, but would become a political leader, who would deliver the Jews from their foreign oppression.

Another theme that had come to the fore in the Judaism of Jesus' time was apocalyptic belief. Those Jews who could not foresee a political solution to their problems turned to supernatural expectations in the form of apocalypticism. We find relatively little of this in Hebrew scripture. Apocalyptic ideas formed an important part of Zorastrianism, the religion of Persia, where it was believed that at key periods in human history, supernatural beings were sent to earth, and that the existing system of human affairs would be brought to an end, with a final judgement. It is not known exactly when such ideas percolated into Jewish thought: the Jews had contact with the Persians when the latter conquered the Babylonians and the Persian king Cyrus allowed the Jews to return to their homeland. Jews later came into contact again with the Persians when they fought together to oppose the Romans in 40 BCE. Some of the later parts of Hebrew Scripture refer to cosmic intervention into human history, for example the second half of the book of Daniel. One well known passage is the following:

> In my vision at night I looked, and there before me was one like a son of man, coming with the clouds of heaven. He approached the Ancient of Days and was led into his presence. He was given authority, glory and sovereign power; all peoples, nations and men of every language worshiped him. His dominion is an everlasting dominion that will not pass away, and his kingdom is one that will never be destroyed. (Dan. 7:13-14)

Christians are familiar with a passage in Joel—quoted by Peter on the first Day of Pentecost (Acts 2:17-21)—which, although written several centuries before the rise of Jewish apocalypticism, contains some of the imagery associated with it:

> And afterwards, I will pour out my Spirit on all people. Your sons and daughters will prophesy, your old men will dream dreams, your young men will see visions. Even on my servants, both men and women, I will pour out my Spirit in those days. I will show wonders in the heavens and on the earth, blood and fire and billows of smoke. The sun will be turned to darkness and the moon to blood before the coming of the great and dreadful day of the Lord. (Joel 2:28-31)

Jesus and the Gospels

Those who are familiar with the canonical Gospels will immediately recognize how Jesus of Nazareth fits into this religious and cultural background, and we shall now examine this biblical evidence. Two of the four Gospels—Matthew and John—are traditionally attributed to immediate disciples of Jesus. The author of Matthew claims to be a former tax-collector who responded to Jesus' call to follow him (Mt. 9:9-12). John does not name himself explicitly as the author of the fourth Gospel, but suggests at the end of his book that he is Jesus' closest disciple ('the disciple whom Jesus loved'; Jn 21:24). Luke was not one of Jesus' twelve apostles: he appears to have been Paul's travelling companion on his later journeys. The reason for this assumption is that the Book of Acts is a sequel to Luke's gospel, and Luke uses the first-person plural ('we') in recounting these travels (Acts 16–21), and Paul occasionally refers to him in his letters (Col. 4:14; Phlm 23). It is believed that Luke was a Gentile, not a Jew, unlike the other Gospel writers.

The remaining Gospel writer is Mark. It is generally believed that he is John Mark, to whom Luke refers in the Book of Acts. He was the cousin of Barnabas (Col. 4:10), who accompanied Paul on his early journeys. Paul seems to regard Mark as unreliable, and Mark accompanies Barnabas on his travels instead (Acts 12:25). Mark was not one of the twelve apostles, and the question arises as to how he gained his information about Jesus. According to traditional Christian piety, Mark followed Jesus around during his mission, and some readers of his Gospel have claimed to detect pieces of detail that indicate eye-witness testimony. Although Mark makes no claim to have witnessed at first hand the events he describes, some Christians have claimed that he places himself incognito in the narrative in at least two places. Jesus sends two of the disciples into Jerusalem to make preparations for the Passover, and tells them that they will find a man carrying a water jar, and that he will guide them to an upper room that is ready for them (Mk 14:15). Tradition has it that this man was none other than John Mark. The meal turns out to be the Last Supper, which heralds Jesus' arrest in the nearby Garden of Gethsemane. In describing the fracas that breaks out during the arrest, Mark adds the following, somewhat curious, point of detail, which all the other Gospel writers omit: 'A young man, wearing nothing but a linen garment, was following Jesus. When they seized him, he fled naked, leaving his garment behind' (Mk 14:51).

The Last Supper, Greek Orthodox icon. Authors' collection.
Photograph: George Chryssides

Why, it has been asked, should Mark mention this, except to indicate to the reader that he was there in the Garden during the incident? However, these attempts to link Mark with such events in Jesus' life are mere conjectures, and serious historians cannot rely on conjectures, but provable facts.

There is a further tradition about Mark's relationship to the events he describes. The early Church Father Papias tells us that he was the apostle Peter's amanuensis, and transcribed the events that Peter later recounted.

> This also the elder used to say. Mark, indeed, having been the interpreter of Peter, wrote accurately, howbeit not in order, all that he recalled of what was either said or done by the Lord. For he neither heard the Lord, nor was he a follower of His, but, at a later date (as I said), of Peter; who used to adapt his instructions to the needs [of the moment], but not with a view to putting together the Dominical oracles in orderly fashion: so that Mark did no wrong in thus writing some things as he recalled. For he kept a single aim in view: not to omit anything of what he heard, nor to state anything therein falsely. (Papias; quoted in Stevenson 1957: 52)

It should be noted that these two traditions about Mark are somewhat contradictory. The first asserts that he was an eye-witness, the second that he received someone else's testimony, and thus a secondary rather than a primary source. However, Papias was writing in 156 CE, long after these events, and he does not tell us how he gained his information: perhaps he too was making a guess, based on his personal impression of Mark's Gospel.

Most Christians are aware of the overlap between the Gospel writers' material, but are probably vague about the details, and are unlikely to know which stories are to be found in which Gospel. Some churches organize Bible study groups in order to advance their members' knowledge of the Bible, and Mark's Gospel is a favourite starting point. Mark's Gospel is the shortest, and probably the earliest. Although Christians commonly believe that at least two of the Gospel accounts (Matthew and John) are first-hand accounts of Jesus' ministry, scholars have questioned this. When we compare Matthew's account of his call to discipleship with Mark's version, we find that Mark gives the erstwhile tax-collector's name as Levi, not Matthew (Mk 2:13-14), and we find different lists of the twelve apostles in different Gospels (Mt. 10:2-4; Mk 3:14-19; Lk. 6:13-16. John mentions that there were twelve disciples, but does not list them.) Did 'Matthew' appropriate an apostle's name in order to lend authority to his Gospel? John's Gospel is an extremely developed theological reflection on the life of Jesus, and seems to reflect a longer passage of time between the described events and the time of writing. The estimated date of writing is generally agreed to be between 90 and 100 CE, and despite the fact that the tradition ascribing authorship to the beloved disciple goes back to the second century, most scholars are agreed that John is unlikely to have penned the work. Conservative Christians, however, point to the tradition that John lived to a very old age, and argue that a late date does not necessarily disprove Johannine authorship.

Much has been written on issues of authorship and the nature of the synoptic problem. It is sufficient to say, however, that many historians are unconvinced that the Bible presents eye-witness testimony regarding the life of Jesus. Furthermore, the Gospel writers do not present the kind of biography to which twenty-first century readers are accustomed. Instead, they collate small fragments of material, in many cases a couple of hundred words or less, describing incidents in Jesus' life that are not closely linked with the material before and after. Scholars refer to such a piece of material as a *pericope*. Literally this means 'cut around': in other words, Matthew, Mark and Luke are presenting the reader with little 'cut-outs' of material, which they have pieced together like a patchwork to form their Gospels. (John is somewhat different, however, and provides more by way of continuous material.) We also find that there are large gaps in Jesus' life story. A present-day biography would go into details about the subject's family background, childhood and education, for example, but we get almost none of this in the Gospel records. There is only one recorded incident relating to Jesus' childhood: his family lose him on a visit to the Jerusalem Temple, and he is presently found asking precocious questions to the scholars (Lk. 2:41-52). We are told that Jesus' father Joseph was a carpenter, and Jesus' audience once describe him in this way (Mk 6:3), but we are left uncertain whether his early adult was spent pursuing his father's trade, or whether he trained as a Jewish rabbi—a title that he is given more frequently (e.g. Mk 9:5).

Because of the fragmentary nature of the Gospel narrative, exactly chronology seems unimportant to the Gospel writers, and different Gospels arrange events differently. For example, Matthew places Jesus' 'cleansing of the Temple' (an incident in which Jesus drives out the vendors and money-changers from the Jerusalem Temple) at the end of his ministry, after the triumphal entry into Jerusalem (Mt. 21:12-13), while John places it at the start (Jn 2:13-17). Jesus' sayings seem to be arranged according to theme, rather than temporal sequence: for example, analogies between the kingdom of God and growing seed are found in one single chapter (Mk 4). It would seem strange if Jesus only explained God's kingdom in this way on one single occasion. Of all the material about Jesus, the most continuous piece of narrative recounts the last week of Jesus' earthly life, his trial and crucifixion. Scholars refer to this section of the Gospels as the 'passion narrative'. (The original meaning of 'passion' is suffering, from the Latin *passus*, meaning 'suffered' or 'allowed'. We sometimes use the word in this somewhat archaic sense when we say, 'I'll suffer it', which connotes unpleasantness combined with acceptance. Christianity teaches that Christ accepted his suffering: being divine, he could have escaped undergoing the anguish and affliction that were necessary for the world's redemption.)

Scholarship and the Life of Jesus

Some Christians, particularly in the evangelical Protestant tradition, believe that it is possible to harmonize the various Gospel accounts and to resolve any apparent chronological difficulties. Particularly in the nineteenth and early twentieth centuries, several attempts were made to construct lives of Jesus, piecing together this fragmentary information from the Gospels, and making it into a seeming coherent biography, although without material about Jesus' childhood and adolescence. This was done both by scholars and by popular writers. Albert Schweitzer's *The Quest of the Historical Jesus* (1906/1910) gives an overview of various scholars who have offered such attempts, and finishes with his own. A number of popular writers made attempts to write lives of Jesus in the late nineteenth and mid-twentieth centuries. Charles Dickens wrote *The Life of our Lord* in 1849. Dorothy L. Sayers' *The Man Born to Be King*—a series of radio plays, published in 1943—proved enormously popular in the English-speaking world. Even Enid Blyton made her contribution with various accounts of Jesus' life for children, with her *A Story Book of Jesus*, published in 1956.

Others accept that the Gospels are not biographies as we understand them today, and that it was not the intention of the Gospel writers to present a blow-by-blow account of Jesus' ministry. *The Catechism of the Catholic Church* sums this point up in following way, with which the vast majority of Christians—not just Roman Catholics—would agree:

> Many things about Jesus of interest to human curiosity do not figure in the Gospels. Almost nothing is said about his hidden life at Nazareth,

and even a great part of his public life is not recounted. What is written in the Gospels was set down there 'so that you may believe that Jesus is the Christ, the Son of God, and that believing you may have life in his name.' The Gospels were written by men who were among the first to have the faith and wanted to share it with others. (*Catechism* 514-15)

We shall examine some of the more scholarly approaches to the historical Jesus in chapter 12. With a few exceptions, post-Enlightenment scholars have tended to be sceptical about the possibility of recovering much information about the historical Jesus of Nazareth, and have tended to suggest a distinction between the historical figure, whom the present-day Christian cannot know, and the 'Christ of faith' who transcends the world and is freely accessible to the believer. Most present-day Christians tend to veer towards theological conservativism on such matters: although they may not necessarily believe in the complete inerrancy of the Gospels, or even know their contents particularly well, they would subscribe to the view that Jesus of Nazareth was born some two thousand years ago, that he taught and performed healing miracles, that—most importantly—he was crucified and rose again in physical form within three days.

One popular book that argued the case for Jesus' literal resurrection was Frank Morison's *Who Moved the Stone?*, published in 1930 and still in print. Morison, a journalist whose real name was Albert Henry Ross (1881–1950), relates how he was a sceptic and, as a young man, started to write a book debunking the historicity of the New Testament's claims about Jesus. As his research progressed, however, he came to the conviction that Jesus truly rose from the dead, and that alternative explanations were not feasible. A shorter book, *Man Alive!*, by Anglican clergyman Michael Green, appeared in 1967, and was also a popular defence of Jesus' physical resurrection. Both writers consider the possibilities that the disciples stole Jesus' body, as the chief priests instructed the soldiers to allege (Mt. 28:13), and that Jesus was not really dead, but merely comatose when placed in his tomb. Green powerfully argues that someone who had been so physical harmed as Jesus had been would still have been extremely weak, with serious wounds, when he appeared to his disciples, and would scarcely have been the source of inspiration that the accounts of his resurrection appearances imply.

Such arguments assume, of course, that there is a historical core of information about Jesus' trial, his scourging by the Roman soldiers, his crucifixion and burial, and some of the apparitions experienced by the disciples. Many present-day scholars would regard such assumptions as question-begging. However, rank-and-file believers confine themselves to popular Christian literature, preferring a faith by which to live, which they can anchor with a belief in history.

From Jesus to Christ

Christianity is firmly a historical faith. However, for Christians it is not sufficient merely to know historical facts about Jesus of Nazareth. Although he was certainly a teacher and an exemplar, the importance of Jesus is that he is the Christ, the bringer of salvation. The branch of theology that deals with Christ's nature is known as Christology, although probably this term is unfamiliar to the average Christian believer. Christology deals with who Christ was, examining both his divine and human characteristics, and how they interact. The word 'Christ' derives from the Greek word *christos*, which translates the Hebrew *mashiach*, or 'messiah', and Jesus' immediate followers believed and taught that he was the messiah. *Mashiach* in Hebrew literally means 'anointed one': the important figures in Jewish political and religious life, notably kings and priests, were anointed on taking up office, and were held to be God's divinely appointed representatives. In claiming that Jesus was the messiah, his disciples were affirming that he was God's chosen one, who could grant them liberation. Because of messianic associations with kingship, Jesus is typically referred to as 'king', and indeed Matthew and Luke trace his family tree back to King David, generally reckoned to be the greatest king of the nation of Israel (Mt. 1:6; Lk. 3:31). 'Son of David' is a title that he sometimes receives in the Gospels (see, e.g., Mt. 1:1; 9:27; 12:23).

One very important incident in the Gospels was at the northern town of Caesarea Philippi, when Jesus posed the question to his disciples, 'Who do people say that I am?' Peter's reply was, 'You are the Christ' (Mk 8:27-30). Strangely, the incident concludes with Jesus instructing them to tell no-one of this. This caused some scholars to develop the notion of the 'messianic secret'—an idea originating with William Wrede (1859–1906). Wrede's ideas are now largely rejected, but continue to be influential. He suggested that Jesus did not claim to be the messiah, but that Mark added this detail to explain why Jesus did not seem like the messiah of Jewish expectation, and that the disciples did not proclaim him as messiah until after his death. Wrede argued that the Christians' belief in the resurrection served to vindicate their messianic claims. Certainly, if Jesus had political aspirations as a messiah, these failed: when Jesus died, the Jews were still under Roman rule and subject to heavy taxation. In affirming the messiahship of Jesus, the Christians re-interpreted the concept, regarding Christ as their redeemer, not from political oppression, but from sin, delivering them from Satan's rule, and offering them membership of the kingdom of God.

The concept of messiah therefore links with Christ's redeeming work, and an important title that is given to him is 'Saviour'. John's Gospel particularly emphasizes Christ's role in taking away human sin. He is 'the Lamb of God, who takes away the sin of the world' (Jn 1:29). In the Jewish religion of Jesus' time, atonement for sin was linked with a sacrificial system. On the Day of Atonement, an animal was to be sacrificed as an offering to God, and lambs, goats and bulls were regularly sacrificed at the pilgrim festivals, and doves were used to atone for personal sin or for the cure of certain diseases (Lev. 14:30-31; 23:4-44). The coincidence of Jesus' death and the Passover caused John and subsequent generations of Christians to identify Jesus with the Passover lamb. The Passover lamb was not actually sacrificed to God, but was killed and eaten as part of the festival meal; although this lamb was not offered as a token of atonement, Christians nonetheless made associations between Jesus the 'lamb of God' and the atoning sacrifices in the Jewish tradition.

The association between Jesus and sacrifice had several implications for Christians. If Christ was himself the sacrifice for the world's sin, then, they concluded, the sacrificial system of the Jerusalem Temple had been superseded. For the Christian, Christ was the sacrifice; therefore it was unnecessary to perform the sacrificial rites associated with the Jewish law. As Paul wrote, 'Christ, our Passover lamb, has been sacrificed. Therefore, let us keep the Festival, not with the old yeast, the yeast of malice and wickedness, but with bread without yeast, the bread of sincerity and truth' (1 Cor. 5:7-8).

The allusion to yeast relates to the Jewish practice, which still survives, of using unleavened bread at Passover time, and of hunting out and removing all traces of yeast in one's household before the Passover period. Yeast symbolises impurity, and Paul associates it here with sin. Likewise, the Passover lamb had to be 'without defect' (Num. 28:19), and Christ, being sinless, was the pure and blameless sacrifice for the world's sin (Heb. 9:14).

Jesus is not regarded as a passive victim in his sacrifice for the world's sin. When Pontius Pilate says to Jesus, 'Don't you realise I have power either to free you or to crucify you?' Jesus replies, 'You would have no power over me if it were not given to you from above' (Jn 19:10-11). Christianity embraces the paradox that, although Jesus' crucifixion was a grave sin on the part of his accusers, it was nonetheless in accordance with God's will, being necessary for the world's salvation. The writer to the Hebrews therefore portrays Jesus, not just as the sacrificial victim, but as the high priest, who initiates the sacrifice of atonement. As a favourite Christian hymn, often used at the Eucharist, puts it:

> thou within the veil hast entered,
>   robed in flesh, our great High Priest;
> thou on earth both Priest and Victim
>   in the eucharistic feast.
> (*Hymns Ancient and Modern*, New Standard Edition, no. 262)

The reference to the veil is an allusion to part of the crucifixion story. Matthew records that at the moment of Jesus' death the curtain ('veil') of the Jerusalem Temple was torn in two (Mt. 27:51). The Temple had a curtain, dividing its most sacred area—the 'Holy of Holies'—from the rest, disallowing public access or even view. Even the High Priest was only permitted to enter once a year, on the Day of Atonement. The reference to the veil is intended to indicate that Christ's death broke down the barrier separating humanity from God, being the atoning sacrifice that superseded the traditional Jewish priestly activity. As the writer to the Hebrews states, 'Therefore, brothers, since we have confidence to enter the Most Holy Place by the blood of Jesus, by a new a living way opened for us through the curtain, that is his body, and since we have a great priest over the house of God, let us draw near to God with a sincere heart in full assurance of faith' (Heb. 10:19-22).

Another title frequently given to Jesus is 'son of man'—by far his most common title in the Gospels. However, its precise meaning is uncertain, and continues to be debated amongst scholars. Sometimes Jesus appears to use the expression as a self-reference, for example when he says, 'For the Son of Man came to seek and to save what was lost' (Lk. 19:10). The phrase emphasizes Jesus' humanity, and occurs frequently in the prophecies of Ezekiel, for example when God instructs him, 'Son of man, stand up on your feet and I will speak to you' (Ezek. 2:1). Here 'son of man' appears to be a circumlocution for 'man', and its purport is to emphasize Ezekiel's humanity: he is being cut down to size, as it were, in God's presence. Elsewhere in the Bible, however, the expression 'son of man' seems to denote a superhuman rather than a human figure. The verse in Daniel, mentioned above, tells of the son of man coming in the clouds and approaching the Ancient of Days (Dan. 7:13)—plainly not a human figure. Christians applied the Jewish expectation of a coming 'son of man' to Jesus, and many Christians hold a literal belief that human history will be dramatically interrupted and brought to an end by the return of Jesus Christ, the 'son of man', who will come in the clouds of heaven.

The expected Son of Man's coming is associated with judgement. Matthew's Gospel offers a picture of the Son of Man, having come as a king in all his glory, judging the nations of the world, according to their deeds (Mt. 25:31-46). Depending on whether they have shown compassion for the hungry, the thirst, the stranger, the sick or the prisoner, they will be divided into 'sheep' and 'goats'—metaphors used to designate the just and the unjust. The 'goats' are commanded to depart from the Son of Man's presence, 'into the eternal fire prepared for the devil and his angels', while the 'sheep' enjoy eternal life. Some Christians take this picture fairly literally, holding that some form of everlasting punishment awaits the unfaithful—perhaps not a literal fire, but maybe eternal separation from God, which is equally undesirable. (Opinion among Christians, as expressed in poll results seem to vary considerably on this issue; Ontario Consultants on Religious Tolerance 2007.)

Not only is Jesus described as the 'son of man', for the Christian he is also the Son of God. Of course, all Christians regard themselves as sons and daughters of God, in the broad sense of belonging to God's family and recognizing his parental guidance and authority. However, the phrase 'Son of God', as applied to Jesus, designates a unique office. The Christian faith ascribes divine parenthood to Jesus, traditionally teaching that his birth was through the union of God's Holy Spirit and the Virgin Mary. Jesus' sonship, however, does not begin with the Virgin Birth, but is eternal: Christianity teaches that Jesus is the 'firstborn over all creation' (Col. 1:15). According to the story of creation, Adam and Eve were created by God at a point in time—the seventh day of creation (Gen. 1:27)—but Jesus Christ is held to have existed from eternity. The Nicene Creed describes him as 'begotten of the Father before all worlds'.

Jesus is thus conceived as God the Father's co-creator of the world. This notion relates to another title ascribed to Jesus: the Word (*logos* in Greek; Jn 1:1). It is God's word that brings about creation. God says, 'Let there be light', and light appears (Gen. 1:3), and it is God's speech that brings into being each successive stage of creation. By calling Jesus 'the Word' John is identifying Jesus as the co-creator of the universe. 'Word' has more obvious associations with speech, and the prophets spoke 'the word of the Lord': thus Jesus is regarded as the one who proclaims God's word, and in whom God's word of prophecy is complete. John's concept of the *logos* is also associated with divine wisdom; according to the Book of Proverbs, wisdom has a voice: 'Does not wisdom call out? Does not understanding raise her voice?' (Prov. 8:1).

God's word and God's creative energy thus become focused on and united in the person of Christ. It is not difficult to see how the ideas of 'Son of God', eternal co-creator, divine Word and divine wisdom, paved the way for the title 'God the Son' to be accorded to Jesus. Christianity soon came to confer full deity to Jesus: his status as the Son does not imply that he is subordinate or inferior to God, but that he is of equal stature with God the Father. Together with the Holy Spirit, the Father and the Son are one united and undivided Trinity. The doctrine of the Trinity, and the relationship between the three 'persons' that comprise it are not easy to grasp. Suffice it to say here that, for the Christian, no status is too high to be accorded to Jesus. As a well known hymn puts it,

> The highest place that heaven affords
> is his, is his by right,
> The King of kings, and Lord of lords,
> and heaven's eternal Light.
> (*Hymns Ancient and Modern*, New Standard, no. 141)

There are many other titles that are given to Jesus Christ. John records seven occasions on which Jesus predicates the words 'I am' with a description of himself: 'the bread of life', 'the light of the world', 'the gate', 'the good shepherd', 'the resurrection and the life', 'the way, the truth and the life', and 'the true vine' (Jn 6:35; 8:12; 10:7, 11; 11:25; 14:6; 15:1), all of which are metaphors indicating the role Jesus has for his followers. Above all, however, Jesus is the saviour or redeemer of the world. The Christian regards him as the one who has conquered sin and death, and who offers new life and hope of resurrection in God's kingdom. Reflecting on Christ's person is no mere attempt at abstruse theology: it points to the message of redemption, which the Christian faith proclaims.

Jesus' status is frequently summed up in the phrase, 'Jesus Christ, Son of God, Saviour'—a phrase that is represented by the ancient Christian symbol of the fish. The fish symbol is frequently displayed in churches, and has become popular in Christian paraphernalia that are frequently marketed, particularly items of jewellery, or car bumper stickers. The symbol originated because of an acronym in Greek. The Greek word for 'fish' is *ichthus*. If one bears in mind that *ch* and *th* are single letters in the Greek alphabet, the acronym runs as follows.

I	*Iesous* (Jesus)
CH	*Christos* (Christ)
TH	*Theou* (of God)
U	*Uios* (Son)
S	*Sōter* (Saviour)

Whatever the uncertainties about the pedigree and historical reliability of the Gospels, and however much or little can be truly known about the historical Jesus, the acronym sums up the essence of all Christians' belief in Jesus, as the expected Messiah (the Christ), the Son of God, and the world's saviour.

4

Paul's Contribution to the Christian Faith

Although Christianity is plainly founded on the life and teaching of Jesus, Christianity would not have survived in its present form—indeed it would possibly not have survived at all—if it had not been for the early apostle Paul. His contribution to the Christian faith is such that one present-day scholar describes him as 'the most influential theologian of all time' (Hooker, in Bowden 2005: 897). Despite the fact that Paul was not an immediate follower of Jesus and indeed had never met him, his impact on the emergent Christian faith was manifold. In Christian art, Paul is usually depicted as a short man, bald, and with a stoop. Although this traditional portrayal goes back to the second century, and the fourth-century Church historian Eusebius affirms its authenticity, such representations are probably due to imagination rather than historical fact.

When Paul was drawn into the Christian fold, the Christians were gaining momentum as a distinctive Jewish sect who still observed the Jewish Law, and worshipped with their fellow Jews in the synagogues, although they sometimes made themselves unpopular by proclaiming Jesus as the expected messiah. Judaism had its diaspora—its dispersed following outside Judaea—where the Jewish scriptures were read in Greek rather than Hebrew, since Greek was the language of the educated, in which scholarly writing was typically published. Paul himself was a member of the Jewish diaspora, and when he quotes from the Jewish scriptures in his own writings, he invariably uses the Septuagint (the Greek edition of Jewish sacred writings). With the influx of Gentiles into Jerusalem, as well as the rise of Jewish diaspora communities outside Judaea, some Gentiles were converting to the Jewish faith, and some of them had begun to encounter the early Jewish-Christian communities.

Paul describes himself as 'the apostle to the Gentiles' (Gal. 2:7), and his major achievement was to make Christianity a religion that could be appropriated by the Gentile world, and not simply by Jews. Paul is renowned for his work within the early Christian communities, building up these churches and endeavouring to resolve emergent problems. His contribution to the rise of Christianity included his extensive letters to early Christian communities, which work out a complex theology which continues to influence twenty-first century Christians. As well as being a writer, Paul was a seasoned traveller, making three extensive missionary journeys throughout the Middle East, establishing communities in various major cities.

We learn about Paul through his own writings, and from the Book of Acts, which was written by Luke as the sequel to his Gospel. At times there are difficulties in reconciling Luke's account with Paul's: until recently it was assumed that Luke afforded reliable and at times first-hand testimony regarding Paul, but recent scholars have come to question this. In particular, Hans Conzelmann, John Knox (a twentieth-century scholar, not to be confused with the sixteenth-century Protestant reformer), and the Jewish scholar Hyam Maccoby have called into question Paul's own veracity. The scholarly debates continue, but the generally accepted account of Paul is as follows.

Paul's original name was Saul, and he was born in Tarsus, a coastal city in Asia Minor, now modern Turkey. Saul of Tarsus was a tentmaker by trade, and studied to become a Jewish rabbi: Paul tells us that his teacher was Gamaliel, a well-respected Pharisee who on another occasion advised the Sanhedrin to be lenient in dealing with Peter and other disciples when they were arrested in Jerusalem. Saul was not as tolerant of the Christians as Gamaliel, however, for he was present when the early apostle Stephen was stoned to death, apparently being entrusted with the task of looking after their coats during the stoning. (Stephen is often cited as the earliest Christian martyr; Acts 6:8–8:1.) Saul continued his opposition to the Jerusalem Christians by tracking them down in their homes, and securing their imprisonment (Acts 8:1-3). He then turned his attention to Damascus, in Syria, and sought the Jerusalem High Priest's authorization to purge the Jewish communities of Christians there. Armed with letters of introduction to the Damascus synagogues, giving him powers of arrest, he was travelling on the Damascus road with three companions when he experienced a sudden vision. A flash of light appeared to come from heaven, causing him to fall to the ground, and he heard a voice saying, 'Saul, Saul, why do you persecute me?'

(Acts 9:4). On enquiring who was speaking to him, he received the reply, 'I am Jesus, whom you are persecuting.' The voice instructed Saul to continue into Damascus, where he would be told what next to do. On getting back on his feet, Saul discovered that the brightness of the flash had blinded him, and he had to be led into the city, where he was sought out by Ananias, an early Christian leader who, Luke tells us, had received a vision, instructing him to find the place where Saul was lodging, and to restore Saul's sight. Ananias was initially apprehensive, knowing Saul's past reputation, but he obeyed; Saul's eyesight was restored and he was baptized into the Christian faith.

The famous Damascus Road incident is often referred to as 'the conversion of Saint Paul', Paul being the new name by which he was called, following his acceptance of Christ. Although the word 'conversion' is used in this regard, it should be remembered that Saul did not change religions: the Christians were not at that point separate from their Jewish roots. The former persecutor of the Christians now became the victim of a Jewish plot against him, and Luke reports that he had to escape from the city by being lowered down in a basket through a gap in the city wall. From there, Saul went to Arabia, where he spent two years before being sought out by Barnabas, who found him in Tarsus, and brought him back to the Christian community in Antioch. Luke reports that this was where the early disciples were first called 'Christians' (Acts 11:26)—the name that has lasted for almost twenty centuries. Barnabas was to become Paul's travelling companion on his first missionary journey.

Paul's first missionary journey, accompanied by Barnabas and Mark, went from Antioch, a place to which numerous Jews escaped to avoid persecution, on to the port of Seleucia, where he departed from Cyprus, visiting Salamis and Paphos. From there Paul sailed over to Asia Minor (present-day Turkey), arriving at Iconium, and from there to Lystra. It was at Lystra that Paul was hunted down by some traditional Jews, and stoned. Paul was presumed dead, but revived and travelled on to Derbe, and back to Antioch. Paul's second journey was not with Barnabas: these two apostles quarrelled because the latter wanted Mark to accompany them. Apparently Mark had left them in Pamphylia on the first journey, and Paul regarded this as desertion. Instead, Paul decided to travel with Silas on a much more extensive journey than the first. After travelling once more through Syria, where they were joined by Timothy, who resided at Lystra. On reaching Troas, Paul received a dream, which he regarded as a celestial vision: a Macedonian man appeared to be standing and imploring the disciples to come and preach the gospel in

Macedonia. Paul immediately accepted the call, and the remainder of the journey took Paul and Silas into Macedonia, and from thence down the east coast of Greece, encompassing Thessalonica, Beroea, Athens, Corinth and Cenchreae, before returning to Asia Minor. Paul's third journey was largely a return to places previously visited on the second one, but taking a different route through Asia Minor and Greece.

In the course of these journeys Paul would find any platform that was available to him to preach the gospel. Local synagogues provided an obvious forum, but Paul also preached in market places and in well known debating places such as Mars Hill in Athens. Paul can be credited with setting up Christian communities in most of the places he visited, although in a few locations—Thessalonica is probably one such example—believers were already present, and found support from Paul's preaching. The book of Acts recounts Paul's adventures, which included arrest, imprisonment, beatings and shipwrecks. Paul's final journey ended in Rome. He was arrested at the Temple in Jerusalem and brought before the Jewish Sanhedrin. Being a Roman citizen, however, Paul insisted on trial under Roman law, and was brought to Caesarea to have his case heard by Antonius Felix, who was governor of Judaea. Felix procrastinated, and two years passed before his successor Porcius Festus allowed Paul's case to be brought before Caesar in Rome. Paul was taken to Rome, via Malta, where he survived a further shipwreck, and the story ends with Paul's situation still unresolved. Luke ends his account by depicting Paul in rented accommodation, preaching to anyone who came to visit him. Paul expressed an intention to go on to Spain, but there is no record of his having done so. The Church historian Eusebius, writing in the fourth century, relates that Paul was finally beheaded during Nero's reign, possibly between 60 and 62 CE.

The above account of Paul's journeys is somewhat of a thumbnail sketch. It is difficult to match up Luke's account with Paul's own version of his travels which we find in his letters. One important incident was the so-called Council at Jerusalem (Acts 15), which Luke places between Paul's first and second journeys, but the exact occasion is disputed by historians. This 'Council' was a meeting between Paul and Barnabas, and several other Christian leaders, including Peter and James. The meeting appears to have been occasioned by a number of traditional Jews, who wanted to insist that Christianity, being a form of Judaism, required Gentile converts to undergo circumcision as an initiatory requirement. After much debate, the assembly concluded that circumcision was inappropriate, and that Gentile converts should 'abstain from food polluted by idols, from sexual immorality, from the meat of strangled animals and from blood' (Acts 15:20). This requirement seems to be based on the Noahide Covenant—a set of requirements believed to have been given by God to Noah, and which a god-fearing Gentile should obey in order to be assured of a place in the world to come. (Noah predates the establishment of Israel as a nation; hence the commandments that he received are regarded as binding on all humanity.) The requirements for Jews, of course, were much more stringent, entailing full compliance with the 613 commandments of the Torah. The Noahide list proscribed idolatry, murder, theft, adultery, blasphemy and eating of flesh taken from live animals, and required righteous Gentiles to adopt a system of just laws. The Noahide Covenant is contained in the Talmud, which is a much later piece of writing (around 500 CE), and may not have assumed this form by the first century. Nonetheless, it is plain that the question of the degree of Gentile compliance with the Torah was an important issue, and the Council of Jerusalem may have been instrumental in formulating these Noahide laws.

Paul's Letters

The issue of the Christian's relationship to the Jewish law is a key theme in Paul's writings, to which we now turn. Paul's letters were written to various early Christian communities, and were composed between 50 and 56 CE. They are therefore the earliest Christian documents that we possess, predating the Gospel records. One letter—to Philemon—addresses an individual rather than a community, and concerns a runaway slave who came to Paul: Paul requests Philemon, the slave-owner, to reinstate him. The other letters, to the communities, offer encouragement to fellow-leaders, offering advice on problems, such as rival factions and the falling away of members. They offer guidance on practical behaviour, in terms of lifestyle in general, and also within the Church, including Paul's somewhat controversial views on the behaviour of women. Other liturgical issues include the celebration of the Lord's Supper—Paul's term for the Eucharist. Such practicalities apart, the bulk of Paul's writings are theological, dealing with issues of interpreting Jewish scripture, attitudes to the Law, the role of the Gentiles, the nature of Christ and the reconciliation with God that he offers through faith in him. Newness of life, both now and after death, is also an important theme, and the nature of the resurrection receives extended treatment particularly in his first letter to the Corinthians.

We do not possess the entire collection of Paul's letters. Paul refers to a letter written to the Laodicaeans, which he invites the Colossian Christians to read (Col. 4:16), but which became lost. There is reason to suppose that 1 Corinthians was not the first letter Paul wrote to the Corinthian church, since he appears to refer to a previous one (1 Cor. 5:9), and it has been hypothesized that 2 Corinthians is an amalgam of two distinct pieces of correspondence (Bruce, in Black and Rowley 1962: 931). The authenticity of some of the letters attributed to Paul has also been questioned. The letters to Timothy and Titus acknowledge the existence of designated office-bearers, such as overseer (*episkopos*) and congregational servant (*diakonos*), which assumes a rather more developed Church than is likely during Paul's lifetime. The authorship of the letter to the Ephesians has been questioned, both on account of its style and because of its themes: it has little to say about Christ's cross, and seems much more positive about marriage and family life than we find elsewhere in Paul's writings. Some doubts have been cast on Colossians, on account of its apparently 'high' Christology: the author describes Christ as 'the image of the invisible God, the firstborn over all creation'—a description that is not found elsewhere in Paul's writings. The Letter to the Hebrews makes no claim to Pauline authorship, and its style and contents differ markedly from Paul's writings. Some older versions of the King James Bible bear the title 'The Epistle of Paul to the Hebrews', but this heading is purely editorial.

There is some disagreement among scholars about the order in which Paul wrote his letters, but one reasonable conjecture is that the letters to the Thessalonians came first, with Romans as the culmination of Paul's ideas. A possible chronology is as follows:

50 CE	1 and 2 Thessalonians
53 CE	Galatians
53 CE	Philippians
53 CE	Colossians
53 CE	Philemon
54–56 CE	1 and 2 Corinthians
56 CE	Romans

This chronology excludes Ephesians, which more conservative scholars, such as F. F. Bruce, suggest was written around 60 or 61 CE, while those who doubt its authenticity have suggested a wide range of possible dates, from 70 CE to as late as 170 CE.

Four of the letters attributed to Paul are sometimes described as the 'captivity epistles', since their author refers to himself as being in bondage.

These are Philippians, Colossians, Ephesians and Philemon. This does not mean they were necessarily written from Rome, as is sometimes assumed, since Paul was arrested and imprisoned on more than one occasion. Paul would typically use an amanuensis, not because he was chained, or because of pressure of work, or because his eyesight might have been failing—all of which have been popularly suggested—but rather because it was normal practice at that time for a scribe to write a draft on a wax tablet, transcribe it on to parchment and then take it to the author for approval. The author would often add a final message in his own handwriting, as Paul at times appears to do. For example, the letter to the Galatians ends with Paul stating, 'See what large letters I use as I write to you with my own hand!' (Gal. 6:11).

Key Themes in Paul's letters

It is perhaps surprising that Paul has little to tell his readers about the historical Jesus. In the entirety of his letters, such information is minimal. We are told that Jesus was a descendant of King David (Rom. 1:3), that he had brothers, one of whom was called James (1 Cor. 9:5; Gal. 1:19), that he celebrated the Last Supper on the night of his betrayal (1 Cor. 11:23-26), that he was crucified (1 Cor. 2:2), died and was buried, and that he rose again on the third day (1 Cor. 15:4-6). Paul makes reference to a number of resurrection appearances, including an appearance to over five-hundred people—an incident that is not recorded in the Gospels (1 Cor. 15:6). There is reference to the ascension in Ephesians (4:7-13), as well as to an expected second coming (1 Thess. 4:13-18), which will be followed by Christ exercising his role as the judge of the world (Rom. 2:16). Clearly, some of these points are more Christological than historical, reinforcing the idea that Paul is much more interested in the 'Christ of faith' than in the historical Jesus.

We cannot be certain whether Paul simply did not know the details of Jesus' life, or whether he assumed that such information would already be known to the early Christian communities, or whether he thought it was unimportant. Whatever the explanation, Paul's writings make no mention—apart from the Last Supper—of any incidents in Jesus' life: there are no stories of healings, no accounts of controversies with the scribes and Pharisees, no parables, no sermons, not even an account of Christ's passion. The only hint we receive about Jesus' teaching is in the final chapter of Galatians, where Paul tells his readers that bearing each other's burdens is fulfilling the law of Christ (Gal. 6:2). Paul sums up the

Jewish Law as the law of love (Rom. 13:8-10; Gal. 5:14), but does not attribute this summation to Jesus: it was in fact a well known summary of the Law by Jewish rabbis of the period, including the famous Rabbi Hillel (trad. 110 BCE–10 CE). Whereas Jesus' teaching was substantially about the kingdom of God, Paul makes only minimal reference to the concept (Rom. 14:17; 1 Thess. 2:12).

Paul's aim was not to disseminate or reiterate Jesus' teachings, but rather to proclaim the Christ of faith. In Rudolf Bultmann's words, 'the proclaimer becomes the proclaimed' (Bultmann 1952: 33). In other words, Jesus proclaimed the kingdom of God, but Paul proclaimed Jesus himself. Unacquainted himself with the historical Jesus, Paul's own familiarity was with the Christ of faith whom he experienced on the Damascus Road. Paul counts his vision as one of the post-resurrection appearances: 'last of all he appeared to me also, as to one abnormally born' (1 Cor. 15:8). Paul certainly regarded his Damascus Road experience as a post-resurrection experience, equivalent in authenticity to those of the disciples who knew Jesus 'from a worldly point of view' (2 Cor. 5:16). The experience entitles him to claim to be an apostle, like the other disciples who claimed to have seen him after his resurrection (1 Cor. 9:1), although perhaps the fact that Paul has to assert his apostolicity indicates that there were those in the early Christian communities who questioned his status.

The Nature of Christ

For Paul, Jesus is no mere human figure. Paul preaches a cosmic Christ—a Christ who rules the world and who is the consummation of human history, not a mere historical character confined to a specific place and time. The whole of creation, he declares, has been longing for his coming, in order to obtain liberation from its captivity (Rom. 8:20-21). The entire human race became defiled through Adam's sin, but Christ comes as the 'second Adam', recapitulating Adam's role, but, unlike Adam, he fulfils God's will perfectly, offering newness of life to humanity. Adam's punishment for sin was death (Gen. 2:17), a sentence that was inflicted on all of his progeny, but, as Paul writes, 'as in Adam all die, so in Christ all will be made alive' (1 Cor. 15:22). Paul confidently affirms Christ's resurrection, assuring his readers that, as one who has conquered death, he is the guarantor of the general resurrection of all humankind. He is God's messiah, who offers redemption, and who has ascended into heaven, where he intercedes for humanity (Rom. 8:34), and from whence he will return. Paul fully expected Christ's second coming, confidently affirming that he will return very soon (1 Thess. 4:13–5:11).

When Christ returns, he will come as the world's judge (2 Cor. 8:10), receiving the homage and submission of all, as the ruler over God's new kingdom:

> Therefore God exalted him to the highest places,
>   and gave him the name that is above every name,
> that at the name of Jesus every knee should bow,
> in heaven and on earth and under the earth,
> and every tongue confess that Jesus Christ is Lord,
> to the glory of God the Father. (Phil. 2:9-11)

This cosmic Christ was 'in the form of God' (Phil. 2:6), and the Son of God (2 Cor. 1:19), although Paul stops short of affirming that Jesus Christ is God himself. His life on earth was as a normal human being, having laid aside his divine attributes and powers, in order to become fully human, and to accept death on the cross (Phil. 2:6-8).

The key event in Jesus' earthly life which secured humankind's redemption was crucifixion. Through his death, Jesus assumes the punishment that was prescribed for Adam's sin. As Paul writes, 'We preach Christ crucified', and adds that this was 'a stumbling-block to the Jews and foolishness to the Greeks' (1 Cor. 1:23). For traditional Jews, the notion of a crucified messiah was a contradiction: the messiah was expected to lead the Jewish nation to victory. As for the Greeks, the idea of a bodily resurrection was incomprehensible: Paul's attempts to persuade the Athenian philosophers about Christ's resurrection from the dead were met with derision (Acts 17:32).

The Nature of the Resurrection

Paul identified his Damascus Road experience as an encounter with the risen Christ—hence the Christian faith is about a relationship with a living person, not mere veneration of someone who has died for a worthy cause. Although Paul does not mention an empty tomb, unlike the Gospel writers, Paul affirms the resurrection of the body, and identifies Christ's resurrection as the pivot of the Christian faith: 'If Christ has not been raised, our preaching is useless and so is your faith' (1 Cor. 15:14). Christ's resurrection is the 'firstfruits'—the harbinger and the guarantor of the general resurrection from the dead, for which Christians may hope. If there were no resurrection, Paul believes, one's ultimate goal should be no more than seeking after the hedonistic pleasures pertaining to one's physical life. There would be no salvation from sin, whose consequence is death, if nothing lay beyond our earthly existence: 'For the wages of sin is death, but the gift of God is eternal life in Christ Jesus our Lord' (Rom. 6:23).

Paul envisages Christ's return as the herald of this general resurrection. Christ will come down on a cloud from heaven, to the sound of a trumpet, and the archangel's voice (presumably Paul is referring to the archangel Michael) will command the dead to return to life. The 'dead in Christ' will be the first to rise—that is, those who have actively been Christ's followers, but have not lived to witness this final end to human affairs. Then the living faithful will be caught up to meet him in the air, and will remain with Christ for all eternity (1 Thess. 4:13-17). Paul believes in a bodily resurrection, rather than in the immortality of a disembodied soul—a later idea that found its way into Christianity as a result of Greek philosophical influence. The resurrection, however, is not the mere resuscitation of corpses. Paul insists that 'flesh and blood cannot inherit the kingdom of God' (1 Cor. 15:50). Paul distinguishes between a 'natural body' and a 'spiritual body' (1 Cor. 15:44). The former is the physical, carnal body that we possess during our earthly existence, and which is subject to physical ('fleshly') desires, and subject to death. The believer's physical body, however, is not totally annihilated on death, but becomes transformed into a 'spiritual body'. Adam's body was created from the dust of the ground, but the 'new man' and new woman, who are 'in Christ' will be given a body that is from heaven.

If one were to inquire what this spiritual body is like, Paul's answer is that one cannot imagine from the standpoint of earthly existence what its character will be. All one can affirm is that it is a 'glorious' body, imperishable, incorruptible, not subject to sin and death, and made in the likeness of Jesus Christ, whose body is now a heavenly, not an earthly one (1 Cor. 15:35-56). Paul writes triumphantly:

> Where, O death, is your victory?
> Where, O death, is your sting?

The sting of death is sin, and the power of sin is the law. But thanks be to God! He gives us the victory through our Lord Jesus Christ. (1 Cor. 15:55-57)

The Law

In the passage quoted above, Paul mentions the Law in connection with sin and death. The Law is a key theme in Paul's writings, to which we now turn. We have already mentioned the controversy about whether Christianity was to be regarded as a form of Judaism or whether it was a separate form of spirituality. Both Paul and Jesus' immediate disciples were Jewish, and the prospect of casting away their Jewish identity was no light matter. The Jews are typically described as 'God's chosen people', although this description has frequently been misconstrued. The 'chosenness' of the Jews consists of their presumed obligation to obey the Law's requirements—an obligation that was not fully binding on the Gentiles—in exchange for which the Jews were the beneficiaries of God's 'covenant'. A covenant was an agreement that God is held to have made with various patriarchs, notably Noah (Gen. 8:21; 9:4), Abraham (Gen. 15:5; 17:11), Jacob (Gen. 35:11-12) and especially Moses, who received the entire written Torah from God at Mount Sinai (Exod. 19:5-6).

A covenant dictates obligations, but also offers a promise. In the case of the Jews, the promised benefit for keeping God's Law was that they would become a great nation, inheriting their own 'promised land'. (When Moses received the Torah—the first five books of the Jewish-Christian Bible—on Mount Sinai, the Jews were still wandering through the Sinai desert, having escaped from oppression in Egypt.) At a later stage in Jewish history, covenant keeping became associated with messianism: there arose a belief, still prevalent in some Jewish circles today, that if all Jews faithfully kept two successive Sabbaths the messiah would come. Having received the Law from God through Moses, the Jews were the special custodians of God's word, entrusted with its observation and interpretation (Rom. 3:2).

These were the presumed benefits of being Jewish. However, embracing Judaism in order to join the Christian fold was a disincentive to espousing Christianity. In particular, the initiatory rite of circumcision and the keeping of the food laws were perceived as particularly onerous, as indeed were the many detailed prescriptions for maintaining purity and living one's daily life. However, if Christianity were to supersede Judaism, this would raise a cluster of problems. What was the role of the Jews in God's plan for humankind's salvation? Were they no longer God's chosen people? God had made promises to the patriarchs and to Moses: was God now intending to renege on these, by offering salvation to the Gentiles, through faith rather than Torah observance? Was the

Law utterly to be disregarded? Although some of the ritual requirements might seem inappropriate to Gentiles, the Law also dealt with social responsibilities and personal morality. Was not at least some of the Law needed in order to maintain social cohesion and personal integrity? These are the questions with which Paul wrestles in much of his writing, particularly (but not exclusively) in the letters to the Galatians and the Romans.

Paul argues, first, that God has not cast away his people, for he continues to will that all Israel should be saved (Rom. 11:11-24). In commending Christ to the Jews, Paul is not recommending that they abandon their Jewishness. On the contrary, the Jews have been entrusted with God's word (Rom. 3:2), and were the first to be offered the benefits brought by Jesus Christ, who himself belonged to the Jewish faith. Many of the Jews had been blinded to the truth of the gospel, but Scripture gave the assurance that there would always remain a faithful 'remnant'. It was because of the Jews' wide-scale rejection of Christ that God now offered salvation to the Gentile as well as—not instead of—the Jew. The Gentiles inherit God's salvation by a process of 'ingrafting'. Paul uses the analogy of an olive tree. A gardener will break off branches from an olive tree, in order to graft in new ones; thus branches from a wild olive tree can become a profitable part of a fully cultivated one. The broken-off branches represent the unfaithful Jews, and the wild olive branches the Gentiles. Paul also envisions the possibility of original branches being grafted back in—Jews who at first rejected the gospel, but reconsidered and accepted it (Rom. 11:11-24). The Gentiles thus inherit God's promises by being 'grafted on' to God's people.

Paul perceives a number of problems concerning living by the Jewish Law. The commandments of the Torah are many and detailed, and thus it is difficult—indeed impossible—to be righteous by the Law's own standards. The Law therefore highlights sin; indeed, Paul claims that it can even be the cause of sin, since laws multiply offences rather than simply control behaviour. The Law also underlines one's carnal nature. Paul tells the Romans that he wants to keep God's Law but, no sooner has the desire to keep the Law arisen, than he finds another law at work: his physical body rebels against the divine law, and the desire to sin arises. 'When I want to do good,' he writes, 'evil is right there with me,' enslaving him to this 'law of sin' (Rom. 7:21-25). Those who are more adept at keeping the Law face a different danger, however: the risk of self-righteousness (Gal. 6:12). Since righteousness has been brought about by Christ's death and resurrection, one should not boast about one's own efforts: 'Let him who boasts boast in the Lord' (1 Cor. 1:31). Since the Law gives rise to sin, and 'the wages of sin is death', the Law becomes the agent of death, Paul reasons. For Paul, the Law is also dead in the sense of being inanimate, first written in tablets of stone, which Moses received on Mount Sinai, and brought down from the mountain top to the Israelites. The people could see the stone tablets, but having sight of them was in no way equivalent to having a direct experience of the living God, which Moses alone was permitted.

It might seem to follow from Paul's scathing attack on the Law that Paul is advocating its total abandonment. Was Paul really suggesting that the Law should be done away with, and that one should do as one pleases? Paul attempts to counter the possible accusation of antinomianism. Paul asks, 'What shall we say, then? Shall we go on sinning, so that grace may increase?' (Rom. 6:1). It has sometimes been suggested that there was a school of thought within early Christianity that advocated profligate lawbreaking, reasoning that if Christ's grace cancelled out sin, then the believer would receive all the more grace, the more he or she sinned. There is no evidence of such a current of opinion within the early Church, and it is more probable that Paul is merely asking a rhetorical question as a means to developing his line of argument. Paul argues, first, that Christ offers newness of life and 'death to sin' (Rom. 6:1-4), which can hardly involve increased sinfulness. We have noted Paul's concern that the Law helps to generate carnal desires but, equally, believing that 'everything is permissible' would involve giving free reign to one's fleshly appetites. Those who cannot control their desire for food or for sex have not achieved mastery over their bodies. Christ brought us back from the bonds of sin; therefore, Paul reasons, our bodies do not belong to ourselves, but to God, and should be respected as such (1 Cor. 6:12-20).

Paul has a further and perhaps more compelling argument against antinomianism. Jewish Scripture speaks of a covenant that God made with Noah, Abraham, Jacob and Moses, but it also speaks of a 'new covenant'. This covenant was proclaimed by the prophet Jeremiah, who wrote:

> 'The time is coming,' declares the LORD,
> 'when I will make a new covenant with the house of Israel
> and with the house of Judah.
> It will not be like the covenant
> I made with their forefathers
> when I took them by the hand to lead them out of Egypt,
> because they broke my covenant,

> though I was a husband to them,'
> declares the LORD.
> 'This is the covenant I will make
> with the house of Israel
> after that time,' declares the LORD.
> 'I will put my law in their minds
> and write it on their hearts.
> I will be their God,
> and they will be my people.
> No longer will a man teach his neighbour,
> or a man his brother, saying, "Know the LORD,"
> because they will all know me,
> from the least of them to the greatest,' declares the LORD.
> (Jer. 31:31-34)

This passage is quoted by the writer to the Hebrews (probably not Paul; Heb. 8:8-12), who applies it to Christ, the mediator of this new covenant (Heb. 9:15), and early Christian communities regarded such prophecy as predicting what the coming messiah would accomplish. Paul may also be alluding to this passage when he writes, 'He has made us competent as ministers of a new covenant—not of the letter but of the Spirit; for the letter kills, but the Spirit gives life' (2 Cor. 3:6).

The new covenant to which Jeremiah refers has two important aspects. First, as the writer to the Hebrews points out, the new covenant is superior to the old one (Heb. 8:6). God has therefore not reneged on his promise to the Jews, but exceeded the terms of his agreement with them. Second, this new law is on God's people's hearts and minds. Paul tells his Roman readers that the Gentiles have God's law written within them, as Jeremiah described.

> Indeed, when Gentiles, who do not have the law, do by nature things required by the law, they are a law for themselves, even though they do not have the law, since they show that the requirements of the law are written on their hearts, their consciences also bearing witness, and their thoughts now accusing, now even defending them. (Rom. 2:14-15)

The expression 'a law unto themselves'—the King James translation of the phrase—popularly connotes lawlessness, but this is precisely what Paul does not mean here. He is referring to an unwritten law code, not set in tablets of stone, but in one's heart—the voice of conscience. The Gentiles' position with regard to God's law is that they have no excuse for their moral deficiencies, since one does not need stone tablets or a set of scriptures to determine God's will. Conscience exists within everyone. Paul argues that this voice of conscience, which forms part of the new covenant, comes directly from God, not mediated through a human lawgiver. It is more alive, being received by living human beings straight from a living God without intermediaries.

What, then, does Paul perceive as the value of the Law? The Torah is more than a mere list of commandments. Even a superficial acquaintance with the first five books of the Bible will show that these books have a strong narrative component, and not merely an ethical-legal one. As mentioned above, the Torah recounts God's creation of the world, how sin entered into it, and how God covenanted with the patriarchs, beginning with Noah and Abraham. Paul points out that it was a whole 430 years after God's covenant with Abraham that Moses was commissioned to transcribe and codify God's commandments. For Paul, therefore, the Law is predominantly about God's purpose and promise, rather than his legal requirements. As a rabbi, Paul's role was to interpret not only the Mosaic law code, but the entirety of the five books of the Torah, the narrative as well as the legal code.

When one considers the story of Abraham, Paul points out, Abraham's important quality is faith. The Book of Genesis recounts the story of God promising Abraham (Abram) a son, after his wife Sarah had proved to be infertile. The book states, 'He believed God, and it was credited to him as righteousness' (15:6; quoted in Gal. 3:6). In later incidents, God promises Abraham, 'To your offspring [seed] I will give this land' (Gen. 12:7; 13:15; 24:7). Paul points out, with rabbinical precision, that the word 'seed' is singular, not plural, and hence must refer to a single specific individual, namely God's messiah, Jesus Christ. The Law thus fulfils the function of pointing to Christ. Until Christ's coming, the Law is there because of human weakness, since men and women lack complete and reliable knowledge of how to live. The Law acts like a school pupil's tutor, to be dispensed with when Christ comes, and faith in him is found (Gal. 3:24-25).

Paul also interprets the Torah allegorically, believing it contains important hidden meaning beneath its surface. We have already mentioned his comparison between Adam and Jesus Christ. In the Letter to the Galatians (4:21-28) he makes another significant comparison, again involving the story of Abraham. The Book of Genesis records that since Sarah was unable to bear children, Abraham entered into a sexual relationship with Hagar, their servant, which resulted in the birth of Ishmael. When Abraham and Sarah, at the advanced ages of 100 and 90 respectively, miraculously parented their only child Isaac, Hagar was dismissed and sent out to wander in the desert. (One must not become sidetracked on the moral issues pertaining to Abraham's behaviour: the story is for didactic purposes, and God's providential oversight transcends human behaviour.) Paul tells his readers to take the story figuratively: Hagar represents the Law, and Sarah the promise. Hagar is the slave, while Sarah is the free woman. Ishmael was born naturally, while Isaac was born miraculously, as a result of divine promise. Hagar, Paul states, corresponds to Mount Sinai and Jerusalem, the respective locations of the giving of the Torah and of the centre of the Jewish religion, which is enslaved to the Law. Sarah represents 'the Jerusalem that is above', where there is freedom. When God's promise materializes (Isaac, and later Christ), then the slave (Hagar, representing the Law) must be got rid of. As children of the free woman rather than the slave, Christians are enjoined to dispense with the Law, and as children of free parents, not slaves, enjoy the full inheritance of the gospel, as they have been promised.

Although all this may seem extremely contrived and dubious exegesis of Scripture, it was nonetheless characteristic of early Christians (and indeed later ones) to see such cryptic allusions to Christ in God's word. Needless to say, the vast majority of twenty-first century Christian biblical scholars, and any Jewish rabbi—past or present, would not take such liberties with Scripture. Nevertheless, the notion that the Old Testament foreshadowed the New has always been prevalent within the Christian faith, and Paul finds such a role for the Torah.

Justification by Faith

If salvation cannot be gained through compliance with the Jewish Law, how then is it obtained? Paul's answer is that one obtains peace with God through being 'justified' by faith in Jesus Christ (Rom. 5:1). This statement, which lies at the heart of the Christian faith, needs some explanation. The word 'justification' is not self-explanatory. To 'justify' means 'to make straight': probably the best-known use of the term is in the context of 'justifying a margin' when one is typing—a 'justified' margin is a straight one. The word 'justify' was used in the law courts: to be justified meant to be acquitted, and thus Paul's term signifies that the believer is no longer held guilty of his or her sins. The analogy between straightness and righteousness is also used in the Old Testament, when the prophet Amos has a vision of God measuring a wall with a plumb-line (Amos 7:7-9): the plumb-line represented the nation of Israel, who did not measure up to God's standards. In everyday parlance we talk about people being 'straight' and 'crooked'.

Becoming 'straight' by God's standards, according to Paul, cannot be done through human effort, through compliance with the Law—since that is impossible—but rather through faith in Jesus Christ. Jesus is the perfect individual, who complied fully with the demands of the Law while he lived on earth, in contrast to Adam, who brought sin into the world. Despite being without sin, Jesus vicariously accepted the punishment for sin, namely death, by his atoning sacrifice on the cross (Eph. 5:2). Paul describes Christ as a 'sacrifice of atonement' (Rom. 3:25), portraying him as the one who supersedes the sacrificial system of the Jews. Paul also speaks of Christ as redeemer (Rom. 8:23)—a metaphor drawn from the context of the slave trade: believers are transformed from slaves to become the true heirs of God's inheritance. In other places, Paul speaks of 'reconciliation' (2 Cor. 5:18): the believer is no longer alienated from God, but at peace with him (Rom. 5:1). Obtaining justification through faith means that God now treats those who accept Jesus Christ in faith as if they were righteous, even though their past actions have been sinful (Rom. 5:19). It is as if God has deleted the law code with which humanity has failed to comply (Col. 2:13-14).

If justification does not require obedience to the Law, then it is reasonable to ask what this implies about the believer's behaviour. If one is saved through faith and not works, then does this mean that one can do as one pleases, and simply rely on faith for salvation through Jesus Christ? We have already considered and rejected the possible allegation that Paul is antinomian. Paul's answer to this question is that justification is merely the beginning of one's new spiritual life; as well as being justified, the believer must be 'sanctified' or made 'holy'. The Gentiles, Paul declares, are 'sanctified by the Holy Spirit' (Rom. 15:16). To be holy does not mean to be sanctimonious, but rather to be 'set apart'. A holy book, or a holy or sacred object, is something that is to be treated in a special way. Thus, the believer is set apart from 'the world'. He or she remains in the world, but sets oneself apart from worldly standards. Paul recommends to his readers that they eschew the company of those who have worldly standards, even going so far as to argue that members of the Christian community who maintain standards should be expelled from the congregation (1 Cor. 5:9-12).

This sanctifying process is the work of the Holy Spirit, Paul affirms. Although Paul uses the three-fold formula, 'Father, Son and Holy Spirit' on one occasion (2 Cor. 13:14), Paul's theology only contains the seeds of later trinitarian doctrine. For Paul, Jesus Christ is the Son of God, the messiah and the saviour of the world, and the Holy Spirit is the life-force of God, or God's active energy in the world. God's Spirit works within the believer, who therefore has the 'mind of Christ' (1 Cor. 2:16), receiving the knowledge and thoughts of God (1 Cor. 2:11).

Paul contrasts the Spirit of God, who is the agent of sanctification with the 'spirit of the world'—the agent of worldliness and worldly thoughts. Paul is not suggesting that the 'spirit of the world' has real independent existence like the Holy Spirit, although there is a genuine struggle between the forces of good and evil, which at times he compares to a cosmic battle (2 Cor. 10:3-6). The Letter to Ephesians (which may or may not be Paul's writing, but is certainly based on Paul's teaching) contains a famous passage which describes a battle in which the Christian is urged to put on God's armour, consisting of the 'belt of truth', the 'breastplate of righteousness', the 'shield of faith', the 'helmet of salvation', and 'the sword of the Spirit, which is the word of God' (Eph. 6:10-18). Whatever the reality of 'the powers of the dark world', a contrast exists between those whose lives are not empowered by God's Spirit and those who are. Paul reasons that, if the believer has God's Spirit, then he or she is God's temple, and therefore to be treated as sacred (1 Cor. 3:16). Paul writes:

> Therefore, I urge you, brothers, in view of God's mercy, to offer your bodies as living sacrifices, holy and pleasing to God—this is your spiritual act of worship. Do not conform any longer to the pattern of this world, but be transformed by the renewing of your mind. Then you will be able to test and approve what God's will is—his good, pleasing and perfect will. (Rom. 12:1-2)

This implies that the Christian has no place for vices such as arrogance, pride, greed, drunkenness, idolatry, dishonesty and sexual immorality (1 Cor. 5:11). Living in the Spirit rather than by the Law certainly does not entail that 'anything goes' regarding the Christian's lifestyle. Paul gives instruction on the need to comply with civil authorities (Rom. 13:1-7), the importance of maintaining peace within one's spiritual community and avoid schism (1 Cor. 1:10-17), and the duty to ensure that one does not cause those of weaker conscience to 'stumble' by one's own inappropriate behaviour. On this last matter, Paul discusses the example of eating food that has been offered to 'idols' in the Greek temples (1 Cor. 8). While Paul appears to have no inherent objection to doing so, he feels that 'weaker' members, who still believe that such a practice should be avoided, may follow the more liberal believers and feel remorse about so doing.

The Spirit is also the bearer of virtues. Paul enumerates the gifts (or 'fruits') of the Spirit as 'love, joy, peace, patience, kindness, goodness, faithfulness, gentleness and self-control' (Gal. 5:22-23). Paul identifies the most important Christian virtue as love. The commandments of the Mosaic Law, he writes, are summed up in one single rule, 'Love your neighbour as yourself' (Rom. 13:10), stating that 'love is the fulfilment of the law'. On this matter Paul concurs with Jesus' own summary of the Law, which was characteristic of first-century rabbis (Mk 8:28-31). The Holy Spirit also brings various spiritual gifts, which are distributed in different measures to various members of Christian congregations. These gifts include wisdom, knowledge, faith, healing, miracle working, prophecy, discerning of spirits, speaking in tongues and interpreting tongues (1 Cor. 12:8-10). Not all Christians agree that such talents should be found in twenty-first century congregations, although they would accept that the Holy Spirit affords a variety of gifts within each Christian community, complementing each other, and to be used for God's purposes.

Paul—An Evaluation

It is hard to over-estimate Paul's contribution to Christianity's development. Paul's great achievement was to devise a version of the Christian faith that had an appeal to the Gentile world. Without Paul, Christianity might simply have remained a Jewish sect that believed in Jesus as the messiah, and to which one could gain admission through the Jewish rite of circumcision. Such a sect might have lasted little more than a decade or two. By emphasizing the importance of the Christ of faith rather than the Jesus of history, Paul prevented Christianity from being tied to a specific time and place. This 'cosmic Christ' is presented as a Christ who can be experienced by all, without historical or geographical boundaries. Paul did more than simply devise a theology around this Christ of faith; he actively travelled throughout the Mediterranean, preaching this Christ to Jews and Gentiles alike, and establishing Christian communities at various key locations. His journeys' end at Rome was significant; by proclaiming the Christian faith within the Roman Empire, he secured the spread of Christianity with the spread of Rome's power.

Paul's contribution to the Christian scriptures is highly significant. He has contributed the largest number of books to the New Testament, even discounting the pastoral epistles and Ephesians. In terms of wordage, he is only rivalled by Luke, although, unlike Luke, Paul's writings are largely his original work, whereas much of Luke is derivative from other sources. In Roman Catholic and Anglican churches, Paul's writings are read on most Sundays, and there are several famous passages in his writings that are well known to most Christians. These include the words of institution of the Lord's Supper (1 Cor. 11:23-26), which are frequently used at Christian eucharists; his celebrated 'hymn to love' (1 Cor. 13), which is a favourite reading at wedding ceremonies, his account of death and resurrection (1 Cor. 15:12-58), and the famous 'armour of God' passage in Ephesians, among others.

Many passages from Paul are made known through Christian hymnody, for example, 'Fight the Good Fight', 'Soldiers of Christ Arise', and the well known line of 'Abide with Me', which runs 'Where is death's sting? Where, grave, thy victory?' Many other examples could be cited. A less favourable image is projected in some of Britain's town centres, where it is not uncommon to see an evangelist with sandwich-boards bearing the text, 'The wages of sin is death'. Such people, most of whom belong to small independent congregations, may be keeping Paul's words in the public eye, but the majority of Christians find such figures a source of embarrassment.

Paul is much commemorated in Christian art, both in painting and architecture. In Corinth, the famous Greek Orthodox Cathedral of Saint Paul bears his name as a testimony to his visit to that city, and the Saint Paul Column in Valetta, Malta, marks the spot where Paul is believed to have been shipwrecked. The Roman Catholic, Orthodox and Anglican traditions annually celebrate the festival of the Conversion of Saint Paul on 25 January, and the Feast of Saint Peter and Saint Paul on 29 June. The joint celebration of Saint Peter and Saint Paul recounts a Christian tradition that the two apostles were martyred on the same day in 67 CE and the association of these two figures is an acknowledgement of their supreme importance in establishing the Christian Church (see chapter 9). The naming of eight Roman Catholic popes with Paul's name is a further acknowledgement of the importance that Christianity attaches to Paul.

Paul's journeys continue to be of interest to Christian pilgrims. A footpath in modern Turkey, known as the Saint Paul Trail, enables trekkers to retrace Paul's first missionary journey: it runs from Perge, near Antalya, to Yalvaç, Isparta—a distance of over three-hundred miles. A second branch of the trail runs from Aspendos. Other travellers can visit numerous ancient sites relating to Saint Paul, including Saint Ananias'

House in Damascus, where Paul is said to have been after being blinded after his conversion, and Mars Hill in Athens, where Paul preached to the Greek philosophers. In every city to which Paul journeyed, there exists some memorial to his work. Many books have been devoted to Paul's journeys, the most popular of which is undoubtedly H. V. Morton's *In the Steps of Saint Paul* (1936). More recently Edward Stourton has authored a similarly titled book, *In the Footsteps of Saint Paul* (2004).

In this chapter we have presented, as far as possible, the agreed facts about Paul and the way he has been appropriated in Christian devotion. We have not touched to any significant extent on the enormous amount of scholarly material that addresses more controversial issues relating to him. For example, what were his relationships with Jesus' immediate disciples, especially Peter? Were they friends or opponents? To what extent was Paul influenced by Gnostic ideas, or by the Graeco-Roman religions? The Jewish writer Hyam Maccoby alleges that, coming from Tarsus, he may have been more familiar with these than with the original Jesus movement, and that the Lord's Supper, which he believes is foreign to Judaism, derives from the Mysteries. Other debated questions relate to authorship. Which writings are genuinely Pauline, and which are pseud-onymous, and have there been interpolations in some of the authenti-cally Pauline literature? How does one adjudicate on discrepancies been Luke's account of Paul and his own testimony about incidents in his life? While such questions help to earn the living of hundreds of biblical scholars, theologians and historians, the vast majority of practising Christians are content to celebrate Paul as a saint who built up the early Christian community, and as a biblical author, whose work has a timeless dimension, continuing to inspire and encourage Christians in the twenty-first century.

5

The Bible

Christians attach great importance to their sacred scriptures, known collectively as the Bible, or the Holy Bible. It is read publicly in churches, and privately by devout followers of the faith. It is not a single book, but an anthology of 66 books, arranged into two parts: 39 books comprising the Old Testament, and 27 comprising the New Testament. To these the Roman Catholic Church recognises a further 15, known as the Apocrypha. The word 'canon' is the technical name used by scholars for a body of sacred texts that is formally designated as authoritative. 'Canon' is the Greek word for a measuring rod, alluding to the Scripture's function as a standard or a measure. Scripture serves to define the standard by which Christians ought to live their lives, it defines their history in divine providence, and it defines their doctrines.

Christians disagree regarding the degree of precision with which the Bible defines such matters: Christian fundamentalists hold that the Bible is inerrant in all matters of history, science, ethics, theology and prophecy, while more liberal Christians will acknowledge that the Bible portrays a broad picture of God's dealings with his people and the standards by which they should live. Fundamentalists and liberals, however, would agree that, although Scripture is in some sense inspired by God, the Bible is more than an inspiring book, of which there are many, but an authoritative book. As the (Protestant) Westminster Confession of Faith states of the books of the Bible, 'All...are given by inspiration of God, to be the rule of faith and life' (*Westminster Confession*, I, ii). Fundamentalist Christians regard the Bible as a book that God almost literally dictated to a number of secretaries, while more liberal Christians perceive the Bible as a collection of books by fallible human beings, each of whom had his distinctive perspective on God's dealings with humanity and how the world is redeemed through Christ.

Christianity is distinctive in appropriating the scriptures of its parent religion in their entirety. Although Islam acknowledges the scriptures of the Jews and the Christians, Muslims hold that they became corrupted through time, and that the Qur'an corrects the errors and misconceptions that found their way in to their original message. By contrast, Christians do not reject the canon of Jewish Scripture or deny that it has been defectively transmitted, but perceive it as fulfilled or completed in Jesus Christ. It should be remembered that the first Christians, and of course Jesus himself, were Jews: they worshipped in the local synagogues, where the law and the prophets were read. Jesus himself is portrayed as going to the synagogue in Nazareth, and publicly reading and expounding the prophet Isaiah (Lk. 4:1-21). The Christian term 'Old Testament', understandably, is not used by Jews, on account of its apparently negative connotations. However, the term 'old' need not be construed as pejorative: it connotes its ancient character, rather than its being outmoded or superseded. Being the scriptures of the Jews, the Old Testament was originally written in Hebrew, while the New Testament was written in Greek, which was the language of the educated in first-century Palestine and beyond.

The term 'testament' needs some explanation. Although the term connotes the notion of giving evidence, it is a mistranslation of the original Greek word *diathēkē*, which means 'covenant'. The Old Testament recounts God's entering into covenant relationships with Noah, Abraham, Jacob and Moses, in which these early Jewish leaders are promised material prosperity as a reward for obedience. The prophet Jeremiah, writing at the time of the Babylonian exile, says that God 'will make a new covenant with the house of Israel and with the house of Judah' (Jer. 31:32): God's law will be written on people's hearts, rather than on the stone tablets of the Mosaic Law. Christianity appropriated the notion of the 'new covenant': the writer to the Hebrews claims that 'The law is only a shadow of the good things that are coming—not the realities themselves' (10:1) and, quoting Jeremiah, says of Jesus that 'the covenant of which he is mediator is superior to the old one, and it is founded on better promises' (8:6). It is to this 'new covenant' that the New Testament testifies.

The Bible is arranged in several sections. The Old Testament consists of the Books of the Law (the Torah—Genesis, Exodus, Leviticus, Numbers and Deuteronomy), the Prophets (Nevi'im), and the Writings (Ketuvim): Jews know these collectively as the Tanakh, which is an acronym of Torah, Nevi'im, Ketuvim (TNK). This threefold distinction does not seem a particularly logical one, however. The first five books are not exclusively law books: indeed only Leviticus, Deuteronomy and parts of Numbers consist of law codes, although there are sections of ancient Hebrew law scattered throughout the rest. Genesis and Exodus tell the story of the Jews encompassing the creation of the world, Adam and Eve's expulsion from the Garden of Eden, Noah and the flood, the tales of the ancient patriarchs (Abraham, Isaac and Jacob), the Israelites' captivity in Egypt and the exodus under the leadership of Moses. The 'Prophets', likewise, do not exclusively consist of prophecy. The first book in this section is Joshua, which continues the exodus story with the conquest of the promised land of Canaan, and the books of Judges, Samuel and Kings continue the historical narrative up to the Babylonian exile of the fifth century BCE. The unarguably prophetic books consist of Isaiah, Jeremiah, Ezekiel and the twelve 'minor prophets'. The Writings are an assortment of literature including poetic works (Psalms, Song of Solomon and the Lamentations of Jeremiah), 'wisdom' literature (Proverbs, Ecclesiastes and Job), and other historical literature consisting of Chronicles (the content of which replicates Samuel and Kings), and Ezra–Nehemiah, which tells of the rebuilding of Jerusalem and its Temple after the return from exile in Babylon. This seemingly illogical typology of Jewish Scripture does not reflect different genres of literature, as the names appear to imply, but rather different stages of compilation and acceptance within the Jewish community. The Torah was canonized first, followed by the Prophets, with the Writings coming last. Interestingly, Jesus is recorded as speaking of 'the law and the prophets', a possible indication that the Writings still awaited formal acceptance—although he certainly appears to have been familiar, for example, with the Psalms.

Although Jews and Christians share this substantial body of scriptures, the Jewish canon of Scripture was not finalized until 90 CE. (Some Jewish scholars, such as Michael Hilton, contend that the finalization of the Jewish canon may even have been later.) This is substantially after the commencement of the Christian era, and is perhaps surprising. Hilton suggests that the Christians' acceptance of this final part of the Jewish canon was due to the disputations between Jews and Christians: such debates needed to rest on agreed scriptures between the two communities. The arrangement of Hebrew Scripture into these three majors sections is clearly indicated in Hebrew versions of the Tanakh, but not in Christian Scripture, where the order of the books has been altered.

The New Testament scriptures begin with four Gospels, attributed to Matthew, Mark, Luke and John. The first three Gospels have considerable overlaps, and even identical wording in many places, indicating a close literary dependence. They are therefore known as the 'synoptic Gospels', meaning 'seeing together' or 'seeing with the same eyes', signifying that they are not three independent sources, but draw on the same material. The precise nature of this literary dependence has exercised the minds of biblical scholars from the 1830s onwards, with no universal agreement. Most scholars in the Protestant tradition regard Mark's Gospel as the first of the three, while Roman Catholics have tended to view Matthew as the primordial piece of writing, which Mark and Luke copied in part. Although the academic debate is complex, most Christians are at least aware of the shared content of these Gospels.

Christians popularly hold that Matthew and John were disciples of Jesus and therefore provide eye-witness testimony of his life and teaching. Mark and Luke were certainly acquaintances of Paul (Col. 4:10, 14). As we have seen (chapter 2) there are two traditions relating to Mark, one that he was a close follower and eye-witness of Jesus, and the other that he was Peter's amanuensis; and Luke may have accompanied Paul on at least one part of his missionary journeys. (Luke writes in the first person in Acts 20 and 21.) Present-day biblical scholars are more cautious about such identifications, recognizing that several early Christian writers were pseudonymous, and noting, for example, that John makes no explicit claims to be Jesus' closest disciple. He writes about a special 'disciple whom Jesus loved', generally assumed to be John, but this fourth Gospel places Jesus in a complex metaphysical and theological context, indicating that it was written later than the others, and suggesting that it is unlikely to be the creation of a Galilean fisherman.

The Book of Acts is a sequel to Luke's Gospel. He repeats and amplifies the story of Jesus' ascension, continuing with his account of the coming of the Holy Spirit at Pentecost, and continuing with an explanation of the growth of the early Church, with special reference to Paul and his missionary journeys. This book is followed by a series of letters (sometimes called 'epistles') to early Christian communities, the first thirteen of which bear Paul's signature. Three of these letters (1 and 2 Timothy and Titus) presuppose a highly organized church hierarchy, and this observation has caused some scholars to doubt their authenticity; likewise Ephesians is often regarded as a pseudonymous piece of writing. The Book of Hebrews is popularly attributed to Paul, no doubt because in older Bibles it bears the heading. 'The Epistle of Paul the

Apostle to the Hebrews'. This attribution is purely editorial, however: no such claim is to be found inside the book, and it is questionable whether it should even be called a 'letter'. It is a theological treatise about Christ's role as a high priest, who is presented paradoxically as the priest and the sacrificial victim, and who offers access to God's throne in heaven. The remaining letters consist of one attributed to James, two to Peter, three to John, and one to Jude, who tells his readers that he is the brother of James. These letters are sometimes known as 'the general epistles', since they are not directed to any specific readership, in contrast with Paul, who invariably writes to a particular Christian community at a named location.

The New Testament ends with the Book of Revelation, sometimes known as the Apocalypse, attributed to John, who was writing from the island of Patmos, at a time when the Church was undergoing persecution from the Romans. The book consists of a series of visions experienced by the author, couched in obscure imagery, and ends with a vision of the coming heavenly city descending to earth, with the promise of Christ's imminent return to redeem the faithful. Because of the book's obscurity, most of its content tends to be ignored by the majority of Christians, apart from the final chapters describing the 'New Jerusalem'. More extreme Protestant groups, however, as well some new religious movements, regard its content as prophetic, pertaining to events in our present times, leading up to an imminent apocalypse with a final battle of Armageddon, which will be fought on earth between Saint Michael and his angels and the hosts of Satan. The book refers to the number of the beast (666) and his mark (Rev. 13:16-18), and various explanations have been offered regarding their identity: since the book states that no one can buy or

Detail from Jan van Eyck's Ghent Altarpiece (1432): The Adoration of the Lamb. The painting alludes to Rev. 5:6-10, where Christ is depicted as 'the Lamb'. The artist has portrayed his 'throne' as an altar.
Source: commons.wikimedia.org (in the public domain)

sell without the beast's mark, some of Christianity's more extreme edges have seen this as a prediction of present-day management information systems and barcodes!

The Formation of the Canon

The Protestant Reformers held that the books of Christian Scripture bore their own self-authenticating marks of authority. John Calvin wrote,

> As to the question, How shall we be persuaded that it came from God without recurring to a decree of the Church? it is just the same as if it were asked, How shall we learn to distinguish light from darkness, white from black, sweet from bitter? Scripture bears upon the face of it as clear evidence of its truth, as white and black do of their colour, sweet and bitter of their taste. (Calvin, *Institutes*, VII, 2)

Although Christian fundamentalists may sometimes claim that there is a self-evident quality that distinguishes the 66 books of Christian Scripture from any other piece of writing, any such distinguishing features were not evident to the early Church, since initially there was a certain amount of disagreement as to which books should be included, and which excluded. Other pieces of early Christian writing came into existence in the first two centuries of the Christian era, and there were therefore choices to be made.

There were three principal reasons for Christians not confining themselves to Jewish Scripture. First, Christianity had broadened out as a faith for Gentiles as well as Jews, and, as the Christian population grew, it generated its own distinctive writings, initially those of Paul, who wrote to encourage and strengthen these early Christian communities. Second, as time passed it became apparent that Jesus was not going to return to earth in the lifetime of his immediate followers. New generations of Christians were being born, or being brought into the faith by conversation, and were therefore unacquainted with the Jesus whom the first disciples knew. Jesus' message and accomplishment had to be passed on. Initially this was done through an oral tradition, but oral traditions are ephemeral and liable to alteration; hence the need for more permanent written records. Third, the Christian message went beyond that of the Jewish faith: it required a separate proclamation, as well as written apologetic material that aimed to demonstrate how Jewish expectations were fulfilled in Jesus Christ.

As Christianity developed beyond being a form of Judaism, some early Christians questioned whether Jewish Scripture should play any role at all in its message. One early Christian writer, Marcion (d. c. 160), recommended that Christians should abandon Jewish scriptures, and use only the Gospel of Luke and ten of Paul's letters. Luke was favoured on account of the fact that he was the only Gentile Gospel writer. Marcion contrasted the Christian faith, which he argued was a gospel of love, in contrast with Jewish belief, which bound its followers to the letter of the law. Marcionism never became part of mainstream Christianity: the early Church fathers Tertullian and Irenaeus attacked him, and his writings are now lost in their entirety. At a popular level, many present-day Christians—particularly in the Protestant tradition—make Marcion's contrast between law and gospel, and many a sermon has been preached portraying the Pharisees unfavourably as nit-picking legalists who had an obsession with meticulously observing the letter of law, rather than showing Christian love. We have already questioned this interpretation of Jesus' relationship with the Pharisees (see chapter 3); however, Protestant Reformers maintained this contrast, drawing on St Paul's teaching that one is justified through faith, not through works.

The initial justification for Christianity's retention of the Jewish scriptures was its contention that they pointed to Christ. They showed how God had dealt with his people throughout the ages, entering into a covenant relationship with them, making promises to Noah, Abraham, Jacob and Moses on behalf of his people. As Christians studied the Jewish scriptures, they claimed to perceive implicit references to Christ. For example, God promises 'Abraham will surely become a great and powerful nation, and all nations on earth will be blessed through him' (Gen. 18:18). Jews have taken such passages to refer to the prosperity of God's chosen people, and specifically their acquisition of their promised land. While not denying that this was the immediate and obvious import of the verse, Christians claimed to perceive a 'greater fulfilment' of the promise in the coming of Christ. Since Christ's death was an expiation for the sins of the whole world, opening the door to eternal life, there was an important new sense in which the earth's nations would be blessed through him. Other areas for reinterpretation of Hebrew Scripture included prophecy. One of the best known examples is Isaiah's prophecy, 'The virgin will be with child and will give birth to a son, and will call him Immanuel' (Isa. 7:14), often taken by Christians to be an allusion to the Virgin Mary giving birth to Jesus. (Scholars have questioned the appropriateness of the word 'virgin', which is a rendering of the Greek *parthenos*. The original Hebrew means 'young woman', which is not quite as specific.) Other examples include the so-called 'suffering servant' passages in Isaiah: these are passages, familiar to most Christians, in which the prophet writes God's servant who is despised, rejected and made to suffer, but who redeems God's people through suffering.

> He was despised and rejected by men,
> a man of sorrows, and familiar with suffering.
> Like one from whom men hide their faces
> he was despised, and we esteemed him not.
> Surely he took up our infirmities
> and carried our sorrows,
> yet we considered him stricken by God,
> smitten by him and afflicted.
> But he was pierced for our transgressions,
> he was crushed for our iniquities;
> the punishment that brought us peace was upon him,
> and by his wounds we are healed.
> We all, like sheep, have gone astray,
> each of us has turned to his own way;
> and the LORD has laid on him
> the iniquity of us all. (Isa. 53:3-6)

There are many such examples of Christian interpretations of the Old Testament. Many Christians are familiar with such passages through their liturgical use, particularly at Christmas and Holy Week. The famous oratorio 'The Messiah', by George Frideric Handel (1685–1759), sets to music several Old Testament passages that are given a Christian messianic application.

Apart from such cryptic allusions to Jesus Christ, the role of the Old Testament in Christian thought may seem problematic. Christianity accepts the Old Testament within its canon of Scripture, but yet many of its ideas seem at variance with Christian thought, and even in places repugnant to one's moral sense. Jewish scriptures prescribe the observance of festivals, dietary laws and ritual practices that have been superseded within Christianity—for example, observance of the festivals of Passover, Weeks (Pentecost) and Tabernacles, the avoidance of pork and shellfish, laws about cleansing after recovery from infectious diseases, how to treat mildew on one's clothes, and a host of other detailed regulations. The Old Testament prescribes death by stoning for adultery, homosexuality and disobedience to one's parents, among a variety of other offences. How can Christians accept scriptures that advocate practices with which they disagree?

Christian fundamentalism has a problem in reconciling the two sets of scriptures, and tends to ignore such problematic Old Testament passages, rather than seeks to explain them. Some Christian denominations such as some Seventh-day Adventists, observe Jewish food laws, avoiding pork and shellfish, for example, keep the seventh day (Saturday, the Jewish sabbath) as the day of rest and worship rather than Sunday, and observe the principal Jewish festivals. More liberal Christians are inclined to view the Old Testament as a record of God's dealings with the Jewish people, reflecting the moral and spiritual insights of their times, many of which fell short of perfection, but indicate a striving towards better ways of living and demonstrating one's religious faith. Christians within the Protestant tradition contend that the Jewish law is not so much to be obeyed, but to demonstrate how impossible it is to obey it, and hence that God must make some other means of salvation, such as Christ's vicarious atoning sacrifice. The Book of Concord—or Concordia—of the Lutheran Church ('Concordia' means 'agreement', or literally 'one heart') identifies three main purposes served by the Jewish law. First, it inculcates discipline, curbing sin in society. Second, it demonstrates one's sinful nature, since humanity is unable to fulfil the demands of the law. Third, it provides an insight into God's nature, and gives rules for personal living, in the light of the gospel. This third point entails that, although neither Christians nor present-day Jews may put into operation all the societal laws and penalties that are prescribed in Hebrew Scripture, passages like the Ten Commandments continue to have important application to men and women in twenty-first-century society. The Church of England's *Thirty-Nine Articles* identifies a special category of the Old Testament's contents, which it describes as 'moral', reasoning thus:

> The Old Testament is not contrary to the New: for both in the Old and New Testament everlasting life is offered to Mankind by Christ, who is the only Mediator between God and Man, being both God and Man. Wherefore they are not to be heard, which feign that the old Fathers did look only for transitory promises. Although the Law given from God by Moses, as touching Ceremonies and Rites, do not bind Christian men, nor the Civil precepts thereof ought of necessity to be received in any commonwealth; yet notwithstanding, no Christian man whatsoever is free from the obedience of the Commandments which are called Moral. (Article VII)

The New Testament

In addition to the Old Testament, Christianity adds the New. In selecting the books that should comprise the New Testament, the early Church had choices to make, for the 27 books that became canonized were by no means the only accounts of Jesus' life and of the early Christian community. A number of early gospels were purportedly written by Jesus' disciples, including Philip, Peter, Bartholomew and Thomas. The last mentioned was discovered in 1945 as part of the Nag Hammadi documents, and is a collection of sayings attributed to Jesus.

A number of these apocryphal gospels contain childhood miracles attributed to Jesus. A gospel attributed to Thomas (not in the Nag Hammadi discovery) depicts Jesus in his father Joseph's carpenter's shop. Joseph has sawn a wooden beam, but cut it too short, whereupon Jesus is able miraculously to stretch it out to its proper length. No doubt many early Christians found such stories bizarre and unedifying, and hence not worthy of inclusion in their canon of Scripture. Other writings came to be judged heretical. In particular, two early, related, heresies were identified and excluded: docetism and gnosticism. The word 'docetism' is derived from the Greek word *dokein*, meaning 'to seem'; hence the docetics claimed that Jesus only *seemed* to be human, but was not really so. Gnosticism relates to the Greek *gnosis*, meaning 'knowledge'—understood to mean secret knowledge. According to the gnostics, physical matter was evil, and hence could not have been created by a wholly good god. The world therefore must be illusion, and hence had to be transcended by means of special knowledge that would enable the soul to transmigrate to the realm of light or truth. If this were the case, then it would follow that Jesus, being the perfect divine being, could not assume the tarnished or illusory form of physical matter.

An oft-cited example of an early gnostic is in the Bible itself. The Book of Acts relates the story of Simon the Sorcerer, who was popularly held to be 'the divine power known as the Great Power' (Acts 8:10). Simon allegedly could work magic, but became converted to the Christian faith by the apostle Philip, and was baptized. However, he perceived that Philip could work even more amazing miracles, and was particularly impressed by new converts receiving the gift of the Holy Spirit from Peter and John, and he offered the apostles money for the power to transmit this gift to others. Peter was affronted, and the account ends with Simon retracting his request. The story serves to illustrate the early Christian belief that spiritual gifts are available to those whom God appoints, not special spiritual commodities that are available for purchase. Mainstream Christianity firmly rejected the view that one could buy one's way to salvation, or that salvation was attainable through the mastery of progressive esoteric knowledge, as Simon was attempting to achieve.

Doctrinal soundness was one important criterion that the Church used in determining its scriptures. Other criteria included the prestige of the author. Although modern scholarship has questioned whether all the letters attributed to Paul are authentic, and whether the canonical Gospels that bear Matthew's and John's names were really written by men who belonged to Jesus' inner group of twelve disciples, having such prestigious names in the opening salutation was enough to convince early Church leaders that such writings were worthy of serious consideration for inclusion. If it is the case that, for example, books that bear such names as John or Paul were not actually written by these individuals, it does not follow that there were forgers who set out to deceive the early Christian community. Some of the early disciples had their 'schools'—Paul himself alludes to this (1 Cor. 3:1-14), although not altogether with approval—and it is possible that disciples of John and Paul used their teacher's name in acknowledgment of the source of their ideas.

As well as the ideas of the books that were considered for inclusion in the canon, there were practicalities too. A number of books were lost, for reasons that are unknown. It is possible that they were destroyed in turbulent times, or perhaps their ideas were not considered sufficiently important for the text to have been copied and preserved. Several such writings are mentioned in both the Old and the New Testaments: for example, reference is made to the Book of the Wars of the Lord (Num. 21:14) and the Book of Jashar (Josh. 10:13; 2 Sam. 1:18)—among several others—although these books have never been found. Obligingly, someone has composed a letter purporting to be Paul's lost letter to the Laodicaeans, but the manuscript is only found in Latin, and scholars have dated it as coming from the mid-sixth century (James 1924: 478). The letter is short, consisting of a mere 20 verses, and is singularly bland and uninformative, speaking vaguely of the author's suffering in bonds, and wishing his readers joy and peace. One can hardly imagine any reason to direct the Colossians to it; presumably the sixth-century Latin-speaking author composed it to fill a literary gap.

Various ecclesiastical authorities endeavoured to present lists of the Church's authoritative writings. It was Athanasius, Bishop of Alexandria, in his 39th Festal Epistle, who first defined the list of New Testament writings that corresponds exactly to the list of books to which present-day Christians are accustomed. Athanasius enjoyed considerable prestige within the fourth-century Christian Church, and only one mainstream authority subsequently defined a slightly different list. This was Didymus the Blind (c. 313–c. 398), who omitted Philemon, and 2 and 3 John.

Some Christians may wonder why the Book of Revelation gained inclusion, and indeed general support among most of the early Church Fathers. Despite its many bizarre interpretations by extreme fundamentalists, it is distinctive in speaking to early Christian congregations who were experiencing persecution by the Roman Empire. Whether the persecution to which the author alludes was that of Nero (54–68 CE) or under the later emperor Domitian (81–96 CE) continues to be disputed among biblical scholars. Nonetheless, it depicts the Church as being in opposition to the state, and engaging in civil disobedience against it. The author's encouragement to the 'seven churches' in Asia to stand firm and maintain their faith against opposition is an important counterbalance to Paul, who, writing to Christians at a different time and place, urged obedience to 'the powers that be', claiming that state authority was ordained by God (Rom. 13:1-7). Christianity does not involve blind obedience to civil authority.

The Apocrypha

Some Christian Bibles include a collection of writings placed between the two Testaments. These are known as the Apocrypha, and consist of 1 and 2 Esdras, Tobit, Judith, the remaining chapters of Esther, the Wisdom of Solomon, Ecclesiasticus (not to be confused with Ecclesiastes, which is part of the Old Testament), Baruch, a Letter of Jeremiah, the Song of the Three, Daniel and Susanna, Bel and the Dragon, the Prayer of Manasseh, and 1 and 2 Maccabees. In Roman Catholic translations of the Bible, these books (with the exception of Esdras) are interspersed among the Old Testament scriptures. 'Apocrypha' literally means 'hidden away', although the books of the Apocrypha are not secret writings. They are fairly accessible, and indeed are occasionally read publicly even within Christian denominations that do not officially accept them. They are not considered apocryphal in the colloquial sense of the word: they are not reckoned to be false, but simply not to be regarded as authoritative by those traditions that reject them.

The Apocrypha emerged within Jewish circles, and formed part of the Septuagint—the Greek version of Hebrew Scriptures. The Septuagint included a number of texts that were originally written in Greek rather than Hebrew, and hence came to be regarded as inferior Scripture.

When the Jewish Council of Jamnia met in 90 CE to define its canon, they rejected these pieces of Scripture. When St Jerome later translated the Septuagint into Latin (the famous Vulgate), he included the Apocrypha, but regarded it as having a subordinate status. The rest of the Church overruled Jerome, however, and the books of the Apocrypha came to form part of the Roman Catholic and the Eastern Orthodox Churches' canons.

The Apocrypha is not accepted by Protestantism. The rejection of these writings does not amount to a prohibition: they may be read, but, as the Westminster Confession of Faith puts it, 'are of no authority in the Church of God, nor to be any otherwise approved, or made use of, than other human writings' (*Westminster Confession*, I, iii). Referring to the Apocrypha, the Church of England's *Thirty-Nine Articles* state, 'And the other Books (as *Hierome* [Jerome] saith) the Church doth read for example of life and instruction of manners: but yet doth it not apply them to establish any doctrine' (*Articles of Religion*, VI).

There are not many points of doctrine that turn on the acceptance of the Apocrypha's authority. However, one example is the tradition of praying for the dead—practised by Roman Catholics, but strongly disapproved of by the vast majority of Protestants. The practice finds justification in the Second Book of Maccabees, where Judas Maccabeus engages in combat with Antiochus Eupator's army. After securing victory at Adullam, his troops collect the bodies of the fallen, and find that they had been wearing pagan amulets. They pray that this sin might be forgiven, and that they should have a favourable resurrection (2 Macc. 12:38-45).

Despite its non-canonical status within Protestantism, it is occasionally used by Protestants. The famous passage that begins, 'Let us now sing the praises of famous men, the heroes of our nation's history' (Ecclus. 44:1; NEB), is frequently read during Remembrance Day services. The verse that reads, 'But the souls of the just are in God's hand, and torment shall not touch them' (Ecclus. 3:1; NEB), is indicated, with some other verses from the Apocrypha, as a possible sentence to be used at an Anglican funeral service.

Just as this supposedly 'hidden' body of Scripture gets used publicly, conversely there are passages in the canonical scriptures that are rarely, if ever, read or preached from. Lengthy genealogies, lists of ancient legal instructions and passages of unclear meaning form part of Judaeo-Christianity's sacred Scripture. Some passages are sexually explicit—so much so that one author has compiled a volume entitled *The X-rated*

Bible, which is an anthology of sexually explicit extracts. Other parts of Scripture recount the Israelites' military expansionism, justifying the acquisition of territory as a mark of divine favour on behalf of God's chosen people. Some scriptural passages commend vengeance: the Mosaic Law advocated 'life for life, eye for eye, tooth for tooth' (Exod. 21:23). At times the psalmist pleads with God to exercise divine vengeance:

> O LORD, the God who avenges,
> O God who avenges, shine forth.
> Rise up, O Judge of the earth;
> pay back to the proud what they deserve. (Ps. 94:1-2)

All this seems quite contrary to standards of human rights, justice, forgiveness, and all the virtues that we associate with Christianity. Yet the Bible states that 'All scripture is inspired by God and profitable for teaching, for reproof, for correction, and for training in righteousness' (2 Tim. 3:16; RSV).

Although the majority of Christians own their own Bible, only a small proportion have read it in its entirety, and hence are only vaguely aware of such difficulties. Even fewer would claim to have answers to these problems. However, even those who claim to believe in the inerrancy of Scripture would not concede that, if such events formed part of Israel's history, the Israelites therefore taught and acted acceptably. Present-day biblical scholars frequently talk of *Heilsgeschichte*—literally 'salvation history'—meaning that the Bible does not depict perfect people who faithfully carry out God's will at all times, but rather a community that strives, with God's help and guidance, towards the achievement of salvation. God's people (in Hebrew Scripture, the Jews, and subsequently Christ's Church) are a people in need of redemption, precisely because of their endemic sin. The Bible therefore portrays a community that, at least until the Messiah's coming, is unredeemed, and only on the path towards salvation: indeed, on many occasions God's people are seen straying widely from the path, to which they need to be brought back. The Bible's 'salvation history' consists of a developing understanding of the nature of God and his demands. Even Moses' injunction to mete out 'eye for eye, tooth for tooth' was itself a development of a preceding under-standing of justice, where the taking of one life was typically avenged by the taking of several lives—perhaps the offender's entire family as well as the offender. Of course, most Christians are familiar with Jesus' own interpretation of this passage: 'Do not resist an evil person. If someone strikes you on the right cheek, turn to him the other also' (Mt. 5:39).

As far as the canonicity of the Bible's 66 books is concerned, we can sum up Christianity's stance in the following way. First, canonical writings are regarded as having *authority*. They have a special status for the Christian, but this does not necessarily mean that they are to be regarded as historically true, or that they condone the deeds of its characters. Authority means more than simply being 'inspiring'. The Bible recounts the way in which humankind is brought to salvation, and herein lies its authoritative status. Second, the authority of the Bible does not preclude Christians finding other books inspiring. Christian literature is a growing industry; many churches have their own bookshops, and Christians are encouraged to deepen their faith through reading. Third, even if Christians do not always understand the import or relevance of a biblical passage, they can be certain that it was written for a definite purpose. In the ancient world, parchment was scarce and expensive, and it is therefore unlikely that a writer would waste valuable writing materials on subject-matter that lacked any serious point. While some members of the clergy may avoid preaching about difficult biblical themes, Christians typically hold that understanding of the Bible can grow. As the refrain of a popular Protestant hymn puts it, 'The Lord has yet more light and truth/To break forth from his word.' Although Christians have found new insights on the Bible, and biblical scholarship continues to progress, the major Christian traditions have not revised their canon of Scripture, or added to it, ever since it was initially defined.

The Arrangement of the Bible

Some explanation of the order in which the books of the Bible appear may be of interest. Initially, the books of the Bible were written on parchment, and joined together as scrolls. In the early Jewish synagogue, each major book would make up a single scroll. The Ark—the repository of the scrolls—would therefore contain an assortment of scrolls, and any question of their order therefore did not arise. During the second and third centuries of the Common Era, Christians came to prefer the codex to the papyrus, the codex consisting of pieces of parchment stitched together in the style of a modern book, normally with a cover. When a codex encompassed several books, as in the case of the Bible, then decisions were needed about the appropriate order in which they were placed.

The Jews arranged their Scripture according to their broad threefold categorization, placing the Torah (Law) first, followed by the Nevi'im

(Prophets), then the Ketuvim (Writings). The Christians rationalized this ordering. In common with the Jews, the Christian Bible begins with the five books of the Torah (also known as the Pentateuch, literally meaning 'five containers', referring to the five scrolls). Thereafter, the Christian Bible continues the history of the Jews, placing Joshua, Judges and the two books of Samuel and Kings next. The book of Ruth is lifted from the Ketuvim, and placed between Judges and 1 Samuel, since Ruth is stated to be the great-grandmother of King David (Ruth 4:13-22), whose life is recounted in 1 Samuel. The Christian Bible thus emphasizes chronology, rather than traditional Jewish divisions of Scripture. For the same reason, the two books of Chronicles (again part of the Ketuvim) are removed from their Jewish scriptural context and placed after 2 Kings, since they cover the same chronological period as the four preceding history books. Ezra, Nehemiah and Esther continue the Jews' history and therefore come next. The Book of Job follows, being a story, but without any historical context. (The story is about a man who continues to trust God despite a series of calamities. In reality, it is mainly dialogue between Job and his 'comforters', ending with an exchange between Job and God, raising questions about the problem of suffering.) What now follows is the remainder of the Writings (Psalms, Proverbs, Ecclesiastes, Song of Solomon), arranged in order of size, the longest going first. The prophets come next, again starting with the longest—Isaiah—first. Lamentations is placed next to Jeremiah, breaking the rule about the descending size order, since it purports to be penned by the same prophet. Daniel is counted as a book of prophecy, although it is half narrative, containing tales like the 'fiery furnace' (Dan. 3), the writing on the wall (Dan. 5) and the lions' den (Dan. 6), and half apocalyptic. Finally, the twelve 'minor' prophets appear: they are so-called not because they are less important than the other prophetic writings, but because they are shorter than the 'major' prophets. In the Jewish synagogue they occupied a single scroll, and were arranged in order of size.

As has already been mentioned, the Roman Catholic and Greek Orthodox Bibles intersperse this material with the books of the Apocrypha. There are slight differences between Roman Catholic and Eastern Orthodox: the latter renames the books of Samuel and Kings, calling them 1–4 Kingdoms, and also includes a book called Odes, which includes the Prayer of Manasseh, as well as other material.

The ordering of the New Testament is less complex. The Gospels are placed first, since they recount the key message of the life, teaching, death and resurrection of Jesus Christ. Matthew was presumed for centuries to have been the first Gospel, and hence appears first, although this judgement is now questioned by most Christian scholars. The remaining Gospels follow the order in which they were reckoned to have been written. Acts contains the post-gospel Christian narrative: it is a continuation of Luke's Gospel, and tells of the story of the early disciples' work after Jesus' ascension, with special reference to Paul's missionary work. Paul's letters are appended, again in descending order of size. Hebrews comes next, being of indeterminate authorship, then the letters of James, Peter and John. Jude is placed last, being the shortest epistle, and the Book of Revelation concludes the canon, being of an entirely different genre from the preceding material, and ensuring that the Bible ends with the final outcome of the Christian faith—triumph over the world's sin and suffering, in the New Jerusalem, which will come down from heaven, heralded by Christ's return.

Bible Translation

Christians today attach great importance to the availability of the Bible in the language of the people. At the inception of Christianity, the Hebrew scriptures were also available in *koinē* (colloquial) Greek, having been translated in Alexandria during the first three centuries BCE. This version of the Old Testament is known as the Septuagint (often abbreviated as LXX)—literally meaning 'seventy'. According to legend, King Ptolemy II of Egypt commissioned 72 scholars to translate the scriptures. They were assigned to 72 independent cells for 72 days, and miraculously emerged with 72 identical translations. Although this seems unlikely, the legend underlines the authority with which the Septuagint was regarded. Until the Christian era, its readership was the diaspora Jews who lived in the Mediterranean.

During the fourth and fifth centuries CE, at the behest of Pope Damasus, St Jerome (c. 382–420) translated both the Old and the New Testaments into Latin, which had become the official language of the Western Church. Jerome's translation of the Old Testament was from the original Hebrew, not the Septuagint. The Vulgate was the version used in the Roman Catholic Church, and read publicly during the Mass, until the Second Vatican Council (1962–1965) brought about a number of liturgical reforms. In England, only relatively small extracts of the Bible were available in Anglo-Saxon before the 1066 Norman Conquest. The psalms, translated by Aldhelm around 700 CE were principally for use by monastic orders. The Lindisfarne Gospels, now on display in the

British Museum, were written around the same time, and King Alfred secured the translation of the Ten Commandments and the 'Book of the Covenant' (Exod. 21–23, which outline the Israelites' social responsibilities and the celebration of Jewish festivals). Because Roman Catholicism held that the ultimate authority resided in the Church, translation of the Bible was discouraged. In 1199 Pope Innocent III formally banned unauthorized translations.

The first English translation of the entire Bible was by John Wycliffe (Wyclif, c. 1330–1384). It was made from the Vulgate, and hence contained the Apocrypha as well as the Old and New Testaments. As previously mentioned, the subsequent Protestant Reformers did not acknowledge the Apocrypha as part of the canon, and—perhaps more importantly—recognized the importance of translating the Bible from its original languages, rather than from Latin, which was at first remove from the original texts. The scholar Desiderius Erasmus (1469–1536) undertook pioneering work in reviving the study of the Greek New Testament, and preparing a definitive version of the Greek text that would be fit for translation. This was published, together with his own translation of the Latin, in 1516. The first English translation of the Bible from the original Hebrew and Greek was that of Myles Coverdale (1488–1569), published in 1535. The English Bible which was used in Protestant churches, however, was the one commissioned by King James I. This is known as the King James Version (KJV), or the Authorized Version: it was published in 1611, and was the work of 54 scholars, who translated it from its original languages.

From the time of the Protestant Reformation, the KJV was consistently read at public worship, being displaced very occasionally when an adventurous member of the clergy read a passage from a modern translation such as James Moffatt's. Moffatt's *A New Translation* of the New Testament appeared in 1913, followed by the Old Testament in 1924. The use of the KJV declined substantially, however, with the advent of the New English Bible, when the New Testament edition appeared in 1961, followed by the Old Testament in 1970. Within Roman Catholicism, the only authorized English translation was the Douai-Reims (the New Testament was published in 1582, and the Old Testament in 1609–1610), which was a translation from the Vulgate, and continued to be used up to the twentieth century.

At the time of writing, it is reckoned that there are some 350 different English translations of the Bible, with a further thousand or so independent translations of the New Testament or other parts of the

Bible, such as the Psalms. The most widely used of these within Protestant denominations have been the Revised Version (1881–1885)—a revision of the KJV, the Revised Standard Version (1946–1952), the New Revised Standard Version (1989), the New English Bible (1961–1970), the New International Version (1978) and the Good News Bible (1976, rev. 1994). Within Roman Catholicism, the Ronald Knox Translation (1945–1949) was the first modern version, translated from the original Greek and Hebrew Texts. After the Second Vatican Council, the favoured version for liturgical and private use was the Jerusalem Bible (1966), followed by the New Jerusalem Bible (1985). The New American Bible (1970) is another Roman Catholic version. In previous generations Christians used to go to church carrying Bibles, but the practice has largely died out, one possible reason being that they cannot be certain which version will be read during the service. Many congregations now print out the passages on a service sheet. Tastes differ regarding translations, and there is normally no fixed rule regarding the translation that may be used. Some Christians favour literal translations, of which the Revised Standard Version and The New International Version are examples, while the Good News Bible, which is more of a paraphrase of the original texts, has proved tremendously popular in the Free Churches, especially in more evangelical circles.

It is worth emphasizing that each successive translation does not take the reader increasingly further from the original text. This is a misconception that is shared by certain inexperienced Mormon missionaries (the Mormons continue to use the King James Version), and by some Muslim critics of the Christian faith. It should be evident that a new English translation is not based on previous English translations, but is generally produced by an editorial panel of scholars who are renowned for their expertise in biblical studies and the relevant ancient languages, and whose first task is to reconstruct as authentic a form of the original text as possible. As scholarship increases, new translations that are based on the Hebrew and Greek are likely to be more rather than less accurate renderings of the original. There are occasional exceptions: for example, Kenneth Taylor (1917–2005), who produced the Living Bible (1965, 1971) was a Baptist layman who was not conversant with Greek and Hebrew, and based this paraphrase of the Bible on the American Standard Version (1901). Taylor's idea was to produce a livelier rendering of the Bible than the more scholarly translations. His rendering of 1 Samuel 20:30 ('Thou son of a perverse rebellious woman' in the ASV) was originally, 'You son of a bitch!', but he had to tone this down to 'You fool!' in a subsequent edition.

Taylor's rendering of the Bible reflects a concern that traditional religious language does not communicate effectively with present-day men and women, and especially the younger generation. A number of 'trendy' paraphrases of Scripture have therefore emerged. One example is *The Unvarnished New Testament* (1991) by Andy Gaus. The word 'unvarnished' is meant to indicate that it is more straightforward than traditional translations that are encumbered by centuries-old theological jargon. Instead of using a word like 'sin', Gaus talks about 'doing wrong', for example. Another similar endeavour is John Henson's *Good as New: A Radical Retelling of the Scriptures* (2004), which bore an endorsement from no less a figure than the Archbishop of Canterbury. Henson does not paraphrase the entire Bible, only the Gospels and Paul's letters. The Book of Ephesians, whose authenticity is questioned by many scholars, is headed, 'Letters from Paul's Team', and begins, 'This letter comes from the Mission HQ of Paul' (401). Not everyone was happy with Henson's inclusion of extracts from the Gospel of Thomas, however, which is non-canonical.

A further concern about traditional translations is that most of them fail to use inclusive language, privileging the masculine gender over the feminine. Some attempts have now been made to remedy this. *The Inclusive New Testament* (1994) is an updated version of the Good News Bible. *The New Testament and Psalms: An Inclusive Version* (1995), another similar attempt, does away with references to God as 'king', substituting 'ruler' and 'sovereign', and the phrase 'son of man' becomes 'the human one'.

Other endeavours to popularize the Bible have included the *Reader's Digest Bible* (1982), which condensed the Bible's narrative. Another attempt to disseminate the basic biblical story was *The 100-minute Bible*, launched in Canterbury Cathedral in 2005: this slim volume condenses the essential biblical story to 20,000 words, which its authors believe can be read in a mere 100 minutes. Unsurprisingly, Christians have made full use of modern information technology in disseminating their scriptures. About 100 different translations are available online, some are downloadable as e-books, and other translations and commentaries are available as CDs, including talking books.

Despite the plethora of modern translations, there are still a few Christians who prefer the King James Version of the Bible. The 'King James Only' movement spans a variety of Protestant denominations mainly, but not exclusively in the USA. These KJV-only believers hold that the KJV is the only version of the Bible that should be used for public worship and private devotion. Reasons for favouring the KJV are various. The more moderate KJV-only supporters merely prefer the traditional dignified language of the 1611 edition, while more extreme advocates believe that it is the most accurate translation, that it is the only translation to use authentic Hebrew and Greek texts, that the translation is divinely inspired, or even that all other translations are the work of the devil!

Uses of the Bible

The existence of a canon of Scripture entails that it is necessary to read publicly from these writings in Church. At every Church service, at least some part of Scripture is read. In the Eastern Orthodox, Roman Catholic and Anglican traditions, the relevant passages to be used are prescribed, with only limited choice at best. In Protestant non-conformist churches, biblical readings are selected by the officiant. The idea of having a common lectionary ensures uniformity throughout the tradition. At the time of writing, a common lectionary is shared by the Church of England and Roman Catholics, thus serving to underline the notion that there is one Church. Christians in both these traditions will find that, when they worship in a church away from the home, the readings (and perhaps some of the associated hymns) are the same as those that are being used in their home church. A common lectionary also helps to ensure that worshippers are exposed to a good selection of the Bible's material, and that worship leaders do not simply home in on a limited number of their own favourite texts and themes.

The Free Churches tend to resist the idea of hierarchical authority dictating what biblical passages must be read. In some congregations, particularly in the Pentecostal tradition, high importance is attached to the prompting of the Holy Spirit. Since one cannot foretell how the Holy Spirit will prompt a congregation, it is argued that one should not be constrained by a predetermined lectionary. In some Pentecostal churches, readings are not always even planned in advance: opportunities are afforded to attendees to read whatever passage they believe the Holy Spirit has prompted them to share with the rest of the company.

In whatever way Bible readings are chosen, however, these readings must come from the authoritative writings themselves. At times other inspiring books may be read from, but these can never be a substitute for Scripture. While the Apocrypha may be used, even by those denominations that do not accept it as authoritative, it should not be used in place of the Old or New Testaments. One of the authors once attended a service in the Church of Scotland, at which the only Bible reading was from Ecclesiasticus (in the Apocrypha). At the end of the service, a small queue of worshippers assembled to complain to the minister! An important point about the canon is that authoritative Scripture must not be displaced by other writings. The canon of Scripture is 'closed'—that is to say, there is a finality about Scripture. Scripture contains all that is needed for spiritual nourishment and for salvation.

Private Devotion

Christians are encouraged not merely to hear the Bible during public worship, but to read it for themselves. Some churches organize Bible study groups, in which a specific book is selected, read in instalments and discussed. Individuals are also encouraged to read the Bible as part of their private devotion. The vast majority of Christians in developed countries own a copy of the Bible, but only a very small handful would claim to have read it in its entirety. In practice, only a small proportion of Christians read the Bible with any regularity, as several surveys have demonstrated. In England and Wales, only 16 per cent of regular churchgoers claimed to read the Bible personally on a daily basis — only 3 per cent of the English and Welsh populations. An additional 25 per cent claimed to read it at least once a week, while 14 per cent had not read it in the past year, and, perhaps surprisingly, a further 18 per cent stated that they had never read it at all (Bible Society 1997; cited by Kemp 2007). A survey of US Presbyterian churches had similar findings. Fourteen per cent of respondents claimed to read it daily, a further 38 per cent weekly, 43 per cent monthly, and 12 per cent never in the past year (Marcum 1995). An Australian survey of 22 denominations purported to find slight interest in the Bible, with 21 per cent claiming to read Scripture daily, with a further 14 per cent a few times each week (Grimmond 2008).

Differences in interest in the Bible appear to relate to countries and to denominations. Ownership of Bibles (where Christianity is the country's dominant religion) is highest in the USA (93 per cent), France lowest (48 per cent), and Britain and the Netherlands in the middle (67 per cent; Wooden 2008). The Catholic Biblical Federation surveyed nine countries and found that readership was highest in the USA (75 per cent having read the Bible in the past 12 months), with Spain coming bottom (a mere 20 per cent). Pentecostalists appear to come top, with 72 per cent claiming to read it daily, while 59 per cent of Roman Catholics stated that they rarely consulted the Bible. Despite its apparent neglect in private devotion, the majority of Christians believe that it nonetheless influences their lifestyle (CathNews 2008). Another survey in England and Wales revealed that 75 per cent of its sample of 3,660 churchgoers felt that it influenced their daily living and provided encouragement. Some 39 per cent believed that the Bible had affected a decision they had made in the past week (Christian Today 2008).

Christians who do read the Bible privately tend to read passages randomly, rather than employ a definite programme of study, such as following a lectionary, or selecting a book to read sequentially. Several Christian organizations have devised programmes for daily Bible reading. The Scripture Union was founded in 1867 in the UK for this purpose, and it provides daily Bible notes for adults and children, directing them to its selected portion for the day, and offering a brief commentary. The International Bible Reading Association (IBRA) took its rise in 1882, and serves the World Church, circulating half a million sets of Bible notes to its supporters. In 1990 the IBRA organized the first of several 'Bible reading marathons' on the Mount of Olives in Jerusalem, where the Bible was read in half-hour relays, starting at the beginning of Genesis, and ending with the final verse of Revelation.

Mention should be made of the work of the Gideons in promoting Bible reading. Many readers will no doubt have discovered a Gideons' Bible in a hotel bedroom. Gideons' Bibles are not distinctive translations of Scripture: today they are usually editions of either the Good News Bible or the New International Version. Gideons International began in 1898 with three itinerant lay businessmen in Jamesville, Wisconsin, who hit on the idea of depositing Bibles in hotels to provide spiritual sustenance for travellers, who might have little else to do on a sometimes lonely journey. The first Bibles were placed in 1908, and the work of the Gideons was later extended to hospitals, prisons and schools. During the Second World War, they sent copies of the New Testament to the armed forces. Gideons' Bibles do not provide any commentary on the text of the Bible, but indicate where to find well known passages, and where to turn to in a variety of states of mind, such as weariness, guilt or discouragement. The name Gideon refers to the Old Testament leader in the book of Judges who conquered the Midianites, and whose followers carried pitchers and torches into battle (Judg. 7)—hence the pitcher-and-torch symbol on the Gideons' Bible cover.

Conclusion

The Bible remains the world's best-selling book, although it probably has the highest ratio of ownership to readership than any other volume. Most Christians possess a copy, and will at least be familiar with the basics of the Gospel narrative, and some of the favourite Old Testament stories, such as Joseph, the Exodus from Egypt, and Daniel in the lions' den. Their knowledge of Hebrew chronology is likely to be somewhat vague, and there are books that are seldom used, for example, some of the minor prophets. Nevertheless, the Bible is reckoned to have authority, and there are no signs that the Church wants to revise the canon of its sacred texts.

6

Christian Belief

Of all the world's religions, Christianity is the one that has been the most concerned about belief. While some other faiths pride themselves on being 'a religion without dogma', Christianity has taken pains to define its teachings in a variety of creeds and confessions of faith. There have been times when Christians have taken such pains to defend orthodox doctrines, when they have made a point of defining unacceptable heresies, and even excluding those who have subscribed to them.

Despite the seeming complexity of Christianity's various creeds, the basic message of Christianity is simple enough. Saint Paul wrote, 'If you confess with your mouth, "Jesus is Lord," and believe in your heart that God raised him from the dead, you will be saved' (Rom. 10:13). Many Christians, particularly in the Protestant evangelical tradition, insist that the path to salvation is simple: the sinner merely needs to seek forgiveness, believe in Jesus Christ as saviour and Lord, and 'ask him into one's heart'. In its early days, converts to the Christian faith who sought to be baptized were simply asked to affirm the 'Lordship' of Jesus Christ, as instructed by Paul.

The description of Jesus as 'Lord' highlights the fact that Christians throughout the ages have typically regarded Jesus as more than a human teacher. Christianity does not accept the view that Jesus saved the world through his moral influence, allowing his followers to substitute good deeds for bad. The Christian concept of sin is such that it cannot be counterbalanced by a compensatory surfeit of merit. Traditional Christianity in the West has taught the doctrine of 'original sin'. (This doctrine is not shared by Eastern Orthodoxy, however.) According to Christian teaching, humanity's problem is not that men and women have committed misdemeanours that can be cancelled out by means of apologies, restitution or compensation, or by undertaking charitable works, so that one's balance of good deeds outweighs one's wrongdoing.

It is not like a bank balance, where one's credits and debits are weighed together: the seriousness of sin is such that no human compensation is ever sufficient. Christianity teaches that sin (in the singular) is a condition, rather than an accruement of bad deeds. Traditionally, it is taught that sin entered the world at the moment when Adam and Eve disobeyed God in the Garden of Eden. From that moment, they subjected themselves to the authority of Satan, who tempted them into disobedience, and the condition of sinfulness was transmitted to all subsequent generations, through their offspring.

'Original sin' should not be construed as the first sin (Adam and Eve's disobedient act), but rather the condition of sinfulness, which all humans inherit. According to Saint Augustine, this sinful nature was inherited at the very moment of conception—although many Christians might not care to be quite as specific. Many take the Genesis story literally, believing that sin came into the word in this very literal way, while others regard it as a myth, which serves to demonstrate the condition into which all human beings are born, the seriousness with which God regards it, and how we are incapable of pulling oneself up by one's bootstraps to surmount the problem.

One meaning of applying the word 'Lord' to Jesus Christ is that Christ is the Christian's 'master'. The Greek term *kurios* ('Lord') in the New Testament was to designate human authorities. It was assigned to emperors, masters of servants and slave owners. Paul exploits this last denotation by telling his Roman readers that 'though you used to be slaves to sin...you have been set free from sin and become slaves to righteousness' (Rom. 6:17-18). Acceptance of Christ therefore designates a change of authority, the new master being 'God in Christ Jesus' instead of Satan. The word 'Lord' was also a term of respect, equivalent to the English word 'sir'. The Gospels record that the disciples frequently used the word when addressing Jesus, and the word exclusively refers to Jesus in the New Testament, except when it forms part of the expression 'Lord God', principally in the Book of Revelation. In the first century, the term 'Lord' came to have super-human connotations. Emperors in the ancient world were typically regarded as divine and worthy of homage. Christians in the early Roman Empire declined to participate in 'emperor worship', insisting that their master was Jesus Christ, not an earthly ruler. As reverence grew for Jesus, he came to be given the title 'Son of God', and the term 'Lord' connoted a divine rather than a mere human status. Mainstream Christianity has insisted that Jesus Christ was no mere human being: while being fully human during his earthly lifetime, he was—and is—fully divine.

As early Christianity progressed, its statement of faith needed to go beyond the simple affirmation that Jesus Christ is Lord. Christianity needed to distinguish itself from other rival faiths, and also, importantly, to define orthodox beliefs in contrast to a number of theological positions which it came to regard as heretical. At a popular level, few Christians are aware of the ancient disputes between the 'orthodox' and the 'heretical', and it is not our intention to rehearse the historical background to the ancient creeds. Readers who are interested in the more detailed historical origins of the creeds can find this in most histories of Christianity, and in reference works. Those who are embarking on the Christian faith, and who seek baptism, are not required to understand the theological complexity of the creeds. In common with ancient practice, baptismal candidates typically affirm that they turn to Christ as Saviour and Lord, and repent of their sins. An ancient creed, such as the Apostles' Creed or the Nicene Creed may feature as part of the baptismal service, but it is not usual for candidates to be tested for any prior understanding of them. As Christians sometimes point out, it is not necessary to understand precisely how Jesus Christ accomplished his saving work; it is sufficient that he has done it. The authors have sometimes heard Christians compare accepting salvation with taking medicine: we do not need degrees in pharmacy for our medicine to work, since the medicine itself does all that is needed.

The Apostles' Creed

The Apostles' Creed is the simplest of the creeds that are widely used within the Church. Its name relates to a legend that the creed was the work of the twelve apostles, each of whom contributed a clause. (There was disagreement as to which apostle supplied which lines, however.) This seems unlikely: it is doubtful that Christian theology had developed thus far at the time of the apostles, and the first reference that is found to it is in the writings of Saint Ambrose, around 390 CE. It probably did not reach its final form until around 700 CE. The Apostles' Creed appears to derive from an even simpler creed, now seldom used in Christian churches, known as the Old Roman Creed, which may go back to the second century. It runs as follows:

I believe in God the Father almighty

> And in Christ Jesus, his only Son, our Lord, who was born of the Holy Spirit and the Virgin Mary, crucified under Pontius Pilate and buried, on the third day he rose from the dead, ascended to heaven, sits at the right hand of the Father, thence he will come to judge the living and the dead.
>
> And in the Holy Spirit, the holy church, the forgiveness of sins, the resurrection of the body. (Quoted in Bowden 2005: 300)

Because the origins of the Apostles' Creed lie in the Roman Church, the Apostles' Creed is used by Roman Catholics and Protestants, but not within Eastern Orthodoxy, although it contains nothing that is inconsistent with Orthodox theology. The Apostles' Creed expands on the clauses of the Old Roman Creed, and runs as follows:

> I believe in God, the Father almighty,
> creator of heaven and earth.
> I believe in Jesus Christ, his only Son, our Lord,
> who was conceived by the Holy Spirit,
> born of the Virgin Mary,
> suffered under Pontius Pilate,
> was crucified, died, and was buried;
> he descended to the dead.
> On the third day he rose again;
> he ascended into heaven,
> he is seated at the right hand of the Father,
> and he will come to judge the living and the dead.
> I believe in the Holy Spirit,
> the holy catholic Church,
> the communion of saints,
> the forgiveness of sins,
> the resurrection of the body,
> and the life everlasting.
> Amen.

This is the 'contemporary' version; the traditional English version, which is still used in some churches, has slight differences, for example, 'He descended into hell,' instead of 'He descended to the dead.' The contemporary version makes the meaning less obscure.

Some comments about the content of the Apostles' Creed may be appropriate. The creed consists of three unequal sections: God, Jesus Christ, and the Holy Spirit. Belief in God and God's creative power needs no elaboration in the creed: this belief is shared by Christians with its parent religion, Judaism. Belief in Jesus Christ, however, occupies the bulk of the creed, since this is Christianity's distinctive message, and highlights the conviction that Christ is the world's redeemer. The creed offers a reminder of the miraculous birth attributed to Jesus: the angel Gabriel announces to Mary that she will give birth to a son, despite her being a virgin (Lk. 1:26-38). The theological significance of the story is that is that the manner of Christ's birth enables him to be free of original sin. According to Roman Catholic teaching, Mary's mother (Saint Anne) conceived her without sin. This doctrine is referred to as the 'immaculate conception', and the doctrine was formally defined as a dogma by Pope Pius IX in 1854. Belief in the doctrine, and its celebration in the liturgical calendar, was widespread for centuries previously. The immaculate conception should not be confused with the virgin birth, the former relating exclusively to Mary, and the latter to Jesus, although many Christians may not clearly distinguish the two. The doctrine of the immaculate conception tends to be rejected by Protestants, and Eastern Orthodoxy tends to hold that Mary was sinless throughout her life, while not embracing a theology involving original sin.

The creed's reference to Pontius Pilate—also reiterated in the Nicene Creed—may seem surprising. Pilate is portrayed as the somewhat weak Roman Governor of Judaea to whom Jesus is brought after his arrest, and who tries to pass the buck, first to King Herod (the ruler of Galilee) then to the irate crowd, and finally to the chief priests. He is renowned for his symbolic act of taking a bowl of water, 'washing his hands' of any responsibility for Jesus' death (Mt. 27:1-25; Mk 15:1-15; Lk. 23:1-25; Jn 18:28–19:16). The reference to Pilate, however, serves to anchor Jesus firmly in human history: he is not a mythical dying-and-rising god, as was found in the Graeco-Roman mystery religions, but a real human being, whose time and place can be identified. The affirmation that Jesus was crucified also indicates a real human death. Some early Christian groups suggested that Jesus, being God, could not have undergone a physical death, but only appeared to do so: either he was still alive when taken down from the cross, or else someone—perhaps Simon of Cyrene, who helped to carry his cross to Golgotha (Mt. 27:32)—was put to death in his place. As well as rejecting the divinity of Christ, Muslims deny that Jesus died on the cross: 'They did not kill him, nor did they crucify him, but they thought they did' (Qur'an, sura 4:154). Mainstream Christianity has consistently rejected such suggestions, insisting that, when Jesus was interred, he was not merely in a coma or drugged, but underwent a real death.

The line, 'He descended to the dead', is not self-explanatory. This clause alludes to a couple of verses in 1 Peter: '[Christ] was put to death in the body but made alive by the Spirit, through whom also he went and preached to the spirits in prison who disobeyed long ago when God waited patiently in the days of Noah while the ark was being built' (1 Pet. 3:19-20).

The writer's point is that Jesus Christ does not merely offer salvation to those who were alive during his lifetime, and later generations who heard the gospel message. It would seem particularly unfair if those who, through no fault of their own, lived in a previous era, were denied eternal life. Thus, Peter's letter and the Apostles' Creed portray Jesus as descending to this underworld, to offer hope to the dead as well as the living. The reference to Noah reminds the reader that the flood that God sent was a judgement for the human wickedness that was rampant at the time of the story (Gen. 6:5-7). Although all except Noah's family perished, the pre-Christian generations are not irrevocably condemned, but can benefit from Christ's atoning work. The old-fashioned line, 'He descended into hell,' does not indicate that the spirits were in a lake of eternal sulphurous fire. The Jews of Jesus' time and before tended to view the world of the dead as a shadowy half-life—not particularly pleasant, but not a world of torment.

An Easter garden, St Peter's Roman Catholic Church, Cardiff. Many Roman Catholic and Anglican churches display miniature 'Easter Gardens' from Easter Sunday until Pentecost, as a reminder of Christ's resurrection.
Photograph: George Chryssides

Belief in Christ's death and resurrection is, of course, the heart of the Christian message. As Saint Paul writes, 'And if Christ has not been raised, our preaching is useless and so is your faith' (1 Cor. 15:14). The doctrine of the resurrection highlights a number of key points in Christian teaching. First, the resurrection emphasizes that Jesus' death was not the end, and that the Christian message is one of hope, not despair. Much is made in Christian preaching of 'the cross'. Jesus' last recorded words on the cross were, 'It is finished' (Jn 19:21). Most scholars agree that the Greek word used by John (*tetelestai*), does not so much connote, 'This is the end,' but rather, 'It is accomplished.' This is no mere point of scholarly erudition: most mainstream clergy are aware of this, and it is a point frequently made in sermons, especially on Good Friday.

The crucifixion is generally proclaimed as Christianity's central salvific event. As one of the best known Passiontide hymns puts it,

There is a green hill far away,
without a city wall,
where the dear Lord was crucified,
who died to save us all.
(Cecil Frances Alexander, *Hymns Ancient and Modern*, New Standard, no. 137)

Christianity proclaims Christ's death as a 'ransom sacrifice': the hymn continues by referring to Christ as paying the price for sin, and thus unlocking the gates of heaven. The crucifixion is the sacrifice from which humankind benefits, but the resurrection adds triumph, turning apparent defeat into victory. Death and resurrection connotes newness of life: Paul in particular associates Christ's death and resurrection with the initiatory rite of baptism: 'having been buried with him in baptism and raised with him through your faith in the power of God, who raised him from the dead' (Col. 2:12).

The creed moves on from the resurrection to the ascension. At a practical level, the ascension story writes the earthly Jesus out of the Gospel narrative. If Jesus rose from the dead, then where is he now? Why was he not seen as constantly with his followers as he was before the crucifixion? More importantly, the account of the ascension demonstrates the power and authority that Christians ascribe to Jesus:

Therefore God exalted him to the highest place
and gave him the name that is above every name,
that at the name of Jesus every knee should bow,
in heaven and on earth and under the earth,
and every tongue confess that Jesus Christ is Lord,
to the glory of God the Father. (Phil. 2:9-11)

117

Christians are divided on how literally to take the ascension story. Few, if any, would hold that Jesus physically ascended to some realm in extra-terrestrial space: heaven is a spiritual realm, not a physical one. Whatever happened, the ascension marks the transition from Christ's post-resurrection earthly existence to his rule in the kingdom of heaven, where he is believed to reign.

The Apostles' Creed describes Christ's work as culminating in a final judgement of the world. Many Christians believe in a 'second coming', in which Christ will literally return on the clouds. According to Mark's Gospel, Jesus says, 'At that time men [and women] will see the Son of Man coming in clouds with great power and glory. And he will send his angels and gather his elect from the four winds, from the ends of the earth to the ends of the heavens' (13:26-27).

Other Christians (possibly a minority of laypeople, but the majority of theologians) would view apocalyptic language as symbolic—an attempt to find language for something that cannot be wholly put into words. What we can be sure of, they might argue, is that the earth cannot endure forever in its present form. If it is not destroyed through some cataclysmic natural disaster, global warming, nuclear holocaust, or depletion of its natural resources, it will finally end by running into the sun—by which time humanity will well and truly have become extinct. Christian belief is that none of these scenarios will simply put humanity out of existence into eternal oblivion. History, Christians believe, has a *telos*, and will reach a final culmination in God's kingdom, over which God and Christ rule, and, unlike one's earthly existence, this kingdom will be unending.

There is some uncertainty about the nature of the final judgement. Traditionally, the last judgement is portrayed as a grand cosmic event that ensues after Christ's second coming. According to Matthew (25:31-46), Christ will sit on his throne and divide human beings into 'the sheep' and 'the goats', on the basis of the deeds they have accomplished during their lives. Those who have fed the hungry, given a drink to the thirsty, clothed the destitute and visited the sick and the prisoners, inherit Christ's kingdom, while 'the goats', who have failed to commit such acts of compassion, are sent 'into the eternal fire prepared for the devil and his angels' (Mt. 25:41). This scene has typically been portrayed in Christian art: Michelangelo's 'The Last Judgement', displayed in the Vatican's Sistine Chapel, where Christ is depicted in the air, having returned in heaven's clouds, gathering up his saints, while the less fortunate are depicted at ground level, looking appropriately miserable, being led away to everlasting punishment.

As with other apocalyptic discourse, much of the language and religious art depicting the last judgement is symbolic. Michelangelo may have depicted sinners roasting in a furnace, but few Christians would maintain that this is literally what they might expect in an afterlife. The average rank-and-file Christian talks little about hell and eternal damnation; those who preach in churches are more inclined to explain eternal punishment as some kind of (unspecified) separation from God, which is a thoroughly undesirable state. As the *Catechism of the Catholic Church* (1994) states, 'The chief punishment of hell is eternal separation from God, in whom alone man can possess the life and happiness for which he was created and for which he longs' (*Catechism*, 1035).

Whether a benevolent God would mete out an unending punishment on sinners has been questioned in recent years, for example by scholars such as John Hick. Hick favours a universalist position—the doctrine that, in the end, all humankind will be saved and experience eternal life. Amongst other ideas, he draws on the Roman Catholic notion of purgatory. Roman Catholicism teaches that those 'who die in God's grace and friendship, but still imperfectly purified' (*Catechism*, 1030)— probably the vast majority of humanity, in effect—will undergo a state of purification before entering God's presence in heaven. In popular parlance, the word 'purgatory' connotes excruciating torment, but this is not its meaning when used theologically. 'Purgatory' is related to 'purging' or purification and, as the *Catechism* explains, it 'is entirely different from the punishment of the damned' (*Catechism*, 1031).

The Holy Spirit

We move now to the third section of the Apostles' Creed, which refers to the Holy Spirit. At first glance, this section appears to be an assortment of relatively unrelated points; however, as we shall show, the Holy Spirit links closely with the Church, the saints, the forgiveness of sins, and the resurrection. In the past, Christians have referred to the third member of the Trinity as the 'Holy Ghost'; some continue to use this expression, but the name 'Holy Spirit' is now increasingly favoured. Originally the English word 'ghost', like the German *Geist*, simply meant a (living) soul or spirit, and it was only in the twentieth century that it came to acquire 'spooky' connotations, becoming associated with haunting and Halloween celebrations. The term 'Holy Ghost' is characteristically used in the Church of England's *Book of Common Prayer*, as well as the Douay Rheims and King James versions of the Bible, and some older Christian hymns. While some Christians continue to use the expression, the name 'Holy Spirit' has increasingly gained popularity, and avoids the somewhat sinister associations of the older term.

Christians believe that God has appeared in a variety of ways: as creator of the universe, in Jesus Christ his Son, and in the Holy Spirit. According to John's Gospel, in the evening of the first Easter, Jesus appeared to his disciples, showed them the wounds on his hands and side to demonstrate that he was indeed their crucified leader, and then breathed upon them, saying, 'Receive the Holy Spirit' (Jn 20:19-23). The Greek word for 'spirit' is *pneuma*, which also means 'air', 'wind' or 'breath' (as in current English words like 'pneumatic'). The Spirit is therefore the form of God that gives life to Christ's followers; as the Nicene Creed puts it, he is 'the Lord and giver of life'. Christ's giving of the Spirit does not mean that the Holy Spirit came into existence by Jesus' action: God's Spirit has been active right from the moment of creation. The writer of Genesis explains that 'the Spirit of God was hovering over the waters' (1:2).

In Christian art, the Holy Spirit is frequently portrayed as a dove. This symbolism relates to the story of Jesus' baptism (Mt. 3:13-16): when John the Baptist brought Jesus up from the water at the River Jordan, 'he saw the Spirit of God descending like a dove and lightning on him.' Since artists cannot depict what is invisible, the image of the dove indicates the Holy Spirit's presence: thus, pictures of the Annunciation typically include a dove, to make the theological point that Mary was conceiving Jesus through the Holy Spirit. The reference in Matthew's account makes reference to lightning, indicating that the Spirit brings power. Fire is often associated with the Holy Spirit, since the story of Pentecost (Acts 2:1-13) recounts that, when the Holy Spirit descended on the disciples, they appeared to have forked 'tongues of fire' resting on their heads. The Spirit's dynamic nature transformed this group of despondent and fearful disciples into confident supporters of the risen Christ, who were empowered to preach with conviction and to perform miraculous wonders (Acts 2:42-43).

The Holy Spirit is said to impart numerous spiritual gifts to believers. Traditionally, there are said to be seven 'gifts of the Spirit'. A well-known Pentecost hymn incorporates the lines:

> Thou the anointed Spirit art,
> who dost thy sevenfold gifts impart.

Paul supplies two lists of spiritual gifts, one in 1 Corinthians, and a second in Romans. The former is in fact a nine-fold list, which itemizes wisdom, knowledge, faith, healing, miracle-working, prophecy, discernment of spirits, speaking in tongues and the interpretation of tongues (1 Cor. 12:7-11). The latter is a seven-point list, which overlaps the former, but does not explicitly mention the Holy Spirit: prophecy, service, teaching, encouragement, generosity, leadership and mercy (Rom. 12:6-8). These lists of virtues have suggested to some Christians, particularly those in the Pentecostal tradition, that they should be prophesying, practising spiritual healing ('faith healing'), and speaking in tongues. Others— probably the majority—are wary of them, believing that certain members of the early Church may have attempted them, but that they subsequently died out, and should not be revived. In support of this position, some would cite Paul's famous chapter in which he predicts that prophecy, glossolaliation, and knowledge will pass away, but that love endures as the abiding, greatest virtue for the Christian (1 Cor. 13).

There is another seven-point list of the Spirit's gifts, which is used at the sacrament of confirmation in the Roman Catholic Church. It is derived from the Old Testament, being based on a passage in Isaiah, where he speaks of God's chosen messenger who will come from the ancestor Jesse. (Jesse was the father of King David, and Christians have traditionally understood the passage as a messianic prophecy.) Isaiah tells his readers that 'the Spirit of the Lord will rest on him' and that he will possess the virtues of wisdom, understanding, counsel (sound judgement), strength, knowledge, piety and 'fear of the Lord' (Isa. 11:1-3. The penultimate point in the list is not found in modern Bibles, however: it occurred in the ancient Greek and Latin translations, once employed by the Church, and remains as part of the Roman Catholic confirmation liturgy.)

The preceding discussion indicates that there is a close connection between the Holy Spirit and the 'holy catholic Church'. The Church's birth is often defined as occurring at Pentecost, 33 CE, when the Holy Spirit descended on the disciples, and the Holy Spirit is believed to continue to inspire and guide the Church, continuing to grant its 'gifts' to believers, as the candidate for confirmation is reminded. Comment should be made about the word 'catholic', which is used to describe the Church in the Apostles' Creed. One of the authors had once had a Sunday School teacher—in the Church of Scotland—who avowedly refused to recite this line of the creed, on the grounds that she was a Protestant, not a Catholic! No less a figure than Martin Luther was concerned by the phrase, and wanted to revise it to read, 'I believe in the holy Christian Church'. The word 'catholic' in this context, however (usually spelt with a small 'c') is not to be confused with 'Roman Catholic'. The word 'catholic' literally means 'general', being derived from the Greek phrase *kata holou* ('according to the whole'). The creed therefore refers to the fact that, despite its divisions, the Church is a unity, and that being a Christian entails belonging to the universal Church, as opposed to a single congregation or denomination. (This point will be explored further in chapter 7.)

The universal Church consists of the dead as well as the living, hence the Creed's reference to the communion of saints. In this context, a saint is not to be understood as the kind of spiritual adept who has been canonized by the Church, like Saint Benedict or Saint Francis, but rather all those who have followed Christ and who are members of his kingdom. Paul often begins his letters by referring to his recipients as 'called to be saints' (Rom. 1:7), and the idea that all Christians are saints is expressed in Christian hymnody. One well known example is the American gospel hymn, which runs:

> We are traveling in the footsteps
> Of those who've gone before,
> But we'll all be reunited,
> On a new and sunlit shore.
> Oh, when the saints go marching in
> When the saints go marching in.
> Oh Lord, I want to be in that number
> When the saints go marching in.
> (Lyrics007 2007)

The song was made particularly popular in the 1930s by Louis Armstrong, and in New Orleans it became used as a funeral march, and known as the 'jazz funeral'.

If Christians feel that there is a discrepancy between sainthood and the quality of their earthly lives, it is the forgiveness of sins—the next clause in the Creed—that enables the gap to be bridged. According to Christian teaching, all humanity is subject to sin. The condition of original sin causes a proneness to wrongdoing, and there is no one on earth who can claim not to have sinned. The root meaning of the original Hebrew words *'asham* and *pashaḥ* (usually translated as 'guilt' and 'trespass') is 'missing the mark' and 'rebellion', respectively. The concept of sin thus has connotations of crookedness and deviation. Adam's sin resulted in death, and this penalty subsequently accrues to every member of humanity: as Paul wrote, 'The wages of sin is death' (Rom. 6:23). Sin is a serious matter, which God cannot overlook, yet at the same time humanity is in no position to redeem itself. Accordingly, Jesus Christ comes as the 'Second Adam' (1 Cor. 15:22), through whom all who have faith in him are 'justified' (Gal. 3:24; see chapter 4). The forgiveness of sins therefore involves straightening what is crooked. It is an act of grace that, on the one had acknowledges that sin is not trivial enough for God merely to ignore, but yet for God to take the initiative in annulling or atoning.

If sin is forgiven, its penalty—death—no longer accrues. Hence, becoming a saint in God's kingdom entails survival after death, and so the Apostles' Creed ends by referring to 'the resurrection of the body and the life everlasting.' The expression 'the resurrection of the body' should be noted. Many Christians espouse a soul–body dualism, and will explain that death involves physical decay and bodily annihilation, while the soul is the eternal part of the human self, which is capable of living on after death and into eternity. The notion of the immortality of the soul entered Christianity in its early centuries, principally through its dialogue with Greek philosophy, which typically maintained a thorough-going dualism of soul (or mind) and body. Mind–body dualism gained momentum in the West under the influence of philosophers such as René Descartes (1596–1650). The New Testament, particularly the teaching of Paul, does maintain this kind of dualism. Paul prefers to speak about a 'spiritual body', which is not the same as one's physical body. As Paul asserts, 'flesh and blood cannot inherit the kingdom of God, nor does the perishable inherit the imperishable' (1 Cor. 15:50). This does not mean, however, that the perishable body is left behind, for the New Testament affirms a physical resurrection. Rather, as Paul states, 'the perishable has been clothed with the imperishable, and the mortal with immortality' (1 Cor. 15:54), one's physical body being transformed into a 'spiritual body'. Asked what a spiritual body is like, Paul implies that this cannot be fully known in our present existence: all we can say is that it will be imper-ishable, glorious, powerful, unlike one's present physical body, which is perishable, corrupt and weak. This is Paul's theology, as we understand it, but there are Christians who would maintain a sharper soul–body dichotomy, and believe in an immortal disembodied soul.

What does the Christian expect God's eternal kingdom to be like? Jesus' own teaching is not entirely explicit, and is ambiguous about whether the kingdom of God is something present or future. Some of Jesus' teachings, like the 'sheep' and the 'goats' mentioned above, suggest that the kingdom of God is a destination to which the 'righteous' are assigned after a final judgement. In other places, the kingdom seems more immediate: when the Pharisees ask Jesus when they might expect the kingdom of God, Jesus' reply is, 'The kingdom of God does not come with your careful observation, nor will people say, "Here it is," or "There it is," because the kingdom of God is within [or, among] you' (Lk. 17.20-21).

The Greek word *aiōnos*, which is translated as 'eternal', can be construed as meaning 'of endless duration', or else 'of the highest level'. Christian theologians are divided as to whether eternity is a continuation of time, or whether eternity is something 'time-less', in which there is no such thing as time.

Is the kingdom of heaven a place? Certainly the vast majority of Christians agree that it is not a physical space, like a world on another planet. Jesus frequently describes the kingdom of God (or kingdom of heaven) as somewhere one can 'enter' (e.g. Mt. 19:24); Peter is given its keys (Mt. 16:19), and those who enter will see Abraham and all the ancient prophets (Mt. 8:11; Lk. 13:28), and eat and drink with them. The Book of Revelation concludes with Saint John's vision of the New Jerusalem, a city of enormous dimensions, each gate of which was made out of a single pearl, and whose streets were of pure gold (Rev. 21).

However, Jesus warned against supposing that after-death existence bore too close a resemblance to the physical world. At a popular level, Christians sometimes mention pearly gates with Saint Peter as the custodian and angels playing harps but such talk is more likely to be frivolous or at best figurative, rather than literal theological discourse about an afterlife. Most Christians would agree that the life they expect after death is not fully imaginable. As Paul writes, quoting Isaiah:

> No eye has seen,
> no ear has heard,
> no mind has conceived
> what God has prepared for those who love him.
> (1 Cor. 2:9)

However, Paul adds, 'but God has revealed it to us by his Spirit' (2:10), thus indicating that there are spiritual truths that can only be expressed by 'spiritual words' (2:13).

The Nicene Creed

The Nicene Creed is a somewhat longer statement of the essentials of the Christian faith, and tends to be used at the Eucharist, or Mass, in the Roman Catholic, Eastern Orthodox and Anglican traditions. It is a statement of faith that finds acceptance in all the mainstream traditions, even those who do not refer to it explicitly, or use it liturgically. The only point of divergence concerns the phrase 'and the Son', which we have placed in parentheses below. This point of doctrine is not accepted by the Orthodox churches, for reasons that will be explained in chapter 10. The Orthodox Churches acknowledge this creed, claiming that it was agreed ecumenically by the whole Church, before its major divisions appeared. The creed runs as follows:

> We believe in one God,
> the Father, the Almighty,
> maker of heaven and earth,
> of all that is,
> seen and unseen.
> We believe in one Lord, Jesus Christ,
> the only Son of God,
> eternally begotten of the Father,
> God from God, Light from Light,
> true God from true God,
> begotten, not made,
> of one Being with the Father;
> through him all things were made.
> For us and for our salvation he came down from heaven,
> was incarnate from the Holy Spirit and the Virgin Mary
> and was made man.
> For our sake he was crucified under Pontius Pilate;
> he suffered death and was buried.
> On the third day he rose again
> in accordance with the Scriptures;
> he ascended into heaven
> and is seated at the right hand of the Father.
> He will come again in glory to judge the living and the dead,
> and his kingdom will have no end.
> We believe in the Holy Spirit,
> the Lord, the giver of life,
> who proceeds from the Father [and the Son],
> who with the Father and the Son is worshipped and glorified,
> who has spoken through the prophets.
> We believe in one holy catholic and apostolic Church.
> We acknowledge one baptism for the forgiveness of sins.

We look for the resurrection of the dead,
and the life of the world to come.
Amen.

There are small variations in the English translation from the original Greek. The version above is in modern English; older versions such as those in the *Book of Common Prayer*, use somewhat more archaic vocabulary, such as 'begotten of the Father before all worlds' rather than 'eternally begotten of the Father'. It is not our intention to comment on each section of the Nicene Creed, since there is considerable overlap between Christianity's classical statements of faith, but we shall bring out some of the distinctive features of this statement.

Although it is referred to as the Nicene Creed, the name is somewhat of a misnomer. Less commonly, it is called the Creed of Chalcedon, which is a more accurate description, since the version set out above is the final confession of faith that emerged from the Council of Chalcedon in 485 CE. The Council of Nicaea, which tends to gain the credit of the creed, was convened in 325 CE, and produced a rather different creedal formula. It ran:

We believe in one God the Father All-sovereign,
maker of all things.
And in one Lord Jesus Christ, the Son of God,
begotten of the Father, only-begotten,
that is, of the substance of the Father,
God of God, Light of Light, true God of true God,
begotten not made, of one substance with the Father,
through whom all things were made,
things in heaven and things on the earth;
who for us men and for our salvation came down
and was made flesh,
and became man, suffered, and rose on the third day,
ascended into the heavens,
and is coming to judge living and dead.
And in the Holy Spirit.
And those that say 'There was when he was not,'
and, 'Before he was begotten he was not,'
and that, 'He came into being from what-is-not,'
or those that allege, that the son of God is
'Of another substance or essence'
or 'created,'
or 'changeable'
or 'alterable,'
these the Catholic and Apostolic Church anathematizes.

This creed (sometimes called the Creed of Nicaea) is seldom, if ever, used today, partly because it was superseded by the Creed of Chalcedon (popularly known as the Nicene Creed), and partly because the sentiments expressed in the last line sound so uncharitable and intolerant. However, these words indicate the strength of feeling on the part of the early Church leaders who engaged in controversial theological issues concerning the person and status of Jesus Christ.

By far the largest section of both the Creed of Nicaea and the Nicene Creed is the one that relates to Jesus Christ. This is due to two principal factors. First, Jesus Christ is at the heart of the Christian faith, being the long-awaited messiah and the world's redeemer. Second, several controversies arose concerning the person of Jesus Christ, and the Church found it necessary to define orthodoxy and rebut what it regarded as heresy. Outside theological seminaries, few Christians are aware of these controversies, which are complex and somewhat confusing to the non-specialist. The controversy that led to the Council of Nicaea was between two early Church leaders, Athanasius and Arius, and related to the question of how Jesus Christ could be simultaneously divine and human. Arius' explanation was that Jesus Christ was 'of like substance' (*homoiousios*) with the Father, and that he was the first-begotten one. Christians refer to Jesus as the 'Son of God', and Arius reasoned that, since sons are younger than their fathers, there must have been a time—aeons ago—when only God the Father existed, before the Son was begotten.

Athanasius argued that this interpretation of Christ's nature did less than justice to his divinity. To claim that he was merely 'of like substance' with the Father, and that there was a time before which he did not exist, made Jesus less than God, a mere semi-divine being. Jesus Christ, according to Athanasius, was 'of one substance' (*homoousios*) with the Father, fully God in every sense. The dispute between Athanasius and Arius has sometimes been said to be a dispute about a mere letter: there is only an iota of difference between the Greek words *homoiousios* and *homoousios*. However, a single letter can radically change the meaning of a word, and Athanasius' account of the person of Christ won the day. The Emperor Constantine convened a Council at Nicaea in 325 CE, and Athanasius' position prevailed.

Although present-day Christians may be unaware of the history of the creed, its theology shines through, principally in lines like, 'true God from true God, begotten, not made, of one Being with the Father'. Hymns and prayers are frequently the interface between popular Christianity and scholarly debate. One hymn, attributed to St Thomas à Kempis

(c. 1380–1471) ends with the lines, 'Consubstantial, co-eternal/While unending ages run', and the second verse of the famous Christmas carol, 'O come, all ye faithful', describes Jesus Christ with the words, 'God of God/light of light ... Very God/Begotten, not created'. The Eastern Orthodox churches continue to use the following prayer: 'You became a pillar of Orthodoxy, strengthening the Church with divine dogmas, O Hierarch Athanasios. For by preaching that the Son is one in essence with the Father you put Arius to shame. O venerable Father, to Christ our God pray earnestly, entreating that great mercy be on us bestowed' (Troparion, *Tone 3*; cited by Greek Orthodox Diocese of America 2010). Athanasius and Arius are certainly not forgotten.

Other theological controversies surrounding Christ's nature were debated at three other ecumenical councils—the Council of Constantinople (381 CE), the Council of Ephesus (431 CE), and the Council of Chalcedon (451 CE). Apollinarius (c. 310–c. 390), the Bishop of Laodicaea, and once one of Athanasius' close friends, proposed that Jesus had a divine mind and a human body, a position that the Council of Constantinople rejected. Nestorius (c. 386–c. 451), Archbishop of Constantinople, questioned the appropriateness of the title 'Mother of God' being applied to the Virgin Mary, preferring to call her 'Mother of Christ'—a controversy culminating in the Council of Ephesus. Eutyches (c. 380–c. 456), a presbyter at Constantinople, contended that Jesus was not born fully divine, but became so after his incarnation. The problem the Church found with these explanations of Christ's nature was that they implied that Jesus was either not wholly divine, not wholly human, or some kind of hybrid between God and man.

Although histories of Christianity have tended to lose interest in the so-called heretics after their condemnation by Christian orthodoxy, they neither died off nor died out. The Nestorians fled to Persia and Bahrain, reaching China in 635 CE. In the twelfth century they became the state religion of Khitans, and survived as one of several religions in Genghis Khan's empire. More recently they experienced a revival as the Assyrian Church of the East, also known as the Assyrian Orthodox Church (which is not a form of Eastern Orthodoxy). They prefer not to be called Nestorians, regarding the term as having become pejorative. Other classical heresies appear in modern forms, not always as direct descendants of the factions who were ousted by the ancient Councils. The idea that Jesus became divine after his birth—a doctrine sometimes referred to as 'adoptionism' (implying that God adopted Christ as his son)—is found, for example, among present-day Jehovah's Witnesses, who claim that, at his baptism, Jesus was accepted by God, whose voice was heard from heaven, saying, 'You are my Son, whom I love' (Mk 1:11). Jehovah's Witnesses, as well some Unitarians, regard Christ as a being who has 'divinity' but not 'deity': in other words, he is the supernatural being who is closest to the Father, but is not God himself—an Arian position.

The expression 'Mother of God' merits brief comment. Those who are unacquainted with the term may find it strange, since it appears to imply that God had a mother, and that God was only two or three years old when Jesus was a toddler at the beginning of his earthly life. However, the expression is intended to emphasize Christ's full deity, which, according to Christian teaching, did not merely come to him in adulthood—as Eutyches claimed—but imbued his entire being. The phrase *theotokos* ('bearer of God') features extensively in Greek Orthodox liturgy and theology, and Roman Catholicism is prone to using the expression 'Mother of God' as a title for Mary. 'Mary, Mother of God, have mercy upon us' is a simple and much-used prayer.

The Trinity

We have noted that the Apostles' Creed, the Creed of Nicaea and the Nicene Creed are divided into three sections, relating respectively to the Father, the Son and the Holy Spirit. None of these creeds explicitly mentions the doctrine of the Trinity, or states that they are persons in one godhead. However, it is apparent that creeds are moving towards a recognition of the traditional Christian belief in the 'tri-unity' of God.

The first creed that explicitly affirms the doctrine of the Trinity is the Athanasian Creed. Although traditionally attributed to Athanasius, it is now agreed that it was compiled much later—most probably in the sixth century CE. This creed is sometimes known as *Quicunque vult* ('Whoever wants') on account of its opening line, 'Whoever wants to be saved should above all cling to the catholic faith.' The creed goes on to state:

> Now this is the catholic faith: We worship one God in trinity and the Trinity in unity, neither confusing the persons nor dividing the divine being.
>
> For the Father is one person, the Son is another, and the Spirit is still another.
>
> But the deity of the Father, Son, and Holy Spirit is one, equal in glory, coeternal in majesty.
>
> What the Father is, the Son is, and so is the Holy Spirit.

Some of the earlier Church fathers had been approaching a trinitarian position. Tertullian of Carthage (c. 160–225) had written of a triad comprising God, the Word and Wisdom, and Origen of Alexandria had affirmed the 'eternal generation of the Son', contending that 'there never was [a time] when he was not.' Three Cappadocian bishops are normally given credit for being the first exponents of the Trinity: Basil of Caesarea (c. 330–379), Gregory of Nyasa (c. 330–c. 395) and Gregory of Nazianzus (329–389). Saint Augustine (354–430) wrote an entire book entitled *De Trinitate* ('On the Trinity'), arguing that what is true of any one member of the Trinity is true of all, apart from their 'procession'. In other words, the Father, the Son and the Holy Spirit are all equally uncreated, infinite, almighty, and so on. However, while it is true that 'the Son proceeds from the Father', one could not legitimately substitute 'Father' for 'Son' and vice-versa.

One way of explaining the doctrine of the Trinity is to conceive each member as forming part of a triangle, and the following diagram is sometimes to be found in churches, often embroidered on to altar falls.

It is commonly written in Latin, to indicate that the explanation is in line with an ancient tradition.

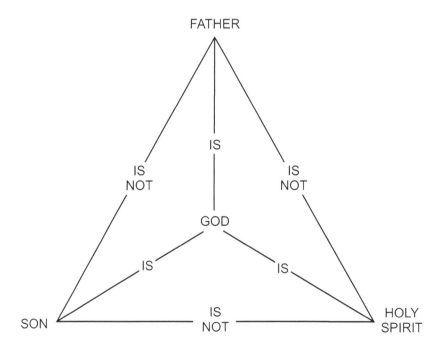

The relationship between the three persons of the Trinity becomes clearer if we recognize that the meaning of the theological term 'person' differs from the word's colloquial meaning. When we read commonplace instructions like, 'Only three persons allowed in this lift,' we understand the word to mean individual, distinct people. However, the Latin word *persona*, which is normally translated 'person', originally meant 'role' or 'mask'. In the ancient world it was commonly used in the context of the theatre, where actors could assume multiple parts by wearing a different mask to signal their appearance as a different character. As a rough analogy, one might consider (say) the actor John Gielgud, who variously played the roles of the Shakespearian characters Macbeth, Romeo and King Lear (and of course many more). At one level, these three characters are distinct (Macbeth is not Romeo, who is not King Lear), but at another level, it is the one actor—Gielgud—who is each of the three.

Like most analogies, this illustration has its limitations. It is not claimed that God was merely acting out the roles of Father, Son and Holy Spirit: Christianity teaches that God is wholly and fully each of the three. Unlike the actor, who can only portray one part at any one time, it is not mainstream Christian teaching that God fulfilled the roles of Father, Son and Holy Spirit at different points in human history. Christianity rejects the notion, for example, that there are three ages: one of the Father (the Old Testament age), one of the Son (the period of Christ's incarnation) and one of the Holy Spirit (the period of the Church). Such ideas carry obvious problems, such as how the universe was sustained if God was wholly and exclusively incarnate in Jesus Christ. One religious group, the Muggletonians (founded in 1651), so-called after one of its founder-leaders, Ludowicke Muggleton (1609–1698), suggested that when God became incarnate he handed over his heavenly duties to the prophet Elijah. Perhaps unsurprisingly, such speculations have not found much acceptance within the Christian faith. God's three persons are not so distinct that they amount to three separate gods; however, they are not identical to the point of being totally indistinguishable. Thus, it was not God the Father who died on the cross, but God the Son. The Son sends the Holy Spirit, but is not himself the Holy Spirit.

If all this sounds complicated, it is important to mention that Christianity frequently mentions the concept of mystery in the context of Trinitarian doctrine. It is by no means the only religion to claim that, in talking about eternal matters, one is dealing with concepts that cannot be fully grasped by the human mind, or expressed in words.

Even members of the clergy, who have undergone extensive training in theological seminaries, have not infrequently admitted to being nervous about preaching on Trinity Sunday!

Other Statements of Faith

In addition to the classical creeds discussed above, various strands of Christianity have defined their distinctive doctrines in confessions of faith and in catechisms. This is particularly true of denominations whose inception stemmed from the Protestant Reformation. A confession of faith is a structured statement of belief, normally more extensive than the creeds. A catechism sets out the tradition's beliefs and practices in question-and-answer format. Traditionally, candidates for baptism or confirmation were expected to learn the answers by rote, and to prove their eligibility by being 'catechized'—that is, responding correctly to the questions posed in the catechism. Few Christian churches today continue this practice, however.

The earliest confession was the Augsburg Confession (1530) to which the Lutheran churches subscribe. To this confession a number of further statements were added—Apology of the Augsburg Confession (1531), devised by the Protestant Reformers Philipp Melanchthon and Martin Luther; Luther's Small Catechism (1529), written for the instruction of children; and the Formula of Concord (1577)—and collated as the Book of Concord (1580). In the Presbyterian traditions, the Westminster Confession of Faith (1647) defined their doctrines, accompanied by *The Larger Catechism* (1648) and *The Shorter Catechism* (1648). In practice, *The Larger Catechism* proved to be too long for catechetical purposes, comprising nearly two-hundred questions, with substantial answers stretching to lengthy paragraphs. Its purpose was 'for catechising such as have made some proficiency in the Knowledge of the Grounds of Religion' (p. 1), while *The Shorter Catechism* was much more widely used, being 'a Directory for catechising such as are of weaker Capacity' (p. 1).

In Roman Catholicism, the *Decrees and Canons of the Council of Trent* (1564) defined its doctrines in response to the Protestant Reformers. In more recent times, the two Vatican Councils (1869–1870 and 1962–1965) have had an important role in formulating the Church's teaching. Papal decrees have also been used to define doctrines, for example the Immaculate Conception (1854) and the Assumption (1950). (The Dogma of the Assumption is the belief that the Virgin Mary was transported directly to heaven at her death.) The Second Vatican Council did not define new doctrines, but 'reformulated' existing teachings, in more up-to-date language.

Eastern Orthodoxy tends to take the view that the ancient creeds are definitive, and that the Church should be the custodian of tradition, rather than seek to be doctrinally innovative. However, a small handful of confessions of faith have emerged from Orthodoxy: those of Peter Mogila, Metropolitan of Kiev (1643) and Dosítheos, Patriarch of Jerusalem (1672). The Synod of Jerusalem adopted both in 1672. Additionally, the Holy Synod approved the *Catechism of Philaret* (Metropolitan of Moscow) in 1839. Although formally adopted, little regard is given to them, since the Nicene Creed is regarded as definitive. As previously noted, the Apostles' Creed is not used within Orthodoxy, being a product solely of the Western churches.

Attitudes to Orthodoxy and Heresy

The formulation of creeds and confessions was an attempt to ensure that the Church proclaimed the true teachings that were necessary for salvation. In previous epochs, these doctrines were imposed by Church authorities, and conviction of heresy carried serious penalties, including excommunication and even being burnt at the stake. The vast majority of present-day Christians are not proud of their history of inquisitions and witch hunts, and Christians are more likely to acknowledge one's right to freedom of thought and conscience. In fact, a sizeable proportion of Christians do not appear to accept the tenets of the creeds in their traditional form. A recent survey of the Church of England revealed that only 97 per cent of clergy and laity believed in God, 80 per cent in Jesus' bodily resurrection, 62 per cent of laity and 60 per cent of clergy in the Virgin Birth (Gledhill 2005). A recent research project on reincarnation revealed that significant numbers of Christians believed in reincarnation, presumably oblivious to the fact that the Council of Constantinople in 553 CE had declared such belief to be heretical (Walter and Waterhouse 1999: 187-97).

More tolerance is extended to the laity than to the clergy in such matters. Although present-day heresy trials are rare, safeguards and even sanctions exist to prevent clergy disseminating unacceptable teachings. The 'heretic' may find that he or she is not accepted for theological training; in the Presbyterian tradition, presbyteries have been known to refuse admission to clergy who cannot accept traditional teaching;

and those responsible for the training of clergy can be relieved of their teaching duties, as happened to the Roman Catholic theologian Hans Küng, who questioned traditional views of authority and infallibility. Very occasionally, a member of the clergy is removed from office: one former Methodist minister, known to the authors, was disciplined in this way; his offence was questioning the existence of God!

It might be asked why people who cannot accept Christianity's traditional tenets remain within the Church, especially as members of the clergy. The laity are not theologians by training, and often may not understand what traditional Christian doctrine is. They may explore extraneous ideas, such as reincarnation, and genuinely not perceive incompatibilities with Christian teaching. Neither clergy nor laity are obliged to accept Christian doctrine in its literal, original form. As the Lutheran theologian Rudolf Bultmann (1874–1976) insisted, it is not possible to be a Christian in the modern world and embrace a first-century worldview that accepts that the earth is flat, that human illness can be due to demon possession, or that corpses can be brought back to life. Roman Catholic theology acknowledges that the faithful's under-standing of the truth can grow 'through the contemplation and study of believers who ponder these things in their hearts', and 'theological research [which] deepens knowledge of revealed truth' (*Catechism*, 94; parenthesis as original). Protestantism acknowledges the legitimacy of 'demythologizing' ancient teachings, separating the 'substance of the faith' (the kerygma, or 'proclamation') from the 'myth'. In the Church of England, candidates for ordination are not required to accept all of the *Thirty Nine Articles*, but to indicate 'general assent'. In Catholic and Protestant traditions, many clergy tend to regard the creeds and confessions as 'historical formularies' rather than dogmas hewn in stone tablets. By contrast, Eastern Orthodoxy is more inclined to hold on to the doctrines of the ancient Church, regarding the Council of Chalcedon as the culmination point of doctrinal orthodoxy.

In conclusion, Christianity traditionally stands by its creeds and, as with the canon of Scripture, shows no signs of revising or replacing them. However, although the creeds that are acknowledged by one's tradition are to be believed, they are also subject to interpretation, and in the twenty-first century they have been subjected to a wide variety of interpretations, particularly in the Protestant tradition.

7

The Church

In everyday language we use the word 'church' to mean a building in which Christians worship on a Sunday. Etymologically, the word derives from the Greek word *kuriakon* (the derivation is more obvious in the Scottish word 'kirk' and the German *Kirche*), meaning 'something belonging to the Lord', or 'the Lord's house'. This is usually the definition that first appears in a dictionary ('a building for public Christian worship'; Dictionary.com 2010). However, from a theological perspective, a further meaning is more important: 'the whole body of Christian believers' or 'Christendom' (Dictionary.com 2010). One of the authors, in his youth, was frequently reminded by a Christian minister, that the word 'Church' simply meant 'all Christians everywhere', and that this definition included Christians of the past and the generations of Christians that were as yet unborn, as well as present-day Christians. To distinguish this concept of 'Church' from the church building or congregation, 'Church' in this sense is generally spelt with a capital 'C'. It is also worth noting a further way in which the word 'church' is used. Sometimes it can refer to a denomination or a tradition. To ask the question, 'What church do you belong to?' can either elicit the answer, 'Saint Michael's' (the congregation), or the denomination ('I belong to the Church of England,' or 'I am a member of the United Reformed Church').

The first Christians did not use their own distinctive church buildings. Initially they formed a part of the Jewish community, and proclaimed Jesus Christ in synagogues. Jesus himself, being a Jew, worshipped in synagogues and at the Jerusalem Temple. Faced with mounting hostility in the synagogues, Christians took to meeting privately, often at the home of one of the believers, where they would pray, study Scripture, and share a common meal in memory of Jesus. Christian worship was prohibited within the Roman Empire until 313 CE, under the Emperor Constantine, and it was only after that time that Christians were enabled to construct their own purpose-built premises. The construction of church buildings began in the fourth century, and the oldest churches are probably the Church of the Holy Sepulchre in Jerusalem (around 330 CE), which Roman Catholics and Eastern Orthodox Christians traditionally regard as the site of Jesus' crucifixion, and the Church of the Nativity in Bethlehem. In 2005, the remains of an even earlier church were found inside Megiddo prison during an archaeological dig.

In the New Testament, the word that is most commonly translated as 'church' is *ecclesia*, which literally means 'assembly'. The word 'assembly' or 'congregation' was traditionally used within Judaism to designate God's people, Israel, who were instructed to hold assemblies at designated times. The early Christians believed themselves to inherit God's promises to Israel (Gal. 3:29), and hence desired to meet together as God's people. As the sociologist Émile Durkheim (1858–1917) pointed out, religion is essentially a social activity, and it would not be possible to follow the Christian faith to any significant extent without being of this wider community, the Church, and meeting with others for worship and the celebration of the sacraments.

One Holy Catholic and Apostolic Church—'One'

The Church (with a capital 'C'), therefore, existed before the first purpose-built church building, and it essentially consists of God's people, rather than of bricks and mortar. As we noted earlier (chapter 6), the Nicene Creed affirms the Christian belief in 'one holy catholic and apostolic Church'. Each of these adjectives is significant.

'One'

First, the 'oneness' of the Church. Part of Sabine Baring-Gould's (1834–1924) famous hymn 'Onward Christian soldiers' reads:

> We are not divided,
>   All one body we,
> One in hope, in doctrine,
>   One in charity. (*Hymns Ancient and Modern*, 333)

This may seem to be wishful thinking, in view of the thirty-four thousand Christian denominations that exist in the twenty-first century. Christianity's apparent diversity has caused at least one pair of writers to question whether Christianity is not one religion, but several (Thomas and Coakley 1987: 8-9). However, there are numerous respects in which the Church can claim to be 'one'. Its various denominations can all claim a common origin, basing their faith on the saving work of Jesus Christ, and on his teaching and example, regarding him as the head of the Church. They all share the same body of Scripture, despite some minor disagreement (as previously noted) on the precise definition of the canon. Although there are doctrinal disagreements, all the various branches of the Church affirm their belief in the ancient creeds, with only the *filioque* clause being a point of divergence between the Eastern and Western churches. Despite some differences in ethical teaching, all the churches are committed to Jesus' fundamental ethic of loving one's neighbour. Baring-Gould also mentions 'one hope': again, despite divergences in interpretation of the concept, the Christian Church presses forward towards a hope of establishing God's kingdom on earth and in heaven.

The oneness of the Church is symbolized by the fact that there is 'one baptism' (Eph. 4:5). A person who undergoes baptism is not baptized into the Church of England or the United Reformed Church or the Catholic Church, but into 'the Church' as a whole. If someone has been baptized in, say, the Church of England, and then seeks confirmation in the Roman Catholic Church, the latter would not normally require re-baptism, since that man or woman has already been baptized into the Church—that is to say, the worldwide 'catholic' Church, which transcends traditions and denominations. Organizations like the Jehovah's Witnesses, who insist that only their own baptism is valid, and require members to undergo their own distinctive rite, place themselves outside the Church, as indeed the Jehovah's Witness would seek to do in any case. (Having said this, there are exceptions which will be explored in the next chapter.)

A New Testament metaphor describing the Church's oneness is the human body. 'You are the body of Christ,' Paul writes, 'and each one of you is a part of it' (1 Cor. 12:27). This metaphor is multifaceted. First, it highlights the point that, since God is 'without body, parts, or passions' (*Thirty Nine Articles*, I), he needs a physical means of acting within the world. The Church fulfils this role, acting as God's instrument on earth, endeavouring to carry out his will. Second, as Paul also points out in the same passage, a human body has many parts, with different functions, and likewise the Church consists of men and women with different characteristics, abilities and functions. Paul enumerates these as 'first of all apostles, second prophets, third teachers, then workers of miracles, also those having gifts of healing, those able to help others, those with gifts of administration, and those speaking in different kinds of tongues'

(1 Cor. 12:28). Branches of the Church differ on how literally to take Paul here. Certain forms of Pentecostalism believe that Paul is enumerating various fixed offices within a congregation, which must be filled. The majority of Christians favour the view that Paul is merely speaking of the diversity of Christian believers, and not all of these functions (particularly those of miracle working and speaking in tongues) need literally to be found in any congregation. The metaphor of the body also suggests that, in the midst of the plethora of Christian denominations, they may not regard themselves as competing 'bodies of God', but are one single body, sharing common aims and characteristics amidst diversity.

'Holy'

The second adjective describing the Church is 'holy'. Christians are perhaps disinclined to use this word, particularly with reference to themselves, since it has acquired pejorative connotations. The expression 'holy Joe' describes someone who is self-righteous, sanctimonious, or fanatically obsessed with religion. However, there are many contexts in which the word 'holy' is typically used in the context of the Christian faith, for example 'Holy Bible', 'Holy Communion', 'holy orders', 'holy matrimony', holy water', and 'holy place', the last of which can either designate a church building or a place of pilgrimage. The word 'holiday' is derived from the words 'holy day', and used to designate a festival in the Christian calendar, such as a saint's day or a major festival such as Christmas, Easter or Whitsun.

Central to the concept of holiness is the idea of being set apart. Thus, a holy place like a church is specially consecrated to mark the fact that it is importantly different from other, secular buildings. Events take place within a church that do not typically occur in the outside world, such as worship, prayer, and the celebration of the sacraments. The Holy Bible is a special book for the Christian, being imbued with greater authority than any other piece of writing, and read at every service of worship. Some particularly pious Christians go so far as to insist that it is placed the top of any pile of books that they carry. Those in holy orders are similarly set apart from the world. In some instances the setting apart is physical, for example in monastic orders, where the community of monks and nuns lives physically apart from the world. The use of special attire by clergy and other officiants serves to indicate that they are acting in a special sacred capacity, which transcends their everyday human identities.

There is a respect, however, in which all members of the Church are 'holy', theologically speaking. The idea goes back to ancient Israel, when God tells Moses that the Israelites are 'a kingdom of priests and a holy nation' (Exod. 19:6). They are to 'be holy because I, the LORD your God, am holy' (Lev. 19:2). Obviously, at a literal level, not every Israelite was an ordained priest: what was meant was that the Jews were God's chosen people, set apart by him for a particular purpose in God's plan of salvation for humankind. According to Christian teaching, the Church has assumed this role: 'But you are a chosen people, a royal priesthood, a holy nation, a people belong to God, that you may declare the praises of him who called you out of darkness into his wonderful light' (1 Pet. 2:9-10). Paul, in his introduction to the letter to the Romans, addresses his readers as 'all in Rome who are loved by God and called to be saints' (1:7).

Just as a priest is God's representative, chosen to fulfil his assigned role, and commissioned to fulfil a special set of obligations from the laity, so the Christian is regarded as someone who is 'called' by God; being inherently sinful, they have not earned this chosenness through their own merits but through divine grace. They are also set apart in the sense of refusing to conform to worldly standards of behaviour: Christians often paraphrase the words of John's Gospel, saying that they are 'in the world, but not of the world' (Jn 17:13-14). Christians are therefore under no obligation to separate themselves off from society—although there have been some that have formed their own communities (for example, the Amish and the Hutterites)—but to 'shine as a light in the world' (*Book of Common Prayer*). Christian hymnody picks up the themes of priesthood and consecration in lines like 'Take my life and let it be/consecrated, Lord, to thee' (*Hymns Ancient and Modern*, 249) and 'Jesus, whom their souls rely on/Makes them kings and priests to God' (*The Church Hymnary*, 421).

Mention should be made of the 'special' saints whom the Church formally recognizes as such. In the early Church, special recognition was given to the Christian martyrs, who had made the supreme sacrifice for their faith. When persecution under the Roman Empire declined in the fourth century, honour was extended to certain Christian figures who had exhibited outstanding virtues or attainments. Saints were assigned a special day in the festival calendar, shrines associated with their lives or with their place of burial were defined as locations for their veneration, stories of their lives were collected and written down (these are known as 'hagiographies'), and relics were often collected and displayed at appropriate locations: for example, what purports to be St Stephen's hand is displayed at his Basilica at Budapest. Veneration of saints was particularly popular during the Middle Ages; during this period saints were informally defined, and local custom dictated who counted as a saint. In 1234, the procedure was tightened up, when Pope Gregory IX prohibited any canonization of saints without papal permission.

'Canonization' is the procedure carried out within Roman Catholic Church, whereby a person of outstanding qualities is accorded sainthood. Just as the canon of Scripture is a definitive list of authorized writings defined by the Church, the canonization of saints places them on a formal list, ensuring that their lives conform to the standard (the 'canon') that is required for sainthood. Canonization involves a two-fold process. First, there is 'beatification' (literally, declaring the person to be 'blessed'), which begins at a local level. Enquiries are made into the life of the candidate for beatification, in order to ensure that the person was virtuous, led a holy life, performed charitable deeds, held orthodox beliefs, and performed at least one miracle. Evidence of one miracle is required for beatification, while two are normally expected for sainthood. Once beatified, the individual is eligible to receive local honour, but does not yet receive the title 'saint', and does not receive due recognition from the whole Church. The process of beatification and canonization is carried out by the Congregation of Rites, established in 1588. It is a lengthy and formal process, requiring meticulous documentation. Until the late twentieth century, one of the cardinals assumed the role of 'devil's advocate', presenting evidence against the case for the candidate's canonization. This part of the procedure was dropped in 1983, when Pope John Paul II reformed the process with his *Divinus perfectionis magister* (*The Divine Teacher of Perfection*).

In Eastern Orthodoxy, the creation of saints has been less arduous and formal. Orthodoxy defines six categories of saints, who are recognized as a result of tradition. These are: apostles, prophets, martyrs, Church Fathers, celebrated monastics, and those Christians (clergy or laity) whose lives are recognized as exemplary. In Orthodoxy, particular importance is attached to the depiction of saints in icons, which are placed in large numbers around the church building, often with a picture on the ceiling or dome depicting Christ the *pantokrator* (the judge of all). The effect of this arrangement is to place the worshipper at ground level, the saints in an intermediate position, and Christ above all, replicating the spiritual positions of the worshippers, the saints, and Christ respectively. The saints play an intermediary role spiritually, interceding on behalf of the faithful.

In the Anglican tradition, saints' days are celebrated, but saints are not normally asked to intercede for men and women. Congregations characteristically have a patron saint, after whom the church is named, usually a founder-leader of the early Church, such as Saint Peter, Saint John or Saint Barnabas. Saint Michael is a 'supernatural' saint, the leader of God's heavenly hosts of angels, who will do battle with Satan and his forces at Armageddon (Rev. 12:7-9): many congregations are called after him. Annually the saint has a 'patronal festival' when he or she is particularly remembered within the congregation that bears the saint's name. Protestantism shows a preparedness to acknowledge the existence and the status of saints, but only a few are celebrated in any way, and they do not have any mediatorial role. It is not so common for Protestant churches to be named after a saint, although the names of the twelve apostles and early Church leaders such as Paul and Barnabas are sometimes used: they are more likely to derive their names from their geographical location (for example, 'Hatherton United Reformed Church'). National saints, such as Saint Andrew, Saint David and Saint George can have their special day commemorated. A few Protestant churches take their names from local saints such as Saint Columba, the Irish saint who established a Christian community in Iona in 563 CE.

This may be an appropriate juncture to mention a further way in which Christians understand the Church. In several places in Scripture, the Church is described as the 'bride of Christ'. Jesus sometimes compares himself with a bridegroom (Mt. 9:15; 25:1-13), whose marriage will take place at the end of time. The Book of Revelation tells of the New Jerusalem—the community of the saints who have been brought to heaven—coming down 'as a bride beautifully dressed for her husband' (21:2), and goes on to speak of the 'marriage of the Lamb' (12:9). This last phrase may seem obscure to those who are unfamiliar with the Christian tradition. As we have noted (chapter 3), 'the Lamb' is a title given to Christ, and this imagery also describes the union of Christ with his Church. Traditionally, it has been common to speak of the Church in the feminine gender for this reason. (The present authors have not adopted this convention, regarding it as somewhat old-fashioned and potentially confusing.)

Like the concept of God's holy people, the bridegroom-bride imagery has its roots in Hebrew Scripture: 'As a bridegroom rejoices over his bride, so will your God rejoice over you' (Isa. 62:5). The Song of

Solomon—although it never explicitly mentions God, perhaps surprisingly—was included in Jewish Scripture, since its dialogue between a lover and his beloved was regarded an allegory of God's love for his people. A typical theme of the ancient Hebrew prophets is that God's people have been unfaithful, and in several places they are compared with adulteresses and harlots (e.g. Hos. 3:1). This imagery is intended to convey the closeness of the ideal relationship between God and his people (Israel and the Church respectively), the love that God gives, and the faithfulness that is expected. Just as marriage involves faithful and exclusive allegiance to one's spouse, so the relationship between God and the Church is portrayed as one demanding exclusive faithfulness.

This, of course, is the ideal, and most, if not all, Christians would have to admit to being very unfaithful followers of Christ. In the Sermon on the Mount, Jesus instructs his listeners to 'Be perfect, therefore, as your heavenly Father is perfect' (Mt. 5:48). Most members of the Church are aware of the requirement, but recognize that there is a disparity between the ideal and the real. At times within the Church there have been movements to promote Christian holiness. The so-called 'Holiness Movement' which was spearheaded by John Wesley (1703–1791) and Charles Grandison Finney (1792–1875), and which resulted in the rise of the 'Holiness Churches', was one such attempt. It was a revivalist movement, encouraging growth in grace, and emphasizing the theological concept of 'sanctification'. Justification, as we noted (chapter 6) is the condition in which the convert repents, is free from sin, and made right or straight. Sanctification is a further, lengthier process, by which one is progressively made holy ('sanctified') through the work of the Holy Spirit.

'Catholic'

The third major characteristic of the Church is that it is 'catholic'. We have already noted that the expression 'Catholic Church' does not mean 'Roman Catholic Church', although sometimes the phrase is loosely used with this meaning. The word 'Catholic' is juxtaposed to 'Roman' in this sense because the Roman Catholic Church is the only branch of the Church that has a unified worldwide organization. Other churches tend to be nationally organized, for example the Eastern Orthodox churches, whose presence is predominantly in a single country. 'Catholic Church' means 'whole Church', and the Church, as opposed to the churches, transcends all its denominational expressions. However, the Church as a whole (not merely Roman Catholicism) is a worldwide body, and traditionally it has believed itself to have a worldwide mission. The last recorded words of Jesus, according to Matthew, were, 'Therefore go and make disciples of all nations' (28:19), and the Book of Revelation describes 'a great multitude that no one could count, from every nation, tribe, people and language, standing before the throne and in front of the Lamb' (7:9). They are the ones who have become citizens of God's heavenly kingdom, and St John describes them (symbolically) as wearing white robes, waving palm branches, and singing praises to God and to the Lamb.

The Church's catholicity is not merely in the future, but in the present, and it is pertinent to ask what gives unity to such a multitude of traditions and denominations. The writer and monk Saint Vincent of Lérins (d. c. 445) proposed the expression *quod ubique, quod semper, quod ab omnibus credituni est* ('what is believed in all places, at all times and by all people') as a means of distinguishing between true and false expressions of the Christian faith. Later theologians have followed Saint Vincent by contrasting the 'substance of the faith' with its temporal expressions. Although there is much doctrinal disagreement among Christians, there is nonetheless a consensus on Christianity's basic tenets. In the authors' experience, one often finds more theological diversity among members of a single congregation than one does between members of different denominations. Common to all Christians is a belief in the way in which God has brought salvation to humankind through Jesus Christ, his incarnation, sacrificial death and resurrection, his Lordship, the work of the Holy Spirit, and the hope of eternal life. Common to all Christians are the ancient creeds that express this means of salvation, and common to all is the belief that God is a Trinity of Father, Son and Holy Spirit.

There is no legal restriction on who may use the word 'church' as part of its name, and there are many claimants that the majority of Christians would wish to disown. Examples include Church of Jesus Christ of Latter-day Saints (the Mormons), the Church of Scientology, the Unification Church (popularly known as the 'Moonies'), the Church Universal and Triumphant, the World Church of the Creator (a white supremacist organization), and even the Church of Satan. (Not all of these, of course, would claim to be part of Christianity, and some of these will be discussed in chapter 17.) How does one decide who are genuine claimants of a Christian identity? The basis of membership of national Councils of Churches and of the World Council of Churches is that one is part of 'a fellowship of churches which confess the Lord Jesus

Christ as God and Saviour according to the scriptures, and therefore seek to fulfil together their common calling to the glory of the one God, Father, Son and Holy Spirit' (Bowden 2005: 365).

Several points emerge from this seemingly broad statement. Of key importance is Christ's deity and his redeeming work. It is not sufficient to regard Jesus as a great teacher, or even as a perfect example. Belief in the Trinity is regarded as essential for acceptance as part of the wider Church: organizations like the Unitarian Church, who applied for membership of Churches Together in Britain and Ireland (CTBI), have been rejected on this ground. The reference to Scripture requires an acknowledgement of the authority of the Old and New Testaments, although not necessarily belief in their literal inerrancy. The member church must be 'part of a fellowship of churches': this means that the denomination in question must have previously shown some interest in ecumenical activity. Independent churches without external links, or groups that claim to be the sole custodians of truth, would not be eligible.

'Apostolic'

We turn now to the fourth descriptor of 'Church': apostolic. Just as it is important to distinguish 'Catholic Church' from the Roman Catholic Church, it is also important to distinguish between 'the apostolic Church', referring to the Church as a totality, and a particular denomination like the Apostolic Church, which is a Pentecostal denomination, founded in Wales in 1920. To confuse matters further, the expression 'Apostolic Church' is sometimes used by church historians to refer to the Church in the apostolic age—that is, the period in which its branches were presided over by the twelve apostles. Some denominations, like the (Pentecostalist) Apostolic Church, try to emulate the Church that they presume to have existed at the time of the apostles, and have endeavoured to restore a system of church government including present-day apostles and prophets, as well as evangelists, pastors, teachers, elders and deacons (Eph. 4:11). Most denominations do not use such a system of government, arguing that the Letter to the Ephesians refers to gifts of the Holy Spirit, rather than formal organizational offices.

As a description of the worldwide Church, the term 'apostolic' harks back to the story of Peter's 'confession'. Jesus asks his disciples who people believed he was, and gets a variety of answers: John the Baptist, Elijah, Jeremiah, one of the prophets. He then asks who they think he is, whereupon Peter replies, 'You are the Christ, the Son of the living God' (Mt. 16:16). Jesus gives this response to Peter: 'I tell you that you are Peter, and on this rock I will build my church, and the gates of Hades will not overcome it. I will give you the keys of the kingdom of heaven; whatever you bind on earth will be bound in heaven, and whatever you loose on earth will be loosed in heaven' (Mt. 16:18-19).

Until this point in the Gospel narrative, Peter has been called Simon—his given name. Jesus gives him a new name, Peter, the significance being that the Greek *petros* means 'rock'. Peter's profession that Jesus is the Messiah (the Christ) is the foundation on which the Church is to be built. Different traditions impose different interpretations on the incident: the Roman Catholic Church holds that Jesus was making Peter his successor, the first head of the Church, and thus the first Pope. Protestantism disputes this, claiming that the Church's foundation was not Peter, but rather his confession of faith that Jesus is the Messiah. In the story, Peter is given authority: the words 'bind' and 'loose' are somewhat old-fashioned words for 'prohibit' and 'allow', implying that the emergent Church has the powers to determine the facets of human behaviour that are permitted or forbidden. Peter is also given the 'keys of the kingdom', implying that it is only through the Church that one can gain salvation, and hence entry into the kingdom of heaven.

The Visible and the Invisible Church

Despite our explanation of the Church's catholicity, it is plain that, on a visible, empirical level, the Church is extremely diverse and divided. There are organizations that are on the fringe of Christianity— Mormons, Jehovah's Witnesses, Christadelphians, Unitarians, and, more recently, the Unification Church, The Family International (formerly the Children of God), Christian Science, and many more—most of whom claim to have a Christian identity, but who are denied such an identity by the mainstream churches, as well as local and national Councils of Churches. Additionally, mainstream churches themselves contain a variety of members: a few have been designated as saints; many more lead upright lives, pray regularly and study the Bible; others make the Christian faith a 'Sunday only' activity; others again are simply nominal members; and, sadly, there are those who belong to churches but whose lives are thoroughly reprehensible—adulterers, paedophiles, fraudsters. How does one decide who genuinely belongs to Christ's Church and who does not?

In practice, churches rarely exercise discipline over their members. Unlike a business firm, members are not appraised, disciplined or dismissed if their conduct is judged to be unsatisfactory. A few lay office-bearers are paid employees of churches, notably the Director of Music, other musicians and singers on occasions, and sometimes caretakers. They are subject to normal secular employment law, are often given contracts, and are therefore legally accountable for their behaviour. Volunteer office-bearers are in a different position. Because of recent concern relating to child abuse, most churches now take precautions to ensure that those who work with children do not have criminal records, and they may be removed from that office for inappropriate behaviour, for example a treasurer who mishandles money or a Sunday School teacher who puts children at risk.

Theoretically, there are three levels at which sanctions can be applied within the Church, in accordance with a saying attributed to Jesus:

> If your brother sins against you, go and show him his fault, just between the two of you. If he listens to you, you have won your brother over. But if he will not listen, take one or two others along, so that 'every matter may be established by the testimony of two or three witnesses'. If he refuses to listen to them, tell it to the church; and if he refuses to listen even to the church, treat him as you would a pagan or tax collector (Mt. 18:15-17)

Since in all probability Jesus never intended to found a Church, many scholars think that this saying may well come from a later period, and attributed to Jesus retrospectively. Whether or not Jesus actually pronounced this judgement, it is reflected in a three-fold way of dealing with misconduct. The first step is informal: instances of misbehaviour are resolved at a personal level. In Roman Catholicism and in some Anglican churches, provision is made for confessing one's sins to a priest, who is empowered to pronounce absolution (that is, declare that the penitent's sins are forgiven), and to assign a penance to the sinner. In the Anglican tradition, priests are ordained to 'teach and admonish', although they do less of the latter than the former. The ensuing stages are much less common. The second of these is the invocation of church law, whereby the offender is excluded from receiving the sacraments. This is a serious matter, since the sacraments are the visible signs of God's grace; however, Paul reminded the Corinthian church that 'anyone who eats and drinks without recognizing the body of the Lord eats and drinks judgment on himself' (1 Cor. 11:29). The third step is expulsion which involves social exclusion: the offender is prohibited from social contact with other members of the congregation, who are required to 'shun' him or her.

In Roman Catholicism, a distinction is made between 'greater' and 'lesser' excommunication—*vitandus* ('to be avoided') and *toleratus* ('to be tolerated') respectively. In the case of the former, all associations with other members are to be avoided, the offender is stripped of all offices that he or she possessed, and may not attend public worship. If the guilty party is a priest, all his powers are voided and, if he attempts to dispense a sacrament, it is null and void. The penalty for the *toleratus* is less severe: he may not receive or administer the sacrament, but may attend public worship for the express purpose of hearing the sermon. Either individuals or groups may be subject to these disciplinary procedures. These scenarios are now rare, however. They were more common in medieval times, and during the Protestant Reformation, when witches and heretics respectively were the targets. In the Church of England, excommunication was more common after the Restoration, although it sometimes occurs today in Anglican churches overseas. 'Greater excommunication' in Roman Catholicism is a penalty reserved exclusively for those who do violence to the Pope himself. Two points should be noted about excommunication, however. First, the possibility of restoration must always be open to the offender: Christianity teaches the continued possibility of repentance and forgiveness. Second, although in excommunication the offender is deprived of the sacraments, it is never stated that he or she no longer remains in a state of grace, or that his or her soul has been severed from communion with God. The Church on earth cannot make such judgements on God's behalf: God alone is believed the judge of who his true followers are.

In practice, negative sanctions tend to be enforced only by 'high commitment' organizations, usually outside the mainstream. Christadelphians and Jehovah's Witnesses practise 'disfellowshipping' (excommunicating) recalcitrant offenders, and denominations such as the Churches of Christ practise 'discipling'—also known as 'shepherding'. This practice entails close spiritual supervision by a more senior member, who will give instructions about how to live the spiritual life, how to pray and study the Bible, when to fast, and how much time to devote to church activities, including evangelizing. Such practices are controversial, and have attracted much criticism from mainstream Christians.

More commonly in the mainstream, spiritual encouragement is more the norm than the imposition of negative sanctions for misbehaviour. Much Christian discipline is self-discipline: it is left to the individual as to how much time he or she spends on prayer, study and devotion. There is much Christian literature—at least in the West—to aid spiritual practices and to develop one's understanding of the faith. In Roman Catholicism, use is made of the rosary to encourage devotion to God, to Christ and to the Virgin Mary. We have already mentioned confession as a means of discipline, but one does not only approach a priest or a minister only after committing sin: priests, ministers and lay leaders frequently offer counselling to help a Christian through a difficult personal decision or a difficult period in his or her life.

For the majority of Christians any external responsibility for their spiritual life lies with their priest, vicar, minister, pastor, or whoever has oversight of their congregation. However, Christianity affords opportunities for a rather stronger commitment than simply being a layperson who can call for spiritual direction. The monastic life offers a more intense spiritual commitment than a normal secular existence. Being a monk or a nun involves undergoing ordination: the monastic life is a special type of spiritual life, to which its members experience a calling. It is an alternative form of ordination to the priesthood and, unlike the priesthood, its members are not empowered to administer the sacraments, hear confessions, or pronounce absolution. Monks and nuns live in self-contained single-sex spiritual communities, and commit themselves to a life of prayer, devotion and poverty.

The 'invisible' Church

This survey of the Church that we have provided above leaves a picture of a diverse organization with high ideals but varying degrees of commitment. Metaphors such as 'the body of Christ' and 'the bride of Christ' suggest a readily identifiable entity, but yet it appears to have blurred edges, with a number of organizations claiming to be Christian, and whose Christian identity is contested. How, then, does one decide who belongs to the true Church? This is a question to which Saint Augustine of Hippo (354–430) gave much attention. Although many Christians have heard of his *Confessions*, which tell of how he was a sinner and at one time a heretic, and who found his way into the Christian fold, his more substantial work *De Civitate Dei* (*City of God*) provides an extended analysis of the nature of the true Church.

Augustine was writing in a climate of controversy. Various groups of Christians had been accused or convicted of heresy. Under the Roman persecution, some Church leaders had been compelled to hand over copies of scriptures to be destroyed by the Roman authorities, and had subsequently been taken to task for their complicity by their fellow-Christians. These problems were exacerbated by certain heretics and traitors who subsequently had a change of heart, and who sought readmission into the mainstream Christian fold. Were they still members of the Christian Church, or had they forfeited their right to belong, requiring re-baptism? Moreover, there were *bona fide* Christians who had been baptized or ordained by these heretics and traitors. Was their baptism or ordination valid, or did it need to be repeated within the mainstream Church? What about receiving the Eucharist? Rank-and-file Christians did not necessarily know about the lives and doctrines of the officiants, so might some of the rites in which they had participated lacked validity and denied them the means of grace? Such conundrums are not confined to the archives of Church history: they continue to resurface in the twenty-first century.

The word 'city' in Augustine's title *City of God* is of key importance. Prompted by the sack of Rome by the Goths in 410 CE, the work was written over the period 413–426, and provides an analysis of the Church and the State, and their respective functions and destinies. Although it is entitled *City of God*, Augustine's thesis is, as it were, a tale of two cities, which he refers to as the 'earthly city' and the 'heavenly city' respectively. The earthly city is the civil society in which we all dwell, whether Roman, Goth, or a member of a twenty-first century nation state, and it contains Christian and non-Christian alike. The heavenly city is the New Jerusalem, of which the Book of Revelation speaks (21–22), and which is the culmination of the Christian's hope. Those who are members of the true Church belong to this heavenly city, and have only a temporal existence in the present earthly society: their real citizenship is in God's kingdom.

Both Saint Paul and the author of Hebrews allude to this idea when they write, 'But our citizenship is in heaven. And we eagerly await a Saviour from there, the Lord Jesus Christ, who, by the power that enables him to bring everything under his control, will transform our lowly bodies so that they will be like his glorious body' (Phil. 3:20-21), and, 'For here we do not have an enduring city, but we are looking for the city that is to come' (Heb. 13:14). The earthly city is the political state on earth, which contains heavenly citizens, as well as those who do not belong to the heavenly city. Augustine compares them respectively to Cain and Abel, the first children born to the primal ancestors Adam and Eve. Cain and Abel both brought ritual offerings to God, but

God accepted the offering of Abel, not of Cain (Gen. 4:1-16; the Bible does not clearly explain the reason for God's judgement). Consumed with anger and jealousy, Cain killed Abel, and was condemned by God to wander throughout the earth. Cain thus represents the earthly city for Augustine, while Abel—the righteous—represents the Church, the 'heavenly city'.

One should not infer from Cain's evil deed, however, that the earthly city is inherently unrighteous. The earthly city is not wholly bad: earthly government is necessary for human well-being, and aims at establishing peace, justice and concord among its citizens. Earthly societies, however, are ephemeral: political systems change, and empires can fall, as did Rome, unlike the City of God, which is an enduring city. Although Augustine has much to say that is unfavourable to Roman lifestyle, he points out that the members of the heavenly city look the same, and observe the same customs as the unrighteous inhabitants. From a human standpoint, they are not wholly distinguishable. Only God knows for certain who belongs to which city, and this will become clear at his final judgement of the world. If anyone thinks that they can clearly tell who belongs to which city, they should reflect that they do not necessarily know the motives of those who perform worthy deeds. Perhaps they are doing them for earthly honour, and perhaps they are clandestinely perpetrators of less commendable actions. As for those whose deeds are reprehensible, there always remains the possibility of repentance and receiving divine grace. Jesus taught that one should not be too ready to judge others (Mt. 7:1).

Jesus told a parable about the indistinguishability of the good and the bad, to which Augustine alludes (Mt. 13:24-30; *City of God*, Book XX, 5). A farmer sowed wheat in a field, but later discovered that an enemy had later sown weeds, under cover of darkness. The farmer's servants enquired whether they should attempt to uproot the weeds, but the farmer declined, preferring to let the wheat and the weeds grow together until the harvest, when it would be possible to uproot the weeds without damaging the good crop. The parable illustrates the relationship between the members of the two cities: they intermingle and are often hard to distinguish, but at the end of time God will be able justly and reliably to decide who are the true members of the New Jerusalem.

Augustine provided a number of insights on the nature of the Church, which were new at the time. One important contribution to Christian thought is his concept of the Church's invisible nature. Previously, the various disputing parties within the Christian faith had been looking for visible signs of authenticity and orthodoxy, such as its creed, or its methods of ordination and baptism. Augustine suggested that these were no more than visible signs of Christianity, but did not necessarily determine which Christians were destined to everlasting life—a decision which could only be made by God. It should be emphasized, however, that Augustine did not want to abolish such external symbols: like his predecessors, he continued to affirm the importance of baptism as the means of entry to the Christian fold, the need to celebrate the Eucharist, and the necessity of an ordained clergy. By insisting on these visible tokens of the Church's presence, Augustine is acknowledging a distinction which continues to be made, between the 'visible Church' and the 'invisible Church'. The visible Church is the aspect of Christ's Church that one sees on earth—its buildings, its members, its clergy, its sacraments—while the invisible Church is the totality of Christ's followers—past, present and future—whose identity is only known to God. Clearly there is considerable overlap between the visible and invisible Church, but human judgements have to be made with great care. Of course the Church still has to maintain discipline over its earthly members: Augustine may not have resolved the problems of how this might be done, but he has suggested a theology of the Church which continues to influence Christians.

Allied to the distinction between the visible and invisible Church is a further distinction to which Christians commonly allude: the 'Church militant' and the 'Church triumphant'. The visible Church on earth is a body that moves through history, moving towards a final victory, when evil will be defeated, and Christ's perfect kingdom established. While some Christians have come to dislike the militaristic imagery in such metaphors, metaphors about armed combat against sin and against Satan are commonplace in Christian Scripture. The Book of Revelation describes a cosmic battle in which Michael and his angels wage war against the dragon (Satan; 12:7) and the letter to the Ephesians urges Christians to 'put on the full armour of God' (6:11). Of course, these are not calls to physical armed conflict, but to the war against sin and evil. The writer to the Ephesians continues by enumerating the pieces of divine armour, which are 'the belt of truth', 'the breastplate of righteousness', shoes fitted with readiness to proclaim the gospel, 'the shield of faith', 'the helmet of salvation', and 'the sword of the Spirit, which is the word of God' (6:13-17).

Augustine made a further important contribution to Christian theology. He is the first Christian writer to perceive the Church as a body with a history. In its early years, Christians expected the swift return of Jesus Christ, as they had predicted, and a decisive end to human affairs. Although Christians throughout the ages have continued to expect an imminent Second Coming, the concept of the Church as a body that moves through history and influences affairs in history is something that Christians were brought to acknowledge through Augustine's writing. At a popular level, of course, only a small handful of Christians are directly acquainted with Augustine's theology. However, once again, Christian hymnody provides a bridge between theological ideas and popular understanding. There many hymns about the Church that convey the idea of the Christian community being a pilgrim people, on a journey towards a celestial goal, and consisting of a totality of believers, the living and the dead, transcending individual congregations and denominations. One favourite hymn that is used in the Western traditions is Samuel John Stone's 'The Church's One Foundation/Is Jesus Christ her Lord', and brings together several of the ideas discussed here. The hymn's penultimate verse runs:

> Mid toil and tribulation,
>   and tumult of her war,
> she waits the consummation
>   of peace for evermore;
> till with the vision glorious
>   her longing eyes are blest,
> and the great Church victorious
>   shall be the Church at rest.
> (*Hymns Ancient and Modern*, 170)

The notion of the terrestrial Church as part of a journey towards a celestial city is further conveyed in John Bunyan's (1628–1688) spiritual classic, *The Pilgrim's Progress*. This allegorical tale has been described as 'the most influential religious book ever written in the English language' and it has undergone many editions and translations. Bunyan wrote it in Bedford prison, where he was incarcerated for persistent preaching without a licence. The story is of a man, formerly called Graceless, but now called Christian, who seeks the Celestial City. He carries a heavy irremovable burden, which he must first shed in order to undertake the journey. He first finds the Wicket Gate, which puts him on the straight and narrow path, and arrives at the 'Place of Deliverance', where his burden is lifted. After climbing the Hill of Difficulty, he arrives at Home Beautiful, where he is given armour to enable him to fight the arch-demon Apollyon. As he continues his journey, Christian meets various opponents and obstacles, as well as helpers, until he finally arrives at the Celestial City.

The various incidents correspond to points in a real-life Christian's journey: the Place of Deliverance is Christ's cross, which removes the burden of sin; Home Beautiful is a Christian congregation (the Church on earth), and the armour is the spiritual panoply that is mentioned in Ephesians, including God's word, the Bible. Bunyan's book has two parts: in the second, his wife Christiana, their sons and a young woman called Mercy, embark on the same journey, and arrive at the Celestial City, thus demonstrating that it is possible for women as well as men, young as well as old, to reach God's eternal abode. Western Christians who have not read Bunyan's allegory will almost certainly know the hymn 'Who Would True Valour See?'—the only hymn Bunyan wrote—which forms part of the book, and alludes to several of its incidents.

The Church on Earth

Thus far we have considered the theology of the Church and its universal character, especially its invisible nature. We now turn to the more visible aspects of the Church, and how it operates on earth. The physical design of churches takes many forms; its characteristics vary according to tradition, and there can be local idiosyncrasies. Churches are often built on the highest point of the locality they serve, and Roman Catholic, Anglican and Protestant churches frequently have a spire or a tower, which, until the advent of skyscraper buildings, made the church the highest and most instantly recognizable point in a locality. The spire or tower often houses a bell: traditionally this had the purpose of calling the faithful to worship, since in bygone times the church served the locality, and only a minority used watches. Bell-ringing today is more to keep up a tradition and to remind those in the locality of the Church's continued presence. Where there are several bells in a church tower, skilled ringers can chime out tunes or sequences: this is called 'ringing the changes', and the art is known as campanology.

Outside the church, graveyards are commonly found: these exist for obvious practical reasons, enabling burial to take place at the same location as the rites of passage for the departed. The graveyard also serves as a reminder that the Church consists of the dead as well as the living. In the twenty-first century, many churchyards are now full, and no burial ground can be offered. If members of the deceased's family are already buried there, the designed ground may be shared, otherwise alternative means of disposing of the body must be sought.

In the Roman Catholic, Eastern Orthodox and Anglican churches the church building is typically designed so that the altar is at the east end, with the congregation facing it. This convention arose in the West, causing the people to face Jerusalem during worship, but tends to be followed worldwide. Frequently the main baptismal font is located at the entrance—symbolizing the fact that baptism is the means of entry to the Church. However, many churches locate the font at the front. The church is often cruciform in shape—an obvious reminder of Christ's sacrifice. When there is a full congregation, the people occupy the larger (western) area, known as the nave. The side areas are known as transepts, and can be used for various purposes: overspill from the congregation, an area for the choir or organ, or a small 'lady chapel'. Lady chapels can be found in various locations in a church, where there is sufficient semi-enclosed space to contain a few worshippers. These chapels are for private prayer and devotion, and at times they can be used for smaller, more intimate services. They are called 'lady chapels' since they are frequently dedicated to the Virgin Mary, but some are dedicated to other saints.

The main area used by the priests and other officiants is the chancel. This houses the altar—the focal point of the service, from the sacrament is administered. It is frequently bounded by an altar rail, preventing the congregation from entering the chancel itself, and enabling them to kneel or stand, while the priest and eucharistic ministers administer the sacrament. Sometimes the choir sit in the chancel, but the organ is always placed at the side, the back or in a gallery, since nothing must obstruct the congregation's view of the altar, since the sacrament is of key importance. To one side of the chancel (usually the South) is a lectern, from which the scriptures are read, and on the other is the pulpit, from which the sermon or homily is traditionally delivered. In Eastern Orthodoxy, the area between the priest and the people is separated by a large, usually ornate, screen known as an iconostasis (literally, 'icon stand'). The priest conducts a substantial part of the service from behind the screen, bringing out the sacrament to the congregation.

The design of Protestant churches is simpler, and less uniform. Their aim is more to serve a practical purpose, being accessible to the community and to enable them to hear God's word. There is little concern for the direction that the building faces and, while some Protestant churches maintain a cruciform shape, the majority are plainly rectangular. The pulpit is frequently central, since greater emphasis is placed on preaching

Interior of St Michael the Archangel, Rushall, Walsall (Church of England). The church is cruciform in shape, with the altar as the focal point.
Photograph: George Chryssides

than on the sacraments. At the front there is normally a table from which the sacrament is dispensed: it is known as a 'communion table', never an altar, since altars are held to be for sacrifices, and Protestants deny that any sacrifice takes place during Holy Communion. Although the communion table is given prominence, Protestants feel no compunction about giving the pulpit greater centrality, or about obscuring its view, for example by placing the organ console directly in front of it. In the Methodist tradition, it is common to have a central pulpit, with a large high organ—and sometimes the choir—positioned behind it, thus highlighting the emphasis that it is given to music and singing.

First and foremost, the Church consists of people. In most branches of Christianity, a distinction is made between laity—the vast majority of Christians—and clergy, who undergo an extended period of study and training, and are formally ordained to their offices. A few branches of Protestantism are entirely lay movements, taking literally the Reformation principle of 'the priesthood of all believers'. While denominations with an ordained clergy can draw on a national, or even international, pool of trained leaders, lay-led congregations tend to draw on the resources of their own members for their leadership. Any training is informal and acquired through experience, since it is believed that one's words and actions are prompted by the Holy Spirit. Such denominations tend to be theologically very conservative, and suspicious of formal training and scholarship—especially modern critical scholarship—believing that this stifles the work of the Spirit, and can introduce dangerous ideas that call into question God's word, which is to be thoroughly trusted.

The titles given to clergy vary according to denomination. In Eastern Orthodoxy and Roman Catholicism they are referred to as 'priests'. A priest is an intermediary between God and the people, a representative of both. In worship he (not she) brings the needs of the people before God in worship, and brings God down to them, through the sacraments and through preaching. Traditionally, in Roman Catholicism, it is believed that the priest has the power to bring about the miracle of transubstantiation at the Mass, changing the bread and the wine into Christ's body and blood. He is able to hear confession and pronounce absolution, declaring that one's sins are forgiven. According to biblical teaching only God can forgive sins (Mk 2:7), thus the pronouncement of absolution involves the priest acting as God's proxy.

In Protestantism the leader of a congregation is usually known as a 'minister', meaning a servant. Jesus told his disciples, 'I am among you as one who serves' (Lk. 22:27). In most denominations (but not all) they can be male or female. Protestants do not regard their ministers as intermediaries, or having supernatural powers, either to change the nature of the communion elements, or to pronounce forgiveness of sins. Their central role is preaching, and they are also available to their members for personal and spiritual counselling. The lay-led denominations tend to prefer the title 'pastor' for their leader, rather than 'minister'. There is no theological reason for this: a congregation is often compared to a flock, and the pastor is therefore the one who leads the flock, ensuring that they find the appropriate pastures for spiritual nourishment.

Anglicanism typically assumes a medial position between Roman Catholicism and Protestantism. The leader of a congregation is usually known as a vicar: a vicar is God's representative on earth, and hence the clergy act on God's behalf to offer the sacraments to the congregation, and to pronounce absolution for sins. In some parishes, the incumbent is known as the 'rector' rather than the 'vicar': the reasons are purely historical, and their function and status are identical. Normally Anglican and Protestant clergy assume the title 'Reverend' in front of their name. (It should be noted the 'Reverend' is always adjectival: it is inappropriate to refer to a member of the clergy as 'the Reverend' as if the word were a noun.) However, some Anglican clergy, particularly in the High Anglican tradition, prefer the title 'Father', in line with Roman Catholicism. Technically Anglican clergy are priests: they perform a priestly role, and at their ordination they are 'ordained priest'. Other officiants within the Anglican tradition are deacons and curates. One is 'ordained deacon' before being ordained as priest: a deacon may assume the title 'Reverend' and can wear a clerical collar, like a vicar. Normally the deaconate is a step on the path to full ordination, lasting around a year. The deacon may baptize and conduct weddings and funerals, but may not preside over the Eucharist. A curate is a member of the clergy who assists the vicar within a parish; he or she has the full liturgical capabilities, but does not have full oversight of the laity.

The members of the clergy mentioned above are all part of a wider, more complex organization. In Roman Catholicism, priests are accountable to their bishop, who has responsibility for the diocese (bishopric)—a fairly wide geographical region. The bishop is normally associated with a cathedral, belonging to a city, from which the diocese takes its name (for example, the Diocese of Liverpool). Further up the ecclesiastical hierarchy are archbishops, cardinals, and ultimately the Pope himself. Anglicanism follows this pattern to some degree, having bishops and archbishops (but not cardinals or a Pope). There are only two archbishops—of York and of Canterbury—and the latter is given the title 'Primate of All England'. Eastern Orthodoxy has an archbishop with overall authority for each branch of the Orthodox Church, with bishops and priests accountable to him.

The Protestant churches adopt one of two systems: synodical and congregational. A synod is a church court which meets to determine policy, and is part of a hierarchy of such courts. In the Church of Scotland, for example, each congregation has a Kirk Session, which consists of its Elders (senior members who oversee the spiritual life of assigned members). Delegates from each congregation (usually one elder and the minister) attend meetings of the presbytery, which is the local Church court and which meets at regular intervals. Presbyteries are grouped into synods, of which there are twelve in Scotland. Over and above the synods is the General Assembly, which meets annually to receive reports and to determine the denomination's policies. In Congregationalism, each individual congregation has the authority to decide its own affairs; this is done at the 'church meeting', which any member can attend and at which he or she may vote. Although this is the highest authority, a

Congregational Federation exists in England to promote the church's mission at a national level, and to ensure that its ministers receive appropriate training. The United Reformed Church was formed in 1972, when the majority of the Congregationalist churches in England merged with the English Presbyterian Church. As a consequence, there remains a hierarchy of church courts—Elders' Meeting, District Council, Synod and General Assembly—but, curiously, they have no more than an advisory role, with the ultimate authority still residing within individual congregations. There are also many independent churches throughout the world, which do not wish to be part of any wider federation, but simply to determine their own affairs.

There is a further category of religious 'specialists' within Christianity, namely those in monastic orders. The idea of monasticism, of a group of men or women living together and devoting their lives to shared prayer and work, goes back to fourth-century Egypt, where some of the hermits who had moved out into the desert began to organize themselves into groups. The movement spread within a century to the West, where the first monastic communities were set up in France and then Italy. The new communities needed a framework, and a number of rules were drawn up to regulate their communal life. The best known of them is that of Saint Benedict, who is often described as 'the father of Western monasticism'; his Rule has remained the basis for monastic life for centuries to come and is still widely followed. It was not the first rule to be devised, but it proved to be an exceptionally successful one.

Monasteries began as small simple communities which divided their time between regular hours of prayer and work to support themselves. As time went on, they became increasingly large and prosperous, attracting grants of money and property from landowners in return for the spiritual benefits they offered. New groups emerged that sought a simpler or more secluded way of life, such as the Cistercians, who built their monasteries in remote rural areas, or the Carthusians, who lived largely solitary lives within their communities. In complete contrast to these, military orders such as the Templars emerged at time of the Crusades. The enormous diversity of Western monasticism has no parallel in the Eastern churches, which have never developed separate orders.

The Benedictine rule included an emphasis on stability, which meant that monks remained permanently in the community where they made their profession. At the beginning of the thirteenth century a new movement began: groups of men not tied to one place, who travelled through towns and villages preaching to those who were not being reached by the contemporary church. These Franciscan and Dominican friars were a radical departure from conventional monasticism, and the later Middle Ages also saw the rise of generally less tightly regulated groups, such as Augustinian canons and beguines—semi-monastic communities of women in the Low Countries.

The Reformers rejected the idea of monasticism, for which they found no basis in the Bible; they believed that every Christian was called to lead a godly life in the world, and that work and family life were no bar to holiness. In Catholic countries new orders with new purposes continued to be founded; Jesuits in the sixteenth century, for instance, and Daughters of Charity in the seventeenth. In the nineteenth century the Church of England saw a revival of religious orders as a result of the Oxford Movement, which spread throughout the Anglican Communion; a few were also founded in Lutheran churches.

Despite episodes of suppression during the eighteenth and nineteenth centuries in several countries, religious orders continued to flourish and now range from strictly enclosed communities of women who never leave their convent to teachers, nurses and missionaries. Many orders also have lay associates, such as Benedictine oblates and Franciscan tertiaries, who share the ideals of the community while living an ordinary life.

Conclusion

The Church on earth manifests itself in its various traditions and denominations, the majority of which have laity and clergy, and some of which offer the possibility of monastic life. Despite its many divisions, theologically there is only one Church—the community of the faithful who will progress to God's kingdom at the final eschaton. Present-day Christians frequently find the diversity of traditions and denominations is often a source of embarrassment, since it appears to contradict the notion of the Church's oneness. The ensuing chapters will explore the Church's diversity by examining its various strands of tradition, the problems this diversity poses, and attempts by Christians to express the Church's unity at an earthly physical level.

8

Christian Worship

Every religion provides a means for the follower to be in touch with the transcendent, and Christianity is certainly no exception. Christian worship admits of a wide variety forms, encompassing the silence of the Quaker meeting, the near-spontaneous exuberance of a Pentecostal service, and the extremely formal worship of the traditional Orthodox, Roman Catholic and Anglican Eucharist. The formality of certain types of worship involves ornate opulent buildings with elaborately robed clergy and attendants, trained choirs, and a meticulously defined sequence of liturgical movements, the burning of candles and incense, with set prayers from a service book. By contrast, the more extreme ends of Protestantism are lay-led, with a spontaneous reliance on the promptings of the Holy Spirit. At a Quaker meeting, anyone may break the silence in order to 'give ministry', and many a Pentecostalist service allows members of the congregation to speak in tongues, give a testimony about how God has worked in their lives, and actively to associate themselves with the prayer or even the sermon by interjecting with 'Amen' or 'Hallelujah', as they feel moved.

Despite these enormous variations, Christian worship has numerous points in common. With the exception of the Quakers, who largely worship in silence, worship generally consists of hymns, prayers, the reading of Scripture and the preaching of God's word. In the Eastern Orthodox, Roman Catholic and Anglican traditions the main service is usually a Mass (more frequently called the Eucharist by Anglicans), while forms of Protestantism celebrate holy communion, but not necessary every Sunday. The purpose of worship is to pay homage to God, in his triune form of Father, Son and Holy Spirit, to feel his presence and receive guidance for life. Worship also serves to deepen one's faith and to further one's understanding of Christian teaching and Christian living—a function that is served by the regular reading and preaching from the scriptures. As we pointed out in chapter 2, the movement through the liturgical calendar reminds the faithful of the Christian story, and enables them not simply to be hearers, but to be actors, participating in it, and appropriating it for themselves.

Unlike Eastern religious traditions, but in common with the other Abrahamic religions, Christian churches do not portray God in pictorial form. Although it is not unknown for Christian art to use anthropomorphic representations of God on occasion—for example, in portraying the Trinity in painting or sculpture—such images are not used liturgically, since God is invisible and beyond human comprehension. Since the cross is the means of salvation for the Christian, most churches will have a cross or crucifix as the central focus. Eastern Orthodoxy often depicts an eye as the central feature of the iconostasis: although God is invisible, he is all-seeing. If an Orthodox church has a dome, it is common to depict Christ the *pantokrator* (the Judge of all) on it, as a reminder that there are no aspects of one's life that are not seen by God and judged by him. Worship is of course addressed to God, and since the persons of the Trinity are equally divine, worship may be addressed to any of these three persons. Prayer to the saints and to the Virgin Mary, invoking their aid as intermediaries, is common within Eastern Orthodoxy and Roman Catholicism, but is utterly avoided in Protestant circles, since it is held that the only mediator between God and humanity is Jesus Christ. Worship is never addressed to other supernatural beings such as angels.

Worship is typically conducted in a church building, but Christian rites do not normally require sacred space for their validity. The Bible records the apostles baptizing converts in the open air, at any place where water was available, and such practice still holds good. A baptism can be conducted at someone's home, although many clergy prefer to use the church building, since baptism is the admission to the Christian community, and the community can be present there to welcome the new member. God is omnipresent, and the Church is the community of God's people rather than bricks and mortar, and therefore any form of worship can be conducted anywhere, indoors or out of doors, with the obvious exceptions of consecrations or dedications of church buildings and their artefacts. Since God is accessible at all times as well as all places, there is no restriction on the times at which worship can be given. Some Christian churches are kept open during daytime hours for private devotion, since they provide an appropriate atmosphere and facilities for such purposes, but this is for the convenience of the worshipper, who can carry out his or her devotions at any time or place.

Public worship is by definition congregational, and there are therefore designated times and places for services. Although many churches hold services during the week, Sunday remains the principal day for Christians, being the day of Christ's resurrection. The choice of Sunday may also have been influenced by early Christians' desire to distinguish themselves from Judaism; the Church's earliest followers continued to observe the Jewish Sabbath, but assigned a further day to meet as emergent Christian communities. A few Christian communities, such as Seventh-day Adventists, continue to use the Sabbath (Saturday) as their main day for worship. There is no uniform time at which Sunday services occur. In Britain and the United States, eleven o'clock used to be a favoured time—a custom which perhaps owed its origins to a largely bygone agrarian society, where essential farming work could first be completed, enabling farm workers and their families to attend. The twenty-first century has moved beyond this way of life, of course; while some churches still retain this older tradition of mid-morning worship, other congregations have taken the view that it is no longer realistic to expect Christians to give up an entire morning. Since there are competing demands on people's time, they believe it may be preferable to hold worship earlier in the day, enabling people to be free for employment, study or recreational activities. Some larger congregations may offer a choice of times: this is particularly true of Roman Catholicism, where in many churches the Mass is celebrated at hourly intervals, starting perhaps at eight o'clock and continuing until noon. The Eastern Orthodox liturgy, being somewhat lengthy, cannot readily be repeated in this way. Other churches, such as those in the north of Scotland, still remain in agricultural communities, and exercise greater strictures regarding Sunday observance; hence the traditional time for worship remains.

Church services normally consist of prayers, reading from Scripture, singing and, more often than not, a sermon. In Orthodoxy, singing is normally unaccompanied and performed by a choir. Since the mid-nineteenth century in other traditions, the organ has been the most popular musical instrument, although recent times have seen the revival of congregational music groups and the use of lighter 'pop' music in place of (or sometimes alongside) traditional hymns. With the exception of Protestantism, readings are normally determined by a pre-defined lectionary, ensuring consistency among congregations and due coverage to all the most important passages in the Bible. Orthodox services are conducted entirely by the priests, while in other traditions the officiant is usually an ordained priest or minister, with laity contributing at least one reading and perhaps one of the prayers—normally the intercessions.

Prayer takes a variety of forms. It can be extempore, prepared or set. Charismatic Christians (those who emphasize the gifts of the Holy Spirit) tend to prefer extempore prayer, believing that God, being their Father, should be addressed in a natural, spontaneous way, and that prayer should come from the heart rather than from someone else's cold words on paper. Approved prayer books are used by Orthodox Christians, Roman Catholics and Anglicans, containing prayers appropriate to the place in the service and to the point in the liturgical calendar. Some Protestant ministers write their own prayers in advance and use them in worship, or draw on various books of prayers that are available. Prayers fall into various categories. Prayers of adoration extol God's attributes, while prayers of confession acknowledge one's sins to God. Public worship normally begins with these two types of prayer, since recognition of God's nature, and getting one's heart right with God are held to be preconditions of sincere worship. Prayers of thanksgiving, as the name implies, show gratitude for the benefits that God has provided. Petition is prayer for oneself, which may be specific benefits or for developing virtues. Intercession is prayer for others, and is usually divided into sections: the Church, the world, the local community, the sick and the suffering, and (where tradition approves) the communion of saints. Since human needs constantly change, there is more scope for innovation and creativity within the intercessory prayers. Since the prayers offered in worship are not composed by the whole congregation, those who attend are normally afforded the opportunity to identify themselves with the prayer, by saying a communal 'Amen', or a set response, such as 'Lord, in your mercy hear our prayer.' It is usual for the Lord's Prayer—the prayer Jesus taught his disciples (Mt. 6:10-14; Lk. 11:2-4)—to be recited communally:

> Our Father, who art in heaven,
> hallowed be thy name.
> Thy Kingdom come,
> thy will be done,
> on earth as it is in heaven.
> Give us this day our daily bread.
> And forgive us our trespasses,
> as we forgive those who trespass against us.

And lead us not into temptation,
but deliver us from evil.
For thine is the kingdom, the power and the glory.
For ever and ever. Amen.

The above is the traditional English form; some churches prefer more modern wording. (Roman Catholics normally omit the doxology at the end.)

Sacraments

Christianity identifies a number of rites as having special significance, and designates them as 'sacraments'. A sacrament is a symbolic set of actions, which conveys Christ's redemptive work, and thus serves as a 'means of grace' to the believer. Two such rites are agreed to be sacraments by the vast majority of Christian denominations: baptism and the Eucharist. To these the Roman Catholic Church acknowledges a further five: confirmation, penance, anointing the sick (formerly called 'extreme unction'), holy orders, and matrimony. Eastern Orthodoxy agrees on Roman Catholicism's sevenfold list, itemizing them thus: baptism, chrismation, Holy Eucharist, confession, holy unction, matrimony and priesthood. Orthodoxy prefers to call them 'mysteries', on the grounds that they point to things that are not fully comprehensible to the human mind, and the means by which they are deemed to be efficacious are not fully understandable.

The Roman Catholic Church concurs with the association between sacrament and mystery, noting that *sacramentum* is one of the Latin terms used to translate the Greek *musterion*. The *Catechism of the Catholic Church* states that *sacramentum* 'emphasizes the visible sign of the hidden reality of salvation which was indicated by the term *mysterium*' (*Catechism*, 774). The Anglican tradition offers a similar definition in its 1928 *Book of Common Prayer*, defining them as 'an outward and visible sign of an inward and spiritual grace given unto us, ordained by Christ himself, as a means whereby we receive the same, and a pledge to assure us thereof' (*Book of Common Prayer*, 1928). *The Shorter Catechism*, acknowledged by Protestant churches, states, 'A sacrament is an holy ordinance instituted by Christ; wherein, by sensible signs, Christ, and the benefits of the new covenant, are represented, sealed, and applied to believers' (*The Shorter Catechism*, question 92).

Some brief comment on these definitions may be helpful. They concur in acknowledging that they give sensory expression to the invisible. (The reference to 'sensible signs' above means signs that are detectable by the five human senses.) Although the Roman Catholic *Catechism* uses the word 'visible', sacraments can be experienced by all the five senses. They can be seen, in a manner similar to viewing a theatrical performance; one can hear the spoken words and the singing; baptismal water is felt by the candidate; the bread and wine are handled and tasted; and the use of incense makes use of one's sense of smell, although this last aspect of worship tends to be consistently avoided in Protestant worship. Protestantism insists that, for a rite to qualify as a sacrament, it must provide—or at least symbolize—the means of grace, and it must have been instituted by Christ. Protestants will point out that Christ specifically commanded his disciples to baptize (Mt. 28:19), and that his words at the Last Supper are reported as, 'Do this in remembrance of me' (1 Cor. 11:24). Jesus gives no such instructions that his followers should be chrismated, confess their sins (although James recommends mutual confession—Jas 5:16), anoint the sick, be joined in marriage, or belong to holy orders. Jesus was present at a wedding in Cana in Galilee, but he did not preside over it: he was the welcome guest, who miraculously created wine when the hosts had run out (Jn 2:1-11).

A small handful of Christian denominations do not celebrate sacraments, the best known of which are the Quakers and the Salvation Army. The Quakers desired to rid themselves of all external manifestations of religion. The Salvation Army likewise holds that grace should be internal rather than external; it also regards the sacraments as having proved divisive in the course of Christian history, and regrets the fact that women have been largely excluded from celebrating communion. A further objection relates to the use of wine: the Salvation Army is aware of dangers of alcoholism, and hence believes that its use at communion could prove to be a temptation to the weak. Neither of these two organizations, however, declares that it is wrong for other Christians to use sacraments.

The Oxford Dictionary of the Christian Church identifies three requirements for a sacrament to be regarded as 'valid': it must have the right matter, the right form, and the right intention. The 'right matter' refers to the substances that are used in the sacraments: water for baptism, and bread and wine for the Eucharist. Occasionally, Christians have returned from Israel with water from the River Jordan—the river in which Jesus was baptized—and the River Jordan is often used as an especially appropriate venue for baptism. Such preferences are predominantly sentimental, however, and there is no special efficacy conveyed by holy rather than ordinary water. A member of the clergy told one of the authors that on one occasion he had decided to conduct a modern Eucharist, the climax of which was the congregation processing out of the church to consume coffee and rolls in the hall. Whatever the merits of this liturgical innovation, the event could in no sense qualify as a sacrament, since the appropriate matter must be recognizably bread and wine!

The second of this trio relates to the manner in which the sacrament is conducted, and the rules relating to this may vary slightly from one denomination to another. In most denominations the officiant at a Eucharist must be an ordained member of the clergy. Where this is the rule, the sacrament cannot proceed if, for example, the priest is incapacitated and an appropriate substitute cannot be found. (In the Anglican tradition, it is possible to use elements that have already been consecrated and stored in an aumbry, which can be distributed by a deacon. The service is then described as 'Holy Communion' rather than a Eucharist, and the words of consecration are not pronounced, since the bread and wine have already been consecrated in the appropriate way.) If an inappropriate baptismal formula is used, then the candidate is not considered to be properly baptized. This can occur, for example, where someone undergoes baptism in a Unitarian congregation, where the officiant may or may not use the trinitarian formula, 'I baptize you in the name of the Father, the Son and the Holy Spirit.' If the officiant leaves out the threefold name, or simply welcomes the child into the world (as some Unitarian ministers have done), a child's parents may find such a rite helpful, but it is not a sacrament of baptism.

The third point—the right intention—does not require an explicit statement of intention, like Muslim prayer. It merely entails that a baptism or a Eucharist must be intended to be such. For example, actors making a film that included a scene depicting a baptism or a Eucharist would not be receiving a sacrament, not even if the actor portraying the priest had himself or herself undergone ordination. Someone who was quite unfamiliar with Christianity and who had strayed into a church and gone up to the altar would not be receiving communion, for no intention would be present. Of course, it is normally part of the eucharistic liturgy for the congregation to acknowledge their unworthiness to receive the sacrament, and members may possibly receive the Church's sacraments for all sorts of baser reasons. Parents have been known to present children for baptism because they think it is 'lucky', or because they may think it is socially respectable. Unworthiness, ulterior motivation and ignorance, however, do not invalidate a sacrament. It is Christian belief that God offers grace to the partaker, which may come in unexpected ways.

It is sometimes asked whether the clergy's integrity has any bearing on the validity of sacraments. Clergy do not lead blameless lives, and occasionally there are scandals in which Christian clergy are unmasked as sex offenders, fraudsters or even bank robbers! It may seem strange to learn that, notwithstanding their behaviour, their sacraments still have validity. The reason for this is that their congregations come to receive the sacraments in good faith, and, however reprehensible the behaviour of some leaders, they can at least be assured that they are not deprived of the means of grace through ignorance of their clergy's secret lives.

The concept of a 'valid' sacrament is simply a matter of what a sacrament actually is. Validity is not the same as efficacy, or legality, which are two further concepts relating to sacraments. To describe a sacrament as efficacious is to comment on how well it has functioned. Christians may well report that there are times when a Eucharist is inspiring and uplifting, while on other occasions it feels as if it offers little or no benefit. One's subjective feelings do not affect the sacraments' 'validity', which is unaffected by one's feelings. (One might consider the analogy of a book: a boring book is still a book, despite arousing negative feelings, but a CD is still not a book, no matter how interesting one finds it. 'Validity' is about definition, not about reaction.) Whether or not a sacrament's efficacy is subjective or objective is a matter that continues to divide Christian theologians. An 'objective' view, which implies that sacraments 'work' independently of the recipient's feeling might seem to imply that they have quasi-magical efficacy, while a 'subjective' view might suggest that the benefit accrues only through the recipient's state of mind, rather than from the divine grace that is said to operate through such rites. We do not intend to resolve this issue, but merely to note it. No doubt many Christians would plead ignorance of how grace works, and the devout would continue to receive the eucharistic elements, undeterred by any lack of confirmatory feelings.

A sacrament can also be legal or illegal, depending on whether it violates Church law. A minister who is disciplined by suspension from his or her duties, but continues to celebrate the sacrament, acts illegally in doing so. Such examples are rare, but they do occur on occasions, although they do not invalidate the sacrament, and may be efficacious. Ordinations can also be invalid: someone who has been ordained as a priest or bishop without the backing of the denomination is described as an 'irregular' priest or bishop. Such ministers are more likely to operate within a schismatical Christian group, rather than to offer their services in mainstream Christian denominations. Again, although acting illegally, their sacraments may still be valid sacraments, and provide the faithful with the means of grace.

In most denominations, the sacraments require the presidency of a fully ordained priest or minister in good standing. In the lay-led branches of Protestantism, a lay pastor or an elder may be authorized to celebrate communion, while some of the Free Churches empower designated elders to preside when an ordained minister is unavailable. In the Anglican tradition, deacons may conduct baptisms, although where there is an 'emergency'—for example if a baby is about to die—any member may baptize. Protestants tend not to acknowledge the idea of 'emergency baptism', since they regard it merely as a symbol, believing that God is capable of providing the means of grace without the need for its 'sensible signs'.

Baptism

The rite of baptism goes back at least to the time of first-century Judaism, when Jesus presented himself to John the Baptist as a baptismal candidate and was baptized in the River Jordan. In the Jewish tradition immersion in water was prescribed as a remedy for ritual impurity, but it seems that a number of Jewish reformers offered baptism as a means of complete rededication of one's life. Gentile converts to Judaism are still expected to take a ritual bath (*mikveh*) as a symbol of purification. Since water was the means of gaining entry to Judaism, it was natural that Gentile converts to Christianity should be required to undergo baptism as the means of entry to the emergent Jewish-derived faith. There is some uncertainty as to whether Jesus himself baptized anyone (Jn 4:1-2), but certainly his close disciples did, and the Bible records his clear instruction that they should do so (Mt. 28:19).

Baptism is therefore the means of entry to the Christian faith. The Book of Acts recounts that on the day of Pentecost, after the Holy Spirit descended on the disciples and Peter preached to the crowd that had assembled in Jerusalem, three thousand converts were added to the newly founded Church, and underwent baptism (Acts 2:41). Early baptismal practice appears to have been by immersion: the candidate would stand in water up to his or waist, and water would be poured over the head. Immersion differs slightly from submersion (or 'total immersion'), whereby the officiant completely submerges the candidate in the baptismal water. It is possible, although not certain, that Paul refers to this latter method when he uses the expression, 'buried with him [i.e. Jesus] in baptism' (Rom. 6:4).

As subsequent generations of Christians were born, it became common practice to baptize children, and not merely adult converts. While there are various accounts of adult baptism (sometimes called 'believers' baptism'), there are no explicit references to infant or child baptism (paedobaptism) in the New Testament, as Christians in the Baptist tradition will frequently point out. However, those who favour infant baptism may reply that Luke refers to the baptism of the entire household of Lydia of Thyatira (Acts 16:15), and that Paul's injunction that children should obey their parents (Col. 3:20) implies that he regarded children as part of the Christian community. In Protestant churches the baptismal service sometimes incorporates the story of parents bringing children to Jesus (Mt. 19:13-15), who tells them that the kingdom of heaven belongs to them. However, in common with first-century rabbinic practice, Jesus blesses them; he does not baptize them. The practice of baptizing children acknowledges that children as well as adults form part of the Church. Despite the lack of clear biblical precedent for child baptism, it was certainly common practice by the third century.

The methods of baptism and the appropriate age for the candidate are matters that continue to divide Christians. The Baptist, Adventist and Pentecostal denominations favour the baptism of adults by total immersion, arguing that, not only was this the original first-century Christian practice, but that it ensures that the candidate understands what is taking place, and that baptism is therefore an expression of a faith that is genuinely present. In these denominations baptism is synonymous with gaining membership within the denomination, and entitles the candidate to receive the further sacrament of holy communion. By contrast, infant baptism cannot be an expression of faith on the child's part, since infants are frequently baptized when they are only a few months old. Infant baptism is therefore a welcoming of the child into the wider Christian family, a dedication of the child by the parents, and an opportunity for the parents to affirm their faith again publicly and to promise to bring up their child in the Christian faith. (One might wonder how many parents actually do this, particularly when they rarely attend church on any other occasion, but this at least is the official purpose of the baptismal ceremony.) In the Roman Catholic and Protestant traditions, child baptism is typically carried by sprinkling or pouring water on the head (technically known as 'affusion'). Although there is no prescribed method for administering the water, it is common practice for the officiant to pour or sprinkle the water three times on the child, signalling the threefold name in which baptism is done. Alternatively, some clergy make the sign of the cross in water on the child's forehead.

It may appear as if adult baptism is by immersion and child baptism by affusion, but this would be an oversimplification. Someone who converts to Christianity as an adult will normally receive baptism by affusion, where this is the denomination's normal practice. Some clergy may offer the convert a choice regarding the method. However, there are practicalities to consider, since only churches that regularly administer total immersion contain an appropriate baptismal font. In the Eastern Orthodox tradition, babies, as well as adult converts, are baptized by immersion, not affusion.

The rite of baptism may be conducted as part of congregational Sunday worship, or it may be performed as a special service. Special baptismal services, which are largely attended by the candidate's friends and family, are sometimes done for pragmatic reasons: there may be so many attendees that they could not fit into the church building together with the regular congregation. Where this is the case, representatives from the regular congregation are encouraged to attend, so that the child is received into a wider Christian community. Although the minimal requirements for a baptism are the administration of water using the trinitarian formula, a baptismal service normally consists of reading from Scripture (normally one of the Gospels) and prayer. Candidates are asked questions regarding their commitment to the Christian faith; in the case of infant baptism, questions are put to the parents. The service ends with the instruction to 'fight valiantly'.

The symbol of water has obvious connotations of washing or cleansing, and hence baptism signifies the washing away of sin. The *Catechism of the Catholic Church* notes that in the story of Jesus' baptism, the heavens opened (Mt. 3:16), arguing that the heavens were closed by Adam's sin and that full access to God is reopened by Jesus Christ and symbolized in the rite of baptism. Baptism is associated with the receiving of the Holy Spirit, as is evidenced in the story of Jesus' baptism, and also in his words to Nicodemus, to whom he says, 'no one can enter the kingdom of God unless he is born of water and the Spirit' (Jn 3:5). Saint Hilary of Poitiers (c. 300–368) wrote, 'Everything that happened to Christ lets us know that, after the bath of water, the Holy Spirit swoops down upon us from high heaven and that, adopted by the Father's voice, we become sons of God' (quoted in *Catechism*, 537). At Jesus' baptism the voice from heaven declared, 'This is my beloved son.' Likewise, the person receiving baptism becomes the adopted son or daughter of God.

Water also has associations with the history of God's people. Water was the medium through which God's Spirit worked to bring the world into being (Gen. 1:2); crossing the waters of the Red Sea delivered the Israelites from bondage in Egypt (Heb. 11:29); traversing the Jordan brought God's people into the promised land (Josh. 1:10); and water is connected with the means of salvation offered through Noah when, obeying God's command, his ark brought human and animal life to safety through water (1 Pet. 3:19-21). These associations signify that the baptismal candidate is a new creation (2 Cor. 5:17), reborn to a new life, and saved by Christ's redeeming work. The concepts of incorporation and 'engrafting' are sometimes used in connection with baptism (*Catechism*, 1213; *Shorter Catechism*, question 94). Just as water was the means by which the Gentile was incorporated into the Jewish community, so the believer becomes part of the body of Christ, which is the Church.

Baptism also signifies thanksgiving and dedication. In the case of infant baptism, baptism is a rite of passage celebrating birth, and provides the opportunity for the parents to express thankfulness for a new life, and to dedicate the child to God. Where baptism is administered to adults, the candidate is afforded the opportunity to express thanks publicly for the salvation Christ offers, and to dedicate his or her life to the Christian faith. In the case of infant baptism, the thanksgiving is for a new physical life that is born, whereas in adult (believers') baptism, the thankfulness is for the new spiritual life that the candidate has found. A further association between new life and baptism is made by Saint Paul, when he associates baptism with Christ's death and resurrection: 'We were therefore buried with him through baptism into death in order that, just as Christ was raised from the dead through the glory of the Father, we too may live a new life' (Rom. 6:4).

The association is more obvious in the practice of baptism by total immersion, where the descent into the baptismal water parallels the descent into the ground at a burial, and the coming out of the water recapitulates Christ's resurrection. The candidate is thus participating in Christ's redeeming work, declaring that his or her sinful 'old self' is now dead, and that there is now the prospect of a new redeemed life.

Baptism signifies one's birth into the Christian life and, just as physical birth is a once-only event, baptism should not be repeated.

Asking a Christian to repeat his or her baptism would be tantamount to denying that previous spirituality was not truly Christian, but worthless. Some more traditional forms of Eastern Orthodoxy, however, believing that they alone constitute the true church, have required converts to be baptized (they would not say 're-baptized'), and there have been Protestant evangelical missions who have encouraged followers to be baptized again as a token of renewed commitment—especially if their baptism was in their infancy, and unremembered. Such movements tend to arouse disapproval in most mainstream circles, since in effect they call into question the validity of the baptisms of most other members of the Church.

Baptism is also irrevocable. In recent times there have been secular movements who have either advocated 'de-baptism' or demanded the destruction of their members' baptismal records (*Telegraph*, 14 January 2007). From the Church's standpoint, destroying a baptismal record would be similar to destroying a birth certificate. Through baptism, the candidate has been offered the means of grace, and this offer is believed to stand, whether or not the recipient confirms it or becomes apostate. This is held to be true even where civil law might require such destruction, for example by the Data Protection Act, since baptismal records constitute personal data. If such apostates were to reappraise their position and return to the Church, re-baptism would not be required, since divine grace is regarded as uncancellable, unlike the physical records of it, which are delible.

Confirmation and baptism

No Christian would claim that a ritual, however important or meaningful, provided instant transformation of sinners into perfected saints. It is common practice for clergy to remind baptismal candidates that baptism marks the beginning, not the end, of a spiritual journey. In the case of young children, who cannot understand what is taking place at their baptism, and probably do not even remember it, the Roman Catholic and Protestant churches provide a further opportunity for candidates to profess their commitment to the Christian faith. In the Roman Catholic and Anglican traditions this is known as 'confirmation'. The adherents, who have already been baptized and offered the means of grace, are now 'confirming' that they wish to appropriate these for themselves. Candidates for confirmation should have reached 'the age of discretion' (*Catechism*, 1307). This does not necessarily mean adulthood; in fact it is quite common for children of eight or nine to be confirmed in the Roman Catholic tradition, and not much older in Anglicanism. More often than not, in the authors' experience, it is adults who become confirmed: they may be new converts or, more probably, men and women who once were baptized and who have decided to make a commitment later in life.

The confirmation service is normally conducted by the local bishop. Originally the rite was conducted immediately after baptism—a practice which still prevails in Eastern Orthodoxy—but in Christianity's early centuries there were too many candidates for baptism for it to be possible for a bishop always to be present. The solution to this difficulty was therefore for priests to baptize, and for confirmation to await the bishop's availability. Eastern Orthodoxy combines the two rites, performing these in the context of the Eucharist, thus signifying that these three sacraments form a unity, and all three are needed to symbolize Christ's grace. Confirmation—or 'chrismation'—confers the right to receive the Eucharist, and it would be pointless to undergo the first two rites if one were not intending to receive the sacramental bread and wine in common with one's fellow Christians. There is normally a period of instruction preceding confirmation, to ensure that the candidates are familiar with the basics of the Christian faith, and understand its commitments. The rite involves the renewal of one's baptismal vows and the candidates being anointed on the forehead with oil ('chrism' means 'oil'). Anointing with oil has a wealth of connotations: in ancient biblical times it was used to appoint priests and kings, setting them apart for God's special purposes; it signifies abundance as well as healing; it marks the forehead in the way a slave was marked with his or her owner's name; and, especially, oil was administered by hosts to their guests as a sign of welcome—the last point signifying that in confirmation (or chrismation) the candidate is now welcomed as a guest at Christ's table of holy communion. For this reason it is normal practice to incorporate a Eucharist into the confirmation service, thus enabling the candidates to receive their first communion.

In Protestantism confirmation is not acknowledged as a sacrament. In denominations where becoming a full member of the Church is not accomplished through adult baptism, there is normally a short joining ceremony, sometimes referred to as 'admission' rather than 'confirmation', in which the candidates take vows of commitment and thus become eligible to receive the sacrament of Holy Communion. As in Roman Catholicism and Anglicanism, classes are held for first communicants.

The Eucharist

The other principal sacrament observed by the vast majority of Christians is Holy Communion, or the Eucharist, which is the symbolic re-enactment of the Last Supper, which Jesus celebrated with his disciples before his betrayal and arrest. The sacrament is given different names in different traditions, and the use of the correct terminology is important. The majority of Protestants, for example, do not take kindly to the suggestion that their communion service is a Mass, since this latter term is firmly associated with Roman Catholicism, which they reject. Protestants prefer the term 'Holy Communion', and Anglicans now tend to use the word 'Eucharist', although some churches in the Anglo-Catholic tradition describe the sacrament as a 'Mass'. In Eastern Orthodoxy the term 'Holy Eucharist' is used. The expression 'The Lord's Supper' is sometimes employed, being the phrase Paul uses (1 Cor. 11:20), and in some of the smaller Protestant denominations, for example the Brethren, 'The Breaking of Bread' is the preferred term, although both elements (bread and wine) are used. The word 'Mass' derives from the final words of the old Latin missal, *Ite, missa est* ('Go, it is the dismissal'). 'Eucharist' derives from the Greek *eucharistein*, meaning 'to thank', since, among other things, the sacrament is an act of thanksgiving for Christ's sacrifice. Although the term is not offensive to Christians in the Protestant tradition, it would probably be unrecognized by many of them. In discussing this sacrament, it is therefore difficult to decide on the appropriate terminology to use. We have elected to use the 'Eucharist', despite its unfamiliarity in Protestant circles; at least the word has the merit of being uncontentious, it spans a variety of traditions, and, unlike the term 'Communion' it does not have a variety of other meanings.

The Orthodox and Roman Catholic churches have traditionally celebrated the Eucharist at least once a week. Practising Roman Catholics are expected to attend Mass at least one on a Sunday (although they are not actually obliged to receive the sacrament). In Orthodoxy the sacrament is available weekly, but in practice only a small handful of worshippers go up to the altar to receive it. The norm is for the average worshipper to receive the bread and wine about three or four times in the course of the year. Orthodox Christians are expected to fast from the previous night—a practice that is too arduous to be a frequent expectation. In Anglicanism, Matins (Mattins) used to be the principal form of Sunday worship, and did not involve communion, which would typically be celebrated twice a month. Patterns of worship changed in the 1970s, when the Eucharist came into prominence as the major Sunday service.

Protestants have tended to celebrate Holy Communion less frequently. This is partly because Protestantism has tended to emphasize the preaching of the word rather than the celebration of sacraments. However, infrequent celebration can enhance rather than diminish the significance of communion. In the Church of Scotland, where communion was typically quarterly, it was common practice for communicants to be visited beforehand by their designated elder who would provide members with their 'communion card', to be presented at the door on Sunday. Often there would be a 'preparatory service' on the preceding Friday evening, since receiving the sacrament should not be undertaken lightly. The collected cards were used to check the frequency with which members communicated, and those who persistently failed to attend without good reason could even be struck off the congregational roll—a sanction which required re-joining the church! Attendance at communion tended therefore to be high, and an important climax of the service was the entry of the elders, formally dressed, bearing the communion elements, while the congregation sang the metrical 24th Psalm, 'Ye gates, lift up your heads on high.' Some Church of Scotland congregations now celebrate Holy Communion more frequently, but practice varies nationwide.

Although church services are open to the public, receiving the sacrament is only permitted to those who are in good standing within that branch of the Church. The criteria of eligibility vary according to tradition and denomination. Orthodoxy and Roman Catholicism only allow their own members to communicate, while Anglicans will allow anyone who belongs to a trinitarian church. Protestants tend to be liberal in their inclusivity, the criteria usually being determined by the presiding minister. The minister may invite anyone who is a member of any branch of Christ's church, or extend the invitation to 'all those who love the Lord.' One United Reformed minister known to the authors frequently intimated that anyone who had made the decision to follow Jesus Christ, 'even from this very moment', could receive the bread and wine. In Roman Catholic and Anglican churches, those who are ineligible to receive the elements can come forward to the altar to receive a blessing from the priest or minister.

In the Eastern Orthodox, Roman Catholic and Anglican traditions, the Eucharist has a similar structure. In all traditions, the service is conducted in the language with which the congregation is familiar; before the Second Vatican Council (1962–1965), the Roman Catholic

Mass was in Latin. There is a short introductory section, which includes the *Kyrie Eleison* ('Lord have mercy')—a set of responses linked with a prayer of confession. It is important for Christians to express penitence for their sins before participating in the sacrament. Paul writes, 'Therefore, whoever eats the bread or drinks the cup of the Lord in an unworthy manner will be guilty of sinning against the body and blood of the Lord. A man ought to examine himself before he eats the bread and drinks of the cup' (1 Cor. 11:27-28). It should not be thought that members of the congregation are invited to confess specific sins that they have committed. The confession is a general one. Those who are burdened with guilt on specific matters can confess their sins to a priest outside the service.

The first principal part is called the Liturgy of the Word or, in the case of the Orthodoxy, the Liturgy of the Catechumens. The service proceeds with readings from Scripture—normally from the Old Testament, the Psalms, an 'epistle' (the term includes the books of Acts and Revelation), and a Gospel. The last of these is essential: it is the high point of the service, at which a large copy of the Gospels is often carried in procession to the lectern, or into the congregation: this may be accompanied with candles and incense. The congregation stands while hearing the Gospel. The reading is done exclusively by clergy in the Orthodox tradition, where it is customary for the priest to intone the Gospel passage rather than read it like an ordinary book. Roman Catholics and Anglicans now involve the laity in reading from Scripture, although the reading of the Gospel tends to be reserved for the clergy. These ritual accompaniments to the reading of the Gospel emphasize its significance, allow the congregation to demonstrate respect for their Scripture, and illustrate the importance of not reading it in an over-casual way. Carrying it into the congregation symbolizes that God's word is brought to the people. The lectionary is set in advance for each day, and shared in common with all churches in that tradition. Protestants do not normally observe a fixed lectionary, the Bible passages being selected by the presiding minister. After the Bible is read, a sermon is given, to explain the word of God and show its relevance to members' lives. The congregation responds to God's word by affirming their faith in the creed (normally the Nicene Creed). This is followed by prayers of intercession, and this concludes the Liturgy of the Word.

The Liturgy of the Sacrament follows—the second principal part. This consists of prayers, some ancient hymns of praise, such as the Sanctus ('Holy, holy, holy, Lord God of hosts; heaven and earth are full of your glory'), Christ's words of institution of the sacrament, and the officiant's invitation to partake. The high point of the Eucharist is the receiving of the bread and the wine. Once again, there are variations in practice, according to tradition. Before the liturgical changes made by the Second Vatican Council, communicants in the Roman Catholic Church received the communion wafer (the 'bread') only, the wine being reserved for consumption by the clergy. The wafer is known as the 'host'—from the Latin *hostia*, meaning 'sacrificial victim'—and it is so named because it is believed to be, in a real sense, the body of Christ. In all traditions now, the elements are received 'in both kinds'. It is customary in the Roman Catholic and Anglican traditions for a communion wafer to be used rather than ordinary baker's bread. If the Last Supper was a Passover meal, the bread Jesus used would be unleavened, and thus the wafer, being unleavened, is a reminder of Jesus Christ as the Passover lamb that was killed and eaten at this Jewish festival. Since leaven connotes impurity, and its absence in the communion bread signifies the purity of Christ. Orthodoxy takes a different view, denying that the Last Supper was a Passover meal: Orthodox scholars point out that the biblical word for the eucharistic bread is *artos* (1 Cor. 11:23), meaning a loaf, not *azumē*, which means unleavened bread. In the Orthodox rite the bread is crumbled into the wine, and the priest administers the mixture to communicants on a long spoon. Protestants use normal bakers' bread, probably because of its ordinariness, and because they wish to distance themselves from practices associated with the Roman Catholic Mass. Methodists use either type.

The bread and wine are received by the communicants going up to the altar rail, where they either stand or kneel—except in Protestantism, where a kneeling gesture might indicate veneration of the elements. In most Protestant churches the communicants remain in their seats, while the bread and the wine are brought round to them by office-bearers. Because some Protestants disapprove of alcohol, small individual glasses are used, and the wine is unfermented. Congregationalists encouraged members to wait until all were served with the bread and wine respectively, then everyone ate and drank together, and some former Congregationalist churches (now part of the United Reformed Church) continue this practice.

All Christians would agree that the Eucharist is a thanksgiving for Christ's redeeming work, and that it is a memorial of his death, Jesus' instruction being, 'Do this in remembrance of me.' Although the Eucharist is not a meal that satisfies physical hunger, the quantities of bread and wine being minute, the notion of commensality is important in a religious community. To share a table with someone is usually a token of friendship and equality: societies that have a caste system demonstrate this by denying commensality to those of a different status. Paul observes that, where a common meal is celebrated, the shared common ingredients become part of each person's physical body, and thus in a very literal sense food sharing makes for corporate identity. To quote Paul, 'Is not the cup of thanksgiving for which we give thanks a participation in the blood of Christ? And is not the bread that we break a participation in the body of Christ? Because there is one loaf, we, who are many, are one body, for we all partake of the one loaf' (1 Cor. 10:14-17). The import of Paul's argument is that the Church is one body, and each individual Christian is part of this unified body. This is the theory, at any rate: as has been mentioned, denominations frequently deny Holy Communion to other Christians, and the Eucharist has often been a reminder of disunity rather than unity within Christianity—a problem with which the ecumenical movement continues to grapple.

More controversial are the various theologies surrounding the Eucharist. The majority of Christians agree that it is a thanksgiving, a memorial and a means of defining one's identity. What the various Christian traditions are disagreed on is what—if anything—happens to the bread and wine during the Eucharist. Roman Catholicism traditionally holds that there is a real (although not physical) change in the eucharistic elements, transforming them into the body and blood of Christ, while Protestants consider that belief in any such miraculous change is mere superstition. The Orthodox position is to affirm that some real change takes place in the elements, but the nature of the change cannot be specified: the sacrament is a mystery. Protestants have frequently endorsed a doctrine of the 'real presence', affirming that Christ is present when the sacrament is celebrated, but not as the result of any miracle performed by a priest. Certainly the claim that, when the Eucharist is celebrated, Christ is present with the faithful, is something that can be agreed by all Christians.

Rites of Passage: Marriage

Most religions provide a means of bringing the key events of one's life into a religious context, endowing them with significance and meaning. Christianity is no exception. We have already discussed how most Christian denominations mark the birth of a child with baptism, and how coming of age is linked with confirmation or admission to the Church. The next life-cycle event for many people is marriage, which Christians celebrate within the context of their religion. Even those whose connection with the Christian faith is tenuous often wish to celebrate a religious rather than a merely civil wedding.

Christian marriage is viewed as one of God's main purposes in creation. God deliberately creates humans as male and female (Gen. 1:27), creating Eve out of Adam's rib, signifying that a husband and wife form a unity: 'For this reason a man will leave his father and mother and be united to his wife, and they will become one flesh' (Gen. 2:24). Marriage is therefore strictly between a man and a woman, although some Christians have begun to consider the appropriateness of blessing ceremonies for gay and lesbian partnerships.

Jesus' first recorded miracle is in the context of a wedding party, when he turns water into wine at Cana in Galilee (Jn 2:11). In the Old Testament, God's love for his people is frequently described as akin to a marriage relationship, and the New Testament extends this idea by comparing Christ's love for his Church ('the bride of Christ') as a matrimonial relationship. Marriage is therefore regarded as a serious commitment: until recently the ceremony was described as the 'solemnization of matrimony', and the expression 'holy matrimony' indicates that marriage is a way of life that is ordained by God. The words of the service remind the couple that marriage is not to be entered into lightly, and provision is normally made for counselling before the wedding. In the United Kingdom it is customary for the established churches to read 'banns of marriage'. These are declarations of the couple's intention to marry, and these are normally announced on three occasions before the wedding. This is partly a matter of law, although it is probably more appropriate to a bygone era in which members of a congregation were drawn from the local community, who would be able to vouch for the couple's eligibility to marry. If banns are not read in church, they must be displayed in the Registry Office for a period.

Marriage normally takes place at the local church to which at least one of the marriage partners is associated. In the Church of England, the local parish is obliged to marry anyone residing within the parish and who is eligible for matrimony. Normally both partners will be at least nominal Christians, and marriage of partners of the same Christian tradition tends to be preferred. This is not an absolute rule, however. Roman Catholics may marry outside Catholicism, and Eastern Orthodox Christians outside their tradition, but it is expected that children will be brought up as Roman Catholics and Orthodox respectively.

Church weddings work in tandem with the State's requirements. In Britain, the United States, and some European countries, a church wedding constitutes a legally binding marriage. Where this is the case, the couple sign a register as part of the ceremony. If a civil ceremony is additionally required (as it is in countries such as France, Belgium, Bulgaria, the Netherlands and Turkey), this normally takes place before the church ceremony. A member of the clergy must preside over the religious ceremony: the conduct of weddings by deacons is permitted in the Anglican tradition, but

Wedding at All Saints' Church, Highgate, London.
Photograph: George Chryssides

in Roman Catholicism and Eastern Orthodoxy a fully ordained priest is needed. The ceremony involves readings, prayers and possibly a short homily, followed by the declaration of marriage vows. The word 'covenant' is sometimes used to describe the marriage promises, and just as a physical sign accompanied the covenants made between God and the ancient patriarchs, rings are often exchanged as a tangible sign that the couple have entered into a lifelong contract. Celebration of the Eucharist may be incorporated into a marriage service—this is called a 'nuptial Mass' in Roman Catholicism—but this practice is not so common. In Eastern Orthodoxy, the couple may receive communion within the Divine Liturgy, and then proceed with the wedding ceremony at the end of the service. Eastern Orthodoxy has the additional practice of placing 'wedding crowns' on the couple. These are worn for eight days after wedding, then ceremonially removed by the priest.

Marriage is for life: the words of the ceremony require commitment to marital fidelity 'as long as you both shall live' or, in the more traditional words, 'till death us do part'. Christians typically believe in a life after death in which there will be a reunion of one's loved ones, and that distinctions between male and female may exist in the afterlife. However, unlike Mormons and Unificationists, they do not believe that marriage itself endures beyond the grave. The Sadducees reportedly asked Jesus a question about the position of a woman who consecutively had seven husbands, to which Jesus replied, 'At the resurrection people will neither marry nor be given in marriage; they will be like the angels in heaven' (Mt. 22:30).

Holy Orders

Entering holy orders is sometimes perceived as an alternative to holy matrimony. In Roman Catholicism it is an expectation that a priest is unmarried and celibate, and hence would be unlikely to be a candidate for both the sacraments of marriage and of holy orders. (There are some exceptions: some Roman Catholics priests have left the priesthood and subsequently married, and some married Church of England clergy who transferred to Rome after the decision to ordain women in 1992 became Roman Catholic priests despite their matrimonial status.) In Eastern Orthodoxy, a priest should be married, since Paul's letter to Timothy states, 'Let deacons be the husband of one wife' (1 Tim. 3:12, RSV). This they take to be a positive requirement, rather than a restriction on the number of wives a priest ('deacon') is allowed. An Orthodox bishop, however, may not be married; hence Orthodox clergy must decide whether or not they will marry, before proceeding to ordination. In the Anglican and Protestant traditions, marriage of the clergy is permitted, and tends to be the norm.

Death and Funeral Rites

Death is the final event that is placed in the context of religion. Despite the fact that the Christian faith offers assurance of life beyond the grave, death remains a daunting prospect for many. The living cannot know what it is like to die, and hence the administering of the sacrament of extreme (or holy) unction is to assist the dying person through this uncharted territory. The practice of anointing the sick need not imply that he or she is seriously ill or in danger of death. In early Christian circles the practice was associated with healing. James writes, 'Is any one of you sick? He should call the elders of the church to pray over him and anoint him with oil in the name of the Lord. And the prayer offered in faith will make the sick person well; the Lord will raise him up. If he has sinned, he will be forgiven' (Jas 5:14-15).

With the exception of the Lutherans, Protestantism has largely rejected the formal practice of anointing the sick, and Protestants might point out that it is not the anointing that brings health, but the prayer. Christians of any tradition would not normally expect either prayer or anointing to guarantee a cure: faith offers healing, rather than curing, and healing involves holistic well-being, which is associated with feeling forgiven. Christianity continues to have its spiritual healers, some of whom claim to have healed in cases where the medical profession has failed. However, Protestants who practise spiritual healing—mainly evangelical and charismatic Christians—are more likely to do it by the laying on of hands rather than by anointing. Oil is sometimes used for healing in charismatic and Pentecostal circles, but not in any prescribed ritual manner; healings are done in a more spontaneous way than by following a liturgical manual. In the Orthodox, Roman Catholic and Anglican traditions, the formal practice of holy unction serves as a means of assisting the dying believer from this life to the next. The rite itself, of course, does not have quasi-magical powers to guarantee eternal life, and it is not believed that those who die without undergoing this rite of passage (for example, in the case of a fatal accident, or a sudden death) are denied entry to the kingdom of heaven.

Death itself is marked within all forms of Christianity, and even those whose connections with the Christian faith are tenuous often want the death of a loved one to be placed within the context of religion. The more committed Christians will want the funeral to take place in a church, but others may be content with a short service at a crematorium or graveside. Eastern Orthodoxy insists on burial rather than cremation, but the other traditions usually permit choice. Those who prefer a church funeral will frequently follow it with a committal (the internment or a short crematorium service), but in recent times the practice of disposing of the body before the church service has developed. Normally funerals are conducted by clergy, but in Anglican and Protestant traditions approved laypeople may perform the funeral rites. Roman Catholics frequently celebrate Mass as part of the funeral service (known as a Requiem Mass), a practice that is shared, although not so commonly, by some sectors of Anglicanism, particularly the Anglo-Catholic tradition.

The Christian funeral focuses on resurrection and eternal life, rather than death. Death is the consequence of sin, but Adam's sin is cancelled out by Christ's redeeming work. Although Christians have traditionally believed in two types of eternal destination—heaven and hell—funerals are conducted on the assumption that eternal life is a possible expectation for the departed. There are occasions when the deceased is plainly not part of the Christian Church, and Roman Catholic Canon Law states,

> Church funeral rites are to be denied to the following, unless they gave some signs of repentance before death:
> 1 notorious apostates, heretics and schismatics;
> 2 those who for anti-christian motives chose that their bodies be cremated;
> 3 other manifest sinners to whom a Church funeral could not be granted without public scandal to the faithful. (*Code of Canon Law*, Can. 1184)

Such denials are rare, but such prohibitions do not wholly belong to the Church's historical archives. In 2002 the Roman Catholic Diocese of Brooklyn denied the Mafia boss John J. Gotti a Requiem Mass. Notwithstanding his life of crime, he was given a Christian burial, however, and a requiem was held at a later date. To deny full funeral rites is not a punishment of the sinner, but rather an acknowledgement, in the words of Pope Leo the Great (448), 'We cannot hold communion in death with those who in life were not in communion with us' (Thurston 1908). Normally a priest or vicar is under an obligation to provide a burial for anyone who belongs to the parish, but in the Protestant tradition, where the parish system does not generally apply, the appropriateness of conducting funerals is often at the minister's discretion. In 2007 the Revd Gary Simons, Pastor of HighPoint megachurch in Arlington, Texas, refused to conduct the funeral of a naval veteran on the grounds that he was gay. Other clergy, conversely, may be accused of being excessively liberal: for example, the vicar of St George's, Malvern (Australia), Canon Dr Colleen O'Reilly, came under fire for providing a funeral service for Pamela Bone, a well known agnostic journalist, who in no sense belonged to the Church. Those who are responsible for funerals are faced with the dilemma of how to offer the bereaved the help they need, while continuing to make sense of their tradition, which presupposes that the deceased is part of the Christian community who attend the funeral.

The practice of holding memorial services is favoured by many sectors of Christianity. Eastern Orthodox churches frequently celebrate brief memorials for the dead, usually after the Divine Liturgy. This is done on the third, ninth and fortieth day after the death (the funeral itself is often on the third day), and on the first anniversary. Thereafter, memorials may be held on anniversaries at the family's request. Additionally, there are a number of 'Soul Saturdays' on which the dead are remembered.

Prayers are offered for the departed, and a popular practice to distribute *koliva* to the congregation. This is a sweetened cake, made from grain, recounting Jesus' saying about death and resurrection: 'Unless a grain of wheat falls to the ground and dies, it remains only a single seed. But if it dies, it produces many seeds' (Jn 12:24).

It is customary in Roman Catholicism and in high Anglicanism for the names of the departed to be recorded in a Memorial book. The names are read during public worship on the anniversaries of their death, at the end of the intercessory prayer, and they are commended again to God. In Roman Catholicism, prayers may be offered to assist the deceased's passage through purgatory.

Protestants largely reject prayer for the dead, holding that the departed are now in God's hands, and cannot be affected by the actions of those who remain on earth. *The Larger Catechism* states,

> Q. 183. For whom are we to pray?
> A. We are to pray for the whole church of Christ upon earth; for magistrates, and ministers; for ourselves, our brethren, yea, our enemies; and for all sorts of men living, or that shall live hereafter; but not for the dead, nor for those that are known to have sinned the sin unto death. (*The Larger Catechism*)

Conclusion

In a previous chapter (chapter 2), we noted how the Church's key events were brought into the context of Christian worship. In this chapter we have focused on the more regular forms of worship, as well as the life-cycle events that are brought into the context of the Church. Despite all the differences in its theology and its liturgy, and changes that have taken place over the centuries, Christian worship enables the believer to pay homage to God as the Trinity, to present the invisible in visible form, to enable worshippers to receive guidance for life and in particular to mark and celebrate the key events in their lives.

9

The Roman Catholic Church

The Roman Catholic Church is the world's largest Christian organization. Roughly half of all Christians worldwide are Roman Catholics, and its total membership at the time of writing is 1.1 billion, making it the religion of one sixth of the world's population. We have referred to Roman Catholicism as a tradition rather than a denomination, since the latter term implies that it is one of several legitimate expressions of the Christian faith. Traditionally, Roman Catholicism has rejected this, claiming to be the one and only true Church, denying even the name 'church' to other Christian bodies, which it has regarded as having broken away from the true body of Christ, which offers the sole means of salvation. Until very recently, Roman Catholicism's position was summed up in the phrase *ex cathedra nulla salus*—'no salvation outside the Church' (that is, the Catholic Church). It has been remarked that the Vatican's web site contains no external hyperlinks—a reminder that anyone who seeks salvation has no need to look outside the Church (Vatican 2010).

The first recorded use of the expression 'Roman Catholic' was by the Roman Emperor Theodosius in 380. Referring to those who accepted the authority of Bishop Damasus of Rome and Bishop Peter of Alexandria, he said, 'We authorise the followers of this law to assume the title Roman Catholic Christians; but as for the others, since in our judgment they are foolish madmen, we decree that they shall be branded with the ignominious name of heretics, and shall not presume to give their conventicles the name of churches' (*Theodosian Code* XVI.i.2; in Bettison 1943: 31).

Roman Catholicism is unique in being a single worldwide Church; indeed the word 'Catholic' means 'worldwide'. Protestantism has many different varieties, and Eastern Orthodoxy is made up of several autocephalous national churches. The Roman Catholic Church can legitimately claim to be the world's largest multinational organization, having one single central authority based in the Vatican at Rome. In addition to the vast majority of Roman Catholics who observe the Church's Latin rites, Roman Catholicism also includes the lesser known churches whose liturgy is Orthodox in style, but who are in communion with the Roman Catholic Church and are subject to papal authority. Examples include the Ukranian Catholic Church and the Coptic Catholic Church.

Roman Catholicism came to centre on Rome for several reasons. The Bible records Paul's final years as a prisoner in Rome, where, according to tradition, he was martyred. Legend has it that the apostle Peter was also martyred in Rome, and on the same calendar date. (Saint Peter and Saint Paul typically share a festival in the liturgical year.) Peter's particular significance lies in his confession of faith that Jesus is the Messiah, thus eliciting Jesus' response, 'You are Peter, and on this rock I will build my church' (Mt. 16:18). Traditionally it has been taught that in this incident Jesus ordained Peter as the first head of the Church, and he became the first in an unbroken line of popes in apostolic succession to the present day. Pope Benedict XVI is believed to be the 264th in this lineage. Many present-day Roman Catholics, however, are not so inclined to attach importance to a one-to-one line of succession, but rather to believe that Jesus was succeeded by a number of apostles who collectively were succeeded by other leaders whose line of succession leads up to the entire present-day Church. The Pope represents the whole Church, rather than acts as an autocratic individual who dictates its doctrines and practices. As the succession of early Christian leaders developed, the See of Rome tended to gain importance, since Rome was the centre of the empire that penetrated much of Europe, taking Christianity with it. It was the Roman emperor who presided over the early ecumenical Councils. The Bishop of Rome thus gained increasing authority, extending beyond his own geographical province.

The Roman Catholic Church is organized along the lines of a nation-state. Its scale surpasses that of any of the world's political systems, and Vatican City constitutes a state in its own right: although set in the middle of Rome, it is not subject to Italian government or legislation. The Church is governed by two bodies: the Roman Curia (Court of Rome), and the College of Bishops. The former is located in Vatican City, and is the bureaucratic complex of its Secretariat, Congregations, Tribunals, Councils and Commissions. The oldest of the nine Congregations is the *Congregatio pro Doctrina Fidei* (Congregation for the Doctrine of the Faith; CDF), which originated in the Counter-Reformation, and used to be called the Office of the Inquisition. Although the Inquisition has acquired notoriety, its original, and indeed present, purpose has been to ensure sound doctrine and hence the salvation of souls. It is the final court of appeal in any trials for heresy, but adjudicating on specific cases and imposing sanctions is only a portion of its work.

The work of the Congregation for Divine Worship and the Discipline of the Sacraments (*Congregatio de Cultu Divino et Disciplina Sacramentorum*) includes ensuring that the sacraments are conducted legally and validly, and that liturgical texts are updated and disseminated. In connection with the former, it can consider whether specific marriages and ordinations were valid. It also regulates the cults of saints and relics. Other Congregations deal with issues such as evangelism, canonization of saints, the affairs of the Eastern Catholic Churches, and so on. The Tribunals consider appeals from the lower courts within the Church, relating to penitential, ecclesiastical and sacramental matters, while the Councils deal with specific concerns of the Church, such as ecumenical affairs, family life, justice and peace, and inter-religious dialogue. The Commissions deal with more predominantly internal, mainly theological matters.

The hierarchy of the Roman Catholic Church consists of the Pope, Cardinals, Archbishops and Bishops, all of whom have authority over the priests and the laity. There has been much discussion within the Church as to whether this hierarchy is pontifical or episcopal—that is to say, whether its structure is a kind of 'line management', with the Pope's role being equivalent to that of a Chief Executive Officer, or whether decisions in the Church are taken in a 'collegiate' or collective way, with the Pope having a role more akin to that of a chairman, who convenes his College of Cardinals. The Roman Catholic Church's government is complex. A rudimentary explanation might be that the priest is the religious official who is responsible for a parish, exercising pastoral care over his flock, administering the sacraments (except ordination), and teaching the Christian faith to the people. The bishop has oversight over the diocese, while an archbishop oversees a province (a cluster of dioceses) and thus has authority over his bishops. The cardinals are the rank immediately below that of the Pope, and their duties include the election of new popes. All these roles are male: women may not be ordained to holy orders. Those who belong to holy orders may not marry, and are required to live a strictly celibate life.

The above explanation is complicated by a number of factors. A priest may be one of a number of clergy who are responsible for a parish. In such situations the priest who 'governs' is known as the pastor, and is assisted by at least one curate. The priest is the 'cultic officer', who has the powers to administer the sacraments and to teach, although he requires 'faculties' from his bishop for both these functions. Although the parish priest is a teacher, a distinction is sometimes made between the 'teaching church' and the 'listening church', and the priest belongs to the latter. The former is comprised of bishops and higher-ranking officials, and collectively they constitute the living Magisterium (literally, direction or guidance, but usually explained as 'teaching authority'). What this means is that the bishops, archbishops and cardinals are guarantors of sound doctrine; the Roman Catholic Church has never acknowledged that any bishop has fallen into doctrinal error. Having undergone extensive training, the priest should of course be expected to teach sound doctrine, but his teaching does not carry the same authority as that of higher-ranking clergy. A bishop is empowered to give an imprimatur to theological books, affirming that such books contain sound doctrine, free from theological error. A priest is not so empowered; an academic who is also a priest might give an endorsement for someone's book, but this would merely be his personal opinion, and would carry no ecclesiastical authority.

The priesthood is wider than the totality of parish priests. Additionally, there are ordained priests who undertake specialized work, such as university lecturing, journalism or ecclesiastical administration. It may seem surprising that priests in academic posts are still accorded a 'listening' rather than 'teaching' role, since many of them are likely to be more knowledgeable than bishops, and since in many cases they are responsible for teaching ordinands in Roman Catholic seminaries. However, the nature of academia is to innovate, and there have been times when Roman Catholic scholars have expressed ideas that have failed to meet with the hierarchy's approval. While they may still be allowed to teach their own students—although at times some have been barred from doing so (for example, Hans Küng)—their teachings may not be disseminated to the wider Church as 'true doctrine'.

The word 'bishop' is the English translation of the Greek *episcopos* ('overseer'), a term that is used on five occasions in the New Testament (Acts 20:28; Phil. 1:1; 1 Tim. 3:2; Tit. 1:7; 1 Pet. 2:25). Initially the office involved oversight of a small group of Christians, and a city's community sometimes had several overseers. As Christianity grew, the office became more onerous and professionalized. Bishops have authority to 'teach, sanctify and govern'. Their authority exceeds that of the priests, since it is the bishops who are held to be in apostolic succession to the original twelve apostles. The New Testament records that the apostles met as a body; hence the body of bishops is referred to as the College of Bishops. The bishops are thus the custodians of the faith entrusted to the early apostles, and consequently have a teaching rather than a mere listening role. A bishop normally oversees a diocese, and the duties of a diocesan bishop include the care and oversight of the priests, and endowing with the authority ('faculties') to perform their priestly roles. The bishop's governing role includes the ordination of priests, and the confirmation of catechumens; the latter, but not the former, may be delegated to a priest. The bishop is also responsible for the consecration of churches and altars, and he presides over the Mass of the Chrism during Holy Week. At this Mass, holy oil is dedicated and distributed to parish priests, who use it for confirmation, anointing the sick and at baptisms. The seat of a diocesan bishopric is a cathedral, so-called because it contains a *cathedra*—a special seat or 'throne' exclusively reserved for the bishop as a symbol of his authority. Out of the College of Bishops, the Synod of Bishops is elected: this congregation of bishops was created by the Second Vatican Council, and is convened periodically by the Pope. The Synod has an advisory role, and does not make resolutions, although the Pope has the power to express the collective opinion of the Synod into a decree or resolution of his own.

An archbishop is an elevated bishop, who has oversight over an archdiocese (an unduly large diocese). The prefix 'arch' derives from the Greek word *archē*, meaning 'first'. The office of archbishop therefore carries greater responsibility and prestige than that of bishop. Technically, it is not a separate rank from bishop, and candidates for this office do not undergo another ordination unless, exceptionally, they are elevated directly from the status of priest to that of archbishop. One talks about an archbishop being 'installed' or 'enthroned', rather than ordained to office. An archbishop has oversight over other bishops, or he may be the head of a department of the Roman Curia. Being made an archbishop is occasionally an honour conferred on aged priests of distinction.

The office of cardinal is next in rank to that of the Pope. There are three orders of cardinal: Cardinal Bishop, Cardinal Priest and Cardinal Deacon, each order reflecting the background from which the officiant is drawn. The word 'cardinal' derives from the Latin *cardo*, meaning 'pivot', thus indicating the key role of the office. The Sacred College of Cardinals offers advice to the Pope, either collectively, or from individual members who have areas of specialism. Additionally, like a bishop, a cardinal may be the head of a large diocese, or have responsibility for a department of the Curia. Cardinals are chosen by the Pope, in consultation with the College, at a consistory. Cardinals are also well known for their key role in choosing a new pope when the Supreme Pontiff dies. Pope Sixtus V (reigned 1585–1590) limited the number of cardinals to 70 (six cardinal bishops, 50 cardinal priests, and 14 cardinal deacons), but Pope John XXIII broke the tradition, and subsequently there has been no restriction on the total number. Not all cardinals may vote in conclave, however, but only those who are less than 80 years old on the day of the Pope's death. In theory, any male baptized member of the Roman Catholic Church may be chosen as Pope, but the office has always been filled by a member of the conclave. The conclave's deliberations are secret, and the cardinals remain in confinement until a successor is agreed. The only communication with the outside world is maintained by burning straw: black smoke indicates that a decision has not yet been reached, and white smoke indicates that a decision has been made. The cardinal protodeacon—the most senior member of the cardinal deacons—then appears at the Basilica of St Peter to pronounce the famous words, *Habemus Papam* ('We have a Pope').

The Pope is the leader of the Roman Catholic Church. The word 'Pope' derives from the Greek *papas* and the Italian *papa*, meaning 'father'. He is known as the 'Supreme Pontiff', the title 'Pontiff' being derived from 'Pontifex Maximus', the title first given to Julius Caesar, and subsequently applied to the line of Roman emperors. The full title is *Summus Pontifex Ecclesiae Universalis*: Supreme Pontiff of the Universal Church. He is the Bishop of Rome, his office being derived from the succession of bishoprics in the city, and he is also referred to as the 'Vicar of Christ', meaning that he is Christ's representative on earth. Such titles seem to highlight the Pope's importance, but he also has the official title *Servus Servorum Dei* ('Servant of God's Servants'). After the Second Vatican Council, successive popes have dispensed with some of the symbols of office that have connoted high status. The tiara (the papal three-layered jewelled crown) is no longer worn. Despite having been crowned with a tiara, Pope Paul VI descended from his throne at the conclusion of Vatican II, and laid his tiara down on the altar, as a gesture of humility. It has never since been worn by a pope, although some traditionalists would like to see its re-introduction. Subsequent popes have dispensed with a coronation, preferring an installation ceremony in which he was given a pallium as a symbol of office. A pallium is a white woollen band, which is placed over the Pope's shoulders, and which looks like the letter

'Y' at both front and back. It signifies the Pope's role as the successor to the Good Shepherd, who cares for his flock, the Church. Another dispensation of pomp was the disuse of the sedan chair, in which popes were ceremonially carried until the reign of John Paul II, who introduced the 'pope-mobile'—a vehicular mode of transport using modern automobile technology. The papacy thus attempts to combine authority with humility. On being elected as Pope Benedict XVI, Cardinal Joseph Ratzinger said, 'Dear brothers and sisters, after the great Pope John Paul II, the cardinals have elected me, a simple and humble labourer in the vineyard of the Lord.' The professed origin of the papal office in the apostle Peter is important to this servile role. John's Gospel records that after his resurrection, Jesus asked Peter to reaffirm his love for him, giving him the instruction, 'Feed my sheep' (Jn 21:15-19).

The papal office is for life. For almost 600 years until the present day, every pope has continued in office until his death. The last pope to resign was Gregory XII, in 1417, although at the time his office was contested by two other claimants. Popes do not retire, and cannot be dismissed. A pope may resign, so long as he does so without being pressurized to do so, and his resignation does not depend on any office-bearer of Church accepting it. The *Code of Canon Law* (1963) states, 'If it should so happen that the Roman Pontiff resigns his office, it is required for validity that he makes the resignation freely and that it be duly manifested, but not that it be accepted by anyone' (Roman Catholic Church 2010, Canon 332.2).

For some time before John Paul II's death, there were rumours that he might abdicate, since he was suffering from Parkinson's disease and becoming increasingly frail. Although John Paul II did not do so, his last will and testament revealed that he had contemplated abdication in the year 2000, but decided to continue until his death in 2005. No formal provision is made for incapacitated popes. In the case of an incapacitated bishop, an auxiliary bishop can take over his responsibilities, but in the case of a pope, a designated cardinal can do no more than act as a substitute for day-to-day duties. It was frequently commented that, in John Paul II's final years, the Church was effectively without a leader to give it definite direction.

The Pope is often associated with infallibility, and some comment is therefore needed on the Church's teaching on the matter. The doctrine of papal infallibility was not formally defined until the First Vatican Council of 1870, although the belief in the supremacy of papal authority is many centuries older. Papal infallibility does not mean that the Pope never makes a mistake, or that his actions are perfect, beyond criticism.

The Roman Catholic Church acknowledges that the Pope is human, and subject to error, and that there have been bad popes as well as good ones. It is often assumed, particularly by Protestants, that the doctrine of papal infallibility makes unduly extravagant claims about the lineage of popes. It is therefore salutary to read in *The Catholic Encylopedia* that 'what is claimed for the pope is infallibility *merely*, not impeccability or inspiration' (Toner 1910; authors' emphasis). Papal pronouncements are not inspired, like Scripture; popes are not present-day prophets with new revelations; and they are not automatically endowed with sainthood after death.

The doctrine of papal infallibility is bounded by three important conditions. First, he must be giving 'solemn teaching': that is to say, he must be making an important statement on behalf of the entire Church. Such papal pronouncements are called *ex cathedra*—from the 'throne' or papal seat. Before Cardinal Joseph Ratzinger assumed office as Pope Benedict XVI, it was well known that he had published theological writings making known his personal views, with which not everyone in the Church agreed. His installation as Pope did not mean that his opinions *ipso facto* became those of the wider Church, since academic writings are not *ex cathedra* pronouncements. Second, an infallible papal pronouncement can only be on matters of faith and morals, thus ensuring that only topics of great importance are involved. Less important subjects such as liturgical practice would not be subject to papal infallibility. Third, he must be acting 'as supreme universal pastor'. In other words, he must not merely be offering guidance to a particular sector of the Church, but offering it to the whole Church, with the insistence that it should be accepted. The required response from the faithful is assent.

A pope does not normally make infallible pronouncements on his own, or on a whim of the moment. He seeks advice and weighs the evidence, and his pronouncement is normally made in association with the College of Bishops. As explained above, it is not merely the Pope who is the successor of Peter and the Vicar of Christ. The authority of the apostles is held to have been transmitted to the bishops, who are also Christ's vicars, the custodians of sound doctrine, and the teachers of the Church. It is the Pope who calls and convenes the College of Bishops, and his papal prerogative in doing so is also subject to infallibility. Papal infallibility is therefore not a power imbued in one man, but rather a collegiate authority: the Pope sums up the authority of the Church, rather than channels his authority down.

The Church's authority comes from the past as well as the present. In particular, the decisions of the ecumenical councils are held to be binding on the Church for all time. An ecumenical council is one to which to which the Pope invites all the Church's bishops, who are obliged to attend. It has three essential hallmarks: convocation, direction and confirmation. The Pope must call the bishops together; he must convene it, defining and directing its proceedings, and he must confirm the decisions that are reached. The council must always secure the Pope's assent. It is important to note that the term 'ecumenical' in this context has little to do with the 'ecumenical movement' of the twentieth and twenty-first centuries. Other Christian denominations are not involved in its decision-making, but only the Roman Catholic bishops. Before the Great Schism of 1045, ecumenical councils incorporated the Eastern as well as the Western churches. Hence even greater importance is attached to the decisions reached by the first eight of these councils, which include the Councils of Nicaea, Constantinople, Ephesus and Chalcedon, where the Nicene Creed was formulated. No subsequent pope or Council of Bishops would be likely to suggest that the tenets of the historical creeds might be changed, or that God was not a Trinity.

Roman Catholics hold that there is nothing absurd in ascribing infallibility to one person in this way. The Pope, as Christ's representative, leads the Church with the assurance its people cannot alight on an error when it acts as Christ's body. Jesus' promise to Peter was, 'on this rock I will build my church, and the gates of Hades will not overcome it' (Mt. 16:18). This statement is understood to be an assurance that the Church cannot be overcome by the powers of evil. Jesus also said, 'I am with you always, to the very end of the age' (Mt. 28:20), guaranteeing his continued presence with the apostles and the emergent Church. Roman Catholics maintain that it is therefore reasonable to believe that his presence remains with his Church, manifested by his representatives in the form of the Pope and his bishops. The doctrine of infallibility also provides assurance to believers that the Church's teaching is eternal and unchanging. While some present-day sects are accused of 'flip-flopping' by asserting their position on an issue and then backtracking on it, this cannot happen to official Catholic teaching. This does not mean there is no room for debate on theology and ethics. On the contrary, there are many matters which remain undecided, and on which personal conscience and judgement may be exercised. However, once the Church has formally pronounced on a teaching, such pronouncements stand firm. Just as any discipline has its authorities, so the Church is the authority on religious and moral matters. Many Roman Catholics acknowledge that the Pope and his bishops embody much more learning and experience than themselves, and hence provide more reliable answers to such questions than rank-and-file believers. Saint Ignatius of Loyola (1491–1556) wrote, 'We should always be disposed to believe that that which appears white is really black, if the hierarchy of the Church so decides.'

The Church's Magisterium acts as the custodian of the faith. The core of the faith is technically referred to as the 'apostolic deposit'—that is to say, the truths that Christ conveyed to the apostles, with which they are entrusted. The apostolic deposit is not a collection of books, such as scriptures, or a list of doctrines, such as the creeds, both of which developed at a later stage. While scriptures and creeds are undoubtedly important in Roman Catholicism, it is emphasized that the apostolic deposit precedes both. This apostolic deposit is expressed both through tradition and through Scripture, and it is the task of the Magisterium to present the deposit of faith to the whole Church. This deposit is living, rather than a tradition that simply belongs to the past. One Roman Catholic source has likened it to a river's current (Bainvel 1912). It has its source in apostolic teaching, and runs through the Church from age to age, and from place to place, enabling ensuing generations to draw from it. The Church's living Magisterium not only draws on it, but—to continue the analogy—can find new receptacles in which to transport it and to make it intelligible to the present day.

As well as presenting the truth through teaching, the Magisterium has the additional role of imposing the truth. Imposition of the truth is often associated with its more unpleasant forms, such as the Spanish Inquisition; however, upholding truth and suppressing heresy is more commonly achieved today through pastoral oversight and theological training. Professors of theology who teach in the Church's seminaries are not themselves part of the Church's 'teaching authority'. Their study of religion is scientific and critical, often furthering the frontiers of knowledge rather than expounding the Church's apostolic deposit. However, the Church still maintains oversight of the training of its ordinands. The Church has also sought to impose truth by means of the *Index librorum prohibitorum*—the 'Index of Prohibited Books', sometimes called the Index Tridentinus, the Index of Pius IV, or simply the Roman Index—first published in 1559 under Paul IV's papacy. The list was revised over the centuries, but common to all the revisions was the prohibition of heretical works, works promoting superstition, immoral and obscene writings, and translations of Scripture that were judged to be inappropriate. In recent times, students had a general exemption from the Roman Index's requirements, since academic study typically involved reading the works of 'infidels' such as Voltaire or David Hume. The demise of the Roman Index was yet another consequence of the Second Vatican Council.

Scripture remains a further source of authority in Roman Catholicism. As we have seen, the Roman Catholic Church accepts the Old and New Testaments, in common with Eastern Orthodoxy and Protestantism, but also affirms the Apocrypha as canonical. Scripture is held to be divinely inspired: it gains its authority not simply by being *inspiring* to those who read it, which would be a subjective human reaction. Scripture, unlike other human writings, is God's word, and is in divine rather than human language. Unlike the Protestant tradition, the Roman Catholic Church does not accept Scripture as the sole source of authority, pointing out, with justification, that the Church's tradition preceded the existence of Scripture. It preceded any individual piece of Scripture by at least two decades, and it preceded the agreed set of canonical writings by over three centuries. Hence tradition is primordial, not Scripture.

The Bible's truths are divinely guaranteed, and belong to the Church. As the custodian of the Bible, the Church has the responsibility of 'guarding' it, making sure that it is translated appropriately for the time and place, and ensuring that it is disseminated and interpreted. Studying the Bible is recommended, for outsiders as well as insiders. However, it is inappropriate for outsiders to cite the Bible against the Roman Catholic Church, since such critics lack the authority for correct interpretation. The Vulgate—the Latin version of the Bible—was used liturgically until recent times, until the Second Vatican Council permitted Scripture to be read in the language of the people. The Douay-Rheims translation, completed in 1611, was the official English translation, although, being derived from the Vulgate, it was a translation of a translation, not of the original texts. In the twentieth century, an interest in biblical archaeology gained momentum, and the discovery of ancient papyri, such as the Nag Hammadi documents, raised scholarly critical questions about the Bible. This prompted Pope Pius XII's *Divino Afflante Spiritu* ('Divine Spirit')—the Encyclical Letter on the Promotion of Biblical Studies (30 September 1943). This encouraged the translation of the Bible from its original texts: the use of the Vulgate was essential for the Western Church, not for the East. The Encyclical recommended the training of priests in biblical studies, and the exposition of the Bible in public worship. The Pope welcomed the academic critical study of Scripture, affirming that insights into understanding the Bible could come from other disciplines, and even from those outside the Church.

The tendency for Roman Catholicism historically to restrict the dissemination of Scripture to the laity was well intentioned. It was an attempt to safeguard the Church's teachings, and to ensure that the Bible was not subjected to bizarre interpretations or to unduly sceptical criticism. With the publication of the Jerusalem Bible in 1966, the laity has been able to use an up-to-date English translation, derived from the original texts at first-hand. The Jerusalem Bible bears the Church's official imprimatur, *Nihil obstat* ('Nothing obstructs'), indicating that the faithful may read it freely.

The Catholic Life

This weight of authority exists to ensure that those who belong to the Roman Catholic Church know and practise their faith thoroughly, and the Catholic faith applies to one's whole life. As the Codex Iuris Canonici (1983) states, 'To the Church belongs the right always and everywhere to announce moral principles, including those pertaining to the social order, and to make judgments on any human affairs to the extent that they are required by the fundamental rights of the human person or the salvation of souls' (CIC, can. 747, para. 2; cited in *Catechism* 1994: 2033).

Of course, rank-and-file believers have different degrees of commitment and knowledge of their tradition, and there exist those who, in conscience, do not agree with all of the Church's pronouncements. However, the Church sets some minimal requirements for its members in the form of five 'precepts'. These are:

(1) You shall attend Mass on Sundays and holy days of obligation.
(2) You shall confess your sins at least once a year.
(3) You shall humbly receive your Creator in Holy Communion at least during the Easter season.
(4) You shall keep holy the holy days of obligation.
(5) You shall observe the prescribed days of fasting and abstinence. (CIC, can. 1246-1248; 989; 920; 1246; 1249-1251; cited in *Catechism* 1994: 2042-2043)

Additionally, Codex Iuris Canonici states that, 'The faithful also have the duty of providing for the material needs of the Church, each according to his abilities' (CIC, can. 222; cited in *Catechism* 1994: 2043).

According to Canon Law, the 'holy days of obligation' are Sundays, and the following ten festival days:

The Immaculate Conception of the Blessed Virgin Mary (8 December)
The Nativity of our Lord Jesus Christ—better known as Christmas (25 December)
Holy Mary, the Mother of God, her Immaculate Conception (1 January)
The Epiphany (6 January)
Saint Joseph (19 March)
The Ascension (Thursday of the sixth week after Easter)
The Body and Blood of Christ (Corpus Christi) (Thursday after Trinity Sunday)
Saint Peter and Saint Paul the Apostles (29 June)
The Assumption of the Blessed Virgin Mary (15 August)
All Saints (1 November)

Before 1911, there were 36 'days of obligation' or 'days of precepts', but Pope Pius X reduced these to eight. Two were re-instated in 1917, resulting in the present list.

One might think it a simple matter to itemize the Church's festival days, but there are inevitable complexities about this list. First, this list applies to the Western churches; the Eastern Catholic churches only observe the Nativity, Epiphany, the Ascension, the Dormition (the same festival as the Assumption) and the Holy Apostles Peter and Paul. Second, although the above is the canonical list, these ten festivals are only observed within Vatican City and in Ticino, Switzerland. Observance varies from country to country, and there can also be diocesan variations, at the discretion of the bishop. For example, in The Netherlands only Christmas and the Ascension are celebrated, while Germany observes ten, but a somewhat different ten from the canonical ones. German churches add Easter Monday, Pentecost Monday, 'Second Christmas Day' on 26 December, but drop Saint Joseph, Saint Peter and Saint Paul, the Immaculate Conception, and some—but not all—dioceses observe Epiphany, Corpus Christi and the Assumption. All very complicated!

It may be wondered why these lists of festivals do not include Easter, Pentecost and Trinity. The answer is that these three major festivals always fall on a Sunday, the dates being defined by reference to Easter, which must be observed on the day of Christ's resurrection. The 'days of obligation' do not necessarily fall on a Sunday. However, if they do, then they simply coalesce with Sunday observance, and are celebrated at the Sunday Mass. At the discretion of the bishop, some festivals can be 'transferred' to an adjacent Sunday, rather than observed on a separate day. In 2007 it was announced that Corpus Christi should be observed on the adjacent Sunday, rather than its traditional Thursday, presumably with the expectation that more Catholics would observe it on their regular day of worship.

On the days of obligation (including Sundays), Roman Catholics are encouraged to rest from work, to enjoy home life and to engage in cultural, social and religious activities. Mass is said in Church on these days. The Church acknowledges that not everyone is in a position to observe the festival, however, perhaps because of poverty, employment contracts, and the need to maintain essential public services around the clock. The Church advises the faithful to set aside at least some time for leisure, and reminds employers and public authorities of their obligation to ensure that their workers are allowed sufficient time for rest and worship. This emphasis on joy and recreation explains why Ash Wednesday and Good Friday are not listed among these festival days. They are 'prescribed days of fasting and abstinence', falling in the season of Lent, in which one should display penitence, and observe solemnity. Devout Roman Catholics—as well as those who belong to the Anglo-Catholic tradition—will attend a Mass on Ash Wednesday, the first day of Lent. The Mass ends with the priest imprinting ash on the forehead of each member of the congregation as they come forward to the altar. Ash is a sign of mourning —for sin and for Christ's passion, which will be commemorated during the Lenten season. The use of ash as a sign of repentance was an ancient Hebrew custom, accompanied by fasting and the wearing of course cloth (see, e.g., Isa. 58:5; Mt. 11:21).

The Mass

A common feature of Sunday worship and the observance of holy days is the celebration of the Mass. It should be noted that attending Mass differs from receiving Holy Communion. The faithful should at least attend, even if they do not receive the sacrament, although, as we have noted, receiving the sacrament during the Easter season is a requirement. Unless a member is incapacitated, it is a reasonable assumption that anyone who is unwilling to celebrate the Church's most important festival by participating in the Church's most important rite does not have a serious interest in the faith.

We have already described the ritual components of the Mass (chapter 8), but further comment is needed on the specifically Catholic understanding of it. According to Roman Catholic teaching, by consuming the elements of bread and wine, the faithful are in reality partaking in a real sense of Christ's body and blood. During each Mass a miracle takes place in which ordinary bread and wine are literally transformed into the body and blood of Christ. This doctrine, which asserts that a real change occurs to the eucharistic elements, is known as 'transubstantiation'. The belief has been much criticized by Protestants, who have alleged that it is unscriptural and superstitious. However, the Roman Catholic Church teaches that the doctrine derives from its tradition, and that there is more than a hint of it in Scripture. John's Gospel recounts that Jesus refers to himself as the 'bread of life', and says, 'unless you can eat the flesh of the Son of Man and drink his blood, you have no life in you. Whoever eats my flesh and drinks my blood has eternal life, and I will raise him up at the last day. For my flesh is real food and my blood is real drink' (Jn 6:53-55).

Jesus' words of institution at the Last Supper were, 'This is my body' and 'This is my blood' (Mt. 26:26, 28), and Roman Catholicism takes this literally. The change is believed to take place when the priest utters these words during the Mass, and the occurrence of the miracle of transubstantiation is indicated by an acolyte ringing a bell, signifying that Christ is literally present in the form of the bread and wine.

Belief in a literal transformation of the eucharistic elements does not mean a physical transformation. Roman Catholics would agree that the change is invisible, not visible. Critics have sometimes challenged Catholics to subject the consecrated bread and wine to chemical analysis to determine whether they have undergone a change. We are not aware of any occasion on which such an experiment has been conducted: to do so would involve a breach of liturgical procedure, which dictates that all the bread and wine must be consumed during the Mass, and not taken away. However, the vast majority of Roman Catholics would not expect chemical analysis to determine that the bread had physically become human flesh or that the wine had turned into blood. The question therefore arises as to what it means to say that there is a literal, but not a physical transformation of the elements.

The traditional explanation of transubstantiation derives from Aristotelian philosophy, as interpreted by Saint Thomas Aquinas (1225–1274), who is undoubtedly the most influential theologian in the Roman Catholic tradition. As part of the Church's response to the Protestant Reformation it was re-affirmed at the Council of Trent (1545–1563). The doctrine relies on a distinction between an object's 'substance' and 'accidents'. Let us imagine, for example, a table. When asked to think of a table, we might think of our kitchen table, which, let us suppose, is wooden, three-feet tall, oblong, and with four legs. Do any of these features make it a table? Tables need not be wooden; they can be made of metal or plastic. They need not be any particular height; a nest of tables is a set, each of various heights. It is not the shape that makes the object a table; as we know, tables can be square, round or oval. The number of legs does not make a table a table, for there can be three-legged tables, or even tables without legs, such as a communion table. One might try identifying other properties in one's quest for the essence of a table. Might it be its function—we can put objects on a table? This does not work either, for it is not a distinctive feature of a table: we can put things on stools, chairs and desks. If we look to the physical word to find what is common and peculiar to all tables, there is no physical feature that constitutes a table's 'table-ness'. Hence, the argument runs, the table's essence must be metaphysical rather than physical. There must be some metaphysical substance common and peculiar to all tables, which underlies them, determining their essential nature, and enabling us to refer to them all as tables. The physical properties we have considered—its raw materials, its height, its shape—are all 'accidents' of the table, since none of them are essential to the table's real essence.

Applying this philosophical distinction between substance and accidents to the bread and wine used in the Mass, the Roman Catholic doctrine of transubstantiation entails that the elements that are brought to the altar are truly ordinary bread and wine, but during the Mass their substance is altered, so that they become Christ's body and blood. Since substances are invisible, no empirical change can be observed during the Mass, and the physical properties of the bread and wine remain. This explains why any chemist who analysed the transubstantiated bread and wine would find no difference: scientists deal with physical properties, not metaphysical or spiritual ones. By participating in the Mass, the faithful are therefore literally, but not physically, eating Christ's body and drinking his blood.

This understanding of the Mass has a number of implications. Since the essence of the sacramental materials is Christ's body and blood, the priest is not offering up ordinary bread and wine, but Christ himself. Thus, the Mass is viewed as a sacrifice, in which Christ is being offered up to the Father. The use of stone altars, which is typical in Roman Catholic churches, reinforces the idea of the Mass as a sacrifice: religions that sacrifice animals use stone altars, for hygienic reasons. Sacrifices in religion are propitiatory, calling on God to look more favourably upon the participant, by atoning for sin. The Mass is therefore held to have a genuinely propitiatory function, mediating grace to the participant. It is spiritual food, offering genuine spiritual nourishment. Because the food one eats becomes part of one's body, the partaker in the Mass experiences union with Christ and union with God. The Church acknowledges that there are significant differences between the sacrifice of the Mass and Christ's sacrifice on the cross. The latter was a single, violent event, whereas, 'The holy sacrifice of the Mass is the ever available unbloody sacrifice of the New Testament, in which the sacrifice of the cross is made present' (*A Catholic Catechism*, 188-89).

Although this discussion of the Mass may seem somewhat abstruse and theological, such explanations of transubstantiation are by no means confined to theological tomes. The Catholic Enquiry Centre in Britain offered the Thomist explanation of transubstantiation in a recent course for enquirers (although it did not explicitly cite Aquinas), and materials used for the education of Catholic children provide fairly detailed explanation of the Mass as a sacrifice. The above quotation, in fact, is taken from a catechism, with commentary, designed for school use.

Whether Roman Catholics in the twenty-first century continue to accept Thomist accounts of the sacrament is a different matter. A Gallup survey of American Catholics in 1992 revealed that only 30 per cent believed in transubstantiation (Traditio 2005). Many present-day Roman Catholics perceive the difficulties of Thomism. The existence of underlying 'substances' is unverifiable, and in a scientific age they are more likely to be conceived of as molecular structures, or as sub-atomic particles. Although one can find examples of substances changing their accidents (a tree is leafy in summer but bare in winter), there is no other example in nature of a set of accidents that have changed their substance. Accordingly, alternative explanations of what happens at the Mass have been offered. Some of the younger laity simply view the Mass as a symbol of Christ's sacrifice, while some Catholic theologians have devised more systematic and detailed explanations. For example, one Catholic scholar (Nichols 2005) has suggested that it is the 'mode of existence' of bread and wine that change. They do not exist 'in themselves' but in context, and their introduction into the Mass makes them 'subsidiary entities', engrafted, together with the participants into the presence of Christ's resurrected and glorified body. Another suggestion, along similar lines, is 'transignification'. How we describe an object depends on its context and significance. For example, someone might buy a watch and decide to give it to a friend for her birthday. There are quasi-ritual components in an act of giving, such as wrapping the watch, adding a gift tag, and indicating to the recipient that it is the giver's intention to give her the watch. The watch thus becomes a gift, although the physical character- istics of the watch itself remain exactly the same. Similarly, the ritual action of the Mass transforms the bread and wine into Christ's body and blood for the purpose of the rite, without effecting any physical change in them.

It is not our intention to discuss the merits or deficiencies of alter- natives to Thomism, but merely to indicate that Roman Catholics are not necessarily committed to understanding the Mass in terms of medieval thought. Theological discussion of the sacrament continues, unhampered by traditional dogma, in a quest to make the meaning of the Mass intelligible in the twenty-first century. As well as offering interpretations which they believe make more sense, exponents of these new accounts will sometimes argue that reappraising and reinterpreting transubstantiation is more conducive to ecumenism, affording interpre- tations on which Orthodox and Protestant Christians might also be able to agree.

The Virgin Mary

The 'days of obligation' we discussed earlier are connected not only with the Mass, but with veneration of the Blessed Virgin Mary, whose importance in Roman Catholic teaching and devotion is considerable. Of these special days, most dioceses will celebrate at least one festival pertaining to Jesus and one other relating to Mary. Mary is regarded as the Queen of Heaven, where she reigns with Christ; she is the *theotokos* ('God-bearer'), the Mother of Christians, ranked above the angels and saints. She is held to be worthy of devotion; she may be prayed to and asked to make intercessions on one's behalf, but devotion stops short of adoration, since worship is reserved for God alone. 'Hail, Mary!' is a customary salutation to the Blessed Virgin, being the greeting used by Gabriel at the Annunciation (Lk. 1:28). The words 'Hail, Mary!' may be recited using a rosary, or extended into the traditional 'Hail Mary' prayer:

> Hail, Mary, full of grace, the Lord is with thee.
> Blessed art thou among women, and bless is the fruit of thy womb, Jesus.
> Holy Mary, Mother of God, pray for us sinners now and at the hour of our death. Amen.

In Scripture, the portrayal of Mary occurs around Jesus' birth and death. The angel Gabriel announces that she will miraculously become the bearer of the Christ child; she journeys with Joseph to Bethlehem, where Jesus is born; the shepherds and the Magi find Mary with Jesus (although the Magi worship Christ alone, not Mary); Mary, with Joseph, take Jesus into Egypt to escape Herod; she is next depicted taking Jesus to the Temple for dedication. She is barely mentioned during Jesus' ministry, but reappears at the crucifixion, waiting at the cross with other women, she is believed to be one of the women who accompany Joseph of Arimathea to Jesus' burial place (Lk. 23:56), and who also discover the empty tomb from which Jesus has risen. Although it is not stated in the Bible, it is Roman Catholic teaching that Mary was in the upper room when Jesus appeared to his disciples after the resurrection, and that she was also present at the same place on the day of Pentecost and was one of the disciples on whom the Holy Spirit's 'tongues of fire' descended.

It may be asked why Roman Catholic tradition has come to offer more devotion to Mary than to Peter, James and John, who receive much greater coverage in the Gospels, and who had a much more active role in promoting the Christian faith within the early Church. There are several reasons. First, it is Mary's conception by the Holy Spirit that provides the assurance of Jesus' divine and human origins. Second, Mary performs the role as a kind of counterpart of Eve: theologically, Jesus Christ is cast in the role of the second Adam, sent to redeem humanity from Adam's sin. However, sin entered the world through a woman's sin as well as a man's; indeed, Eve, not Adam, was the first to disobey God. It therefore seems appropriate in the Roman Catholic tradition that a woman as well as a man should perform an important role in the world's redemption. Third, Christianity's other traditions tend to focus on men rather than women, and it has sometimes been remarked that there is a need for feminine objects of devotion as well as masculine ones. At the Council of Ephesus (431), there appears to have been great adulation at the acceptance of the title *theotokos* for Mary. Ephesus was renowned for its pagan goddess worship, and this may have favourably disposed Ephesian Christians towards a female object of veneration in the form of the Virgin Mary.

All three main Christian traditions accept Mary's role in mothering Jesus, and are committed to accepting the doctrine of the Virgin Birth. Roman Catholicism, however, goes further in Marian veneration, by teaching Mary's 'perpetual virginity', claiming not only that she was a virgin when Jesus was conceived, but that she remained so throughout the rest of her life. Those outside the Roman Catholic Church often find this doctrine surprising, particularly since the Bible mentions that Jesus had brothers and sisters (Mk 6:3). However, the Catholic Church's response is that the word *adelphos*—usually translated as 'brother'—can equally mean a close relative. Mary is also held to be sinless, through her immaculate conception (see chapter 6).

Also connected with Mary is the Dogma of the Assumption (sometimes called the Dormition). It is believed that, on her death, Mary was directly taken up ('assumed') into heaven, without having to await the resurrection of the dead. Two rival sites in Jerusalem are claimed as her tomb—the Hagia Maria Sion Abbey (formerly called the Church of the Dormition), and the Church of the Tomb at Gethsemane—but neither claim to house her remains, and no parts of her body are produced anywhere as sacred relics. Only secondary relics exist, most notably the veil that Mary is said to have worn during childbirth, and which is located at Chartres Cathedral. The absence of any tomb or primary relics confirms that, when Pope Pius XII announced the Dogma of the Assumption *ex cathedra* on 1 November 1950, he was not devising some new teaching about the Virgin Mary, but merely formalizing what was believed throughout the centuries.

Although Mary is held to have been taken up into heaven, she also continues to bring gifts to the faithful. Apart from the spiritual help she affords in answering prayer and interceding on behalf of the faithful, a number of Roman Catholics have claimed visions of the Blessed Virgin.

Virgin Mary's House, near Ephesus, Turkey. According to one tradition, the apostle John obeyed Jesus' dying instruction to look after his mother Mary (Jn 19:25-27), and brought her to Ephesus.
Photograph: Margaret Wilkins

Below the house, pilgrims affix their petitions to the Blessed Virgin. Some are written on luggage labels, or napkins from the nearby café. The shrine is venerated by Christians and Muslims alike.
Photograph: George Chryssides

Such visions are often referred to as 'apparitions'. The locations of these apparitions have often become the origin of shrines, where the faithful come on pilgrimage, to pay homage to Mary, or to seek benefits such as healing in particular. The earliest recorded apparition of this kind was on the Esquiline Hill in Rome in 352, when on a hot night in August an elderly couple reported a vision of Mary, who requested the building of a shrine. The following morning the Esquiline Hill was covered in snow. The church that was built is known as Saint Mary Major, the Church of Saint Mary of the Snow. Similar apparitions have been reported throughout the ages. The shrine at Walsingham in England was established in 1061, after Richeldis de Faverches, the lady of the manor, received a series of visions of the Virgin Mary, culminating in her being transported to Mary's home in Nazareth, where she was asked to memorize the dimensions of the house and build a similar one at Walsingham. Problems occurred during the early stages of construction, prompting Richeldis to pray for further help. The following morning, the completed house miraculously appeared some two-hundred yards from the original site: apparently Richeldis had misjudged the location. The house was destroyed during the English Reformation, but the village of Little Walsingham remains a pilgrimage site for Anglicans and Catholics. Another notable shrine originating from apparitions is Our Lady of Guadeloupe, Mexico, who appeared to Juan Diego in 1531. Later apparitions include Our Lady of La Salette, who appeared to two shepherd children in 1846, and the Basilica of Our Lady, Queen of Ireland, at Knock (1879).

Apparitions can be associated with prophecy as well as healing. Our Lady of Fatima at Portugal (1917) is believed to have predicted World War II, the rise of communism, and imminent persecution of the Roman Catholic Church. More generally, it is believed that, just as Mary heralded Christ's first coming, she also appears in more recent times as the harbinger of his Second Coming. Also associated with shrines are talismans, which are believed to have supernatural properties, and which are available for purchase. The Shrine of the Miraculous Medal in Paris, France, originated from apparitions to Saint Catherine Labouré in 1830, culminating in the Virgin Mary directing her to coin a number of medals, each bearing the letter 'M' below a cross, with two hearts and the bottom representing the hearts of Mary and Jesus. An image of the Virgin appears on the medal, together with the prayer, 'O Mary, conceived without sin, pray for us who have recourse to thee'. These medals are held to have the powers to convert, to protect and to work miracles.

This discussion of apparitions would be incomplete without reference to Saint Bernadette of Lourdes, which is the world's best known and most popular Roman Catholic shrine. On 15 February 1858 a 14-year-old peasant girl named Bernadette Soubirous began to have apparitions at a grotto on the outskirts of Lourdes, France. The visions were of a small woman dressed in white with a blue sash, who requested Bernadette to drink of the water, to persuade the priests to build a chapel, and for pilgrims to visit the grotto in procession. By 1860 the bishop was convinced of the authenticity of these apparitions—18 in all—and in 1862 Pope Pius IX authorized them. At first, the waters of the grotto were used by the local people, but the shrine's fame grew, now drawing the faithful from all over the world. Some five million pilgrims currently visit the shrine each year, some out of piety, but mainly for the purpose of attaining healing by drinking the holy water or bathing at the *piscenes.* Pius XI authorized the building of the Cathedral at Lourdes in 1870 and established the Feast of Our Lady of Lourdes (18 February). Bernadette was beatified in 1925 and canonized in 1933. Many miraculous cures have been claimed at Lourdes. As a safeguard against fraud and spurious claims, Pope Pius X established the Lourdes Medical Bureau, which continues to investigate claimed cures, and has affirmed many miracles. Lourdes has also given rise to sceptics, however—both inside and outside the Church—and has certainly had its share of hoaxes, unapproved healings, and cases of illness that have returned after the pilgrim's visit. Healings are by no means guaranteed at Lourdes, or indeed at any other healing shrine; it is believed that God heals those he chooses, and has his reasons for withholding cures.

Cults of shrines associated with apparitions cannot be dismissed simply as 'folk religion' or popular superstition. Popular faith and piety closely intertwines with the religious hierarchy within the Catholic Church, who have subjected claims to apparitions and the miraculous to careful scrutiny. Apparitions constitute 'private revelation', in contrast with 'public revelation', which the Church believes was completed in the Apostolic era. Apparitions are afforded only to a selected few, and their acceptance relies on human faith and human testimony, in contrast with the teachings of the Bible and the Catechism, which are available to the whole Church, and approved by its teaching authority. Consequently, there is no obligation for any Catholic to accept the authenticity of any of these apparitions, to make pilgrimages to any of these shrines, or to observe the feasts of the saints associated with them. Visions do not replace or add to any of the Church's traditional teachings; they may not contradict Scripture, or surpass the revelation already granted to the Church. Although these shrines are Marian, their function should be to bring the believer closer to Christ, not to Mary. Because of the potential problems associated with private revelations, the Church is therefore careful to control them, and to determine which forms of piety are legitimate and which are not. This is done initially through the diocesan bishop, who decides whether to authorize the apparition; then, as piety grows, a shrine may gain in legitimacy and prestige by attested miracles, papal visits, the establishment of an associated Feast Day, and perhaps ultimately the beatification and canonization of the initial recipient of the apparition.

We have mentioned the titles 'Mother of God', 'Our Lady' or 'Madonna', and 'The Immaculate Conception' which the Catholic tradition ascribes to Mary. Three further titles have aroused discussion within the Church in recent times, and deserve brief mention: Mediatrix, Co-Redemptrix and Advocate. As we have pointed out, Mary is particularly associated with Christ's incarnation, crucifixion and resurrection; hence Roman Catholicism particularly associates her with her Son's redeeming work. If she had not accepted Gabriel's commission as God-bearer, no such redemption could have taken place. Such associations are not new: Saint Antonius (c. 250–c. 350) is quoted as saying, 'All graces that have ever been bestowed on men, all came through Mary.' A number of papal encyclicals in the nineteenth and twentieth centuries affirmed Mary's mediatorial role, and belief in the doctrine was strengthened when Pope Benedict XV created the Feast of Mary Mediatrix of All Graces as an optional festival to be observed on 15 December. The title Co-Redemptrix has been traced back as far as Irenaeus (c. 130–c. 200), who described Mary as *causa salutis* ('cause of salvation'). In 1904 Pope Pius X issued an encyclical, *Ad Diem Illum* ('To that day'), stating that Mary 'has been associated by Jesus Christ in the work of redemption'—a notion that has been reiterated by various subsequent popes. In 1993 a petition was started in an attempt to persuade Pope John Paul II to make the doctrine official by an *ex cathedra* pronouncement. By the end of 2000 it had attracted over six million signatures from 148 countries. In 2008 five cardinals petitioned Pope Benedict XVI to make official the doctrines of the Co-Redemptrix and Mediatrix. *Vox Populi Mariae Mediatrici* is a lay movement, which provides petitions for signing by Roman Catholics more widely. Until now, popes have resisted such pressures. The current official position is that 'the Blessed Virgin is invoked in the Church under the titles of Advocate, Helper, Benefactress, and Mediatrix'

(*Catechism*, 969), and that such offices do not detract from Christ's unique mediatorial role. *Lumen Gentium*, proclaimed by Pope Paul VI as part of the Second Vatican Council (21 November 1964), stated that Mary's influence, 'flows forth from the superabunderance of the merits of Christ, rests on his mediation, depends entirely on it and draws all its power from it' (*Lumen Gentium*, 60; quoted in *Catechism*, 970).

The Second Vatican Council

No account of Roman Catholicism would be complete without mention of the Second Vatican Council. When Pope Pius XII died in 1958 there was uncertainty as to who should succeed him. Much to his surprise, Cardinal Angelo Roncalli (1881–1963) was appointed—he had even bought a return ticket for his journey to the conclave—and it was thought that, being 76 years old at the time, he would merely be a stop-gap. He assumed the papal name of John XXIII. It was not anticipated that he would call the Second Vatican Council, which would revolutionize the Church. The First Vatican Council had met in 1870, where it dealt with papal infallibility. It was scheduled to deliberate further on the nature of the Church, but was suspended indefinitely on account of Italy's annexation of Rome.

The Second Vatican Council addressed the 'organic structure of the Church', dealing with its internal organization, its media communication, its sacraments, ecumenical issues and interfaith matters. The last two of these will be discussed in the final chapter. A total of 2,520 bishops attended its opening session, and additionally some Orthodox and Protestant observers were present. The most visible changes that were effected by the Council were in its sacraments, particularly the Mass. The Mass was to be celebrated in the language of the people, rather than in Latin, and Scripture should be available in one's mother tongue, and studied. The liturgy was simplified, and participation by the laity was encouraged. Previously the laity had learned how to chant responses; now laity could more actively participate, as cantors and readers of Scripture. Altars were moved away from the walls, enabling the priest to go behind the altar, and to face the congregation during the Mass, rather than acting as a faceless intermediary supplicating God on the people's behalf. The whole Church was renewed and brought up to date.

John XXIII died when the Council was still progressing; it lasted for four autumns, from 1962, through to 1965. John's successor, Pope Paul VI continued to preside over the Council, bringing its work to fulfilment. Inevitably, the Council's work was criticized both by liberals and traditionalists. Some liberals argued that its reforms did not go far enough; for example, issues like the celibacy of the clergy and women priests were not addressed. Traditionalists held that the Council was wrong in reappraising the Catholic Church's historical claim to be the one and only true Church, claiming that its doctrinal and liturgical changes made too large a concession to modernism, Protestantism and secular ideology. Some wanted the restoration of the Tridentine Mass; Archbishop Marcel-François Lefebvre (1905–1991) in particular gained much media attention in this regard (see chapter 17). Whatever the criticisms, the Council marked a watershed in the Catholic Church's history, demonstrating that its commitment to tradition and authority did not preclude major change.

10

Eastern Orthodoxy

To many people mention of Orthodoxy conjures up pictures of something foreign and exotic: a white-washed monastery on a Greek island or the onion-shaped domes of Saint Basil's Cathedral in Moscow, towering over Red Square. But in the course of the twentieth century a whole variety of Orthodox communities took root both in Britain and the United States, first as a result of emigration from traditionally Orthodox countries and more recently as a consequence of increasing interest in the distinctive forms of faith and practice developed in the eastern half of the Christian world.

Orthodox Worship

The interior of an Orthodox church may look unfamiliar to those who are more familiar with Western Christianity. The first thing that will probably strike the visitor is the iconostasis—the screen that divides the sanctuary from the main body of the church. Raised up a little above the level of the rest of the interior, with a double door or gate in the middle and smaller ones on either side, and covered with ranks of icons, it dominates the building. Behind it stands the altar, which for most of the time is concealed from view by the closed doors of the iconostasis. There are usually no pews, though some churches may have chairs. Russian and other Eastern European churches are more likely to have nothing but a bench or a few chairs against a wall for those who are unable to stand the whole time.

The experience of Orthodox worship, too, is likely to feel unfamiliar to a Western Christian. Anyone who attends the Sunday liturgy in an Orthodox church will probably find that there is already a service going on when they arrive, as Matins is celebrated before the eucharistic liturgy begins. People come in gradually, not at any fixed time. Worshippers are

The Orthodox Church of the Nativity of the Mother of God, Walsall, England (interior). The building is adapted from a disused Anglican church, with an iconostatis separating off the chancel area.
Photograph: George Chryssides

free to move around, perhaps to pray or light a candle before one of the icons on stands that one finds as one enters the church. It is quite acceptable to slip into the church quietly and out again, and this can be done without causing any distraction. Even where there are chairs, which is common in Greek churches, sitting and standing during worship are not as tidily regimented as they tend to be in Western Christianity. Formality and informality, though, work in different ways in Orthodox churches; while it is perfectly acceptable to move around quietly, it is not considered appropriate to sit with one's legs crossed or stand with one's hands behind one's back. Worshippers cross themselves frequently during the service (but from right to left, not left to right as in the West).

The music is provided by an unaccompanied choir (though some Greek churches in the United States have organs) singing the traditional music of the jurisdiction to which the church belongs; most of the service is chanted or sung. The congregation in most churches is largely silent, and their responses are made by the choir. They do not necessarily follow the liturgy in the same way that a Western congregation would. It is perfectly in order to light a candle in front of an icon, or say one's own prayers, for much of the time. No hymn books or prayer books are needed, because there are no congregational hymns and few people, except newcomers, feel the need to follow a printed order of service (though one of the authors has been in one church in Athens which had small copies of the liturgy in the back of each chair).

Much of the liturgy itself will be very familiar to many Western Christians, as it follows the same pattern as a Roman Catholic mass or Anglican Eucharist, though over time other elements have been introduced into the basic shape of the liturgy which make it longer than its Western counterparts. The usual liturgy is that of Saint John Chrysostom, though on Sundays in Lent and on some other occasions the more elaborate Liturgy of Saint Basil is used. The hymns that are sung as part of the liturgy are rich and complex, the oldest of them dating back to the fifth and sixth centuries, and written in a variety of poetic forms. The music to which they are sung is equally rich and varied; the Byzantine chant, from which most Orthodox churches derive their music, has eight tones which vary from week to week and throughout the liturgical year. Visually, too, there are things to observe: vestments are basically not very different from those used in the West, but the two traditions have developed a little differently and Orthodox vestments are typically richer and more elaborate than most modern Western ones. There is nothing corresponding to the changing liturgical colours used in the West for vestments and drapery (see chapter 2). The Orthodox church divides liturgical colours into two categories, dark and bright, for solemn or joyful occasions, so colours will vary within those categories and different churches will have their own customs to decide what colour is worn for a particular day.

The language used in worship will depend on the jurisdiction to which the church belongs. As the Orthodox churches sent out missionaries into new areas, they translated the liturgy into the language spoken by the people among whom Christianity took root. Greeks use Byzantine Greek, not far removed from the Greek of the New Testament, though pronounced like the modern language. In Russian churches, Old Church Slavonic is the language into which the liturgy was translated when Russia became Christian, not too difficult for speakers of Russian to understand. In churches where the majority of members are English speakers, English is generally used, often with some prayers in the language of the jurisdiction to which the church belongs.

Communion is given only to Orthodox, and is not necessarily received every week. Careful preparation is expected of communicants, including confession and a complete fast from midnight before receiving. The priest gives each communicant the consecrated bread and wine, and even babies and small children receive. There is nothing like the Western gap between baptism and confirmation or first communion; babies are chrismated when they are baptized and are full members of the church right away, and so may receive communion. Everyone present, Orthodox or not, is invited to share the antidoron, the remainder of the specially baked bread from which the portion consecrated for the communion has been taken, and which is blessed and distributed at the end of the liturgy.

The Two Halves of the Christian World

How did the churches of the East and West come to develop in such different ways? The answer goes back to the days of the late Roman Empire, when at the end of the third century the Emperor Diocletian divided the increasingly unwieldy empire into two parts, East and West, for greater ease of government. Though the empire was later reunited for a time, the final political split between East and West came at the end of the fourth century.

As the Roman Empire gradually disintegrated, the eastern and western halves were shaped by different conditions. In the western part, incursions by tribes from outside its borders brought new populations into Europe, where they were absorbed and Christianized; meanwhile the eastern half became the Byzantine empire, ruled from Constantinople, which had its own external threats to deal with, fighting Persians, Arabs and Bulgars, and its own preoccupations. The Christian world was split not just by different political and social conditions, but also by language; the western half spoke Latin, and later the cluster of languages that developed from Latin, while the eastern half spoke Greek, and then the languages of the areas into which Eastern Christianity expanded.

For some centuries Christendom was more or less held together by the series of major gatherings, known as the seven ecumenical councils, which were called at intervals to debate important matters of doctrine. The first, at Nicaea, now Iznik in modern Turkey, was called by the emperor Constantine in 325, and declared Arianism a heresy (see chapter 6). The last time the Orthodox churches and the churches of the West met together was at the second council of Nicaea in 787. The division between the churches of Western and Eastern Europe was a reality long before the eleventh century, though the Great Schism of 1054 is the conventional marker for the formal split, when Pope Leo IX's legates placed a papal bull excommunicating the Patriarch of Constantinople on the altar of Hagia Sophia during the liturgy, while the Patriarch in his turn excommunicated the legates. (A bull is an official papal document; its name derives from the Latin *bulla*, meaning a lead seal. Such documents bore the papal seal depicting the heads of Saint Peter and Saint Paul.)

The Development of Christianity in the East

From the seventh century onwards the shape of Christianity in the East was changed by the rapid rise and spread of Islam, which took root in the ancient heartlands of Christianity in North Africa and the Near East. Many of the inhabitants of these areas converted to the new faith, and those who remained Christians found themselves in a minority, technically protected but also forced to pay extra taxes and sometimes disadvantaged in other ways. Of the four great ancient patriarchates of the East, three—Alexandria, Antioch and Jerusalem—were now under Muslim rule; only Constantinople, together with Rome, the patriarchate of the West, remained as Christian centres.

Although Christianity retreated in the Eastern Mediterranean world, it began to spread north and east as missionaries from the Orthodox churches went out to work among the pagan Slav tribes. The Bulgars accepted Christianity in the ninth century and the Russians of Kiev in the tenth, and Orthodoxy spread as far west as the shores of the Baltic. As missions grew into churches, the shape of Orthodoxy changed; the flourishing church in Russia (which today is the largest of the Orthodox churches) gained its own primate in the eleventh century, and became independent of Constantinople in the fifteenth century, as an autocephalous church (that is, a church governed by its own leadership but in full communion with other Orthodox churches).

As the churches in the West and the East spread Christianity among new populations with very different cultures, theological differences also began to appear. The most important of these was the dispute over the version of the Nicene Creed that began to appear in Western churches, which describes the Holy Spirit as 'proceeding from the Father and the Son'. In the East the creed still keeps its original text, which simply says, 'proceeding from the Father'. The phrase 'and the Son' was first added to the creed in Spain at the end of the sixth century to exclude the Arians who were numerous there at the time, and then spread north into France. Rome resisted it until the beginning of the eleventh century but finally adopted it, and so it became the norm in the churches of the West; but in the East it is regarded as both scripturally and historically wrong, and is a major obstacle to any attempts at reunion. (The Latin for 'and the Son' is *filioque*, hence the dispute between East and West is known as the *filioque* controversy.)

To add to political divergence and theological dispute, the low point in relations between the two halves of Christendom was reached in 1204. The Fourth Crusade was originally intended to strike at the Muslim rulers of Egypt, the centre of the Islamic world at the time, but instead a series of complications and an alliance with a claimant to the Byzantine throne diverted it to Constantinople. Seeing the wealth of the capital of the Byzantine Empire, the crusaders decided to besiege and plunder it instead of going on to their original destination. They indulged in an orgy of looting, desecration of churches, and killing, and the bitterness and distrust that the attack provoked among Christians in the East is still alive to this day. Eight centuries later, in 2004, Pope John Paul II expressed his deep regret for the atrocities committed by the crusaders to the Patriarch of Constantinople.

Renewed Contacts between East and West

Despite the memories of the Fourth Crusade, political imperatives sometimes led to attempts at reunion of the churches. In 1274 the then Pope and Byzantine Emperor attempted to heal the schism at the Council of Lyon, at which the Orthodox delegates recited the Nicene Creed with the addition of the *filioque* clause. However, the clergy were not as enthusiastic as the emperor about the reconciliation; the Patriarch of Constantinople resigned, and when the emperor died a few years later his successor repudiated the agreement. Another attempt at reconciliation was made in 1438–1439, as Constantinople came under increasing pressure from the advancing Turks; this time the emperor and the Patriarch of Constantinople came to Italy, and negotiations at the Council of Florence, with the Greeks making most of the concessions, finally resulted in an agreement signed by all but one of the Orthodox delegates. However, it received almost no support from the general population in the Greek empire, and lapsed after the fall of Constantinople a few years later.

There was little support from the West for the shrunken Byzantine Empire, either, when Constantinople was besieged by the Turks and fell in 1453. There were some efforts to put together a coalition to recapture the city, but they came to nothing. Meanwhile, refugee scholars from the East helped to trigger the revival of Greek learning as they took refuge in Western countries, bringing their books and their language with them. Not only did they bring the works of classical Greek authors, but also those of the Greek theologians of the early Church as well as biblical manuscripts. The rediscovery of Greek scholarship in the Renaissance had far-reaching implications for Christianity in the West; it made possible the study of the New Testament in its original language, and a much greater knowledge of the early Church as Greek patristic literature became available. Books in Greek were being printed in Venice by the end of the fifteenth century, and the Dutch scholar Erasmus published the first Greek New Testament in Basel in 1516. The new scholarship helped to give encouragement to those who wanted to reform the church in the West; we know that some of Henry VIII's bishops studied patristic writings to see what they said about the ordering of the Church.

There was a series of scholarly contacts between Greeks and the Church of England in the seventeenth century; many Anglicans were attracted by the idea of a church with ancient traditions but without any equivalent of the papacy. There were Greek students at Oxford in the seventeenth century (though this connection apparently led to trouble, with some of the Greeks, far from home, behaving badly, and was terminated at the beginning of the eighteenth century). The Metropolitan of Samos visited England to raise funds for the first Greek Orthodox church in London, which was built in 1677 for the Greek community in London but soon closed by the Bishop of London, who apparently disapproved of the presence of icons. However, the Greek community in London prospered and in 1877 the building of the church which is now the Cathedral of Saint Sophia was begun, while Greek communities in Manchester, Liverpool and Cardiff also built their own churches. Since then other Orthodox communities have arrived, most notably the Russian émigrés who fled from the Russian revolution. Although Greeks and Russians form the major communities in the UK (the situation in the USA is rather different and will be discussed below) several Orthodox traditions are now represented. A number of Serbian Orthodox came after the Second World War (their main church, in Birmingham, was built with the help of the Quaker Cadbury family), and there is now an Antiochian Orthodox presence in the UK originally confined to the Arab community in London but now attracting a number of British converts in other parts of the country. There are Romanian Orthodox churches in London and Leeds and a Bulgarian one in London, and with the enlargement of the European Union bringing in workers from Eastern Europe these communities may grow too.

The Orthodox Churches in More Recent Times

Most of the Orthodox nations have experienced occupation by outsiders, or religious persecution at some point in their history. The Greeks lived under the rule of the Ottoman Empire for centuries and commemorate their New Martyrs, those who died for their faith since the fall of Constantinople; while the Orthodox in Slav lands faced a long struggle with the Tatars, and more recently the difficulties of life under communism and the problems of maintaining faith in an officially atheist state. So Russia also has its New Martyrs, those who suffered for their faith under communist rule, and Serbia theirs, those killed in the conflicts of the twentieth century.

This history of difficulty and oppression has left its mark on Christianity in Orthodox countries. Orthodoxy is frequently identified with nationality: Greece, for example, was governed under the Ottoman *millet* system, which divided non-Muslims into religious groups, each headed by a religious leader. The leader of the Greek millet was the Ecumenical Patriarch of Constantinople, whose position gave him political as well as religious authority, and so religion and nationality came to be closely linked. This link between religion and ethnicity still persists; churches and monasteries in Greece often have Greek flags flying outside them.

Although Greece is now a modern European country and a member of the European Union, in many ways it remains a very traditional society where ethnicity is closely tied to religion, so that it is a general expectation that a Greek person will be Orthodox. Only small numbers of Greeks belong to other Christian groups or to other faiths, and although they are not on the whole discriminated against, no other religious group has the legal advantages that the Orthodox Church enjoys. Similarly, in Russia Orthodoxy is seen as the religion of the Russian people, even if it is a matter of culture rather than faith. The authors of this book know a Russian academic who decided to be baptized after the fall of communism, not because he had any strong Christian beliefs, but because he felt that as a Russian being Orthodox was part of his heritage. The Orthodox Church has largely regained its position as the spiritual home of Russians, and seeks to limit the freedom to evangelize of other forms of Christianity as well as of new religious movements. In many cases this may be entirely understandable, for example in the case of Western evangelical groups, who disregard Russia's long Christian history and look upon post-communist Russia as a mission field for their own versions of Christianity.

One interesting aspect of the reaction against communism and restoration of the place of Orthodoxy in Russian society is the canonization of Tsar Nicholas II and his family, first by the Russian Orthodox Church Abroad in 1981, and then in 2000 by the Russian Orthodox Church inside Russia. Shot by the Bolsheviks in 1918, their bodies were reburied in the Cathedral of Saints Peter and Paul in St Petersburg in 1998, and they are now the object of much popular veneration. Whatever Nicholas's shortcomings as a ruler (and the decision to canonize them met with a considerable amount of opposition), the family's example of patient suffering in captivity and death has earned them the title of 'Passion-bearers'. The conservative and nationalistic outlook illustrated by the canonization of the imperial family is not confined to Russian Orthodoxy, but has played a role in the recent history of other Eastern European countries as their communist governments began to lose their grip on power. In Serbia, for instance, Orthodoxy sees itself as the bearer of Serbian national traditions, and Orthodox clergy were heavily involved in the resurgence of Serb nationalism during the last years of communist rule that contributed to the disintegration of Yugoslavia.

The pattern of emigration, whether enforced or voluntary, from Orthodox countries to America and Western Europe has given Orthodoxy a new problem. Traditionally church government coincides with national government, but in the Orthodox diaspora each ethnic community built its own churches in the country in which its members were living. Now, though, instead of being traders or exiles in another country whose first allegiance was to their homeland, Orthodox Christians have settled and become citizens of their new countries, and their churches are no longer communities for those passing through but permanent parishes. Instead of one Orthodox church in each country, there are several, with overlapping parishes and dioceses, from a variety of national backgrounds; but as their members become increasingly assimilated into the mainstream of society, and new converts from other ethnic backgrounds join, the hope is that eventually there will be one Orthodox jurisdiction in every country where there are Orthodox Christians instead of ethnic groupings.

The situation in the USA is more complicated, with a wider range of Orthodox traditions represented. The history of Orthodoxy in North America begins with Russian missionary work in Alaska, both while it was still a Russian territory and after it was sold to the USA in 1867, and continues with the arrival of immigrants from the countries of Eastern Europe from the end of the nineteenth century onwards. The Orthodox of Russian origin eventually formed the Orthodox Church in America (OCA), which was granted autocephaly by the Patriarch of Moscow in 1970. However, there was another Russian Orthodox body in America, the Russian Orthodox Church outside Russia (ROCOR; also known as the Russian Orthodox Church Abroad) formed by émigré White Russians escaping from the revolution of 1917 and independent of Moscow, which they regarded as compromised by collaboration with the Soviet government. ROCOR and OCA have a history of difficult relationships, but ROCOR was eventually canonically reunited with the Moscow Patriarchate in May 2007 and the two groups are now in full communion.

Apart from the Russians, Americans of Greek origin are served by the Greek Orthodox Archdiocese of America, while other jurisdictions reflect the countries of Eastern Europe from which their members originally came; the website 'Orthodoxy in America' lists twelve separate Orthodox jurisdictions in the USA.

Ecumenism and the Orthodox Churches

The idea of closer relationships and increased cooperation between churches which has developed so strikingly in the West during the twentieth century has not had nearly as much influence in the East. Many Orthodox are not in the least enthusiastic about the idea of ecumenism, or about the quest for Christian unity. Quite apart from the legacy of bitterness left by difficult relations with the West over the centuries, there are profound theological and organizational differences. One of the difficulties in dialogue with the Roman Catholic Church is that both Orthodox and Roman Catholics claim that theirs is the one true Church. Even if one can get past this to imagining a future union of the two bodies, the issue of the papacy is another major point of contention. For the Orthodox, Rome is one of the original patriarchates of the church, like Jerusalem, Antioch and Alexandria, and though it can claim primacy it has no right to claim any jurisdiction over the other patriarchates. The Orthodox therefore rejects papal claims to supremacy over the whole church.

Theological differences also play a part, and many conservative Orthodox regard all non-Orthodox Christians as heretics, split off from the true church since the Great Schism of 1054. They insist that the only basis for closer cooperation can be the recognition by other Christians that the Orthodox Church is the only true Church, and the only basis for unity is for them to become members of an Orthodox church.

Even though the then Ecumenical Patriarch of Constantinople, Athenagoras, lifted the anathemas pronounced against the Roman Catholic Church in 1054, in 1965, after a meeting with Pope Paul VI, there was widespread disapproval of the ecumenical movement among Orthodox. The monks of the very conservative monastery of Esphigmenou on Mount Athos, for example, declared themselves out of communion with the Ecumenical Patriarch in response to his action, and when he held a joint prayer service with the Pope in 1972 they flew black flags to mark their disapproval. In 1983 the bishops of ROCOR issued an anathema against ecumenism. Many Orthodox refuse to join in prayer with other Christians in any context. Others have no problem with it: one of the authors of this book used to sing in a Russian Orthodox Church, where the choir at Saturday vespers, which was in English, consisted of Roman Catholics, Anglicans and a Baptist, as well as a couple of Orthodox.

When the current Ecumenical Patriarch Bartholomew invited Pope Benedict XVI to Istanbul in 2006 and attended a Mass celebrated by the Pope, many Orthodox were scandalized. However, Patriarch Bartholomew, who studied and taught in Rome at the beginning of his career, is very active in promoting better relationships between Orthodoxy and other Christian churches, as well as with other faiths, and has served as a president of the Word Council of Churches. Despite their reservations about ecumenism, most Orthodox churches are members of the WCC, apart from the small Estonian Church, and those of Georgia and Bulgaria, which used to be members but withdrew in 1997 and 1998 respectively. At the time of writing all the other Orthodox churches belong to it, though there is now a campaign within the Russian Orthodox Church to adopt observer rather than full member status. This may be due to the increasing self-confidence of the Orthodox churches of the former Soviet Union since the fall of communism, and their tendency to see contacts with Western churches in the light of intrusive Protestant evangelism in recent years.

There was hope for closer ties between Anglicanism and Orthodoxy in the past (the Fellowship of St Alban and St Sergius was founded in 1928 to foster contact between Orthodox and Western traditions and to encourage them to learn more about each other), but the decision of many Anglican churches to ordain women to the priesthood and now the episcopate has been a major difficulty between the two churches.

Monasticism

Orthodox monasticism is organized along very different lines from its Western equivalent. For a start, the separate orders which exist in the West have no counterpart in the Orthodox churches, and neither does the Western distinction between contemplative and active communities. In general, monks and nuns remain within their communities with little contact with the world outside, though some may serve as spiritual directors. Most monks are not ordained; a few are, so that they can serve their communities as priests. Monasteries vary in the emphasis they put on different aspects of the spiritual life: some are more liturgical, some more ascetical. Some communities produce books and materials for worship and study. There is no formal system of associating lay people with monastic life, as with Benedictine oblates or the Franciscan third order, but lay people can attach themselves to a monastery in various ways, traditionally by living close to it, and now through the internet, as many monasteries have their own websites.

The life of an Orthodox monk or nun is a frugal and disciplined one, with a constant round of daily prayer. Admittance to the monastery and training within it are much less tightly regulated than in the West, and the progression from novice to fully professed member of the community depends on the individual and not on any set timetable. There is no formal ceremony for becoming a novice; the aspiring monk or nun simply comes to live in the community, and stays until he or she is thought ready to join it formally, if ever. Receiving the tonsure marks the next stage of commitment, which may last for years, and only then after that are formal vows made. Monks and nuns normally remain for the rest of their lives in the community in which they make their profession. Monastic life is less tightly organized than in the West, though the rhythm of worship and work within the community remains constant. Some monks and nuns may feel called to a life of more intense prayer and contemplation, and in some cases they may, though only after years of living in community, withdraw into solitary life as hermits.

Mount Athos, the Holy Mountain, with its monasteries and hermitages, is the central point of Orthodox monasticism. It has its own website, which says, 'As an institution Mount Athos is, and has been, the chief standard bearer of Orthodox Christianity.' The monks who live there are not just Greek but are drawn from all over the Orthodox world, and it is self-governing and under the authority of the Ecumenical Patriarch, though technically part of Greece. Women, famously, are forbidden even to set foot on it (though now anyone can do a virtual tour of the mountain thanks to a set of six CD-ROMs, available from its website). Despite the strictness of the life and the isolation of the communities dotted along a mountainous peninsula far away from the mainstream of Greek society, Mount Athos is attracting an increasing number of young and well educated men. Even Mount Athos, though, is not without its problems; one of its twenty monasteries, the Esphigmenou, a centre of particularly conservative religious practice, which has been in dispute with the Ecumenical Patriarch for years, has been threatened by government action, and even at one point besieged by Greek police.

Orthodox monasteries are not confined to traditionally Orthodox countries, but have sprung up in Western countries, too, wherever Orthodox Christians have settled. The oldest, and perhaps the best known, community in England is the Monastery of St John the Baptist at Tolleshunt Knights in Essex, founded in 1959 by Elder Sophrony, a Russian monk who had spent many years on Mount Athos. Although it is unusual in being a double monastery, housing both monks and nuns, it is very much in the classic Orthodox ascetic tradition and, though its founder died in 1993, the community is flourishing.

Although monasteries exist first and foremost as places where men and women may dedicate themselves to a life of prayer and self-discipline, historically they have produced many spiritual guides. The tradition of the spiritual father (or mother), is distinct from the official ordained ministry of the church, though it may overlap with it, and the parish priest is regarded as a spiritual father to his parishioners. Typically monastic spiritual guides are people who are identified by others who recognize their holiness and seek them out to ask for their guidance. In Russia the starets (Russian for 'elder') tradition of spiritual direction flourished especially in the nineteenth century, when there were a number of outstanding spiritual guides. One of the great Russian saints of the nineteenth century, Saint Seraphim of Sarov, was a monastic hermit who after years of seclusion threw open his doors to anyone who chose to come to him for spiritual direction; and thousands made their way to his remote hermitage.

Icons and Prayer

While the churches of the East and West have been cautious about drawing closer, many Christians in the West have begun to appropriate spiritual resources from Orthodoxy. The most noticeable imports, often taken out of context and used in ways unfamiliar in their original setting, are icons. In the East the role of icons in the church and in the home is a very specific one; the icon is not merely a picture, it is an expression of divine reality. Icons are painted (the proper term is 'written') with prayers according to traditional and precise rules. Their proportions and lack of perspective are intentional; they are not meant to be realistic depictions of individuals. They are about the spiritual, not the material, and are meant to lead the eye and heart into contemplating the spiritual universe, a window into heaven. Saints are present with the believer in these representations, both in church, where their images surround the worshipper, and at home. The bright light, which casts no shadows, represents the uncreated light of Mount Tabor, the light of the Transfiguration. The colours used are often symbolic; for example, a red garment symbolizes divinity, and a blue one humanity, so Christ wearing a blue cloak over a red tunic symbolizes his taking on of humanity in the Incarnation, while Mary's red cloak over a blue robe hints at her role as *theotokos*, the one who gave birth to God.

As Orthodoxy becomes increasingly naturalized in the UK and more people of British origin join the Orthodox churches, icons of the Celtic and Saxon saints of the British Isles who lived before the Great Schism of 1054 have become popular. They are regarded as belonging to the one undivided church; hence one will find icons of Saint Aidan, Saint Patrick, Saint Swithin and other British saints in many UK Orthodox churches—particularly one with a high proportion of ethnically British members, just as Greek saints tend to predominate in Greek churches and Russian ones in Russian churches.

Eastern Christian art has developed very differently from that of the West, though some nineteenth century Orthodox art employs shading and perspective and has plainly been influenced by Western religious art. There is no tradition of sculpture in Orthodoxy, but a very highly developed tradition of painting, not just of individual icons, but of wall painting. Murals in churches and monastery chapels often depict the whole universe, with the eye being led up through the ranks of saints and angels round the walls to Christ the Pantokrator, the ruler of all, in the dome, his hand raised in blessing.

Another practice with a long history, dating back in its simplest form to the early days of monasticism in the Egyptian desert, which has become popular in the West, is the Jesus Prayer. The most commonly used form is a repetition of the words 'Lord Jesus Christ, Son of God, have mercy on me, a sinner', often linked to the rhythm of one's breathing. It is meant to be a way of 'praying continually', as recommended by St Paul in his first letter to the Thessalonians (1 Thess. 5:17). Some authorities suggest that it should not be undertaken without the guidance of a spiritual director, though it has to be said that people in the West who use the prayer tend to disregard this advice. *The Way of a Pilgrim*, published in Russia towards the end of the nineteenth century, first appeared in English in 1930, an account of a young man who wanted to know how to pray continually. The account of his journey through nineteenth-century Russia, praying the Jesus Prayer as he went, sparked Western interest in the prayer. Less widely known in the West is the ancient monastic tradition of hesychasm which lies behind it, a tradition of withdrawal into inner silence and contemplation to concentrate entirely on the prayer, which is discussed and elaborated in the *Philokalia*, a collection of writings on the practice of ascetic prayer.

Another linked tradition sometimes adopted in the West is the use of the prayer rope, made by tying knots in a length of woollen or silken cord. Like icons, the ropes are made with prayer, usually tied by monks or nuns. (The Mount Athos website sells a wide selection of prayer ropes made by monks on the Holy Mountain.) The elaborate knots are tied by hand; the story is that a monk tying his prayer rope was constantly interrupted by the devil, who undid the knots he had tied, until an angel appeared and showed him how to do knots in the form of interlocked crosses, at which the devil gave up in despair. A small metal ring or a bead of some material is inserted between every ten or more knots as a way of keeping count. The rope can be kept in one's pocket or at home and used to say short, repeated prayers—the Jesus Prayer or some other brief prayer, or intercessory prayers. Again, it is a way of praying continually; the action of passing the rope knot by knot through one's fingers at each repetition of a short prayer aids concentration and stops the attention from wandering.

Asking for the help and intercession of the Mother of God and the saints in prayer is very much a part of the life of the Orthodox Christian. The saints are not very far away; their presence is made visible in icons, and their assistance is freely available to those who ask for it. One of the authors was once told by an Orthodox nun about an experience she had had of the presence of saints: she was a member of a small community of only three, and one evening she was the only one present to say the office. She was tired and really did not want to say it on her own, but dutifully went into the convent chapel and began to read the prayers—and suddenly felt, she said, that the chapel was full of saints, all encouraging her and praying the office with her. Saints may also be tangibly present in the form of their physical relics; Orthodox believe that holiness persists in the remains of someone who has been a vessel of God's grace, so that their physical remains are venerated, and the graves of saints are a focus for prayer. Objects that have been consecrated for use in the liturgy also share in this holiness; they must be treated with reverence and not handled casually or by unauthorized people.

The Liturgical Year and the Sacraments

Most Orthodox churches still use the Julian calendar, which means that the Church's year is now thirteen days behind the civil year and (for example) Christmas is celebrated on 7 January according to the Gregorian calendar. The Greek government adopted the Gregorian calendar for civil use in 1923, and a year later the Greek Orthodox Church agreed to use a modified form of it which did not interfere with calculating the date of Easter in the traditional way. So Greeks celebrate Christmas on the 25 December, but Easter at the same time as the other Orthodox churches. As a result of the introduction of the Gregorian calendar a number of conservative Orthodox decided to withdraw into a separate communion in 1935, and are known as the Old Calendarists; they still have a number of parishes and monastic communities. Other Orthodox churches—as well as the monasteries of Mount Athos—still use the Julian calendar but remain in communion with the Church of Greece.

The great festivals of the church, Christmas, Easter (Pascha) and Pentecost, are of course the same, though they may fall on different dates from their Western counterparts because of the different calendar or the different method of calculating Easter. Other festivals began to develop while observances were still fluid as the East and West slowly drew apart, so different practices are preserved; for example, the Orthodox keep All Saints Day on the Sunday after Pentecost while the churches of the West keep it at the beginning of November. Orthodox Easter is fixed according to the Julian calendar, which repeats every 28 years, so the calculation of the dates of Easter in the East and West has differed since the introduction of the Gregorian calendar in the West in 1582. Orthodox Easter may sometimes coincide with Western Easter, but is usually at least a week, sometimes several weeks, later.

The Orthodox churches celebrate a yearly cycle of twelve major festivals. Easter/Pascha itself is not one of them, because it is the Feast of Feasts, and so stands apart from the others. Pentecost is the greatest of the twelve great feasts of the year, which follows the same outline as the Western liturgical year, though with different emphases; the Transfiguration, for example, is given much greater prominence in the East. Since the liturgical year in the East begins on 1 September, the first festival of the new church year is the Nativity of the Theotokos on 8 September.

The rhythm of the liturgical year is brought home by the elaborate scheme of fasting and abstinence observed by many devout Orthodox, a scheme so elaborate that a calendar is needed to keep track of what is permitted on each day. Four periods in the year are designated as fasts: the Great Lent, which is the longest and most severe; the Apostles' Fast (from after Pentecost to the feast of Saint Peter and Saint Paul on 29 June), the Dormition Fast (the first two weeks of August leading up to the Dormition of the Theotokos on the 15th), and the Nativity Fast, parallel to Western Advent but longer, beginning on 15 November. All Wednesdays and Fridays are also kept as fast days, except during particularly joyful seasons, such as Bright week, the week after Easter. There are different degrees of fasting, depending on the day, and the most rigorous entails abstinence from meat, fish, dairy products, oil and wine. Of course fasting is modified in case of illness, and the details are usually decided on after discussion with one's parish priest; the Orthodox concept of 'economy', the power to use discretion in the strict application of rules for the greater spiritual good, comes into play here. The idea behind it is self-discipline and not suffering. Many Orthodox believers take fasting very seriously indeed, though it is stressed that it is as much a mistake to spend too much time agonizing over details as it is to neglect fasting altogether. The idea behind it is to loosen one's ties to the everyday world of selfishness and consumerism, and one of the authors once heard an Orthodox priest describe the simple vegan food of the strictest fast as 'the vegetarian food of paradise', linking it back to the Garden of Eden, where God said to Adam and Eve, 'I give you every seed-bearing plant on the face of the whole earth and every tree that has fruit with seed in it. They will be yours for food' (Gen. 1:29).

Orthodoxy recognizes seven sacraments, sometimes referred to as 'mysteries': baptism, chrismation, the eucharist, holy orders, penance, anointing and matrimony. Babies are baptized by triple immersion in the name of the Trinity, and are immediately chrismated, anointed with holy oil, as a sign that they are sealed with the Holy Spirit. There is no separate rite of confirmation, in which a child or young person takes on adult membership of the church; a baby who has been baptized and chrismated is already a full member of the church, and as such may receive communion. People who have been baptized in other churches are usually received into the Orthodox Church by chrismation. Some conservative Orthodox will baptize them again, on the grounds that the only true sacraments are within the church, and only the Orthodox churches constitute the one true Church, so baptism administered by any other body is not a true baptism. However, the general rule is to apply the concept of economy and accept the previous baptism as valid.

The eucharist is regarded with great reverence by Orthodox Christians, who maintain an absolute fast, not even drinking water, on the morning when they intend to receive it. While many Western Christians are encouraged to receive the sacrament every Sunday, in Orthodoxy the stress is much more on the seriousness of receiving it, and communicants are expected to prepare themselves for it very seriously. Although only Orthodox may receive, at the end of the liturgy it is customary to distribute bread from the specially made loaf from which the consecrated bread was cut, and everyone may share in that.

Men are ordained as deacons, priests and bishops; deacons may choose to remain as permanent deacons, or more usually go on to be ordained to the priesthood. Priests are permitted, and generally expected, to marry, and the priest's wife typically has an important though informal role in the parish. Bishops are drawn from the monastic clergy; priests may also be monks, but if they intend to marry they must marry before they are first ordained as deacons, and a priest whose wife has died is not permitted to marry again, though he may enter a monastery and thus be eligible to be made a bishop.

Penance and anointing of the sick are close to their Western counterparts. The sacrament of penance is intended to repair the relationship between the sinner and God, and the confession is made to God, with the priest there to act as a witness. He may suggest penances or give other advice to help the penitent deal with the particular sins he or she has confessed.

Marriage is understood in a slightly different way from that of the Western churches. Instead of the Western view that the couple minister the sacrament to each other, Orthodoxy sees marriage as consecrated by the priest in the name of the community rather than as an exchange of vows between two people. Though marriage is intended to be indissoluble, human weakness may damage it to the point where repair is no longer possible, and divorce and remarriage are permissible, again in the context of economy. Ideally, though, marriage is seen as a spiritual path in its own right.

Orthodoxy and Tradition

Tradition is immensely important in Orthodoxy. It is handed down from the time of the early Church and preserved in the writings of the earliest theologians who systematized the Church's beliefs, in the teachings of the seven ecumenical councils, and in the canons of the Church. From a Western point of view, Orthodoxy can look rigidly conservative. The hard times which Orthodox churches have endured in the past and the effort that they have had to make to keep their faith and their traditions alive is also a factor in their continuing conservative outlook. This conservatism and reluctance to accept change is particularly evident in Russia, where many believers still have a profound distrust of the state long after the end of Soviet repression, and resist what they see as alien and threatening innovations. Millenarianism is reported to be widespread in many Russian dioceses, where believers feel that such things as the increasing computerization of records may be one of the signs that the end of the world is near.

Even where it has taken root in the West, however, Orthodoxy remains profoundly conservative in its social as well as its theological attitudes. The joke that Orthodoxy does change, but takes a couple of millennia to do it, reflects its resistance to outside influences, a resistance which is frequently part of its attraction for Christians from Western traditions. A number of Anglicans opposed to the ordination of women, for example, have become Orthodox. Women in the Orthodox Church are not even allowed to go through the doors of the iconostasis into the sanctuary (which strictly speaking is reserved to members of the clergy, though laymen may be permitted to enter under certain conditions).

One of the authors once talked to a Greek woman who was shocked at the very thought of women arranging flowers on the altar of an Anglican church. Female altar servers are as unthinkable as female priests, though women deacons may assist in baptism, chrismations and anointing the sick; women may sing in the choir, read the epistle and be involved in the administration of the parish.

This conservative tradition extends to the version of the Old Testament used by the Orthodox; they use the Septuagint, the translation made into Greek in the third and second centuries BCE, rather than a translation of the Masoretic Hebrew text, standardized in the early Middle Ages by Jewish scholars and the text used by Jews and Western Christians. The Septuagint's readings are often different from those of the Masoretic text, reflecting an earlier Hebrew variant of the text which no longer survives.

Orthodox theology, too, has developed along conservative lines and under very different circumstances, untouched by the Western scholasticism of the Middle Ages and the debates of the Reformation, There is a much lesser degree of systematization than in the West; but this does not mean that Eastern Christian theology is not very precise indeed. Its precision is different from that of the West, and it does not attempt to analyse religious experience in the same way. It seeks to experience the divine rather than describe it, and is much more content to accept that there are areas which human reason cannot penetrate, and much that one cannot understand and express about the mystery of God.

The Other Churches of the East

There is a further group of churches which is much less visible in the West: the churches that are often referred to as the Oriental Orthodox. The split between the Copts, Armenians, Ethiopians, and Syrians and the Greek-derived Orthodox churches goes back much further than the Great Schism which divided the Christians of Europe; in fact it dates back to the Council of Chalcedon in 451 and the arguments there over whether Christ had one single divine/human nature or whether his divine and human natures were separate. Those who believed he had one single nature, the 'monophysites', or 'Nestorians' (after Nestorius, Patriarch of Constantinople, whose theological ideas were condemned at Chalcedon), were regarded as heretics by their Orthodox neighbours, and the two groups split apart and subsequently developed separately. Increasingly today there is a realization that the theological difference is not so great as has been supposed for centuries, and a certain amount of rapprochement has begun between the Orthodox and Oriental Orthodox churches.

These churches are among the most ancient Christian communities. Armenia was the first country to convert to Christianity as a whole, and all of them have long and ancient traditions. Many have spent much of their long histories surviving invasions and foreign rule and have lived as minorities, often under difficult conditions, up to the present day. The deportations and massacres suffered by the Armenians of Turkey after the First World War are the most horrific example in the last century, but other communities live under sustained pressure. The Copts in Egypt face marginalization and occasional violence, while in Iraq the invasion of 2003 has led to perhaps up to half of the ancient Assyrian Christian community leaving the country as a result of attacks by Islamists. Many of these Christians now live in lively and growing diaspora communities in Western countries.

Despite the conditions many of them live under now, the Oriental Orthodox churches have not just been remarkably successful in surviving and flourishing, but, historically at least, in spreading Christianity. The extraordinary missionary journeys of the early Nestorians, who took Christianity as far east as China and Mongolia from the seventh century onwards, have left archaeological traces across the far East and possibly influenced Buddhism in China, though the communities they founded there died out long ago.

The various Oriental Orthodox churches, though they share so much in common and are in communion with one another, are not very organized among themselves, and there are a number of differences and disputes between them. However, things have begun to change since 1965, when representatives from the churches met in Addis Ababa to discuss matters of common interest, and now the leaders of the Coptic, Syrian and Armenian churches meet regularly. All the Oriental Orthodox churches are members of the World Council of Churches.

11

Protestants

No one who is familiar with the Roman Catholic Mass or Eastern Orthodoxy's Divine Liturgy can fail to observe the radical difference in worship on visiting a Protestant church. The building itself is less elaborate. There may be stained glass, depicting scenes from the Bible, but often the windows are plain. There are no statues, and no crucifixes: instead a plain cross often dominates the sanctuary. There may be a biblical text painted on a wall, or occasionally a picture—not a carving. All this is in conformity with one of the Ten Commandments, 'You shall not make for yourself an idol' (Exod. 20:4). An 'idol' is regarded as something three-dimensional—hence the avoidance of statues—while two-dimensional art is acceptable. The plain cross is also regarded as a reminder of the resurrection: the cross is empty, since Christ is alive.

The design of Protestant churches is less rule-governed than in Catholicism or Anglicanism. There is no requirement that worshippers should face East, or that the shape of the building should be cruciform. The focal point of the sanctuary is frequently, although not always, the pulpit, signifying the Protestant emphasis on the preaching of God's word. In large Methodist churches, the organ is often positioned behind the pulpit, sometimes with a choir area, emphasizing the importance of music and singing in that tradition. In Roman Catholic and Anglican churches, it is important that nothing obstructs the worshipper's view of the high altar; hence other church furniture is positioned to permit this. In the Protestant tradition, practicalities rather than liturgy tend to dictate the positioning of objects such as lecterns and organ consoles, and it is not unknown for the organ console to be positioned directly in front of, or behind, the communion table.

In the Protestant tradition, the service itself is much simpler. There is no national or international liturgical uniformity, such as a prescribed order of service and fixed lectionary. The service proceeds according to the practice that is determined locally, usually at the officiant's discretion, and the officiant determines what readings from the Bible are selected, what the subject matter of the sermon will be, what prayers will be used, and whether prayer is extempore, prepared beforehand, taken from published worship resources, or a combination of these. Hymns, readings, prayers and the sermon tend to be interspersed with hymns—normally four or five at principal Sunday services—and their positioning seems designed to create breaks, rather than to aid the liturgy's progression. Protestants themselves sometimes joke about the 'hymn sandwich' service, and there have been occasional attempts to break this

St Paul's Church of Scotland, Pilrig Street, Leith, Edinburgh. The pulpit occupies the central position, behind the communion table. Notice the use of plain crosses, not crucifixes. LCD monitor screens are often used to replace hymn books. Photograph © Andrew Hayden 2010. Reproduced with permission.

pattern. No higher authority than the officiant and the congregation is needed to effect such changes: Protestantism is flexible.

Protestant clergy tend to avoid elaborate robes. There is considerable variation in liturgical dress, but commonly the minister will wear a black cassock underneath a black preaching gown, with an academic hood on top. This last item signifies the minister's role as the teacher, the one who expounds God's word. The service is often conducted entirely from the pulpit, with clergy making little use of other church furniture and liturgical movement during the service. It used to be common, although the practice is dying out, for the minister to select a verse from the Bible as the text from which to develop the sermon. Frequently, the sermon is the culmination point of the service, followed by the final hymn, so that the congregation departs with God's word in their minds. Because of the emphasis on God's word, holy communion is not celebrated at every service, the sacraments being subordinate to the Bible. The frequency of holy communion, again, varies according to local practice.

These are broad generalizations. At a conservative estimate, there are at least thirty thousand different Protestant denominations. The Lutheran tradition is somewhat different to what we have just described. The Lutheran service is much closer to the Roman Catholic liturgy, despite Martin Luther being generally regarded as the father of Protestantism.

The Protestant Reformation

Although this book is not a history of Christianity, Protestantism cannot be properly understood without some knowledge of the fifteenth and sixteenth century Protestant Reformation. The origins of the Reformation are usually traced to Martin Luther (1483–1546), although, as we mentioned in our discussion of the Bible (chapter 5), there were precursors, such as Desiderius Erasmus and John Wycliffe.

Luther studied philosophy and theology at the University of Erfurt in Germany, which was then part of the Holy Roman Empire, and obtained his Master's degree in 1505. He intended to proceed to a career in law, but found legal studies unsatisfying. On 2 July that year, while returning to university from a visit home, he was caught in a lightning storm and almost struck by a thunderbolt. This terrifying experience precipitated the young Luther's decision to abandon law and to enter an Augustinian friary. Luther became ordained to the priesthood in 1507, and began a teaching career at the University of Wittenburg in 1508, where he obtained his doctorate in theology in 1512. While a student of philosophy, Luther believed that he had learned the use of reason, but not the love of God, which came through revelation. One day, while studying Paul's letter to the Romans in his room in the monastery tower, his attention fastened on the verse that read, 'For in the gospel a righteousness from God is revealed, a righteousness that is by faith from first to last, just as it is written: "The righteous will live by faith"' (Rom. 1:17).

This incident in Luther's life is often referred to as the 'tower experience', and on several occasions Luther identified it as a key turning point in his life. The verse highlighted two important insights. First, it is the gospel that highlights God's righteousness, in contrast with one's own unrighteousness as a sinner; second, it highlights the role of faith as the means by which men and women are made righteous in God's sight. Paul's contrast between faith and works struck home to Luther. The theologians of the Middle Ages had emphasized law and works, and Luther himself had entered wholeheartedly into a monastic life replete with prayer, fasting, confession of sins and pilgrimage. This had only served to reinforce a deep-down anger rather than love that Luther felt towards this righteous God.

A further incident that proved decisive in the history of the Protestant Reformation was Johann Tetzel's arrival in Wittenberg in 1516. Teztel was a Dominican friar, and the papal commissioner for indulgences. According to Roman Catholic teaching, an indulgence is 'a remission before God of the temporal punishment due to sins' (*Catechism*, 1471). It is held that sins attract unhealthy attachments requiring purification, and, if purification does not take place on earth, then it will take place in Purgatory. Because Jesus Christ, together with the Virgin Mary, the saints and the martyrs, have accumulated merits, these can be procured by the faithful from the Church, which serves as the custodian. The Church was empowered to make conditions for the obtaining of indulgences, and Tetzel's condition was the payment of money, for the restoration of Saint Peter's Basilica in Rome—a major and expensive project. Tetzel was reputed to have said, 'As soon as the coin in the coffer rings, the soul from purgatory springs.' Luther held that forgiveness could only be obtained directly from God, and was so incensed by Tetzel's indulgence-peddling that he was prompted to write his 95 Theses—points of criticism of the Roman Catholic Church—and to pin them on the door of the Castle Church at Wittenberg that very day. Pinning important information on the church door was the standard form of public communication at that time. The Theses were written in Latin, but they were swiftly translated into German, and circulated widely, through the use of the newly-devised printing press. Luther's pinning of the 95 Theses to the Castle Church door is celebrated annually among German Protestants as Reformation Day, on 31 October.

The Archbishop of Mainz did not reply directly to Luther's Theses, but had them checked for heresy, and forwarded to the Vatican. It was not until 1520 that Pope Leo X issued the papal bull *Exsurge Domine* ('Let the Lord arise'), which identified 41 of the 95 Theses as heretical, demanding that Luther recant. Luther's response to the bull was not to recant any of his assertions, but to burn the papal letter publicly, an act for which he was excommunicated. The following year, 1521, the Holy Roman Emperor Charles V convened a Diet (general assembly) at the town of Worms, to determine how Luther should be dealt with. Johann Eck, assistant to the Archbishop of Trier, and at one time an ally of Luther, asked Luther to verify that the writings were indeed his, and to state whether he still stood by them. Luther is said to have responded in the famous words, 'Here I stand, I can do no other. So help me, God.'

The Edict of Worms, finalized on 25 May 1521, declared Luther to be a heretic, banned his writings, and condemned him to death. However, Frederick III of Saxony, having assured Luther of safe passage to and from his trial, had arranged for him to be abducted on the way back, and to be taken to Wartburg Castle. Luther remained there, incognito, for nearly a year, during which time he translated the New Testament from Greek to German.

Although the 95 Theses referred principally to the selling of indulgences, the issue was linked to several of Luther's other key teachings. As we have seen, Luther came to believe that salvation was not attainable through good works, or to be obtained through the Church's rites, but rather the sinner was justified through faith, and through faith alone (*sola fide*). (Luther has sometimes been criticized for adding the word 'alone', which is not to be found in Paul's writings.) Luther believed the doctrine of *sola fide* to be biblical, holding that Scripture was the sole authority in matters of faith, not papal or ecclesiastical authority. Scripture taught that Christ's sacrifice was 'once for all' (Heb. 10:2) and hence the Church was not re-enacting Christ's sacrifice at the Mass, or acting together with Christ and the communion of saints as the body who brought salvation anew each time the faithful participated. For Luther, the Mass was not a sacrifice; Christ was not being offered up again to the Father, and he objected to the doctrine of transubstantiation. Unlike some of the more radical Protestant Reformers, however, Luther did not view the Mass merely as a memorial of Christ's sacrificial death, but held that there was a 'real presence' of Christ in the Eucharist: the words, 'This is my body', were not merely to be understood symbolically. According to Luther, Christ is present 'in, with and under' the eucharistic elements—a doctrine that is sometimes referred to as 'consubstantiation'. Although Luther and Lutherans have held that something objective takes place during the sacrament, the sacrament is not effective without faith. The traditional Roman Catholic view is that sacraments work *ex opere operato* (operative by performance): in other words, spiritual benefits are obtained simply by participation in the rite itself, irrespective of the worshipper's or the priest's state of mind, or whether they feel inspired or uplifted by the rite. The contrasting Protestant view is not that the effects of the sacrament are entirely subjective, depending exclusively on the worshipper's feelings, but rather that spiritual benefits accrue through divine grace, and the sacraments operate as signs that this inner grace is mediated through Christ's own sacrifice on the cross.

Allied to the concept of *sola fiducia* (grace alone) is the Protestant doctrine of 'the priesthood of all believers', a doctrine to which Luther gave considerable emphasis. According to Luther, every believer has equal access to God. He or she does not need special intermediaries, such as priests to pronounce forgiveness for one's sins, or saints to offer petitions to God on one's behalf. In the Book of Revelation, 'four living creatures' and the 24 elders who surround Christ's throne sing, 'You have made them [people from every nation] to be a kingdom and priests to serve our God, and they will reign on earth' (Rev. 5:10).

The doctrine of the priesthood of all believers does not entail that Protestants have no distinction between clergy and laity, or that any member of the laity can fulfil the functions that are traditionally associated with priesthood. The complete abolition of a separate rank of clergy is only to be found at the more extreme edges of Protestantism, for example the Quakers, the Brethren, and various independent Protestant churches. In the case of the Brethren, there is not complete democratization of spiritual functions, since each congregation is overseen by a number of elders, who are specially appointed to govern the spiritual life of the community, and who have the exclusive prerogative of preaching and presiding over the Lord's Supper. In common with some other fundamentalist Protestant denominations, spiritual leadership is exclusively male, thus debarring more than half of their members from office. These unequal roles are not incompatible with the Protestant principle of the priesthood of all believers, however. The doctrine does not imply democracy or equality, but rather the idea that each individual has direct access to God and to the means of salvation, through faith and by divine grace. Spiritual leaders—whether they are called ministers, pastors or elders—do not have the powers to influence affairs in heaven, unlike the priest, whose presumed powers to dispense the sacraments and to pronounce forgiveness help to determine one's eternal destiny. In Protestantism, spiritual leaders do not exercise power over their congregations that affect the afterlife, but teach the word of God, as found in Scripture.

Because of their rejection of the mediatorial role of priests, Protestants resolutely avoid referring to their leaders as priests, and are often offended if they are referred to as such. The word 'minister' is often preferred; literally the word means 'servant', indicating that the clergy's role is a supportive one rather than a position of power over the laity. The term only alludes to Christ's own role, as recounted in Scripture: although equal with God, he became a servant (Phil. 2:6), he is typically identified with the 'suffering servant' to whom Isaiah refers (see, e.g., Mt. 12:8), and he performed the menial task of washing his disciples' feet before the Last Supper (Jn 13:1-17). Protestant vocabulary also excludes terms that signify sacerdotal functions, for example the word 'altar'. Altars are places of sacrifice, and the word connotes the Roman Catholic doctrine of the sacrifice of the Mass. Hence, the term 'communion table' is preferred.

Varieties of Protestantism

The spread of the Reformation in Europe was somewhat uneven: Germany and Scandinavia largely adopted Lutheranism, while Switzerland and The Netherlands became influenced by more radical varieties of Protestantism. France, Belgium, Spain, Portugal and Italy remained Catholic. In the twenty-first century, Roman Catholicism remains the strongest form of Christianity in Italy, Poland, the Iberian peninsula, France, Crotia, Hungary, Lithuania and Austria, with Protestantism having the strongest foothold in Scandinavia. Germany is now fairly equally divided between Protestants and Catholics, while The Netherlands, once a bastion of Reformation ideas, is a mixture of Protestant and Independent churches, increasingly rivalled by secularism. Outside Europe, Australasia and the USA have gained a predominance of Protestants, largely through immigration from Protestant countries. Africa, almost half Christian, has a slight prepon- derance of Protestants over Catholics, if one counts Anglicans as the former. In Latin America, Protestantism is more common in the North than in the South.

The form of Protestantism that derives most directly from Luther is Lutheranism. The denomination is the least visible in the English-speaking world, but it is the strongest form of Protestantism worldwide. The World Lutheran Federation, founded in 1947, consists of 140 member churches from 79 countries, comprising 68.3 million Christians. The name 'Lutheran' was first used as a pejorative term by Luther's opponents at the Leipzig Disputation in 1519, but subsequently gained acceptance by Luther's followers. In the face of confrontation between the opposing parties, the Elector of Saxony favoured Luther and his supporters were permitted to establish their own churches. Approval was formally given at the Diet of Speyer in 1526. Following the Peace of Augsburg in 1555, each territory was permitted its own official church, headed by its own ruler. Christianity's Lutheran varieties took root in Scandinavia (Norway, Sweden, Denmark and also Finland). In Germany, where the denomination's head is a state official, Christian affiliation is divided fairly evenly between Catholic and Protestant.

In terms of present-day Lutheran belief, there is considerable variation. Officially, the Lutheran Church's faith is enshrined in the Book of Concord, compiled by Jakob Andreae and Martin Chemnitz, and adopted in 1580, marking the fiftieth anniversary of the presentation of the Augsburg Confession to the Emperor Charles V on 25 June 1530. The Book of Concord is a collection of ten doctrinal statements. It includes the ancient ecumenical creeds (Apostles', Nicene and Athanasian), indicating that the Church's tradition goes back to ancient times, sharing common roots with mainstream Christianity as a whole. The remaining texts are specifically Protestant: the Augsburg Confession, and the Apology (or Defence) of the Augsburg Confession (written by the Protestant Reformer Philipp Melanchthon), the Small and the Large Catechisms, and the Smalcald Articles (all by Luther), the Treatise on the Power and Primacy of the Pope (by Philipp Melanchthon), and the Formula of Concord.

The Augsburg Confession was principally the work of Philipp Melanchthon (1497–1560), and other Protestant Reformers (Martin Luther, Justus Jonas and Johannes Bugenhagen), having been commissioned by Elector John of Saxony. The Confession covers a wide range of Christian doctrines, beginning with the nature of God, sin and justification, the Church and its sacraments, ecclesiastical and civil government, and the alleged abuses of the Catholic Church. The Confession was brought to the Diet of Augsburg (although Luther himself did not attend), but in the meantime some Roman Catholic theologians had composed a set of responses entitled the Confutations, countering the Confession's position. The Confutations secured acceptance, rather than the Augsburg Confession. Melanchthon's Apology was a defence of the Confession, in reply to the Roman Catholic document. The Small and Large Catechisms present the fundamentals of the Christian faith, as understood by the Lutheran Reformers, in question-and-answer format. Lutherans will at least be familiar with the Small Catechism, which is sometimes referred to as the Layman's Bible. The Smalcald (or Schmalkald) Articles were written by Luther in 1537 for the Schmalkaldic League—a group of Lutheran princes—in preparation for an ecumenical council. Luther was unable to attend in person, owing to illness. Melanchthon, who was concerned that a document of Luther's authorship would prove divisive, dissuaded the League from accepting the document. Instead, Melanchthon was asked to prepare a statement about papal power and authority; this was the Treatise on the Power and Primacy of the Pope, which was adopted at the gathering. The document is noteworthy for its description of the Pope as the antichrist—a notion that gained momentum during the Protestant Reformation, and continues to be supported in extreme Protestant circles. The Smaldcald Articles state, 'Therefore, even though the bishop of Rome had the primacy by divine right, yet since he defends godless services and doctrine conflicting with the Gospel, obedience is not due him; yea, it is necessary to resist him as Antichrist. The errors of the Pope are manifest and not trifling' (Smalcald Article 57).

The final Lutheran document, the Formula of Concord, was presented to Elector August of Saxony in 1577. It contains yet another statement of Lutheran doctrine, and was signed by over fifty political leaders of various rank, and over 8,100 pastors and theologians. Not all Lutherans agreed with the statement, however, and roughly one third of Lutherans did not endorse the Formula.

The Book of Concord is held to be an elucidation of the teachings of the Church as found in the ancient creeds and, particularly, in Scripture. It is therefore sometimes referred to as 'the normed norm', meaning that, although it is to be regarded as the definitive statement of faith, its authority does not reside in itself, but in the higher authority of God's word, as found in the Bible. Despite the authoritative status of the Book of Concord, however, divergent attitudes to its authority have emerged. The rationalism of the European Enlightenment caused a liberalization of attitudes to these statements of faith in the eighteenth century, followed by a move back towards conservativism in the nineteenth. Currently there exists a spectrum of theological stances. There are conservative Lutheran churches—in particular the Evangelical Lutheran Churches—who regard the Book of Concord as definitive, and give 'unconditional subscription', while others, influenced by theological liberalism, regard these statements of faith as historically conditioned and works of human opinion. A number of liberal scholars have been Lutherans, gaining a reputation extending much wider than the Lutheran Churches themselves. Examples are the theologian Paul Tillich (1886–1965), the biblical scholar Rudolf Bultmann (1884–1976) and Dietrich Bonhoeffer (1906–1945), who was famed not only for his theological and biblical scholarship, but for his resistance to the Nazi regime, for which he was imprisoned and finally executed in a German concentration camp. Scholarship and theological education are therefore important in the Lutheran tradition. Clergy are required to undergo theological education, including acquiring familiarity with biblical languages. Although most clergy are male, there are women ministers. Clergy have an important teaching role, although lay members of a congregation may be invited to preach or lead worship from time to time.

Lutheran worship observes a similar structure to the traditional Roman Catholic Mass, although the term 'Mass' itself is avoided except in Sweden, where the word 'Lögmessa' is used. The eucharistic liturgy is generally referred to as Holy Communion, or sometimes the Sacrament of the Altar, the Lord's Supper, or the Holy Supper. Lutheran churches encourage frequent communion, although it is necessarily available on a weekly basis. Other varieties of worship include Matins, and Morning and Evening Prayer. Services are invariably in the language of the people. Notwithstanding the scathing criticisms of Rome that the Reformers made, the communion service is modelled on the Roman Catholic Mass. As the Apology to the Augsburg Confession states, 'At the outset we must again make the preliminary statement that we do not abolish the Mass, but religiously maintain and defend it' (Article XXIV [XII]: Of the Mass, para. 1).

The communion service begins with the Kyrie Eleison ('Lord, have mercy'), and includes an introit, Gloria, Credo and Agnus Dei, as in Roman Catholicism. (The Gloria is a song of praise, based on the angels' song at Jesus' nativity [Lk. 2:14], and the Agnus Dei ['Lamb of God'] calls upon Christ for mercy and peace.) Art and music have an important role. Much of the service is sung; indeed, in some Lutheran churches the only spoken word is the sermon itself. Luther wrote many hymns, many of which remain in use. (Several of Luther's hymns are used within the Protestant tradition more widely, not merely within Lutheran churches.) Some of the chorales to which these hymns are set are also attributed to Luther, but scholars now doubt whether Luther himself composed music. Certainly, some very famous church composers have themselves been Lutherans, for example Dietrich Buxtehude, J. S. Bach and Felix Mendelssohn. (Mendelssohn was born a Jew, but converted to Christianity.) Lutheran hymns are intended to be didactic, and the liturgy seeks to combine the sacrament with the preaching of the Word. Traditionally, the sermon is based on a biblical text or theme, which the preacher proceeds to expound. The word 'evangelical', which very often forms part of the name of Lutheranism's branches, serves to indicate that the church's role is the preaching of the Word, rather than proselytizing zeal. (In fact, of all the major branches of Christendom, Lutherans have probably done the least in terms of foreign mission.) The sacramental nature of Lutheranism is underlined by the positioning of the altar, which is invariably the focal point.

There exists a variety of styles of worship. In some Lutheran churches, the officiant (who is referred to either as the priest or pastor) wears robes similar to those of a Catholic priest, for example an alb, a chasuble or a stole, whereas other Lutheran clergy wear a black robe, with white 'preaching bands' at the neck. Some churches have introduced more modern music in worship, hoping that this will with help to attract and retain the younger generation.

There are also variations in the methods of church government. Some Lutheran churches are episcopal, with a bishop or archbishop presiding over a congregation, while others have adopted a synodical structure whereby a church court makes decisions on behalf of its member congregations. Different congregations have different degrees of congregational autonomy. In the USA there are two contrasting forms of Lutheranism: the Evangelical Lutheran Church in America (ELCA) and the Lutheran Church—Missouri Synod (LCMS). The ELCA was formed in 1988 by a merger of the American Lutheran Church, the Association of Evangelical Lutheran Churches and the Lutheran Church in America. It is governed by a bishop and a synod which meets every two years. It is the more liberal of the two strands of Lutheranism, being open to modern theological and biblical scholarship. It accepts women's ordination, and is more tolerant of homosexuality and abortion. It is also open to ecumenical relationships, accepting the validity of ordination and the sacraments of other denominations. The LCMS, by contrast, is more conservative: only men can receive ordination, and it 'believes that the Bible requires full agreement in doctrine before it is possible to join in altar and pulpit fellowship with other churches.'

Anglicanism

A second major strand of Christianity that stems from the Protestant Reformation is the Church of England. 'Church of England' and 'Anglicanism' are not synonymous, the former being a sub-set of the latter. The Church of England, as its name implies, exists in England, while Anglicans are those who are outside England, but in the same tradition, and in full communion with the Church of England. In Scotland, Anglicans belong to the Scottish Episcopal Church, Welsh Anglicans belong to the Church in Wales, and there is the Episcopal

Church in the USA, the Anglican Church of South Africa and so on. Each of these Churches is an Anglican 'province', headed by its own archbishop, with its various dioceses and parishes. The Church of England has two provinces—Canterbury and York—each with its own archbishop; however, in addition to his role as the senior bishop of the Diocese of Canterbury, the Archbishop of Canterbury is Primate of All England and, additionally, the senior bishop within the worldwide Anglican communion.

Although there has been a Church in England since at least the third century, the Church of England as it is now known stems from King Henry VIII's (1491–1547) controversies with Pope Clement VII, who refused to give Henry an annulment of his marriage to Catherine of Aragon. Henry VIII consequently usurped the role of Supreme Head of the Church of England, thus bringing to an end papal authority over the Church. For his defiance Henry was excommunicated by Pope Paul III in 1534. The impetus for the English Reformation was therefore political, rather than doctrinal and liturgical, and it might be asked whether the Church of England should be regarded as Protestant at all. The Church of England regards itself as 'catholic and reformed', and falls in a middle position between Roman Catholicism and the more thorough-going forms of Protestantism that took their rise in Scotland and in Switzerland under John Calvin (Jean Cauvin, 1509–1564).

The replacement of papal authority by monarchical authority resulted in a relationship between Church and state that is not found anywhere else in the world. The Church of England is not exactly a state Church, but is termed 'the established Church'. The monarch's role as 'supreme governor' is not quite the same as being the head of the Church of England. The monarch does not convene church courts, direct policy, or even attend the General Synod (the principal Church court, which meets annually). The monarch, however, being Supreme Governor, must belong to the Church of England; he or she may not be a Roman Catholic or a member of one of the Free Churches. The monarch formally approves senior appointments, notably bishops and archbishops. Normally, this is accomplished by the Church recommending names to the Prime Minister, thus creating a somewhat circular process in which the Church makes a recommendation to the Prime Minister, who recommends to the Queen, who recommends the appointment to the Church. Although appointments effectively are normally made by the Church, it was rumoured that Prime Minister Margaret Thatcher vetoed at least two nominations during her period of office.

The Church of England is in fact part of the British legal system. It is not an independent voluntary organization, but is linked to the state in a way in which other denominations are not. This special link has several implications. A number of bishops (now only the most senior, not all) have seats in the House of Lords, although, curiously, until 2001 clergy themselves were disqualified from becoming Members of Parliament. Some major church policies may require state approval: for example, when the General Synod approved the ordination of women to the priesthood in 1992, the decision was subsequently ratified in Parliament, where some MPs who opposed the decision sought to block the necessary parliamentary endorsement. The British Parliament's involvement in ecclesiastical matters was demonstrated in 1928–1929, when it succeeded in blocking the introduction of a new prayer book. It is doubtful, however, whether this would happen in the twenty-first century, although Parliament still has the right.

The Church of England is involved in major civic events that require religious legitimation. A monarch's coronation is performed at Westminster Abbey; the Archbishop of Canterbury presides over it, and undertakes the task of crowning the new king or queen. The coronation forms part of a eucharist. Leaders of other denominations may be invited to attend, but any role they perform in the service is by invitation rather than right. Royal weddings, likewise, are conducted in a suitably prestigious Anglican building, as are royal funerals. The sociologist Émile Durkheim (1858–1917) noted that religion served to legitimate society's *status quo*, and these are examples.

At a local level, the Church of England is organized into parishes— geographical areas over which the parish church has responsibility. In times past, the church had responsibility for local government, and had a Parochial Council which had responsibility for local affairs such as keeping law and order. (The vicar of Dibley, in the television situation comedy, regularly convenes such a Council, but this is anachronistic: local authorities, not parish churches, now determine matters such as naming streets.) The parish system today offers any parishioners the right to be married (provided they are legally eligible, of course), to have their children baptized, or to have a funeral. The parish is also the area over which the vicar or rector has pastoral oversight. It is not merely the members of the Sunday congregation who can seek pastoral support or confess their sins; the parish church serves all who live in the locality. The vicar may offer his or her services as a chaplain to local schools, or conduct services of worship in a local care home. Parishes are organized into dioceses, over which a bishop presides; if the diocese is large, the bishop may be assisted by one or more 'suffragan bishops'. As noted above, the dioceses are grouped under the two provinces of York and Canterbury.

The Church of England is sometimes described as a 'broad church'. This description indicates that it contains a variety of theological views and styles of worship. It is sometimes said that there are three major strands within Anglicanism: the Catholic, the Evangelical and the Liberal. Anglo-Catholics (sometimes referred to as 'High Anglicans') adopt a style of worship that is close to that of Roman Catholicism. Key parts of the service are sung rather than said, chants may be used, incense is burned, emphasis is given to saints' days, and homage may be paid to the Virgin Mary. The Anglo-Catholic tradition received impetus from the Oxford Movement, which took its rise in the 1830s, and was so-called because it was led by clergy associated with the University of Oxford. Famous names associated with the movement are John Henry Newman (1801–1890), John Keble (1792–1866) and Edward Bouverie Pusey (1800–1882), among others. They are also known as the Tractarians, on account of a series of publications called *Tracts for the Times* (1833–1841). Supporters of the Oxford Movement contended that the doctrines defined at the (Roman Catholic) Council of Trent (1545–1563) were compatible with the Church of England's *Thirty-Nine Articles*, and they viewed Anglicanism, Roman Catholicism and Orthodoxy as three branches of the one catholic Church. Some of the leaders of the Oxford Movement, including Newman himself, converted to Roman Catholicism. Newman aspired to the status of cardinal, and was beatified after his death.

The Evangelical tradition is more likely to emphasize personal conversion and the necessity of spreading the gospel to those who have not accepted it. The study and preaching of the Bible is supremely important, and evangelicals are more likely to take the Bible literally, perhaps even adopting a fundamentalist stance. There is more emphasis on spontaneity and exuberance, with worship drawing on modern popular musical composition. The service's music may be led by a 'praise group', using instruments such as guitars, drums and an electronic keyboard, rather than the traditional organ. The expression 'happy clappy' is sometimes used to refer to this type of worship. Spontaneity may involve a departure from some of the traditional liturgical components, such as the use of a fixed lectionary.

The Liberal strand steers a middle course. Services are more formal and restrained, but avoid the features of High Anglicanism that tend to be associated with Roman Catholicism. Apart from the hymns, most of which are traditional rather than 'trendy', the service is said rather than sung. There is more emphasis on deepening the spiritual life and on social outreach than on personal conversion, and clergy and congregations in this tradition may be more amenable to liberal ideas about the Bible.

Identifying these three strands is a broad generalization. Churches do not formally identify themselves as belonging to any one of these three categories. In sociological terminology, these are 'ideal types' or theoretical constructs, rather than actual examples in real life. A congregation that predominantly belongs to one of these traditions may incorporate features of the other. For example, a High Anglican church may decide occasionally to introduce a more 'happy clappy' 'Youth Mass', or incorporate some popular religious songs into the service. Any of the three traditions may decide to use music from Taizé, an ecumenical religious community in France that has disseminated its own distinctive worship material. An evangelical congregation may attract worshippers who do not necessarily espouse biblical inerrancy; people may attend simply because it is their parish church. Conversely, High Anglican and Liberal congregations may have their share of biblical fundamentalists in their ranks. Individual churches, too, may alter over time, as congregations change and their leaders are replaced.

Until the 1970s, the principal Anglican service of worship was Matins (also known as Morning Prayer, or Lauds). This consists of general confession of sins and pronouncement of absolution, followed by various canticles (which may be said or sung), readings from the Old and New Testaments, the Apostles' Creed and prayers. Matins may include a sermon, but there is no communion. The Eucharist was celebrated as the main act of worship once or twice a month. Additionally, a worshipper might attend Evensong (also known as Compline) in the early evening. Evensong consists of prayers, readings from each Testament, a psalm (said or sung), the Apostles' Creed and sometimes a sermon. Apart from the sermon, the services followed the precise wording set out in the 1662 *Book of Common Prayer*.

The *Book of Common Prayer* is one of the principal products of the English Reformation. The first *Book of Common Prayer* was commissioned by King Edward VI, and edited by Thomas Cranmer, the Archbishop of Canterbury. It first appeared in 1549. Further revisions resulted in a 1552 version, but this was never used, since Queen Mary had come to the throne, and ordered the nation to revert to Roman Catholicism. Cranmer was burnt at the stake for his efforts at reform. On the accession of Elizabeth I, Protestant reforms were reinstated. However, owing to the turbulent political times, it was not until the end of the Civil War that the *Book of Common Prayer*, revised once again, was introduced in 1662, and remained the Church's principal service book until the late twentieth century. The *Book of Common Prayer* was the first prayer book that contained the written text of all the daily and Sunday services. It should be remembered, however, that this did not mean that every attendee had access to the text. Books were scarcer and more expensive in the seventeenth century, and literacy rates were lower, unlike the twenty-first century, when congregations may borrow copies of the service book on arrival at church.

The aims of the *Book of Common Prayer* were to ensure the uniformity of worship throughout the realm, to make the Church's liturgy available to the people in their own language, and to provide forms of worship that were free from the features of Roman Catholicism which the Reformers rejected. Before the Reformation it had been common practice for the laity to receive the sacrament only once a year (at Easter), or at the occasional Nuptial Mass, or if they were seriously ill. At the Mass, it was therefore quite common for the priest alone to receive the eucharistic elements. The *Book of Common Prayer* sought to ensure that all who had been confirmed, and not simply the officiant, received the sacrament. The celebrant was instructed to give advance notice that communion would be celebrated on a particular Sunday, and to emphasize the importance of accepting the invitation to participate. If members were reluctant to come forward to receive the bread and the wine, the celebrant might issue the following invitation, usually given after the sermon:

> Dearly beloved brethren, on—I intend, by God's grace, to celebrate the Lord's Supper: unto which, in God's behalf, I bid you all that are here present; and beseech you, for the Lord Jesus Christ's sake, that ye will not refuse to come thereto, being so lovingly called and bidden by God himself. Ye know how grievous and unkind a thing it is, when a man hath prepared a rich feast, decked his table with all kind of provision, so that there lacketh nothing but the guests to sit down; and yet they who are called (without any cause) most unthankfully refuse to come. Which of you in such a case would not be moved? Who would not think a great injury and wrong done unto him? Wherefore, most dearly beloved in Christ, take ye good heed, lest ye, withdrawing yourselves

from this holy Supper, provoke God's indignation against you. (*Book of Common Prayer*, 170)

The *Book of Common Prayer* purposely avoided vocabulary that connoted Roman Catholic theology. Words like 'Mass' and 'altar' were removed; the Kyrie and the Gloria were omitted, and there were no allusions to the rite being a sacrifice, and no instruction that the communion wafer should be elevated.

In the second half of the twentieth century, there was a growing awareness that the language of the *Book of Common Prayer* had become archaic. This was ironic, since it was originally designed to enable worshippers to use the language of the people. New translations of the Bible enabled congregations to hear Scripture read in modern speech, but it became clear there was a need to revise the language of the liturgy also. Accordingly, the 1970s heralded a number of experimental liturgical innovations, resulting in *The Alternative Service Book 1980*. As well as containing the principal services and rites of passage in modern language, the book also contained an ordinal—a manual for ordaining deacons, priests and bishops. This was used widely until 2000, when it was superseded by *Common Worship*, which covers the same ground, but without the ordinal. At the time of writing, this remains the most widely used service book in the Church of England, although the *Book of Common Prayer* is still occasionally used, and many older church members prefer it. The Prayer Book Society was established in England in 1975, to ensure the preservation of the prayer book. Members regard it as particularly important that the younger generation, who have not been familiarized with it, do not allow it to be a mere historical document.

It may be asked to what extent the Anglican tradition can be regarded as Protestant. The eucharist follows the style of the Roman Catholic Mass, its government is episcopal, and its bishops and priests claim a line of apostolic succession. Unlike Roman Catholicism, Anglicans do not hold that they constitute the one true Church, or that they exclusively offer the means of salvation. On the other hand, the Anglican Church does not accept papal authority, and it rejects the traditional Roman Catholic theology of the Mass. Unlike the Roman Catholic priesthood, clergy may marry, and most of them are married and have families. There are some respects in which Anglicanism adopts a middle position between Protestantism and Catholicism: for example, the term 'vicar' is normally preferred to 'priest', with the exception of the High Anglican tradition, but the ordination ceremony refers to candidates being 'ordained priest'. The Anglican Church observes saints' days, but discourages the veneration of relics, and the saints are not prayed to. Regarding the number of the sacraments, Anglicans do not wholly reject the Roman Catholic belief that there are seven, sometimes identifying two 'major' sacraments (baptism and eucharist) and five 'minor' ones. In some respects, Anglicanism moved closer to Catholicism as its history progressed; for example, in the nineteenth century it became a worldwide communion, and it also re-established monastic orders. Roman Catholicism also moved through time: as we have seen, its worship is now in the vernacular, and members receive both the bread and the wine at the eucharist.

Congregationalists and Presbyterians

Lutheranism and Anglicanism are the more conservative expressions of the ideas of the Protestant Reformation. However, the Reformation had more radical forms, of which Presbyterianism and Congregationalism are two of the principal examples. England, in fact, became Presbyterian for a short period, during the Commonwealth, but with the restoration of the monarchy in 1660 episcopacy was restored. When the *Book of Common Prayer* was approved in 1662, Charles II introduced the Act of Conformity, requiring the prayer book to be used throughout England. Some two-thousand clergy refused to comply, and they were removed from office. Their removal became known as the Great Ejection. Those who declined to use the *Book of Common Prayer* became known as Non-Conformists—an umbrella term that spans a variety of denominations who have defined their own forms of worship.

There are at least seven-hundred Presbyterian denominations worldwide today, and it is only possible to give broad generalizations. The term refers to their system of church government: the session or elders' meeting at congregational level, the presbytery (sometimes called a synod) with authority over a group of churches locally, and a General Assembly overseeing the denomination as a whole. Ministers and laity are usually appointed in equal proportions to attend presbyteries and assemblies. At local level, the elders are sometimes assisted by a 'deacons' court' or management committee, which oversees the congregation's fabric, while the elders attend to its spiritual life.

The names of Presbyterian denominations tend to relate to the country in which they reside. In Switzerland, The Netherlands and Germany, the name 'Reformed' is preferred to 'Presbyterian' and is juxtaposed to the country's name. In Bohemia, Hungary, Scotland and England, national names prefaced the description 'Presbyterian'. The Protestant Reformers in France adopted the name 'Huguenots' in the sixteenth century and were the first national Presbyterian church. Presbyterian churches in the USA, Canada, Australia and New Zealand arose through emigration during the nineteenth century, while Presbyterianism in developing countries was largely the result of the Christian missionary enterprise during the same period. In 1875, a worldwide association of Presbyterian denominations was formed, named The Alliance of the Reformed Churches throughout the World holding the Presbyterian System. In 1970 this body merged with the International Congregational Council, to form the World Alliance of Reformed Churches (WARC).

The key historical figures shaping the ideas of the Reformed tradition were Huldrych Zwingli (1484–1531) and John Calvin in Switzerland, and John Knox (c. 1513–1572) in Scotland. Zwingli preached his first sermon in Zürich, where he departed from the normal practice of basing his address on a text from the day's lectionary passage. Instead, he read from the beginning of Matthew's Gospel, expounding it with his own commentary. He repeated this practice on successive Sundays, until his exposition of Matthew was finished, whereupon he proceeded to explain the Acts of the Apostles sequentially. Zwingli's departure from convention underlined the radical Reformers' belief in the importance of the Bible as a source of doctrine. Indeed, all the various Reformed confessions and catechisms are invariably regarded as being subordinate to Scripture, which is the supreme standard of doctrine. Zwingli's understanding of the sacraments differed from Luther. He could not accept the doctrine of Christ's 'real presence' at the communion, contending that it was absurd to believe that Christ's body could be omnipresent. Instead, he argued that the word 'is' in Christ's words, 'This is my body', meant 'signifies', and that the service was to be understood as a symbolic re-enactment of the Last Supper. Zwingli and Luther never succeeded in resolving their disagreements about the sacrament, although Zwingli wholeheartedly supported Luther's anti-papal stance.

Simplicity in worship was a key concern for the radical Reformers. There is no fixed form of worship, the order of service being determined by the pastor or minister, subject to the approval of the congregation's session. The service is frequently conducted from the pulpit, with little, if any, use of other church furniture, apart from the communion service, where necessity dictates that the minister descends to the area behind the communion table to preside over the sacrament. The service consists of prayers, reading from Scripture and a sermon, interspersed with hymns. Zwingli himself, although an accomplished musician, forbade the use of any music during worship, but other Reformers were not so extreme. However, there was a desire to avoid the elaborateness of the choral music that had often been associated with the Roman Catholic Mass, and which seemed designed to demonstrate the virtuosity of the musicians rather than to instruct the congregation. John Calvin wrote a number of hymns, believing in the didactic value of music. Probably his best known is his metrical version of Psalm 100 ('The Old Hundredth'). The music of the *Genevan Psalter* (1539) was kept simple: each tune had no more than an octave's compass, and each syllable was matched with no more than one single note. Twenty-first century Reformed churches use a variety of hymnals, drawing on various sources, but of course with words consistent with Reformation theology.

The theology of the Reformed tradition is expressed in a number of confessions of faith, and catechisms. These include Zwingli's *Sixty-seven Articles* (1523), the *French Confession* (1559), the *Scots Confession* (1560), the *Westminster Confession* (1646), the *Shorter Catechism* (1649), and the *Larger Catechism* (1649), among others. A confession of faith serves some of the functions of a creed, but it is invariably longer, and is not used liturgically. It serves to explain in some detail the principles of the Reformed faith, with scriptural proof-texts. Candidates for the ministry may be asked to sign their acceptance of their denomination's favoured confession of faith as a standard of doctrine subordinate to Scripture, thus ensuring that they are prepared only to teach sound doctrine.

Much of the Reformers' theology is associated with John Calvin, who spent much of his life in Geneva. In collaboration with William Farel, Calvin wrote *Articles on the Organization of the Church and its Worship at Geneva* (1537), which set the ways the Church was to be reformed in accordance with Reformation principles. The *Articles* contained a confession of faith, a statement of how the eucharist was to be understood, directions regarding excommunication of wayward and dissenting members, instructions on singing, and marriage laws. Calvin's theology, however, is more substantially contained in his four-volume *Institutes of the Christian Religion*, first published in Latin in 1559, and subsequently in French the following year. The *Institutes* is a comprehensive piece of systematic theology, encompassing the themes of how God can be known, the authority of Scripture, the atoning work of Jesus Christ, divine grace and redemption, the nature of the Church, and life after death. This important volume contains the doctrine that is probably most associated with Calvin and Calvinism, namely predestination, which requires brief explanation.

According to Calvin, when Adam and Eve sinned in the Garden of Eden, they fell from grace, becoming 'totally depraved', being unable to redeem themselves from their fallen state. Any human effort, such as trying to perform good deeds, is quite insufficient to atone for sin. Because of their 'total depravity', even good works become sins in God's sight. The only way in which men and women can attain salvation is through divine grace, and this comes solely through faith in Jesus Christ. Because salvation is not through our own efforts, it is not possible to take the initiative in exercising faith in Jesus Christ: this, too, would be a work. Thus it can only be God who takes the initiative in offering grace. However, since some men and women have faith and others do not, God must therefore offer faith to some and not to others, and must have reasons for doing so, even if these are not apparently to humankind in their earthly lives. God knows the future and, being omnipotent as well as omniscient, could change it if he so desired. God must therefore will the future, electing some to salvation and others to damnation. The notion that God consciously decides who are the 'damned' as well as the 'elect' is sometimes known as 'double predestination'. God has decided these matters at the moment of creation. Being in control of the universe, these were not contingency plans once Adam and Eve sinned: Calvin writes of 'eternal election'. Calvin regarded this position as being based on the teaching of Saint Paul, who wrote, 'For those God foreknew he also predestined to be conformed to the likeness of his Son, that he might be the firstborn among many brothers. And those he predestined, he also called; those he called, he also justified; those he justified, he also glorified' (Rom. 8:29-30).

He also writes of 'objects of his wrath, prepared for destruction' (Rom. 9:22). If God has really decided from eternity the eternal fate of every man and woman, this raises a number of obvious questions. Why bother to do good deeds if salvation does not depend on them? Why send missionaries to convert others if God has already sealed their destiny? Calvin is not unaware of these issues. If God has predestined those in distant lands to receive divine grace, he argues, he will also predestine the means by which they receive it, which must include the opportunity to hear the gospel. As for good deeds, they can only emanate from faith, otherwise—as Calvin stated—they are sins.

If these ideas sound unpalatable, it is worth noting that by no means everyone in the Reformed churches agrees with Calvin. Calvin is studied in Reformed theological seminaries, but not uncritically, and the Reformed Churches' basic standard of authority is neither Calvin, nor the various Protestant confessions and catechisms, but the authority of the Bible. Even the concept of biblical authority is open to interpretation; while some Christians in this tradition regard it as inerrant, there are others who regard it as a set of human attempts to understand God's word and feel uncomfortable with Calvin's theology, despite its undoubted historical influence on their tradition. Calvinism is an attempt to understand the seriousness of sin, divine grace, and how salvation is God's gift, not something that men and women have earned. This is perhaps the idea that all Reformed Christians would share.

Congregationalists

A further strand of Reformed Christianity consists of the Congregationalists. Their origins can be traced back to Robert Browne (1550–1633). Browne was born in Tolethorpe, near Stanford, Lincolnshire, and studied in Cambridge. After a brief period of school teaching, he gained charge of a congregation in Norwich. From 1580 Browne circulated a number of pamphlets against the established Church. In 1582 he published three books including *A Brief Treatise of the Reformation without Tarrying for Anie*. The expression 'without tarrying for any' became associated with Browne and his supporters, who were nicknamed Brownists, but also attracted the names 'Separatists' and 'Independents'. Initially these independents were not congregations, but radical Protestants— sometimes referred to as Puritans—who were dissatisfied with the effects of the English Reformation, whose structures remained episcopal and whose worship followed the *Book of Common Prayer* as if it were holy writ.

The first separatist congregation had its origin in Scrooby, Lincolnshire, in 1606, led by John Smyth (c. 1554–1612) and John Robinson (c. 1575–1625). Smyth is generally regarded as the precursor of the Baptist churches, his congregation having split with Robinson's. Faced with mounting persecution, Robinson took his congregation to Leyden in The Netherlands, where he was later joined by Browne. However, The Netherlands did not prove a conducive environment for Robinson's congregation, whose theology differed from that of the Dutch Reformers, and in 1620 a number of the congregation set sail for Southampton, and then to New England. These voyagers became known as the Pilgrim Fathers, and were the pioneers of Congregationalism in America.

The key feature of Congregationalism is the autonomy of each local congregation, and its original absence of central authority made it more of a movement than a single Christian denomination. It was based on the principle that Christ's visible body is fully manifested in each congregation, and Congregationalists declared themselves to have 'no head, priest, prophet or king, save Christ', and to be 'without pope, prelate, presbytery, prince or parliament'. In England, these Independent churches emerge from a refusal to accept Charles II's Act of Uniformity (1662), and hence are a sub-set of the Non-Conformist churches.

Historically, Congregationist doctrine has been based on Reformation principles. They accepted a slightly modified form of the *Westminster Confession*, known as the *Savoy Declaration* on account of a meeting of 'elders and messengers' at the Savoy Palace, London, in 1658. In common with Calvinists they affirmed the authority of Scripture, the doctrine of the Trinity, salvation by faith alone, and the authenticity of two sacraments (baptism and communion), not seven. Each Congregational church determines its own affairs, including the appointment of elders, deacons and ministers (sometimes called pastors); even the minister is subject to congregational decisions. Worship has no prescribed form, normally consisting of hymns, prayers, Bible reading and a sermon.

Congregational independence has associated problems. Congregationalists have emphasized the importance of trained ministers, rather than leaders drawn from the ranks of each congregation, and this raises issues about the training of clergy. In England the situation was compounded by the exclusion of dissenters from universities—a situation that caused Non-Conformists to set up their own colleges. The Congregational Union of England and Wales was set up in 1832 to co-ordinate affairs of Congregationalists nationwide. (In 1965 the body became the Congregational Church of England and Wales.) Such affairs included mission, worship resources and the training of clergy. In 1955 The National Association of Congregational Christian Churches (NACCC) was founded in the USA, although some Congregationalist congregations did not join, but preferred to remain in the Conservative Congregational Christian Conference (CCCC), which was established in 1948 in an endeavour to stem the rising tide of theological liberalism. Similar umbrella organizations have been formed in other countries. It may be thought that there is a contradiction between congregational autonomy and national bodies with apparent supervisory oversight.

However, any decisions of these councils are advisory only, and congregations may disregard them. There is no obligation, for example, for a congregation to use the denomination's hymnary or other worship material.

In the second half of the twentieth century, ecumenical interests prompted Congregational churches to enter into negotiations with Reformed churches, and in the USA in 1957 the General Council of Congregational Churches merged with the Evangelical and Reformed Church to form the United Church of Christ. In 1972 in England Congregationalists merged with the English Presbyterians, becoming the United Reformed Church (URC). In 1981 the Reformed Association of the Churches of Christ entered into the consolidation, and in 2000 the Congregational Union of Scotland came into the URC. Other ecumenical mergers occurred in different countries worldwide. Invariably, there are those who object to the terms of ecumenical mergers, and numerous congregations declined to come into these unions. Congregationalism therefore lives on in groupings of independent churches retaining congregational autonomy. In the USA, the National Association of Congregational Christian Churches (NACCC) represents the interests of some of these, while in England the Evangelical Fellowship of Congregational Churches was set up in 1967 as a stance against theological liberalism, and remained in existence after the 1972 merger. Likewise, despite ecumenical unions, Presbyterians also remain: either these churches did not enter into ecumenical negotiations, or else they seceded, forming groups of churches retaining a Presbyterian structure. In some cases the Presbytery embraces only a small handful of congregations. Worldwide, however, some fifty million Presbyterians continue to exist. The number of adherents to Congregationalism is more difficult to determine, since it is difficult to know which congregations to count. Adherents claiming Congregationalist affiliation might be between two and three million, while the total membership of independent churches worldwide may be around 303.3 million.

Baptists

Like the Congregationalists, the Baptists have congregational autonomy, but are brought together by national and international associations, such as the American Baptist Association, the Baptist Union (in the UK), and—worldwide—the Baptist World Alliance. The main feature associated with the Baptists is believer's baptism, although they are not unique in their insistence that membership should exclusively be by immersion, and confession of one's faith at an age at which one is capable of understanding Christian belief and practice. (Adventists and Pentecostalists also admit adults to membership through baptism by immersion.)

Historically, the rise of the Baptist churches is associated with the Anabaptist movement of the Protestant Reformation in Europe. The prefix *ana* is the Greek word meaning 'again', and the Anabaptists urged that paedo-baptism was insufficient and had to be complemented by the adult rite. In England, their origins are traced to John Smyth, who emigrated to The Netherlands, where in 1609 he baptized himself, together with 36 others. Not all Baptists are happy to acknowledge these origins, however. Some claim that they anticipated the Protestant Reformation, pre-dating Martin Luther, who opposed rather than supported them. Some Baptists have also claimed that their version of Christianity is the primordial one, based on New Testament principles, that the early Jerusalem Church baptized adults by immersion on confession of faith, and that the existence of Baptist congregations was perpetuated throughout history up to the present day. The view that there have always been historical landmarks of Baptist practice came to be known as 'landmarkism', and the doctrine implies that the Baptist Church predates Roman Catholicism, Eastern Orthodoxy and also Protestantism.

There exist two main types of Baptist church: the General Baptists and the Particular Baptists. The latter are Calvinist in theology, and are dominant in the USA and UK, teaching that Christ's atoning work was for the elect only. The former hold that salvation is offered to all—a doctrine that is sometimes called Arminianism, after the Dutch theologian Jacobus Arminius (1560–1609). The sixteenth-century European Anabaptists gave rise to a number of Baptist groups who set themselves up in communities—for example, the Amish, the Hutterites and the Mennonites.

A number of key principles are associated with the Baptist movement. Baptists have emphasized the freedom of religion and freedom of conscience. They do not acknowledge a creed, holding that Christian doctrine should be derived from the authority of the Bible. Baptists have drawn up a number of Confessions, and each Baptist Association has formulated its own. However, no external body has the right to impose a statement of belief on a congregation. Freedom of religion entails a belief that Church and state should be separate, and that there should be no state interference in religious matters. In England and in America Baptists championed the right of freedom from the state, and in America, Baptist leaders such as John Leland, were influential in achieving the First Amendment's inclusion in the US constitution: 'Congress shall make no law respecting an establishment of religion, or prohibiting the free exercise thereof.' On the recommendation of the Baptist World Alliance, congregations are invited to celebrate annually a Human Rights Sunday.

Like the other Non-Conformists, Baptist worship has no universal set form, but is determined by local practice. Communion is celebrated, normally once a month, or even once a quarter, at the congregation's discretion. There is usually a trained leader (a minister or pastor) for each congregation, although there is disagreement about whether he or she should be formally ordained. The Reformation principle of 'the priesthood of all believers' is held to imply that all Christians are equal, and that any act of ordination should not confer special powers to the minister; hence some churches simply 'admit' the minister to the congregation.

The Southern Baptists are not only the largest Baptist denomination, but the largest Protestant denomination in the USA. It is also one of the most conservative. Originating in Augusta, Georgia in 1845, the Southern Baptist Convention (SBC) split from the Northern Baptists over the issue of slavery, which the Southern Baptists supported. Southern Baptists tend to regard the Bible as inerrant, using it to justify practices such as the subordination of women: women may not assume a teaching role, and they are opposed to women's ordination. The SBC is opposed to homosexuality, and is unequivocally anti-abortion. It is not in favour of ecumenism, and does not belong to the National Council of the Churches of Christ or the World Council of Churches, although it is a member of the Baptist World Alliance. In 1995, however, the SBC took the step of denouncing racism—a reversal of its historical stance on race.

Adventism

A further strand of Protestantism is Adventism. At its inception, Adventism was not a separate denomination, but a current of thought running through nineteenth-century American Protestantism. Particularly influential was William Miller (1782–1849), a Baptist preacher in Vermont. Adventists were keen to interpret some of the more cryptic prophetic writings, especially Daniel and Revelation. (They believe in the inerrancy of Scripture.) Miller's belief that Christ would return in 1843 stemmed from his interpretation of Dan. 18:14: 'Unto two thousand and three hundred days; then shall the sanctuary be cleansed.' The word 'day' in connection with biblical prophecy was typically interpreted as 'year', drawing on Ezekiel's words, 'A day for a year, a day for a year, is what I have given you' (4:6). Different Adventists made different and complex calculations relating to Daniel's prophecy, but Miller's calculations led him to believe that the end of human affairs could be expected in 1843. Following a series of articles which he wrote for the Baptist newspaper, *The Vermont Telegraph*, Miller gained support at a national level. When the date passed uneventfully, Miller acknowledged his error, but continued to preach that Christ's return was nonetheless to be expected soon. His follower Samuel S. Snow undertook some recalculation, alighting on the date of 22 October 1844. Again, the date passed uneventfully, and became known as the 'Great Disappointment'.

Following Miller's failed predictions, Adventism went in different directions. Apart from the disillusioned followers who left the movement, some Adventists favoured recalculation, while others 'spiritualized' the expected events. Particularly important in this regard was Hiram Edson (1806–1882), who claimed to receive a vision that Miller's 1844 predictions were correct, but related to spiritual rather than physical events: Christ had begun his heavenly rule, rather than an earthly. This interpretation was endorsed by Ellen G. White (1837–1915) who became the founder of the Seventh-day Adventist Church. It is important to recognize that the terms 'Second Adventism' and 'Seventh-day Adventism' have different meanings: the former refers to a belief in Christ's second advent (or second coming), while the latter refers to the seventh day of the week—Saturday—the day on which Seventh-day Adventists worship. The term 'Second Adventism' is generally applied to those Adventist groups who do not trace their origins to Ellen G. White, and who continue to worship on Sundays.

The Seventh-day Adventist Church was formally established in 1863, with 3,500 members. It affirmed the continuing Spirit of Prophecy, evidenced in Ellen G. White's visions and writings, the authority of which was secondary to Scripture. There is no official creed that serves as a test of membership. One early Adventist minister, J. N. Loughborough (1832–1924) wrote, 'The first step of apostasy is to get up a creed, telling us what we shall believe. The second is, to make that creed a test of fellowship. The third is to try members by that creed. The fourth to denounce as heretics those who do not believe that creed. And fifth, to commence persecution against such' (*Review and Herald*, 8 October 1861).

In the course of their history, Adventists have formulated statements of 'Fundamental Beliefs', but with the main purpose of dealing with inquiries. Twenty-five such principles were set out in 1872, and these were expanded to 28 in 2005. Principal beliefs include the inerrancy of Scripture, Christ's imminent second coming, and his 'investigative judgement', which began in 1844. According to Adventist teaching, Christ has begun the process leading to humankind's final judgement, examining the deeds of those who died to determine their eligibility for immortality. Adventists have typically rejected the notion of eternal torment, and instead believe in 'soul sleep'—a state of oblivion that awaits the unredeemed. When Christ returns, he will resurrect the righteous, who will reign with him for a thousand years, while the earth will become desolate, inhabited only by Satan and his angels. After that time, the unrighteous will be raised for final judgement, when the New Jerusalem will descend from heaven to earth, surrounding Satan, his angels and the unrighteous with fire, which will consume them, cleanse the earth and free it eternally from sin.

The keeping of the Sabbath is important. In accordance with Jewish custom, it begins on the Friday evening, and in many homes is brought in with a Sabbath meal. Most Adventists refrain from secular activities, such as watching television or participating in sports, and from unnecessary work. The Jewish Law is still regarded as having an application in Christian times, particularly the Ten Commandments. Many Adventists also conform to Jewish dietary laws, avoiding pork and shellfish, while many are completely vegetarian, believing that a vegetarian lifestyle is healthier. Ever since its inception, Adventism has been concerned with health and diet, and the Kellogg brothers—John Harvey Kellogg (1860–1951) and Will Keith Kellogg (1860–1951), famed for their commercial marketing of cornflakes—were Adventists.

The Methodist Churches

Another significant strand of Protestantism is Methodism. Although the Methodists originated from within the Church of England, they consider themselves unequivocally Protestant, not merely 'catholic and reformed'. The denomination's origins go back to John Wesley (1703–1791) and his brother Charles Wesley (1707–1788). While students at Christ Church in

Oxford, they became members of a society known as the 'Holy Club'—a group of men who met together for prayer and Bible study, setting great emphasis on the cultivation of deep inner faith. As a young man, Wesley came to attend the Moravian Society in London. (The Moravians are a Protestant denomination, founded by Jan Hus [John Huss, c. 1372–1415] in fourteenth-century Bohemia—now the Czech Republic—and who expanded internationally through missionary activity.) At a Moravian gathering in 1738, Wesley underwent an experience about which he said, 'I found my heart strangely warmed.' He regarded this as a conversion experience, in which the Holy Spirit entered his life to sanctify it.

One of the Holy Club's members was George Whitefield (1714–1770) who spearheaded the Great Awakening—a large-scale religious revival in Britain and America in the 1730s, which involved large open-air rallies, and which was a major influence on the Holiness Movement and the formation of the Holiness Churches, which include the Wesleyan Church, the Free Methodist Church, the Church of the Nazarene and the Salvation Army. After returning to England from America, George Whitefield invited John Wesley to preach at one of his open-air rallies, and this invitation heralded a lifetime of open-air preaching up and down the country. Preaching was done in the open air, partly because Whitefield and Wesley had been excluded from the pulpits of the Church of England, and also because of their desire to attract people, particularly from the working classes, who did not normally attend Sunday worship. It is estimated that, during his lifetime, John Wesley travelled some 250,000 miles and preached some 40,000 sermons. Wesley intended to promote his evangelism in America, and wanted the Bishop of London to ordain ministers for this purpose. When the bishop declined, Wesley conducted his own ordinations, despite the fact that, not being a bishop, he was not empowered to do so. This heralded the Wesleys' break with the Church of England. His first Conference, with a hundred nominated members, was set up in 1784.

Methodism has its own distinctive structure. Its central governing body is known as the Connexion, which holds an Annual Conference. Methodist congregations are grouped into circuits, and a group of circuits forms a district. Districts have Chairs to convene their proceedings, while circuits have a Circuit Leadership Team, comprising a Superintendent Minister and (lay) Circuit Stewards. Congregational ministers are normally expected to remain for a period of four years: this is a measure to prevent their work simply becoming routine, and to inject new ideas and approaches into congregational life.

Different Methodist congregations adopt different styles of worship, some in 'high church' and some in 'low church' tradition. Their *Book of Offices* is their liturgical manual. Two sacraments are celebrated (baptism and communion), although it is acknowledged that these are only two out of many other means of grace. The Methodist liturgical calendar has its own distinctive features. There is an annual Covenant Service, in which the congregation renews its 'covenant' with God. The Covenant Prayer is recited, which runs as follows:

> I am no longer my own but yours.
> Put me to what you will,
> rank me with whom you will;
> put me to doing,
> put me to suffering;
> let me be employed for you,
> or laid aside for you,
> exalted for you,
> or brought low for you;
> let me be full,
> let me be empty,
> let me have all things,
> let me have nothing:
> I freely and wholeheartedly yield all things
> to your pleasure and disposal.
> And now, glorious and blessed God,
> Father, Son and Holy Spirit,
> you are mine and I am yours.

The Covenant Service is usually held in September, when it marks the beginning of the Methodist liturgical year (although some congregations hold it at the beginning of the calendar year). When held in September, this marks the beginning of Kingdomtide, which is a period of thirteen weeks leading up to Advent. During this period Methodists intensify their charitable work to the poor—sometimes referred to as 'social holiness'. Methodism is also particularly associated with singing, which plays a major part in worship. John and Charles Wesley were prolific hymn writers (the latter wrote some 6,500 hymns during his lifetime), and Charles Wesley's son and grandson—Samuel Wesley and Samuel Sebastian Wesley—were organists and composers. Their hymns and music are used throughout Western Christianity, and are by no means confined to Methodism.

In common with other Protestant denominations, Methodists affirm the Apostles' and the Nicene Creeds, although these are not normally used liturgically. They believe that salvation is for all, not merely for a body of predestined 'elect' people: thus Methodists tend to be Arminian, rather than Calvinist in their theology. There are exceptions: Calvinistic Methodists are found in Wales, for example, and are also known as the Presbyterian Church in Wales. Early in the twentieth century, there were several Methodist denominations, principally the Wesleyan Methodist Church, the Primitive Methodists and the United Methodist Church. (The last of these is not to be confused with the American denomination of the same name, which remains in existence.) Primitive Methodists believed that through time Methodism had departed from the Wesleys' original intentions, and they wanted greater emphasis placed on simplicity in worship, the role of the laity, political engagement and mission to the poor. In 1932, these three strands came together as the Methodist Church of Great Britain. The United Methodist Church, as the name implies, was a union of a number of other smaller Methodist denominations, formed in 1907.

The Salvation Army

One of Methodism's offshoots is the Salvation Army. Founded by William Booth (1829–1912), who was a Methodist minister, and his wife Catherine Booth (1829–1890), the organization was founded in 1865 as the East London Christian Mission, and sought to offer salvation to the poor. It offered help to alcoholics, prostitutes, drug addicts and the destitute, offering—in William Booth's words—three Ss: soup, soap and salvation. In 1879 the Mission was organized along military lines, with military ranks and uniforms. Its motto is 'Blood and fire', referring to Jesus' sacrifice on the cross and to the Holy Spirit's descent as 'tongues of fire' to the early apostles. Thus, in line with the Holiness Movement, the Salvation Army attaches importance to securing conversions, to personal sanctification and to offer social and spiritual care especially to the disadvantaged members of society. In 2008 the Salvation Army reported operating in 115 countries, claiming over a million 'senior soldiers', with approximately 360,000 'junior soldiers', and nearly 200,000 adherents. Its international work now includes offering aid for national disasters such as floods and earthquakes, as well as ministering to individuals' needs.

The Salvation Army, Walsall, England
Photograph: George Chryssides

Pentecostalism

A further consequence of the Holiness Movement is the rise
of Pentecostalism. Pentecostalism emphasizes the early disciples'
experience in the upper room on the Day of Pentecost, where the Holy
Spirit descended and enabled them to 'speak in tongues'. Pentecostalism
emphasizes a 'second blessing' that is held to follow water baptism.
John the Baptist said concerning Jesus, 'He will baptize you with the
Holy Spirit and with fire' (Mt. 3:11). Pentecostalists claim that the
phenomenon of speaking in tongues—'glossolaliation'—goes back to
the early Church, and Paul discusses it at length in 1 Corinthians (chs
12 and 14). The modern Pentecostalist movement, however, goes back
to the early twentieth century, and its origins can be traced to Charles
Parham (1873–1929), who was Director of Bethel Bible College in
Topeka, Kansas. Parham taught that 'baptism in the Spirit' was a
spiritual gift, a second work of grace, providing sanctification after
conversion and baptism. In 1901, Agnes Ozman, one of his students,

began to speak in an unknown tongue. Initially the phenomenon was ridiculed by others, until the Azusa Street Revival in Los Angeles in 1906. This famous event was led by William J. Seymour (1870–1922), a pastor in the African Methodist Episcopal Church, who was influenced by Parham's teaching. Seymour's congregation began to have ecstatic experiences, causing them to glossolaliate. The congregation included a mixture of black and white participants—unusual in America at the time—illustrating Pentecostalism's blend of Wesleyan Holiness with African-style worship. This exuberance and spontaneity in worship continued for several years, and the phenomenon spread internationally, reaching Scandinavia, Europe, Latin America and Africa. Initially the phenomenon occurred within mainstream churches, where it is still sometimes found. However, mainstream Protestants tended to disapprove, and frequently expelled supporters of Pentecostalism, causing them to form their separate denominations.

Pentecostalists are among the largest groups of Protestants. There are at least 115 million adherents worldwide—indeed, some estimates are more than double that number. One source reckons that some eleven thousand different Pentecostal denominations exist globally. While some congregations are small, some of them are 'mega-churches', with a capacity for thousands of worshippers. The largest is Yoidi Full Gospel Church in Korea, claiming over 780,000 members. Pentecostalists do not belong to national Councils of Churches, or to the World Council of Churches, although they are party to more evangelical ecumenical organizations, such as the World Evangelical Alliance. Their resistance to ecumenism is mainly due to the liberal stance of other denominations, particularly in regard to modern biblical scholarship and to their liberal stance on moral issues, such as homosexuality.

The words 'Full Gospel' and 'Foursquare Gospel' feature frequently in the names of Pentecostal denominations. The 'Full Gospel' consists of five basic tenets associated with the Holiness Movement: Christ as Saviour, Christ as Sanctifier, Christ as Healer, Christ as Baptizer in the Holy Spirit, and Christ as the Coming King. These key principles are associated with those Pentecostal Churches who are in the Wesleyan Holiness tradition. In 1910, a dispute arose concerning the second of these principles, when William H. Durham (1873–1912), who became the pastor of the First Pentecostal Church in Chicago, proposed his 'finished work' theory. According to Durham, sanctification was not an on-going perfecting process, otherwise Christ's redeeming work was not fully accomplished. Sanctification, he argued, meant being set apart as holy, rather than becoming perfected. Those who followed Durham therefore frequently adopt the term 'Four Square' as part of their names, indicating the acceptance of four, not five of these characteristics of Christ. Examples of these churches include the Assemblies of God, the Pentecostal Church of God, the International Church of the Foursquare Gospel, and the Open Bible Standard Church.

There is a further type of Pentecostalism, known as Oneness Pentecostalism or 'Jesus Only' Pentecostalism. This branch of Pentecostalism is non-Trinitarian, and took its rise in 1906 with the foundation of the Pentecostal Assemblies of the World (1906), consisting largely of Black Pentecostals. Early leaders included pastors R. E. McAllister, Frank J. Ewart, Glen A. Cook, and Garfield Thomas Haywood. Oneness Pentecostals point out that the early Church's practice was to baptize in the name of Jesus Christ, rather than to use a threefold Trinitarian formula (e.g. Acts 2:38; 8:14). Although Jesus referred to 'the name of the Father and of the Son and of the Holy Spirit' in his Great Commission (Mt. 28:19), Oneness Pentecostals point out that he uses the word 'name' in the singular, and that, as Paul states, 'in Christ all the fullness of the Deity lives in bodily form' (Col. 2:9).

The distinctive feature of Pentecostalism, which marked it off from its Holiness roots, was glossolaliation. This phenomenon is not always exhibited during worship, however, but is often experienced when the exuberance of Pentecostal worship reaches its climax. Pentecostalism tends to rely on spontaneity, informality, participation and experiential worship, and tends to be relatively unstructured. Services will certainly include hymns, readings from the Bible (which is regarded as inerrant), prayers and usually a sermon. Members of the congregation may come forward during the worship to read a Bible passage that they feel the Holy Spirit has led them to share. Prayers may be contributed directly by the congregation, and they are invariably extempore. Members frequently participate by adding their personal 'Amen', 'Hallelujah' or some other brief indication of assent to parts of prayers, or at points in the sermon, thus appropriating the sentiments expressed, rather than allowing the leader to deliver a monologue. Worship is invariably lively, often with clapping, shouting and sometimes dancing.

Healing is also of great importance in Pentecostalism. Pentecostals firmly believe that the age of miracles is not dead, and that Christ's healing powers can still be exercised by his followers. It is not uncommon for a Pentecostal service to conclude by inviting those who need healing to come forward for the laying on of hands. Use is sometimes made of 'prayer cloths', which are taken to the sick to mediate healing. This practice echoes Luke's account of Paul's healings in Ephesus, where cloths and garments that Paul had touched were taken to the sick, resulting in miraculous cures and the casting out of demons. Pentecostals observe three 'ordinances' (they do not call them sacraments): baptism, communion and foot washing. Baptism is administered to adults, by immersion, on profession of faith. Communion makes use of baker's bread and grape juice, rather than alcoholic wine, and both elements are brought to the congregation, the 'wine' being administered in individual glasses. Foot washing is a rite to instil humility, in accordance with Christ's own example, when he washed his disciples' feet in the upper room before the Last Supper (Jn 13:4-17). These ritual acts are known as ordinances, since they were instituted and commanded by Christ. Jesus said, 'you also should wash one another's feet' (Jn 13:14): this is taken to be an instruction to continue performing this act.

Although Pentecostalism is a movement in its own right, ecstatic activities such as speaking in tongues and casting out demons have found their way into other branches of Christianity, including Roman Catholicism, and Pope John Paul II expressed approval of the Catholic charismatic revival which arose during his period of office.

Conclusion

Protestantism is characterized by its diversity, and inevitably it has only been possible to cover its best known varieties. In general, the radical forms of Protestantism are characterized by their free style of worship, their acknowledgement of Scripture rather than ecclesiastical authority as a source of doctrine, and an emphasis on divine grace as the means of salvation, rather than works. Many of the Protestant denominations claim that their governance is in accordance with early Church practice, although, as we have shown, there is considerable diversity as to how the various offices mentioned in the New Testament are to be interpreted. Unlike Eastern Orthodoxy and Roman Catholicism, Protestant denominations do not claim exclusivity, acknowledging each other as legitimate forms of the Christian faith. While evangelical Protestants frequently claim that personal conversion is essential for salvation, it is not usually claimed that any one denomination exclusively offers spiritual re-birth. Organizations claiming to be the sole ark of salvation, such as the Jehovah's Witnesses, tend to be regarded as inauthentic expressions of the Christian faith, and frequently incur hostility. Because of their mutual respect, Protestant denominations have been able to work ecumenically and, as we have seen, made some progress in coming together institutionally.

12

Challenges to Christianity

The past two centuries witnessed enormous changes in the Christian religion. The intellectual climate of earlier parts of this period, at least in Europe, is sometimes referred to as the European Enlightenment, or simply the Enlightenment. The timescale and the prevalent ideas are contested. Some regard it as beginning in the seventeenth century, tracing it back to René Descartes' *Discourse on Method* (1637) and Thomas Hobbes' *Leviathan* (1651). New ideas seldom have an absolute beginning in time, and defining the Enlightenment is not as important as identifying a number of ways in which the Christian faith, as traditionally understood, was called into question.

The period was characterized by two key principles: freedom and reason. Until the Enlightenment, the authority of the Church held sway, and doctrines were accepted as matters of faith. True, the Protestant Reformation was a questioning of authority, but it was a questioning of one particular source of authority, namely papal authority. The Protestant principle of the priesthood of all believers did not entail a democratization or relativity of truth, but rather the directness of access of all believers to divine authority. Protestant churches maintained their own authoritative structures, with the Bible as the supreme standard of authority, with the minister or pastor as the authoritative teacher and interpreter of God's word, and—with the exception of the Congregationalist and independent churches—a hierarchy of leaders or church courts, each exercising its own authority.

The emphasis on reason caused some key thinkers to abandon religion entirely. The French Free-Thinkers included Denis Diderot (1713–1784), Jean le Rond d'Alembert (1717–1783) and Voltaire (François-Marie Arouet; 1694–1778), whose *Encyclopédie* included an article entitled 'Libre-Penseur', defending atheism. In Scotland, David Hume (1711–1776) argued that religion, not being based on reason or empirical observation, might be dismissed as 'sophistry and illusion'. Other thinkers of the period did not go so far, of course. Descartes himself used reason to establish God's existence, as did Immanuel Kant (1724–1804). Equally important in the Enlightenment period was the rise of empiricism. While purporting to rely on deductive reasoning to prove the existence of the self, God and the world, Descartes' *Meditations* concluded with the contention that the human mind was immune from deception so long as it relied on 'clear and distinct ideas'. This notion was later developed by John Locke (1632–1704), who contended that the human mind began as a *tabula rasa* on which sensation and reflection provided ideas by means of the senses. Locke's empiricism was developed further by George Berkeley (1685–1753), who was an Anglican bishop in Ireland, and later by Hume.

Reason and sensory observation are, of course, particularly associated with the sciences, and the Enlightenment period saw an advancement of science. By this time the Church had already come to terms with Galileo Galilei (1564–1642), and Nicolaus Copernicus (1473–1543), who had demonstrated, contrary to the traditional belief, that the earth was not the centre of the universe around which the celestial bodies moved. This was a conclusion that cut humanity down to size: if this were the case, was the earth really the centre of God's providential plan? Science in the Enlightenment era included further advancements in astronomy, mathematics, physics, chemistry and medicine, heralding the eclipse of alchemy and astrology. Advances in these disciplines did not have a direct effect on religion, but were part of the *Zeitgeist*, encouraging scientific critical thought to become transposed to the field of religion and religious scholarship. Joseph Priestley (1733–1804), the first scientist to isolate oxygen, was as much a theologian as a scientist: a Unitarian by commitment, much of his writing was directed to arguing for the unreasonableness of the doctrine of the Trinity.

Also associated with the Enlightenment era was its emphasis on human rights. Thomas Hobbes' influential work *Leviathan* challenged the accepted doctrine of the Divine Right of Kings by proposing a 'social contract' model of the state, whereby citizens came together and agreed to forfeit some of their natural rights in order to enjoy the security afforded by the state. A similar theory was later advanced by John Locke, who contended that each human had inalienable natural rights to life, liberty and property. These two thinkers wanted to take religion in different directions, however: Hobbes argued that uniformity of religion was necessary for a stable civil society, while Locke's essay *A*

Letter concerning Toleration (1689) urged the case for religious diversity. Locke's toleration did not extend to atheists or to Roman Catholics, however, since he believed that covenants and oaths could have no binding force on atheists, and that Roman Catholics had effectively subjected themselves to the 'service of another prince', namely the Pope. The concern for human rights manifested itself during the Enlightenment period in a number of famous declarations of human rights, notably the *US Declaration of Independence* (1776), written principally by Thomas Jefferson; the *US Bill of Rights* (1789), consisting of the first ten Amendments, including the First Amendment granting freedom of religion, and the *French Declaration of the Rights of Man and of the Citizen* (1789).

All these figures and key events in themselves had little effect on Christianity in Europe and America, but collectively they marked a transition from an era that relied on faith and subjection to authority. Belief in the veracity of the Bible was largely unquestioned, and popular piety revered the Church's saints, venerating their relics, and accepting the Church's accounts of their lives, including astonishing miracles associated with them. In his *Enquiry concerning Human Understanding* (1748), Hume included a chapter arguing forcibly against miracles, emphasizing their unscientific nature, and contending that they lacked proper verification by reliable witnesses. While the Enlightenment's principles encouraged freedom and diversity, its supporters' regard for reason prevented them from allowing religious faith to go unchallenged.

Charles Darwin and the Challenge of Evolution

One of the most serious and divisive challenges to Christianity arose in the nineteenth century with Darwin's theory of evolution. Although many conservative Christians perceive Charles Darwin (1809–1882) as an enemy of the faith, Darwin did not set out to attack Christianity, and he was not an outsider. Darwin was baptized in the Church of England, went to a Church of England boarding school, and studied at the University of Cambridge with a view to entering the Anglican priesthood. Like the majority of church members, he accepted the inerrancy of the Bible. Darwin appears to have lost his faith later in life, however, describing himself as an agnostic in 1879. Nonetheless, when he died he was given a state funeral, and he was buried in Westminster Abbey. Darwin was not the first evolutionary theorist; ideas of human and societal evolution and progress were very much part of the nineteenth-century European *Zeitgeist*, and promoted by thinkers like Jean-Baptiste Lamarck (1744–1829). Darwin's contribution was to apply evolutionary ideas to biology, and to contend that species evolved and adapted over time.

Darwin's seminal work, *On the Origin of Species*, was published in 1859, and was the work of much research, carried out on a global scale. In December 1831 he embarked on his famous round-the-world expedition on the HMS Beagle, returning in October 1836. During this time he noted the variety of species, their geographical distribution and distinctively local features. The geologist Charles Lyell (1797–1875) met Darwin on his return, and the two scientists became lifelong friends. Lyell's geological research confirmed Darwin's theories: fossils that he discovered suggested that earlier examples of species had different physical characteristics, and in some cases were millions of years old, thus allowing ample time to evolve and adapt. Some Christians subscribe to the popular, but erroneous belief that Darwinism entails that humans are descended from apes. Darwin never suggested this, but rather contended that all species derived from common ancestors. The terms 'natural selection' and 'survival of the fittest' are typically associated with Darwin, who held that species either changed their attributes in order to adapt to new environments, or else became extinct if they were unable to do so. The fact that certain species are only found in certain geographical locations, coupled with the fact that there are geographical differences among the same species, indicated to Darwin that transmutation took place as species migrated. Darwin's theories proved particularly important for subsequent developments in biology, and later findings in biology and in geology have tended to confirm Darwin's and Lyell's research. With the discovery of DNA in 1953 by James Watson and Francis Crick, molecular biologists have been able to ascertain that humans and chimpanzees have a mere one to two per cent difference in the units that comprise their genetic structure. With the help of radioactive dating, mineralized skeletons have been reckoned to be some 550 million years old, with vertebrates dating from around 370 million years ago. The earth itself is reckoned to have become a solid body some 4.5 billion years before our time.

Darwinism proved to be particularly worrying to Protestants, being a threat to the authority of Scripture. Since Protestantism relied on the principle of *sola scriptura*, Darwinism appeared to erode its sole basis of authority, for a number of reasons. It contradicted the biblical account of creation, which told that the world was created in six days: according to Darwin and Lyell, it took millions of years for different species to evolve. Although the Bible does not explicitly name a date for the creation of the world, the genealogical information provided in various places, if collated, suggested that the world was less than six millennia old. A favoured date for creation's inception was reckoned to be 4004 BCE. James Ussher, the Bishop of Armagh, had defined the date of creation as 22 October 4004 BCE, and he even specified the time—six o'clock in the evening. (Ussher is often ridiculed for this seemingly impossible precision. However, he is assuming that creation must have begun on the first day of the first Jewish new year, taking into account that the Jewish day begins at dusk, not midnight or dawn. The reference to fruit in the Garden of Eden story is a further detail suggesting an autumn date to biblical literalists.)

Evolutionism also implied that *homo sapiens* was not a special creation, as the Bible implies. The Genesis narrative suggests that men and women were the pinnacle of creation, created especially for God's purpose, with dominion over and responsibility for creation. Christianity has had little to say about the role of animals in the divine purpose. Although some of the saints such as Francis of Assisi have shown kindness to them, it is typically assumed that they do not have souls, and will not gain admission to the kingdom of heaven, since they are incapable of acquiring faith, and cannot understand or accept the gospel. Since evolutionism seems to imply that there is no sharp demarcation between humans and animals, it appears to undermine the notion that salvation is a special privilege afforded to elected human beings.

The idea that humanity had a divine purpose linked up with the whole question of God's existence. The teleological argument for God's existence (better known as the Argument from Design), relied on a comparison between the fabrication of material objects with a purpose, and humanity, who is destined to fulfil God's purpose. An oft-cited proponent of this argument was William Paley (1743–1805), renowned for his 'watchmaker' analogy. Paley's argument, in brief, was that, if we found a watch lying on the ground we would assume, on account of its complexity and interrelationship of its parts, that it was an artefact that had a maker, who created it for a definite purpose—unlike a stone, which has no such apparent design or function. The human body has even greater complexity, and its parts, such as the eye, have even greater complexity and clear functions; hence there is all the more reason to believe that the human body, and indeed the whole world, has been created by a divine watchmaker, whom we call God. Interestingly, Darwin was familiar with Paley's work, and took aboard the idea of things and creatures being adapted for particular purposes. By contrast, however, Darwin's evolutionary theory taught adaptation, but only for survival, not for any more ultimate divine purpose.

Although evolutionary theory does not afford the sole ground of criticism of Paley, as David Hume pointed out in his *Dialogues concerning Natural Religion*, evolutionary theory undermines the argument by affording an alternative explanation. An organism's complexity may not necessarily be attributable to a divine watchmaker, but may be the result of a lengthy process by which it evolves. Other organisms that are less fitted for a purpose and do not adapt adequately to their environment simply fail to survive. Because of natural selection, the less remarkable examples of life forms simply die out, and we are left with the better ones, which are more fit for purpose. Evolutionary theory provided an explanation for the world's existence without recourse to a creator God. Not only did evolution offer an alternative explanation for design in the universe, but it presented definite obstacles to belief in a providential divine plan. 'Survival of the fittest' entailed that there were many forms of species that died off through failure to adapt. This seemed a tremendous waste. If an omnipotent benevolent God designed and created the universe, why had he created aspects of it for no apparent purpose, simply to become extinct?

Because of its apparent threat to the Christian faith, four US states—Arkansas, Mississippi, Oklahoma and Tennessee—passed laws in the 1920s prohibiting the teaching of evolution in schools. This gave rise to the Scopes trial, sometimes known as 'the monkey trial' of 1925 and described as 'the world's most famous court case'. John T. Scopes was a high school teacher who was accused of teaching evolutionary theory to his pupils, in contravention of state law. Whether Scopes actually did so is unclear: he claimed merely to have been using a standard textbook, which explained what Darwin's ideas were. Scopes's defence was financed by the American Civil Liberties Union (ACLU), and it received extensive media coverage. Not only was it the first US trial to be broadcast on national radio, but it was also the subject of the play *Inherit the Wind* (1955), a Hollywood film in 1960 and a number of television films. The outcome of the trial was that Scopes was found guilty, and ordered to pay a 100-dollar fine. He was later acquitted on appeal, but only on the grounds that the penalty was excessive.

The controversy over evolution raised important issues regarding religion and education in US schools. The First Amendment of the American Constitution required a separation of Church and state, and in 1947 the Supreme Court ruled that such separation applied to individual US states, and not merely to Congress. This judgement therefore entailed that the teaching of any subject, including science, should not favour one particular set of religious ideas above others. On the one hand, to teach evolutionary theory as scientific fact apparently disparaged belief in biblical inerrancy, while on the other hand, promoting creationism over evolution would give those with a literal belief in the Book of Genesis a privileged status. One apparent solution to the problem was to define the alternative to Darwinism in such a way as to imply that it was a rival scientific theory rather than a religious alternative, and creationism assumed the alternative name of 'Creation Science'. A number of states passed laws during the 1970s and 1980s requiring that equal time should be given to teaching evolution and to 'creation science'. However, in 1987 the Supreme Court ruled that such laws were in violation of the First Amendment, since they were designed to promote Christian biblicism over evolutionary theory. A subsequent initiative to substitute the expression 'Intelligent Design' for 'Creation Science' was challenged in 2004 in Pennsylvania, where the judge ruled that the term was simply a re-labelling of creationism and religiously motivated. A further attempt at challenging evolution is the use of disclaimers in textbooks. In various US states, biology textbooks bear a warning, such as the statement that evolutionary theory cannot explain the origins of life, or that the material is controversial and should be critically assessed. (The exact wording varies according to the state.)

In Britain, the conflict between evolutionism and creationism was nothing like as fierce as it was in the USA. There were several reasons why this was so. First, there has been a greater propensity in the States towards creationism and biblical fundamentalism. One 2005 survey concluded that some 64 per cent of American citizens believed that humans were directly created by God, compared with 22 per cent in Britain (Williams 2006). (Statistics vary in different surveys, depending on what respondents understand by evolution and direct creation, but there is undoubtedly a markedly greater tendency to toward biblical literalism in the USA.) Second, Britain has not attempted to separate Church and state, as the USA has done. Having established churches in Britain ensures a greater linkage between religion and society, and various Education Acts have made religious education a compulsory school subject, although there has been provision for parents withdrawing their children, if they wish. This situation has tended to encourage lively debate rather than an enforced silence on the topic. This does not mean that relationships between creationists and evolutionists are amicable in Britain. On the contrary, there has been much hostility to Darwin from the evangelical Protestant camp, and a substantial amount of popular literature has been written, defending the Bible against evolutionary theory.

Popular evangelical Protestantism has devised a number of defences against Darwin. One line is to question the scientific in favour of evolution. Proponents of evolution have been accused of exaggerating the time scales involved in the production of phenomena such as stalactites, volcanic rock formations and fossils (Grohman 2010). The oldest plant life, it is argued, is no more than 4,300 years old, consistent with the creationist notion that we really live on a young earth. Faced with problems such as light taking millions of years to travel from stars to reach the earth, some fundamentalists will question whether light always travels at the speed that scientists agree. Some will attempt to show that conventional scientific theory is false. For example, scientists believe that the earth is slowing down, at the rate of about a second (or slightly less) each year. Creationists will point out that, if this were the case, then 300 million years ago it must have revolved at the rate of ten revolutions per second, which is absurd (Nordquist 2006). The flood in Noah's time brought about many changes in the earth, they have argued, and the flood explains why fossils of fish and sea shells are sometimes discovered near the tops of mountains; they were left there when the flood waters receded. Regarding fossils, some fundamentalists have even argued that they were actually created in such a way as to look old, and that their apparent age is either a test of faith by God, or a temptation by the devil to lure humanity into error. Some more conciliatory fundamentalists have contended that, although God's six-day creation is as described in the book of Genesis, there is no indication that the earth's situation, as recounted in the second verse ('Now the earth was formless and empty') immediately followed God's initial creative act, described in the first ('In the beginning God created the heavens and the earth'). Thus, millions of years could have elapsed in between, allowing ample time for fossils to form, and for primeval mud to give rise to rudimentary life forms. Another attempt to reconcile evolution and creation is to question whether the word 'day' in the account of the six-day creation is to be taken literally. Elsewhere, the Bible states that a day is a thousand years in God's sight (Ps. 90:4), so perhaps the earth really took six thousand years to create. If this were there the case, then the earth would not be millions of years old, but around seven millennia, thus allowing a limited amount of evolutionary development to take place.

Challenge from within

There was another type of challenge that Christianity faced during the Enlightenment period, not unrelated to Darwin. Although evolutionism had raised questions about the Bible's veracity, such questions were already being considered by biblical scholars. Already, the Bible had been subjected to 'lower criticism'—that is to say, the scholarly endeavour of adjudicating on textual variants, and establishing the original text of the scriptures, as far as possible. The text of the Bible was originally disseminated through copying manuscripts by hand. Despite meticulous checking, it was inevitable that mistakes would occur, as scribes could lose their concentration, try to amend the text of damaged manuscripts, or sometimes even add their own occasional explanatory glosses. Textual criticism remains an important branch of biblical studies, and involves comparing different manuscripts, ascertaining their age and, most importantly, establishing their pedigree. Biblical criticism of this kind was to be welcomed, particularly in Protestant circles, since its aims were to determine which version of the text should be translated into their mother tongues, and to ensure that Christians obtained as accurate a version of the Bible as was humanly possible.

'Higher criticism', however, raised different sets of questions, which militated against belief in biblical inerrancy. The term 'higher criticism' was first used by William Robertson Smith (1846–1894) in his *The Old Testament in the Jewish Church* (1881), although the term is not so commonly used today. 'Lower criticism' was a task which could be uncontroversially agreed to be necessary. Manuscripts differed, and Bible translation could not proceed without adjudication on which textual variants were to be accepted. 'Higher criticism' was more contentious, since it raised questions that undermined the traditionally received view, that the Bible was a work of divine authorship, that its authors were who they claimed to be, that it was a harmonious unity, whose various books were written under divine inspiration, and preserved virtually intact (barring occasional scribal errors) throughout the ages.

The rise in historiography as a science causes scholars to raise critical questions about their source material. For example, who was the source's author? When and where was the material written? How did he (probably not she) gain access to the material? What are his sources of information? Is there a bias that may cause the material to be less than objective? What was his background? What was his purpose in writing, and who were his likely readers? How do we resolve apparent contradictions within a piece of writing? Can we truly believe a book that is replete with miracles, claiming, as the Bible does, that Jesus cured the sick, walked on water, fed a large crowd with five loaves and two fishes, and even raised the dead? The reluctance—even refusal—to accept miracles was one of the axioms of much Enlightenment thinking, and therefore cast aspersions on the Bible's accuracy and authority. Of course, there are Christians who contend that the Bible is a special book, whose authenticity is guaranteed by divine authorship, and that the remarkable phenomena that it reports should not surprise us, since Scripture records the works an omnipotent God, who is well capable of performing miracles on behalf of his people. However much such claims may be debated by theologians and philosophers of religion, special pleading in favour of one particular set of sources is not part of modern critical historiography. For the professional historian there are no special books, no divinely guaranteed sources that should be regarded as more trustworthy than the rest, no acts of faith that exempt certain favoured sources, such as scriptures, from the brunt of historical criticism.

A variety of types of scholarly criticism arose from Enlightenment thinking. Textual criticism already had its niche, having been an important consideration in the Bible translation of the Protestant Reformation. Historical criticism was of key importance in establishing how the story of the Israelites and the early Christians unfolded. Although historical criticism has been applied to all periods of biblical history, inevitably a key question was what can be known of the historical Jesus—a topic that is still keenly debated. Source criticism became a further area for academic scrutiny. What sources did the various authors use? Is it possible to identify and, in some cases, attempt to reconstruct them? Allied to source criticism is redaction criticism, which addresses issues relating to the processes that the text has undergone in the compilation process. Texts may have been combined, expanded, contracted, or altered in various ways in the course of time, and it is the task of biblical criticism to attempt, as far as possible, to establish these facts.

These developments in biblical scholarship were occasioned by a number of observations about the Bible. There are apparent incon-sistencies in the biblical narrative. For example, in the first chapter of

Genesis we are told that God created plants and trees before the creation of humanity (Gen. 1:11-12), but in the second chapter, after having been told that 'God had finished the work he had been doing' (Gen. 2:1), we find that Adam and Eve are in an environment in which 'no shrub of the field had yet appeared on the earth' (Gen. 2:5). In the subsequent story of the great flood, God instructs Noah to take all birds and animals into the ark in pairs (Gen. 6:19-20), yet we later read of animals entering the ark in sevens (Gen. 7:2-4). Again, there are apparent anachronisms. The Ten Commandments, purportedly given to the Israelites in the Sinai desert, after their flight from Egypt, require God's people to ensure that the sabbath is kept by their manservants, maidservants, animals, and 'the alien who is within your gates' (Exod. 20:10). Moses' followers sound more like a settled community, with masters and servants, working animals ploughing fields, and securely bounded city limits. It seems unlikely that a wandering tribe would transport city gates with them! The Book of Deuteronomy ends with an account of Moses' death—a fact that is difficult to explain if Moses is reckoned to be the author of the first five books of Hebrew Scripture. The writer even states that 'to this day no one knows where his grave is', and, 'Since then, no prophet has risen in Israel like Moses' (Deut. 34:6, 10), suggesting that the account was written some considerable time after Moses' demise. Other anachronisms appear in the New Testament. Jesus instructs his disciples to 'take up their cross' (Mk 8:34-35), but any allusion to the cross hardly makes sense before Jesus' crucifixion. Teaching about dispute resolution, Jesus recommends a system where the final court of appeal is 'the church' (or the congregation; Mt. 18:17), yet during his earthly ministry there the Christians had not emerged as a distinct community.

Additionally, numerous biblical scholars drew attention to linguistic issues relating to the Bible. Of particular importance was the various words that were used to refer to God. Although it can be argued that varying one's vocabulary is a feature of good writing style, it seems puzzling that God appears to be given different names, and not merely different descriptions. Particularly problematic are the names 'Elohim' and 'Yahweh' (or 'Jahweh'). Elohim is in fact a Hebrew plural, not a singular noun, which is surprising when one remembers the Jews' insistence that God is one, not many. The name 'Yahweh', by contrast, is singular. This was the sacred name which Jews have refused to utter, and has come into English as 'Jehovah', probably as the result of a misunderstanding about the joining of Hebrew consonants and vowels. In most English Bibles, the word 'Yahweh' is rendered as 'the LORD', with the word 'LORD' entirely in upper casing, to indicate the Hebrew original. The meaning of the word 'Yahweh' has been much debated among scholars: it appears to be connected with 'being', since God declares his name to Moses as 'I AM' and 'I AM WHO I AM' (Exod. 3:14). These two names of God—Elohim and Yahweh—do not therefore appear to be interchangeable names, coming from similar origins, but are more likely to be the result of different pieces of writing being brought together by a later editor.

The scholars who are best known for their work on redaction criticism are Karl H. Graf (1815–1869) and Julius Wellhausen (1844–1918). Their hypothesis, known as the Graf-Wellhausen Hypothesis, involves much more than a crude apportioning of extracts according to divine names. The hypothesis is the result of noting variations in style, examining the consistency of the narratives, noting repetition of material, and accounting for seemingly different key interests of the author (for example, some parts relate principally to the priesthood, while others are more interested in political history). Taking these considerations cumulatively, Graf and Wellhausen concluded that Torah was edited from at least four different sources, which are now generally referred to in Bible commentaries and scholarly writing as 'J', 'E', 'D' and 'P'. Letters are used to identify them, since of course we do not know the names of the original authors. 'J' and 'E' stand for the Jahwist and the Elohist respectively, indicating the respective favoured words for God, which, arguably, they used.

'D' is the Deuteronomic source, whose author appears to combine the two divine names as 'Yahweh Elohenu' (translated as 'the LORD our God'). This source consists of most of the Book of Deuteronomy (the fifth book of the Torah). The Second Book of Kings relates that a book of the Law—generally assumed to be this book—was found by Hilkaiah the High Priest in the Jerusalem Temple when repair work was being carried out. The Temple secretary brought the book to King Josiah, who was distressed by its content, recognizing that there was much of the Jewish Law that he and his people had neglected, as a result of the book's loss (2 Kgs 22:1–23:25). The book was ceremonially read in public—an act that typically affirmed a piece of Scripture's canonicity. While conservative Christians accept this story at its face value, scholars who accept D's separate identity contend that the story of the discovery is more likely to be a fictional one—a myth whose purpose lies in the book's legitimation. The letter 'P', finally, stands for 'Priestly Code', consisting of most of Leviticus, together with some parts of Exodus and Numbers. P's interest lies in the priesthood, its duties, rites and meticulous regulations, such as the food laws, how infectious skin diseases should be diagnosed and cleansed, and even how to deal with mildew. (It is perhaps unsurprising that many Christians would rate Leviticus as the Bible's least interesting book!)

In past generations, such problems were addressed by harmonization of the biblical material. Andreas Osiander (1498–1552)—a German Lutheran scholar who helped further the Protestant Reformation—wrote a *Harmony of the Gospels* (1537), one of the earliest attempts to reconcile discrepancies in the Gospel narrative. For example, in the Gospel of John, the 'cleansing of the Temple' is one of the earliest incidents in Jesus' ministry, in which Jesus expels the vendors and money-changers from the Temple precincts (Jn 2:13-16). However, the synoptic Gospels place the incident at the end of his ministry, after the triumphal entry into Jerusalem (Mt. 21:12-13; Mk 11:12-19; Lk. 19:45-46). Some present-day fundamentalists contend that there must have been two such incidents; Osiander in fact claimed that there were three. Another much-cited discrepancy relates to the story of Jairus' daughter (Mt. 9:18-26; Mk 5:21-43; Lk. 8:40-56). Mark and Luke record that Jairus approaches Jesus and tells him that his daughter is dying, whereas Matthew states that a synagogue ruler (who is unnamed) tells Jesus that his daughter is already dead. All accounts agree, however, that the girl had died by the time Jesus arrived, and that Jesus miraculously brought her back to life. Harmonizers have contended, again, that there were two separate miracles; perhaps Jairus' daughter became gravely ill and died on a further occasion after the first miracle, and once more had her life restored by Jesus. Another more recent attempt has been to suggest that the Gospel writers left out a considerable amount of detail in a complex incident; Mark and Luke record Jairus' words at an early point in the event, while Matthew's account of the ruler reporting the daughter's death quotes later words of Jairus, after the news has been broken to him (Hutchinson 1996).

Apparent inconsistencies are not confined to the narrative parts of Scripture. Discrepancies in ethical teachings, laws and theology can also be identified. For example, at certain points the Bible appears to teach pacifism: Jesus says, 'My kingdom is not of this world. If it were, my servants would fight' (Jn 18:36). In the Sermon on the Mount, he preaches the importance of not seeking revenge, overcoming evil with good, restraining one's anger (Mt. 5:21-24), and 'turning the other cheek' (Mt. 5:38). However, when the Last Supper has finished, and the disciples are about to depart with him to the Mount of Olives, Jesus instructs them, 'if you don't have a sword, sell your cloak and buy one' (Lk. 22:36). The prophet Isaiah looks forward to an age of peace, which he describes as follows:

> They will beat the swords into ploughshares
> and their spears into pruning hooks.
> Nation will not rise against nation,
> nor will they train for war any more. (Isa. 2:4)

Yet the Old Testament is full of stories about battles in which God encourages his people to be victorious, and King Saul is even ordered at one point to commit genocide: 'Now go, attack the Amalekites and totally destroy everything that belongs to them. Do not spare them; put to death men and women, children and infants, cattle and sheep, camels and donkeys' (1 Sam. 15:3). When Saul does not carry out this instruction completely, the prophet Samuel informs him that God has now deposed him (1 Sam. 15:26).

Of equal concern are apparent theological discrepancies. Although the vast majority of Christians conceive of God as an invisible spirit, the Bible does not seem wholly consistent. Jesus tells the Samaritan woman that God is a spirit (Jn 4:24), and in the prologue to his Gospel, John declares that 'no one has ever seen God' (Jn 1:18). Yet God appears to walk in the Garden of Eden (Gen. 3:8), and, following a struggle with a mysterious man at Peniel, the patriarch Jacob concludes, 'I saw God face to face, and yet my life was spared' (Gen. 32:30). Moses is allowed to see God's hand and his back, but not his face, for he is told that seeing God's face is fatal (Gen. 33:21-23). Apparent theological discrepancies also relate to life after death. Paul describes the resurrection as a future event, depicting the dead as having fallen asleep, awaiting Christ's return, to be awakened by 'the last trumpet' (1 Cor. 15:12-56). When Jesus tells a parable about a beggar called Lazarus and an uncaring rich man, the two characters die and find themselves in heaven and hell respectively, where they both encounter Abraham. However, affairs in heaven and hell appear to be happening simultaneously with events on earth, for the rich man implores Abraham to send Lazarus back to warn his brothers of their need for repentance (Lk. 16:19-31).

Some discrepancies amount to more than pairs of texts that militate against each other. It is not our purpose to identify all the various real or supposed inconsistencies in Scripture, let alone consider possible resolutions of them. Suffice it to say that at least one current website—'The Secular Web'—has a page identifying at least 350 scriptural discrepancies, and the list is by no means exhaustive. Equally important are broader issues, where the emphases of different scriptural authors diverges, and where broad questions receive different answers. One example is the importance attached to Christ's resurrection by the four evangelists and Paul, in contrast with the author of Hebrews, who never mentions the resurrection of Jesus, but to whom the ascension assumes greater importance. Another is how the 'kingdom of God' is to be understood: is it present or future, earthly or heavenly, brought about by human effort or by supernatural intervention?

If the Bible could not be accepted as an inerrant book, but contained discrepancies, even contradictions, then questions arose regarding its portrayal of Jesus Christ. To what extent could it be relied on? The rise of historiography as a scientific study had its effect on Christian scholarship regarding the historical Jesus. If scholars were not to subject the Bible to special pleading, then it must be treated—at least for the purposes of academic study—as any other book that purports to provide information about the past. One must seek external corroboration, raise critical questions about authorship and bias, and make judgements about the credibility of the material. The rise of science raised questions about whether books that so frequently affirmed miraculous happenings were believable. Could Jesus really have been a remarkable miracle worker, and if miracles are to be discounted, then who was he, and what did he achieve on behalf of humankind? In particular, Christianity appeared to be founded on the miracle of Christ's resurrection; as Paul wrote, 'if Christ has not been raised, our preaching is useless and so is your faith' (1 Cor. 15:14).

Modern Scholarly Interpretations of Jesus

Before the European Enlightenment it was widely accepted that the Bible was a special book and could be relied on, among other matters, for reliable information about the life of Jesus. Scholars who wrote about Jesus largely confined themselves to harmonizing the Gospel narratives, and resolving problems of chronology. It was Hermann Samuel Reimarus (1694–1768) who is generally regarded as the father of critical scholarship relating to the historical Jesus. Reimarus was not himself a believer, viewing Jesus as a political leader whose aspirations were unsuccessful. The kingdom of heaven (or the kingdom of God), about which Jesus frequently spoke, was a political regime over which he would rule as king: the inscription on his cross referred to his claim to be King of the Jews. Jesus' failure, he claimed, was evident from his final words on the cross: 'My God, my God, why have you forsaken me?' (Mt. 27:46). Faced with this obvious failure, his disciples reappraised his achievement, contending that his kingdom was spiritual rather than physical. Reimarus' essay, *The Aims of Jesus and His Disciples*, was only published posthumously (Voysey 1879): he no doubt feared that he might lose his post at the University of Hamburg, where he was an orientalist.

Subsequent critical studies followed. Heinrich Eberhard Gottlob Paulus (1761–1851) was somewhat less radical than Reimarus. A Lutheran, he felt more able to accept the Gospel narrative, although he had an aversion to miracles, which he believed could be explained away rationally. For example, the story of the feeding of the crowds of four and five thousand people were probably not miraculous events, but rather occasions on which Jesus and his disciples shared their food with some of the crowd, setting an example for others likewise to share. Jesus' healing miracles could be explained psychologically; at other times Jesus is portrayed as making rather primitive forms of medicine, such as mud (Jn 9:6).

Centrally important to the development of the quest for the historical Jesus was D. F. Strauss (1808–1874), who wrote a large two-volume work entitled *The Life of Jesus Critically Examined*. Strauss was unhappy with some of the earlier attempts to rationalize the miracles. An example he discusses is the raising of Jairus' daughter (Mk 5:21-43; Lk. 8:40-56). The Gospel writers recount that Jairus, a synagogue president, approaches Jesus to heal his daughter. As Jesus travels to his home, he is met by people from the house who inform him that the girl has died. Jesus responds, 'The child is not dead, but asleep', and commands the girl to get up, which she does. Previous rationalists suggested that Jairus' daughter was not dead, but—as Jesus said—simply sleeping; hence the 'raising' was no miracle. However, Strauss argued that such an explanation still left a miraculous residue to be explained: if Jesus knew that the girl was not dead, without first seeing her, then he must have possessed supernatural clairvoyant powers. Strauss's innovation to critical scholarship was to introduce the concept of *mythos* (myth)—a term that now has wide currency in the study of religion. According to Strauss, such stories are not to be understood as historical incidents, but rather as stories with a supernatural significance to which the narrative points.

From a scholarly perspective, Strauss was enormously influential. However, for the average Christian a 1,400-page work peppered with

Greek and Latin quotations was quite a daunting task. A much more popular work was *The Life of Jesus*, by Ernst Renan (1823–1892), which was widely read, and which remains in print. Renan was professor of Hebrew and Semitic Languages at the University of Paris at the time of writing, but his book is written in the style of a novel, offering a chronological account of Jesus' life. Although Renan researched his material, he added much fanciful detail, providing imaginative descriptions of Galilean skyscapes and cornfields. Renan presents Jesus as a deluded visionary. Once a supporter of John the Baptist's revivalist moment, he broke away and found his own group of disciples, aiming to restore theocratic rule in Judaea. Initially his preaching consisted of gentle sayings and colourful parables, but he became bolder after incurring opposition from the Jewish authorities, eventually claiming to be the messiah. His enemies, aided by a Judas of Kerioth (Judas Iscariot) the traitor in Jesus' ranks, facilitated his arrest, and Jesus was tried for blasphemy and insurrection, and crucified. Joseph of Arimathea, a wealthy supporter, offered a large tomb for Jesus' burial, but the tomb was found empty on the Sunday morning. Renan gives no explanation for the empty tomb, but puts down the resurrection story as the product of Mary Magdalene's vivid imagination. In the spirit of the eighteenth- and nineteenth-century European Enlightenment, no miracles feature in Renan's account: the raising of Lazarus, he suggests, was faked in order to impress Jesus' opponents.

Of key importance in these attempts to re-construct the historical Jesus was Albert Schweitzer (1875–1965). Schweitzer was a truly remarkable figure. A Lutheran, he was a prominent church musician, making professional recordings of several of the organ works of J. S. Bach, as well as Felix Mendelssohn and César Franck, as well as writing on the art of organ building. Schweitzer also spent much of his life in Lamaréné in Africa as a medical missionary. His significant major work on Jesus of Nazareth was written as a young man in 1906, *The Quest of the Historical Jesus*. The book is a survey and critique of the contributors to the Jesus debate, from Reimarus to Wrede, concluding with Schweitzer's own interpretation. Schweitzer contends that previous attempts at identifying the Jesus of history reflected more of their authors' social environment than authentic history. Instead, Schweitzer sees Jesus as an apocalyptist, who predicted an imminent end to human affairs, for which his hearers must prepare. This imminent end would bring in God's kingdom, but it would be preceded by a period of tribulation. Jesus, believing himself to be the messiah, held that he should inaugurate the tribulation period by personally undergoing suffering on the cross. However, the end did not come and, as an apocalyptist, Jesus was a deluded one.

This may seem a very negative conclusion to reach. However, Schweitzer acknowledged that Jesus still had meaning for today's world, because 'a mighty spiritual force stems from Him and flows through our time also. This fact can neither be shaken nor confirmed by any historical discovery. It is the solid foundation of Christianity' (Schweitzer 1910: 397). Schweitzer's *Quest* concludes with a much-quoted passage:

> He comes to us as One unknown, without a name, as of old, by the lakeside, He came to those who knew Him not. He speaks the same word: 'Follow thou Me!' And sets us to the tasks which He has to fulfill for our time. He commands. And to those who obey Him, be they wise or simple, He will reveal Himself in the toils, the conflicts, the sufferings which they shall pass through in His fellowship, and, as an ineffable mystery, they shall learn in their own experience who He is.
> (Schweitzer 1910: 401)

Schweitzer's conclusions suggested a distinction between the Jesus of history and the Christ of faith, and caused biblical scholars and theologians to consider how much history was really necessary for a living faith. Several concluded that the Christian faith involved a relationship with a living person—the Christ of faith—rather than the acquisition of information about a long-departed historical character of whom there are few certainties. The Danish philosopher and theologian Søren Kierkegaard (1813–1855) had previously advocated a faith that travelled light on historical facts. He wrote, 'If the contemporary generation had left nothing behind them but these words: "We have believed that in such and such a year the god appeared among us in the humble figure of a servant, that he lived and taught in our community, and finally died," it would be more than enough' (Kierkegaard 1962: 130).

As the Lutheran scholar Rudolf Bultmann (1884–1976) was later to write, any study of the historical Jesus must be 'more than a walk through a museum of antiquities' (Bultmann 1926: 11). Bultmann was among a number of—principally German—scholars who embarked on what came to be called the 'New Quest' for the historical Jesus. Having abandoned the prospect of successfully constructing biographies of Jesus, the key question that they addressed was how much information in the Gospels, however fragmentary, could be regarded as authentic material relating to Jesus' life and teaching. Bultmann made an important distinction between what he called *kerygma* ('proclamation') and myth. The term 'myth' follows Strauss's use: the trappings that surround the core message of the gospel, and which have accrued through the early Church's life situation. Bultmann's method of studying the Gospels was to categorize the different types ('forms') of literature which comprised them, to consider what aspects of the early Church's life-situation might have given rise to them, and thus to penetrate the oldest strand of tradition. Bultmann concludes that Jesus was a rabbi who interpreted the Jewish Law in a radical way. For example, the Law applies not only to one's actions, but to one's thoughts. In the Sermon on the Mount, Jesus says, 'You have heard that it was said, "Do not commit adultery." But I tell you that anyone who looks at a woman lustfully has already committed adultery with her in his heart' (Mt. 5:27).

Like many of his contemporaries, Jesus preached an eschatological gospel: Satan's rule was about to end, and God's kingdom about to begin. Jesus also, Bultmann concludes, did not regard God's kingdom as a political ideal, or a special privilege reserved for the Jews: Gentiles too will be admitted to the kingdom. Jesus' message is therefore one of obedience and hope.

Bultmann's pupil Ernst Käsemann (1906–1998) developed the former's ideas by suggesting that Gospel material relating to Jesus could be regarded as authentic if it were not attributable either to the teachings of the Jewish rabbis of his time or to the early Church. If we can find material that is distinctive, then it is likely to be authentic. Other scholars, such as Günther Bornkamm (1905–1990) and Norman Perrin (1920–1976) emphasized 'redaction criticism'—that is to say, examining the process by which material about Jesus may have developed within the Church for its purposes. Perrin advocated the principle, 'If in doubt, discard': in other words, historians should only accept material that has certainty, not dubiety. These scholars tended to conclude that the sayings attributed to Jesus were more likely to be authentic than the deeds, the latter often being merely a framework for the former.

The 'Third Quest'

Towards the end of the twentieth century, yet another form of quest for the historical Jesus emerged. This is sometimes called the 'Third Quest'—a term devised by N. T. Wright, currently Bishop of Durham. The phrase is contested, but it helps to identify a new trend in the quest for the historical Jesus. Its key characteristics are that it regards Jesus as an end-time prophet, and sees his role within the context of first-century Judaism. Indeed, Christian scholarship has now been significantly influenced by the work of some Jewish scholars, who have helped to place Jesus within his Jewish context. Wright identifies some twenty scholars whom he regards as pursuing this Third Quest; hence we can do little more than give a brief impression of their diversity.

The Roman Catholic scholar John P. Meier has written a four-volume work entitled *A Marginal Jew: Rethinking the Historical Jesus* (1991–2009). Meier sees Jesus as a prophetic figure whose source of inspiration was John the Baptist, and whose preaching focused on the kingdom of God, which he believed had already come, and which would bring about a significant change in human affairs. Jesus, he believes, was a healer, and his healing miracles were a sign that God's rule had begun. Meier holds that the quest for the historical Jesus has been beset by scientific scepticism, and that it has tended to avoid proper acknowledgement of Jesus' apocalyptic message. Miracles need not be ruled out, he holds, particularly Jesus' miraculous resurrection; and a key line in the Lord's Prayer is, 'Your kingdom come.' Not everything that is true, Meier argues, is historically verifiable, and historical research cannot provide everything that can be learned through faith. Jesus is the 'marginal Jew' because he does not conform to the norms and lifestyle of the average Jewish man. He is a prophet and a thaumaturge, and he associates with those who are on the margins of society, as well as Samaritans, but not, as far as we know, the Essenes or the Zealots.

In common with Meier, E. P. Sanders (b. 1937), in his *Jesus and Judaism* (1985), sees Jesus as an eschatological prophet concerned with the restoration of Israel. Against popular tradition, Sanders does not believe that Jesus opposed the Pharisees: in common with them, he interprets and obeys the Jewish Law. Jesus created an eschato-logical Jewish movement which challenged the political authorities. His 'cleansing of the Temple' was a symbolic as well as a provocative act, which demonstrated his opposition, and which led to his arrest and subsequent execution.

John Dominic Crossan (b. 1934) likewise emphasizes the social revolutionary elements of Jesus and his followers, and agrees that the disturbance that he caused at the Jerusalem Temple led to his downfall. The kingdom that Jesus proclaimed was not a future supernatural kingdom to be ushered in by an apocalyptic event, but rather a way of life to be experienced in the present. He came from a peasant family, probably having no formal education, and possibly illiterate. He was an egalitarian, and wanted to break down hierarchical and patriarchal insti-tutions: he was concerned with the 'nobodies' rather than the elite. His mission had two distinctive aspects. First, there was 'magic': Crossan accepts the stories of miraculous healings and exorcisms as authentic, holding that Jesus cured illness, but not disease. He ensured the reintegration of leprosy victims to society, rather than effected their cure. True to his egalitarian principles, Jesus did not seek authorization to perform such cures, he did not charge for them, and he offered them to all, irrespective of social status. Second, Jesus' egalitarianism was demonstrated by 'open commensality': he incurred criticism for dining with all, and his 'parable of the great supper' (Lk. 14:15-23) tells of a host whose invitation to a banquet was declined by his respectable acquaintances, and who therefore invited 'the poor, the crippled, the blind and the lame' to take their places. Crossan agrees that the disturbance at the Temple was a challenge to authority that led to Jesus' trial and execution. Crossan's academic writings include *The Historical Jesus* (1991) and *The Birth of Christianity* (1998), and he has also authored a number of more popular works, including *Jesus: A Revolutionary Biography*, *The Essential Jesus* and *Who Killed Jesus?*

Another prominent contributor to the Jesus debate is Marcus J. Borg (b. 1942). It has been questioned whether Borg should be classified as belonging to the 'Third Quest'. He is less concerned with methodology than the other contributors, holding that the Jesus of history can be accessed through an overall cumulative impression of the Gospel evidence, rather than from assessing the authenticity of individual sayings and incidents. He also downplays the role of eschatology in Jesus' teaching, contending that the material about the coming Son of Man belongs to a later tradition. Borg's key ideas are expressed in *Jesus: A New Vision* (1987). Central to his understanding of Jesus is his characterization of him as 'a spirit person'. Many religions recognize special individuals as having extraordinary relationships with the world of the spirit: the shaman, the exorcist, the mystic, the prophet. Jesus, Borg believes, was one such person: his life and teaching are Spirit-driven, as is evidenced by the account of his baptism, where the Spirit descends upon him (Mt. 4:16). His relationship with the supernatural realm is evidenced by four particular characteristics: he was a man of prayer, a healer, a sage and a social prophet.

Borg draws attention to the intimacy of Jesus' prayer. He addresses God as Father, even using the term 'Abba', which was the intimate term used by children to address their fathers (the equivalent of 'Dad' in English). At times he spends an entire night in prayer (Lk. 6:12), which suggests that his prayer was contemplative or meditative rather than discursive. Jesus was not unique in being a healer (Mk 9:38), and his opponents never question the genuineness of his miracles. This suggests authenticity to Borg, who finds little problem in acknowledging the miraculous in the Gospel narrative. As a sage, Jesus uses traditional conventions of proverbs and parables, teaching a message of trust in a compassionate God. As a social prophet, Jesus looks for the renewal of Israel. His decision to appoint twelve principal disciples was a symbolic act, showing his desire to reconstitute the twelve tribes of Israel. Jesus aimed to challenge the social inequality that existed between peasant and urban life, the latter's wealth being evidenced in the Temple authorities and the land owners. Borg believes that it was Jesus' activities as a social prophet that led to his execution: in common with Sanders and Meier he sees the cleansing of the Temple as the provocative act that precipitated the final events of his life. Borg doubts whether Jesus' death was followed by a physical resurrection, arguing that the resurrection stories are somewhat confused, and that in all probability they were added later. For Borg, this does not mean that Christianity cannot proclaim a risen Christ: men and women have been able directly to experience the presence of Christ from the days of the early Church to the present day, and hence the resurrection must amount to more than a story about a corpse's resuscitation.

It is unsurprising that present-day feminism should make its impact on the Jesus debate. One of the most prominent Christian feminist scholars is Elisabeth Schüssler Fiorenza (b. 1938). Of her many publications, the most relevant in this context is *In Memory of Her: A Feminist Theological Reconstruction of Christian Origins* (1984). Fiorenza comments on the uncontestable fact that Jewish society was patriarchal. However, the contribution of women in early Christianity, she contends, has been downplayed, and Jesus himself challenged the patriarchal system of his time. He speaks to the Samaritan woman at a well (Jn 4:1-42) who becomes persuaded of Jesus' messiahship, and thus it is a woman who becomes the first recorded Gentile convert. Jesus appears to have a female disciple in Mary of Bethany (Lk. 10:38-42); it is mainly women supporters who wait at the foot of Jesus' cross (Jn 19:25-27), who attend his burial (Lk. 23:55-56), and who are the first witnesses to the resurrection (Jn 20:10-18). This is notwithstanding the fact that women's testimony was accorded less weight than men's, according to Jewish Law. Fiorenza conceives of Jesus as the embodiment of divine wisdom (*sophia* in Greek), who is portrayed in the Book of Proverbs as a woman. Although himself a man, Jesus is thus the incarnation of the female principle of God. It was later Christianity, Fiorenza believes, that became patriarchal, generating the myth that Jesus called twelve male disciples, and requiring women to adopt a passive, silent role during worship (1 Cor. 14:34-35).

Tom Wright presents a much more traditionalist view of Jesus. Wright's approach is to consider how the Jesus movement emerged from a background of first-century Judaism to a large, successful, international movement whose followers worshipped Jesus. In order to answer this, one must ascertain the worldview or mindset of the Jews of Jesus' time. The Jews, he argues, still felt as if they were in exile, being under Roman rule. They looked forward to a time when Israel would be restored and God would once again dwell among his people in Zion. The rebuilt Herodian Temple was a source of national pride, but was in fact 'idolatrous nationalism'. Preoccupied with pride in their Temple, observance of its sacrificial rites, and endeavouring to maintain their national identity through exact details of Torah observance, they lost sight of the need for repentance and faith. Jesus' aim was to bring about a restored Israel, but not one that would be recognizable through material success: Jesus preached about impending national disaster, and predicted the Temple's destruction (Mk 13:1-2). A key component of Jesus' message was therefore a 'deliverance eschatology': the restored Israel was comprised of those who accepted Jesus' invitation, having faith in him to secure avoidance of the imminent tribulations, attaining God's kingdom in heaven. An important part of Jesus' plan was to embrace suffering, undergoing 'messianic woes' and taking upon himself Jerusalem's fate. The 'Son of Man' motif in the Gospels is not to be construed as a heavenly deliverer descending from the clouds to establish a messianic kingdom on earth; rather, the Son of Man is God descending to his people to take them from earth to heaven. Wright's approach is to offer his theory as a hypothesis: he disagrees with the approach that commences with small fragments of evidence and considers whether sayings and incidents are authentic. Rather, he believes one should start with a theory that appears to be consistent with the general body of evidence, and to consider whether the theory fits. If Wright's theory is correct, Jesus was not a failed apocalyptist, as Schweitzer suggested. On the contrary, he was a successful one, proclaiming a 'deliverance eschatology'; he is the true messiah who leads his people to deliverance beyond the earthly world, not within it. Wright believes that Jesus' controversies with the Pharisees focused on eschatological and political matters, rather than on points of legal interpretation or religious observance, and that his trial by Caiaphas (the Jewish High Priest) centred on the issue of whether he claimed to be Israel's messiah—a claim which would be blasphemous to Jews and provocative to the Romans, thus meriting his execution.

One final attempt to discover the historical Jesus deserves mention: the 'Jesus Seminar'. The Jesus Seminar was set up in 1985 by Robert W. Funk (1926–2005) and Dominic John Crossan. Funk's major writings include *The Five Gospels: The Search for the Authentic Words of Jesus* (1993) and *Honest to Jesus: Jesus for a New Millennium* (1996). The reference to five Gospels rather than four in his 1993 title indicates that the Seminar considers the Gospel of Thomas in addition to the canonical Gospels. The Seminar consists of some two hundred Bible scholars who circulate papers and meet at regular intervals to debate the authenticity of sayings and incidents attributed to Jesus. The distinctive feature of the Seminar is that it incorporates a voting system. Members are issued with coloured balls—red, pink, grey and black—which they place in a container to indicate the degree of authenticity they ascribe to passages from the Bible, apocryphal gospels and early Christian sources. A scholar who places a red ball indicates confidence in the authenticity of the material: to be classed as 'red' the material should be verifiable and corroborated by other evidence. Being found in more than one Gospel, for example, is deemed to increase the likelihood of authenticity. Pink indicates that the material's authenticity is likely, but not certain; grey means unlikely although possible; and black means improbable and likely to be fictitious.

The Five Gospels summarized the work of the first six years of the Seminar, which dealt with Jesus' sayings. No sayings that were extraneous to these Gospels received any 'red' verdicts, and the coloured balls exhibited the following distribution with regard to the five Gospels:

	Total	*Red*	*Pink*	*Grey*	*Black*
Matthew	420	11	60	115	234
Mark	177	1	18	66	92
Luke	392	14	65	128	185
John	140	0	1	5	134
Thomas	201	3	40	67	91

The pattern that emerges may be clearer if we add together the reds and pinks and then the greys and blacks, and express the findings as percentages, thus:

	Total	Red and pink	Grey and black
Matthew	420	16.9	83.1
Mark	177	10.8	89.2
Luke	392	20.2	79.9
John	140	0.7	99.3
Thomas	201	21.4	78.6

The conclusion that John's material is historically the least reliable may not be surprising, since his work is more metaphysical and theological than narrative. The verdict on Thomas is perhaps unexpected: he is regarded as the most reliable source, if only fractionally. Luke seems to be best for factuality, and Mark worst, despite the fact that Mark is generally regarded as the original synoptic source.

Of course, the Jesus Seminar is controversial. Conservative Christians believe implicitly that the Bible is inspired by the Holy Spirit, and hence any studies that undermine its reliability must be flawed. Others have criticized the composition of the seminar participants. Are they a representative sample of scholars of different shades of opinion? In any case, is an 'average' conclusion necessarily the correct one? Some Christians have accused the Seminar of gimmickry: scholars have traditionally considered questions of biblical authenticity by debate, not by coloured balls. Whether or not accusations of gimmickry are fair, at least Funk and Crossan's ideas have gained publicity for the seminar, and brought questions of the historicity of the Gospels and the quest for the historical Jesus into the public arena.

Most of the critical study of the Bible took its rise in Germany. However, in 1860 seven English scholars published a volume entitled *Essays and Reviews*, edited by Benjamin Jowett (1817–1893), an Oxford classicist and theologian. This collection appeared only four months after Darwin's *Origins of Species* and, although many more Christians have heard of Darwin than of Jowett, *Essays and Reviews* initially sold many more copies than Darwin: some twenty-two thousand copies were bought in its first two years of publication, in contrast with Darwin, whose now more famous work sold a mere two thousand. Seven clergy and academics, including Jowett, contributed essays that were largely supportive of the liberal scholarship that had taken rise in Germany. An essay by Frederick Temple (1821–1902), later to become the Archbishop of Canterbury, was positioned first in the volume. It was entitled 'The

Education of the World', and argued the case for independent thought, unhampered by dogma or tradition. Temple contended that this was not an abandonment of faith, but the reverse. He wrote, 'He is guilty of high treason against the faith who fears the result of any investigation, whether philosophical, or scientific, or historical' (Jowett 1861: 47).

Jowett's own essay—'On the Interpretation of Scripture'—appeared last. '*Interpret the Scripture like any other book*' (1861: 377; italics Jowett's), was the key theme, and he endorsed the critical attempts to explain Scripture that had recently gained momentum, arguing that a more liberal approach to Scripture could enhance mission, education and preaching. Jowett perceived positive benefits of a critical approach to Scripture, and a need to appropriate its findings, although Jowett was cautious about disseminating the results of the new scholarship. He wrote,

> One consideration should be borne in mind, that the Bible is the only book in the world written in different styles and at many different times, which is in the hands of persons of all degrees of knowledge and education. The benefit of this outweighs the evil, yet the evil should be admitted—namely, that it leads to a hasty and partial interpretation of Scripture, which often obscures the true one. A sort of conflict arises between scientific criticism and popular opinion. The indiscriminate use of Scripture has a further tendency to maintain erroneous readings or translation; some which are allowed to be such by scholars have been stereotyped in the mind of the English reader; and it becomes almost a political question how far we can venture to disturb them. (Jowett 1861: 379)

Other contributions included Baden Powell's (1796–1860) 'On the Study of the Evidences of Christianity'. The name Baden Powell is commonly associated with the Boy Scouts organization, which was founded by his son Robert Stephenson Smyth Baden-Powell (1857–1941). Baden Powell's essay focused on whether miracles could provide evidence in favour of the Christian faith, but he argued that our antecedent knowledge of the world precluded belief in them. His essay also expressed support for Darwin's *Origins of Species*. Rowland Williams' contribution, 'Bunsen's Biblical Researches', was an appreciation of the work of Christian C. J. Bunsen (1791–1860), the German scholar and diplomat who had undertaken pioneering work on biblical studies as well as Egyptian chronology.

The collection of essays caused a furore, not merely on account of the ideas they expressed, but because the contributors were British and not German, and because all of them were churchmen. Traditional views regarding the Christian faith were here coming from inside, not outside the faith, and higher criticism had now gained a foothold in Britain, not just Germany. The essayists became popularly known as 'the Seven against Christ', and their ideas were severely attacked by Samuel Wilberforce, then Bishop of Oxford. Wilberforce wrote an article in *The Quarterly Review* in 1861 condemning the new scholarship, and the Archbishop of Canterbury followed this up with a letter to *The Times*, with 25 bishops as co-signatories, threatening the authors with disciplinary action. Two of the essayists—Jowett and Williams—were tried for heresy and deposed.

The Rise of Fundamentalism

The new ideas divided opinion considerably, particularly within Protestantism. A number of conservative biblical scholars regularly attended the annual Niagara Bible Conference between 1878 and 1899. The conference principally dealt with millenarianism, but attendees came to discuss the new learning and how to respond to it. Out of this conference emerged the American Bible League, founded in 1902, and between 1901 and 1915 a series of twelve books, entitled *The Fundamentals: A Testimony to the Truth*, written by R. A. Torrey and A. C. Dixon, was circulated free of charge among clergy and ordinands, financed to the tune of 250,000 US dollars by Lyman Stewart, the director of the Union Oil Company, California. Three million copies in all were distributed. In 1910 the General Assembly of the Presbyterian Church defined five 'fundamentals', which were held to lie at the foundations of the Christian faith. These five tenets were

1. The inerrancy of the Bible
2. The Virgin Birth of Christ
3. Christ's substitutionary atonement
4. Christ's bodily resurrection
5. The authenticity of Christ's miracles

The list assumed slightly different forms in other Christian circles. In some versions, 'The deity of Christ' was inserted between the first and second principles, omitting the fifth, and adding 'the bodily return of Christ' after 'the physical resurrection'. The five points, in whatever form, became known as the 'five principles of fundamentalism'.

The word 'fundamentalism' has been used in a somewhat nebulous way in recent times, and is often regarded as a pejorative term, connoting extremism, uncompromisingness and even violence. Although the term is imprecise when applied to certain Muslims, Sikhs or Buddhists, it has a definite meaning within Christian Protestantism. (Occasionally the term is applied to those Orthodox Christians who place strict emphasis on tradition, or to ultra-conservative Roman Catholic organizations such as Opus Dei.) Many conservative Christians are happy to accept the label 'fundamentalist', and at least one organization—the National Federation of Fundamentalists, founded in the USA in 1920—adopted the word as a self-description. Others preferred the term 'fundamental' to 'fundamentalist', and the former tended to be used where certain Protestant churches and organizations wished to declare their biblical conservatism, for example the Independent Fundamental Baptist Church, the Independent Fundamental Churches of America, and the World Christian Fundamentals Association.

The five principles were formulated as a counter to 'modernism'. Belief in the inerrancy of the Bible signals a rejection of evolution, as well the views of the higher critics that the Bible contains embellishments, contradictions, unbelievable miracles and a biased view of Jewish history. Fundamentalists regard the Bible as true in all matters of history, doctrine and ethics. The explicit reference to miracles or the Virgin Birth was an emphatic denial of the liberal interpretations of Scripture that regarded miracles as exaggerations overlaying otherwise genuine historical incidents, and the tendency to regard Jesus as a human teacher rather than a divine saviour. The reference to penal substitution underlined the fundamentalist belief that Jesus did not save the world merely by moral influence, as some liberal scholars appeared to suggest, but rather that his death was truly an atoning sacrifice for the sins of the world.

Those fundamentalists who adopted the five-point list ending with the bodily return of Christ were emphasizing fundamentalism's millenarian roots. Fundamentalism is typically associated with apocalypticism, since Christ's return on the clouds of heaven is a belief which the Bible affirms. The Book of Revelation ends with Jesus saying 'I am coming soon.' (Rev. 22:20). Many fundamentalists contend that, as the Bible claims, the second coming is near, and that humanity is currently witnessing the signs that herald the end: wars, earthquakes, famines, persecution, breakdown of family relationships, false messiahs (Mk 13:3-31). The version of apocalypticism that is typically adopted by present-day fundamentalists is known as pre-millennialism: that is to say, human history is believed to precede Christ's millennial rule, as described in the Book of

Revelation: Satan is to be bound and locked in the Abyss for a thousand years, following Christ's return, and there will be a thousand-year period in which Christ will rule over a peaceful earth. When this period has elapsed, Satan will be unleashed and permitted to continue his deception of the world, then finally be consumed by fire from heaven (Rev. 20:1-10). Fundamentalists lean towards a very literal interpretation of biblical apocalypticism, to the extent that some American churches have been built with retractable roofs to allow the congregation to rise 'to meet the Lord in the air' (1 Thess. 4:17). Within the past twenty years various novels have been written by fundamentalist authors, depicting fictional characters who have to live through the 'Rapture' and the events that lie beyond it. The most popular series of novels is by Tim LaHaye and Jerry B. Jenkins, the first of which is entitled *Left Behind: A Novel of the Earth's Last Days*, first published in 1995, and subsequently made into a film. The series remains controversial, however, and not all conservative Christians welcome its portrayal of either the Christian faith or the last days.

Inevitably, universities were more tolerant of modernism than the churches. In 1891 Charles A. Briggs (1841–1913) was appointed to the newly created post of Professor of Biblical Theology at Union Seminary, New York. His inaugural lecture argued that there were three sources of authority in the Christian faith: the Church's tradition and reason, as well as the Bible. He also endorsed the claims of liberal scholarship, asserting that Moses was not the author of the Pentateuch, and that Isaiah did not write the second part of the book bearing his name, as well as questioning the veracity of messianic prophecy. For these claims he was tried for heresy the following year, and, although he was acquitted, he was suspended from the denomination in 1893. However, he retained his academic post.

Churches, however, were rather less tolerant of proponents of modernism. In 1910 the Presbyterian Church of the United States adopted the five principles of fundamentalism, requiring clergy to accept them. The five points became known as the 'five fundamentals'. The five points did not go unchallenged, however. On 21 May 1922 Harry Emerson Fosdick, who was minister of First Presbyterian Church, New York, preached a sermon entitled 'Shall the Fundamentalists Win?', in which he urged that the Presbyterian Church should be sufficiently liberal to accommodate both fundamentalists and modernists. Copies of the sermon were circulated to clergy countrywide, and Fosdick's sermon helped to popularize the modernist approach to Christianity. William

Jennings Bryan, the leading prosecutor in the Scopes trial, forcibly argued for Fosdick's resignation. Fosdick resigned his position in 1924, but was almost immediately appointed as pastor of Park Avenue Baptist Church—a prestigious congregation attended by no less a figure than John D. Rockefeller. The Presbyterian Church's General Assembly reviewed its position, however, and appointed a commission who reported back in 1927, concluding that it was inappropriate to identify five principles, with a prescribed interpretation, as compulsory, and that there should be no need to require clergy to subscribe to anything more than the historical statements of faith, such as the creeds and the Westminster Confession. The Church, it was argued, should be wide enough to accept fundamentalists and liberals within its borders. In 1929 the Presbyterian Church also reorganized the governing bodies of Princeton Theological Seminary, depriving the fundamentalists of overall control.

As liberal scholarship gained momentum, universities and seminaries were more inclined to encourage higher criticism of the Bible. For most Protestant denominations this was acceptable, since there was value in the more conservative candidates understanding the scholarship that they rejected. Indeed, the authors have known fundamentalist students who have regarded a liberal theological education as a test of their faith, from which it can emerge triumphant. Although most of the major Protestant denominations have accommodated both ends of the theological spectrum, there are exceptions, such as the Southern Baptists, who have their own theological seminaries. Smaller denominations such as the Salvation Army, the Brethren, the International Churches of Christ, as well as various forms of Pentecostalism, do not have an ordained clergy, regarding personal commitment as more important than academic training. Where denominations allow a spread of theological opinion, fundamentalists have formed their own organizations to promote theological conservatism, such as the Evangelical Alliance in Britain, or the Inter-Varsity Fellowship, which promotes conservative Christianity among younger people.

Fundamentalism has gained public visibility through a number of 'televangelists'—pastors and preachers who conduct much of their ministry through television. Of particular note is Jerry Falwell (1933–2007), a Southern Baptist pastor who led one of America's megachurches in Lynchburg, Virginia. In 1979 Falwell founded the Moral Majority, a politically right-wing Christian organization aiming to promote conservative Christian values within US politics. The Moral Majority performed a significant role in the election of Ronald Regan as

US President in 1980. The Moral Majority continued until 1989, when it was succeeded by the Christian Coalition, under the leadership of Pat Robertson (b. 1930), another of America's televangelists. In 2004 Falwell revived the Moral Majority, renaming it the Moral Majority Coalition. The Moral Majority and its successors have opposed abortion, the practice of homosexuality, and the proposed Equal Rights Amendment to secure equal rights for women under all US state law. Family life is emphasized, and the Moral Majority advocated censorship of radio and television programmes that appeared to promote alternative lifestyles. Supporters also opposed the Strategic Arms Limitation Talks (SALT) between the USA and the (then) USSR in 1979: the Moral Majority is also emphatically opposed to communism.

Not all fundamentalists are politically organized, or even politically active. The authors have encountered a variety of fundamentalist opinions about politics. There are those who have expressed the view that 'a Christian should leave politics severely alone', on the grounds that Christ's kingdom is 'not of this world', while others have contended that Christians should be socially responsible, and hence have a duty to vote. Some fundamentalists contend that their faith transcends party politics, and that Christians should favour electoral candidates who are Christians, in order to secure a Christian voice in parliament. Christian fundamentalists tend to regard homosexuality as sinful, and oppose abortion. They are also prone to adopt a somewhat staid lifestyle: many (although not all) avoid tobacco, alcohol and gambling. (The authors have known fundamentalists who even prohibit playing cards, on account of their associations with gambling.) Family life is regarded as the ideal, with the husband as the head of the household; feminism is not favoured. Some fundamentalists avoid dancing, cinemas and theatres.

In general, fundamentalists believe in a clearly defined, unified form of Christianity, considering it unacceptable to espouse a form of the Christian faith that allows the believer to pick and choose the elements of belief or lifestyle that he or she adopts. Fundamentalists tend to be exclusive, regarding themselves as embracing the only true form of the Christian faith, and often denying the name 'Christian' to those who have not undergone a personal conversion experience or do not accept the inerrancy of God's word. However, because the Bible is a lengthy and complex book, and its meaning is not always transparent and unambiguous, it is inevitable that fundamentalists tend to be selective in the passages they use and at times offer competing interpretations. In particular, fundamentalism has not satisfactorily resolved the question of how to treat the Old Testament. If, as the evangelist Billy Graham put it, 'The Bible is a book written by God through thirty secretaries' (quoted in Hick 1973: 52), then God must have dictated the Old Testament as well as the New. Should the Christian therefore keep the ancient Jewish festivals and observe its dietary laws? Is the death sentence the appropriate punishment for rebellious children, adulterers, homosexuals and spiritists (Lev. 20)? Many fundamentalists will claim that faith in Christ replaced the Jewish law, but does this mean that its demands were nonetheless appropriate for their time and place? Whatever explanation is given for the penalties, fundamentalists will insist that the proscribed actions remain sins, and that the sacrificial rites of ancient Judaism are superseded by Christ's once-and-for-all atoning sacrifice on the cross.

Twenty-first Century Responses to Challenge

Fundamentalism is a particularly Protestant phenomenon, and highlighted the apparent conflict between modern science and modern historiography on the one hand, and biblical authority on the other. The battle between liberals and fundamentalists remains unresolved, although both camps are determined that religion must not simply be bad science. The fundamentalists continue to argue against the intellectual innovations of Lyell, Darwin and modern liberal biblical scholarship, while more liberal Christians seek for a co-existence between scholarship and science, and a view of the Bible and the Church that distinguishes between authority and inerrancy. While some denominations, such as the Southern Baptist Convention, are committed to biblical fundamentalism, most Christian congregations allow a range of views to flourish.

13

Ethics and Lifestyle

Religious believers sometimes say that their faith is 'not just a religion, but a way of life'. If they mean that God requires more than a few perfunctory rituals, then this is true of the vast majority of religions, since few, if any, fail to give guidance for living. Christians in fact were known as those 'who belonged to the Way' before they acquired the name 'Christian' (Acts 9:2). Those who contrast 'religion' and 'way of life' are no doubt equating religion with its ritual components, and Christian ritual is perhaps more visible than Christian conduct. Christians can be seen going to worship on a Sunday, and churches are visible as landmarks, although often closed on other days of the week. Nonetheless, the Welsh priest and poet George Herbert (1593–1633) wrote the lines of a well known hymn, which run:

> Seven whole days, not one in seven
> I will praise thee.
> (in Tobin 1991: 137)

It can be difficult to determine what precisely is the way of life that Christianity affords, however, since Christianity does not prescribe special obligations, unlike certain other faiths that have food laws, or require wearing some kind of special dress. It is not easy to comprehend how a Christian lifestyle really differs from that of a morally upright non-believer, or makes moral requirements that would not be accepted by any other religious faith.

Of course, some strands of Christianity and some individual Christians adopt distinctively lifestyles. As we have seen, the Adventist tradition observes some of the Jewish food laws, such as the avoidance of pork and shellfish. Some Christians are vegetarian, but this is a matter of personal choice, since it is fairly clear that Jesus ate fish and meat. Other Christians avoid alcohol, some of whom have even suggested that Jesus only drank unfermented wine—a somewhat unlikely suggestion. Some Christians are pacifists, but Christians have certainly had their share of participation in military conflict. Matters of dress remain optional, apart from those who are in religious orders, who are expected to wear garments that are appropriate to their tradition. There is certainly much debate about ethics among Christians, as is evidenced by the many volumes of scholarly writing on the subject: moral theology and Christian ethics have become branches of study within universities and seminaries. Yet there is no consensus on burning issues such as sexual morality, war and peace, abortion and euthanasia, or political and economic systems.

If the Christian lifestyle seems to lack distinctiveness, this is not because of apathy or neglect. The early Christians' decision to abandon the distinctive requirements of the Jewish law, they committed themselves 'to abstain from food polluted by idols, from sexual immorality, from the meat of strangled animals and from blood' (Acts 15:20). One anonymous early Christian writer (possibly 100–150 CE) wrote the following, in a letter to Diognetus, who is thought to have been a well respected follower of traditional Greek religion:

> For Christians are not distinguished from the rest of mankind by country, or by speech, or by dress. For they do not dwell in cities of their own, or use a different language, or practise a peculiar life. This knowledge of theirs has not been proclaimed by the thought and effort of restless men; they are not champions of a human doctrine, as some men are. But while they dwell in Greek or barbarian cities according as each man's lot has been cast, and follow the customs of the land in clothing and food, and other matters of daily life, yet the condition of which they exhibit is wonderful, and admittedly strange. They live in countries of their own, but simply as sojourners; they share the life of citizens, they endure the lot of foreigners; every foreign land is to them a fatherland, and every fatherland a foreign land. They marry like the rest of the world, they breed children, but they do not cast their offspring adrift. They have a common table, but yet not common. They exist in the flesh, but they live not after the flesh. They spend their existence upon earth, but their citizenship is in heaven. They obey the established laws, and in their own lives they surpass the laws. They love all men, and are persecuted by all. They are unknown, and they are condemned; they are put to death, and they gain new life. They are poor, and make many rich; they lack everything, and in everything they abound. They are dishonoured, and their dishonour becomes their glory; they are reviled, and are justified. They are abused, and they bless; they are insulted, and repay insult with honour. They do good, and are punished as evildoers; and in their punishment they rejoice as gaining new life therein. The Jews war against them as aliens,

and the Greeks persecute them; and they that hate them can state no ground for their enmity.

In a word, what the soul is in the body Christians are in the world. The soul is spread through all the members of the body, and Christians through all the cities of the world. The soul dwells in the body, but is not of the body, Christians dwell in the world, but they are not of the world. The soul, itself invisible, is detained in a body which is visible; so Christians are recognised as being in the world, but their religious life remains invisible. (quoted in Stevenson 1974: 58-59)

Jesus said, 'You are the salt of the earth' (Mt. 5:13). The saying implies a somewhat unobtrusive approach to ethics. It is better for his followers to act as a catalyst for actions and causes that help to bring about the kingdom of God, rather than devise new codes of ethics that mark out the Christian as visibly different from others. Jesus emphasized the importance of acting discretely, without the need for human recognition. He scathingly criticized hypocrites, who prayed in synagogues or street corners to attract public gaze for their piety, recommending that his followers should pray in private, but with sincerity. 'Then your Father, who sees what is done in secret, will reward you' (Mt. 6:5-8). This last remark might seem to imply that Christians undertake good works with the ulterior motive of being rewarded after death. However, such incentives rarely seem to feature either in Christians' discourse about right or wrong or in preaching. On the contrary, Christianity is more likely to emphasize the importance of divine grace in endeavouring to keep God's law, and the need for prayer, and importance of forgiveness for failing to live up to the required standards.

Christian ethics enjoins nothing less than perfection. Jesus said, 'Be perfect, therefore, as your heavenly Father is perfect' (Mt. 5:48). By contrast, Christians themselves may seem far from perfect. The Crusades and the Spanish Inquisition are frequently cited as atrocities that were committed in the name of Christianity, and the Roman Catholic Church incurred criticism for failing to speak out against the Third Reich. Hitler himself was a Roman Catholic. At an individual level one does not have to look far to find instances of Christians committing adultery, being less than honest, showing racial prejudice. The issue of paedophile priests seriously damaged the reputation of the Church's clergy—a scandal for which inadequate disciplining was exercised, and for which the authorities in various sectors of the Church are now endeavouring to make amends. It is futile to ask whether Christianity has caused more harm than good, or whether Christians lead better lives than others, since there is no means of verifying our answers. The greatest sinner might have been ever worse if his or her life had been untouched by a religious faith. As the Roman Catholic novelist Evelyn Waugh once wrote, 'I always think to myself: "I know I am awful. But how much more awful I should be without the Faith." One of the joys of Catholic life is to recognize the little sparks of good everywhere, as well as the fire of the saints' (Letter to Edith Sitwell; cited by Person 2005).

Even if attaining perfection seems an unrealistic expectation, the concept of *theosis* (becoming like God) lies at the heart of Orthodox ethics. Athanasius wrote, 'The Son of God became man, that we might become God' (*De Incarnatione*, I). While there remains an ultimate ontological difference between the individual soul and God, one's aim is to participate in the life of the Trinity, having been restored to an even closer fellowship with God than Adam and Eve enjoyed before the Fall. Becoming like God, with all his perfection and holiness, is of course an aim of which every Christian falls short. This is attributable to sin, and Paul wrote, 'all have sinned and fall short of the glory of God' (Rom. 3:23). The Greek word for sin is *hamartia*, which literally means 'missing the mark', and the notion of sin is thus a falling short of the ideal standard that is respected. To become truly Godlike will inevitably involve struggle (Orthodoxy uses the word *praxis*—'practice'), which entails membership of the Christian community, participation in the sacraments, and prayer from the heart. The last of these does not mean the sincere recitation of a short prayer, but rather an entire life in which the prayer-like state of constant communion with God is never absent. 'Praying without ceasing,' Paul wrote (1 Thess. 5:17, NASB). Human struggle alone cannot achieve *theosis*; one also needs divine grace. Athanasius explained *theosis* as 'becoming by grace what God is by nature' (*De Incarnatione*, I). This final state is unlikely to be attained in one's earthly life, but remains a hope when God's kingdom has fully come.

Roman Catholicism and Protestantism tend not to use the term *theosis*, but acknowledge that perfection remains the Christian's goal. The *Catechism of the Catholic Church* (2013) states, 'All are called to holiness: "Be perfect, as your heavenly Father is perfect."' And, 'Grace is the help God gives us to respond to our vocation of becoming his adopted sons. It introduces us into the intimacy of the Trinitarian life (*Catechism*, 2021).

Protestantism is more prone to using the term 'sanctification', a concept that was particularly emphasized in the Holiness Movement, inspired by John and Charles Wesley. In some of Charles Wesley's hymns we find reference to humanity becoming divine, for example:

He deigns in flesh to appear,
Widest extremes to join;
To bring our vileness near,
And make us all divine:
And we the life of God shall know,
For God is manifest below.
(Wesley, 1745, no. 5)

Sources of Christian Ethics

If asked where one might find guidance for appropriate Christian behaviour, Christians would probably cite the Ten Commandments (Exod. 20:1-17; Deut. 5:6-21) and Jesus' Sermon on the Mount (Mt. 5–7). Although Christianity broke its ties with Judaism, it should be remembered that Jesus is described as a Jewish rabbi, and he certainly provided interpretations of the Torah for his hearers. He had no quarrel with the Ten Commandments:

You shall have no other gods before Me.
You shall not make for yourself an idol...
You shall not misuse the name of the LORD your God...
Remember the Sabbath day by keeping it holy.
Honour your father and your mother...
You shall not murder.
You shall not commit adultery.
You shall not steal.
You shall not give false testimony against your neighbour.
You shall not covet. (Exod. 20:3-17)[1]

The Ten Commandments are sometimes known as the 'Decalogue' (literally, 'ten words'), and it is held that Moses received them from God at Mount Sinai, when the Israelites were travelling to their promised land. Jesus referred to them when a rich man asked him what he needed to do to gain eternal life (Mt. 19:26), although he indicated that his followers needed to go beyond simply keeping the Law.

The Sermon on the Mount is a lengthy discourse, which Jesus reportedly preached on a mountainside near Tiberias in Galilee. In all

---

1. This is the traditional Protestant list. Roman Catholics combine the first two commandments, and divide the final one, distinguishing between coveting property and coveting one's wife, servants and livestock.

probability it was not delivered as a single sermon, but is a collection of sayings brought together by Matthew in his Gospel. The discourse covers aspects of moral behaviour, words of comfort and consolation (the Beatitudes), and guidance on the spiritual life, particularly prayer and fasting. How Jesus' teaching relates to the Mosaic Law is not wholly clear. Jesus makes a series statements like, 'You have heard that it was said, "Eye for eye, and tooth for tooth." But I tell you, Do not resist an evil person. If someone strikes you on the right cheek, turn to him the other also' (Mt. 5:38-39).

Scholars sometimes refer to this series of apparent contrasts between Jesus' teaching and that of Moses as the 'antitheses', and it is popularly believed that Jesus was asserting his own authority as being superior to Moses. Although this is a popular interpretation of the sermon, frequently endorsed from church pulpits, we think this is an unlikely interpretation, for several reasons. Jesus prefaces his moral teachings with the words, 'Do not think that I have come to abolish the Law or the Prophets; I have not come to abolish them but to fulfil them. I tell you the truth, until heaven and earth disappear, not the smallest letter, not the least stroke of a pen, will by any means disappear from the Law until everything is accomplished' (Mt. 5:17-18).

It is also very unlikely that a respected Jewish teacher would have had the temerity to contradict Moses and the Torah, or that his hearers would have permitted him to do so. The Greek word that is normally translated as 'but' in the so-called Antitheses could equally be translated as 'and'; it provides continuity, not contrast. It is much more likely that Jesus selected sayings from the Torah and interpreted them, suggesting that his hearers should not merely comply with its minimal require-ments, but obey the Law in a radical and thorough-going way. Thus, the prohibition on murder proscribes 'murderous' thoughts such as anger, as well as insulting behaviour. Avoiding adultery involves purifying one's thoughts, so as to avoid looking lustfully at someone. Retribution should not merely be limited to an 'eye for an eye': an injured party should show magnanimity rather than seek revenge.

The Sermon on the Mount contains, as an opening section, a series of aphorisms known as the Beatitudes (Mt. 5:3-12). The name derives from the Latin word *beatus* ('happy'), since each line identifies a category of person who is happy or blessed: the poor in spirit, the mourners, the meek, seekers after righteousness, the merciful, the pure in heart, the peacemakers, and those who are persecuted for righteousness. The import of this section is partly to offer consolation to those who suffer the misfortunes that are mentioned, and partly to identify a number of virtues that Christ's followers should cultivate: righteousness, mercy, purity, peace. Orthodoxy includes mournfulness as a virtue, adding an explanatory gloss to the text, so that it reads, 'Blessed are those who mourn for the sins and evils that prevail in the world.'

The idea of enumerating virtues has given rise to a school of thought that interprets Christian ethics as a form of 'virtue ethics'. This form of ethics is traceable back to the ancient Greek philosophers, notably Plato and Aristotle. St Thomas Aquinas (1225–1274), drawing on this tradition, identified four 'cardinal virtues': temperance, fortitude, prudence and justice. The adjective 'cardinal' derives from the Latin *cardo* ('hinge'): they act as a pivot for all other commendable qualities of character. To these four, the Roman Catholic tradition added a further three, derived from Saint Paul: faith, hope and love (or charity; 1 Cor. 13:13). Love is the supreme virtue that Christianity extols: Paul commends it as the greatest of the three, and Jesus, when asked to summarize the Jewish law, identified love for God and love for one's neighbour as the greatest commandments, on which 'all the Law and the Prophets hang' (Mt. 22:37-40).

As a counterpart to the cardinal virtues, Christianity came to develop a list of 'seven deadly sins' (sometimes called 'cardinal sins' or 'capital vices'). The list, as we know it, was formulated by Pope Gregory I ('Gregory the Great'; c. 540–604): lust, gluttony, greed, sloth, wrath, envy and pride. Dante Alighieri (1265–1321) used the same list in his *Divine Comedy*, and Aquinas gave them extensive discussion. Although the sevenfold list is not biblical, there are two scriptural passages that attempt to enumerate vices. One comes from the Book of Proverbs: 'There are six things the LORD hates, seven that are detestable to him: haughty eyes, a lying tongue, hands that shed innocent blood, a heart that devises wicked schemes, feet that are quick to rush into evil, a false witness who pours out lies and a man who stirs up dissension among brothers' (Prov. 6:16-19). Paul provides a somewhat longer list of vices in his letter to the Galatians:

> The acts of the sinful nature are obvious: sexual immorality, impurity and debauchery; idolatry and witchcraft; hatred, discord, jealousy, fits of rage, selfish ambition, dissensions, factions and envy; drunkenness, orgies, and the like. I warn you, as I did before, that those who live like this will not inherit the kingdom of God. (Gal. 5:19-21)

On 11 March 2008 Pope Benedict XVI announced an updated set of seven deadly sins, arguing that people in the twenty-first century had lost their sense of sin, and needed to be reminded of its seriousness. Pope Benedict's list included 'bioethical' violations (birth control is one example), 'morally dubious' experiments (for example, stem cell research), abuse of drugs, environmental pollution, widening the divide between rich and poor, inordinate wealth and the creation of poverty. In contrast with the traditional list, these are social sins rather than individual sins, and at least some could be 'mortal sins'.

In addition to Scripture and these lists of virtues and vices, Roman Catholicism and Eastern Orthodoxy regard the tradition of the Church as prescriptive for Christian behaviour. In both traditions the decisions of Church councils is regarded as definitive, although Eastern Orthodoxy only acknowledges the ecumenical councils that took place before the 1054 East–West split. Both traditions acknowledge the work of the Holy Spirit in individuals, enabling them to discern right and wrong. Roman Catholicism regards its Western councils as authoritative, as well as pronouncements by successive popes. A summary of the Roman Catholic Church's decisions on moral matters can be found in various compendiums, the most accessible of which is the *Catechism of the Catholic Church* (1994). In deciding whether one is acting rightly or wrongly, three broad considerations should be taken into account: the object, the end and the circumstances. The 'object' refers to the type of act that is involved, for example, killing, stealing, lying. The second refers to the intended consequence, although it is emphasized that the end does not justify the means. The third refers to the context: for example, an action is not commendable if it is done simply because of social pressure.

Roman Catholicism makes a distinction between mortal sins and venial sins. A venial sin is one that is readily forgivable, although not permissible. A mortal sin, by contrast, is grave, causing separation between the sinner and divine grace, resulting in death to the soul. If such sins are not confessed to a priest, then, according to traditional Roman Catholic teaching, one's soul is condemned to eternal separation from God in hell. Mortal sins should not be confused with the 'deadly sins' mentioned above. The latter are propensities rather than deeds, and can serve as the cause of both venial and mortal sins. There is no formally defined list of mortal sins, although violation of the Ten Commandments would normally be regarded as a mortal sin; however, three formal conditions must be satisfied for a sin to be a mortal one.

It must be serious; it must be committed knowingly; and it must be with 'consent' or 'decision'—that is, deliberate. In stating that it must be committed knowingly, it should be remembered that ignorance of God's law is not an excuse. If the penalty for mortal sin seems harsh, it should be remembered that hell is the state of eternal separation from God, and that this state has been freely and consciously chosen by those who commit such sins. The distinction between these two types of sin does not mean that all mortal sins are equally grave: clearly, first-degree murder is more serious than theft or adultery. Also, there can be mitigating factors, for example, mental illness or emotional disturbance. The God who will judge the sinner is believed to be a just God. Towards the end of the twentieth century, some Roman Catholics questioned whether the distinction between these two categories of sin was still pertinent. However, in 1993 Pope John Paul II issued the encyclical *Veritatis Splendor* ('The Splendour of Truth') in which (among other matters) the categories of moral and venial sins were re-affirmed.

Mortal sins must be confessed to a priest. Confession must always be preceded by prayer and examination of one's conscience. The penitent must name the sin, stating what it was, when it was committed, how often, and against whom. The priest will then pronounce absolution and prescribe an appropriate penance for the sinner. Eastern Orthodoxy does not distinguish formally between mortal and venial sins, but teaches that there are serious sins that bar the member from receiving Holy Communion. In both traditions, one should not receive the sacrament until confession and absolution have occurred.

Issues in Christian Ethics: The Status of Animals

Christian ethics draws substantially on the story of creation, which portrays humanity as its culmination point. Adam and Eve, the first man and woman, are created on the sixth and final creative day. God creates Adam 'from the dust of the ground' (Gen. 2:7) and breathes life into these first human beings, creating them 'in his own image' (Gen. 1:27). They are instructed to exercise 'dominion' over the plants, animals, fish and birds that God has created, and 'to be fruitful and increase in number' (Gen. 1:28). The creation story ends with God's observation that everything he has made is good (Gen. 1:31); hence Christians conclude that when the world's creation was complete there existed an ideal state of affairs, until sin entered the world by Adam and Eve's disobedience.

The instruction that Adam and Eve should have dominion over creation is not taken to mean that humans can do what they like with the created world, but rather that they exercise responsible stewardship over the earth's resources. Animals therefore are typically held to exist to serve humanity's needs, and the majority of Christians have no objection to using them as beasts of burden, for food or for medical experimentation. The Bible recounts that Peter received a divine vision of a net descending from heaven, bearing all kinds of animals, birds and reptiles, and that he hears God's voice instructing him to 'kill and eat' (Acts 10:9-23). The story is not so much intended to rebut vegetarianism, but rather to indicate that the Christian is no longer subject to the Jewish dietary laws. It is important to recognize that Christian ethics does not consist exclusively of prohibitions, as religious ethical systems are often construed, but is an ethic that offers permissions. The creation story teaches that humans and animals are distinct creations, in contrast with Eastern traditions which teach that animals and humans are on the same cycle of reincarnation. Animals therefore may more readily be subjected to human welfare, according to Christianity. Christians may use animals for food or clothing, and even for scientific experimentation, so long as they do not 'cause animals to suffer or die needlessly' (*Catechism of the Catholic Church*, 2418). Whether animals should suffer through vivisection, to test perfumes or to provide clothing are matters of conscience for Christians, on which there are no agreed answers. Interestingly, there is no absolute Christian prohibition on hunting hares or foxes. Historically the Roman Church forbade its clergy to hunt, but, it seems, mainly because of the noise that it involved, not because it was judged to be cruel (Fanning 1910). Generally, kindness to animals is a principle to which Christians subscribe, and saints such as Francis of Assisi and Philip Neri provide role models for them.

It is possible that Christians are experiencing some reappraisal of traditional attitudes to animals. One theologian who has gone against the trend of sanctioning animal exploitation is Andrew Linzey (b. 1952). Linzey is a priest in the Church of England, and has the distinction of being the first academic to hold a post in Ethics, Theology and Animal Welfare. He is the founder of the Oxford Centre for Animal Ethics. Unsuprisingly, he is a vegetarian. Linzey has written prolifically on the theme of Christianity and animal welfare, which he regards as one of the major moral issues of our time. He has called into question the traditional Christian view of animals, which believes that dominion over animals permits exploitation, that holds that animals do not have souls, that human beings are superior, that animals are for human use, and that animals have no rights. Linzey argues that domination over animals entails moral responsibility for their well-being, and that human superiority lies in its ability to be generous and altruistic. The world which we inhabit is God's world, not humanity's, and hence animals exist for God's glory rather than human use. Animals are not objects, but are sentient beings to be treated with respect and shown justice. The Bible portrays Jesus as having been born in a stable, among animals, and hence feels their plight as well as that of humanity. Animals, too, are portrayed as sharing in God's coming kingdom, where humans and animals will live in harmony, without mutual hostility. As Isaiah wrote,

> The wolf will live with the lamb,
> the leopard will lie down with the goat,
> the calf and the lion and the yearling together;
> and a little child will lead them. (Isa. 11:6)

Respect for Human Life

Whether or not Christians share Linzey's respect for animals, Christians are agreed that respect for human life is of paramount importance, since men and women are created in God's image. What respect for life actually entails, however, is much more complex. Certainly, killing in cold blood would be a violation of the sixth of the Ten Commandments, 'Thou shalt not kill' (Exod. 20:13). Yet, despite this injunction, the Old Testament in particular contains many accounts of battles and executions, even genocides, carried out in God's name. Such acts are not confined to those who belonged to the 'old covenant'. Christians have gone to war, often against each other with both sides praying for victory; the armed forces have their chaplains who have blessed warships and bomber planes; the Roman Catholic Church did not condemn Adolf Hitler, himself a Roman Catholic, during Germany's Third Reich; Christian authorities have tracked down and burned heretics and 'witches'; and Christianity has gained notoriety through propagating the gospel against Islam during the Crusades.

Christians are far from perfect, and many Christians look on their religion's past with some embarrassment and regret. However, throughout its history Christianity has not been a religion advocating unequivocal non-violence, although one or two denominations are against the trend: for example, the Amish and the Quakers are strictly non-violent. Jesus may have taught that one should 'turn the other cheek' and that one should not resist evil people (Mt. 5:39), but he did not discourage his disciples from taking a couple of swords into the Garden of Gethsemane (Lk. 22:38). The seventh commandment is more accurately translated in modern versions of the Bible as 'You shall not murder' (Exod. 20:13) and for the majority of Christians it is necessary to decide when, not whether, the taking of life is justified. In general, Christianity has taken the view that killing is regrettably necessary for just causes, particularly where non-violence might lead to further and greater loss of life, which is how Christians have justified self defence (personal or national), capital punishment and war.

Historically, Christianity has regarded the taking of life in such as circumstances as not merely permitted, but required for the protection of society. The *Thirty Nine Articles* of the Church of England state, 'The Laws of the Realm may punish Christian men with death, for heinous and grievous offences. It is lawful for Christian men, at the commandment of the Magistrate, to wear weapons, and serve in the wars' (Article XXXVII).

In countries where Christianity is the dominant religion, it has fulfilled the role of legitimating the state's affairs, rather than challenging them. In England, until the early parts of the twentieth century, Christian clergy were associated with civil executions. They would often add 'Amen' after a judge had passed the death sentence on the accused, and a prison chaplain would accompany the prisoner to the gallows, reciting the burial service. During the nineteenth century, some Methodist ministers took children to observe public executions, believing that watching such scenes would be morally improving. When proposals were afoot in Britain to abolish the death penalty, the Church of England expressed opposition. It supported moves to abolish public executions, which ended in 1868, perhaps in the hope that if the public did not witness hangings it might be less squeamish about them. In the 1950s Archbishop of Canterbury Geoffrey Fisher argued for acknowledging degrees of murder, retaining the death penalty for the more serious offences. Abolitionists in the nineteenth and twentieth centuries tended to be secular reformers, such as Jeremy Bentham, and minorities like the Quakers. After 1969, when the death penalty was finally abolished in England, Christians tended to be won over, but it was not until 1988 that the Lambeth Conference finally condemned the death penalty. The death penalty continues to exist in North America, notwithstanding its largely Christian identity, and in 2000 the Southern Baptist Convention voted in favour of its retention.

War is another area in which the taking of life is regarded as permissible. Although Jesus Christ is given the title 'Prince of Peace', and although peace is part of the Christian vision of the coming kingdom of heaven, most Christians have regarded war as a necessary evil. Traditionally, the Roman Catholic Church formulated a number of principles for a 'just war'. War must be a last resort: non-violent means of achieving one's goals must not be feasible. It must be sanctioned by a legitimate authority, for example a state that has made a formal declaration of war; violent action initiated by terrorists is unjustifiable. There must be a just cause, not merely a desire to expand one's territory or achieve world domination. There must be a reasonable chance of success, and the deleterious effects of a war must be offset by the legitimate advantages achieved. The intended victims of hostilities should be combatants, with due care being taken to avoid civilian casualties. Finally, the aim of a war should be the re-establishment of peace.

With the advent of nuclear weaponry and the use of the atomic bomb at Hiroshima and Nagasaki, not all Christians are convinced that any war can be a just war in the present-day world. Accordingly, a number of peace organizations have grown up, either founded by Christians or substantially supported by them. One such movement is Pax Christi International, a Roman Catholic organization established in 1945 with the aim of promoting reconciliation at the end of the Second World War, and which particularly opposes the use of nuclear and cluster bombs. Originally established in Europe, it is now an international network, operating with other denominations and other faiths. In 1963 Pax Christi International took as its charter Pope John XXIII's papal encyclical *Pacem in Terris* ('Peace on Earth'). Although Pope John XXIII by no means advocated pacifism, he strongly denounced the arms race, calling for its cessation and arguing that expenditure on armaments was an enormous waste of human resources. He also expressed his concern for the observance of human rights, particularly those of the disadvantaged, as a means for preventing armed conflict.

Other Christians have supported Christian CND (CCND), the Christian wing of the Campaign for Nuclear Disarmament, established in 1960. Christian CND supports Abolition 2000—a global network of two thousand organizations, operating in 90 countries, aiming for nuclear disarmament. South African Archbishop Desmond Tutu is one of the signatories to the Abolition 2000 statement, which aims 'to achieve for the 21st Century a signed agreement committing the world to the permanent elimination of nuclear weapons according to a fixed timetable'. Of particular note for his work within CND is Bruce Kent, now its Vice-President, and who was the organization's General Secretary from 1980 to 1985, and its Chair from 1987 to 1990. Kent served in the Royal Tank Regiment from 1947 to 1949 before studying to enter the Roman Catholic priesthood. Kent has done much lecturing and writing, as well as campaigning for peace. In 1987 he left the priesthood, after Cardinal Basil Hume counselled him against involvement in political campaigning during that general election year in Britain.

Some Christians are opposed to any kind of war. Although the Peace Pledge Union now defines itself as a secular organization, it originated in 1934, when Dick Sheppard, a canon at St Paul's Cathedral, London, wrote a letter to *The Manchester Guardian* (now *The Guardian*) calling on all men (not women) who were opposed to war to send him a postcard bearing an undertaking to 'renounce war and never again to support another'. The support was massive, and the organization supported a substantial number of conscientious objectors to the Second World War. The Peace Pledge Union has been somewhat uncomfortable with the linkage between Remembrance Day and Remembrance Sunday with armistice and the practice of red poppies. The idea of selling white poppies in aid of peace, as an alternative to the slightly older practice of wearing red ones, was put into practice in 1926. However, congregations who have been asked to distribute white poppies have sometimes been quite affronted at what they perceive as an unpatriotic suggestion.

Suicide and Euthanasia

Other controversies regarding life-and-death issues relate to suicide, euthanasia and abortion. The prevailing belief throughout Christianity's history is that there is no moral difference between taking one's own life and taking someone else's. In his *City of God* Saint Augustine pointed out that the fifth of the Ten Commandments is, 'Thou shall not kill', making no specific reference to other people, unlike the seventh, which specifically mentions one's neighbour in the context of bearing false witness. All life is held to be created by God, and hence a Christian should regard his or her own life as sacrosanct, as well as the lives of others. Suicide implies that life is not worthwhile, in contradiction to the belief that men and women are created in God's image, and hence that life is of value, even when the body is in a state of suffering or degeneration. Roman Catholic teaching points out that suicide is contrary to the love of self, which is implicit in Jesus' commandment to love one's neighbour as oneself. The Orthodox Churches emphasize Christianity's central teaching that Christ attained victory over death, and hence death is a foe to be conquered, not a solution to the problems of being alive.

Historically, suicide has been regarded as a grave offence. Even John Wesley wrote that he would like to see the bodies of suicides chained and hung up for public view to emphasize the Church's disapprobation and as a deterrent for others who might be contemplating self-murder. The Church's disapproval went so far as to deny the suicide a Christian funeral. The *Book of Common Prayer* specifies that The Order for the Burial of the Dead 'is not to be used for any that die unbaptized, or excommunicate, or have laid violent hands upon themselves' (*Common Prayer*, 216.) Traditionally, the Roman Catholic and the Orthodox Churches took a similar view, but all three traditions now recognize that suicide can be the result of serious mental disturbance, from suffering or from extreme fear. In all three traditions, Christian burial rites are no longer denied, although Orthodox clergy like to be satisfied that the suicide was not of sound mind. For the Orthodox, someone who commits suicide deliberately has no further opportunity for repentance. By contrast, the Roman Catholic belief in purgatory allows for God to provide some means of repentance after death, and hence we 'should not despair of the eternal salvation of persons who have taken their own lives' (*Catechism*, 2283). One situation for which sacrificing one's own life is positively commended is martyrdom. The martyr follows the example of Jesus Christ, who sacrificed his life for others, and it has been traditionally believed that the martyr is assured of a place in heaven. This is why saints and martyrs are not prayed for in Roman Catholicism, where it is customary to pray for the dead.

There is relatively little societal debate about suicide. Euthanasia, by contrast, has proved to be a much more controversial issue. Advances in modern medicine have made it possible not only for men and women to live longer than before, but modern technology can provide the means to keep alive those whose medical conditions would have caused them to die in earlier times. This new situation has enabled matters of life and death to fall more often into the hands of humans, rather than to be left to God. While Christians have largely welcomed medical advance, Christianity's various traditions have almost unanimously rejected artificial human attempts to interfere with the dying process. Euthanasia, or 'assisted suicide', has proved much less acceptable than suicide, and has been condemned by Orthodox, Catholics and Protestants alike. The Greek Orthodox Archdiocese of America stated in a 1996 Supreme

Court case, 'The Orthodox Church opposes murder, whether it be suicide, euthanasia or whatever, and regardless if it is cloaked in terms like "death with dignity"' (Robinson 2009). In his 1995 papal *Evangelium Vitae* ('The good news of life'), Pope John Paul II stated,

> Human life is sacred because from its beginning it involves 'the creative action of God', and it remains forever in a special relationship with the Creator, who is its sole end. God alone is the Lord of life from its beginning until its end: no one can, in any circumstance, claim for himself the right to destroy directly an innocent human being. (*Evangelium Vitae*, 53)

Similar quotations can also be found in many Protestant sources, all of whom have several objections to euthanasia.

Christian opposition, as with suicide, stems from the notion of human life having been given by God and having unique worth. In the biblical story of Job, all Job's children die at a celebration in a house that is blown down by a storm. In his ever-resigned manner, Job comments,

> Naked I came from my mother's womb,
> and naked I shall depart.
> The LORD gave and the LORD has taken away;
> may the name of the LORD be praised. (Job 1:21)

The Christian position is that matters of life and death should be in God's hands, not those of humans. Those who are dying are of no less worth than healthy human beings, and have an equal right to live. Many Christians also fear that the practice of euthanasia could mark the beginning of a slippery slope: if one terminates the lives of those whose state is purely vegetative, should one go on to end the lives of those who are in extreme pain, or who are terminally ill? Further, Christian leaders have frequently regarded the period before death as spiritually important, allowing the dying person to prepare for death. Christians have also remarked that expressions like 'quality of life' and 'the right to die' are unbiblical, and that acceptance of euthanasia would involve Christianity succumbing to the ideals of secularism. The Churches have typically disallowed any distinction between 'active' and 'passive' euthanasia. Withholding further medical treatment, for example, is perceived as being little better than refusing to feed a patient. It is accepted that palliative care might involve the prescription of drugs that will shorten the patient's life: this is generally viewed as acceptable, provided that it is not the doctor's intention to kill him or her. While remaining opposed to euthanasia, Christians are not obliged to prolong life at all costs. The *Catechism of the Catholic Church* states, 'Discontinuing medical procedures that are burdensome, dangerous, extraordinary, or disproportionate to the expected outcome can be legitimate; it is the refusal of "over-zealous" treatment. Here one does not will to cause death; one's inability to impede it is merely accepted' (*Catechism*, 2278).

Despite the official opposition to euthanasia, there are Christians who would like to see changes, both in legislation, and in the Church's stance. The controversial Roman Catholic theologian Hans Küng co-authored *Dying with Dignity: A Plea for Personal Responsibility* (1995), in which he argued that the Christian virtues of love and compassion entailed a concern for the quality of a person's life rather than an absolute respect for the 'sanctity' of life. Küng argues that assisted suicide would help the weakest and most vulnerable members of society—patients who are helpless in their condition, and often in severe pain. Küng's position has been endorsed by the Modern Churchpeople's Union, an organization within the Church of England, dedicated to promoting liberal theology, which submitted evidence to the Parliamentary Select Committee on Assisted Dying for the Terminally Ill Bill (2005). This evidence cited the work of Robin Gill, an Advisor to the Archbishop of Canterbury, and who edited *The Churches and Euthanasia* (1998) in which he revealed that 66 per cent of weekly worshippers in the Church of England favour assisted dying, and 88 per cent of those who worshipped at least once a month.

Members of the Modern Churchpeople's Union (MCU) question the traditional arguments against euthanasia. The claim that matters of life and death are in God's hands does not remain true where modern medical treatment demands decisions about where to use one's resources and which patients' lives have priority over others. While palliative care is undoubtedly beneficial, they point out that there are other indignities that the terminally ill suffer. Jesus' 'golden rule' surely demands that one alleviates the misery of those who are terminally ill and who wish to die. Indeed, many doctors who favour assisted suicide would be quite willing to accept similar treatment for themselves in such circumstances. The MCU's Memorandum, submitted to the Select Committee on the Assisted Dying for the Terminally Ill Bill in 2006, cited the line in Ecclesiastes, 'a time to be born and a time to die' (Eccl. 3:2), arguing that prolonged deaths are often at inappropriate times and places—alone, in hospital, when an assisted death could ensure that the dying person was surrounded by family and friends, and could receive spiritual help by being offered holy communion or the last rites, ensuring a distinctively

Christian death. The authors quote the verse from Ecclesiasticus, 'Death is better than a miserable life, and eternal rest than chronic sickness' (30:17).

Abortion

It is popularly thought that the debate about abortion is a Catholic-versus-Protestant issue. This is not the case. Disagreement about the issue is really between the majority of religious believers (not merely Christians) and secularists who believe in abortion on demand. All churches deplore abortion, but all churches, including the Roman Catholic Church, acknowledge that there can be instances where it is regrettably justifiable, even necessary. Common to all Christian churches is a recognition that an unborn foetus is a human life, and hence worthy of respect as a human being. Even from the early days of the Church abortion has been prohibited. The *Didachē*, probably written around 100 CE, states, 'You shall not kill the embryo by abortion and shall not cause the newborn to perish' (2.2). Although the Bible does not explicitly proscribe abortion, Christians typically point to biblical verses such as, 'Before I formed you in the womb I knew you' (Jer. 1:5). Christians generally believe that human life begins not at birth, but at the moment of conception. This was taught by Augustine and by Thomas Aquinas, and it is implicit in biblical statements like, 'Surely I was sinful at birth, sinful from the time my mother conceived me' (Ps. 51:5).

The *Catechism of the Catholic Church* states, 'Human life must be respected and protected absolutely from the moment of conception. From the first moment of his existence, a human being must be recognised as having the rights of a person—among which is the inviolable right of every innocent being to life' (*Catechism*, 2270). This statement was quoted and formally endorsed in a resolution put before the Church of England's General Synod in 2005. Other Protestant denominations have condemned abortion, as have the Orthodox churches. In 2000 the Russian Orthodox Church reaffirmed its opposition to the practice in its report *The Church and the Nation*. In Roman Catholicism abortion is an excommunicable offence *latae sententiae* ('of implicit decision'): in other words, such an act is of itself a declaration that one has committed a mortal sin that has placed oneself outside the church. The prohibition on abortion also proscribes being an accessory to such acts; one may not arrange for a woman to have an abortion, and Roman Catholic nurses should not participate in surgical procedures that involve it. Christians have engaged in organized opposition to abortion: in Britain, Life—a Roman Catholic organization—is possibly the best known, and the American Life League is the largest in the United States. Anti-abortion campaigning is by no means confined to Roman Catholics, and examples of Protestant organizations include Presbyterian Pro-Life and Baptists Pro-Life in the USA. Opposition to abortion tends not to be organized ecumenically across the three main Christian traditions, but in Britain the Society for the Protection of Unborn Children (SPUC) has a division known as SPUC Evangelicals, which belongs to the Evangelical Alliance.

A foetus should not be brought into existence for the purposes of research, nor should a Christian attempt to influence the characteristics of the foetus, for example trying to select its sex. As a person, the foetus is entitled to medical treatment, hence there is no objection to subjecting an unborn child to scans or other medical checks. However, the aim of such procedures must be the unborn child's welfare. The underlying intention of carrying out such tests is all-important: they should not be used to determine whether or not the parents want an abortion if the foetus has a serious deformity. The Roman Catholic Instruction *Donum Vitae* ('The Gift of Life') states, 'a diagnosis which shows the existence of a malformation or a hereditary illness must not be the equivalent of a death-sentence' (1987: I, 2).

The churches are officially agreed that abortion is morally no different from murder. What they are less agreed on relates to extenuating circumstances which might exceptionally justify it. There is general consensus that an abortion is legitimate if the unborn child is so seriously deformed that he or she would only survive for a few hours. Carrying out an abortion to save a mother's life is generally regarded as permissible. Roman Catholic teaching imposes some conditions here: abortion must not be the desired intention in such situations, and the death of the embryo or foetus must be the result of any treatment to the mother, rather than a direct action that leads to her recovery.

More controversial among Christians is whether an abortion is legitimate if the mother has been a rape victim, or if the child is likely to have a serious deformity. The Southern Baptist Church, conservative as it is, resolved in 1971 that legislation should 'allow the possibility of abortion under such conditions as rape, incest, clear evidence of severe fetal deformity, and carefully ascertained evidence of the likelihood of damage to the emotional, mental, and physical health of the mother' (cited at Southern Baptist Convention 2007). The opposing view, in

Roman Catholic teaching, is that, since one would not recommend terminating the lives of disabled children or adults, it would be equally reprehensible to recommend terminating the life of a foetus or embryo on the grounds of disability.

Despite the formal opposition to abortion on the part of every branch of the Church, a significant proportion of Christians seem to favour abortion. On 22 January 1973, the US Supreme Court ruled that abortion should be legal in all fifty US States, the population of which is in all cases predominantly Christian. Statistical research on abortion indicates that in practice there exists a large number of (at least nominally) Christian women who resort to abortion. Worldwide, it is estimated that 42 million induced abortions took place in 2003, and in the United States 1.21 million were carried out in 2005. Of these, 23 per cent identified themselves as Roman Catholic, and 43 per cent as Protestant (Jones, Darroch and Henshaw 2002). This compares with the US Government Census of 2007, which indicates that 23.9 per cent of the US population is Roman Catholic, and 51.3 per cent Protestant. Although statistical information about abortion is contested (see, e.g., Roman Catholic News Agency 2008), these statistics suggest that a large proportion of Christians do not practise their churches' official teaching on abortion, and that Roman Catholics are no less likely than the rest of the US population to resort to abortion. At the time of writing, former British Prime Minister Tony Blair, who converted to Roman Catholicism in 2007, has been challenged by SPUC to declare his stance on abortion, having supported abortion on demand, abortion for schoolgirls as young as 11 years old without parental knowledge or consent, and the destruction of human embryos for stem-cell research.

Marriage and Contraception

Allied to the issue of abortion is contraception. The distinction is blurred on account of the fact that certain forms of contraception, such as the intrauterine device (IUD) and the 'morning after' pill, are abortifacient. For those Christian traditions that disapprove of contraception, such forms are considered more morally reprehensible than contraceptives that simply prevent conception. Opposition to contraception is popularly associated with Roman Catholicism, but much of Orthodoxy has also expressed disapproval. Saint Ignatius Brianchaninov (1807–1867) taught that sex must only be practised for procreative purposes, and any other use is an 'unnatural carnal sin'—a position much more extreme than any traditional Roman Catholic teaching. This extreme view is by no means shared by the Orthodox Church more widely. Some Orthodox leaders have expressed agreement with Pope Paul VI's encyclical *Humanae Vitae* ('Of Human Life', 1960), which prohibited all unnatural forms of contraception, while the Russian Orthodox Church permits the use of contraceptives, provided they are not abortifacient, that the couple are open to the possibility of having a family in the future, and that they have the approval of their priest or bishop.

The Catholic and Orthodox position is based on the premise that marriage and sex are essentially for the purpose of procreation rather than pleasure. God's commandment to Adam and Eve, and repeated to Noah, is to 'be fruitful and increase in number' (Gen. 1:28; 9:7). Marriage itself is not a Christian obligation, but it is a divinely sanctioned institution in which a man and a woman live together, engaging in sexual relationships with the purpose of bearing children. Contraception is therefore viewed as a practice that is inconsistent with this aim. Christians have opposed contraception for many centuries. Augustine wrote, 'Intercourse even with one's legitimate wife is unlawful and wicked where the conception of the offspring is prevented. Onan, the son of Juda, did this and the Lord killed him for it' (*De Bono Coniugali*, 2.2). The biblical reference is to Onan, who was obliged to marry his deceased brother's wife, in accordance with Jewish custom, but practised *coitus interruptus* to avoid raising a family (Gen. 38:9).

Although *Humanae Vitae* may be the best known of the Vatican documents dealing with contraception, an early papal document, *Casti Connubii* ('Of Chaste Marriage', 1930), dealt substantially with issues surrounding marriage and procreation. Pope Pius XI wrote the document in the wake of the Seventh Lambeth Conference, although it is not explicitly mentioned. The 1930 Lambeth Conference had passed several resolutions relating to matrimony and sexual matters, and had given authority to using contraceptive measures 'when there is a clearly felt moral obligation to limit or avoid parenthood and where there is a morally sound reason for avoiding complete abstinence' (Lambeth Conference Archives 1930). In contrast, *Casti Connubii* and *Humane Vitae* only permit the so-called 'rhythm method' of contraception, whereby a couple only engage in sexual intercourse during the 'safe' period in the woman's menstrual cycle. This ensures that the possibility of procreation is always present during intercourse.

The Roman Catholic Church's teaching on contraception has been much criticized, from within as well as without, and the majority of

Catholics appear to have disregarded it. An article in *The Tablet* in 2008 reported a survey in England and Wales of 1,500 Mass-going Catholics. Eighty-two per cent expressed familiarity with the Church's position, while over half admitted to cohabiting before marriage, and 54.5 per cent to using the pill; 69 per cent stated that they had either used condoms or would consider using them. A mere 15 per cent of Catholics surveyed expressed belief that the Pope's teaching was right (Von Hügel Institute 2008: 14-15).

Protestant Christians have typically recommended a much more liberal view of contraception, allowing sex to be engaged in for enjoyment, and not regarding sexual pleasure as in any way secondary to procreation. There exist a few exceptions. The Amish and the Hutterites do not permit contraception, and a very small proportion of evangelical Christians regard God's command to Adam and Eve and to Noah as still binding. One such example is an organization called Quiverfull, which emerged in the mid-1980s, encouraging the rearing of large families, and providing information opposing abortion and all forms of contraception. Its name refers to Ps. 127:5, which compares children to arrows inside a quiver, saying, 'Blessed is the man whose quiver is full of them.'

Christian marriage

Marriage is not a requirement for Christians, but is the norm for the majority. Traditionally, Christians are expected only to have sexual relationships within marriage, avoiding premarital sex, and most certainly adultery. So-called 'open marriages', where a husband and wife agree that extraneous sexual relationships are permitted, are disallowed. Trial marriages, common law marriages and co-habitation are reckoned to fall short of holy matrimony, which is the Church's ideal. Realistically, many churches now accept that couples—including their own members—live together without having undergone a marriage ceremony, and it is now not uncommon for cohabiting partners to want to express their commitment by means of a church wedding. In previous decades, people used to talk unkindly of 'shotgun weddings', when a man felt obliged to marry a woman he had impregnated. In Western society, there are no longer such scandals, and it is not uncommon for brides to be already in a state of pregnancy, or even to have children who attend the ceremony. In 2009 the Church of England offered the possibility of a 'two-in-one' ceremony, which combined marriage with the baptism of the couple's children. Predictably, this aroused controversy, with traditionalists objecting that the Church should sanction children being born out of wedlock, even though in twenty-first century Britain this happens to 44 per cent of all children.

Marriage is a union of male and female, and this tradition has raised the question of how gay and lesbian relationships should be regarded. Traditionally the Church has condemned it: the Vatican document *Persona Humana* ('The Human Person', 1975) condemns it as a 'serious depravity', while acknowledging that it is an innate propensity, the cause of which is not known. Homosexuals may be unable to help their urges, but they must on no account put them into practice. *Persona Humana* points out that homosexuality is contrary to Scripture—a view with which many Protestants would agree, citing the story of the men of Sodom, who demanded Abraham's son Lot to bring out his male visitors for sex (Gen. 19:5). Those adducing biblical evidence also typically cite Paul, who deplores the fact that in Rome, 'men committed indecent acts with other men' (Rom. 1:27).

While many Christians remain largely opposed to homosexuality, the issue has aroused considerable debate among Anglicans and Protestants and proved a divisive issue. Some Christian denominations now regard homosexuality as morally acceptable, for example the United Church of Canada, the United Church of Christ, the Moravian Church and the Quakers. Christians who approve of homosexual relationships frequently argue that one's sexuality is God-given, not chosen, and biblical prooftexts, such as the ones mentioned above, cannot appropriately be used to condemn lesbian and gay Christians. The Bible, they argue, supports many practices that are now regarded as thoroughly reprehensible, such as genocide, slavery and the subordination of women. The Bible reflects the views and values of its authors' times, and it is appropriate for Christian attitudes to change as society advances. Jesus himself, they point out, was not a family man: although there is no evidence to suggest that he was gay, his lifestyle was certainly contrary to the Jewish norm, which regarded marriage and rearing a family as a societal expectation. Some gay and lesbian Christians have claimed to see hints of other homosexual relationships in Scripture, for example in David's love for Jonathan, and Ruth's devotion to Naomi, although it must be said that such suggestions are highly speculative.

In the Anglican tradition, media interest was aroused in 2003 with the appointment of Gene Robinson as Bishop of New Hampshire in the USA. Robinson was the first Anglican priest to declare publicly that he was a practising homosexual. His appointment was challenged by conservatives, some of whom alleged that his website had direct links to pornography. Opposition was so strong that Robinson reportedly had to wear a bullet-proof vest. Less successful in obtaining a bishopric was Jeffrey John in the Church of England. He had been elected as Suffragan Bishop of Reading in 2008, but opposition caused the Bishop of Oxford not to proceed with the appointment.

A number of Christian organizations have been set up to promote gay, lesbian, bisexual and transgender (LGBT) issues. The Metropolitan Community Church, founded by Troy Perry in 1968, is an ecumenical Christian community ministering predominantly to LGBT Christians. More Light Presbyterians (MLP) is an organization within the Presbyterian Church of the USA, which campaigns against the denomination's homophobia. It publishes a directory of churches that have expressed various degrees of acceptance of LGBT Christians. A church is awarded an 'H' symbol for indicating its hospitality to gay people, a 'D' symbol if the congregation has passed a motion of dissent from the denomination's anti-gay policies, and an 'M' symbol if it has decided to endorse MLP's mission statement. Evangelicals as well as liberals can discover that they are gay, and they have their distinctive organizations, such as the Lesbian and Gay Christian Movement, founded in 1976, and the Evangelical Fellowship for Lesbian and Gay Christians. Within the Church of England, an interest group exists called Changing Attitudes. A number of Christian theologians have developed 'queer theologies', which set out to challenge the traditional assumptions about sexuality that have become embedded in its theology.

Many LGBT Christians have looked for more than mere recognition and acceptance, and have sought to have their relationship with same-sex partners blessed in churches. Some denominations are prepared to affirm the sanctity and integrity of homosexual relationships, requiring that those entering such relationships should be faithful, monogamous, loving and mutually respectful, though only a small number of denominations have agreed to perform same-sex blessings. In some countries and in some US states, same-sex unions have the same legal status as marriage—a situation that potentially affords the opportunity to churches to solemnize the union of same-sex couples. Very few denominations currently offer same-sex marriage ceremonies. Examples include the Church of Sweden, and the Mennonites in the Netherlands, although the former prefers not to use the term 'marriage', but the 'blessing of same-sex registered partnerships'. This is not merely a semantic quibble. Same-sex partnerships obviously differ from traditional marriages, and their recognition in churches has to involve adapting the marriage service, which makes explicit reference to husband and wife and to the rearing of children. The churches recognize the need to tread carefully, as they work out a new understanding of human relationships.

Conclusion

Much of the preceding discussion has focused on life, death and sexual relationships. However, the Christian churches have had much to say on race relationships, women's rights, work, poverty and wealth, justice, politics and ecological issues, to name but a few. Christianity covers all of life: as the psalmist wrote,

> The earth is the LORD's, and everything in it,
> the world, and all who live in it. (Ps. 24:1)

14

Mission and Ecumenism

Traditionally, Christians have believed that their faith is the sole means of salvation. If the eternal destiny of the world's inhabitants depends on accepting the gospel, then it is understandable that Christians should want to propagate their faith as widely as possible. The refrain of a Protestant missionary hymn runs:

> The whole wide world,
> The whole wide world,
> Proclaim the Gospel tidings through
> The whole wide world;
> Lift up the cross of Jesus,
> His banner be unfurled,
> Till every tongue confess Him through
> The whole wide world!
> (*Golden Bells*, no.621)

Although J. Demster Hammond wrote this hymn at the height of the Victorian missionary hey-day, the goal of proclaiming the gospel to the entire world is attributed to Jesus himself. Matthew's Gospel ends with Jesus' 'Great Commission' to his disciples: 'Therefore go and make disciples of all notions, baptizing them in the name of the Father and of the Son and of the Holy Spirit, and teaching them to obey everything I have commanded you' (Mt. 28:19-20).

The idea of God's concern for all nations, and not merely his chosen people, predates Christianity. It is found in God's promise to Abraham that 'all the peoples on earth will be blessed through you' (Gen. 12:3), and is reiterated at various points in Hebrew Scripture. In particular, the prophet Isaiah tells of God's servant bringing salvation to all the nations:

> I will also make you a light for the Gentiles,
> that you may bring my salvation to the ends of the earth. (Isa. 49:6)

The expression 'a light to lighten the Gentiles' was applied to Jesus in Luke's Gospel (Lk. 2:32), and forms part of the Nunc Dimittis— Simeon's song when Christ was presented at the Jerusalem Temple, and which continues to be sung in churches. Mission was also linked with eschatology, and it was commonly believed that preaching the gospel to all nations would herald Christ's second coming. Jesus, speaking of the signs of the end in his apocalyptic discourse in Mark's Gospel, says, 'And the gospel must first be preached to all nations' (Mk 13:10).

The word 'mission' means 'sending', and 'apostle' is etymologically derived from the Greek words *apo* ('away from' or 'out of') and *stellō* ('send'), indicating that the Church's mission extends back to Jesus' sending out of the apostles to proclaim God's kingdom. The early apostles, and particularly Paul, initiated the first wave of Christian mission, taking Christianity beyond its Jewish home territory into the Roman Empire. Rome's occupation of Europe facilitated Christianity's propagation, until shortly after its fall, traditionally dated as 4 September 476, when Odoacer deposed the emperor Romulus Augustus. A second wave of missionary activity took place during the ensuing millennium, essentially by the monastic orders. Examples are Saint Augustine of Canterbury (d. 604), who led a mission to England in the sixth century (not to be confused with Saint Augustine of Hippo, who wrote *City of God*), and the Celtic missionaries Saint Patrick (c. 390–c. 460), Saint Brigid (c. 452–525) and Saint Columba (521–597), who brought Christianity to Ireland and Scotland (Chryssides 2010: 73-74).

This second wave of mission was severely impeded by the rise of Islam, which occasioned the Crusades (1095–1291), a period of the Church's history of which it is not particularly proud. The Crusades were military campaigns, aimed at Christian repossession of the Holy Land, rather than attempts to propagate the Christian faith. This aim was unsuccessful, and the decision to sack Constantinople in 1204 during the Fourth Crusade caused the Western churches to forfeit any hopes of reconciliation with Eastern Orthodoxy. The inability of the Crusaders to conquer Islam shut off an important block of territory in the Middle East, preventing Christianity's spread to Asia, at least by land. It was only when Vasco da Gama and Christopher Columbus went on their sea explorations that African, Asians and Native Americans became the targets for evangelization. Although the Protestants have probably been the most enthusiastic of the three main Christian traditions, Protestant missionary work did not take off for around two centuries after Luther's Protestant Reformation. This was due to several factors. First, and most obviously, the Protestants were still in the process of establishing their own denominations and arguing amongst themselves regarding Reformation principles. This did not merely occupy their energies: unless there was a clear agreed message to proclaim, then mission was seriously impeded. Second, by ridding themselves of the monastic orders, Protestants deprived themselves of the traditional way in which Roman Catholicism had propagated itself. Third, unlike Roman Catholicism, the denominations that emerged from the Protestant Reformation were fragmented and divided, with no centralized authority. This impeded the organization of missions and, in the absence of centralized coordination, made missionary activity inefficient.

It was the nineteenth century that saw the rise of the principal missionary organizations that formed the substantial part of the fifth and most recent wave of Christian missionary activity, and which remain active today. The eighteenth century had witnessed the Great Awakening, with the evangelism of John Wesley (1703–1791), George Whitefield (1714–1770) and Jonathan Edwards (1703–1758), who preached the gospel in North America as well as in Britain. Some Christian foreign mission occurred in the eighteenth century. In 1701, the Society for the Propagation of the Gospel in Foreign Parts (SPG) was established by Dr Thomas Bray. Initially its aim was not to convert the indigenous population, but to enable English colonists to congregate and worship in the Anglican tradition. This aim soon widened, with SPG missionaries reaching slaves and Native Americans, although missionizing in India and Africa did not begin until 1820. David Brainerd (1718–1747), a young Presbyterian minister employed by the Honourable Society for Propagating Christian Knowledge travelled on horseback into American Indian territory. Through a translator, Brainerd preached the gospel message, gaining a few converts before he died of tuberculosis at the age of 29.

Methodism did much early pioneering missionary work. Wesley instructed his supporters to 'Do all the good you can, by all the means you can, in all the ways you can, in all the places you can, at all the times you can, to all the people you can, as long as ever you can' (Methodist Church 2010a). Thomas Coke (1747–1814), one of Wesley's supporters, is sometimes labelled 'the father of Methodist mission' on account of his arrival in Antigua in 1786, when a storm blew his ship off course *en route* to Nova Scotia. Various Methodist denominations set up their respective missionary societies, until the Methodist Union of 1932 caused their amalgamation into the Methodist Missionary Society.

The nineteenth-century missionaries went far beyond mere itinerant preaching. William Carey (1761–1834), a weaver's son who became a schoolteacher and then a Baptist minister gained himself the title, 'the father of modern missions'. An oft-recounted story is that Carey, in his mid-twenties, attended a ministers' meeting and proposed that all Christians had a duty to propagate the gospel worldwide. The convenor responded, 'Young man, sit down; when God pleases to convert the heathen, he will do it without your aid and mine.' The ministers belonged to the Particular Baptist Churches, and hence interpreted Calvin's teaching to imply that Christ did not die for all, but only those whom God had chosen. Undeterred by this rebuff, Carey went on to found the Particular Baptist Society for Propagating the Gospel among the Heathen in October 1792; it is known today as the Baptist Missionary Society (BMS World Mission). Carey preached a famous sermon that year, which was divided into two parts: 'Expect great things; attempt great things'—a motto that is now firmly associated with the missionary. The following year Carey departed for India, settling in Serampore, near Calcutta, where he was later joined by Joshua Marshman and William Ward. These three men became known as 'the Serampore trio'. Carey published a 15,000-word treatise, entitled, *An Enquiry into the Obligations of Christians to Use Means for the Conversion of the Heathens* (1792), in which he provided a theological justification for world mission, a history of the Church's mission and a response to objections to it. The pamphlet also includes a large amount of global demographic information, which Carey apparently compiled from his years as a schoolteacher, concerning the population and religious affiliations of the inhabitants of Europe, Asia, Africa and America.

Carey's work in India was not confined to preaching. Considerable effort was exerted on Bible translation, and Carey produced translations of the Bible in Sanskrit and Bengali, as well as some other Indian dialects. This was accompanied by the production of grammars and dictionaries. In order to ensure that the indigenous population could read these translations, their education was a priority, which included Indian women as well as men. Carey also attempted to persuade the Indian government to prohibit infanticide and *sati* (the immolation of widows on their husband's funeral pyre), and worked to oppose the caste system.

Following Carey, numerous other Protestant denominations set up their own missionary societies. The non-denominational London Missionary Society (LMS), now part of Christian World Mission (CWM), was established in 1795. The Church Missionary Society (CMS) in 1799 was set up by evangelical Christians in London; committed to the abolition of slavery as well as world evangelization, its founders included William Wilberforce (1959–1833). In 1804 the British and Foreign Bible Society was founded—the first of several Bible Societies—with the purpose of translating and providing Bibles, in English and in foreign languages. The Society's inception was inspired by the story of Mary Jones (1784–1864), a Welsh girl who, from the age of ten, had an intense desire to own a Bible. She saved up for six years, and made a 25-mile journey barefoot to the nearest supplier to purchase one. The British and Foreign Bible Society merged with several other Bible Societies to form the United Bible Society in 1946. It now adopts the simpler name 'Bible Society', and seeks to remedy 'Bible poverty'—its term for inadequate provision and knowledge of the Bible. In 1954, to mark the 150th anniversary of the Bible Society, the famous children's author Enid Blyton (1897–1968) published *The Greatest Book in the World*, which recounts some of the Society's work.

The China Inland Mission (CIM), founded by James Hudson Taylor (1832–1905) in 1865, was an attempt to take the Christian faith into inland China. Before that time, Christianity had only gained a foothold at the seaports, and in a few places where previous Roman Catholic missions had reached. CIM's distinctive features were its interdenominational nature, and its policy of never explicitly appealing for funds, but relying on prayer for God to provide the necessary resources. Unusually for that time, CIM adopted the policy of recruiting single women for mission work. Following the rise of communism in China, missionaries were forced to leave, and in 1953 the last CIM missionary departed. CIM widened its scope to encompass East Asia, adopting the name of the Overseas Missionary Fellowship (OMF), the name under which it now operates.

These organizations are only a very small sample of literally hundreds of missionary organizations that took their rise in the late eighteenth and early nineteenth centuries. However, the consequence of such a plethora of societies was that they tended to work independently, giving rise to rivalry, animosity and sometimes schism. One might have thought that the British and Foreign Bible Society's seemingly praiseworthy work of disseminating Bibles without contentious notes or commentary would have gained general approval among Christians. This was far from the case. Some leaders of the Church of England insisted that the *Book of Common Prayer* should be bound into the Society's Bibles. Some Bible

Societies in Europe were circulating Bibles containing the Apocrypha in 1826, whereupon the BFBS re-affirmed its policy of excluding books that were not part of the Protestant canon. This alienated the European Bible Societies, but did not go far enough for some Scottish participants, who seceded to form the Bible Societies of Glasgow and Edinburgh. (These later merged to form the Bible Society of Scotland in 1861.) Another controversy related to the inclusion of Unitarians in the BFBS's work, which gave rise to the formation of the Trinitarian Bible Society in 1831 as a splinter group. Meanwhile in India, missionaries objected to William Carey's allegedly contentious translation of the word 'baptize'; when the BFBS supported the objectors, Carey's supporters formed their distinctive Bible Translation Society in 1839. As for the Roman Catholic Church, it was fiercely opposed to Bible Societies in general, despite the inclusion of the Apocrypha by some. On 8 May 1844, Pope Gregory XVI sent out his encyclical *Inter Praecipuas* ('Among the special schemes'), condemning the work of such organizations, and forbidding the faithful to support them, or to read scriptures unaided by the Church's authority. He wrote,

> Among the special schemes with which non-Catholics plot against the adherents of Catholic truth to turn their minds away from the faith, the biblical societies are prominent. They were first established in England and have spread far and wide so that we now see them as an army on the march, conspiring to publish in great numbers copies of the books of divine Scripture. These are translated into all kinds of vernacular languages for dissemination without discrimination among both Christians and infidels. Then the biblical societies invite everyone to read them unguided. Therefore it is just as Jerome complained in his day: they make the art of understanding the Scriptures without a teacher 'common to babbling old women and crazy old men and verbose sophists,' and to anyone who can read, no matter what his status. Indeed, what is even more absurd and almost unheard of, they do not exclude the common people of the infidels from sharing this kind of a knowledge.

It is important to point out, however, that this is no longer the stance taken by the Roman Catholic Church. Addressing participants at an international Bible Societies gathering in 2002, Pope John Paul II greeted them as follows. Ironically, in common with Gregory XVI, he also quoted Saint Jerome:

> The Bible Societies exist to open the inexhaustible riches of Sacred Scripture to all who will listen; and that is a noble Christian service, for which I give thanks to God.

> For many years, your Societies have been engaged in translating and distributing the text of Scripture, an essential part of proclaiming Christ to the world. For it is not just words which we must speak: it is the Word of God himself! It is Jesus Christ, promised in the Old Testament, proclaimed in the New, whom we must present to a world which hungers for him, often without knowing it. It was Saint Jerome who declared that 'ignorance of Scripture is ignorance of Christ' (*Commentary on Isaiah*, Prologue). Your work then is above all a service of Christ. (Pope John Paul II 2002)

Because of the Protestant missionaries' emphasis on reading God's word, there was a need to ensure adequate standards of literacy, and hence Christian mission was frequently accompanied by the provision of education for indigenous communities. Missionary societies typically emphasize that setting up schools to give children an education was not primarily to enable proselytization, but was an expression of the love of Jesus Christ. Missionaries have therefore not merely brought the gospel to developing countries, but also education, medicine and help with agriculture.

Of the pioneering medical missionaries, David Livingstone (1813–1873) and Albert Schweitzer (1875–1965) are particularly renowned for opening up Africa. Livingstone was born in Blantyre, near Glasgow in Scotland, and his former home is now his museum and is open to the public as a tourist attraction. He was brought up as a Congregationalist, one of seven brothers in an impoverished family, and from the age of ten had to work in a cotton mill to assist the family's meagre finances. In 1834, British and American churches made an appeal for medical missionaries to China, and this inspired Livingstone to study. He qualified as a doctor, but the opium war prevented missions to China, and he departed for Cape Town instead in 1841, sponsored by the London Missionary Society. An explorer as much as a missionary, Livingstone did much to open up Africa. 'I shall open up a path into the interior, or perish,' was one of his famous statements, made in 1853. Fiercely opposed to the slave trade, one of his aims was to find a trade route across Africa that would provide a viable alternative to the slave ships that circumnavigated the continent. Unlike other explorers, Livingstone made a point of ensuring that he did not travel with a bodyguard of rifle-bearing soldiers, but carried only a few necessities, bartering for provisions with the people he met, and winning their confidence. This afforded him the opportunity to plant the Christian message.

The London Missionary Society had hoped that Livingstone would do more preaching than exploration, but Livingstone's desire to explore prevailed, and in 1857 he resigned from the Society. In the same year he published his *Missionary Travels and Researches in South Africa* (1857), continuing with his travels. Livingstone appears to have been less successful as an expedition leader, and his subsequent travels were marred by desertions and internal conflicts among his companions. Nonetheless, Livingstone's pioneering work did much to advance the West's geographical and demographical knowledge of Africa.

Albert Schweitzer studied philosophy and theology in his early years, becoming a pastor and subsequently principal of the Theological Seminary in Strassburg in 1903. When the Society of the Evangelist Missions of Paris announced the need for a medical doctor to work abroad, Schweitzer answered the call, despite the fact that the Mission was Roman Catholic and that he had no medical qualifications at the time. Schweitzer embarked on the study of medicine; his wife, Hélène Bresslau, trained at the same as a nurse, and later assisted him as his anesthetist. Having gained his doctor of medicine degree, Schweitzer set out in 1913 for Lambaréné in French Equatorial Africa, where he founded his hospital. During the Great War, Schweitzer and his wife became prisoners of war, until the war ended in 1918. Returning to France, Schweitzer resumed his preaching and writing. An accomplished concert organist, Schweitzer gave recitals, raising funds for the hospital, which was also partly financed from his publications' royalties. He returned to Lambaréné in 1924 where he spent the remainder of his life. Schweitzer was awarded the Nobel Peace Prize in 1953, and donated the $33,000 award to establish a leprosarium on the site.

Criticisms of Mission

Christian mission has not been without its critics. They have frequently been accused of arrogance, imperialism, destroying native cultures, and of gaining converts through ulterior motives, such as obtaining food, education or medical assistance. The missionary hey-day was at the height of the British, French and Dutch empires, and it was easy for Christians to believe that, having brought 'civilization' to many parts of the globe in the form of economic and technological improvement, they could also bring spiritual improvement in the form of the gospel. This belief frequently caused missionaries to disparage the other cultures and faiths that they encountered abroad. William Carey wrote about 'the barbarous and savage manner of their living', describing their plight as 'heathen darkness'. William Ward's *A view of the History, Literature, and Religion of the Hindoos* (1815) is a tirade against what he perceives as the vices of Hinduism. To give one of many samples, he writes the following concerning the lingam (a phallic image frequently found in Hindu temples):

> It is difficult to restrain one's indignation at the shocking violation of every thing decent in this image; nor can it be ground of wonder, that a chaste woman, faithful to her husband, is scarcely to be found among all the millions of Hindoos, when their very temples are polluted with filthy images, and their acts of worship tend to inflame the mind with licentious ideas. (Ward 1917: xxix)

These ideas found expression in missionary hymns that were sung in the West. One Victorian favourite began,

> Far, far away, in heather darkness dwelling,
> Millions of souls for ever may be lost;
> Who, who will go, Salvation's story telling —
> Looking to Jesus, counting not the cost. (*Golden Bells*, 623)

Christian missionaries often found problems with the use of images in temples, particularly those of the Hindu and Buddhist traditions. This was no doubt due to Protestantism's aniconic nature, and missionaries frequently pointed out the distaste with which 'idols' were regarded in ancient Hebrew times. Reginald Heber, whose missionary hymn, 'From Greenland's Icy Mountains' continues to be sung, contains the following lines:

> In vain with lavish kindness
> The gifts of God are strewn;
> The heathen in his blindness
> Bows down to wood and stone. (*Golden Bells*, 622)
> (Many present-day hymn books have now omitted these words.)

Not all missionaries saw the situation in such black and white terms. Others, such as J. N. Farquhar (1861–1929) viewed Christianity as *The Crown of Hinduism*—the title of a now famous book. Influenced by the theory of evolution, he regarded the other faiths of the world as evolving towards the truth of the Christian gospel. Hindus were not in darkness, he argued, but had aspects of the truth, which awaited their 'crowning' by the gospel message. Other missionary writers argued that non-Christian religions were not bereft of Christ, but enjoyed Christ's presence despite their lack of recognition of his name and his work. This theory is sometimes as known as 'anonymous Christianity', and has been espoused by writers such as Raymond Panikkar in his *The Unknown Christ of Hinduism*. Recent Roman Catholic statements, particularly after the Second Vatican Council, have acknowledged that other faiths can incorporate elements of truth, and that their followers are not in total darkness. Pope Paul VI stated in his encyclical *Nostra Aetate* (1965),

> The Catholic Church rejects nothing that is true and holy in these religions. She regards with sincere reverence those ways of conduct and of life, those precepts and teachings which, though differing in many aspects from the ones she holds and sets forth, nonetheless often reflect a ray of that Truth which enlightens all men. Indeed, she proclaims, and ever must proclaim Christ 'the way, the truth, and the life' (John 14:6), in whom men may find the fullness of religious life, in whom God has reconciled all things to Himself.

A further criticism of missionary work is that Christian mission has been guilty of 'ethnocide'—the erosion of the cultural identity of indigenous populations. Christian mission has come under attack for imposing Western standards of culture, education and architecture in the countries in which it has proselytized. Teachers have taught Western history rather than the history of the converts' countries, and churches were built in Western style, in stone rather than wood. Pipe organs were introduced, despite the fact that they are largely incapable of surviving hot dry climates, and where specialist maintenance is difficult to obtain.

Some missionaries were aware of such problems, and sought to correct them. One example was John Livingston Nevius (1829–1893), of the American Presbyterian Mission, who worked in China and subsequently Korea. His approach became known as the 'Nevius method', about which he wrote in his *The Planting and Development of Missionary Churches* (1886) and which involved a five-point plan:

(1) Indigenous converts should continue to live and work in their localities, being self-supporting, witnessing to their fellow-workers and neighbours;
(2) Projects and institutions should only be ones approved by the national church;
(3) The national churches should appoint their own pastors and support them;
(4) Churches should be built, using local materials, and in local architectural style, financed by local members;
(5) Church leaders should receive rigorous instruction on the Bible and Christian doctrine annually.

Nevius was heavily critical of the older system of commissioning new converts and paying them to preach in other localities, believing that this encouraged conversion for ulterior motives. Motivation for conversion has long been a serious issue, both for missionaries and their critics, since offers of medical support or economic development have encouraged the phenomenon of 'rice Christians', as they are sometimes called. While we know of no instance of missionaries making education, food or medical care conditional on a native's acceptance of Christianity, there remain organizations that explicitly state that these benefits provide a welcome opportunity for the propagation of the gospel. Commenting on their work with the victims of the 2004 Indian Ocean tsunami that hit Thailand, Indonesia and Sri Lanka, the missionary organization Gospel for Asia, whose headquarters are in Texas, reports, 'Gospel for Asia has made the commitment to those in the tsunami-hit areas to construct 1,000 homes and provide 500 fishing boats. We are committed to seeing this done in Asia in order that thousands more...will come to know the Lord' (Gospel for Asia 2005). Claiming that the tsunami was 'one of the greatest opportunities God has given us to share his love with people', its founder and president K. P. Yohannan boasted that some 14,500 native missionaries had distributed Bibles and pamphlets to survivors, offering them hope through God's love. Another example is Samaritan's Purse, a relief organization headed by Franklin Graham, the son of the famous evangelist Billy Graham. Its website states,

> Samaritan's Purse is a nondenominational evangelical Christian organi-
> zation providing spiritual and physical aid to hurting people around
> the world. Since 1970, Samaritan's Purse has helped meet the needs of
> people who are victims of war, poverty, natural disasters, disease, and
> famine with the purpose of sharing God's love through His Son, Jesus
> Christ. (Samaritan's Purse International Relief 2010)

Although Graham also views conversion as the organization's ultimate goal, it should be said, in fairness to him, that his approach was somewhat more sensitive. In an interview reported in *Christianity Today*, he said, 'It's not appropriate in a crisis like this to take advantage of people who are hurting and suffering. Maybe another day, if they ask why I come, I'd say I'm a Christian and I believe the Bible tells me to do this. But now isn't the time. We have to save lives' (Moll and Olsen 2005).

Other better known Christian relief organizations prefer to keep relief work separate from mission. Christian Aid, CAFOD (Catholic Agency for Overseas Development) and Tear Fund (The Evangelical Alliance Refugee Fund) view their work to alleviate poverty, injustice and disease, and their response to disasters, as a response to Jesus' instruction to provide support to the hungry, the homeless and the needy (Mt. 25:31-46), and explicitly affirm that help is available to all, irrespective of age, gender, race or religion. CAFOD and Christian Aid work with other faiths, such as Buddhism and Islam, recognizing that they, too, have humanitarian concerns. None of these three organizations seek conversions, although, being essentially Christian charities, they encourage supporters to pray for their work, and email prayer diaries to subscribers.

Because of those organizations that mix humanitarianism with proselytizing, it is understandable that they have aroused concern from some governments in developing countries. In 2006 several Indian states approved anti-conversion laws, preventing proselytizing by 'force, fraud or allurement'. At the time of writing, the government of Sri Lanka is considering a bill entitled 'Prohibition of Forcible Conversions'. Such bills do not exclusively target Christianity, but the work of Christian missionaries has been a major influencing factor in their formulation.

Missions to Jews

The question of missions to Jews deserves special comment, being an issue on which Christians continue to be divided. Theologically, Christians are divided between 'supercessionists' and those who embrace a 'dual covenant' theology. According to supercessionism, the Jews broke the covenant with God, and their covenant has now been transferred to the Christian community, whom they describe as 'the new Israel' or 'the second Israel' (although neither expression occurs in the Bible). If Jews are no longer party to God's covenant, then the only available means of salvation lies in the Christian faith. Accordingly, a number of missionary organizations specifically targeting Jews has arisen. One of the earliest was The Church's Ministry among Jewish People (CMJ), originally founded in 1809 as the London Society for the Promotion of Christianity amongst the Jews. Its founder-leaders included William Wilberforce, Charles Simeon and Lord Shaftesbury. Its work started in east London, where there was a significant Jewish population, and has now expanded worldwide. The Southern Baptist Church has adopted a similar position, and in 1999 instituted specific days of prayer to coincide with the major Jewish festivals, when its members were encouraged to pray for Jews to accept Jesus Christ as the true messiah. Proponents of supercessionism have sometimes used expressions such as 'antisemitism' and 'spiritual genocide' to characterize the position of Christians who hold that

Judaism as well as Christianity offers full salvation. It follows that failing to preach the gospel to Jews is to condemn them to a worse fate than that of the Holocaust.

The alternative 'dual covenant' view does not exempt Jews from being the targets for proselytizing. Jews for Jesus, founded in 1973 by Moishe Rosen (b. 1932), still regards the Jews as a 'covenant people', but insists that acceptance of Jesus as the messiah is essential for salvation. This is the position of the majority of evangelical Protestants. The Lausanne Movement, which originated in part from the Billy Graham Evangelistic Association as an umbrella organization for mobilizing worldwide Christian mission, produced an occasional paper in 1980 entitled 'Christian Witness to the Jewish People', which affirmed the necessity of proclaiming the uniqueness of Jesus Christ as fulfilment of Israel's hope, and welcomed the conversion of between twenty- and thirty-thousand Jews, which they estimated as the number who had transferred their allegiance to the Christian faith in the previous two decades. The Lausanne Declaration inspired a number of other position statements. In 1989 the World Evangelical Alliance formulated the Willowbank Declaration (at Willowbank, Bermuda), which reaffirmed the perceived need for Jews to embrace the Christian faith. However, the signatories declared that it was not necessary for converting Jews to repudiate their Jewish identity, and that it was even acceptable for them to continue to observe Jewish festivals. A further document, from the same source, emerged in 2008—'The Berlin Declaration on the Uniqueness of Christ and Jewish Evangelism in Europe Today'. The Berlin Declaration attempted to be conciliatory in recommending love for Jews, acknowledgement of the grave harms that past Christians have inflicted upon them, and avoiding the contempt and intolerance of the Jewish faith that was often charac-teristic of the past. Nonetheless, the Theological Commission and Task Force who produced the Declaration reaffirmed the necessity of accepting Christ as the sole means of salvation, and that love for the Jews could not be silent about this requirement. The authors wrote,

> We believe that genuine love cannot be passive. Jesus taught that authentic love could not be unfeeling when other human beings are in misery and need. Honest love must include an expression of Christ's good news in word and deed. Therefore, Christians everywhere must not look away when Jewish people have the same deep need for forgiveness of sin and true shalom, as do people of all nations. Love in action compels all Christians to share the gospel with people everywhere, including the Jewish people of Europe. (World Evangelical Alliance 2008)

The issue of 'targeting' specific groups remains controversial amongst missionary organizations. Billy Graham has spoken against it, claiming that he does not 'single out the Jews as Jews nor to single out any other particular groups, cultural, ethnic, or religious' (*Christianity Today* 1999).

Women in Mission

Special mention must be made of the role of women in Christian mission. The earliest modern pioneers tended to be men, but the importance of women in teaching and health care soon came to be recognized. Since women were the homemakers and child-rearers, it was important for the missionaries to reach them. However, they were frequently inaccessible, since they were often confirmed to their homes, and it was culturally inappropriate for men to attempt to gain entrance. Initially, wives of missionaries accompanied their husbands on their assignments, and husbands and wives were often jointly employed by their missionary society. This arrangement enabled the missionaries to act as role models of family life, showing Christian life in practice to the indigenous population. Around the middle of the nineteenth century the role of the single female missionary took its rise, and missionary organizations specially for women were established. One of the earliest was Zenana, founded in London in 1852 by the Baptist Missionary Society. *Zenana* is Persian for 'harem', and refers to the part of the house reserved for women. Zenana missions were missions by women to women in their own homes, initially with the purpose of propagating the gospel, but by the 1880s the work had extended to health care, and to other denominations. In 1871 the Women's Foreign Missionary Society was set up by the Methodist Episcopal Church of the United States (now merged as part of the United Methodist Church), and is one of the oldest surviving women-to-women missions. Although the story of Christian mission tends to be male-dominated, by 1910 more than half the missionaries worldwide were women, if one counts in the wives of male missionaries with the individual female workers.

A number of individual women missionaries have gained popular recognition for their work. Two famous examples are Mary Slessor (1848–1915) and Gladys Aylward (1902–1970). At the age of 29 Mary Slessor travelled to Duke Town, on the River Calabar in Malawi, and travelled inland on her own at considerable personal risk, preaching the Christian faith, treating the sick and helping to open up safe trade routes. Gladys Aylward used her life savings to pay for her voyage to China in 1930, having initially been turned down by the China Inland Mission. She established her Inn of the Eighth Happiness in Yuncheng, Shanxi Province. For a time she worked as a government inspector, with a particular concern for 'footbinding'. This was a practice whereby young girls' feet were constricted, so as to break the arch of the foot, with the aim of producing extremely small feet (ideally around three inches long), which were believed to be particularly alluring. Aylward's work provides one example of women missionaries' ability to address issues particularly affecting women. Other issues included *sati* burning in India and female education. Aylward was made the subject of a major Hollywood film *The Inn of the Sixth Happiness* (slightly renaming her 'inn').

Despite their undoubted courage and achievements, single female missionaries at times have undergone criticism. They were not feminists, but taught the Western, white, colonial values of their epoch, as the male missionaries had done. It is not our task to evaluate the work of the missionaries here, but rather to note that Christian mission has generated a variety of attitudes on the part of twenty-first century Christians. There are those who continue to see Christianity as exclusively offering truth and the means of salvation, while others feel that the missionary enterprise should have shown more respect for indigenous cultures, and the response to other faiths should be dialogue rather than confrontation. Many Christians believe that the proper target for mission should not be the adherents to non-Christian religions, but present-day secularism, the so-called 'cults', Christians who practise forms of occultism, and nominal Christians who lack full commitment (Johnstone and Mandryk 2001: 13-14).

Whatever its problems, Christian mission has certainly been effective in achieving growth. Religious statistics can be difficult to gather and interpret, and in his *Ten Great Religions* (1879), J. Freeman Clarke quotes some radically different estimates for his time, ranging from 120 million to 369 million Christians worldwide (Clarke 1879: 146). While some of Christianity's growth is due to population increase, and in specific countries (such as the United States, Canada, Australia and New Zealand) to international migration rather than conversion of the indigenous population, at a fairly rough estimate, Christianity has grown from the mid-nineteenth century to the early twenty-first century from between 6 and 10 per cent of the world's population to around 33 per cent. Christianity's growth has not been homogeneous: it has secured a greater uptake amongst minor indigenous religions than amongst the larger traditional religions of the world, notably Buddhism, Hinduism and Islam. Africa has been the most receptive to the Christian faith, while the Arab world, India and South-East Asia have proved the most impenetrable. From the 1980s, evangelical Christians have referred to this part of the world as 'the 10/40 window'—meaning the worldwide circumference between 10 and 40 degrees north of the equator—and have particularly targeted it for evangelism.

The Ecumenical Movement

The fragmentation of Protestantism tended to undermine the efficiency and credibility of foreign mission, and it was therefore important to attempt to coordinate their activities. One major event aimed to address the issue of cooperation, how missionaries might be trained and prepared for their work, and how their organizations might cooperate with foreign governments. This was the World Missionary Conference (WMC), held in the Assembly Hall of the Free Church of Scotland from 14 to 23 June 1910, and attended by 1,200 delegates from missionary societies and Protestant and Anglican churches. It was chaired by John Raleigh Mott (1865–1955), who headed the Student Volunteer Movement—a young men's organization for world evangelization. No Roman Catholic or Orthodox representatives attended. Continuation conferences were organized between 1912 and 1913, principally for leaders of Asian churches, replicating the WMC's 1910 agenda.

The WMC had several important outcomes. Concerning mission, the event was followed by a Continuation Committee, which resulted in the formation of the International Missionary Council (IMC) in 1921. (The Committee's work was retarded by the First World War.) Its work continued until 1961, when it was subsumed into the World Council of Churches as the Commission on World Mission and Evangelism. Two other bodies resulted from the WMC: the Faith and Order Commission, which discussed issues relating to doctrine and ministry within the churches, and the Life and Work Commission, which had responsibility for the churches' societal responsibilities. The IMC consisted of a network of Christian denominational councils, together with Western agencies. The former eventually became national Councils of Churches, and became affiliated to the World Council of Churches (WCC), which was formed jointly from the Faith and Order and Life and Work Commissions in 1948.

The WMC was not the first major attempt to unite Protestants. The Evangelical Alliance (a.k.a. World's Evangelical Alliance) was set up in England in 1846, when its inaugural convention was attended by some 800 delegates from 50 Protestant denominations in Europe and America. This ecumenical organization was initially a reaction against the Oxford Movement in the Church of England, and sought to uphold the principles of the Protestant Reformation, interpreted along Calvinist lines. Its nine principles include belief in the inerrancy of Scripture, justification by faith alone, the total depravity of man, and the Trinity. An American branch was founded in 1867, becoming the Federal Council of Church of America in 1908, and representing the country's major Protestant denominations. In England the Evangelical Alliance tended to decline during most of the twentieth century, although in 1958 it was instrumental in the establishment of the Evangelical Missionary Alliance, which aimed to promote interdenominational cooperation with overseas missions. The 1980s saw a revival within the Evangelical Alliance under new leadership, and it is currently a very active umbrella organization for evangelical Christians, with membership open to individuals, churches, Christian organizations and denominations. It is not merely concerned with evangelical proselytising: its motto is 'uniting to change society', and at the time of writing it offers an evangelical Christian perspective on societal issues such as the 2009 world economic crisis and individuals' related debt problems, the war in Iraq and the 2009 'swine flu' pandemic. The Evangelical Alliance of the UK is part of a wider set of networks, including the European Evangelical Alliance, and Global Connections (established in 1941 as the International Missionary Fellowship, and adopting its present name in 2000) with a particular emphasis on world mission. The Evangelical Alliance's founding convention established a week of prayer for Christian unity, which continues to be observed by many churches in the first full week of each new year, and is supported by evangelicals and liberals alike.

Another well known early ecumenical venture was the Young Men's Christian Association (YMCA, sometimes popularly referred to as 'the Y'). It was set up by George Williams (1821–1905), an assistant draper, who once described himself as 'careless, thoughtless, godless, swearing young fellow' but who found the Christian faith, and was appalled at the squalid and sometimes dangerous conditions in which young men worked in London. Together with eleven colleagues in the drapery trade, he set up the YMCA in 1844 to help the moral and spiritual improvement of those working in the drapery and other trades. Williams' organization initially offered prayer and Bible study as an alternative to life on the streets, and widened its scope to 'build a healthy spirit, mind, and body for all'. The Great Exhibition of 1851 enabled Williams and his supporters to distribute leaflets and establish links with other countries, leading to the World Alliance of YMCAs in 1855. The YMCA's work has expanded to include the provision of sports facilities, camping and hostelling, and classes in public affairs and citizenship. The YMCA hostels, which gave public visibility to the organization, were built to provide safe accommodation to travellers in unfamiliar cities, and to offer recreational facilities to keep young men off the streets. In 1894 Queen Victoria conferred a knighthood on George Williams for his work, and he is buried in St Paul's Cathedral, close to the spot where he and the other young drapers started the organization.

The Young Women's Christian Association (YWCA) offers services for women similar to those offered by the YMCA to men. Its origins are somewhat different: the YWCA took its rise in Britain in 1855 from the merging of two women's organizations: the General Female Training Institute, founded by Lady Mary Jane Kinnaird, and the Prayer Union of Emma Robarts. The Industrial Revolution, combined with the effects of the Crimean War, caused female poverty and destitution, and the YWCA sought to promote 'temporal, moral and religious welfare' specifically for women, and now offers guidance to young women on a range of issues, including domestic violence, homelessness, financial management and health care. In Britain the YWCA no longer regards itself as having a specifically Christian identity but, like the YMCA, it is an example of an early ecumenical endeavour, on which Christians cooperated, irrespective of denominational affiliation.

Another early ecumenical organization was Christian Endeavour (CE), founded by Dr Francis Clark, minister of Williston Congregationalist Church in Portland, Maine in 1881. Originally known as the Young People's Society of Christian Endeavour, the organization's focus was youth ministry, affording an opportunity for young Christians who had reached the stage of commitment to grow spiritually. CE's ethos is predominantly evangelical; there are four 'standards': confession of Christ, service for Christ, fellowship in Christ's people, and loyalty to Christ's Church. Christian Endeavour groups are normally associated with local congregations and their activities are mainly devotional. A typical meeting would consist of singing, prayer, Bible reading, a talk based on the Bible passage or on some pre-determined theme, and perhaps reports on mission work or evangelism in which the group has an interest. Meetings tend to be conducted by the young members, although they may invite a more senior speaker, when appropriate. One distinctive feature of Christian Endeavour is 'chain prayer': members are encouraged to contribute short prayers in swift succession, either extempore, or prayers derived from hymns or Bible passages. The practice is designed to encourage members to gain confidence in praying publicly, and to be personally involved in the prayers. Although Christian Endeavour essentially remains an organization for youth, there are now junior and senior branches for those who fall outside CE's original scope. Although groups are congregational, CE provides the opportunity for members of different denominations to meet together at conventions or social weekends.

All these ecumenical attempts, it should be noted, are Protestant, and until recently the Ecumenical Movement has been essentially a Protestant phenomenon. The World Council of Churches (WCC), which was set up at Amsterdam in 1948, was primarily a network of Protestant denominations but, even so, it was an impressive achievement to bring together 147 different church organizations from 44 different countries. At the time of writing, there are approximately 350 denominations from 110 countries. The WCC initially described itself as 'a fellowship of churches which accept our Lord Jesus Christ as God and Saviour', but in 1961 it amplified its basis for membership, stating that it is 'a fellowship of churches which confess the Lord Jesus Christ as God and Saviour according to the scriptures, and therefore seek to fulfil together their common calling to the glory of the one God, Father, Son and Holy Spirit' (World Council of Churches 2006). A significant number of national Orthodox churches have now joined, but the Roman Catholic Church still remains a non-member, although members of the Roman Catholic hierarchy have frequently been involved in consultations, conferences and the compilation of resources.

The World Council of Churches is not a 'super-church', a federation of worldwide churches, or a council in the sense of a governing body that makes binding decisions on its members. It is an organization, with its Administrative Centre in Geneva, governed by an Assembly that comes together every seven years, and by a Central Committee, which meets annually. The WCC's staff are drawn from its member churches, and it aims are to further the common goals that they share. Such goals include the quest for 'visible unity'. This does not mean, as some Christians occasionally fear, the creation of a single merged monolithic organization through negotiations and compromises in which denominations lose their heritage and identity. Rather, the WCC's ultimate goal is 'visible unity in one faith and one eucharistic fellowship' (World Council of Churches 2010b)

The rank-and-file Christian may not be familiar with the WCC's committees, consultations, reports or even its literature, but is faced with practical questions, such as whether it is acceptable to receive communion in a different denomination, whether a visitor from another denomination might be invited to conduct a service and, if so, whether he or she might baptize a child or preside over the sacrament. If someone is ordained by one denomination, could he or she be given responsibility over a congregation belonging to another, and, if so, on what terms? Is it possible to hold joint services for congregations of different denominations, and might there be conditions attached? As we noted in chapter 7, the Church is one at an invisible level, theologically speaking, but the ideal of oneness, in which all churches shared each other's ministry and sacraments without hindrance or controversy is still awaited. The WCC's logo, perhaps somewhat cryptically, highlights the ideal. Its motto *oikoumene* is the Greek word for 'household' or 'inhabited world', indicating that members of Christ's Church are already one single worldwide family. The accompanying logo of the boat whose mast is in the shape of a cross has been associated with the ecumenical movement for some decades, but its precise origins are unknown. The boat has obvious connotations of Jesus' life with his fishermen disciples, and reminds one of the Church being the vehicle in which one sails through life's sometimes troubled seas. The boat also symbolizes the Church as the 'ark of salvation': like Noah's vessel, which accommodated creatures of many different species to escape the flood, the Church is the vessel which accommodates a myriad of Christians, of different persuasions and denominations, to the final goal of eternal life.

The World Council of Churches logo. © World Council of Churches. Reproduced with permission.

In addition to consultations on ecumenical issues such as baptism, eucharist and ministry, the WCC exists to foster cooperation between churches on mission and evangelism, and also global concerns, such as peace and justice. The WCC's work on these matters is much wider than being a debating chamber. There exists a variety of practical projects that the Council has set up: there are too many to itemize in as short an account as this, and readers desiring more details can consult the WCC website. One or two examples will suffice here. The Ecumenical Institute of Bossey, Switzerland, was set up in 1946, and is now run by the WCC, offering seminars and courses, some of which lead to degrees, including provision of postgraduate study. It is accredited by the University of Geneva. Another example of a WCC project is its 'Faith, Science and Technology' programme, which addresses issues such as bio-technology, ecological problems and surveillance technology. A further programme is its 'Ecumenical HIV and AIDS Initiative in Africa (EHAIA), set up in 2002, offering care and support, education, counselling and pastoral training for those who are affected by the AIDS pandemic. The WCC aims to promote 'HIV-competent churches', by which it means the dissemination of reliable information on the problem, provision of clergy, counsellors and carers who competently provide support, and the removal of the stigma that is often attached to the disease. Much prejudice remains, even among Christian clergy; the authors have heard clergy proclaim from the pulpit that AIDS is a divine punishment for sexual misconduct, or express the opinion that practising homosexuals can be physically afflicted—not merely with sexually transmitted diseases—as a judgement for their lifestyle.

The ecumenical movement has progressed significantly over the past century. Different denominations have found it possible to worship together and sometimes to share premises. Inter-communion now presents few problems for Protestant denominations, although other traditions find greater barriers. In general there is now greater understanding and respect among Christians of different persuasions. Occasionally, ecumenism has led to mergers: the Church of North India, for example, was formed in 1970 as a union of the (Anglican) Church of India, Pakistan, Burma and Ceylon, the United Church of Nothern India (which itself consisted of merged Presbyterian and Congregational churches), the Baptist Churches of Northern India, the Church of the Brethren in India, the British and Australian Conferences of the Methodist Church and the Disciples of Christ. In 1972 in England, the English Presbyterian Church and the Congregational Churches combined to form the United Reformed Church.

Roman Catholics and Orthodox Christians, by contrast, are less keen to achieve institutional mergers. The Roman Catholic position is that there is already one and only one united Church, namely the Roman Catholic Church, and that there cannot be a Council of 'Churches' in the plural. Thus, when Roman Catholic teaching refers to unity and ecumenism, it tends to mean the maintenance of unity within its own organization. As the *Catechism of Catholic Church* states,

> Concern for achieving unity 'involves the whole Church, faithful and clergy alike.' But we must realize 'that this holy objective—the reconciliation of all Christians in the unity of the one and only Church of Christ—transcends human powers and gifts.' That is why we place all our hope 'in the prayer of Christ for the Church, in the love of the Father for us, and in the power of the Holy Spirit.' (*Catechism*, 822)

Until the Second Vatican Council, the Roman Catholic Church's view of ecumenism was that the other denominations should be persuaded to return to the fold. Many Roman Catholics would refuse even to enter a Protestant church building, let alone attend a service of worship there. The Vatican II document *Lumen Gentium* ('The Light of the Gentiles'), however, acknowledged the possibility of finding 'many elements of sanctification and truth' outside the Church of Rome. A later encyclical, specifically on ecumenism, was *Unitatis Redintegratio* ('The Restoration of Unity'), issued by Pope Paul VI in 1964. This document, significantly, used the word 'church' in reference to other denominations, and acknowledged that salvation could be found outside the boundaries of Roman Catholicism.

> It follows that the separated Churches and Communities as such, though we believe them to be deficient in some respects, have been by no means deprived of significance and importance in the mystery of salvation. For the Spirit of Christ has not refrained from using them as means of salvation which derive their efficacy from the very fullness of grace and truth entrusted to the Church. (*Unitatis Redintegratio*)

Roman Catholic endeavours at ecumenism were not confined to issuing encyclicals. In 1960 the Pontifical Council for Promoting Christian Unity was established as part of the Roman Curia. In 1964, Pope John Paul II visited the Administrative Centre of World Council of Churches, and, despite the fact that the Roman Catholic Church remained officially outside the WCC, a number of Roman Catholic theologians formed part of the commission that met in Peru in 1982, and produced the consultation document, *Baptism, Eucharist and Ministry*, which set out the key points of agreement and division amongst Christianity's various branches concerning these topics. In 1995 a further encyclical,

Ut Unum Sint ('That they may be one'—an allusion to Jn 17:11) re-affirmed the desire for unity with the Orthodox churches, continuing a process which began in 1979, when the Joint International Commission for the Theological Dialogue between the Catholic Church and the Orthodox Church was set up. Pope John Paul II repeated his now famous dictum in the 1995 encyclical: '[T]he Church must breathe with her two lungs.' (*Ut Unum Sint*, 54). The document makes little reference to 'other Christians' (it does not use the term 'Protestant'), although it shows appreciation for their work and encourages continued dialogue in the hope of eventual full inter-communion.

Objections to Ecumenism

Not all Christians are in favour of the ecumenical movement, and opposition has come from all three traditions, although opponents are a minority. Among Orthodox Christians, the monastic community of Mount Athos holds that the ecumenical movement compromises traditional doctrines, and believes that those who do not embrace Orthodoxy should be the targets of evangelism rather than negotiation. The Greek Old Calendrists still adhere to the Julian rather than the Gregorian calendar, and believe that the seven ancient ecumenical councils forbid any change, which twentieth- and twenty-first-century ecumenism might require. Roman Catholic opposition comes from traditional Catholics, particularly those who believe that the Second Vatican Council was unduly liberal. Such Catholics can point to pre-Vatican II encyclicals, such Pope Pius IX's 1928 *Mortalium Animos* ('Spirit of mortality'), which disparagingly refers to ecumenists as 'motley' 'pan-Christians' and discourages participation in non-Catholic gatherings:

> [T]his Apostolic See has never allowed its subjects to take part in the assemblies of non-Catholics: for the union of Christians can only be promoted by promoting the return to the one true Church of Christ of those who are separated from it, for in the past they have unhappily left it. To the one true Church of Christ, we say, which is visible to all, and which is to remain, according to the will of its Author, exactly the same as He instituted it. (*Mortalium Animos*, 8)

Just as traditional Roman Catholics believe that Christian unity should be achieved by members of other traditions returning to the fold, some evangelical Protestants believe that salvation can only be achieved through their brand of Christianity. Many of these Christians are mindful of the principles of the Protestant Reformation, and have no wish to enter into ecumenical negotiations with a tradition that accepts the authority of the Pope, whom the Westminster Confession of Faith describes as 'that Antichrist, that man of sin, and son of perdition, that exalts himself, in the Church, against Christ and all that is called God' (*Westminster Confession*, XXV,vi), which venerates the Virgin Mary and the saints, and holds to doctrines such as transubstantiation and the sacrifice of the Mass. Some Protestants are actively opposed to Roman Catholicism, one of the most vociferous opponents being the Revd Ian Paisley, founder of the Free Presbyterian Church, which originated in Northern Ireland in 1951. Protestant–Catholic opposition in Northern Ireland is political as much as religious, since Paisley's supporters fear the possibility of a union of the Northern and Southern states, which would result in Roman Catholic domination of the entire island's politics. (In the Irish Republic, abortion is illegal, and contraceptives cannot be sold—in accordance with Roman Catholic canon law.) In 1988, when the Pope addressed the European Parliament, Paisley, who was an MEP at that time, stood up and shouted, 'I denounce you as the Antichrist!', displaying a placard which read, 'Pope John Paul II Antichrist' (Cleland 2008).

Other Protestants are not confrontational in this way, but merely decline to become involved with the World Council of Churches. Pentecostalists have declined to join the WCC for a cluster of reasons. Many of them believe that it is charismatic renewal, as manifested in phenomena such as the 1994 Toronto Blessing, that will revive and unify the church, rather than organized ecumenical activity. (The Toronto Blessing was a charismatic revival movement that began at the Toronto Airport Vineyard Church, and spread internationally.) Some fear the risk of religious syncretism that ecumenism poses, and do not want to be tainted by the theological and moral liberalism that is found in other churches. Many Baptist denominations have not sought WCC membership, lest ecumenical discussions entail compromise; in June 1996 the Southern Baptist Convention passed a resolution resisting ecumenism, and affirming biblical truth as the sole valid means of uniting Christians. Evangelical fundamentalist Christians, however, have normally no problem in participating in Protestant alliances, such as the National Association of Evangelicals, or Promise Keepers (a conservative men's organization), as long as they seek to affirm and promote the Christian faith in its biblical fundamentalist form.

15

Christianity in the Developing World

For centuries Christianity has been the religion which defined European civilization, but now the centre of gravity of the faith is shifting from the northern hemisphere to the southern. It is estimated that there are now nearly 461 million Christians in Africa—some 46.3 per cent of the continent's population—with over 15 countries having Christianity as their dominant religion. With this shift new forms of Christianity are emerging that maintain ancient traditions, yet reflect the very different experiences of the cultures within which they are being formed. To take Africa and South America first, these two very different continents, with utterly different histories, were both evangelized by European missionaries who have left their mark on the faith of succeeding generations. Now both continents are open to the outreach of new waves of evangelism, often from North America, and in their turn are exporting their own forms of Christianity back to the countries from which the original missionaries came. Some of the forms of Christianity practised there are very conservative, both socially and theologically, while others are novel and often syncretistic.

Meanwhile, Christianity is also growing in parts of Asia. In the last third of the twentieth century South Korea has seen enormous growth in the number of Christians, especially Protestants, though there is also a long-established Catholic community. Somewhere between a quarter and a third of South Koreans identify themselves as Christians (estimates vary), and South Korean missionaries are active in many parts of the world. Some accounts claim that Chinese Christianity is experiencing a massive growth (Cox 1994: 220; Orberdorfer 1997: 49-51), though it is hard to be sure when sources are patchy and not always reliable. It seems fair to assume that the Christianity of the developing world will have an increasing influence on the older churches of Christendom. In what follows, we attempt to determine what has shaped it and where it is going.

Egypt and Northern Africa

Although the approach taken in this book is not predominantly historical, it is necessary to examine something of Africa's history in order to understand Christianity's place there. The history of Christianity in Africa is not one history but two quite separate ones: the first is of Mediterranean Africa where the new faith spread rapidly through the towns and cities of the Roman Empire and eventually reached as far south as Ethiopia; the second is that of sub-Saharan Africa, where it took root many centuries later with the arrival of European traders and settlers.

The northern part of Africa has a long Christian history, one that stretches back to the earliest years of Christianity and has continued unbroken to this day, despite Arab invasions and the Islamicization of most of the area. From it emerged one of Christianity's most influential theologians, Augustine, and the beginnings of the monastic movement which shaped the life and mission of the church, so it is worth examining in some detail. One of the first African Christians we hear about is Apollos, who appears in the Book of Acts (Acts 18:23-27). He was a Jewish scholar from Alexandria, the great cosmopolitan city of northern Egypt, who knew of John the Baptist and knew enough about Jesus to go north to Ephesus (in present-day Turkey) to pass on what he had heard. Alexandria had a very large Jewish population, and Christianity thrived there to such an extent that at a very early stage it became one of the major centres of the Christian world, and the seat of one of the patriarchates of the early Church.

From Egypt Christianity spread west through Roman North Africa. The city of Carthage, near modern Tunis, was another major early centre, and from it we have one of the most remarkable documents of the early Church, the account of the martyrdom of Perpetua, Felicity and three fellow-Christians at the beginning of the third century. Part of it was written by Perpetua herself, an articulate and well educated young married woman, and describes her experiences and visions while she was in prison. Not many writings of early Christian women have come down to us, and hers is a very vivid account of how it felt to be persecuted and condemned.

Carthage produced another notable Christian in Tertullian, a formerly pagan lawyer who became Christian and was writing at much the same time as the martyrdom of Perpetua and Felicity. He was a passionate defender of Christianity against the lurid rumours of cannibalism and incest among Christians that were current at the time, and fiercely ascetic; eventually he joined the Montanists, a group whose emphasis on continuing prophecy and strict discipline brought them into conflict with the wider Church. Carthage—and North Africa in general—was a centre of strict and uncompromising religious practice; a century or so later, after the last ferocious persecution of Christians at the beginning of the fourth century, it produced the Donatists, a group who condemned the church authorities for receiving back people who had fallen away during the persecutions and broke away from the mainstream Church to maintain their own rigorous standards.

The same urge to find a stricter and purer way to practise their faith drove many men and women into the deserts of Egypt in the fourth and fifth centuries, after Christianity had become first legal and then popular in the cities of the Roman Empire. For many people the spread of Christianity meant the loss of the demanding standards of the Church under persecution. Those who wanted to lead lives of more dedicated prayer and fasting moved out into the desert, at first living on their own or in little groups, and later increasingly banding together to form the communities which were the beginning of monasticism. These Desert Fathers (and Mothers) have left a legacy of biographies and sayings which reflect a deep ascetic spirituality.

The greatest theologian of North Africa, and one who has had an immense and lasting influence on the Christianity of the West, Saint Augustine, was born in Tagaste, not very far from Carthage, in 354. He lived at a time of great change, as the Roman Empire began to fall apart; when he died in 430 the Vandals, invading from the north, were already besieging Hippo, the city of which he was bishop. There was division and change among Christians, too. The Vandals, who set up their kingdom in North Africa were Arians, and intermittently persecuted their African subjects. A few years later, at the Council of Chalcedon in 451, the church split on the question of the natures of Christ and the Copts of Egypt found themselves on the other side of the split from most of the Christians around them. (Arianism and its influence on the Council of Chalcedon are explained in chapter 6.)

When an Arab army arrived in Egypt in 639, defeating the Byzantine army which attempted to defend the country, it found a divided, weakened Christianity. The Copts had no love for the Byzantine government, which treated them as second-class citizens, and the early Muslim rulers were tolerant of them, apart from imposing an extra tax on them. Later rulers were less tolerant and conversion was encouraged, but even so, many Egyptians remained Christian, and today at least 10 per cent of Egyptians are still Coptic Christians. From Egypt the Arab armies moved westwards. Islam came to dominate North Africa completely, and within a century or so Christianity outside Egypt had disappeared.

Further south, Christianity in Ethiopia developed a life of its own, and is still flourishing today in spite of periods of persecution and difficulty. While the first Ethiopian Christian recorded is the government official (the Bible calls him a 'eunuch') who was travelling home from Jerusalem, when he met the apostle Philip who baptized him (Acts 8:26-40), the country as a whole did not become Christian until the fourth century, when it was attached to the Coptic Church of Egypt and had its bishops appointed by the Patriarch of Alexandria. Apart from the Coptic connection, and a period of Roman Catholic missionary influence in the sixteenth and seventeenth centuries, the Ethiopian Church remained largely cut off from contact with the rest of the Christian world for a long time and has retained some Old Testament customs such as observance of the Sabbath (as well as of Sunday), and a form of the Jewish dietary laws. It also has its own canon of Scripture, which contains not only all the books accepted by the Orthodox churches in general, but a number of extra ones, most of inter-testamental Jewish origin; it claims that its kings were descended from Solomon and the Queen of Sheba, and that the Ark of the Covenant is preserved in the cathedral at Axum.

Sub-Saharan Africa

While Christianity has deep roots in the north of the continent, it arrived much later in sub-Saharan Africa. The first missionaries came with Portuguese explorers and traders in the middle of the fifteenth century, and their earliest success was in the West African coastal kingdom of Kongo. In spite of setbacks Catholicism took root there, though the missionaries were less successful in neighbouring kingdoms. There was a major revival of Roman Catholic missionary work in the middle of the nineteenth century, with the foundation of missionary orders dedicated to evangelizing Africa.

Protestant missionary work started in the eighteenth century, at first carried out by freed slaves of African ancestry sent out from the West. Sierra Leone, settled at the end of the eighteenth century by freed slaves from America who had become Christians there, became a centre of mission. At much the same time the European-led missions began: Moravians from central Europe, Baptists and Anglicans from Britain all sent out missionaries, and so, increasingly, did American churches. The Protestant missionaries in particular were interested in bringing their version of Western civilization to Africa, and opening it up to trade with the rest of the world. David Livingstone, perhaps the most famous of all the nineteenth-century missionaries, spoke of bringing 'Christianity, commerce and civilization' to Africa. There is no doubt that many missionaries were utterly committed to the people they worked among and braved illness and harsh living conditions to bring Christianity to them, but the Western attitudes they brought were not always a benefit, and their work paved the way for the colonization and exploitation of Africa as well as bringing education and a faith which has entered deeply into the lives of many Africans.

As they introduced Christianity, missionaries also brought their denominational differences, making the map of Christian Africa a patchwork of denominations reflecting the origins of those who brought the gospel, and leaving a legacy which has continued to this day. Even within a single denomination, there could be significant differences which have continued to colour the style of Christianity practised in different places. For example, Anglican missionaries were sent out both by the Church Missionary Society and the United Society for the Propagation of the Gospel, and their different emphases are still reflected in differences between African Anglican churches. The Anglicanism of Ghana reflects the more high-church background of the missionaries who worked there and has absorbed African traditional elements into the conduct of liturgy. By contrast the Church Missionary Society's evangelical teaching still strongly affects the Anglicanism of Nigeria and Uganda, where the Bible, conservatively understood, remains central to Christian experience. This is one of the factors which makes the Christianity of that area so resistant to developments in other parts of the Anglican communion, and the consequences of that resistance are becoming increasingly evident in the disagreements within the Anglican Communion today.

New Ways of Practising an Old Faith

While the missionaries brought Christianity to Africa, it was Africans who spread it and made it truly African, and now nearly 40 per cent of Africans identify themselves as Christians. Though the majority of

African Christians belong to worldwide Christian organizations, such as the Roman Catholic Church, the Anglican Communion, or the international Methodist movement, others have developed indigenous forms of Christianity. The independent churches of Africa often took their rise from missionary-founded Protestant churches whose leadership continued to be based abroad, but where African Christians no longer wished to be subordinated to foreign leaders. In turn, some of these African-led churches have now been introduced into Western countries through immigration from Africa, and have brought African Christianity to Europe and America.

The independent churches vary widely from the theologically orthodox to groups that combine elements of Christianity with traditional African religion. Typically they emphasize the experiential side of Christianity: prayer, prophecy, healing and (sometimes very severe) fasting. They tend to take the Bible extremely literally and to relate Jesus' casting out of demons to traditional African beliefs in evil spirits. The Aladura churches of Nigeria, such as the Cherubim and Seraphim Church, lay great emphasis on prayer, while the largely Zulu Zionist churches of South Africa practice spiritual healing and speaking in tongues, and may also permit polygamy, which has often been a source of tension between the mission churches and African converts. At the less orthodox end of the spectrum there are organizations like the Nigerian Brotherhood of the Cross and Star, which uses the language of the Bible but regards its founder Olumba Olumba Obu as a semi-divine being with supernatural powers. Though Christianity in general is growing in Africa, the independent churches form the fastest-growing sector.

Baptism ceremony in the Celestial Church of Christ, Cotonou, Benin.
© 2007 Ferdinand Reus. Licensed under Creative Commons Attribution-Share Alike 2.0 (generic license).

Most of these churches are Protestant, or Protestant-derived; the Roman Catholic Church has been largely successful in keeping the Catholics of Africa together, though there have been a few notable exceptions; one example that recently gained much publicity was the Movement for the Restoration of the Ten Commandments of God, which was started by Catholics who claimed to have received visions of the Virgin Mary, and which ended in the death of most of its adherents in 2000. Visions of the Virgin Mary are not uncommon. Even within the hierarchy of the Church there are sometimes problems; the most notable example is probably that of the Zambian Archbishop Milingo. As Archbishop of Lusaka he practised a form of healing through prayer and exorcism which incorporated traditional African elements, to the point where the Vatican authorities felt it necessary to investigate what was happening. He was recalled to Rome, and finally resigned from his post in 1983.

Remarkable as the interface between Christian orthodoxy and African traditional religion is, it is in the mainstream churches that African Christianity is beginning to have a significant and growing influence on the rest of the Christian world. The Nigerian Cardinal Francis Arinze, a specialist in inter-faith relations with a long and distinguished career, was seen as a serious contender to succeed Pope John Paul II in 2005. The role of the African churches in the Anglican Communion, too, has recently sprung into prominence, with the growing divide between the liberal Anglicanism of the North, especially that of the Episcopal Church in the United States, and the conservative Anglicanism of many of the African churches. Wealthy and influential as the Episcopal Church is, it has comparatively few members, perhaps about two million, while there are now some nineteen million Anglicans in Nigeria and the church there continues to grow. Peter Akinola, the Anglican archbishop of Nigeria, is a strong defender of what he regards as traditional Anglicanism and is outspoken about what his perceived betrayal of the faith by liberals. The consecration of the openly gay Gene Robinson as a bishop of the Episcopal Church in New Hampshire in 2003 was a flash point for African Anglicans. There has been much talk of schism within the Anglican Communion, and in 2008 a number of African bishops boycotted the Lambeth Conference, the gathering of Anglican bishops convened every ten years by the Archbishop of Canterbury. Instead they met in Jerusalem with conservative Anglicans from other parts of the world at the Global Anglican Future Conference (GAFCON). The conference did not precipitate the formal schism in the Anglican Communion that many had predicted, but the tension between the opposing sides has not diminished.

While the Anglican Communion may have the most visible split, worldwide Methodism also faces the same challenges, with a rapidly growing membership in Africa and other parts of the developing world whose attitudes are equally conservative, and who hugely outnumber their parent churches in Britain and the United States. The leadership of the United Methodist Church—which is based in the USA but also includes Methodists from Africa, Latin America and Asia—attempted to introduce more inclusive measures towards lesbian, gay and transgendered people at its General Conference in 2008, but found many of its motions defeated by coalitions of conservative Methodists from America and delegates from developing countries. For them, as with Anglicans, sexuality, and particularly homosexuality, is a touchstone of how seriously one takes the teachings of the Bible.

There are several reasons for the focus on homosexuality, which seems so strange to liberal Western Christians (although not to the conservatives). Many African Christians are only one or two generations away from their forebears who practised the indigenous religious traditions which still flourish in many parts of the continent, and they identify very strongly with the Bible's firm rejection of 'pagan' practices. They lay great emphasis on Saint Paul's condemnation of homosexual practice (Rom. 1:18-32), and are not impressed by the efforts of many Western theologians to view them as products of their first-century context. Just as they take the Bible literally when it speaks of healing and the power of prayer, they do the same with human sexuality, and believe that sexual relationships should be strictly limited to marriage. In some countries, too, such as Nigeria, where Christianity is in competition, and often conflict, with an equally conservative Islam, any hint of more liberal attitudes towards sexuality might suggest acceptance of the Western decadence which local Islamic leaders attack. In some places there are also historical reasons: Ugandans in particular remember the Catholic and Anglican martyrs of the 1880s, some of whom were executed for resisting the homosexual advances of the king.

Equally in line with a conservative approach to the Bible, St Paul's strictures against women teaching and preaching are still very influential in many African churches. Practice varies quite widely among the Protestant churches which belong to international networks such as the World Council of Churches. Some ordain women to all leadership roles, some allow women in subordinate leadership roles, but not as ministers;

some do not ordain them at all despite encouragement from Western partner churches to do so. The Anglican churches of Africa are also divided on this issue. For example, the South African church ordains women as deacons and priests and the Nigerian one does not, but attitudes are slowly changing; in June 2009 the Anglican Church in Ghana announced its intention to begin training women for ordination. In the Anglican Church of Southern Africa women are also eligible to be made bishops, though none has yet been consecrated. As far as the African Independent Churches are concerned, variations are equally wide, but they have generally helped to empower women, many of whom take on more prominent roles than they do in more conservative mainstream churches or as traditional gender roles in wider society allow.

South Africa contrasts with the rest of sub-Saharan Africa in having some of the most liberal official attitudes in the world to social issues such as homosexuality. The contrast reflects its different history. Christianity arrived there in the middle of the seventeenth century, when the first Dutch traders settled at the Cape of Good Hope, bringing their strict Calvinist faith with them and setting up the Dutch Reformed Church there. At the beginning of the nineteenth century, with the arrival of British settlers and missionaries and the abolition of the slavery which had played such a large role in the development of the colony, the original Dutch community, by now the Afrikaners, came to see themselves as a nation under threat from the outside world. Their sense of isolation and separateness eventually developed into the system of apartheid, by which the Dutch Reformed Church was deeply identified, to the point where it set up separate churches for blacks, coloureds and whites. This led to its increasing isolation from other reformed churches worldwide as international opposition to the system of apartheid grew. In 1982 the World Alliance of Reformed Churches expelled the Dutch Reformed Church for continuing to practise apartheid, and it later publicly expressed its repentance for supporting apartheid. In other churches, attitudes to race and colour have varied considerably, both at denominational level, and among individuals. Many insisted on worshipping together despite racial differences. Some churches, especially the Pentecostals, who have a significant presence in South Africa, had a tradition of keeping clear of involvement with politics, though in the final years of the struggle against apartheid this attitude increasingly broke down. Other churches were involved in the struggle from the start, and the movement developed its own distinctive brand of theology, which emphasized God's demand for justice for the poor and marginalized.

Churches in Difficult Places

The struggle against apartheid in South Africa is a reminder of the extent to which Christians in sub-Saharan Africa have been involved in conflict ever since the introduction of Christianity. The martyrs of Uganda, mentioned above, were missionaries and converts who were caught up in the political and social changes that were introduced by the coming of Western missionaries in the 1880s and fiercely resisted by the ruler. Christianity, in bringing Western-style education and widespread literacy, also raised Africans' expectations and so laid the foundations for resistance to colonialism. Many of the leaders of the struggle for independence in Africa were Christians who had been educated in mission schools.

Christians, along with members of other faiths, were prominent in the fight to overthrow apartheid and establish racial equality in South Africa. There are many examples of leaders such as Desmond Tutu, the Anglican Archbishop of Cape Town, who contributed to the final establishment of majority rule. Beyers Naudé spoke out against the policies of his own church—the Dutch Reformed Church—and was forced out as a consequence. In other African countries Christians have often been in the forefront of resistance to oppression, and have sometimes paid heavily for it. In Uganda Janani Luwum, the Anglican Archbishop, an outspoken opponent of Idi Amin's brutal regime, was murdered by the government in 1977 and is regarded as a martyr in the Anglican communion. More recently Pius Ncube, the Roman Catholic Archbishop of Bulawayo, was at the forefront of the opposition to the increasingly repressive regime of Robert Mugabe in Zimbabwe until he was forced to resign in 2007 after the government accused him of having an affair with a married woman.

However, Christians have been oppressors as well as fighters against oppression; Mugabe himself is a Roman Catholic, and he has found supporters in the churches of Zimbabwe. The former Anglican Bishop of Harare, Nolbert Kunonga, is an enthusiastic backer of Mugabe's policies, and Mugabe rewarded him with the gift of an expropriated farm. The bishop's first action on taking possession was to evict the African farm workers and their families. He has now been excommunicated, but still claims to be the legitimate bishop and has attempted to block the consecration of the new Bishop of Harare. The Rwandan genocide of 1994 provides even more disturbing evidence of the lengths to which Christians can go in identifying themselves with oppression and violence; many priests and members of religious orders were deeply involved in the massacres which took place.

Latin America

Unlike the peaceful spread of Christianity throughout sub-Saharan Africa, the rapid and often brutal Spanish and Portuguese conquest of Latin America in the sixteenth century brought Christianity there by force. The Spaniards took with them a feudal system which entitled them to use the conquered Indians' labour. They assumed responsibility for educating, protecting and teaching Christianity to them, but this led to the ruthless exploitation of the Indian population. Large numbers of immigrants arrived from Spain and Portugal to seize the available opportunities in the Americas, and they brought not only European civilization but also European diseases, from which the local population had no immunity. Between sickness and exploitation the Indians suffered greatly, and some of the Dominican missionaries who had emigrated to work among them began to speak out about the conditions in which they were living. One of the Spanish colonists, Bartolome de las Casas, who was also a priest, became increasingly concerned about the ill-treatment of the Indians and returned to Spain to raise awareness of what was happening in the new colonies. Despite much opposition he succeeded in introducing reforms which improved conditions for the Indians, but also led to the importing of slaves from Africa to do the work that the Indians were no longer forced to do.

Catholic religious orders played a major part in the conversion of the Indians. As well as the Dominicans and Franciscans, the Jesuits also sent out missionaries from the sixteenth century onwards. They set up communities for the rural Indians on their estates, and imposed discipline on their converts. Though their attitude towards the indigenous workers on their estates was paternalistic and often overbearing, they made efforts to learn the local languages rather than forcing the Indians to speak Spanish or Portuguese. The Christianity of Latin America was very much that of the Iberian peninsula, run by clergy and church musicians who came out from Europe, but there were real attempts to reach Indians on their own terms; for instance, sixteenth- and seventeenth-century musicians from Spain set non-liturgical religious texts in local languages so that indigenous Christians could sing devotional songs in their own tongue.

One of the most striking examples of the interaction between Christianity and local traditions is the devotion to Our Lady of Guadalupe, whose shrine in Mexico City is one of the most popular pilgrimage places in the Americas. The Virgin Mary is said to have appeared in 1531 to the Indian Christian convert Juan Diego, and asked him, in the local language, to go to the Bishop of Mexico, requesting him to build a church for her where she had appeared. The Spanish bishop ignored the request, whereupon the Virgin encouraged Juan Diego to return and try again, this time with his cloak full of roses, which she had caused to spring up miraculously on the hill where she met him. When he emptied the roses out in front of the bishop, he found an image of the Virgin imprinted on his cloak. The purportedly original cloak, with its miraculous image, is still on display in the huge modern basilica which has replaced the original shrine. Our Lady of Guadalupe is immensely popular in Mexico and has become a national symbol of the country, as well as being given the title of Patroness of the Americas.

Interestingly, the Virgin is not quite a conventional European figure. Her features and some aspects of her clothing can be read as Aztec, and it has been suggested that she may be an adaptation of an indigenous goddess. Juan Diego himself was canonized in 2002, despite some doubts over the historicity of the apparition story. He is the first indigenous South American to be declared a saint, though not the first saint of Latin America; for example, there were several in Lima, Peru, in the early part of the seventeenth century: Saint Rose of Lima, Saint Martin de Porres and Saint John Massias, all Dominicans from Spanish families (though Saint Martin's mother was a freed black slave, and he is the first black saint of the Americas).

There were other unofficial ways in which Catholicism and American Indian culture met and mingled. Missionaries from Europe found a variety of lively indigenous religions, and though they taught and baptized the Indians, their converts did not necessarily pick up exactly what the missionaries believed they were learning from them. The new faith was combined with elements of the old without any great difficulty, especially as its worship was conducted in Latin, a language completely unknown to the new Christians. In many parts of the continent Catholics (not usually Protestants) still take part in rituals that have survived centuries of Christianity, often with local Catholic clergy turning a blind eye to the practices. The slaves' religious practices, brought from West Africa, have also contributed to the religious mix. In turn the syncretistic religions of Latin America have adopted Christian practices, with shamans sometimes modelling themselves on Catholic priests as a way of improving their status, and ancient gods and goddesses taking on the attributes of Christian saints.

The situation is changing in the wake of the Second Vatican Council. The increasing emphasis on the study of the Bible and the saying of the Mass in Spanish have encouraged lay Catholics to become more aware of Christianity's teachings, and hence they are more able to distinguish between them and traditional practices. At the same time, the expanding Protestant churches are much less tolerant of indigenous religious practices than the Catholic hierarchy has been, and discourage their members from taking part in them.

The Rise of Protestantism

For centuries, South America was a staunchly Catholic continent. Anglicanism, Lutheranism and Presbyterianism all arrived in the nineteenth century with immigrants from Europe, but made little impact outside the communities which brought them. Change began in the second half of the twentieth century, when evangelical Protestantism started to spread through many South American countries. It now forms the main non-Roman Catholic version of Christianity there, with the Pentecostal movement as its largest component.

Evangelical Protestantism's rapid growth and impact since the 1960s has been considerable in many Latin American countries. Protestantism has developed from a small handful of organizations into a movement of great range and diversity, and has had a major social and political impact in the continent, especially Brazil and Guatemala. The evangelical churches often work in the poorest and most deprived areas, and encourage an ethic of self-help sand self-respect. Drinking, smoking and drug use are firmly discouraged, and many churches run training courses to help their members learn new skills and find steady employment. In a context where life is often very hard and many people's Catholicism has become purely nominal, membership of a Protestant church can entail a complete change of lifestyle, and bring real social and material as well as spiritual support. Conversion seems to be genuinely life-changing in many cases, but it often demands a high level of commitment, not just weekly attendance at church but also involvement in other aspects of church life, such as prayer groups, choirs and attempting to win others for Christ in one's home and in public. This can often prove too much for less-committed members. There is also the 'revolving door' effect, where people eventually revert to their familiar Catholicism once their immediate needs have been met, and there is evidence in some countries of a levelling-out in the growth of the evangelical churches.

Brazil is still the largest Roman Catholic country in the world, but it has seen enormous growth among its evangelical churches, especially since the 1980s. It has also seen a recent rash of scandals and accusations of financial irregularities. The poverty of many of the church members is in sharp contrast to the luxurious lifestyles enjoyed by some of their leaders. Estevam Hernandes and Sonia Haddad Moraes—the married couple who lead Reborn in Christ Church (Igreja Renascer em Cristo), one of the major Pentecostal churches—recently returned to Brazil after serving a two-year sentence in the USA for smuggling money, and faced investigation in Brazil on charges of fraud, tax evasion and money laundering. At the time of writing, Edir Macedo—the leader of another major Brazilian church, the Universal Church of the Kingdom of God (UCKG)—and some of his colleagues, are being investigated on similar charges, accused of having diverted donations for charitable work into building a business empire. The UCKG's claims include the ability to liberate people possessed by demons and 'cure' homosexuality and disabilities. It has churches throughout the world, including Britain, and America, which practise healing and exorcisms.

Since the 1980s the evangelical movement has had a considerable political and social effect on the life of the continent, sometimes forming its own political parties and often providing effective pressure on politicians. While its influence is generally conservative, in Brazil and some other countries its centre of gravity is moving leftwards, with an emphasis on social justice; evangelicals, especially Pentecostals, frequently work among the poorest members of the community. Protestants there tend to be socially conservative, with a heavy emphasis on personal morality, and their views on such issues as abortion and homosexuality are very similar to the official views of the Roman Catholic Church. At the same time, Catholicism has its own charismatic movement and, though liberation theology is not the force it once was in some countries of the continent, it still retains many supporters, though its emphasis now is much more on social issues rather than the overtly political issues of its earlier years.

Asian Christianity

Christian missionaries in Asia found themselves confronting a very different situation from those in Africa and South America, where they encountered primal religions and pre-literate societies. They had to contend with well established and theologically highly sophisticated religious systems in most of the countries where they worked, and so there are only two Asian countries which are almost entirely Christian. One is the Philippines, colonized by Spain in the sixteenth century and largely Roman Catholic, though with minorities of other Christians and Muslims, while the second is East Timor, colonized by the Portuguese at much the same time, and which is about 90 per cent Roman Catholic. Another former Portuguese colony, Goa, on the west coast of India, still has a very high proportion of Catholics. Spanish and Portuguese missionaries also made their way to Japan and China, where the Jesuits worked with particular success among the educated upper classes, but later political developments undid most of their work. It was not until the nineteenth century that another wave of missionaries, most of them Protestants this time, arrived and attempted the conversion of Asia, with limited success.

One country in which they succeeded in founding a solid base was Korea. Despite persecution by the occupying Japanese in the first half of the twentieth century, Christianity survived. After the division of the country at the end of the Second World War, many Christians in North Korea moved to the south, and as South Korea began to prosper in the 1960s, Christianity grew rapidly. The country boasts some of the world's largest Protestant churches, including the enormous Yoido Full Gospel Church in Seoul, which claims 750,000 members. Christianity only survives underground in North Korea, where religion is discouraged and there are reports of Christians being persecuted and sometimes executed.

North Korea's neighbour China has seen substantial growth, though there are wildly varying estimates of the numbers involved. After Jesuit influence at the imperial court and among the educated upper class faded, Christianity made no further headway until Protestant missionaries began to arrive at the beginning of the nineteenth century. Throughout the nineteenth century both Catholics and Protestants worked in China, founding many medical and educational projects, and their work was successful enough to provoke a backlash in the form of the Boxer Rebellion of 1898–1901, which targeted both missionaries and Chinese Christians; but in its aftermath Chinese Christianity continued to flourish and become increasingly naturalized, with new independent Chinese-led churches springing up during the first half of the twentieth century.

This process was hastened when the Communist Party came to power in 1949 and foreign missionaries were expelled from the country. At the beginning of the 1950s the Three-Self Patriotic Movement (the name refers to its function as a self-governing, self-supporting and self-prop-agating organization) was set up to consolidate the various Protestant churches of the new People's Republic into one body that would be answerable to the communist government. During the repression of all religious groups during the Cultural Revolution (1965–1968), Christianity went underground and Christians met in unofficial house churches; and when liberalization began in the late 1970s, there was a general resurgence of religion and the house churches continued to thrive. However, although its constitution now guarantees freedom of religion, the government of the People's Republic had no intention of permitting unregulated and unregistered churches to continue, and reinstated the Three-Self Patriotic Movement, which together with the China Christian Council was intended to represent all Chinese Protestants, while Roman Catholics were under the official control of the Chinese Patriotic Catholic Association. Despite this, the unofficial churches have survived and flourished, and seem to be growing more rapidly than the official church, often functioning quite openly. There are regular reports of raids on unofficial churches and of cases of persecution of individuals, but Protestant Christianity seems to be growing rapidly and attracting large numbers of educated younger people.

Catholics face a more difficult situation. The Chinese government does not want its citizens to be part of an international movement, or to owe allegiance to any leader outside China, so the Chinese Patriotic Catholic Association has disassociated itself from the Pope, and is regarded as a schismatic movement by the Vatican. Roman Catholics who insist on remaining loyal to Rome face real difficulties, and a number of Catholic clergy have been imprisoned for maintaining their links with the rest of the Roman Catholic world.

No one knows how many Christians there are in China. Official figures include only the members of the official church organizations and ignore those in the unofficial churches. A conservative estimate would suggest 40 or 50 million in a population of 1.3 billion, but other estimates suggest that the number may be as much as 100 million, and growing rapidly.

India

Finally, we turn to India, where Christians are a small but articulate minority (approximately two per cent). There have been Christians in

India for a very long time; the ancient Mar Thoma church in the south of the country claims to have been founded by the apostle Thomas and undoubtedly dates back to early in the Christian era. (There is a legend that the apostle Thomas journeyed to India to preach the gospel, and ended his days there.) The Christian community in Goa goes back to the Catholic missions of the sixteenth century, and the various Protestant churches were founded as a result of missionary work from the end of the eighteenth century onwards. These missionaries founded schools and hospitals, and though some of their early converts were members of the higher castes, many were drawn from the so-called 'untouch-ables', the most disadvantaged members of society who were often shunned by others and relegated to the moat menial jobs. About 70 per cent of Christians in India are from this stratum of society, who now generally refer to themselves as 'dalits'—those who are downtrodden or suppressed.

India is a generally tolerant society, but there are sometimes outbreaks of persecution of Christians by militant Hindus, especially against Western-run churches and Western missionaries who are perceived as aggressively seeking converts among Hindus. On the other hand, Indian tolerance and openness to new forms of spirituality has led to an interpenetration of Hinduism and Christianity; perhaps the best known example is Gandhi's admiration for the Sermon on the Mount (though he spoke less admiringly of some Christians), and Jesus is widely revered among Hindus, though generally regarded as an inspiring teacher or as a philosophical ideal rather than as the historical Jesus of Christianity. At the same time, Christians, especially Roman Catholics, in India have often drawn on Indian religious traditions to naturalize Christianity. The English Benedictine monk Bede Griffiths, who came to India in 1968 and settled in an ashram in southern India, lived as an Indian ascetic, encouraged Christian–Hindu dialogue, and explored ways of drawing on Hindu philosophy and practice. More generally, many Catholic churches adopt traditional Indian customs, using lamps instead of candles at the altar, putting garlands on statues of saints, and using Indian musical forms rather than translations of Western hymns.

The Protestant churches have adopted a different approach. As Indian nationalism developed, many Indian Christians felt that they should no longer be divided by the legacy of denominational differences left behind by missionaries, and Anglicans, Methodists, Congregationalists and Presbyterians in the south of the country united to form the Church of South India in 1947, as India gained its independence. It was followed in 1970 by the foundation of the Church of North India. The Church of South India shares a common liturgy in *The Book of Common Worship*, authorized in 2004, while the Church of North India, though united, is not uniform, and there is a considerable liturgical diversity which reflects the forms of worship that each church has inherited from its past. For instance, worship in the formerly Anglican Cathedral-Church in New Delhi is still predominantly Anglican in character, while other churches are more Protestant in practice, depending on their original denomination.

Christianity as the Hope of the Poor

It is often pointed out that the experience of people living in developing countries is much closer to the life described in the Bible than the experience of most people in the West—subsistence living and vulnerability to poor harvests, injustice, lawlessness, and a need to depend on God, who is the vindicator of the poor against their oppressors. In the last century Christians in developing countries began to use their experience of the world to form the basis of new theologies, which looked at the world from the perspective of the poor and oppressed and questioned the structures which held them in poverty.

The best known of these theologies is liberation theology, which has given its name to the whole movement and was developed in South America throughout the sixties and seventies under the impulse of the Second Vatican Council. Its impact was particularly powerful in Latin America, the continent with the largest number of Roman Catholics in the world. Catholics were encouraged to read their Bibles, and found inspiration in the prophets of the Old Testament who denounced the exploitation of God's people and in the preaching of Jesus, who announced he had come to bring good news to the poor. This emphasis on the God who has a bias towards the poor gave rise both to academic theology and to practical action; many people influenced by the movement formed themselves into base communities, local church communities sometimes encouraged by the local church hierarchy as a way of supplementing the work of the often over-stretched local clergy, sometimes discouraged for being too radical and independent. Meanwhile, academic theologians such as the Brazilian Leonardo Boff (b. 1938) and the Peruvian Gustavo Gutierrez (b. 1928) found their writings met with an unenthusiastic response from the Church authorities; they were seen as too political, too heavily influenced by Marxism and not enough by the traditional teaching and practice of the Church. Though liberation theology continues to be an influence in many Latin American countries it has taken a much milder, less revolutionary form.

The links between politics and religion in the continent are many and complex. One of the most famous figures of recent Latin American history is Oscar Romero, Archbishop of San Salvador, who was shot while he was celebrating Mass in 1980. He was not directly involved with liberation theology, and had in fact been regarded as a conservative for most of his career; but his experience of human rights abuses by the government of El Salvador led him to speak out against them, and for this he was assassinated by a right-wing group. More recently, in 2008, Paraguay elected a bishop, Fernando Lugo, as its president. He resigned as a bishop and has been released from his vows as a priest, but he was elected on progressive policies which reflect the values of liberation theology.

Other theologies of struggle and liberation have sprung up in their own particular circumstances. In South Africa 'black theology' developed in tandem with the Black Consciousness movement during the 1970s as part of the fight against apartheid, applying the ideas of liberation theology to the struggle for justice and equality for all the country's citizens. At about the same time, though in very different circumstances, Christians involved in the *minjung* (common people) movement in South Korea against the authoritarian government of the time developed *minjung* theology, which gave a biblical underpinning to the fight for democracy in a rapidly changing society.

Another comparatively recent development is the dalit theology of India, which first made its appearance in the 1980s. Dalits, the people who are outside and beneath the caste system, make up about a fifth of India's population; they are usually condemned to do the most menial jobs in society and are excluded from participation in the social and religious life of the rest of the community. Many have become Christians partly in an attempt to escape from caste, but even within Christianity they have found continued discrimination against them, though they make up about 70 per cent of Indian Christians. There are very few dalit clergy even now, though there are more in Protestant churches than in the Roman Catholic Church. In fact they face double difficulties, as under India's complex positive discrimination legislation dalits who have converted to other religions (and so in theory have escaped from the caste system) are less favoured than other dalits. It is sometimes said that caste is a social rather than a religious phenomenon. Running, as it does, through the whole of Indian society, it is not readily shaken off, and is very much alive within Hindu Christianity, particularly in the south. It is more prevalent where entire villages have converted to Christianity, with inhabitants largely retaining their previous caste, although it is not so widespread in towns and cities. Christians are not alone in this regard: contrary to common belief, Buddhists, Muslims and Sikhs frequently have caste status in India, too. Caste manifests itself in Christianity largely in connection with matrimony, but, since caste has been historically associated with commensality, there are some churches who require different castes to drink from different cups at holy communion. It is more pronounced within Roman Catholicism, which historically has tended to accommodate Indian social customs; Protestants, by contrast, have endeavoured to challenge them. As a response to their situation, some Christian dalit scholars have developed their own distinctive theology. Dalit theology celebrates the struggle for justice of an oppressed minority; it sees in God a God who suffers with his people and understands Jesus as a fellow-dalit, the suffering servant of all.

Southern Christianity and Northern Christians

While liberation theology has been a familiar concept in the rest of the world for many years now, other and more conservative elements of the Christianity of the developing world are beginning to make an impact in Europe and North America. Churches whose origins lie in Africa are now a familiar sight in our big cities, and though they mainly (but not exclusively) attract worshippers from the African diaspora they often offer a challenge to local Christians in their numbers and enthusiasm. Several of the biggest churches in London are led by African pastors; for example Kingsway International Christian Centre, founded in 1992, has a largely West African congregation, and claims to be the biggest independent church in Europe. Some of these churches are not without their problems. Members tend to contribute generously, while accounts are not always meticulously kept, and several churches have faced allegations of financial irregularities. The practices that some organizations have brought with them, particularly faith healing and exorcisms, are not necessarily regarded as appropriate in the host culture. This is especially true where children are involved, and the police and social services have been involved in a number of cases where violence has been used on children who are thought to be possessed by evil influences.

The Brazilian-based Universal Church of the Kingdom of God, referred to above, has attracted similar publicity, particularly over the case of Victoria Climbie, who was taken to one of its London churches to be exorcized shortly before her death at the hands of her carers in 2000. Despite the problems associated with some of these churches, they form a vibrant and growing section of the UK Christian spectrum.

Within the mainstream denominations, too, the influence of the Christianity of the South is growing. One of the most interesting aspects of this is the movement within the Anglican Communion towards the formation of a united, and possibly independent, conservative evangelical witness. The GAFCON meeting in Jerusalem in 2008, mentioned above, drew representatives not just from African countries such as Nigeria and Uganda, and from the Diocese of the Southern Cone (which covers some 22,000 scattered Anglicans in Argentina, Bolivia, Chile, Paraguay, Peru and Uruguay), but also from the conservative Australian archdiocese of Sydney, and a number of individual bishops from Britain and North America.

The links between Africans and American conservatives are particularly interesting; a number of conservative members of the Episcopal Church have seen in African Anglicanism an antidote to the liberal attitudes which trouble them in the Episcopal Church. Anglican dissidents in North America have found oversight from bishops from more conservative Anglican churches in other countries, instead of their own diocesan bishops whom they perceive as too liberal. Bishops in Uganda, Kenya and Nigeria have provided extended oversight for Episcopalian churches unhappy with the policies of their diocesan bishops over such issues as liberal theology and the social gospel, attitudes towards homosexuality, and in many cases the ordination of women. Congregations who feel that the Episcopal Church is jettisoning orthodox Christianity find sympathetic support among many African Anglican bishops, and also in the Diocese of the Southern Cone; at the time of writing, four Episcopal Church dioceses have sought temporary oversight from there, as have a number of Canadian parishes. This movement has led to a patchwork of jurisdictions in North America rather than the existence of a separate conservative group under one oversight. However, the Anglican Church in North America, representing nine groups who claim between them a total of 615 parishes and up to 100,000 members, was set up in December 2008 as an umbrella organization for parishes and dioceses in the USA and Canada who have sought alternative oversight; they regard themselves as a separate

Anglican province and they aim to gain recognition from the Anglican Communion as the representative body for 'orthodox North American Anglicans'.

It seems inevitable that the shift in the balance of world Christianity from North to South will continue, and perhaps accelerate, in the twenty-first century. The churches of the Northern hemisphere will be increasingly influenced by Christians from the South at every level. In the Roman Catholic Church, for example, the decline in vocations to the priesthood in Europe is being more than matched by the increase in some African countries, and where Europe used to export missionaries to Africa it is likely it will soon import clergy from there. This century may well be the one in which the effective leadership of the Christian world passes from the traditionally Christian countries of the North to the lively and expanding Christianity of the developing world.

16

Christianity as a Folk Religion

For several decades, sociologists of religion have written about 'secular-ization' and the decline in organized religion. Membership and church attendance have certainly dwindled in Britain during the past century, particularly since the 1960s. Steve Bruce writes about 'Christianity falling below the critical mass required to reproduce itself', predicting the demise of the Methodist Church by 2031, by which time 'the Church of England will...be reduced to a trivial voluntary association with a large portfolio of heritage property', and regular 'churchgoers will be too few to show up in representative national survey samples' (Bruce 2002: 74). As we have argued, this is not a global pattern: although this may be true of Britain and some other European countries, this is certainly not what is happening in Africa and in Latin America. However, even in Britain Christianity is by no means dead or even dying outside its institutional boundaries.

Despite the phenomenon of institutional decline, Christianity extends beyond the boundaries of its sacred spaces and Sunday services. In a recent national census, some 71.6 per cent of the population defined themselves as 'Christian'. It could be argued that many of the respondents did not care to define themselves as having 'no religion', could not identify with any of the alternatives (Buddhist, Hindu, Jewish, Muslim and Sikh), and hence were describing themselves as Christian by default. It is certainly true that the statistic of 71.6 per cent is not matched by the numbers of worshippers in church on a Sunday. Nevertheless, we do not believe that their claims to a Christian identity are necessarily spurious. The celebration of rites of passage within a context of Christianity remains popular. A recent survey indicated that 53 per cent of the British population would favour a church wedding if it were possible (Reuters 2008). Some 48 per cent of the population reported having attended a church in the past year for a wedding, and

57 per cent stated that they had attended a church funeral (Church of England 2008). The number of Christian weddings still significantly exceeds civil weddings, and only two per cent of funerals in the UK are non-religious (ScienceMode 2007).

At a popular level, a range of Christian festivals continues to be celebrated, although not always within the context of a church, and not always recognizing the original meaning of the celebration. Sometimes, and particularly at Christmas, many who do not normally attend church will attend a service in order to mark the festival. At other times, non-at-tendees will acknowledge the festival, but mark it in a way that does not involve a Christian congregation. Whether such activity should be considered 'religious' is doubtful, but the marking of such occasions is certainly related to the Christian faith, and certainly would not have taken place without the presence of Christianity. It may be claimed that what we are discussing in this chapter is not Christianity, or even religion, but rather folklore and folk practice. We do not intend here to enter into a discussion about where religion ends and popular culture begins, but merely to examine the relationship between Christianity and such events. In all these examples, we find the phenomenon of what Richard Thomas calls 'a culturally related public symbol' of the Christian faith (Thomas 2003: 128). In other words, those who are not committed to Christianity in its institutional form, and those who do not consider themselves to be Christian at all, might be put off from buying commodities or engaging in celebrations where the symbolism was explicitly religious, for example if it involved the use of icons or the reading of Scripture. By contrast, these popular festivals draw on a different range of symbols, occasionally overlapping explicitly Christian ones, and hence tend to be observed more widely than by institutional Christians.

In two articles in *The Tablet* (1999, 2001), Gordon Heald provides the following data on how the British said they would celebrate Christmas in 2001:

Question: *Which activities will you participate in this Christmas?*

Activity	% respondents
Exchange presents	94
Have a special Christmas Day/Eve meal with your family	80
Decorate inside/outside your home	80
Have a turkey over the festive season	74
Buy Christmas crackers	66

Have an advent calendar	51
Listen to/view the Queen's speech	51
Buy a Christmas tree	49
Make a special donation to charity over Christmas	49
Attend a carol service	41
Make a Christmas cake/pudding	40
Attend nativity/Christmas service	35
Attend religious service on Christmas Day/Eve	26
Visit a pantomime	25
Have a crib in your home	14
Pray at a crib in church	13
Spend it with friends but without your family	13
Work on Christmas Day	10
Have Christmas abroad	4
Spend Christmas alone	4
Do not celebrate Christmas	1

Not all of these ways of celebrating Christmas are religious, of course, and not all of the celebrators would necessarily regard themselves as Christian, and in many cases follow other faiths, such as Islam, Hinduism or Buddhism. For the Muslim, Jesus is one of God's messengers who are named in the Qur'an (although not the final one) and they therefore find no problem in celebrating his birth. Christian clergy may regret the fact that the population's celebrations of Christmas do not acknowledge more explicitly the festival's true meaning, and will no doubt continue to remonstrate against the commercialization of the festival. However, as we pointed out in the opening chapter, religion can be used in a variety of ways, not merely for spiritual edification. The proud parents who see their child perform in a nativity play may gain personal gratification rather than spiritual nourishment, but it cannot be denied that nativity plays have more than a superficial connection with the Christmas story and the meaning of the festival. Indeed, the very fact that the activities to which Heald draws attention coincide with the religious festival is itself an indication of the British public's desire to celebrate Christmas. Even the commercial aspects of Christmas are not totally divorced from its religious meaning. The giving of gifts, for example, can be related to the story of the Magi, who brought their gifts to Jesus.

The figure of Father Christmas or Santa Claus is an interesting amalgam of Christian and pagan mythology. The Norse god Odin was believed to ride an eight-legged horse at Yuletide, being a personification of winter. Also known as Old Winter, the bringer of cold, he could be appeased by offerings of food and drink at this time of year, in an attempt to mitigate winter's severities. Old Winter did not bring gifts or enter houses through their chimneys, however: these are activities associated with the Christian Saint Nicholas of Myra (c. 270–c. 346). Nicholas is also known as Niklaus, Miklaus or Klaus—hence the name Santa Klaus (Santa Claus). Saint Nicholas is particularly associated with giving, and also with children. He had wealthy parents, and is reputed frequently to have used his money to make anonymous gifts to the poor. According to legend, he encountered a poor man who could not afford a dowry for his three daughters and was on the point of having to sell them into prostitution. Saint Nicholas visited the man's home under cover of darkness, and dropped three bags of gold through his window. The three bags of gold are sometimes associated with the three gold balls that are often displayed outside a pawnbroker's shop. A variant of the story recounts that Nicholas delivered the three bags sequentially, on the occasion of each daughter's coming of age, delivering one bag through a chimney. Another version tells of one daughter leaving out her stockings to dry, and finding the gold in one of them. (Hence the later accounts of Santa coming down chimneys, and the custom of hanging up stockings.) In another story, a famine occurs in the island of Myra, causing a butcher to lure three small boys into his home, and then to murder them and pickle their bodies in a barrel of brine, for sale as a substitute for pork. On discovering this crime, Saint Nicolas was able miraculously to bring the boys back to life. This somewhat gruesome story helps to make the connection between Saint Nicholas and children, of whom he is the patron saint.

Saint Nicholas' Day is on 6 December, however, and thus anticipates Christianity's major festival. In some Eastern European countries, especially Croatia, Hungary, Romania and Poland, Saint Nicholas' Day continues to be celebrated by children putting out food for the saint's horse on the eve of the festival, and on the following day finding sweets that he has supposedly left for them. In the seventeenth century, Dutch settlers came to America, arriving in New Amsterdam (now New York), where they named their first church after the Christian saint. The saint became associated with Christmas by adaptation: children were encouraged to write lists to him on 6 December, and receive their gifts on Christmas Eve. The portrayal of Santa Claus as the jolly white-bearded rotund figure clad in red owes much to the American cartoonist Thomas Nast, and later to Haddon Sundblom, who developed this characterization for the promotion of Coca Cola.

The popular celebration of Christmas demonstrates the way in which a religious festival comes into popular culture, becoming an amalgam of the religious and the secular, the spiritual and the commercial. Because of this, the Christian churches have exhibited an ambivalent attitude towards the popular celebration of Christmas. Many churches in the West are quite comfortable with erecting Christmas trees, holding children's parties at which Santa Claus visits and brings gifts to the children, and exchanging cards and gifts. However, the present-day celebrations of Christmas are frequently criticized, on the grounds that the festival has become unduly commercialized, that it has incorporated pagan elements, and that twenty-first century celebrations are not traditional, but only took their rise in the Victoria era and later. Some clergy frequently criticize the commercialization and paganization of Christmas, although of course Christmas Day itself derived from these pagan winter festivals. In France, the practice of burning images of Santa Claus continued up to the late 1950s—a reminder to the faithful that the modern Santa should not be allowed to upstage the Christ child, whose festival it is. In 1969, Pope Paul VI issued a revision of the Church's calendar of saints (*Calendarium Romanum*), which resulted from deliberation about the historicity of the Church's saints and the holiness of their lives. A number of saints were dropped from the calendar. Although Saint Nicholas was not one of the forty saints who were removed, his feast day was made optional, instead of obligatory for the faithful—a slight demotion of this popular figure.

As well as Christmas, a number of additional Christian or Christian-related festivals are celebrated outside the context of the Church. Indeed, one can identify a popular festival calendar, which parallels, but does not totally replicate Christianity's liturgical calendar. This calendar includes (in chronological order) Saint Valentine's Day, Mother's Day (Mothering Sunday), Shrove Tuesday (Mardi Gras), Easter and Hallowe'en (All Saints). One might add Saint David's Day in Wales, Saint George's Day in England, Saint Patrick's Day in Ireland and Saint Andrew's Day in Scotland. Interestingly, Pentecost (Whitsun) is only observed by a British 'Bank Holiday' outside the churches, and there are no distinctive activities that mark the festival. Epiphany is marked by the taking down of Christmas decorations (the twelfth day of Christmas), while Lent, Ascension Day and Trinity Sunday are ignored.

After Epiphany, the next Christian-related festival is normally Valentine's Day, although occasionally Valentine's Day falls inside Lent, and hence is preceded by Shrove Tuesday. It is unclear which saint gave rise to this festival, since there were some fourteen saints called Valentinus (Valentine), three of whom have their saint's day on 14 February: Valentine of Rome—a physician and priest who lived in Rome (d. c. 269); Bishop Valentinus of Interamna (now Terni; d. c. 175), and a third who lived in Africa. Some historians believe that the first and second are one and the same. Little, if anything, is known about any of them, and Valentine's Day is not normally celebrated liturgically.

The origins of Valentine's Day as a festival for lovers are complex and not at all clear. It is possible that the festival was associated with the ancient Roman festival of Lupercalia, which occurred in mid-February, and was a pastoral festival. Alban Butler (1709–1773), the Roman Catholic hagiographer, in his four-volume *The Lives of the Fathers, Martyrs and Other Principal Saints* (1756–1759), attempted to make the connection between Saint Valentine's festival and romantic love by additionally associating mid-February with the festival of the goddess Juno Februato, who was associated with women, marriage and the family. He recounts a practice of holding 'love lotteries' in which boys' and girls' names were placed in jars, and pulled out randomly, to make pairings, which sometimes resulted in marriage. The Christians, who disapproved of such practices, he recounts, substituted saints' days for pagan festivals, and chose Saint Valentine as worthy of greater honour at this time. However, Butler's conjectures are now believed to be without foundation, although his association between love and Valentine's Day was perpetuated, and continues to be made.

The association between Valentine and lovers derives from a legend associated with Valentine of Rome. Emperor Claudius II wanted to recruit soldiers for the Roman army, and prohibited young men from marrying, in case homesickness for wives, homes and families should impair their military prowess. He also opposed the Christian faith, encouraging its persecution. Valentine, a physician-priest, offered help to Christians whose lives were in peril and, although celibate himself, performed secret marriage rites for young men and women, defying the emperor's decree. He was discovered and imprisoned. Valentine became friends with his jailer's daughter—a young woman who was blind. He miraculously restored her sight, whereupon she fell madly in love with the saint. When Valentine was finally led away to be executed, he left her a note, which ended, 'Your beloved Valentine.'

In 469 Pope Gelasius declared 14 February to be Saint Valentine's Day. Since the connections between mid-February and love matches seem to be largely due to Butler's conjectures, we cannot be certain when and how Saint Valentine came to be connected with carnal love. During the Middle Ages, there arose a belief in England and France that birds began to mate on 14 February. Geoffrey Chaucer refers to this in his *Parlement of Foules* (1382):

> For this was on seynt Volantynys day
> Whan euery bryd comyth there to chese his make.

However, Chaucer was commemorating the marriage of King Richard II of England and Anne of Bohemia, which took place on 2 May, not 14 February, and he is therefore probably alluding to the festival day of yet another Valentine—Valentine of Genoa (d. c. 307), whose festival falls on 2 May—a much more plausible date for birds mating.

The associations between Valentine, love and mid-February may well be the result of various confusions and conflations, but they have furthered the celebration of Valentine's Day as we now know it. Although love letters were sometimes sent around this time, commencing in the fifteenth century, the festival was re-invented in the USA in the late eighteenth century, and the invention of the postal service gave added momentum to the exchange of Valentine greetings. The first commercial Valentine card was produced in the 1840s, by Esther A. Howland in the USA.

'Shrove Tuesday' is the British name for the last day before Lent. This name is not recognized in the United States, where French influence has given rise to the name 'Mardi Gras', or 'Fat Tuesday'—the preferred designation in numerous countries. The well known association of the day with pancakes is explained by the need to rid one's household of rich foods before the Lenten fast, and fat, eggs and dairy products, which historically were disallowed during Lent, were disposed of by being made into large pancakes. The term 'Fat Tuesday' thus refers to the utilization of fat, while the word 'Shrove' has greater religious connotations, being derived from the word 'shrive', meaning 'confess'. Shrove Tuesday was a day in which one confessed one's sins to a priest, obtaining absolution and penance, in preparation for Lent. The festival is not celebrated liturgically, and the majority of Christians are only vaguely aware of its religious significance. Embellishments to the festival have been added over the centuries, such as placing coins in the pancakes for revellers to find (a Canadian custom), having pancake races, playing outrageous games and holding carnivals. It is possible, but doubtful, that pancake races had a religious origin. In 1445 a woman is said to have lost track of time while preparing her pancakes, and, hearing the sound of the 'shriving bell' to summon the faithful to worship, she rushed to church, still holding her pan containing the pancake.

Mothering Sunday is the fourth Sunday in Lent, and in Britain and Ireland it is equated with Mother's Day. In many other countries, including the United States, Mother's Day is celebrated on the second Sunday in May. At a popular level, Mother's Day is a festival in honour of one's mother, and was originally the creation of Anna Marie Jarvis (1864–1948) of West Virginia. In 1907, she held a memorial for her mother, two years after her death, and a year later wrote to the office-bearers of Andrews Methodist Episcopal Church in Grafton, asking them to define a day in which to honour all mothers. She subsequently campaigned for Mother's Day to become a national festival, and in 1914 President Woodrow Wilson signed a resolution passed by Congress to celebrate such a festival on the second Sunday in May.

Mothering Sunday's associations with motherhood are different. In Roman Catholic and Anglican churches Mothering Sunday celebrates the Blessed Virgin Mary, and also the 'mother church', which may be the local cathedral, the first mission church in the diocese or the 'plantation church'—that is, a larger church that gave birth to a particular congregation. The 'mother church' may be given recognition by the 'daughter' churches visiting the mother church and engaging jointly in worship there. Because Mothering Sunday and Mother's Day coalesce in the United Kingdom, motherhood in general is celebrated, and the service may involve young children giving flowers to parents or to women attendees in general. The giving of flowers to mothers is also associated with the alternative name 'Rose Sunday', which is sometimes given to the festival. Rose Sunday originated from a papal custom of sending golden roses to sovereigns of Roman Catholic countries, and blessing them on this day. In some Roman Catholic and Anglican churches it is customary for the celebrant to wear a pink (rose) chasuble instead of the usual purple Lenten colours. Mothering Sunday is sometimes referred to as Laetare Sunday, because of a tradition in which the service began with the introit *Laetare Jerusalem* ('Rejoice, O Jerusalem'; Zech. 9:9). It is a Sunday on which, at least in theory, some respite is allowed if one is observing a Lenten fast. For this reason it can also be referred to as 'Refreshment Sunday'. Yet another alternative name is Simnel Sunday; this name alludes to a practice that goes back to medieval times, when servants would be given time off to visit their mothers, and would traditionally bake a simnel cake to bring with them. The word 'simnel' possibly derives from the Latin *simila*, meaning fine flour made from wheat; a simnel cake is a light fruit cake, usually topped with marzipan.

Good Friday and Easter

Although Easter is the high point of the Christian calendar, the festival is probably a Christian appropriation of the pagan festival Eostre. There is little reason to doubt, however, that Jesus' crucifixion took place around this time, occurring during the Jewish Passover period (Jn 18:28)—a festival which itself may have originated from a spring festival associated with a fertility cult. Easter's pagan associations account for the symbols that are popularly associated with the festival, notably the Easter egg and the Easter bunny. The Venerable Bede (672/3–735), author of *The Ecclesiastical History of the English People*, affirmed that the hare or rabbit was the sacred animal of the Saxon goddess Eostre (also called Ostara or Eastre).

The rabbit is associated with fertility, and the myth associated with Oestre reinforces the notion. After an exceptionally long winter, Oestre discovered a bird whose wings had been frozen by the snow. Out of compassion, Oestre miraculously turned him into a snow hare and, since he could not fly, gave him amazing speed of movement. In recognition of his former existence as a bird, the hare was also given the ability to lay variously coloured eggs, but only on one day of the year. The hare eventually displeased Oestre, who banished him to the skies, where he could be seen as the constellation Lepus, from whence he was believed to return annually. We can thus easily see the connections between Easter, fertility and the popular images of bunnies, eggs and chickens that are associated with the festival. Particularly in the United States, it is a popular practice for children to put out carrots for the Easter bunny, and to leave a basket or a nest for him to deposit coloured eggs.

The egg's associations with fertility coalesces in a fairly obvious way with Christianity's Easter story. An egg has all the appearances of being dead, but can burst into newness of life as the chicken breaks through the shell. This idea parallels the Christian story of the dead Jesus returning to life by breaking out of the tomb, whose covering stone rolled away. The custom of rolling Easter eggs—a practice that is performed annually on the lawn of the White House in Washington, as well as elsewhere—is a re-enactment of the stone of Christ's tomb being rolled away. While the practice of painting eggs harks back to the idea that Eostre's hare's eggs are multi-coloured, certain sectors of Christianity have reclaimed this idea by using red as the colour of paint, to symbolize Christ's blood—a practice that is particularly popular in Greece. In Armenia, and also elsewhere, eggs are frequently decorated with pictures of Christ, the Virgin Mary or some other aspect of the Easter story. The practice of hiding Easter eggs for children to hunt for may have a less commendable origin: this custom may originate from the 'burning times', when the Church hunted out witches for execution.

The fertility theme relates to Babylonian culture. Ishtar (a name that is etymologically related to Oestre) set out to rescue her lover Tammuz, a god of vegetation who had been condemned to spend half of the year in the underworld. Ishtar succeeded in gaining entry to the realm, but only on condition that she removed her crown, then her jewels, and finally her clothing, before being permitted to pass through the last entrance. Her entry to the underworld secured Tammuz's liberation, bringing the world's vegetation back to life. The story bears similarities to the Greek myth of Demeter and Persephone, and it has fairly marked associations with the Christian doctrine that Christ's entering the world and being put to death was an act of humiliation, which was a means to restoration and salvation. Paul writes:

> Your attitude should be the same as that of Christ Jesus:
> Who, being in very nature God,
> did not consider equality with God something to be grasped,
> but made himself nothing,
> taking the very nature of a servant,
> being made in human likeness.
> And being found in appearance as a man,
> he humbled himself
> and became obedient to death—
> even death on a cross!
> Therefore God exalted him to the highest place
> and gave him the name that is above every name,
> that at the name of Jesus every knee should bow,
> in heaven and on earth and under the earth,
> and every tongue confess that Jesus Christ is Lord,
> to the glory of God the Father. (Phil. 2:5-11)

Other symbols associated with Easter point to facets of the Church's message. Lilies, which often decorate churches at Easter, symbolize purity, motherhood and hope. The lily is associated with the Virgin Mary: in Christian art it is usual to depict Gabriel bearing a lily at the Annunciation, thus indicating the purity of both Mary and the Christ child. The lily therefore connotes Christ's sinlessness, as well as the freedom from sin that is held to have been accomplished by his death and resurrection. The hope that the lily symbolizes relates both to Christ's resurrection itself, and to the hope of eternal life that results from Christ's atoning work. While the lily bears these Christian connotations, it was also the symbol of Juno, the queen of the gods, and it is possible that Christianity's use of the symbol owes its origins to Roman religion. The symbol of the lamb, which is often associated with Easter, combines fertility allusions (lambing being a feature of spring time) with the lamb as a key component in the Jewish Passover, relating to Jesus as the lamb of God, who is 'our Passover...sacrificed for us' (1 Cor. 5:7). Lambs can also be identified with Christ's followers, since Jesus is portrayed as the good shepherd (Jn 10:14), and his post-resurrection commission to Peter is to 'feed my lambs' (Jn 21:15).

The hot cross bun, traditionally associated with Good Friday, also deserves mention. Bearing the symbol of the cross, it appears superficially to be Christian. However, the consumption of similarly-marked buns probably pre-dates Christianity: cakes divided into four quarters were eaten by the Saxons in honour of the god Eostre, the four divisions representing the four quarters of the moon. If this is so, the Christians claimed the custom for themselves, giving it a Christian interpretation. The cross has obvious significance, particularly on Good Friday, and the stone-like shape of the bun is reminiscent of the stone that was rolled away from Christ's tomb. The spices that are used as ingredients connote the spices that were used for Jesus' burial (Lk. 23:56); and the fruit represents Christ's love, demonstrated by his sacrificial death. The use of yeast signifies rising and resurrection, and the custom of sharing buns is a reminder of giving: Christ offers the gift of new life (Thomas 2003: 127). In medieval times, it was normal practice to make such buns with the dough used to make the consecrated host: a number of Protestant Reformers in England objected to this practice, and sought for the buns to be banned. Elizabeth I, however, permitted their continued production, but only at Easter and Christmas. Formerly, hot cross buns were only sold around Easter, but their re-appropriation by the secular world has now caused them to be available all the year round. Despite attempts by some Christians to persuade supermarkets to supply an explanation of the buns' significance, supermarkets have resisted, no doubt fearing that associating hot cross buns with religion might adversely affect sales.

Hallowe'en

We turn now to the final festival in this secular festival calendar, Hallowe'en. The name is a contraction of 'All Hallows Even', which is the eve of All Saints' Day. Hallowe'en is commonly thought to be a Celtic legacy, derived from the festival of Samhain, which marked the onset of winter, when nature returned to the gloomy underworld. It has been generally assumed that the festival entailed a blurring of boundaries, not merely between autumn and winter, but between the living and the dead, the visible world and the invisible one. In *The Golden Bough* Sir James Frazer claims that Hallowe'en 'under a thin Christian cloak conceals an ancient pagan festival of the dead' (Frazer 1929: 633). Some historians such as John Hutton question whether Samhain was connected with the dead, an aspect of Hallowe'en which may owe something of its origins to the Roman festival of Feralia—the passing of the dead—which gained a foothold in Britain when the Romans conquered the Celts. The lighting of bonfires at this time of year is variously explained as enabling house-holders to rekindle their hearth fires for the incoming winter, as well as to frighten off the spirits who were rampant and were popularly believed to revisit their former homes.

The festival of All Saints was established by Pope Boniface IV during the seventh century. Its original date was 13 May, but a century later it was moved to 1 November, probably as an attempt to supplant a pagan festival. The conflation of the various festivals has fostered the popular celebrations, with their emphasis on the dead, the demonic, witches, lanterns and bonfires. The practice of 'tricking and treating' may derive from a British pre-Reformation practice, where beggars would go around people's homes, offering to pray for their departed relatives in exchange for a 'soul cake' (a small cake made with flour, egg yolks and saffron). It is believed that Irish settlers brought the custom to the USA in the nineteenth century, before which the festival was not celebrated.

Christians are divided in their attitudes to the popular celebrations of Hallowe'en. Some view it as harmless fun, and some churches have even organized Hallowe'en parties as social events. Other Christians, particularly evangelical Protestants, have condemned it strongly, and actively campaigned against its celebration in schools and homes. Common criticisms are that it is occultist, Satanic and that it extols evil, and that its key themes originated within paganism. Such Christians frequently refer to biblical condemnation of occultist practices, often citing the Book of Deuteronomy's prohibition of them (18:10-11; see chapter 16). Although this may not be exactly what Hallowe'en participants do, their activities are regarded as being too close for comfort. As televangelist Pat Robinson stated, 'I think we ought to close Halloween down. Do you want your children to dress up as witches? The Druids used to dress up like this when they were doing human sacrifice... [Children] are acting out Satanic rituals and participating in it, and don't even realize it' (cited by Ontario Consultants 2008). A Christian fundamentalist website states, 'Satan loves Halloween because it glamorizes the powers of darkness, drawing little kids into his realm. And it is paying off, witchcraft is exploding among teens today' (Servant of Jesus Christ 2010). The Christian Right is more concerned with opposing the celebration of Hallowe'en than with factual correctness, and are quite content to conflate Druidism, paganism, witchcraft and Satanism, and to attribute human sacrifices to Druids, for which there is no historical evidence.

Whatever stance Christians take on the celebration of the festivals we have discussed, it cannot be denied that they are connected, albeit tangentially in some cases, with Christianity. One cannot say that Santa Claus has nothing to do with the Christian faith, even though Christian clergy might remonstrate about 'putting the Christ back into Christmas'. The examples typically share a number of features. First, all have pagan associations: they may be pagan in origin, although the precise origins are obscure. This enables the uncommitted to celebrate the festival outside institutional Christianity, while the Church endeavours to reclaim the festival. While the Church has its foundation myths for its festivals, other myths have become interposed in order to legitimate their popular celebration, for example Odin's eight-legged horse and Old Winter descending chimneys, and the Easter bunny. In some cases re-invention has occurred, as is exemplified in the commercializing of Christmas, which began in the late nineteenth century, or the mass production of Valentine cards in recent times. Occasionally a myth dating from centuries after the festival's origins can legitimate a popular practice, as in the pancake race. Christianity usually accommodates, but sometimes disowns the popular celebrations. Thus, it is not uncommon for Easter eggs to be given out in church at Easter, to have Santa Claus visit a church fayre or children's party, or to organize a Valentine's dance. At other times, the Church appears to distance itself from the popular festival, as is manifested in Roman Catholicism's dropping of Saint Valentine from the liturgical calendar, or in the pronounced hostility of evangelical Christianity to Hallowe'en.

We are not trying to argue that the popular festivals are religious, or even examples of surrogate religion, but merely that they owe their origins substantially to Christianity, and demonstrate an inter-relationship between popular culture and religion, revealing a complex intertwining of the Christian faith, paganism and commercialism. In terms of the functions of religion that we distinguished at the beginning of this book, there is no way in which popular celebrations have any salvific dimension. On the contrary, some Christians would argue that their commercialization is likely to take one away from the festivals' true spiritual meaning, and even jeopardize one's spiritual life, as in the case of Hallowe'en.

Christianity and Music

Another notable area in which Christianity interacts with popular culture is music. Most Protestant and Roman Catholic churches use an organ as the method of accompanying congregational singing, or sometimes a harmonium in smaller rural churches. Although the instrument gives the appearance of tradition, the pipe organ took its rise in the middle of the seventeenth century, and only came into prominence in the middle of the nineteenth. Despite the wealth of its repertoire, both as a solo instrument and an accompaniment to singing, its obvious drawbacks are the expense of installation and maintenance, its lack of transportability, and the sheer difficulty of learning to play it. Although a few present-day pop groups have occasionally made use of pipe organs, music in popular culture tends much more to favour synthesizers, guitars and timpani.

At the same time as the organ was gaining popularity, other forms of religious music were taking shape in the United States. The African-Caribbean communities had developed their own religious music during their period of slavery, the best known genre being the so-called 'negro spiritual'. 'Gospel music' arose from the nineteenth-century mass revival movements, as well as the Holiness and Pentecostal churches who favoured the use of instruments that were available from members of the congregation. The gospel hymns tended to be affirmations of personal faith, rather than strict paraphrases of Scripture that were characteristic of the early Protestant Reformers, and typically had a refrain after each verse. 'How Great Thou Art' is one such example. Music from popular songs was also welcomed, with the benefit that those who are unfamiliar with a church's repertoire are already familiar with the tunes. Drawing on secular music is nothing new. The presbyter Arius reputedly set some of his teachings to the popular melodies of his time, and Martin Luther used secular tunes. Some composers, such as Ralph Vaughan Williams, made a point of writing down traditional English folk melodies, which might otherwise have died out, and it is not uncommon to hear folk tunes like 'All through the Night', 'The Bonnie Ash Grove', 'The English Country Garden' or the 'Skye Boat Song' taking on religious instead of secular words within Protestant and Catholic hymnody.

In the early 1970s, three popular musicals caught the public's imagination. *Godspell*, by Stephen Schwartz and John-Michael Tebelah, was released as an album in 1970, performed on Broadway in 1971, and made into a film in 1973. The musical is based largely, although not exclusively, on Matthew's Gospel, recounting Jesus' ministry, death and resurrection, and drawing on several twentieth-century musical genres, such as folk rock, Gospel music and Vaudeville. Andrew Lloyd Webber and Tim Rice produced their *Jesus Christ Superstar* at exactly the same time (album in 1970, Broadway in 1971, becoming a film in 1973). This rock opera focused on the end of Jesus' ministry, leading up to his death, and bringing the role of Judas Iscariot into prominence. Their *Joseph and His Amazing Technicolor Dreamcoat* had its origins slightly earlier, beginning life as a fifteen-minute-long 'cantata' performed at Colet Court, the preparatory school of Saint Paul's in London. In the early 1970s additional material had been added, reaching the same proportions as *Jesus Christ Superstar*. These performances not only attracted Christians who welcomed these innovatory ways of expressing biblical narrative, but appealed to believer and non-believer alike.

The relationship between contemporary religious and popular music is a symbiotic one. Several pop artists who have found Christianity have expressed their faith explicitly in their singing. Early in his career Cliff Richard (b. 1940) became a practising Christian. Initially uncertain as to whether to pursue his profession as a rock singer and sex symbol in the style of Elvis Presley, he decided to continue working with The Shadows, but using his talents for the furtherance of his faith. He has performed at Billy Graham rallies, as well as the 1971 Nationwide Festival of Light, and his 1991 'Millennium Prayer' gained a number one position in the charts, and brought the Lord's Prayer, which was set to the tune of Auld Lang Syne, into the forefront of the public arena. Ironically, the prayer was unfamiliar to many of the support singers, who had the preliminary task of learning its words.

Johnny Cash (1932–2003) learned traditional gospel songs in his early life, and, despite lapsing into drug and alcohol addiction, rediscovered

Christianity after claiming to see a vision of angels when he was at his lowest ebb in 1968. Cash recorded a number of albums of gospel music. His five-disc box set *Unearthed*, released posthumously in 2004, contains *My Mother's Hymn Book*—a collection of gospel songs from his childhood. Bob Dylan (b. 1941) is another example of a pop singer who became a 'born-again' Christian during his career and joined the Vineyard Fellowship, a charismatic evangelical Protestant denomination founded by John Wimber in California. Dylan had a significant role in the development of Christian gospel music, and especially 'gospel rock'. His 'All Along the Watchtower' (1967), recorded by Jimi Hendrix, was based on Isa. 21:5-9. His best known Christian numbers are 'Slow Train Coming', 'Gotta Serve Somebody' (1979) and 'Saved' (1980).

Popular music has, in turn, influenced the Church's music, at least in the Protestant and Catholic traditions. At weddings and funerals it has become increasingly common to play CDs of the favourite records of popular songs that are particularly significant for the wedding couple or the bereaved. Some musicians within the Church, too, have created their own music, drawing on the styles and techniques of popular secular music. The popularity of 'light music' in the 1940s and 1950s prompted Geoffrey Beaumont (1903–1970) to write his *A Twentieth Century Folk Mass* (1956), and he and Patrick Appleford (b. 1925) formed the Twentieth Century Light Music Group, creating a number of modern hymns that continue to be used in churches. The later pop industry caused its own genres to feature in Christian worship, pioneered by the Jesus People of California—groups of hippies who had turned to Jesus but did not relate to the traditional liturgy of the mainstream churches. The popularity of the various styles of pop music has prompted the creation of new types of Christian song. Darlene Zschech's 'Shout to the Lord!' is one of the best known of Hillsong music, originating from the Pentecostal mega-church, Hillsong Church (formerly Hills Christian Life Centre) in Sydney, Australia. The Christian Community Church (3C), also in Sydney, has its own band 'Delirious!', and both churches market their distinctive albums.

The group U2, founded in Dublin by Bono (Paul Hewson, b. 1960), have on occasion collaborated with Cash and Dylan. In the main, their songs address social and political themes, but also give them a spiritual dimension. 'Sunday Bloody Sunday', included in the album *War* (1983), compared the events of 'Bloody Sunday'—also known as the Bogside Massacre of 30 January 1972—with Easter Sunday. Although the group is more socio-political than religious in its message, the group has given rise to the 'U2charist'—the name for a special form of Eucharist that originated in the US Episcopal Church, the first of which was held in Baltimore, Maryland in 2003. The U2charist service uses U2's music in place of (although sometimes supplemented with) traditional liturgical music, and it has gained popularity, spreading as far as the Netherlands and Australia. In October 2004 a U2charist was celebrated at a conference for all clergy in the Baltimore diocese.

Christianity in Literature

Christianity has also been propagated through literature. C. S. Lewis (1898–1963), who wrote a great deal of popular theology, also expressed his Christian faith in children's fantasy literature. His *The Lion, the Witch and the Wardrobe* (1950) was adapted to become the film *The Chronicles of Narnia* (2005). The film tended to mute much of the Christian message, as found in the book, however. Although many people simply understood the story and film as a piece of children's fantasy that also appealed to some adults, there is little doubt that Lewis intended the book to be an allegorical account of creation, evil and Christ's redeeming work. Its prequel *The Magician's Nephew* (1955) explains how Aslan, the lion, created the world of Narnia, and how the evil witch Jadis entered it and exercised her power. In *The Lion, the Witch and the Wardrobe*, four children enter Narnia, and one of them, Edmund, is lured into the wicked witch's castle and betrays the others. In order to rescue the children, Aslan sacrifices himself in Edmund's place, but returns to life to engage in a final battle against the evil witch. The story ends in triumph, with Edmund being suitably penitent.

Lewis's close friend and colleague J. R. R. Tolkien (1892–1973) is less explicitly Christian in his fantasy fiction. Lewis gave Tolkien, among others, the credit for his return to Christianity after lapsing in his adolescence. Tolkien, a Roman Catholic, was disappointed that Lewis joined the Church of England rather than embracing Catholicism, and was unimpressed with *The Lion, the Witch and the Wardrobe* when Lewis showed it to him in manuscript form. Despite its less explicitly religious character, Tolkien acknowledged his *Lord of the Rings* trilogy as an expression of his own religious commitment. He once wrote,

> The Lord of the Rings is of course a fundamentally religious and Catholic work; unconsciously so at first, but consciously in the revision. That is why I have not put in, or have cut out, practically all references to anything like 'religion', to cults or practices, in the imaginary world.

> For the religious element is absorbed into the story and the symbolism.
> (Letter no. 142, quoted by Carpenter 1995: 172)

The obvious general theme is the conflict between good and evil. However, commentators have claimed to find influence of Aquinas and Boethius in Tolkien's writings. The character Frodo at one point comments that shadows cannot create things, having no reality of their own, possibly echoing Boethius' assertion that 'evil is nothing', and the traditional Roman Catholic doctrine of evil as a privation of good, having no independent or substantive existence.

The Media

Christian ideas have been propagated further through film, radio and television. Particularly noteworthy were Cecil B. DeMille's (1881–1959) epics *The Ten Commandments* (1923) and *King of Kings* (1927). These films were produced in the days of the silent movies, and in black and white. DeMille's original *The Ten Commandments* is in two parts: the first is the biblical story, while the second is a modern story of two brothers, one who keeps all the commandments while the other disobeys them all. In *King of Kings* the story-line is indicated in sign cards bearing quotations from the King James Version of the Bible. DeMille also produced and directed *Samson and Delilah*, released in 1949, and based on the story in the Book of Judges. *The Ten Commandments* was remade in 1956, again under DeMille's direction, and this time recounting the biblical narrative without a modern sequel. Having been written for the cinema, fidelity to the biblical narrative was not a prime concern. Moses, for example, has a love affair with Princess Nefretiri (sic) before deciding to liberate the Israelites, and the plot has been criticized for incorrectly identifying the Pharaohs of the period. Notwithstanding such criticisms, the story of the Exodus has proved popular, and was once again re-made as a television mini-series broadcast in 2006 on US television.

DeMille's pioneering work heralded a proliferation of films on biblical themes, the most popular of course being the life of Jesus of Nazareth. Two popular epics of the 1950s were *The Robe* (1953) and *Ben Hur* (1959), the latter being a re-make of the film of the same title, released in 1925. *King of Kings* was re-made and released in 1961, and *The Greatest Story Ever Told* (1965), released by United Artists, was based on a series of half-hour radio programmes broadcast in 1947, and made into a novel by Fulton Oursler in 1949. These endeavours at straightforward portrayal of Jesus' life and death continued with Franco Zeffirelli's *Jesus of Nazareth* (1979), and most recently Mel Gibson's expression of his Roman Catholic piety in *The Passion of the Christ* (2004).

All of these films were serious attempts at conveying the biblical account of Jesus' life, albeit with occasional imaginative embellishments. They were all characterized by a reverence for Jesus, to the extent that in *The Robe* Jesus was only portrayed off-screen, and in *Ben Hur* he did not speak. Later cinematic portrayals were less respectful, and often sought to raise questions about Jesus Christ's nature and about the Christian faith, rather than to attempt uncritical biographies. *The Last Temptation of Christ*, directed by Martin Scorsese in 1988, was an adaptation of Nikos Kazantzakis' book of that title, and explored Jesus' human nature. Judas Iscariot encourages Jesus to become a political activist and overthrow the Romans, and Jesus engages in sexual encounters with Mary and Martha, the sisters of Lazarus, finally marrying Mary Magdalene and raising a conventional family. The film attracted picketing and even physical violence. On 22 October 1988 some French Christian fundamentalists threw Molotov cocktails at a Paris cinema, injuring thirteen people, four of whom suffered serious burns. Several countries banned or censored the film, and, two decades later, it cannot be shown in Singapore or in the Philippines.

The medium of film has been employed to portray Christianity in a modern idiom. The French film *Je vous salue, Marie* (English version, *Hail Mary*, 1985), directed by Jean-Luc Godard, was set in present-day France, where Marie is a petrol station attendant who has a chaste relationship with Joseph, a taxi driver, but is informed by a stranger called Uncle Gabriel that she will become pregnant. The son who is born is, of course, called Jesus, who pursues 'his Father's business.' The film, which included scenes of full frontal nudity, was condemned by Pope John Paul II, and offended many Christians.

Other cinematic presentations have involved parody and satire. *Monty Python's Life of Brian* (1973) portrays Brian as a very ordinary child who is contemporaneous with Jesus but, against his will, becomes hailed as the messiah. The final crucifixion scene ends with the victims singing from their crosses, 'Always look on the bright side of life,' tapping their feet in time to the tune. The central characters of *Dogma* (1999), Bartleby and Loki, are fallen angels who alight on New Jersey. The plot involves their attempt to find a way back into heaven. Believing that they have found a loophole in Roman Catholic teaching, their efforts are resisted by Metatron, the ruler of the angelic realm, who appears to Bethany, an employee in an abortion clinic, and commissions her to prevent their success. Much is at stake since Bartleby and Loki's success would demonstrate that God is not infallible, and would result in the world's annihilation.

Another parody, this time on television and in cartoon form, was *Simpsons Bible Stories* (1999)—the eighteenth episode of the series' tenth season. The episode takes place on Easter Sunday in the Reverend Lovejoy's evangelical Protestant church, where Homer Simpson puts a discarded Easter bunny into the collection plate. The Reverend Lovejoy then insists on reading the entire Bible to the congregation from the beginning, causing the Simpson family to fall asleep. The rest of the episode recounts the dreams of Marge, Lisa, Homer and Bart, which are respectively set in the Garden of Eden, the captivity in Egypt, and the reigns of King Solomon and King David respectively. They wake up to discover that the four horsemen of the Apocalypse have arrived, and Ned Flanders—a staunch fundamentalist—and his family are being taken up into heaven, while the Simpsons are consigned to the fires of hell.

Some films explore ways of revitalizing the Church. *Sister Act* (1992), starring Whoopi Goldberg, portrays Deloris, a pop singer who takes refuge in a convent to escape a criminal gang. She is dismayed at the choir's lacklustre performance, and shows them how to sing in a more modern popular style. *Babette's Feast* (1987) is about a refugee (Babette) who becomes housekeeper to two staid middle-aged sisters in Jutland in the late nineteenth century. Babette has a lottery ticket from her Paris days, which unexpectedly wins her ten-thousand francs, and she decides to use the money to prepare a feast for the villagers, instead of returning to Paris. The villagers gain more than physical enjoyment from the sumptuous meal, which acquires eucharistic qualities as old wrongs are healed and love rekindled. In *Chocolat* (2000), which won numerous awards, a small French village is revitalized by Vianne Rocher, who opens a chocolaterie during Lent, opposite the local Catholic church. Again, physical indulgence serves as a means of improving relationships and bringing healing, despite bringing Vianne into conflict with the religious authorities. Perhaps more challenging is *The Mission* (1986), about an eighteenth-century Jesuit mission in Latin America among the Guarani Indians. The film explores the political situation affecting Spain, Portugal and their colonies, and how the Catholic Church is caught up in such tensions. Altamirano, the papal emissary, orders the closing of the mission in order to facilitate Portuguese colonization, and the ensuing conflict leads to its being burnt down.

Also related to Christianity is the interest in the occult. *The Exorcist*, released in 1973, was adapted from William P. Blatty's 1971 novel of the same name, and centres around twelve-year-old girl Regan MacNeil who is suspected of a brain lesion. When medical treatment proves ineffective, her strange behaviour is attributed to demonic possession, and two priests die in their (successful) attempts to exorcize the child. *The Omen* trilogy (1976, 1978, 1980—remade in 2006) explored the Satanic powers of Damien Thorn in childhood, adolescence and adulthood, in which it transpires that he is the Antichrist, who bears the 'mark of the beast' on his forehead, as described in the Book of Revelation (Rev. 13:18).[1]

Mention should also be made of films relating to Christianity that support conspiracy theories. The central character in *Stigmata* (1999) is Frankie, a hairdresser who develops stigmata despite being an atheist. It transpires that her marks are related to the spirit of Father Paulo Alameida, a former priest who was excommunicated after claiming to discover a lost gospel, the message of which is that belief from the heart is more important that institutional allegiance. The plot is influenced by the discovery of the Gospel of Thomas at Nag Hammadi in 1945. Dan Brown's novels *The Da Vinci Code* (2003) and his earlier *Angels and Demons* (2000) were adapted for cinema and released in 2006 and 2009 respectively. The former relates to the quest for the holy grail, in which it is discovered that the holy grail is not the cup with which Jesus celebrated the Last Supper, but the remains of Mary Magdalene. Opus Dei, the Roman Catholic religious order, is portrayed as sinister and connives in the Church's attempt to withhold this information from their followers. *Angels and Demons* is about the election of a new pope, set amidst a plan by the secret society the Illuminati to assassinate four cardinals who are preferred candidates for the papal office, together with the theft of a phial containing antimatter, the release of which would destroy the entire world. To fend off such disasters, Professor Robert Langdon must consult the Vatican Secret Archives, in particular the original manuscript of Galileo's *Dialogue Concerning the Two Chief World Systems*. Brown has been severely criticized for his lack of research, and much of his information about Christianity's origins and about Vatican affairs is grossly inaccurate.

The popular interest in Mary Magdalene escalated during the 1990s into the twenty-first century. She is a compelling figure because she is

---

1. The Antichrist is not mentioned in the Book of Revelation, contrary to popular belief. Its only occurrences are in John's letters (1 Jn 2:18, 22; 4:3; 2 Jn 1:7).

enigmatic. All biblical references to her, except one, place her in the context of Jesus' crucifixion and resurrection, to which she is the first witness (Mk 16:9). Luke also records that that Jesus previously cast out seven demons from her (8:2), thus effecting a remarkable conversion. The Gospels also mention an unnamed woman who anoints Jesus with expensive ointment at the house of 'Simon the leper' (Mt. 26:6-13; Mk 14:3-9). Since she lets her hair down in front of Jesus, it is assumed that she is a woman of ill repute. There is also an account (usually placed at Jn 7:53-8:11, but probably a misplaced fragment) of a woman who was caught committing adultery, and whom Jesus rescues from a proposed stoning. It was Pope Gregory the Great who contended in a homily in 591 that these three women were one and the same—hence the later Christian portrayals of Mary Magdalene as the 'scarlet woman', with red hair and wearing scarlet clothes.

Given this background to Mary Magdalene, coupled with the feminist interest in promoting the status of women, it is not difficult for speculation to arise that, if Mary Magdalene was an itinerant disciple of Jesus (Lk. 8:2) and sexually seductive, she might have been Jesus' lover, or even his wife. A number of novels have been written to fill in the information that we lack about Mary Magdalene. Fiona Avery's *The Crown Rose* relates that Mary married Jesus and bore him a son. Other popular novels about Mary Magdalene include Marianne Fredriksson's *According to Mary Magdalene* (1999), Margaret George's *Mary, Called Magdalene* (2002) and Kathleen McGowan's *The Expected One* (2006). Other non-fictional works have recently been published, drawing considerably on Gnostic writings, and casting Mary Magdalene as Jesus' apostle and lover. Among such works, perhaps the best known is Lynn Picknett's *Mary Magdalene: Christianity's Hidden Goddess* (2003).

Conclusions

Much more could be mentioned of the influence of Christianity on contemporary Western society. There is radio and television broadcasting, both of acts of worship and discussions of religious affairs. There is its presence in civic affairs: royal weddings and funerals, acts of remembrance at cenotaphs on Remembrance Day, the taking of oaths in court (notwithstanding the availability of non-religious alternatives), the use of religious texts on public monuments are all examples of how Christianity penetrates civil affairs. Place names, street names, and even names of public houses frequently have Christian origins. A high proportion of personal names derive from Christianity, and until recently the term 'Christian name' was used to refer to one's forename.

In making these observations we are not suggesting that patrons of The Lamb and Flag are 'anonymous Christians' or that they are displaying some kind of implicit or latent spirituality. Some of these phenomena are no more than relics of a bygone age: few patrons of The Lamb and Flag are likely even to recognize the biblical allusion behind the name. Also, we are not suggesting that cultural penetration is unique to Christianity: one can find it also, although to a lesser degree in the West, with the other major world's religions, as well as pre-Christian spirituality. Not all of the phenomena that we have mentioned are necessarily supportive of Christianity, and some of them have even attracted disapproval, as we noted in the reaction against *The Last Temptation* and *The Life of Brian*. Where Christians have felt that certain books, films or theatre productions have been unsupportive of their faith, at least these productions have encouraged 'cultural conversation' about the Christian religion, and kept it in public attention. However, some Christians have perceived an incarnational aspect in some of their endeavours to express the Christian faith in a cultural idiom appropriate to the twentieth century. Just as God assumed human form to enter the world as Jesus Christ, so Christ enters into the present-day worldly forms of popular music, theatre and literature.

The Lamb and Flag (stained glass, All Saints' Church, Highgate, London). The symbol alludes to the triumph of Christ (the Lamb of God) by his resurrection. Photograph: George Chryssides

The Lamb and Flag, Oxford. Photograph: © Andrew Oakley, 2009. From Wikimedia Commons, released into the public domain.

A significant amount of popular culture is therefore closely related to Christianity, and at the very least is a legacy from it. Christianity's boundaries go substantially beyond church doors. How one should classify these phenomena in terms of folk religion, folk custom, popular culture, religious inquiry or interest in religious affairs is something that might profitably exercise the minds of scholars of religion. It is a neglected area, but one that should not be ignored. In his *Religion in Modern Britain*, Steve Bruce objects to the notion of a non-institution-alized Christianity by comparing it with someone who claims to be a football fan, but never plays football, attends football matches, reads accounts of them, watches them on television and cannot name any famous footballers. In fairness to Bruce, he makes reference to religious broadcasting and to the nature and prevalence of religious beliefs held by the British public, although he argues that there is overall decline. However, our analysis indicates that twenty-first century Christianity in the West is not like Bruce's imaginary implicit football supporter, even if only a minority of the public attend church or are able to name its founding apostles. There are many ways in which Christian ideas and practices are manifested at a popular level, and are worthy of attention if we are to understand Christianity in a comprehensive way.

17

Christianity at the Edges

Previous chapters have dealt with Christianity's main traditions and their sub-divisions. However, there are a number of smaller organizations who claim a Christian identity that is frequently called into question by mainstream believers. Chapter 15 drew attention to the Brotherhood of the Cross and Star, and to the Movement for the Restoration of the Ten Commandments of God. Better known in the West are the Jehovah's Witnesses, the Church of Jesus Christ of Latter-day Saints (the Mormons), the Unification Church (the 'Moonies'), the Unitarians and The Family International (formerly known as the Children of God). Popularly these movements are referred to as 'sects' or, more recently, 'cults', although scholars prefer to use the term 'new religious movements' (NRMs). Finding a satisfactory term is difficult, however, since not all these organizations are new. Christadelphians, Jehovah's Witnesses and Christian Scientists are now well over a century old, and organizations like the Unitarian Church can trace their origins back to the Protestant Reformation. There are reckoned to be some six-hundred NRMs in Britain, over two thousand in the USA, and possibly as many as ten thousand in Africa today, although not all of these are Christian-derived NRMs. Most of these 'New Christian' groups are Protestant, partly because Protestantism, unlike Catholicism and (to a lesser degree) Orthodoxy, lacks central organizational control as a tradition, and partly because Protestants have consequently tended to have a wide variety of beliefs and practices, some of which have tested the limits of acceptability.

Those NRMs that claim a Christian identity have generally found such a claim to be challenged. There are two main concerns on the part of mainstream Christians. One is doctrinal: the majority of the organizations mentioned in this chapter are reckoned to impart false teachings. If salvation is through faith in Christ's incarnation, death and resurrection, then any religious community who deviates from these beliefs, or innovates with new revelations or scriptures, could risk depriving its followers of the means of salvation. The second concern is that at least some NRMs can cause physical danger. Such concerns were aroused in 1978, when over nine-hundred members of Jim Jones' Peoples Temple in Guyana were persuaded to commit suicide by drinking cyanide. Interestingly, although the Peoples Temple had distinctive character-istics, it was affiliated to a mainstream Protestant denomination, the Disciples of Christ.

Although critics of 'cults' often appear confident that the 'marks of a cult' can be readily detected, in reality Christianity has blurred edges. As we noted in a previous chapter, Augustine highlighted the severe difficulty, if not impossibility, in trying to devise empirical criteria that would distinguish those who belong to the true Church from those who do not. In general, characteristics that suggest that an organization represents authenticity are the affirmation of the traditional creeds, membership of national Councils of Churches and the administration of the sacraments. Yet all of these criteria have their difficulties. We have already noted the controversies surrounding the administration of baptism and holy communion, and not all Christian churches want to belong to national and international ecumenical bodies. There are many small independent churches in Britain and the United States, and even more in Africa. It is not possible even to know who they all are, let alone determine their level of orthodoxy.

The sociologist Max Weber (1864–1920) suggested an important distinction between 'Church' and 'sect', as he called them. The distinction has been much elaborated, refined and discussed since Weber devised it, and we have discussed questions of definitions and typologies of minority religions elsewhere (Chryssides 1999; Chryssides and Wilkins 2006). Weber's insight, however, lay in his acknowledgement that the Church (at least in predominantly Christian countries) is large; it is the religion of the majority, it dominates the culture, accepting or defining its values, legitimating the affairs of the state, and the majority of citizens are born into it. The 'sect', by contrast, tends to be small and supported by only a minority of people (sometimes a very small minority, in some cases as few as two-hundred members), and instead of working in tandem with the state and endorsing its values, the 'sect' often challenges these. For example, the Jehovah's Witnesses made themselves particularly unpopular for their stance against war, suggesting that patriotism was not a virtue enjoined by the Bible, and they are well known for their rejection of conventional forms of medical treatment that involve blood. Weber's claim that members of the 'Church' tend to be born into it, rather than actively deciding to join, has become less true, as NRMs have become older, and second and third (or even later) generations have grown up in them. Certainly, at their inception, they gained membership through proselytizing rather than sexual reproduction, and many of them (although not all) continue very actively to evangelize within their communities. This is witnessed by the house-to-house evangelism of the Jehovah's Witnesses and the Mormons.

Different Types of NRM

Although many Christians are also concerned with the rise of independent NRMs and those which derive from other religions, this chapter will deal exclusively with the Christian-related ones. One of the early commentators on NRMs, J. K. Van Baalan, observed that 'the cults are the unpaid bills of the church' (Van Baalan 1938: 12), a remark that is frequently endorsed by writers on the phenomenon. Some result from mainstream missionary activity, in which missionaries lost control of new converts, enabling them to preach syncretistic versions of the Christian faith without censure. Others have begun by emphasizing issues that mainstream Christianity appears to avoid, for example ideas relating to end-times and the interpretation of apocalyptic literature, which are prominent in several. Others endeavour to carry biblical literalism to a logical conclusion: in particular, Christian fundamentalism leaves unresolved the question of the relationship between the Old and New Testaments, thus raising issues about the Christian's attitude to the Old Testament law. Sometimes these and other groups seek to return to an authentic first-century form of Christianity, noting, for example, that the theology of creeds is not wholly to be discovered in Scripture: hence the rise of Unitarian and Arian movements. Some communities have emphasized the re-discovery of the first-century Christian lifestyle, affording community living, sometimes involving the communal sharing of possessions, as appears to have been early Church practice, at least at one stage in its development (Acts 2:44). Some groups have emphasized forms of early Christian ministry that find little expression within the mainstream churches, for example divine healing or prophecy. Mark's Gospel reports Jesus' final words to his disciples as these: 'And these signs will accompany those who believe: In my name they will drive out demons; they will speak in new tongues; they will pick up snakes with their hands; and when they drink deadly poison, it will not hurt them at all; they will place their hands on sick people, and they will get well' (Mk 16:17-18).

A small number of Christians have taken this literally and made a practice of handling venomous snakes during public worship. Their reasoning is that the entire Bible is God's word and that believers should not pick and choose which passages they put into practice. The snake-handling movement began in the early twentieth century in Appalachia, and churches who adopt the practice, such as the Church of God with Signs Following, can be found in Alabama, Georgia, Kentucky, Ohio and West Virginia. The number of snake handlers is relatively small, and may be in decline. The highest estimate of the total membership of these churches is five thousand and could be as low as one thousand, and only a small proportion of members actually handle snakes (Conkin 1997: 303). Some have died as a result of snake bites, although sustaining injuries or death is usually attributed to lack of faith. About one-hundred members are believed to have died by such misadventure since the movement began, including founder-leader George Went Hensley (1880–1955). It goes without saying that mainstream Christians are appalled by such ultra-literal interpretations of the Bible by these extreme fundamentalists.

'Back to the Bible' Movements

Unitarians

Not all attempts to get back to the Bible involve such colourful and dangerous practice. The Unitarians constitute one of the older heterodox movements, stemming from the radical edge of the Protestant Reformation, and endeavouring to get back to the Bible's original teachings. Michael Servetus (1511–1553), a Frenchman who was burnt at the stake by John Calvin in Geneva, Francis Dávid (1510–1589) in Transylvania (now modern Romania) and Faustus Socinus (1539–1604) all emphasized God's unity rather than tri-unity. John Biddle (1616–1662), an English clergyman who questioned the independent existence of the Holy Spirit, spent most of his life in prison for his heresy. The Unitarian movements developed independently, principally in Poland, Transylvania and England. The scientist and theologian Joseph Priestley (1733–1804) brought Unitarianism to America. The various European strands of Unitarianism only discovered each other in the late nineteenth century.

Historically, the Unitarian movement contended that the creeds and the doctrine of the Trinity were later additions to the Christian faith, not to be found in Scripture, and recommended that reason and conscience were to determine matters of doctrine rather than faith or belief in authority. In accordance with the Protestant Reformation principles, Unitarians rejected the use of intermediaries in prayer and worship, including Jesus himself: adoration must only be given to God himself. Belief in the ability of men and women to use reason and conscience effectively led them to a more positive view of human nature, in contrast with Augustinian and Calvinist emphases on original sin. In the mid-twentieth century, British and American Unitarians came to emphasize the three principles of 'freedom, reason and tolerance', which steered Unitarianism away from a predominantly Christian movement to one that encourages spiritual seeking without the limits of religious boundaries. Many US and British Unitarian churches experiment with new forms of liturgy, drawing on a variety of religious traditions. Many congregations reject any claims to Christianity, believing that reason and conscience are to be found in followers of all but the most dogmatic faiths. Transylvanian Unitarian remains more traditionally Christian, continuing to celebrate the traditional Christian sacraments, which have largely been abandoned in Unitarianism's American, British and Western European forms. Government of Unitarian churches is congregational, and their regional unions and General Assemblies form a federation of local churches.

Adventists and Jehovah's Witnesses

Another tradition whose beliefs are firmly Bible-based is the Seventh-day Adventists (SDA). Adventism featured in an earlier chapter (chapter 11) as a brand of mainstream Protestantism, and they are acknowledged by the World Council of Churches as one of Christianity's 'church families'. The fact that the SDA are not WCC members is largely through their own choice, since they believe that other member churches over-emphasize Christianity's socio-political role at the expense of prophecy, and place insufficient stress on personal sanctification. However, on occasions they have been involved in ecumenical affairs as observers or in a consultative capacity. Half a century ago, mainstream Christians were more wary of Adventism, and it featured in Christian counter-cult literature, such as Horton Davies' *Christian Deviations* (1954) and Anthony Hoekema's *The Four Major Cults* (1963). Although the Seventh-day Adventist

Church has gained greater respect within the Christian tradition, some other organizations that derive from the Adventist tradition continue to arouse hostility.

The Branch Davidians

Of all the Adventist groups, the Branch Davidians have attracted the greatest public attention through David Koresh's group, the majority of whom died in an FBI raid on their compound in Waco, Texas, in April 1993. The Branch Davidian tradition came from Victor T. Houteff (1885–1955), who claimed to be the successor to Ellen G. White's prophetic office when she died in 1915. Houteff was later accused of distorting her teachings, and 'disfellowshipped' (the Adventist term for 'expelled'). Houteff's movement assumed the name of The Shepherd's Rod, or simply The Rod—an allusion to a verse in the prophet Isaiah: 'And there shall come forth a rod out of the stem of Jesse, and a Branch shall grow out of his roots: and the spirit of the LORD shall rest upon him, the spirit of wisdom and understanding, the spirit of counsel and might, the spirit of knowledge and of the fear of the LORD' (11: 1-2). Houteff's supporters earned the name 'Davidian Seventh-day Adventists' on this account, since they taught that a latter-day King David (David was Jesse's son) would arise and lead his new Israel to salvation. Houteff purchased some land on the outskirts of Waco, and named it the Mount Carmel Center.

When Houteff died in 1955, this was a blow to the movement, since it was expected that he would hand over his leadership to Christ at his Second Advent. There arose among the community the expectation that Houteff would be resurrected from the dead after 'a time, times and half a time' (Dan. 7:25)—that is, in three and a half years' time, in 1959. Meanwhile his wife Florence succeeded him as temporary vice-president; she sold off the land, buying a nearby smaller site, on which the 1993 disaster later occurred. Florence attempted to disband the organization in 1962, and left the compound. After a power struggle, Vernon Howell (1959–1993), later to be known as David Koresh, assumed control of the group in 1981. The name 'David Koresh' was allegedly given to him in a revelation in which God told him that he was the modern day King David and King Cyrus (Cyrus is the Romanization of the Hebrew 'Koresh'), whom Isaiah describes as God's 'anointed' or 'messiah' (Isa. 45:1). Koresh was proclaimed as the modern-day messiah, exercising firm control over the community. This control included extensive teaching on the Bible, particularly the Book of Revelation (Koresh claimed to be the opener and interpreter of the 'seventh seal'—Rev. 8:1), and demanded exclusive sexual rights over the women members.

Following complaints to the police about firearms offences and child abuse, the FBI mounted the 51-day siege, which ended with the burning down of the compound on 19 April 1993. Eighty-one members died, leaving only a very handful of non-resident supporters to continue the decimated organization.

Jehovah's Witnesses

Of all the offshoots of Adventism, the Jehovah's Witnesses are probably the best known. The organization, legally incorporated as The Watch Tower Bible and Tract Society of Pennsylvania, owes its origins to Charles Taze Russell (1852–1916). Russell dissociated himself with Adventism, although he had been acquainted with a number of Adventist groups. None of them had satisfied him, until he heard the Adventist preacher Jonas Wendell (1815–1873) preaching. This prompted him to start his own Bible study group in 1870, which grew to become the International Bible Students' Association (IBSA). Although Russell and the subsequent Jehovah's Witnesses do not regard themselves as Adventist, they have much in common with them. Like Adventists, they believe that the final battle of Armageddon is imminent, that biblical prophecies have a present-day application, and a pattern of end-time events can be given dates in accordance with biblical predictions. Russell and his followers also were unable to accept the mainstream Protestant Christian doctrines of predestination and eternal damnation.

In common with Adventism, Russell and his followers had an implicit belief in the inerrancy of Scripture, and his emphasis on the Bible caused him to question certain key doctrines that had become part of mainstream Christianity. One such doctrine was the Trinity, to which he could find no explicit references in the Bible, but which was nevertheless affirmed by the mainstream churches, including the Adventists. The Adventists taught that Roman Catholicism was a corruption of Christianity, equating it with Babylon the Great (Rev. 17:5). Russell went further, claiming that all the churches were corrupt, not just Rome. The IBSA and the Jehovah's Witnesses have been entirely lay-led, unlike most branches of Christianity, including Adventism, which have clergy. Russell also disagreed with the Adventist belief that the earth would be burnt at the end of time, teaching that it would be renewed, to be inhabited by God's faithful who had lived before Christ's ministry.

After Russell died in 1916, a power struggle among some of the early leaders ensued. A number of schismatical organizations emerged as a result, while Joseph Franklin ('Judge') Rutherford (1869–1941) gained control of the Watch Tower organization and its assets. Possibly to distinguish his own organization from the splinter groups, he gave the name 'Jehovah's Witnesses' to the organization in 1931. Rutherford introduced a number of new features that have become the Witnesses' hallmarks. He maintained a firm anti-war stance, causing his followers to be regarded as unpatriotic; to this day Witnesses will not take part in armed combat. Rutherford also wanted to purge the organization of all the 'pagan' practices that had crept into Christianity: the celebration of Christmas and birthdays, and ideas that had entered Christianity through pagan philosophy, such as the immortality of the soul. He also introduced house-to-house evangelism, in accordance with early Church practice (Acts 5:42). During the Rutherford period, Witnesses came to believe that the Watch Tower Society exclusively offered the means of salvation.

Witnesses are publicly perceived as setting dates for 'the end of the world', but continually changing them when they fail to materialize. This is somewhat of a misunderstanding. Two predicted dates—1925 and 1975—resulted in failed expectations, even on the Society's own admission. (Rutherford had predicted that the ancient patriarchs would return from the dead in 1925, and 1975 was believed to mark the end of the sixth millennium, possibly heralding Armageddon.) Some dates have been re-assigned to different events, and Jehovah's Witnesses are now much less prone to associate prophetic dates with earthly political events. One key date proposed by Russell, which Jehovah's Witnesses continue to regard as significant, is 1914. At one time Russell expected God's kingdom to have been established on earth by that date, but later came to assign it to Christ's *parousia* ('presence'), teaching that Christ began his heavenly rule on that date, preparing his kingdom for his faithful ones.

According to Watch Tower teaching, Christ is gathering his faithful—the 'anointed class' of 144,000—into heaven. Initially it was expected that all Russell's Bible students would attain the heavenly kingdom, but of course the number of Witnesses is now well in excess of 144,000. (In 2008, some 17,790,631 people attended the annual Memorial, the service commemorating Jesus' final meal with his disciples. Not all of those were active Witnesses, however.) In 1935 Rutherford declared that there were two classes of individual: those who belonged to the 'heavenly class' (the

144,000) and those who belonged to the 'great crowd' (Rev. 7:9-10). Most present-day Witnesses regard themselves as belonging to the latter class, and expect everlasting life on the renewed earth after Armageddon.

Mention should be made of the Jehovah's Witnesses' stance on blood—another source of public comment. During the Second World War, blood transfusion was becoming a common medical procedure, and the Governing Body defined its stance on the matter. It was perceived as a violation of God's command to Noah: 'you must not eat meat that has its lifeblood still in it' (Gen. 9:4). Two points are worth noting about this injunction. First, the reference is primarily to a food law, and Witnesses typically avoid foods that are made from blood, such as black pudding. Second, Witnesses do not hold that all the Old Testament laws have force. They represent the 'old covenant' and are only binding if they are reinforced by the New Testament. Witnesses find reinforcement for this commandment in the First Jerusalem Council's ruling, that the Gentiles should 'abstain...from blood' (Acts 15:20). It should be noted that the word is 'abstain' here, which is taken to have a wider application than simply eating. As in all matters, the Bible is regarded as the final arbiter, and the Watch Tower Society has never produced any independent creed or set of principles. Its teachings are disseminated to the public principally through its monthly magazines *The Watchtower* and *Awake!*

New Revelations

Apart from the visions claimed by Ellen G. White, all the offshoots that we have so far considered base their teachings entirely on the Bible. However, there exists another type of organization which supplements the Bible and traditional Christian doctrine with new revelations, new scriptures or new prophets. Such movements contend that God's revelation did not end with the early apostles, the canonization of Scripture, or the formulation of traditional creeds and confessions, but continues to be channelled through chosen individuals.

Probably the best known of these is the Church of Jesus Christ of Latter-day Saints (the 'Mormons'). Their founder-leader Joseph Smith (1805–1844) lived in Palmyra, New York, and at the age of 14 could not decide which of the rival Christian churches he should join. While walking in a grove in Palmyra, he was apparently afforded a vision of two figures which he identified as God and Jesus. (Mormons do not accept the mainstream doctrine of the Trinity, holding that God and Jesus are two distinct beings, each with physical bodies.) They instructed him to go back to his home and await further guidance. It was not until three years later that he received a further vision, this time of the Angel Moroni, who directed him to Cumorah Hill, where he would find some gold plates. Smith searched, as instructed, and discovered two plates bearing characters in the language of 'Reformed Egyptian'. Smith interpreted these, with the aid of a seer-stone, dictating his translation to his friend Oliver Cowdery—a task that took 80 days, and which resulted in the Book of Mormon.

The Book of Mormon is believed to have been transcribed in a mere eighty days, and it is one of four principal Mormon scriptures, the others being the Bible, *Doctrines and Covenants* and *The Pearl of Great Price*. According to Mormon teaching, the true and original Church began not with Jesus, but with Adam, whom Jesus baptized in his pre-existent form. Latter-day Saints hold that each individual has a prior existence in spirit form before receiving his or her physical body. This Church quickly became corrupted, and God sent prophets at various intervals to secure its restoration. The Book of Mormon picks up the story with Jared, whose family escaped the 'confounding of languages' at the Tower of Babel, and who travelled to America. The prophet Ether predicted the coming of Jesus, but his words were unheeded by the Jaredites, who became extinct after various civil wars. Some five-hundred years later God commanded the prophet Lehi, a contemporary of Jeremiah, to leave Jerusalem, and he also journeyed to America. Lehi had three sons: Laman, Lemuel and Nephi. Nephi, the youngest, composed two books that recount how Laman and his supporters came into a prolonged conflict with the Nephites. Shortly before the birth of Jesus, peace was restored, and after his ascension Jesus appeared to the Nephites in America. There he delivered various teachings to them, including his Sermon on the Mount. For a further 160 years there was peace, but conflict broke out once more between Lamanities and Nephites. Mormon (attributed dates c. 310–385 CE) was the latter's military leader, as well as a historian, and he collated the Nephites' historical records, summarizing them on the gold plates which Smith discovered many centuries later.

The early Mormon community began in Palmyra, but opposition mounted, and Smith and his followers moved to Kirkland, Ohio in 1831. In 1836 the first Mormon Temple was built there, although it now belongs to one of the Mormon offshoots, the Community of Christ (previously known as the Reformed Latter Day Saints). Faced with further opposition, the early Mormons moved to Nauvoo, but once again came into conflict with local opponents. Joseph Smith and his brother

Hyrum were arrested and imprisoned, and an angry crowd broke into the jail and shot them. Brigham Young took over the leadership, and led the community to a more favourable environment in Salt Lake City, Utah—a journey of 1,400 miles. The State of Utah, and Salt Lake City in particular, is the base of present-day Mormonism.

After translating the Book of Mormon, Joseph Smith and his principal disciple Oliver Cowdery baptized each other, and their action is held to mark the restoration of the priesthood. Mormons have two ranks of priesthood: the Aaronic priesthood, into which boys are baptized at around the age of eight, and the Melchizedek priesthood, for which young men of around eighteen or nineteen are admitted, if their conduct is judged appropriate. Women are not admitted to the priesthood, but may join the Relief Society, founded by Joseph Smith's wife Emma in 1842. Both men and women are eligible to undertake missionary work: for young men this involves dedicating a period of two years, often abroad, where they undertake door-to-door work, endeavouring to spread the faith. Young women are expected only to commit 18 months of their lives to such mission.

Mormon missionaries are normally attached to a local congregation, whose place of worship is their local church. The church is for Sunday worship, which is for preaching, giving testimony and for communion (which is celebrated with bread and water, not wine—Mormons prohibit alcohol). Marriages are also conducted in Mormon churches, and in most countries this ceremony satisfies civic requirements. In addition to the churches are the Temples, which are fewer in number. Unlike the local churches, these are not open to the public, and are only accessible to those members who have a special 'recommend' from their bishop. (The bishop is the overseer of a local congregation.) Visits to temples must be for 'ordinances', namely Endowment, the Sealing of Marriage and the Sealing of Ancestors.

Endowment involves a member making his or her way through the Temple's rooms, progressively reading or being shown the various scenes of humankind's history from Adam onwards, until finally they pass through a veil into the Celestial Room, commemorating Christ's atonement for humanity. Endowment may be undertaken on one's own behalf, or for others. The Sealing of Marriage involves a ceremony in a Sealing Room, in which the couple sit between two large facing mirrors. The infinite number of reflections that the mirrors generate symbolizes the Mormon belief that marriage is for eternity, and the Sealing ceremony is held to secure the eternal partnership of the couple. The Sealing of

Ancestors involves members undergoing baptism on behalf of deceased members of their family, a practice that is believed to be alluded to by Paul (1 Cor. 15:29). A Sealing Room containing a font with three to four feet of water is assigned for this purpose. Mormons attach great importance to ancestors, in order to afford them the opportunity of experiencing life after death. For this purpose they have done much work in facilitating the tracing of ancestors, and have established several Family History Libraries for genealogical research, which may be consulted by the public as well as by the Church's own members. When an unbaptized ancestor is identified, a member in good standing may undergo baptism by proxy on his or her behalf. This enables the deceased to have the opportunity of accepting the message of the Book of Mormon, and to be eligible for eternal life. For the Mormon there are believed to be three realms in which one may live eternally: in descending 'degrees of glory' they are the celestial realm, the terrestrial realm and the telestial realm. Members believe that even if one is assigned merely to the telestial realm its glory greatly surpasses any joys experienced on earth, and is well worth attaining, and infinitely preferable to 'outer darkness', which is the destiny of those who reject the gospel.

The Unification Church

A more recent example of a Christian-derived organization based on new revelations is the Family Federation for World Peace and Unification, formerly known as the Unification Church (UC), and more popularly known as the 'Moonies'. The nickname is derived from the name of the founder-leader Sun Myung Moon (b. 1920), although the church's official legal name is the Holy Spirit Association for the Unification of World Christianity, which Moon founded in Korea in 1954.

Sun Myung Moon was born in North Korea, and claimed to receive a vision of Jesus on a Korean mountainside around Easter 1935. Jesus, he relates, told him that he had been chosen to complete his unfinished mission. After receiving further revelations, Moon taught that this unfinished work was to marry and parent a family, in order to beget sinless children who would complete God's plan for humankind. Adam and Eve had been expected to do this, but owing to their disobedience, sin entered the world and had to be expiated. At various points in human history, God sent 'central figures'—notably Abel, Noah, Abraham, Moses and finally John the Baptist, who was expected to herald Jesus as the messiah. The messiah would restore the Satanic blood-lineage that had stemmed from Adam and Eve after the Fall, and inaugurate the perfect family under God's dominion. John the Baptist at first proclaimed Jesus as the messiah, but later began to have doubts, and became resentful that Jesus' followers outnumbered his own. The testimony of John, being the son of Zecharias, a chief priest (Lk. 1:13; *Divine Principle*, I, iv, 2) would have carried weight, but his disloyalty left Jesus without a foundation for his messianic role. As a result, the Jewish people did not believe in him, and he was led to the cross.

Unificationists deny that Jesus' mission was a failure—an interpretation often given by their critics. It was others who failed Jesus and, in any case, Jesus' death accomplished something important—he opened up Paradise, a realm of the spirit world where the faithful may go, awaiting full entry into the Kingdom of Heaven, when it is finally opened. *Divine Principle*, the key text of the Unification Church, the contents of which Moon dictated to a close disciple, discusses at length where and when the new messiah will be born, to complete Jesus' unfinished work. The discussion revolves around calculations involving allegedly parallel dates for events in the Old and New Testaments, and is too complex to summarize here. Its conclusion is that the messiah would be born in Korea, sometime between 1917 and 1930. Although Sun Myung Moon is not explicitly named as the new messiah in *Divine Principle*, his followers have never doubted this, and in 1992 he publicly disclosed his messianic status. Sun Myung Moon and his bride Hak Ja Han were married in 1960, and this event is regarded as 'the marriage of the lamb' (Rev. 19:7). Both Moon and his wife are regarded as the messiahs, since blessed marriage is the means of salvation. They have parented fourteen children in all, although only ten remain alive.

Sun Myung Moon received public attention for the 'mass marriages' that he has conducted (they are more correctly called 'Blessing' ceremonies), sometimes marrying over five-thousand couples at a single ceremony. Unificationist teaching is that only couples whose marriage has been blessed by the messiahs (Moon and his wife) may enter the Kingdom of Heaven. The Blessing ceremony is not merely available to members, since the Unification Church teaches that entry into the Kingdom of Heaven is through the messiahs' blessed marriage, not through joining the organization. (Marriage must always be heterosexual, and sexual relationships must be confined to marriage, according to UC teaching: the blessing of gay and lesbian partnerships is not contemplated.) Accordingly, various measures have been taken to ensure that the Blessing is available to those outside the Unification Church. To underline this point, the Unification

Church was renamed in 1996 as the Family Federation for World Peace and Unification (FFWPU). Moon recently claimed to have presided over the marriages of 360 million people, which he declared in 2000, though this figure cannot refer to a number assembled in any stadium, but rather to names that are brought before a gathering of those whose marriages have already been enacted. (The selected candidates may not necessarily be aware that such a marriage has been conducted on their behalf.) These names include the dead as well as the living: the Family Federation teaches that everyone will finally enter the Kingdom of Heaven, even Satan himself. Moon therefore claims to journey into the spirit world to conduct ceremonies for the marriage of spirits: it is believed that he has conducted such a ceremony on behalf of Jesus, among many other departed spirits.

The FFWPU's official name implies the goal of unifying world Christianity, and Moon has spearheaded a number of projects whose purpose is to bring Christian leaders, as well as leaders of other faiths, together. His efforts to bring about world peace include the Middle East Peace Initiative (MEPI), established in 2003, which aims to bring together Christians, Jews and Muslims by organizing dialogues, rallies and pilgrimages. However, critics have frequently noted that Moon's peace projects rest uneasily with his ownership of the T'ongil Engineering Factory, which manufactures parts for weapons: Moon is no pacifist. Moon's incursions into the spirit world have also served to alienate the FFWPU from mainstream religions, not merely Christianity. On Christmas Day 2001, Moon allegedly received a message from a deceased Unificationist leader who claimed to have presided over a ceremony in which various leaders of the world's religions, including Jesus, Confucius, the Buddha and Muhammad, testified that he is the true messiah.

Emanuel Swedenborg and the New Church

A less well known Christian organization based on new revelations is the Church of the New Jerusalem, based on the teachings of Emanuel Swedenborg (1688–1772). Although Swedenborgians are small in number (their own estimate is fifty-thousand members worldwide), Swedenborg had a profound influence on Western spirituality: Spiritualism, New Thought and the Transcendentalist Movement all owe a substantial debt to Swedenborg, as do a number of important scholars, such as Immanuel Kant, Carl Jung and William James. Swedenborg was the son of a Lutheran pastor, and spent his life working as an engineer for the Swedish Board of Mines until, at the age of 56, he began to have a series of visions. The first was of Jesus, and subsequent visions were of angels and spirits, heaven and hell and even God himself.

Swedenborg went on to write prolifically on theological and biblical topics. His experience of Jesus led him to believe that in Jesus alone was the Trinity to be found and that Jesus alone deserved worship. Jesus was therefore not the mediator between God and humanity, offering justification by faith alone: Swedenborg taught that faith had to be accompanied by acts of charity, for which men and women would be judged. Swedenborg had no doubts about the authority and inspiration of the Bible, but central to his thought was the notion that Scripture had different levels of meaning—an outer meaning and an 'inner essence'. This inner meaning of the Bible had been explained to him by God in these visions. Swedenborg expounded this hidden meaning of Scripture in his eight-volume work *Arcana Coelestia* ('Heavenly Secrets', 1749–1756). Swedenborg came to believe that the Second Coming had taken place, but invisibly, and that the New Jerusalem had come down from heaven.

Swedenborg had mentioned a new church, but he did not establish any religious community during his lifetime. Five years after his death, five former Wesleyan ministers founded the Church of the New Jerusalem in England on 7 May 1787. This new church experienced some doctrinal schisms in its early history, resulting in two organizations, the larger of which is now known as the General Church of the New Jerusalem (in Britain it is called the General Conference of the New Church—or simply the New Church), and the smaller the Lord's New Church Which Is Nova Hiersolyma. The latter now exists primarily in South Africa, with a worldwide membership of no more than 1,900: Swedenborg believed that the Africans were humanity's most enlightened race, being more in contact with their inner nature. The General Church and the New Church estimate their worldwide allegiance as fifty thousand.

The Swedenborgian churches teach that the Bible is inspired, but contains two parallel 'stories': an outer meaning and an inner essence. Evil originates within humanity, not from a personal Devil, who is regarded simply as a personification, while good originates from God. Humanity has freewill and must choose between the two, recognizing that salvation comes from a life of charity. Swedenborgians reject mainstream theories of atonement, and regard Jesus as the one who reveals God in his three aspects. Worship in the New Church has a similar structure to that of mainstream Protestantism, consisting of hymns, prayers, Bible readings

413

and usually a sermon. However, it is customary to include a reading from Swedenborg in addition to traditional Scripture. In common with mainstream Protestantism, it observes two sacraments: baptism, which may be administered to adults or children, and the celebration of the Last Supper, which it calls 'holy supper'.

Spiritualism

Although Swedenborg is credited with influencing the later Spiritualist movement, it is doubtful whether much of Spiritualism should be considered as Christian. Spiritualism draws on Swedenborg's teachings, combined with the work of Franz Mesmer (1734–1815), who scientifically developed methods of inducing trance and hypnotic states. Andrew Jackson Davis (1826–1910), known as the 'Poughkeepsie Seer', combined these two strands, claiming to have received a vision of the ancient philosopher Galen and Emanuel Swedenborg, who taught and guided him. Spiritualism gained momentum through the famous Fox sisters, who in 1848 heard and interpreted 'rappings' in their home in Hydesville, New York. Interest in their experiences was encouraged by some of the radical Quakers in the area, and the showman Phineas T. Barnum, who was a Universalist, arranged for them to tour parts of the United States.

In 1853 the first Spiritualist church opened in Britain in Keighley, Yorkshire, and Spiritualism had became a worldwide movement by 1860. Two principal umbrella organizations were formed in the late nineteenth century: the National Federation of Spiritualists (NFS) in 1891, which became the Spiritualists' National Union (SNU) in 1902, and the National Spiritualist Association of Churches (NSAC), founded in Chicago in 1893. The NSAC was set up by Harrison D. Barrett and James M. Peebles, who were both Unitarian ministers, together with medium and author Cora L. Peebles, and originally accepted the authority of the Bible. However, in 1957 the issue of the NSAC's claim to a Christian identity was discussed and rejected. The SNU's principles are:

The Fatherhood of God
The Brotherhood of Man
The Communion of Spirits and the Ministry of Angels
The continuous existence of the human soul
Personal responsibility
Compensation and retribution hereafter for all the good and evil deeds done on earth
Eternal progress open to every human soul

It is worth noting that these principles make no reference to Jesus. A small minority of Spiritualist churches identify themselves as Christian, affiliating to the Greater World Christian Spiritualist Association (founded in 1931 as The Greater World Christian Spiritualist League). These churches affirm the leadership and the example of Jesus, rather than his atoning work, on which mainstream Christianity gives the greatest emphasis.

It is a popular misconception that Spiritualist meetings consist of séances, with table-rappings and mediums going into trances. A service in a Spiritualist church runs along the lines of a Protestant service, with hymns, prayers, a reading and an address. The hymns are typically addressed to God, but make no reference to Jesus or Christ. A distinctive feature is a period of time that is set aside for the medium to make contact with spirits and to deliver messages from them to members of the congregation. In Christian Spiritualist churches, reference is of course made to Jesus Christ, and some observe the traditional rites of baptism and communion.

The recent phenomenon of 'channelling', which has attracted particular interest in New Age circles, has some affinities to Spiritualism. A 'channel' is someone who acts as an intermediary between the spirit world and human beings on earth; however, channellers are more inclined to claim a link with one specific spirit (occasionally two) and pass on their messages of guidance. Some of these are committed to writing—automatic writing is often a method used by the channeller—and some channellers have claimed to pass on new teachings of Jesus from the spirit world. Examples include Levi H. Dowling (1844–1911) and psychic Edgar Cayce (1877–1945) who produced accounts of Jesus' life which they claimed to transcribe from 'akashic records' (esoteric records stored in the spirit world). Levi's *The Aquarian Age Gospel of Jesus, the Christ of the Piscean Age*, although first published in 1908, remains in print. More recent channelled writings that purport to come from Jesus include *A Course in Miracles* (1976) by Helen Shucman (1909–1981). Shucman's volume purports to correct errors in the Gospels and in the Church's teaching and, in common with Dowling, absorbs oriental thinking. Such writings have no place in mainstream Christianity, whose attitude is fairly consistently condemnatory.

New Thought and Christian Science

Other Christian-related organizations that originated in the mid-nineteenth century are collectively described as 'New Thought'. Their prime interest lay in healing, principally through the powers of the mind over matter. Phineas Parker Quimby (1802–1866), a student of Mesmerism, is often regarded as the 'father' of New Thought. Two of his students were Emma Curtis Hopkins (1849–1925) and Mary Baker Eddy (1821–1910). Hopkins was not herself a religious teacher, but she taught Charles Fillmore (1854–1948) and his wife Myrtle Fillmore (1845–1931), who founded Unity in 1891. The Unity School of Christianity emphasizes spiritual healing and counselling, and offers prosperity through meditation, the use of 'affirmations' and the avoidance of negative thoughts. Unity acknowledges Jesus, but as the 'Way Shower' rather than the world's saviour. Jesus has demonstrated the divine potential that exists in all of us, and the word 'Christ' refers to the divinity within each individual. The Bible's importance is recognized, but it is interpreted 'metaphysically' as an account of humanity's evolutionary journey towards enlightenment.

Mary Baker Eddy was once a co-worker with Hopkins, but the two split up as a result of a quarrel. Eddy's key book *Science and Health, with Key to the Scriptures* (1875) continues to be an authoritative text. The first Church of Christ, Scientist was founded in Boston, Massachusetts in 1875. Christian Science maintains public visibility through its reading rooms, which can be seen in various cities, at which the public may obtain information.

After experiencing a fall in 1866, Mary Baker Eddy read one of the Bible's healing miracles, and claimed to have successfully obtained healing by yielding her mind to the Divine Mind. Christian Scientists distinguish themselves from New Thought in their insistence that it is God who brings about healing, not the sufferer's exercise of 'mind over matter'. Christian Science is based on a philosophical idealism that regards matter as unreal. The world is spiritual, not material, and hence evil and disease are unreal, and are most effectively addressed by spiritual means, such as prayer. Healing can be sought not merely for illnesses, but for personal trauma, moral dilemmas, and business and financial problems. Christian Scientists meet weekly for worship: the service is conducted by two readers, and consists of hymns, prayers and readings from the Bible and from Mary Baker Eddy's writings. There is no sermon—Eddy's writings need no further elaboration—and the church does not celebrate sacraments such as baptism and communion. There are 26 set themes, which are followed weekly, each theme being covered twice a year. Christian Science believes in one infinite God, but he is not a Trinity. Jesus was the promised messiah, but not God himself: he is a teacher and healer, and—in common with Unity—the 'Way Shower'. Christian Science accepts the traditional beliefs of his virgin birth and resurrection, but does not regard him as the saviour who expiates the world's sins. Because evil is unreal, there is no punishment for it in the form of a hell.

Christian Science's emphasis on health entails healthy living, including avoidance of alcohol and tobacco. Christian Scientists have been much criticized for their attitudes to orthodox medicine, since they recommend spiritual rather than physical therapy. However, Christian Science is not completely opposed to orthodox medicine, and individual members may choose whether to use its remedies. Medicine, however, is believed to address only the unreal material aspects of illness, avoiding the real spiritual issues, which can only be addressed spiritually. The real causes of ailments are fear, ignorance and sin. Although Christian Science contains some of mainstream Christianity's orthodox teachings, its Christology and its attitudes to matter and healing have caused mainstream Christians to distance themselves from it.

Groups with Mainstream Theology

Some of the New Christian groups subscribe to forms of theology that would largely find acceptance within mainstream circles. Examples are The Family International (formerly the Children of God), the International Churches of Christ, and the Jesus Army, among many others. Such groups have proved controversial on account of certain practices, rather than for their doctrines. We have selected these three groups for particular mention, since they have all attracted media attention.

The Family International

The Children of God (CoG) grew out of the so-called Jesus Revolution in the State of California in the late 1960s and early 1970s. A number of communal groups grew out of the ex-hippie counter-culture and had a relatively young following. Members of such groups became known as the 'Jesus people', or sometimes the 'Jesus freaks'. CoG's leader was

David Bradt Berg (1919–1994), known to his followers as Moses David. Initially Berg's group was an apocalyptic one, and organized 'sackcloth vigils' to warn humanity of the world's imminent end. This emphasis shifted in the 1970s, when sexual freedom became more of a dominant theme. The group achieved particular notoriety for its 'flirty fishing' (or 'FF-ing')—the practice of (mainly) female members offering sexual services to seekers. It was popularly believed that the Family of Love, as the organization came to be called in 1978, was undertaking evangelism by seduction; however, members who remember those days have told the authors that their intention was to ensure that seekers' physical needs were satisfied before offering them spiritual teachings.

The Family's theology was, and remains, firmly fundamentalist. Members believe in a literal six-day creation, rejecting theories of evolution, and hold that the Bible offers inerrant truth about Adam and Eve's Fall, God's sending prophets, the coming of Jesus Christ as the messiah, his life and teachings, and particularly his atoning death and resurrection. In common with mainstream Christianity, they celebrate communion. They are not exclusivist, holding that there are many other expressions of the Christian faith that can offer salvation. Where members do not live in communities, or simply find it more convenient to do so, they are quite happy to worship in mainstream churches with other Christians. Communion is celebrated within their communities, but not baptism, since they firmly hold that salvation is by faith rather than by some external rite.

During Moses David's lifetime, teachings were circulated to members by means of the MO Letters, and also in cartoon form: *True Komix* was a principal favourite publication. The former attracted considerable criticism from the media and from mainstream Christians on account of its sexual explicitness. The Family's attitudes to sex have been liberal, recognizing that Adam and Eve were naked and not ashamed of it, and that God's first commandment was, 'Be fruitful and multiply' (Gen. 1:28). The Family initially permitted free sexual relationships among members, not simply one's spouse, pointing out that many of the Bible's heroes did not confine their sexual activity to one partner. Sexual liberation did not extend to homosexuality, however, since The Family believes that Scripture condemns this. The Family does not believe in contraception, and therefore members tend to have considerably more children than average. In the early 1980s the AIDS epidemic caused the organization to rethink its stance. In 1987 FF-ing was banned completely, although the practice of having multiple sex partners continued and is called 'sharing'. Sharing does not entail having indiscriminate sex: in order to 'share' marriage partners, both couples must know about and agree to it. Clandestine affairs are considered to be adultery, and hence in violation of the Ten Commandments.

Although The Family's sexual practices have gained them media attention, members will claim that sex is not their principal concern. More important, they claim, is prophecy. Moses David was sometimes described as the 'final prophet', claiming to have guided by a spirit called Abrahim (not to be confused with Abraham). Maria, David's widow, has sometimes been known as the 'prophetess', but is not regarded as the only one who is capable of receiving prophecies. Any Family member may receive prophetic revelations, but before these are made public Maria must judge their validity and approve them. New prophecies may not contradict anything in the Bible, but often they add detail and colour to the stories that are already in Scripture.

The Jesus Army

Another theologically orthodox organization is the Jesus Army. The Jesus Army is the evangelizing wing of the Jesus Fellowship Church (its official name), and was originally a distinctive British NRM. It is now becoming an international organization, having made the most strides in Africa, but with other branches elsewhere in Europe. The Jesus Army grew from a small Baptist church in Bugbrooke in Northamptonshire, England. Founder-leader Noel Stanton was appointed as the church's pastor in 1957 when the congregation was well in decline. In 1969 Stanton and others experienced 'baptism of the Spirit'—a phenomenon whereby members began to speak in tongues, and to claim spiritual gifts such as healing powers. In the early 1970s bikers and drug addicts found their way into the fellowship, making it a youth movement.

The Jesus Army is noted for its brightly coloured double-decker buses, which come to town centres in England to spread the gospel, and for the combat jackets that its members wear. Many members live in communities which achieve self-sufficiency largely through their business enterprises, principally farming, health foods and selling clothes. Members of these communities share their possessions, in accordance with early Church practice, and many commit themselves to a life of celibacy. Lifestyle is modest and disciplined, with members committed to abstinence from alcohol and tobacco, the avoidance of cosmetics and personal adornments (apart from a distinctive red wooden cross which may be worn as a necklace) and secular entertainments. Televisions and radios are not found in their communities, and even reading newspapers is discouraged. Those who believe that they are not called to lead a celibate life are permitted to marry, but secular-style dating is not allowed. A 'relating procedure' must be followed, whereby the member must apply to an elder, who may permit the couple to spend time together to become better acquainted. The Jesus Army, in common with the Salvation Army, seeks to 'go where others will not go', and particularly aims to help the dispossessed, offering a spiritual home to those who are homeless, or addicted to drugs or alcohol.

The Jesus Army accepts the Bible as literally true, and is thoroughly Trinitarian, affirming Christianity's major creeds, specifically the Apostles' Creed, the Nicene Creed and the Athanasian Creed. Particularly important to the Jesus Army is the notion of covenant: not only do they believe in the biblical covenants, but members formally enter into a covenant in joining the organization. Covenanted membership entails a lifelong commitment, of which there are four different styles. Style 1 covenant membership is non-residential, involving no greater commitment than attendance at a mainstream church; Style 2 involves specific commitments of time and money; Style 3 is residential in one of the New Creation Communities; and Style 4 is distance membership, which is for those who cannot worship with other members, for example if they work in another country, or if they are in prison. (Someone may have joined the community but still have to stand trial for a past crime.)

The Jesus' Army's work seems commendable, and it may be wondered why the organization has proved controversial, arousing attention from the anti-cult movement, and encountering problems in seeking to maintain membership of umbrella organizations, particularly the Baptist Union, from which their membership was terminated in 1986, and the Evanglical Alliance, from which they were ejected the same year, having joined in 1982. The Baptist Union seeks to bring together Baptist congregations, and since the Jesus Army had grown from a single congregation to a wider network, it had made itself ineligible. Other reservations related to its lifestyle and practices: some seekers who had already undergone baptism were re-baptized by the Jesus Army, thus implying that previous mainstream baptism lacked validity. Further criticisms related to authoritarian leadership: the movement practised 'shepherding', which entailed close personal and spiritual supervision of each member by a designated superior. Their practice of administering corporal punishment to children ('rodding') also came under criticism.

In 1999, the Evangelical Alliance reappraised their ban after the Jesus Army had loosened up some of its control on its members.

The International Churches of Christ

A third theologically orthodox movement is the International Churches of Christ (ICC or ICoC). These churches originate from the mainline denomination, the Churches of Christ, and were founded by Thomas ('Kip') McKean (b. 1954) who was appointed as minister of the Lexington Church of Christ, Massachussets in 1979. Under McKean's leadership the church, renamed the Boston Church of Christ, experience phenomenal growth, increasing from 30 to three-thousand members within a mere two years. Growth outside Boston was achieved through the practice of 'planting'—sending out mission teams to other cities, initially Chicago, London and New York. By 2002 the total membership was estimated to be over 135,000, with over 540 congregations worldwide, and the ICoC's vision was to have one of their churches in every town.

The Churches of Christ are restorationist, endeavouring to recapture a primordial form of Christianity, based on a belief in the inerrancy of Scripture, with a lifestyle in accordance with New Testament principles. They accept the traditional creeds of the Church, however, but deny certain other doctrines such as original sin and predestination. Members are admitted through baptism by total immersion; infant baptism is not regarded as valid. Communion is distributed at services, although the preferred name for the rite is the Lord's Supper. The leadership roles of elder, deacon and evangelist are exclusively male, which they believe is in line with first-century Christian practice. The ICoC became controversial on account of the high demands it placed upon its members, who were expected to attend several meetings during the week, to tithe, to study the Bible and to evangelize. Some ICoC members lived communally, although most of them combined practising their faith with pursuing a regular job or life as a student. The most controversial aspect of the ICoC was 'discipling': each member was assigned a 'discipler'—a (male) spiritual superior to whom the member was responsible, and who ensured that the follower was showing sufficient diligence in attending meetings, studying the Bible, praying and often fasting. Members were encouraged to confess their sins to their discipler, who was also empowered to 'rebuke' wayward members.

The ICoC have been criticized for allegedly excessive demands on members. Some students claimed that the church's demands left insufficient time for their studies, and some members who had physically demanding jobs left the organization because they felt that fasting left them weak or that they were arriving for work unduly tired through lack of sleep. In November 2002, Kip McKean resigned, having confessed publicly to arrogance and failure to protect the weak. His resignation caused a decentralization of the movement, with a dismantling of its central leadership and headquarters. Some congregations found their way back into the mainline Disciples of Christ, while McKean went to Portland, Oregon to revive a struggling unaffiliated congregation there. In 2007 he gathered a number of former supporters in Los Angeles, where he set up the City of Angels International Christian Church, and continues to train 'church planters'.

Orthodox and Catholic NRMs

Most of the New Christian sectarian groups come out of Protestantism. However, Eastern Orthodoxy and Roman Catholicism are not without their new forms of expression and schismatical factions. The later parts of the nineteenth century saw the rise of a few British and Celtic Orthodox churches. The British Orthodox Church and the Celtic Orthodox Church are the most prominent, although very small. Their aims are two-fold. One is to seek to re-establish a form of Christianity that pre-dates the 1054 schism. Another is to express the Orthodox liturgy in English, since the traditional use of Greek, Russian and Eastern European languages presents a barrier to potential converts in the English- and French-speaking worlds. These Orthodox Churches claim a tradition deriving from Joseph of Arimathea, who allegedly came to Britain in 37 CE, followed by Saint Aristobulos in 63 CE. The tradition is believed to have been lost through time, until it was re-established in 1866 by Jules Ferrett, who was consecrated by the Syrian Orthodox Church, assuming the title of Bishop of Iona and its Dependencies. His Church was known as the Orthodox Church of the British Isles. It was not until 1994 that the British Orthodox Church (its new name) became part of the Coptic Orthodox Patriarchate of Alexandria. Some of the French members did not want this association, and separated to form L'Église Orthodoxe Celtique (The Celtic Orthodox Church) and were joined in 1988 by some British priests who seceded. There are various bodies professing Orthodoxy in Britain and France: in addition to the British Orthodox Church and the Celtic Orthodox Church there are the English Orthodox Trust, the Orthodox Church of the Gauls and the

French Coptic Orthodox Church. Since Eastern Orthodoxy consists of autocephalous groupings of churches, there is not always unanimity as to whether a group should be regarded as being in communion with the wider church.

Some Orthodox-derived groups are rejected universally, however. In 1993 media attention focused on the New Community of Enlightened Humanity (YUSMALOS), led by Maria Devi Christos (born Marina Tsrigun), which blends Christian and occultist ideas. ('YUSMALOS' is an acronym for 'Jupiter, Uranus, Saturn, Mars, Luna, Orion and Sirius', indicating the organization's astrological interests.) Maria was proclaimed as the new messiah by Yuri Krivonogov, founder of the White Brotherhood, who later became her husband, and who proclaimed himself as the present-day John the Baptist. The group predicted the 'Coming of the Holy Ghost', accompanied by a final Judgement Day, due to take place on 10 November 1993, and it was feared that they were planning a mass suicide by self-immolation. Instead, the group attempted to invade Kiev Cathedral and take it over. Arrests were made, and Tsvigun and Krivonogov received prison sentences of four and seven years respectively. After various name changes, the group is currently known as The Mystic College of ISIS and Her Followers.

In November 2007 the media focused on a group called the True Russian Orthodox Church, led by Pyotr Kuzetsov (b. 1964). Kuzetsov preached that the world would end the following May, and persuaded around 30 of his followers to take refuge in a cave in Russia's Penza region. Again, there were fears of a mass suicide—the group had brought gas cylinders with them—and the authorities were careful to avoid any physical intervention. Members eventually came out in stages, the last members having been brought out by the stench of the corpses of two members who had died. Negotiators included an Orthodox priest, to whom the group was prepared to listen, and members considered themselves to be Orthodox.

The True (Russian) Orthodox Church should not be confused with the Russian True Orthodox Church, also known as the Tikhonites. The various schisms stem from the 1917 Communist Revolution in Russia, when the Russian Orthodox Church came under persecution. Some of the faithful worshipped in a clandestine manner, and became known as the Catacomb Church. Many members were sent to prison and to concentration camps. Some went into exile, becoming part of the Russian Church outside of Russia (ROCOR), which by necessity was administratively separate from the Orthodox Church in Russia. The communists managed to sever two groups away from the Catacomb Church: the Renovationists and the Sergianists. In 1943 Bishop Sergei met with Josef Stalin, who agreed for the two factions to come together under Sergei's leadership to form a state-supervised Russian Orthodox Church. The severely depleted Catacomb Church remained separate, regarding itself as the true Church that had remained faithful. Sergei, they argued, could not validly be appointed by a head of state, but could only exercise episcopal authority if he were appointed in the presence of all the other bishops, lesser clergy and laity.

This somewhat complex history makes it unclear which sectors of Russian Orthodoxy should be regarded as schismatic. If admission to another body's sacraments is the test of a legitimate claim to a mainline Christian identity, this criterion is problematic, since different factions exclude each other, and disagreement exists within the various branches regarding whether those who belong to a different faction should be admitted to holy communion. Once again, Christianity's true boundaries are indeed difficult to determine.

New Roman Catholic organizations

Despite the centrally organized and unified nature of the Roman Catholic Church, it has also experienced dissenting factions. The Old Catholic Church emerged in 1853 in the See of Utrecht which, for historical reasons, did not come under papal authority. In 1870 a number of Roman Catholic groups dissented from the doctrine of papal infallibility, defined by the First Vatican Council. They joined with the Old Catholic Church, forming the Union of Utrecht of Old Catholic Churches. Catholic groups who did not join are known as Independent Catholics or Independent Old Catholics. The two factions are not in communion with each other, or with the wider Roman Catholic Church, although the Union of Utrecht churches are in communion with the Anglicans.

The Old Catholic Church is more liberal than traditional Catholicism, regarding the Pope as *primus inter pares* ('first among equals'). In 1994 its bishops in Germany approved the ordination of women, and the first women priests were ordained in 1996. Similar decisions were soon made by Old Catholics in Austria, Poland and The Netherlands. The Old Catholic Churches are also more liberal in their views on homosexuality, permit the religious marriage of divorcees and allow artificial contraception. They have 'open communion', enabling members of other branches of the Christian Church to receive the sacrament.

The Liberal Catholic Church stemmed from the Dutch Old Catholic Church (now known as the Old Catholic Church of the Netherlands). It was founded in 1916 by James Ingall Wedgwood (1883–1951), who had been reared as an Anglican, but became interested in the Old Catholic Church in England, and received its ordination. The Liberal Catholic Church blends traditional Catholic doctrine and liturgy with Theosophical ideas, including beliefs such as reincarnation. It is not considered to be a form of Roman Catholicism, or indeed Christianity more widely. Owing to two major schisms, in 1941 and 2003 respectively, a number of rival organizations include the name 'Liberal Catholic Church.'

In more recent times, a minority of Catholics objected to the changes brought about by the Second Vatican Council (1962–1965). A few went as far as to claim that Pope John XXIII and subsequent popes had been so liberal that they had forfeited their right to lead the Church, and that the papal see was now vacant, having no legitimate occupant. This very small handful of Roman Catholic organizations are known as Sedevacantists, from the Latin *sede vacante* ('the seat being vacant'), although some groups have in fact nominated their own rival popes. These groups are little known among Christians.

Greater public attention focused on Archbishop Marcel-François Lefebvre (1905–1991), who promoted the continuation of the traditional Tridentine Mass, being opposed to the Second Vatican Council's liturgical reforms. For this purpose he set up in 1970 *Fratenitas Sacerdotalis Sancti Pii X* ('Priestly Fraternity of Saint Pius X'), otherwise known as the Society of St Pius X (SSPX). It was officially granted the status of *pia unio* ('pious union')—a kind of probationary status towards becoming a fully recognized Society within the Church—and it set up its own theological seminaries for training its priests. Lefebvre's sheer hostility to the new Catholic liturgy caused the Church to withdraw the *pia unio* status, but Lefebvre continued regardless, and conducted his own ordinations in 1976. In 1987, Lefebvre, then 81, wanted to take steps to ensure the continuation of his movement. This required a successor to hold the status of bishop, in order to ordain further priests. However, the consecration of bishops requires papal approval, and on 30 June 1988 Lefebvre proceeded to consecrate four bishops, contrary to Pope John Paul II's explicit instructions. This was considered as a schismatical act, and Lefebvre and the four new bishops were excommunicated. Various controversies within SSPX caused further schisms, some groups forming their own organizations, while others returned to the mainstream Catholic Church. In 2009, Pope Benedict XVI remitted the excommunication of the four bishops, although the SSPX is still unacknowledged by the wider Church.

Some organizations have come to be regarded as 'cults', but in reality are within the mainstream. One such example is Opus Dei (literally 'Work of God'), set up in 1928 by Josemaria Escrivá (1902–1975). The organization aimed to encourage holiness within everyday life, and its members, the majority of whom are men and women who pursue secular vocations, integrate their work with a structured daily programme of prayer and meditation. When Escrivá was canonized in 2002, Pope John Paul II described him as 'the saint of ordinary life'. The society became a 'personal prelature' in 1982: this means that it has its own internal ecclesiastical structure, consisting of laity and priests, and which is not dependent on geographical boundaries, unlike the more usual system of dioceses and parishes.

The organization has attracted criticism for being allegedly a secret society, for expressing support for right-wing political systems, and for encouraging self-mortification. In *The Da Vinci Code*, Dan Brown portrays it as a secret society, run directly by the Pope, with monks who engage in self-flagellation, wear cilices (chains with inward-pointing spikes), and are embarked on a quest for the holy grail. This portrayal is wide of the mark. Opus Dei has no monks, the holy grail is not on its agenda, and they do not practise 'corporal mortification'. Its 'personal prelature' status refers to its internal organization, not to direct papal control. Although numeraries (celibate members living in community) are encouraged to use a cilice for limited periods, the majority of members do not do this. Other forms of self-mortification include sleeping without pillows, fasting, and maintaining periods of silence during the day. Although controversial, the organization has full papal approval, being firmly within the Catholic Church. To date, it is the only personal prelature approved by the Pope.

Christian Responses to NRMs

Mainstream Christians have generally been wary of, and sometimes hostile to most of these new expressions of Christianity. Christianity attaches great significance not only to the Bible, but to its historical creeds and its belief in a triune God. Religious organizations that deny the Trinity or the creeds are therefore judged to have placed themselves outside the fold, and their teachings are regarded as unacceptable.

Christians have taken particular exception to the suggestion that Jesus did not fully complete his mission, and that some new messiah, such as Sun Myung Moon, is needed to complete his work. Even the suggestion that Jesus Christ himself had further work to complete after his earthly ministry has been met with disapproval. The Seventh-day Adventists' doctrine (also appropriated by Jehovah's Witnesses) of Christ's 'cleansing of the heavenly sanctuary'—an event which Adventists believe took place in 1844, and Jehovah's Witnesses between 1914 and 1918—has suggested to some Christians that Jesus did not fully complete his atoning work, notwithstanding Jesus' final words to his disciples that he was going to his Father's house to prepare a place for them (Jn 14:2; Davies 1954: 45).

New revelations are also problematical to mainstream Christians, particularly if they are enshrined in new scriptures that are given equal authority to the Bible. *The Book of Mormon* and the other writings appropriated by the Latter-day Saints are regarded as spurious, and their supernatural origins are strongly denied. It is not totally clear whether the FFWPU regards *Divine Principle* as a piece of canonical writing or simply as a piece of new theology. It is taught systematically to seekers and members, and has the kind of centrality that one normally associates with Scripture. Again, the book is firmly rejected by the mainstream.

Interest in the occult also provides ground for criticism. A verse commonly cited against occultist practices is Deut. 18:10-11: 'Let no one be found among you who sacrifices his son or daughter in the fire, who practises divination or sorcery, interprets omens, engages in witchcraft, or casts spells, or who is a medium or spiritist or who consults the dead.' This is regarded as proscribing Spiritualism. Even The Family International, whose theology is mainstream, are sometimes regarded as suspect because of their founder-leader's communications with the spirit Abrahim.

Other criticisms of NRMs relate to their actions. In its early days in the West, the Unification Church was much criticized for deception, in its frequent failure to disclose its true identity when evangelizing and fund-raising, and members who were part of mobile fund-raising teams were subjected to fairly arduous working conditions. We have already mentioned the high commitment required of the ICoC, and of course the mass deaths that occurred in the Peoples Temple, at Waco, and in the Movement for Restoration of the Ten Commandments of God can only be deplored.

Christian opposition has expressed itself in a proliferation of literature designed to demonstrate the unacceptable nature of 'cults'. Such critiques originated in the early parts of the twentieth century, but increased enormously after the mid-1960s, as NRMs began to increase and attract media attention. Whether such critiques discourage seekers from joining NRMs to any great degree is doubtful, but what they did achieve was a clearer articulation of mainstream Christian faith, and a firm indication of how it differed from what these new organizations were teaching. Some Christians went beyond producing literature, and set up counter-cult organizations. One such organization in the USA calls itself the Spiritual Counterfeits Project. The term 'counterfeit' is significant, since such movements may claim to offer the truth, when they are teaching serious error. Arguably, this places the seeker in a worse position than if he or she had discovered a Hindu or a Buddhist religious group: these forms of religion are readily distinguishable from the Christian faith, whereas the 'counterfeits' are not. Holders of counterfeit money are in a worse position than those who are totally impecunious: they believe they possess the real commodity, until their mistake is discovered. In the case of the counterfeit Christian, he or she may discover the mistake all too late!

18

Recent Movements

However much some Christians may want to practise 'the religion of Jesus', it is not possible to roll back the clock and re-live the lifestyle of the first-century Church in early Palestine, even if we could be sure what it was like. A few restorationist groups have attempted to revive first-century Christianity, but even the Amish, who live in their own distinctive communities, and reject modern technology, drive around in vehicles (albeit horse-drawn ones) and wear clothes that would have been unrecognizable by Jesus' first disciples. New issues, new scientific discoveries and new ideologies all exert their impact on the Christian faith and necessitate a response. In this final chapter we shall identify a few features of twenty-first-century society—most of which gained impetus in the second half of the previous century—which are most likely to change the face of the Christian faith.

The Interfaith Movement

Inreasingly, international communication, travel and globalization have brought together different cultures and, with them, their religions. Christian mission seemed a worthy enterprise in the days of the British, French and Dutch empires, when its missionaries went to under-developed countries and combined medical, technological and educational aid with sharing the gospel with the natives. During the 1950s and 1960s, however, the substantial immigration that occurred, particularly in Britain and the United States, meant that 'foreigners' were now on their own doorstep, rather than residing in foreign parts. In not too long, many of them gained Western national identities, and second and third generations were British or American by birth. Could Christians still maintain the superiority of their faith to their new neighbours who espoused other faiths, or should they relate to those other faiths in a more egalitarian way?

Issues of interfaith relationships were not new to the twentieth century. King Akbar and King Ashoka in ancient India did much to promote inter-religious tolerance, for example. The modern interfaith movement, however, stems from the World's Parliament of Religions, which was held in Chicago in 1893. This event was scheduled to coincide with the World Exposition to be held in 1892 in the city, to celebrate the 400th anniversary of Christopher Columbus' 'discovery' of America. A display of exhibits was planned, reflecting humanity's cultural, technological and commercial achievements, but some religious leaders suggested that these attainments were not humankind's pinnacle of attainment, and that the Exposition should be accompanied by a Parliament of Religions. The Revd J. H. Barrows, Pastor of the First Presbyterian Church of Chicago, chaired the planning committee, which was co-led by himself, a Unitarian minister, and a Swedenborgian layperson. The event proved controversial: the Archbishop of Canterbury, the Rt Revd Edward White Benson, expressed his disapproval, contending that it implied granting equal status to each religion, which he could not accept. The organizers of the Parliament simply recommended 'parity of esteem'.

The name 'Parliament' is perhaps somewhat misleading, since the purpose of the gathering was not to make decisions that were binding on all participants. It was more like a major conference or assembly, attended by seven-thousand attendees in all, spanning all the world's major religious traditions (apart from Sikhism), including academics as well as religious leaders. Famous participants included Anagarika Dharmapala, a Buddhist monk who helped to revive Buddhism in Ceylon (now Sri Lanka) in the wake of Christian missionizing, and Swami Vivekananda, a renowned Hindu teacher. One of the ground rules of the assembly was that speakers should not openly criticize each others' faith, but should 'show to men, in the most impressive way, what and how many important truths the various Religions hold and teach in common' (Barrows 1893: I, 18). In particular, participants expressed the wish that the Parliament would further the cause of inter-religious harmony and, more widely, world peace. Despite the aim of seeking ideas in common, there was no attempt to falsely blur significant differences between the various faiths, and while Vivekanada urged that all paths led to God, this view was not shared by the majority of the participants, and in particular by the more conservative Christian contributors, who argued that Christianity offered the only true path leading to salvation.

The Parliament was judged to have been a success, and at the end a wish was expressed that a similar event should be repeated soon. However, no continuing body was set up by the Parliament, although the interest in interfaith dialogue that it aroused continued. One important outcome of the Parliament was the formation of the International Association for Religious Freedom (IARF) in 1900, an organization that is supported predominantly, although not exclusively, by Unitarians. The name is somewhat of a misnomer, since the IARF focuses on interreligious understanding, rather than campaigning for religious freedom. A subsequent event that furthered interest in other faiths was the Religions of Empire Conference, held in London in 1924, as a spin-off from the British Empire Exhibition. Although the West had gained political control of much of Asia, Christians still comprised only one sixth of the Empire's 460 million population, which included 210 million Hindus, 100 million Muslims and 12 million Buddhists (Braybrooke 1996: 11). Sir Denison Ross, who chaired the organizing committee, insisted that the various religions on the programme should be expounded exclusively by their exponents. As he explained,

> Up to the present if you want to know about Buddhism or Mohammedanism[1] you inevitably went to a European authority for knowledge. You may have read deeply in these religions and yet never heard a native explain the tenets of his belief and what they mean to him and the life of his people. At this conference the believer himself will lecture on his own religion. (cited in Braybrooke 1996: 11)

In 1933 a second Parliament of Religions was convened under the aegis of the World Fellowship of Faiths, to mark the fortieth anniversary of the World's Parliament of Religions. It was also held in Chicago, and attracted some forty-four-thousand attendees at 27 sessions.

A further impetus for interfaith activity came from the explorer Francis Younghusband (1863–1942), sometimes described as 'the last great imperial adventurer'. Younghusband led the invasion of Tibet in 1904, resulting in the massacre of between six- and seven-hundred Tibetan soldiers. On leaving Lhasa, he claimed to have received a powerful religious experience, in which he felt that 'the whole world was ablaze' and that he was 'full of good-will as my former foes were converted into stalwart friends'. 'Never again,' he wrote, 'could I think

---

1. 'Mohammedanism', as Braybrooke notes, was the term used by the conference, in common with many scholars in the nineteenth century and the first half of the twentieth. It is no longer considered acceptable, the correct term being 'Islam'.

evil. Never again could I bear enmity. Joy had begotten love' (cited in Braybrooke 1996: 22).

The experience led Younghusband to gain a deep respect for other faiths, and he became one of the founder-leaders of the World Congress of Faiths (WCF), which was established in 1936 with a major conference in London, at which several famous leaders of the world's faiths spoke. On this occasion the WCF was set up as a continuing organization. The WCF's function was not to create a syncretistic new religion out of the variety of faith traditions, but to work for 'world fellowship', accept and welcome the differences among its fellowship, and to draw on the inspiration of all religious traditions to help to solve humanity's problems. The organizers invited the Archbishop of Canterbury, the Rt Revd Cosmo Gordon Lang, to be the Congress's president, and King Edward VIII to preside over the opening session. Both dignitaries obviously felt that holding the Congress was likely to be too controversial. The Archbishop told Younghusband that his presence might imply that Christianity was only one religion among many, although he advised the king that there was no harm in sending a guarded greeting to the gathering.

The name 'World Congress of Faiths' implies an international scope, although its work has largely been in Britain. Subsequently, a number of other interfaith organizations were set up in various countries. One of the best known is the Temple of Understanding (ToU), which was the result of the work of Judith Hollister (1916–2000), and whose headquarters are in New York City. Firmly believing that an appreciation of the insights of the various world faiths was needed to solve the world's problems, she travelled the world in the 1950s, with a letter of introduction from Eleanor Roosevelt, meeting President Nasser of Egypt, Jawaharlal Nehru (Prime Minister of India), Pope John XXIII and Albert Schweitzer, among others. Her dreams of a 'Spiritual United Nations' were fulfilled in 1960, with the founding of ToU. ToU held its first 'Spiritual Summit' in Calcutta in 1968, and continues to bring together members of all faiths, and to educate the public in 'interreligious literacy'.

Interfaith organizations are often small local groups, rather than international organizations, and invite interreligious dialogue at a local level, as well as disseminate information about the world's various faiths. In Britain the Inter Faith Network for the UK was set up in 1987 as an umbrella organization to coordinate the work of various local interfaith groups. Churches Together in Britain and Ireland is one of its member bodies. The year 1993 was designated as the Year of Interreligious Understanding and Cooperation, being the centenary year of the World's

Parliament of Religions. This was an appropriate time for the creation of the International Interfaith Council (IIC) in Britain, which was largely the result of cooperation between the International Association for Religious Freedom and the World Congress of Faiths. Its aims are to encourage communication among interfaith bodies, to maintain a study centre, to organize conferences and other projects, all in order to encourage dialogue and conflict resolution. In March 2001, representatives of 14 international interfaith bodies came together to form the International Interfaith Organisations Network (IION to coordinate the work of international interfaith organizations.

To mark the World's Parliament of Religions' centenary, another 'parliament' was held, this time bearing the name 'Parliament of the World's Religions'. It is sometimes referred to as the 'second' Parliament, but such references fail to take account of the 1933 event. This 1993 Parliament was attended by over eight-thousand people, and was significant for its promotion of the document 'Towards a Global Ethic: An Initial Declaration', the text of which was largely the work of the Roman Catholic theologian Hans Küng. Over two-hundred leaders from over 40 different religious traditions signed this document. The declaration deplores the world's present condition, and affirms 'a common set of core values' to which all religions subscribe, including commitment to non-violence, mutual respect, economic justice and peace.

Christianity has always had a special relationship with the Jewish faith, and hence special emphasis is given to dialogue with Jews. The Council for Christians and Jews (CCJ) is Britain's oldest interfaith organization, set up in Britain in 1942 to promote mutual understanding between the two faiths, and to work for the elimination of prejudice, particularly antisemitism. Initially, discussions avoided theology, the state of Israel and mission but, as confidence grew among participants, these are now legitimate topics for dialogue. Other Christian–Jewish organizations have taken rise, and the International Council for Christians and Jews, founded in 1947 in response to the Holocaust, serves as an umbrella organization coordinating some 38 such bodies. The Holocaust, of course, marked a turning point, both in Jewish and Christian history. In 2005 the United Nations General Assembly resolved that International Holocaust Remembrance Day should be commemorated annually on 27 January, being the date on which Soviet troops liberated Auschwitz-Berkenau in 1945. It is now common practice for Jews and Christians jointly to commemorate the occasion. Jewish–Christian organizations also seek to combat Holocaust denial. In 2009 the CCJ severely reprimanded

Pope Benedict XVI for reinstating Bishop Richard Williamson, who reportedly stated, 'I believe there were no gas chambers', claiming that a mere 300,000 Jews died in the Nazi concentration camps, rather than six million, as is commonly believed.

The discussion of interfaith relations thus far is about groups of Christians and people from various other faiths who have taken it upon themselves to work together to promote interreligious understanding. The official stance of the churches needs some comment. The World Council of Churches formally began its work on interfaith relation-ships in 1971, when its Central Committee met in Addis Ababa and affirmed that interreligious dialogue was to be 'the common adventure of the churches' (World Council of Churches 1990). A further Assembly met in 1975 in Nairobi, and defined this 'adventure' more specifically as 'dialogue in community'. Relationships with other faiths were to be seen not as a matter for theologians or ecclesiastical bureaucracy, but rather as a set of opportunities for rank-and-file members of a variety of faiths to meet together, sharing their beliefs and practices, exploring their common features, gaining understanding and trust of each other, and addressing issues that affected several faith communities and not Christians alone. For example, members of other faiths—particularly Hindus and Sikhs—often needed places to meet for congregational worship as their communities grew substantially, before they were able to construct their own purpose-built premises. Churches commonly received requests for the hire of their halls, sometimes even the church itself, for Hindu and Sikh *kirtans*, and had to decide whether renting out their premises was an act of hospitality or a denial of the Christian gospel. As church attendance declined, many churches were forced to sell their properties in the 1960s and later, and other faiths would make offers to purchase them. Which was preferable: to allow a church to continue to be used in the name of religion—even if it were not the Christian faith—or for it to become a carpet warehouse, a night club or a casino?

During the 1970s a number of major denominations set up bodies with the specific purpose of considering the Church's role in relating to other faiths, and helping local congregations to decide on such dilemmas. However, the different denominations did not want to re-create the problems of the previous missionary era by separately claiming to be Christianity's representatives to other religions. Accordingly, it was decided that dialogue was best planned ecumenically rather than unilaterally, and denominational bodies that bear responsibility for interfaith work generally have representatives from other denominations. The World Council of Churches has an overarching responsibility for overseeing interfaith work, and in 1979 it formulated its *Guidelines on Dialogue with People of Living Faiths and Ideologies*. The *Guidelines* suggest that Christians should approach other faiths with repentance and humility, acknowledging that they have often behaved in the past as if they were 'the owners of God's truth rather than, as in fact they are, the undeserving recipients of grace' (D, 21), and often misconstruing other religions' teachings and spiritual practices. By doing so, they have infringed the ninth of the Ten Commandments, which states, 'You shall not give false testimony against your neighbour' (Exod. 20:16). Instead, their role should include listening, recognizing that 'Partners in dialogue should be free to "define themselves"' (III, 4). In other words, to find out what (say) Islam involves, one gets a more authentic answer by listening to a Muslim, rather than to a Christian.

Interfaith dialogue is more than an attempt to set the record straight when it comes to understanding another religion's tenets. The WCC *Guidelines* affirm that 'Dialogue should be pursued by sharing in common enterprises in community' (III, 7). Religions have commitments to common ideals, such as love, justice and peace, which transcend their religious identities. At times it is desirable for leaders from different religions to express a united stance on significant social or political issues. After the 9/11 bombings, many people associated Al Qaeda with Islam, and Islam with terrorism. Because Osama bin Laden wore a turban, the general public (including Christians), who are often lacking in 'faith literacy', only too readily unleashed their hatred on Sikhs, failing to recognize the difference between Sikhs and Muslims. In such circumstances, joint statements from leaders of different faiths prove more effective than unilateral ones. Following the Al Qaeda attack on New York and Washington on 11 September 2001, representatives from 14 international interfaith organizations made the following joint declaration, deploring the attack and commending interfaith understanding as a way forward in conflict resolution.

> In response to recent tragic events in the United States of America and ongoing conflicts with religious dimensions around the world, our international interfaith organisations offer our inter-religious dialogue expertise and resources to address the current crisis and promote peace building initiatives.
>
> We have direct experience of bringing into peaceful and constructive dialogue the mainstream and marginalized, moderate and

> militant religious voices of our world. Working with the world's faith
> communities, we have found that inter-religious dialogue can help
> heal wounds caused by feelings of injustice, isolation, and inequality.
> (International Interfaith Organisations Network 2003)

If the text of this statement seems somewhat bland and general, its point
lies not so much in its content, but in the fact that it stemmed from
organizations representing a variety of faiths, thus demonstrating that
(in this case) Islam and Christianity should not be seen as being in open
conflict.

Some supporters of the interfaith movement have gone so far as
to promote interfaith worship, and indeed a number of multi-faith
services have been organized from time to time. Members of different
religions, it is argued, worship the same god (or at least ultimate reality),
are committed to many of the same ideals, and can be inspired by
hearing the scriptures of a variety of traditions. Should differences of
theology and tradition preclude common worship? The World Congress
of Faiths set up a working party to address the issue, and a booklet
entitled *Inter-Faith Worship* (1974), edited by Marcus Braybrooke,
summarized the arguments in both directions, but reaching a generally
positive conclusion. Thankfulness, wonder and a sense of community,
it was argued, stood above interreligious differences. Predictably, such
conclusions were challenged, and not merely from the evangelical right
wing. Lesslie Newbiggin (formerly a bishop in the Church of South India,
and subsequently a minister in the United Reformed Church) argued
that God can only be truly worshipped as he is—as a Trinity of Father,
Son and Holy Spirit, not as some vague common denominator of the
world's various traditions (United Reformed Church 1981: 72-75).

Although only a small proportion of practising Christians formally
belong to interfaith organizations, interfaith dialogue informally takes
place in the everyday life of many. As Western society becomes increasingly multi-cultural and multi-faith, most Christians regularly come
into contact with members of different faiths—in the workplace and
socially. In Britain, the National Curriculum for schools requires pupils
between 12 and 14 years old to learn about 'interfaith dialogue: a study of
relationships, conflicts and collaboration within and between religions
and beliefs'.

Not all Christians are committed to interfaith dialogue, however.
While most Christians would acknowledge the right of members of other
faiths to practise their religion, conservative Christians—particularly
evangelicals—continue to take the view that Christianity is the one true

religion, and that their ideal is that the whole world should be 'won for Christ'. They therefore view interfaith dialogue as an activity that compromises the Christian faith, apparently putting all religions on an equal footing, and evading crucial questions about where religious truth is to be found.

The Role of Women

Aother important issue in present-day Western society is the status of women. It is frequently commented that at public worship, congregations contain an appreciable majority of women, but yet the leaders of worship and the Church's hierarchy tends to be male-dominated. The figures in Christian history, as it is usually recounted, tend to be men, and—apart from the Virgin Mary in the Roman Catholic, Eastern Orthodox and High Anglican traditions—there is little female imagery. Even God is normally referred to in the masculine gender, although of course God is 'without body, parts or passions' (*Thirty Nine Articles*, 1). The Church itself is traditionally referred to as 'she', being the 'bride of Christ', although such reference tends to be confined to formal writing rather than common parlance. Traditionally the sex-role stereotyping that has been found in society more widely has been reflected in the churches, with women performing the domestic chores and men in leadership roles. Women have not been totally powerless, however, and for well over a century it has been usual for women to serve as Sunday School teachers, or to serve on Parochial Church Councils (in the Church of England) or participate actively in congregational meetings (in the Protestant tradition). The only holy orders to which women have been admitted have been monastic ones in the Roman Catholic tradition.

Although the various roles traditionally assigned to women have frequently been called 'ministries' (meaning service), women have historically been denied roles as congregational and denominational leadership, permission to preach and, most especially, to preside over the sacrament of Holy Communion. Various reasons have been offered for regarding women as ineligible for the priesthood or ministry. When the Archbishop of Canterbury, the Rt Revd Donald Coggan, wrote to Pope Paul VI in 1975 concerning women's ordination, he received the following reply:

> She [the Church] holds that it is not admissible to ordain women to the priesthood, for very fundamental reasons. These reasons include: the example recorded in the Sacred Scriptures of Christ choosing his

> Apostles only from among men; the constant practice of the Church, which has imitated Christ in choosing only men; and her living teaching authority which has consistently held that the exclusion of women from the priesthood is in accordance with God's plan for his Church. (Pope Paul VI 1975)

Protestants who oppose women's ordination are more likely to cite the instructions given to Timothy: 'I do not permit a woman to teach or to have authority over a man; she must be silent' (1 Tim. 2:12). The passage goes on to point out that Adam was formed before Eve, and that it was Eve who first succumbed to temptation in the Garden of Eden—reasons that continue to be offered in conservative Protestant circles.

Eastern Orthodoxy and Roman Catholicism continue to have an all-male priesthood. The movement for women's ordination has been largely a Protestant phenomenon, although there are campaigners within the Roman Catholic tradition. Although it is sometimes suggested that the ordination of women is a spin-off from the Western feminist movement, the issue goes back as far as the seventeenth century, when Margaret Fell (1614–1702), co-founder of the Society of Friends (the Quakers), published a pamphlet entitled, *Women's Speaking Justified, Proved and Allowed of by the Scriptures, All Such as Speak by the Spirit and Power of the Lord Jesus And How Women Were the First That Preached the Tidings of the Resurrection of Jesus, and Were Sent by Christ's Own Command Before He Ascended to the Father (John 20:17).* (Concise titles were not the order of the day at that time!) From the late nineteenth century, the Quakers have allowed women to hold equal office to men, and to 'give ministry' at their meetings. However, the Society of Friends is non-sacramental, and does not formally ordain members to any office.

There is not a straightforward answer to the question of when the first woman's ordination took place. Some would cite Antoinette Louisa Brown (later Blackwell; 1856–1921), who was licensed to preach in 1851, and made rector of the Congregational Church of South Butler, New York, in 1853. However, on account of the essential congregational character of Congregational churches, this ordination was only performed within a single congregation, not by the denomination as a whole, and Antoinette Brown's ordination was not recognized by Congregational churches more widely. She resigned her post in 1857, returning to her previous work as a speaker and women's rights campaigner. In 1878 she sought ordination again, this time to the Unitarian ministry. In the meantime, the Universalists had ordained another woman—often cited as the first— Olympia Brown (1835–1926) in 1863. This ordination took place sixty years before women were allowed to vote in the United States. When the Salvation Army was founded in 1865, all of its offices were open to women as well as men. However, a woman was not permitted to marry a man of a lower rank—a restriction that remains in force today. Like the Quakers, the Salvation Army is non-sacramental, and hence there are no issues about presiding over sacraments.

The first mainstream woman's ordination was in 1880, when Anna Howard Shaw entered the ministry of the Methodist Protestant Church. This heralded a trickle of women's ordinations. When the (Pentecostalist) Assemblies of God was founded in 1914, its first women clergy were ordained, and the Congregationalist Church of England and Wales began to admit women to its ministry in 1917. The first Anglican woman ordinand was Florence Li Tim Oi in Hong Kong in 1944; this was on an 'emergency' basis only, since no male priest was available, but it paved the way for further women's ordinations. In 1968 the Church of Scotland approved the ordination of women, followed by the Methodist Church in the UK in 1974. In 1971 Joyce Bennett and Jane Hwang became the first regularly ordained Anglican priests in Hong Kong. Three years later, 11 women were ordained priest in Philadelphia, and a further four in 1975 in Washington DC. These ordinations proved controversial, however, since they were carried out without the approval of the General Convention of the Episcopal Church of the USA (ECUSA). Although these ordinations were 'irregular', they set a precedent and drew public attention to the issue. In 1992 the General Synod of the Church of England, after heated debate, obtained the two-thirds majority needed to approve women's ordination, and the first women priests were ordained two years later. In 2009, approximately one sixth of the Church of England's parish priests are women (Ormsby 2009).

While the decision to ordain women to the priesthood was welcomed by the majority of Church of England members, women remain barred from further advancement in the Church. What about the possibility of women bishops, or even archbishops? This bar to career advanced has sometimes been referred to as the 'stained glass ceiling'. Women have been ordained as Anglican bishops in Canada, the United States and New Zealand. In July 2010 the Church of England's General Synod approved the 'Bishops and Priests (Consecration and Ordination of Women) Measure'. At the time of writing, the measure requires approval by its 44 diocesan synods, followed by a further vote, together with parliamentary approval and royal assent.

Opposition to women's ordination

Some traditionalist clergy, particularly in the High Anglican tradition, could not accept the 1992 General Synod decision. Some left the priesthood, and were provided a resettlement allowance. Several hundred others made arrangements to transfer to the Roman Catholic Church, while others who remained in the Church of England mounted organized opposition. In England, Forward in Faith was founded in 1992 as a reaction against the General Synod's decision. Its scope is somewhat wider than opposing women's ordination: it seeks, additionally, to uphold tradition on the Church's liturgy, favouring the retention of the 1662 *Book of Common Prayer*, and the maintenance of traditional ethical values, including opposition to homosexuality. Forward in Faith continues to maintain that women priests are contrary to Scripture, and damaging to ecumenical relations. Its members refused to accept the 1992 General Synod decision, arguing that the ordination of women priests required the agreement of the entire Church, not merely the Church of England. A related organization, Cost of Conscience (CoC), comprised Anglicans worldwide who opposed women's ordination, claiming to safeguard the Church's heritage. Its campaigning enabled 'alternative episcopal arrangements' to be made for churches whose clergy could not accept women's ordination. Those clergy were permitted to separate themselves from their dioceses, no longer being under the authority of their local diocesan bishop, but coming under the jurisdiction of bishops whose dioceses were not geographically defined. These bishops are known as 'provincial episcopal visitors', popularly known as PEVs or 'flying bishops'. They are suffragan bishops (bishops who do not oversee an entire diocese) and visit those parishes who have opted out of regular diocesan oversight. There are three such bishops in England: the Suffragan Bishop of Richborough and the Suffragan Bishop of Ebbsfleet, who work within the Province of Canterbury, and the Suffragan Bishop of Beverley, who works within the Province of York. Additionally, individual dioceses may appoint their own 'flying bishops' to perform such roles locally.

Although Protestantism more widely has favoured women's ordination, denominations with fundamentalist tendencies tend to reject it. The Southern Baptist Church is one such example. Their statement of faith, *The Baptist Faith and Message*, reads, 'While both men and women are gifted for service in the church, the office of pastor is limited to men as qualified by Scripture' (2000: VI). Although theologically conservative lay-led denominations such as the Brethren, as well as independent evangelical churches, are not faced with the issue of ordaining women, women are usually barred from preaching and presiding over the Lord's Supper, but may teach children or speak at women's meetings.

Some conservative Christians have expressed the view that many churches, and in particular their men, have become over-feminized, and that there is a need for men to re-assert traditional male leadership, in homes and in the workplace, as well as in church. The Christian men's movement, Promise Keepers (PKs), states that its mission 'is to ignite and unite men to become warriors who will change their world through living out the Seven Promises' and claims to have reached over five-and-a-half-million men since it was founded in Denver, Colorado, by Bill McCartney, a former football coach, in 1990. The Seven Promises are commitments to which supporters subscribe: worship and prayer; pursuing relation-ships with other men; spiritual and moral purity; building strong marriages in accordance with biblical values; supporting his church and pastor; demonstrating 'biblical unity' amidst racial and denominational diversity; and obedience to the 'Great Commandment' and the 'Great Commission' (Mk 12:30-31; Mt. 28:19-20). Although PKs do not specifi-cally target women's ordination, they reflect a current within evangelical Protestantism that seeks to retain male leadership and authority.

In Roman Catholicism and Eastern Orthodoxy, there is no foreseeable prospect of women's ordination. Despite some grass-roots support for change, Pope John Paul II pronounced definitively in 1994 that the Church had no authority to ordain women (*Ordinatio Sacerdotalis*, 1994), and the official stance of both traditions is that the Church should not conform to the standards of contemporary society, but rather to God's law. According to Catholic teaching, the worth of women is demon-strated by the Virgin Mary's role in the world's redemption (see chapter 9) and their eligibility to be canonized as saints. Women are allowed to enter monastic orders, to write, teach and run missions. Mother Teresa of Calcutta is a famous example. In Orthodoxy, women are not eligible either for priesthood or for monastic orders, although they can assume the role of deacons, who assist priests at baptisms, chrismations and the anointing of sick. This is often to prevent male priests from coming into contact with a female body at these sacraments.

Christianity and the Internet

Twenty-first century Christianity has not merely been influenced by ideologies but by technology. One of the most significant technological advances in the past two decades has been the invention of the internet, which has transformed the face of worldwide communication. The internet has afforded obvious opportunities for churches to advertise their presence, not only to their local communities, but globally. It is often the first point of contact for seekers who want to discover more about the Christian faith, or to find which churches are in their locality. For a seeker, entering a church for the first time, particularly if he or she is unaccompanied, can be a daunting prospect. One is confronted by dozens of unfamiliar faces, who may or may not be welcoming, and one has to know the expected forms of action and rules of behaviour in liturgies that are sometimes complex and unfamiliar. By contrast, the anonymity of the internet enables an enquirer to get to know something about the Christian faith, or about specific denominations and congregations, in a non-threatening way.

All major Christian denominations now have a web presence, enabling the viewer to gain first-hand information. Some congregations in the West remain without a web presence, perhaps because members do not fully appreciate the benefits, are still technophobic, or still lack the facilities to express themselves online. The World Wide Web enables congregations to do more than simply provide information about their beliefs, practices and forthcoming events. Imaginative websites have incorporated cyber-tours of historically interesting churches, children's quizzes, recordings of their choir and so on. Since the web is multi-media, some Christians have developed sites dedicated to hymnody, with recordings of favourite hymns, together with words and music, and advice enabling couples to choose music for the wedding day—often particularly necessary for increasing numbers of wedding couples who are unfamiliar with church music. In Lent 2007, the Church of England gave the season of Lent a technological aspect by introducing a Lenten programme, backed by a special web site (www.livelent.net) entitled *Love Life Live Lent*, providing information about Lent and suggesting a daily Lenten action that a Christian might perform during the season. The actions were not penitentiary, but small acts of kindness or thoughtfulness, such as giving way to another driver, or praying about an item in the news. The programme incorporated a texting service, enabling the actions to be received daily on one's mobile. There was a supporting blog and chat room. For the many Christians who do not use all this technology, the basic course was available by following a small inexpensive illustrated booklet. Other web-based innovations have included the provision of simple thoughts for the day, and 'cyber pilgrimages' enabling Christians to visit holy sites that they could not readily access in physical space and time.

The internet does more than add technological gimmickry to the Christian faith, however. One important feature of the internet is that it has redefined one's communities. Whether social utility networks such as Facebook genuinely enable users to have literally thousands of 'friends' is debatable, but those who use facilities such as chatrooms or discussion lists have often created a community of people they recognize and relate to in a distinctive way. Several Christian cyber-communities have grown up in such a way. One of the most successful has been Ship of Fools, which started life as a Christian magazine, launched in 1977. The magazine ceased publication in 1983, but was revived on 1 April 1998. The reference to fools not only alludes to the frivolous nature of much of its material, but also to Saint Paul's characterization of Christians as 'fools for Christ' (1 Cor. 4:10). As well as bulletin boards that address a range of religious topics, Ship of Fools includes reports from 'mystery worshippers', who visit unfamiliar churches incognito and recount their impressions. This benefits these churches, since they are able to gauge the way in which they appear to outsiders.

Could one have an entire congregation that existed solely online? This was a live issue that the Ship of Fools raised when, sponsored by the Methodist Church, they created the (interdenominational) Church of Fools in 2004. This was an entire cyber-church, with advertised services at pre-determined times, and which was set out in cyber-space like a conventional church building, with an entrance, pews, a chancel, pulpit and communion table. The 'church' also had a crypt containing sacred 'relics', and coffee machines, which are now becoming a feature of some churches that exist in conventional space. Visitors entered the church by clicking on an icon, which provided them with a cartoon cyber-character, which they could manoeuvre around the interior. This character could not only move, but make gestures, such as sitting in a pew, kneeling or raising its arms in a euphoric halleluiah. Services had hymns, readings and a sermon, which appeared as a combination of text and sound. One could 'sing' the hymns by keying in the text of the words (or as much as one could, depending on one's typing speed), and key in 'amens' as a personal endorsement of the prayers. The church's opening sermon was 'preached' by the Bishop of London—an indication that the project was regarded as a serious one. The seriousness with which the project was regarded was underlined by the way in which appropriate behaviour was expected and enforced: for example, anyone whose character knelt in prayer in front of a coffee machine was evicted by cyber-wardens who were constantly on duty.

The driving-force behind the Church of Fools was not merely techno-logical, but theological. The doctrine of the incarnation, 'the Word became flesh' (Jn 1:14), entails that God is believed to speak to his listeners in whatever form is most appropriate to them. For Moses, it was tablets of stone, but in a technological age people are more inclined to use computers as a source of information and inspiration, rather than read the Bible in its traditional format. The Church of Fools encountered a number of problems and had to discontinue its regular services. These problems were largely due to finance, which the Methodist Church could no longer provide. Although the cyber-church could attract an impressive forty-one-thousand visitors in the course of a single day, only 30 internet users could actively participate in the services at any one time, owing to bandwidth limitations. Anyone arriving late could merely assume the identity of a 'ghost': someone who was not publicly visible—unlike the first 30 who could be seen occupying the pews—and could not send in pieces of text. At the time of writing the Church of Fools attempted to revive itself under the name of St Pixels Ltd. St Pixels' aims include offering sacred space on the internet, affording a Christian presence to those of all beliefs or none. Simple Christian worship has been revived, but with sound and text only: worshippers cannot occupy cyber-pews, make physical gestures or move around the sanctuary area.

The cyber-service offered by the Church of Fools simply replicated the type of service one would expect to find in any conventional church: a hymn, Bible reading, sermon and prayers. This has the advantage of maintaining the congregational nature of worship, acknowledging the fact that Christians do not practise their faith merely as individuals, but form a community of believers. Whether it is possible to devise forms of worship that draw on the more distinctive features of online communication is no doubt something that will become apparent as the use of the internet develops, although it is not clear at this stage what these alternative features of worship might be. Although the uses of the internet to which we have referred are innovatory, there are limitations on the rites that can be practised online. It is possible to express simple religious commitment online, accepting Jesus Christ as one's personal saviour by clicking a button, and a number of evangelical Christian websites offer this facility. However, pursuing a sacramental religion is more problematic: it does not seem possible to conduct online baptisms or to celebrate the Eucharist online, since sacraments, by their very nature, draw on elements of the material world and convert them to acquire spiritual significance. Although in theory it would be possible to give instructions to participants to have water, or bread and wine, at the ready while taking part in cyber-worship, the eucharistic elements need to be consecrated, and it is questionable whether this can be done online. One attempt to surmount this problem comes from the (non-mainstream) Open Episcopal Church, led by 'Archbishop' Jonathan Blake, and which offers a 'post the host' facility. Blake consecrates communion wafers and wine and posts them to purchasers, who can then view one of his Masses online and consume the ready-consecrated eucharistic elements at the appropriate point. (Participants can even order non-alcoholic wine and gluten-free wafers!) Such innovations are, of course, controversial. There are practical problems such as the risk of sacred elements getting lost in the post or falling into the wrong hands; the Church has traditionally safeguarded the elements, ensuring that they are used appropriately, and are not taken away by participants who might use them sacrilegiously or superstitiously. Moreover, Christians have held throughout the centuries that the sacraments are communal activities that must be shared by a bodily community. The Eucharist is a fellowship meal, and to celebrate it with individuals in front of their computers might be like inviting one's friends to share an online dinner instead of inviting them to one's home!

Another internet venture has been the creation of online confessionals. The idea of confessing one's sins online has the obvious advantage that the penitent is totally anonymous, unlike the traditional confession box, where the priest may recognize one's voice, or at least knows that he is probably speaking to a member of his congregation. As far as we know, these cyber-confessionals are not sponsored by any of the mainstream churches, and therefore one cannot be sure that online confessions would be dealt with by a qualified priest or counsellor. Some of these sites allow any internet user to 'hear' confessions, with the obvious consequence that prescribed penances may be inappropriate or even facetious. There may be scope for enabling penitents to confess sins online, but, at the time of writing, the idea has not been seriously exploited by churches who encourage their members to confess.

One or two sites purport to offer online ordination, but they are hosted by Christian-related groups that are outside the mainstream, such as the Universal Life Church, the Christian Glory Church and Rose Ministries, and such ordinations would certainly not enable their candidates to preside over the sacraments in mainstream churches.

Although the Christian Glory Church offers marriage certificates, marriage ceremonies (which may not necessarily be religious) can only be legally enacted if they conform to state law. It has been asked whether a religion could exist exclusively in cyberspace, but the absence of the physical body online precludes several important religious activities. Most especially, no ceremony in cyberspace can deal adequately with death rites, which require the bodily presence of the deceased, although many websites offer cyber-memorials, and electronic resources can capture rites of passage and make them more permanently available in a variety of forms, either online or off-line.

The Future of Christianity

Having examined these attempts to reconcile Christianity with twenty-first century movements, ideologies and technological innovations, how might we expect the Christian faith to progress as the rest of the century unfolds? Scholars attempt to describe, analyse and explain rather than predict the future. However, there exist a number of futurologists, both inside and outside the Church, as well as a handful of scholars, who have ventured some predictions about Christianity's future in the remaining part of the century.

First, there are the Christian fundamentalists who claim that Christianity's earthly days are numbered, because little future remains for the world itself, and we can expect an imminent return of Jesus Christ (the 'Rapture'). Present-day scholars often assume that such beliefs are false, frequently commenting on 'failed prophecy', and citing other failed predictions of the past, such as those of William Miller. Scholars of religion, however, equally claim to be non-judgemental, and to bracket their belief or unbelief, and it is certainly to be noted that there exists a sizeable proportion of Christians who entertain a literal belief in an imminent Rapture. It is rare for such Christians to set a precise date for this expected event and, despite, centuries of expectation of an imminent *eschaton*, continue to affirm it. Even if the present century ends without Christ's return, the fundamentalist can always point out that, in God's sight, 'a thousand years...are like a day that has just gone by' (Ps. 90:4). It is unlikely, therefore, that the passage of the twenty-first century will cause conservative believers to reappraise such a doctrine.

At the other extreme, there are those who believe that Christianity will die out, either through neglect, through belief in science, or because of other religions and ideologies. Douglas Hall, Professor of Christian

Theology at McGill University, Montreal, contends in his book *The End of Christendom and the Future of Christianity*, that Christianity has progressively been pushed out to the margins of society. It is no longer the religion of the empire, as it was in the days of King Constantine, and is no longer a significant influence in the present-day world. Christians delude themselves, he believes, if they see any future in their faith. Others have suggested that Christianity might be overtaken by some other faith, such as Islam, which currently appears to be increasing at a somewhat higher rate. Harold Bloom, a professor at Yale University, notes that Mormonism is increasing at the rate of six per cent, and may come to dominate the American West by the year 2020. Feminist theologian Daphne Hampson suggests that feminism will toll the death knell for Christianity, being a stronger ideology.

Others believe that the immediate future presents increased tensions between the conservative and liberal camps within Christianity. Issues such as homosexuality, the ordination of openly gay clergy, and the possibility of holding church ceremonies to solemnize same-sex relationships, will cause inevitable tensions among Christians. Tensions seem set to become more pronounced as Western liberal thinking develops while conservative Christianity continues to grow in Africa. Bishop John Shelby Spong (b. 1931), formerly Bishop of Newark, New Jersey, sees the Church's future in theological liberalism, believing that traditional theism is outmoded in the modern world, and that doctrines such as the Virgin Birth cannot be believed as literal truth; he is also a champion of gay rights within the Church. Some Christians hold that the Church should respect a variety of forms of lifestyle, and should not merely solemnize traditional marriages, but should provide blessings for gay partnerships, especially in countries where such marriages have legal recognition. Acknowledging that marriage partners are frequently 'sequentially monogamous', or want to live together for trial periods before entering into full commitment, perhaps the Church should bless 'trial marriages', and reconsider whether it is realistic to make couples vow to be faithful 'till death us do part'. One Unitarian minister known to the authors substituted the expression, 'as long as our love shall last', in recognition of the fact that most married couples do this.

Others have expressed the opposite view, seeing the future in evangelical conservatism and in charismatic renewal. Some believe that the future lies in smaller 'cellular' churches, some of which might be based in the home rather than in the sanctuary, enabling a more intimate spirituality. Indeed, there are predictions that the remainder of the twenty-first century may see more interest in spirituality, rather than religion, and that people will seek life's meaning in a range of spiritualities, rather than live out a specific religious faith within one single church. Such spirituality might be a kind of 'cafeteria spirituality', as some have called it, or it may be an amalgam of spiritual practices drawn from a range of spiritual traditions, as has happened with the New Age phenomenon. Some Christians have favoured the 'mega-church' rather than the cellular church, believing that it provides more anonymity, is more up-to-date in its communication style, and can exercise more power in the community. As a fully qualified priesthood or ministry becomes more difficult to obtain and to finance, it is suggested that churches may become organized in clusters rather than in single congregations. This is already happening to a significant degree in the Church of England. Particularly within the Protestant tradition, commitment to the priesthood of all believers suggests widening participation by the laity—something that is already evident in both the Protestant and Roman Catholic traditions.

Religions are not predictable with any kind of precision, and it is unlikely that scholars living a century ago could have foreseen Christianity as it is today. Political, social, technological and environmental factors will all play their role in shaping the next century of the Christian faith, and these are largely unforeseeable. Wars, natural disasters, environmental catastrophes will no doubt exert an effect on Christianity, although not in any straightforward predictable way. Much depends on Christian leaders and thinkers and how they respond. Environmental catastrophe, for example, might cause loss of faith, or it might cause humanity to turn to religion for spiritual sustenance. Certainly current tensions between conservative and liberal will continue in the foreseeable future. At present conservative evangelicalism seems to be growing at a popular level, while Christian scholarship tends to favour a more liberal approach to the Bible and to Christian theology. While it is possible that traditionalist-liberal tensions may lead to schism, the ecumenical movement continues to thrive, and relationships between the different denominations and traditions continue to grow. Ordination and the sharing of the Eucharist continue to divide Christians, and there are no signs of an imminent solution to such problems. Regarding the ministry of women, we seriously doubt Hampson's prediction that their role within the Church is the death knell of Christianity. Women themselves are divided on how they want to be treated within Christianity: many denominations afford equal opportunities, while those women who perceive authority as a predominantly male role can still find many churches that support this position.

Some aspects of Christianity are likely to remain unchanged. Although the Bible and the creeds are open to interpretation and, as we have seen, admit of a variety of different understandings, it is unlikely that Christians would attempt to redefine the canon of Scripture, or to devise new creeds that supersede the ancient ones. The 'substance' or 'deposit' of faith is something that remains eternal, however much human understanding of it may vary. Christianity is based on the idea of God entering the world in physical form, and in similar fashion the Christian faith continues to find appropriate ways of expressing itself in a changing physical world. Doing this in a way that speaks to the twenty-first century, but without comprising the substance of its message, is the challenge which it continually faces.

Glossary

absolution: declaration by a priest that God has forgiven the sins of one who has *confessed*.

altar: table on which the *Eucharist* or *Mass* is celebrated. (The term is rejected by Protestants, who prefer to use the term 'communion table'.)

anathema: official condemnation of a person or a teaching.

Anglicanism: the reformed *denomination*, worldwide, that began in England in the sixteenth century.

Antichrist: (1) literally, anyone who opposes Christ; popularly regarded as (2) an evil opponent of Christ who will appear at the end-times.

apostle: first-century disciple of Jesus after his ascension, at which he commissioned them to go out and preach the gospel (Mt. 28:18-20).

archbishop: the chief *bishop* of a province.

benediction: blessing, especially in a *liturgical* setting.

bishop: the leading *priest* of a *diocese*.

bishopric: the area presided over by a *bishop*; same as *diocese*.

bull: an official document issued by a Pope.

canon: ecclesiastical law, rule or standard, especially the authoritative body of Scripture.

canonization: (of Scripture) the formal acceptance of a book as part of the Bible; (of people) the declaration that someone is a *saint*.

canticle: a passage from the Bible used as a *hymn*.

cardinal: senior Roman Catholic official, usually a *bishop*.

catechism: summary of doctrine designed to teach the faith, usually in question-and-answer format.

cathedral: the main church of a *diocese*, where the *bishop* is based.

chancel: the area of a church in which the *altar* or communion table is traditionally placed.

charismatic: a style of worship characterized by free expression and associated with the gifts of the Holy Spirit.

Church: the body made up of all Christians, or a denomination within that body.

civic religion: customs and symbols used by secular society in a way that parallels the use of religious symbols.

communion: (1) *consecrated* bread and wine, believed to be in some sense the body and blood of Christ; (2) service (or part of a service) at which consecrated bread and wine are consumed; (3) community of denominations who can share communion together.

conclave: secluded assembly of Roman Catholic cardinals to elect a new pope.

consecration: making something sacred, e.g. a church building or the bread and wine in the *eucharist.*

confession: declaration of one's sins, especially to a priest.

creed: formal statement summarizing Christianity's principal teachings.

crucifix: representation of Jesus on the cross.

cult: (1) pejorative name for *new religious movements*; (2) loosely organized movement devoted to a particular *saint.*

deacon: (1) one who assists in leading worship (the exact definition varies from one *denomination* to another); (2) (in some forms of Protestantism) member of a board responsible for a congregation's fabric.

dean: senior member of clergy in a *cathedral.*

denomination: group of churches within Christianity, with its own particular organization and tradition.

diaspora: scattered members of an ethnic or religious group outside its country of origin, living as a minority within a culture.

diocese: area over which a *bishop* presides.

disciple (see also *apostle*): one of Jesus' followers.

Dominicans: religious community founded in the thirteenth century by St Dominic with the aim of preaching and combating false teaching.

ecumenical: shared by more than one *denomination.*

episcopal: descriptive of a *bishop* or a church which is led by them.

Episcopalian: name used to designate *Anglican* churches, e.g. in Scotland and the USA.

eschatology: branch of theology relating to the end-times.

established church: the official church of a state, e.g. the Church of England.

Eucharist: service in which bread and wine are transformed (in some way) into the body and blood of Christ.

evangelical: connected with the gospel, especially used of Protestant groups that put a strong emphasis on the Bible and on the need for personal conversion.

evangelist: (1) one of the writers of the four Gospels; (2) one who preaches the Christian message.

Franciscans: religious community founded in the thirteenth century by St Francis with the aim of popular preaching.

friar: member of a *Dominican* or *Franciscan* religious community.

fundamentalist: one who adheres strictly to the presumed 'fundamentals' of the faith. The term is usually associated with belief in biblical inerrancy.

Gentile: someone who is not a Jew.

glossolaliation: speaking in a foreign or unknown language, attributed to the Holy Spirit's activity.

grail: the cup from which Jesus supposedly drank at the *Last Supper.*

Gregorian calendar: the universal civil calendar, introduced by Pope Gregory XIII in 1582, and replacing the *Julian calendar*. The Gregorian calendar is used for calculating the dates of moveable feasts in the Western churches, but not in Orthodoxy.

high church: (largely *Anglican*) formal and often elaborate style of worship.

holy communion: same as *communion.*

host: wafer distributed by the priest at the *Mass*. The name is derived from the Latin *hostia* ('victim').

hymn: song sung to or about God.

icon: painting of a *saint* or a scene from Scripture, used by Orthodox Christians to aid worship.

Jesuits: religious order founded by Saint Ignatius Loyola in 1540 whose members vow obedience to the Pope .

Jehovah: Latinized form of the Hebrew name of God.

Julian calendar: calendar introduced by Julius Caesar in 45 BCE, now largely superseded by the *Gregorian calendar*. The Julian calendar is still used by most Orthodox churches for calculating moveable feasts.

Lamb: title for Jesus, alluding to the lambs slaughtered at Passover in the Jerusalem Temple.

Last Supper: the meal Jesus shared with his *disciples* the night before he was crucified.

lectern: the stand on which the Bible is placed for reading in church.

lectionary: a list which gives the Bible readings and other information for every day of the year.

lesson: reading of part of the Bible as part of worship.

liturgy: the form of *service* used in worship.

Lord's Supper: another (Protestant) name for the *Eucharist*.

low church: (largely *Anglican*) plain and often informal style of worship.

Mass: name for the *Eucharist* mainly within Roman Catholicism. (The term is rejected by Protestants.)

megachurch: church with a very large membership, usually American, suburban and Protestant.

millennial: relating to the *millennium*.

millennium: (1) literally, Christ's thousand-year reign (Rev. 20:3-5); (2) more loosely, the end of the present era.

minister: a member of the clergy (in Protestant *denominations*).

missal: book containing words of the *Mass*.

monastery: a building in which monks live.

monk: man who lives in a religious community and has taken vows to live according to its rules.

monstrance: display case, often of precious metal, in which the *consecrated* bread is displayed at *exposition*.

moveable feast: a festival that is not linked to a specific calendar date. Thus, Easter, Ascension Day, Pentecost and Trinity Sunday are 'moveable', occurring on different dates in different years.

nave: the main area of a church, where the congregation sits or stands.

new religious movement (NRM): religious organization founded in the recent past, usually outside the mainstream.

Non-Conformist: (in England) Protestant group or denomination which does not belong to the Church of England, the *established church*.

ordinal: book containing forms of *service* for *ordination*.

ordination: the process of admitting someone to the office of *deacon*, *priest* or *bishop*.

orthodox: having correct belief. (The term can be used of all traditions.)

Orthodox: A main tradition which separated from Roman Catholicism in 1054.

parish: area served by a church.

Passion: suffering of Christ before his death.

pastor: a congregational leader (in some Protestant churches).

penance: task which a priest imposes on someone who has been to *confession*.

penitence: feeling of sorrow and regret for doing wrong.

pericope: a unit or episode, especially of a Gospel.

Presbyterian: type of Protestant denomination governed by a hierarchy of church courts.

priest: a member of the clergy (in Orthodox, Roman Catholic and some Anglican churches).

psalm: biblical *hymn*, frequently used as part of *liturgy.*

pulpit: raised enclosure from which sermons are preached.

rector: title sometimes given to an *Anglican priest* in charge of a church.

rosary: set of beads used to assist in prayer.

saint: person of outstanding virtue, declared by the Church to be holy, after death.

sect: group which has split off from a larger religious body.

see: seat of a *bishop.*

service: congregational act of worship.

shrine: holy place, especially one dedicated to a *saint.*

speaking in tongues: see *glossolaliation.*

synod: a council of church leaders.

synoptic Gospels: the Gospels of Matthew, Mark and Luke, which share common material.

Thomist: a follower of St Thomas Aquinas, the *Dominican* philosopher and theologian.

tonsure: way of cutting hair to indicate that one is a *monk.*

tradition: practices handed down over generations.

transubstantiation: Roman Catholic doctrine that the bread and wine of the *eucharist* is transformed literally (although not physically) into the body and blood of Christ.

Trinity: Christian doctrine of God as Father, Son and Holy Spirit.

Twelve Tribes of Israel: the descendants of the twelve sons of Jacob (Gen. 35:23-26).

vicar: (Church of England) the usual title for the priest in charge of a church.

Bibliography

Recommended Further Reading

Chryssides, George D. 2010. *Christianity Today*. London: Continuum.

Davies, Noel, and Martin Conway. 2008. *World Christianity in the Twentieth Century*. London: SCM Press.

Hill, Jonathan. 1996. *The History of Christianity*. Oxford: Lion Hudson.

Kim, Sebastian, and Kirsteen Kim. 2008. *Christianity as a World Religion*. London: Continuum.

Taylor, Richard. 2003. *How to Read a Church*. London: Rider.

Works Cited in the Text

Akerley, Ben Edward. 1998. *The X-rated Bible: An Irreverent Survey of Sex in the Scriptures*. Venice, CA: Feral House.

Archbishops' Council. 2000. *Common Worship: Services and Prayers for the Church of England*. London: Church House Publishing.

Athanasius. 1903. *Athanasii De Incarnatione Verbi Dei* (Athanasius on the Incarnation of the Word of God). Trans. T. Herbert Bindley; London: Religious Tract Society.

Augustine. 1957. *The City of God*. Trans. John Healey; 2 vols; London: Dent.

— 2001. *De Bono Coniugali. De Sancta Uirginitate*. Trans. P. G. Walsh; Oxford: Clarendon Press.

Avis, Paul. 2005. 'Church.' In Bowden 2005: 227-36.

Bainvel, J. 1912. 'Tradition and Living Magisterium.' In *The Catholic Encyclopedia*. New York: Robert Appleton Company. New Advent. Accessed 8 June 2010. http://www.newadvent.org/cathen/15006b.htm

Barna Group of Ventura, California (2007). 'Americans Express Their Views of the Virgin Birth of Christ.' Created 17 December; accessed 13 January 2008. http://www.barna.org/FlexPage.aspx?Page=BarnaUpdateNarrow&BarnaUpdateID=286

Barrows, John Henry. 1893. *The World's Parliament of Religions: An Illustrated and Popular Story of the World's First Parliament of Religions, Held in Chicago in Connection with the Columbian Exposition of 1893*. Chicago: The Parliament Publishing Company.

Colgrave, Bertram, and R. A. B. Mynors (eds). *Bede's Ecclesiastical History of the English People.* Oxford: Oxford University Press.

Badham, Paul. 1995. 'Should Christians Accept the Validity of Voluntary Euthanasia?' *Studies in Christian Ethics* (January) 8.2: 1-12.

Bettison, H. (ed.). 1943. *Documents of the Christian Church.* Oxford: Oxford University Press.

Black, Matthew, and H. H. Rowley. 1962. *Peake's Commentary on the Bible.* London: Nelson.

Borg, Marcus. 1987. *Jesus: A New Vision.* London: SPCK, 2nd rev. edn.

Bowden, John (ed.). 2005. *Christianity: The Complete Guide.* London: Continuum.

Braybrooke, Marcus. 1996. *A Wider Vision: A History of the World Congress of Faiths.* Oxford: Oneworld.

Braybrooke, Marcus (ed.). 1974. *Inter-Faith Worship: A Report of a Working Party.* London: Stainer and Bell.

Browne, Robert. 1582. *A Brief Treatise of Reformation without Tarrying for Anie.* Whitefish, MA: Kessinger (repr. 2007).

Bruce, F. F. 1962. 'The Epistles of Paul.' In Black and Rowley 1962: 927-39.

Bruce, Steve. 1995. *Religion in Modern Britain.* Oxford: Oxford University Press

— 2002. *God Is Dead: Secularization in the West.* Oxford: Blackwell.

Bultmann, Rudolf. 1926. *Jesus and the Word.* London and Glasgow: Collins (repr. 1958).

— 1952. *Theology of the New Testament.* Vol. 1; London: SCM Press (repr. 1968).

Bunyan, John. 1678. *The Pilgrim's Progress.* Harmondsworth: Penguin (repr. 2008).

Butler Alban. 1756. *The Lives of the Fathers, Martyrs and Other Principal Saints.* 4 vols.; Dublin: James Duffy (repr. 1886).

Calvin, John. 1559. *Institutes of the Christian Religion.* 2 vols.; London: James Clarke (repr. 1962).

Calvin, John, and William Farel. 1537. *Articles on the Organisation of the Church and Its Worship at Geneva.* In Reid 1954: 47-55.

Carey, William. 1792. *An Enquiry into the Obligations of Christians to Use Means for the Conversion of the Heathens.* Didcot: Baptist Missionary Society (repr. 1991).

Carpenter, Humphrey. 1995. *The Letters of J. R. R. Tolkien.* Boston: Houghton Mifflin.

Catholic Online. 2010. 'First Station: Jesus Is Condemned to Death.' Accessed 15 July 2010. http://www.catholic.org/clife/prayers/station.php?id=1

CathNews. 2008. 'Catholics Forgetting Bible: Survey.' Created 10 September; accessed 27 November 2009. www.cathnews.com/article.aspx?aeid=8944

Chaucer Geoffrey. 1382. *Parlement of Foules.* London: W. B. Clive (repr. 1914).

Christian Glory Church. 2008. 'Get Your Ordination Here.' Accessed 5 June 2009. www.christianglorychurch.com

Christianity Today. 1999. 'Billy Graham: "I Have Never Felt Called to Single Out the Jews": The Evangelist Discusses Targeted Evangelism in One of His Most Quoted Statements.' Accessed 11 June 2010. www.ctlibrary.com/ct/1999/novemberweb-only/53.0d.html

Christian Today. 2008. 'Bible Great to Read but Hard to Apply—Survey.' Created 12 February; accessed 27 November 2009. www.christiantoday.com/article/bible.great.to.read.but.hard.to.apply.survey/16810.htm

Chryssides, George D. 2010. *Christianity Today.* London: Continuum.

Chryssides, George D., and Ron Geaves. 2007. *The Study of Religion: An Introduction to Key Ideas and Methods.* London: Continuum.

Chryssides, G. D., and M. Z. Wilkins. 2006. *A Reader in New Religious Movements.* London: Continuum.

Church Hymnary Trust. 1973. *The Church Hymnary.* London: Oxford University Press, 3rd edn.

Church of England. 1968. *Book of Common Prayer* (1662). Glasgow: Collins.

1980. *Alternative Service Book.* London: Church House Publishing.

— 2000. *Common Worship: Services and Prayers for the Church of England.* London: Church House Publishing.

— 2008. 'Latest Figures Show Changing Trends in Church-going.' Created 31 January; accessed 14 June 2010. http://www.cofe.anglican.org/news/pr1008.html

— *Thirty-Nine Articles/Articles of Religion.* In *Book of Common Prayer*, 388-96.

Church of Jesus Christ of Latter-day Saints. 1830. *The Book of Mormon: Another Testament of Jesus Christ. The Doctrine and Covenants of The Church of Jesus Christ of Latter-day Saints. The Pearl of Great Price.* Salt Lake City, UT: Church of Jesus Christ of Latter-day Saints (repr. 1981).

Church of South India. 2004. *Book of Common Worship.* Bangalore: Church of South India.

Clark, Francis. 1977. *Seekers and Scholars.* Unit 1: 'The Search for Meaning in Life.' Milton Keynes: The Open University Press.

Clarke, James Freeman. 1879. *Ten Great Religions: An Essay in Comparative Theology.* Boston: Houghton, Osgood and Company.

Cleland, Gary. 2008. 'A Confrontational Giant Who Speaks in Stentorian Tones.' *The Age.* Created 6 March; accessed 14 June 2010. http://www.theage.com.au/news/world/a-confrontational-giant-who-speaks-in-stentorian-tones/2008/03/05/1204402552983.html

Congregational Churches in England. 1658. *A Declaration of the Faith and Order Owned and Practised in the Congregational Churches in England.* London: Congregational Churches in England. Accessed 2 July 2010. http://www.creeds.net/congregational/savoy/index.htm

Conkin, Paul K. 1997. *American Originals: Homemade Varieties of Christianity.* Chapel Hill, NC: University of North Carolina Press.

Council of Trent. 1564. *Canons and Decrees of the Council of Trent.* Trans. H. J. Schroeder; Rockford, IL: Tan Books and Publishers (repr. 1978).

Cox, Harvey. 1994. *Fire from Heaven: The Rise of Pentecostal Spirituality and the Reshaping of Religion in the Twenty-First Century.* New York: Addison-Wesley Publishing Co.

Cross, F. L., and E. A. Livingstone. 1978. *The Oxford Dictionary of the Christian Church.* Oxford: Oxford University Press.

Crossan, John Dominic. 1991. *The Historical Jesus: The Life of a Mediterranean Jewish Peasant.* Edinburgh: T. and T. Clark.

— 1994. *Jesus: A Revolutionary Biography.* San Francisco: HarperSanFrancisco.

— 1995. *The Essential Jesus: What Jesus Really Taught.* San Francisco: HarperSanFrancisco.

— 1995. *Who Killed Jesus? Exposing the Roots of Anti-Semitism in the Gospel Story of The Death of Jesus.* San Francisco, CA: HarperSanFrancisco.

— 1998. *The Birth of Christianity: Discovering What Happened in the Years Immediately after the Execution of Jesus.* San Francisco, CA: HarperSanFrancisco.

C.S.S.M. 1925. *Golden Bells: Hymns for Young People.* London: C.S.S.M.

Darwin, Charles. 1859. *On the Origin of Species.* London: Folio Society (repr. 1990).

Davies, Horton. 1954. *Christian Deviations.* London: SCM Press (repr. 1965).

Descartes, R. 1637. *Discourse on Method.* Harmondsworth: Penguin (repr. 2003).

Dictionary.com. 2010. Dictionary. Accessed 8 June 2010. http://dictionary.reference.com

Didachē, The. 1953. *The Teaching of the Twelve Apostles, Commonly Called the Didachē.* In Richardson 1953. Accessed 10 June 2010. www.ccel.org/ccel/richardson/fathers.viii.i.iii.html

Dowling, Levi H. 1989. *The Aquarian Age Gospel of Jesus, the Christ of the Piscean Age.* Romford, Essex: Fowler.

Eddy, Mary Baker. 1875. *Science and Health, with Key to the Scriptures.* Boston: First Church of Christ, Scientist (repr. 1994).

Eu, Hyo Won. 1973. *Divine Principle.* New York: HSA-UWC.

Evans, Craig A. (ed.). 2008. *Encyclopedia of the Historical Jesus.* London: Routledge.

— 2004. *The Historical Jesus.* 4 vols.; London: Routledge.

Fanning, W. 1910. 'Canons on Hunting.' In *New Advent: The Catholic Encyclopedia.* New York: Robert Appleton Company. Accessed 23 July 2009. www.newadvent.org/cathen/07563c.htm

Farquhar, J. N. 1913. *The Crown of Hinduism.* Oxford: Oxford University Press (repr. 1930).

Fell, Margaret (a.k.a. Margaret Fox). 1667. *Women's Speaking Justified, Proved and Allowed of by the Scriptures.* Los Angeles: University of California, William Andrews Clark Memorial Library (repr. 1979).

Fiorenza, Elisabeth Schüssler. 1995. *In Memory of Her: A Feminist Theological Reconstruction of Christian Origins.* London: SCM Press.

Frazer, J. G. 1929. *The Golden Bough: A Study in Magic and Religion.* London: Macmillan, abridged edn.

Funk, Robert W. 1993. *The Five Gospels: The Search for the Authentic Words of Jesus.* New York: HarperCollins (repr. 1997).

— 1996. *Honest to Jesus: Jesus for a New Millennium.* San Francisco, CA: HarperSanFrancisco.

Galilei, Galileo. 1967. *Dialogue concerning the Two Chief World Systems: Ptolemaic and Copernican.* Trans. S. Drake; Berkeley, CA: University of California Press.

General Assembly of Divines at Westminster. 1649. *The Confession of Faith; Agreed upon by the Assembly of Divines at Westminster.* Edinburgh: William Blackwood and Sons (repr. 1969); includes *The Larger Catechism*, 49-113 and *The Shorter Catechism*, 113-32.

Gledhill, Ruth. 2005. 'Clergy Who Don't Believe in God.' *The Times*, 4 July. Accessssed 8 June 2010. http://www.timesonline.co.uk/tol/news/uk/article540199.ece

Gospel for Asia. 2005. 'GFA Tsunami Relief Work Brings Family to Christ.' Created 10 November; accessed 19 May 2009. www.gfa.org/news/articles/gfa-tsunami-relief-work-brings-family-to-christ

Grant, Robert M., and David Noel Freedman. 1960. *The Secret Sayings of Jesus according to the Gospel of Thomas.* London and Glasgow: Collins.

Greek Orthodox Diocese of America. 2010. 'On-line Chapel: Removal of the Relics of St Athanasios the Great.' Created 2 May; accessed 8 June 2010. http://www. goarch.org/chapel/saints/38

Green, Michael. 1967. *Man Alive!* London: Inter-Varsity Fellowship.

Grimmond, Paul. 2008. 'Where Is that Bible?' *The Sola Panel*, 15 September. Accessed 27 November 2009. http://solapanel.org/article/where_is_that_bible

Grohman, Steve. 2010. 'A Creation Seminar.' Created 15 May; accessed 21 July 2010. www.creationseminar.net

Guttmacher Institute. 2008. 'Facts on Induced Abortion in the United States.' Accessed 27 July 2009. http://www.guttmacher.org/pubs/fb_induced_abortion. html#3

Hall, Douglas. 1997. *The End of Christendom and the Future of Christianity.* Valley Forge, PA: Trinity Press International.

Hampson, Daphne. 1990. *After Christianity.* London: SCM Press (repr. 2002).

Hay, David. 1982. *Exploring Inner Space: Scientists and Religious Experience.* London and Oxford: Mowbray (repr. 1987).

Heald, G. 1999. 'Taking Faith's Temperature.' *The Tablet* 253.8313: 1279-80.

— 2001. 'The British Christmas.' *The Tablet* 255.8415: 1857.

Henderson, G. D., and J. Bulloch (eds). 1960. *The Scots Confession: 1560.* Edinburgh: The Saint Andrew Press.

Henson, John. 2004. *Good as New: A Radical Retelling of the Scriptures.* Alresford: O Books.

Hick, John H. 1973. *Philosophy of Religion.* Englewood Cliffs: Prentice Hall, 2 edn.

Hinnells, John R. (ed.). 1997. *A New Handbook of Living Religions.* Harmondsworth: Penguin.

Hinton, Michael. 1994. *The Christian Effect on Jewish Life.* London: SCM Press.

Hobbes, Thomas. 1691. *Leviathan.* Harmondsworth: Penguin (repr. 1985).

Hoekema, Anthony. 1963. *The Four Major Cults: Christian Science, Jehovah's Witnesses, Mormonism, Seventh-day Adventism.* Exeter: Paternoster.

Hume, David. 1777. *Enquiries concerning Human Understanding and concerning the Principles of Morals.* Oxford: Oxford University Press.

— 1779. *Dialogues concerning Natural Religion.* Harmondsworth: Penguin (repr. 1990).

Hutchinson, Roger W. 1996. 'Jairus's Daughter: Dead but Raised to Live Again.' *The Skeptical Review Online*, May/June. Accessed 30 March 2009. http://www. theskepticalreview.com/tsrmag/3jairu96.html

Hymns Ancient and Modern Ltd.. 1999. *Hymns Ancient and Modern: New Standard.* N.p. Norwich: Canterbury Press.

International Interfaith Organisations Network. 2003. 'Introduction to Interfaith.' Accessed 29 May 2009. http://www.interfaithstudies.org/interfaith/network.html

James, M. R. 1924. *The Apocryphal New Testament.* Oxford: Clarendon (repr. 1972).

Johnstone, Patrick, and Jason Mandryk. 2001. *Operation World: 21st Century Edition.* London: Paternoster.

Jones, R. K., J. E. Darroch and S. K. Henshaw. 2002. 'Patterns in the Socioeconomic Characteristics of Women Obtaining Abortions in 2000–2001.' *Perspectives on Sexual and Reproductive Health* 34.5: 226-35. Cited in Guttmacher Institute 2008.

461

Jowett, Benjamin (ed.). 1861. *Essays and Reviews.* London: Longman, Green, Longman and Roberts, 9th edn.

Kemp, Michael. 2007. 'Confidence in the Word.' Appendix A: Bible Reading Research. Last updated March 2003; accessed 28 November 2009. www.citw.org. uk/research.htm

Kierkegaard, Søren. 1962. *Philosophical Fragments.* Princeton: Princeton University Press.

*The Koran.*1956. Transl. N. J. Dawood; Harmondsworth: Penguin.

Küng, Hans, and Walter Jens. 1995. *Dying with Dignity: A Plea for Personal Responsibility.* Transl. John Bowden; New York: Continuum.

Lambeth Conference Archives. 1930. 'Seventh Lambeth Conference, 1930, Resolution 15.' Accessed 10 June 2010. www.lambethconference.org/resolutions/1930/1930-15.cfm

Linzey, Andrew. 1976. *Animal Rights: A Christian Perspective.* London: SCM Press.

— 1987. *Christianity and the Rights of Animals.* London: SPCK.

Livingstone, David. 1857. *Missionary Travels and Researches in South Africa.* London: John Murray (repr. 1912).

Luther, Martin. 1517–1523. *Luther's and Zwingli's Propositions for Debate: The Ninety-five Theses of 31 October 1517 and the Sixty-seven Articles of 19 January 1523.* Trans. Carl S. Meyer; Leiden: Brill (repr. 1963).

Lyrics007. 2007. Louis Armstrong, 'When the Saints Go Marching in.' Accessed 8 June 2010. http://www.lyrics007.com/Louis%20Armstrong%20Lyrics/When%20The%20Saints%20Go%20Marching%20In%20Lyrics.html

Maccoby, Hyam. 1991. *Paul and Hellenism.* London: SCM Press.

Marcum, John P. 1995. 'Bible Reading among Presbyterians.' Accessed 27 November 2009. https://www.pcusa.org/research/monday/biblemm.htm

Meier, John P. 1991. *A Marginal Jew: Rethinking the Historical Jesus.* I. *The Roots of the Problem and the Person.* New York: Doubleday.

— 2009. *A Marginal Jew: Rethinking the Historical Jesus.* II. *Mentor, Message, and Miracles.* New York: Doubleday.

Methodist Church. 1936. *The Book of Offices: Being the Orders of Service Authorized for Use in the Methodist Church Together with the Order for Morning Prayer.* London: Methodist Publishing House.

Methodist Church. 2010a. 'The Methodist Missionary Society.' Accessed 14 June 2010. http://www.methodist.org.uk/index.cfm?fuseaction=opentoworld. content&cmid=2278

Moll, Rob, and Ted Olsen. 2005. 'Tsunami Weblog: Combining the Gospel with Aid.' *Christianity Today*, January 2005. Accessed 19 May 2009. http://www.christianity today.com/ct/2005/januaryweb-only/21.0a.html

Morgan, Donald. 2009. 'Bible Inconsistencies: Bible Contradictions?' Last updated 1 February 2009; accessed 31 March 2009. http://www.infidels.org/library/modern/donald_morgan/inconsistencies.html

Morison, Frank. 1930. *Who Moved the Stone?* London: Faber and Faber (repr. 1971).

Morton, H. V. 1936. *In the Steps of Saint Paul.* London: Rich and Cowan.

Nevius, John L. 1886. *The Planting and Development of Missionary Churches.* Grand Rapids, MI: Baker Book House (repr. 1958).

Nichols, Terence L. 2005. 'This is My Body: How to Understand Transubstantiation.' Accessed 5 February 2009. www.thefreelibrary.com/'This+is+my+body':+how+to+understand+transubstantiation-a0137864220

Nordquist, Dan. 2006. 'Is the Earth Billions of Years Old?' In 'The Little Book of Prophecy and Truth.' Accessed 26 May 2010. www.prophecyandtruth.com/evolve2.htm

Oberdorfer, Don. 1997. *The Two Koreas: A Contemporary History*. Reading, MA: Addison-Wesley.

Ontario Consultants on Religious Tolerance. 2007. 'Religious Beliefs of Americans: About Ghosts, Satan, Heaven, Hell, etc.' Last updated 23 December 2007; accessed 7 June 2010. www.religioustolerance.org/chr_poll3.htm#salv

— 2008. 'Halloween: As viewed by evangelical Christians.' Accessed 1 May 2009. www.religioustolerance.org/hallo_ev.htm

— 2009. 'Euthanasia and Physician Assisted Suicide (PAS).' Accessed 10 June 2010. www.religioustolerance.org/euth8.htm

Open Episcopal Church. 2010. 'Post the Host.' Accessed 3 June 2010. www.postthehost.net

Ormsby, Avril. 2009. 'Agree to Differ over Women Bishops—Anglican Leader.' Reuters UK, 16 February. Accessed 3 June 2009. http://uk.reuters.com/article/reutersEdge/idUKLNE51F03S20090216

Orthodox Church in North America. 2010. 'Orthodoxy in America.' Last updated 16 May 2010; accessed 26 May 2010. www.orthodoxyinamerica.org

Osiander, Andreas. 1537. *Harmoniae evangelicae libri quatuor* ('Harmony of the Four Gospels'). Basle: Froben.

Paley, William. 1817. *Natural Theology, or Evidences of the Existence and Attributes of the Deity, Collected from the Appearances of Nature.* Edinburgh: Oliver and Boyd.

Palmer, G. E. H., Philip Sherrard, Kallistos (Timothy) Ware (trans. and eds). 1979–1984. *The Philokalia.* 4 vols.; London: Faber and Faber.

Panikkar, Raymond. 1964. *The Unknown Christ of Hinduism.* London: Darton, Longman and Todd.

Parliament of the World's Religions. 1993. *Declaration toward a Global Ethic.* Accessed 3 June 2010. www.urbandharma.org/pdf/ethic.pdf

Parliamentary Select Committee. 2005. 'Parliamentary Select Committee on Assisted Dying for the Terminally Ill Bill (UK).' 2005. Minutes of Evidence. Accessed 28 July 2009. http://www.publications.parliament.uk/pa/ld200405/ldselect/ldasdy/86/5020342.htm

Person, James E. Jr. 2005. 'Deadly Satire, Saving Grace: The Faith and Work of Evelyn Waugh.' Catholic Education Resource Center. Accessed 10 June 2010. http://www.catholiceducation.org/articles/arts/al0235.html

Picknett, Lynn. 2003. *Mary Magdalene: Christianity's Hidden Goddess.* London: Robinson.

Pope Gregory XVI. 1844. *Inter Praecipuas* ('Among the Special Schemes'). Encyclical. Accessed 15 May 2009. http://www.papalencyclicals.net/Greg16/g16inter.htm

Pope John XXIII. 1963. *Pacem in Terris* ('Peace on Earth'). Encyclical on establishing universal peace in truth, justice, charity and liberty. Accessed 30 June 2010. http://www.vatican.va/holy_father/john_xxiii/encyclicals/documents/hf_j-xxiii_enc_11041963_pacem_en.html

Pope John Paul II. 1983. *Divinus Perfectionis Magister* ('The Divine Teacher of Perfection'). Apostolic Constitution, 25 January 1983. Accessed 20 July 2010. http://www.vatican.va/holy_father/john_paul_ii/apost_constitutions/documents/hf_jp-ii_apc_25011983_divinus-perfectionis-magister_en.html

— 1993. *Veritatis Splendor* ('The Splendour of Truth'). Encyclical, 6 August. Accessed 30 June 2010. http://www.vatican.va/holy_father/john_paul_ii/encyclicals/documents/hf_jp-ii_enc_06081993_veritatis-splendor_en.html

— 1994. *Ordinatio Sacerdotalis* ('On the ordination of priests'). Apostolic letter of John Paul II to the Bishops of the Catholic Church on reservign priestly ordination to men alone. Accessed 30 June 2010. http://www.vatican.va/holy_father/john_paul_ii/apost_letters/documents/hf_jp-ii_apl_22051994_ordinatio-sacerdotalis_en.html

— 1995. *Evangelium Vitae* ('The good news of life'). Encyclical on the Value and Inviolability of Human Life. Created 25 March; accessed 30 June 2010. http://www.vatican.va/edocs/ENG0141/_INDEX.HTM

— 1995). *Ut Unum Sint* ('That they may be one'). Created 25 May; accessed 30 June 2010. http://www.vatican.va/holy_father/john_paul_ii/encyclicals/documents/hf_jp-ii_enc_25051995_ut-unum-sint_en.html

— 2002. 'Address of John Paul II to the Participants in the International Meeting Sponsored by the Bible Societies.' Monday, 22 April 2002. Accessed 15 May 2009. http://www.vatican.va/holy_father/john_paul_ii/speeches/2002/april/documents/hf_jp-ii_spe_20020422_bible-societies_en.html

Pope Paul VI. 1964. *Unitatis Redintegratio* ('The Restoration of Unity'). Decree on Ecumenism. Created 21 November; accessed 30 June 2010. http://www.vatican.va/archive/hist_councils/ii_vatican_council/documents/vat-ii_decree_19641121_unitatis-redintegratio_en.html

— 1964. *Lumen Gentium*. Proclaimed as part of the Second Vatican Council, 21 November. Accessed 30 June 2010. http://www.vatican.va/archive/hist_councils/ii_vatican_council/documents/vat-ii_const_19641121_lumen-gentium_en.html

— 1965. *Ad Gentes* ('To the Peoples'): On the Mission Activity of the Church. 7 December, 1965. Accessed 30 June 2010. http://www.vatican.va/archive/hist_councils/ii_vatican_council/documents/vat-ii_decree_19651207_ad-gentes_en.html

— 1965. *Nostra Aetate* ('For our time'). Declaration on the Relation of the Church to Non-Christian Religions. 28 October, 1965. Accessed 18 May 2009. www.vatican.va/archive/hist_councils/ii_vatican_council/documents/vat-ii_decl_19651028_nostra-aetate_en.html

— 1968. *Humanae Vitae* ('Of Human Life'). 25 July. Accessed 30 June 2010. http://www.vatican.va/holy_father/paul_vi/encyclicals/documents/hf_p-vi_enc_25071968_humanae-vitae_en.html

— 1975. *Persona Humana* ('The Human Person'). 7 November. Accessed 30 June 2010. http://www.vatican.va/roman_curia/congregations/cfaith/documents/rc_con_cfaith_doc_19751229_persona-humana_en.html

— 1975. 'Response to the Letter of His Grace the Most Reverend Dr. F. D. Coggan, Archbishop of Canterbury, concerning the Ordination of Women to the Priesthood (November 30, 1975).' *AAS* 68 (1976): 599. Accessed 2 June 2009. http://www.vatican.va/holy_father/john_paul_ii/apost_letters/documents/hf_jp-ii_apl_22051994_ordinatio-sacerdotalis_en.html

Pope Pius IX. 1928. *Mortalium Animos* ('Spirit of mortality'). 6 January. Accessed 30 June 2010. http://www.vatican.va/holy_father/pius_xi/encyclicals/documents/hf_p-xi_enc_19280106_mortalium-animos_en.html

Pope Pius X. 1904. *Ad Diem Illum Laetissimum* ('To that Most Joyful Day'). Encyclical on the Immaculate Conception. 2 February. Accessed 30 June 2010. http://www.vatican.va/holy_father/pius_x/encyclicals/documents/hf_p-x_enc_02021904_ad-diem-illum-laetissimum_en.html

Pope Pius XI. 1930. *Casti Connubii* ('Of Chaste Marriage'). Accessed 10 June 2010. http://www.vatican.va/holy_father/pius_xi/encyclicals/documents/hf_p-xi_enc_31121930_casti-connubii_en.html

Pope Pius XII. 1943. *Divino Afflante Spiritu* ('On the Inspiration of the Divine Spirit'). Encyclical: On promoting biblical studies. 30 September. Accessed 30 June 2010. http://www.vatican.va/holy_father/pius_xii/encyclicals/documents/hf_p-xii_enc_30091943_divino-afflante-spiritu_en.html

Powell, Mark Allan. 1998. *The Jesus Debate: Modern Historians Investigate the Life of Christ.* Oxford: Lion.

Promise Keepers. 2008. 'About Us.' Accessed 3 June 2010. http://www.promise-keepers.org/about

The Psalter or Psalmes of David, after the Translation of the Great Bible [*Genevan Psalter* (1539)]. 1615 . London: Robert Barker. Accessed 2 July 2010. www.genevanpsalter.com

Redfield, Robert. 1956. *Peasant Society and Culture.* Chicago: University of Chicago Press.

Reformed Churches (France). 1559. *Confession of Faith Made in One Accord by the French People, Who Desire to Live according to the Purity of the Gospel of Our Lord Jesus Christ. A. D. 1559* [The French Confession of 1559]. Accessed 2 July 2010. http://www.creeds.net/reformed/frconf.htm

Reid, J. K. S. (ed.). 1954. *Calvin: Theological Treatises.* Philadelphia: Westminster Press.

Renan, Ernest (Ernst). 2007. *The Life of Jesus.* Charleston, SC: BiblioBazaar.

Reuters UK. 2008. 'Church of England Law Relaxes Wedding Rules.' 1 October. Accessed 14 June 2010. http://uk.reuters.com/article/idUKTRE4902N720081001

Richardson, Cyril C. (trans. and ed.). 1953. *Early Christian Fathers.* Philadelphia: Westminster.

Robertson, Pat. 1982. 'The 700 Club.' 29 October. Accessed 1 May 2009. http://www.religioustolerance.org/hallo_ev.htm

Roman Catholic Church. 1969. *Calendarium Romanum.* Vatican: Vatican Polyglot Press.

— 1987. 'Congregation for the Doctrine of the Faith: Instruction on Respect for Human Life in Its Origin and on the Dignity of Procreation: Replies to Certain Questions of the Day.' Accessed 26 July 2009. www.vatican.va/roman_curia/congregations/cfaith/documents/rc_con_cfaith_doc_19870222_respect-for-human-life_en.html

Roman Catholic Church (Latin Church). 2010. 'Code of Canon Law.' Accessed 8 June 2010. www.intratext.com/IXT/ENG0017/_P4A.HTM

Roman Catholic News Agency. 2008. 'Agenda-driven Stats: Pro-abortion Guttmacher Institute Produces Bogus Abortion Statistics.' Accessed 27 July 2009. http://www.catholicnewsagency.com/new.php?n=10643

Rose Ministries. 2010. 'Officate Weddings, Start a Ministry and More!' Accessed 14 June 2010. www.openordination.org

Russian Orthodox Church. 1830. *The Longer Catechism of The Orthodox, Catholic, Eastern Church: Also Known as the Catechism of St. Philaret (Drozdov) of Moscow.* Moscow: Synodical Press. Accessed 2 July 2010. http://www.pravoslavieto.com/docs/eng/Orthodox_Catechism_of_Philaret.htm

Samaritan's Purse International Relief. 2010. 'About Us.' Accessed 11 June 2010. www.samaritanspurse.org/index.php/Who_We_Are/About_Us

Sanders E. P. 1985. *Jesus and Judaism.* London: SCM Press.

Schucman, Helen. 1985. *A Course in Miracles.* Tiburon, CA.: Foundation for Inner Peace.

Schweitzer, Albert. 1910. *The Quest of the Historical Jesus.* London: Adam and Charles Black (repr. 1963).

ScienceMode. 2007. 'Funerals without Religion Set for Huge Increase.' 15 September. Accessed 14 June 2010. http://sciencemode.com/2007/09/15/non-religious-funeral-services-growing-trend-in-uk

Servant of Jesus Christ. 2010. 'The Truth about Halloween.' Accessed 2 June 2010. www.servantofjesuschrist.com/articles/halloween.html

Smith, William Robertson. 1881. *The Old Testament in the Jewish Church: Twelve Lectures on Biblical Criticism.* Edinburgh : A. and C. Black.

Southern Baptist Convention. 2000. *The Baptist Faith and Message.* Accessed 3 June 2009. www.sbc.net/bfm/bfm2000.asp#vi

— 2007. 'Southern Baptist Resolutions on Abortion.' Accessed 26 July 2009. www.johnstonsarchive.net/baptist/sbcabres.html

Stevenson, J. (ed.). 1957. *A New Eusebius.* London: SPCK (repr. 1974).

Stourton, Edward. 2004. *In the Footsteps of Saint Paul.* London: Hodder and Stoughton.

Strauss, D. F. 1892. *The Life of Jesus Critically Examined.* London: SCM Press (repr. 1972).

Swedenborg, Emanuel. 1905–1910. *Arcana Coelestia: The Heavenly Arcana Contained in the Holy Scripture or Word of the Lord Unfolded, Beginning with the Book of Genesis.* New York: Swedenborg Foundation.

Synnestvedt, Sig. 1984. *The Essential Swedenborg: Basic Religious Teachings of Emanuel Swedenborg.* New York: Swedenborg Foundation.

Tennessee, State of. 1925. *The World's Most Famous Court Trial (State of Tennessee vs. John Thomas Scopes): Tennessee Evolution Case. A Complete Stenographic Report of the Famous Court Test of the Tennessee Anti-Evolution Act, at Dayton, July 10 to 21, 1925, Including Speeches and Arguments of Attorneys.* New York: Da Capo Press (repr. 1971).

Thomas, Richard. 2003. *Counting People in: Changing the Way We Think about Membership and the Church.* London: SPCK.

Thomas, Terry, and J. F. Coakley. 1987. *The Christian Religion.* Milton Keynes: The Open University Press.

Thurston, H. 1908. 'Christian Burial.' In *The Catholic Encyclopedia.* New York: Robert Appleton Company. New Advent. Accessed 8 June 2010. http://www.newadvent.org/cathen/03071a.htm

Tobin, John (ed.). 1991. *George Herbert: The Complete English Poems.* Harmondsworth: Penguin.

Toner, P. 1910. 'Infallibility.' In *The Catholic Encyclopedia*. New York: Robert Appleton Company. New Advent. Accessed 30 January 2009. http://www.newadvent.org/cathen/07790a.htm

Torrey, R. A., and A. C. Dixon (eds). 2003. *The Fundamentals: A Testimony to the Truth*. Grand Rapids, MI: Baker Books.

Toumanova, Nina (trans.). 2008. *The Way of a Pilgrim: A Treasury of Russian Spirituality*. Mineola, NY: Dover.

Tracts for the Times. 1833–1841. London: Rivington.

Traditio (Traditional Roman Catholic Internet Site). 2005. 'Polls and Statistics: Third Gallup Poll (1992): Belief in Dogma on Holy Eucharist.' Accessed 8 June 2010. www.traditio.com/tradlib/polls.txt

United Reformed Church. 1981. *With People of Other Faiths in Britain*. London: United Reformed Church.

Universal Life Church. 2010. 'Universal Life Monastery.' Accessed 14 June 2010. www.themonastery.org

Van Baalen, Jan Karel. 1962. *The Chaos of Cults: A Study in Present-Day Isms*. Grand Rapids, MI: Eerdmans.

Vatican. 1964. *A Catholic Catechism*. London: Burns and Oates.

— 2010. 'The Holy See.' Accessed 15 July 2010. www.vatican.va

Von Hügel Institute, St Edmund's College, Cambridge University. 2008. 'Sex and the Modern Catholic.' *The Tablet*, 26 July, 14-15.

Voysey, A. (ed.). 1879. *Fragments from Reimarus, Consisting of Brief Critical Remarks on the Object of Jesus and His Disciples as Seen in the New Testament*. London and Edinburgh: Williams and Norgate. Accessed 25 March 2011. http://www.archive.org/details/fragmentsfromrei00reim

Walter, Tony, and Helen Waterhouse. 1999. 'A Very Private Belief: Reincarnation in Contemporary England.' *Sociology of Religion* 60.2: 187-97.

Ward, William. 1817. *A View of the History, Literature, and Religion of the Hindoos: Including a Minute Description of Their Manners and Customs and Translations from Their Principal Works*. Vol. 1. London: Black, Parbury and Allen. Accessed 10 June 2010. www.archive.org/stream/wardshidoos00sethuoft/wardshidoos00-sethuoft_djvu.txt

Waugh, Evelyn. 1955. 'Letter to Edith Sitwell.' www.leaderu.com/ftissues/ft9305/articles/weigel.html

Weber, Max. 1922. *Sociology of Religion*. London: Methuen (repr. 1976).

Wesley, Charles. 1745. *Hymns for the Nativity of Our Lord*. London: William Strahan.

Williams, Peter S. 2006. 'Playing Both Sides of the Pond: British and American Belief in Creation, Evolution and Intelligent Design.' Last updated 13 November 2006; accessed 26 May 2010. www.arn.org/docs/williams/pw_pollingbothsides.htm

Wooden, Cindy. 2008. 'Not an Easy Read: Survey Indicates Bible Hard to Understand.' *Catholic News Service*, 2 May. Accessed 27 November 2009. www.catholicnews.com/data/stories/cns/0802435.htm

World Council of Churches. 1979. *Guidelines on Dialogue with People of Living Faiths and Ideologies*. Geneva: World Council of Churches. Accessed 14 June 2010. www.oikoumene.org/en/resources/documents/wcc-programmes/inter-religious-dialogue-and-cooperation/interreligious-trust-and-respect/guide-lines-on-dialogue-with-people-of-living-faiths-and-ideologies.html#c22032

— 1982. *Baptism, Eucharist and Ministry: Faith and Order Paper No. 111.* Geneva: World Council of Churches.
— 1990. 'Baar Statement: Theological Perspectives on Plurality.' Accessed 14 June 2010. www.oikoumene.org/en/resources/documents/wcc-programmes/inter-religious-dialogue-and-cooperation/christian-identity-in-pluralistic-societies/baar-statement-theological-perspectives-on-plurality.html
— 2006. 'Constitution and Rules of the World Council of Churches, as Amended by the 9th Assembly, Porto Alegre, Brazil, February 2006.' Accessed 14 June 2010. http://www.oikoumene.org/en/resources/documents/assembly/porto-alegre-2006/1-statements-documents-adopted/institutional-issues/constitution-and-rules-as-adopted.html
— 2010a. 'World Council of Churches.' Accessed 14 June 2010. www.oikoumene.org
— 2010b. 'What Is the World Council of Churches?' Accessed 14 June 2010. www.oikoumene.org/en/who-are-we.html
World Evangelical Alliance Theological Commission Task Force. 2008. 'The Berlin Declaration on the Uniqueness of Christ and Jewish Evangelism in Europe Today.' Accessed 11 June 2010. www.worldevangelicals.org/commissions/tc/berlin.htm
Wrede, William. 1901. *The Messianic Secret.* Trans. J. C. G. Grieg; Greenwood, SC: Attic Press (repr. 1971).
Wright, Tom. 2000. *The Challenge of Jesus: Rediscovering Who Jesus Was and Is.* London: SPCK.

Works of Fiction and Creative Writing Cited in the Text

Avery, Fiona. 2005. *The Crown Rose.* Amherst, NY: Prometheus Books.
Barclay, William. 1977. *Jesus of Nazareth: Based on the Film Directed by Franco Zeffirelli from the Script by Anthony Burgess, Suso Cecchi d'Amico and Franco Zeffirelli.* London: Fount.
Blatty, William P. 1971. *The Exorcist.* London: Blond and Briggs.
Blyton, Enid. 1956. *A Story Book of Jesus.* Shaftesbury: Element (repr. 1998).
Brown, Dan. 2001. *Angels and Demons.* London: Bantam.
— 2004. *The Da Vinci Code.* London: Bantam.
Dickens, Charles. 1934. *The Life of Our Lord: The History of Our Saviour Jesus Christ.* London: Albatross (repr. 1947).
Fredriksson, Marianne. 1999. *According to Mary Magdalene.* Charlottesville, VA: Hampton Roads.
George, Margaret. 2002. *Mary, Called Magdalene.* London: Macmillan.
Harris, Joanne. 1999. *Chocolat.* London: Random House.
Kazantzakis, Nikos. 1960. *The Last Temptation of Christ.* New York: Simon and Schuster.
LaHaye, Tim, and Jerry B. Jenkins. 1995. *Left Behind: A Novel of the Earth's Last Days.* Wheaton, IL: Tyndale House.
Lawrence, Jerome, and Robert Edwin Lee. 1951. *Inherit the Wind.* London: English Theatre Guild.
Lewis, C. S. 1950. *The Lion, the Witch and the Wardrobe.* London: HarperCollins (repr. 2005).
— 1955. *The Magician's Nephew.* London: HarperCollins (repr. 2005).

McGowan Kathleen. 2006. *The Expected One*. London: Simon and Schuster.

Sayers, Dorothy L. 1943. *The Man Born to Be King*. London: Victor Gollancz.

Seltzer, David. 1976. *The Omen*. London: Futura.

Tolkien, J. R. R. 1966. *Lord of the Rings*. 3 vols.; London: Allen and Unwin.

Translations of the Bible

(*In most cases, there are numerous editions*)

The Bible: Authorized Version. 1611. Oxford: Oxford University Press.

Gaus, Andy. 1991. *The Unvarnished New Testament*. Grand Rapids: Phanes.

Gold, V. R. et al. (eds). 1995. *The New Testament and Psalms: An Inclusive Version* (based on the Revised Standard Version). Oxford: Oxford University Press.

Henson, John. 2004. *Good as New: A Radical Retelling of the Scriptures.* New York and Alresford: O Books.

Hinton, Michael. 2005. *The 100-minute Bible*. Canterbury: The 100-Minute Press.

The Holy Bible: Containing the Old Testament and the New. Revised A.D. 1881–1885: Newly Edited by the American Revision Committee, A.D. 1901 (The American Standard Version). 1901. New York: Thomas Nelson and Sons.

Holy Bible: New International Version. 1978. London: Hodder and Stoughton.

The Holy Bible: Revised Standard Version. 1952. New York and Glasgow: Collins.

Holy Bible: The New Revised Standard Version. 1989. London: HarperCollins.

The Holy Bible: The Revised Version with the Revised Marginal References. 1881. Oxford: Oxford University Press.

Knox, Ronald A. 1944. *The New Testament of Our Lord and Savior Jesus Christ. Newly Translated from the Latin Vulgate: Translated at the Request of the Lordships, the Archbishops of England and Wales.* London: Burns, Oates and Washbourne.

— 1948. *The Old Testament Newly Translated from the Latin Vulgate: Translated at the Request of the Cardinal of Westminster.* London: Burns, Oates and Washbourne.

The New English Bible, with the Apocrypha. 1970. Oxford: Oxford and Cambridge University Presses.

Reader's Digest Association. 1990. *Reader's Digest Bible*. Pleasantville, NY: Reader's Digest Association.

Taylor, Kenneth N. 1971. *The Living Bible*. London: Hodder and Stoughton.

United Bible Societies. 1976. *Good News Bible: Today's English Version.* London: Collins.

Subject Index

Names Index